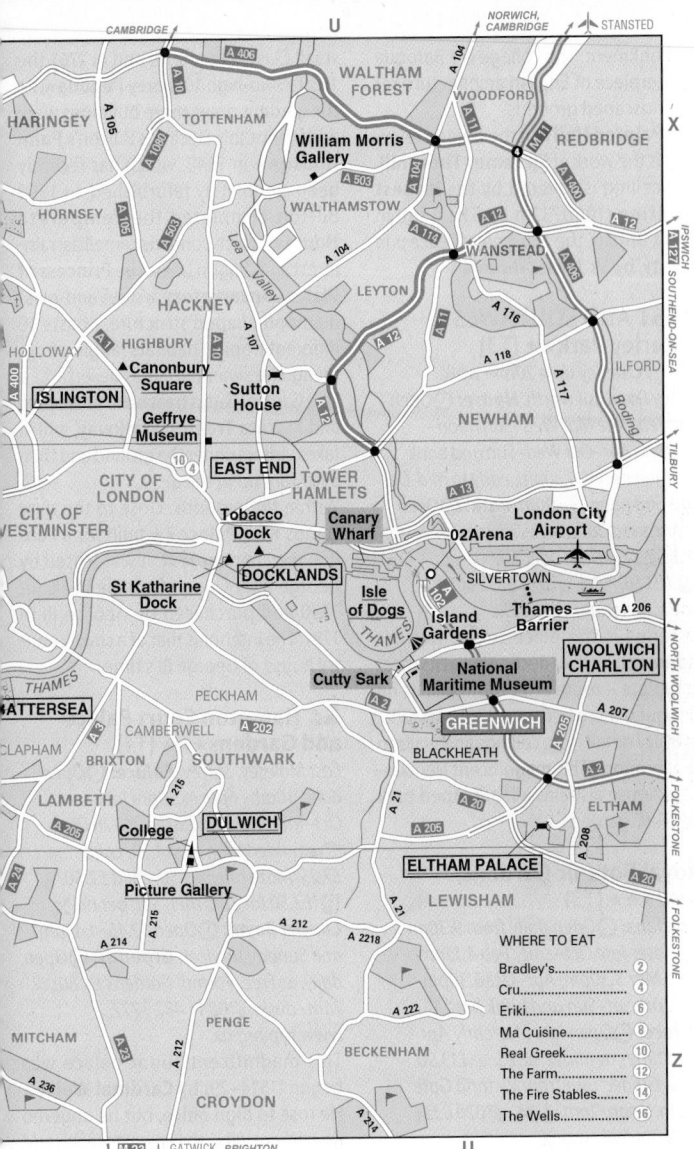

standing astride (thus being in two meridians at once!). Adjacent is the **Astronomy Centre** including three galleries and the state-of-the-art **Peter Harrison Planetarium**.

Old Royal Naval College★★
Painted Hall and Chapel and Discover Greenwich Visitor Centre. ⏰*Open daily, 10am (Sun 11am–2.30pm service in chapel) to 5pm.* 🐾 *Guided tours*

(❧£6). ❧*Entry free.* 📞*020 8269 4791. www.oldroyalnavalcollege.org.*
After demolishing the Tudor Palace (👜*see above*), Wren retained the King Charles Block to which he added three symmetrical blocks named after King William, Queen Mary and Queen Anne. For the Queen's House (👜*see above*) he provided a river vista (150ft/46m) flanked by twin cupolas over the Chapel and the Painted Hall down to a new river

embankment. The college is a Baroque masterpiece of English architecture set in landscaped grounds.

The **Painted Hall**★ in the domed refectory is the work of **Sir James Thornhill**. The ceiling is covered by the **largest painting** (106ft/32m by 51ft/16m) in Great Britain, the *Triumph of Peace and Liberty*, by Sir James Thornhill.

WEST AND SOUTHWEST
Osterley Park★★ (T3)

NT. ⊖Osterley then 20min walk. Jersey Road, Isleworth. House: ⊙Open late Feb–late Mar Wed–Sun noon– 3.30pm. Apr–Oct Wed–Sun and bank hol Mon noon–4.30pm; early to mid-Dec Sat–Sun noon–3.30pm. Park: ⊙Open year-round daily 8am–7.30pm/dusk. ⊙£8.25. Gardens only, £3.60. 🅿 (£3.50)&✗. ℘020 8232 5050. www.nationaltrust.org.uk.

Osterley is the place to see **Robert Adam** rich interior decoration at its most complete – room after room just as he designed them between 1761 and 1780, in every detail from ceilings and walls to the furniture. This magnificent Neoclassical house also has a landscaped park and 18C gardens.

Royal Botanic Gardens, Kew★★★ (T3)

Gardens: ⊙Open daily from 9.30am. ⊙Closes late Oct–early Feb 4.15pm; Feb–Mar 5.30pm; Apr–Oct 6.30pm (7.30pm Sat–Sun and bank hols). Palace: ⊙Open late Mar/early Apr– Sept times as above. ⊙£5. ⊙£13.90 🕭 *Guided tour from Victoria Gate 11am, noon, 2pm.* &✗. ℘020 8332 5655. www.kew.org.

The **Royal Botanic Gardens**, the finest in the land, are a wonderful place to visit at any time of year. However, this 300-acre/121ha garden is not just a pleasure garden but the offshoot of laboratories engaged in the identification and conservation of plants from every corner of the earth, for economic, medical and other purposes.

The gardens were begun in 1756 by **Sir William Chambers**. The same architect designed the **Orangery**★, the three

small Classical temples and in 1761 the 163ft/50m-high 10-storey **Pagoda**★. As the gardens grew, more buildings were added, notably Decimus Burton's **Palm House**★★ in 1848, which has recently been completely refurbished. In 1899 Burton completed the **Temperate House**★, which contains camellias, rainforest and dragon trees. The **Princess of Wales Conservatory**, a steel-and-glass diamond-shaped structure, boasts 10 different tropical habitats ranging from mangrove swamp to sand desert.

Kew Gardens' latest treat is the **Rhizotron** and **Xstrata Treetop Walkway**, which takes visitors under the ground and then 59ft/18m up in the air.

Within the grounds, close to the river stands **Kew Palace**★★ built for a London merchant in 1631. It was leased by George II for Queen Caroline in about 1730 and purchased by George III in 1781. The interior is that of a small country house of George III's time.

♠♦ Hampton Court Palace and Gardens★★★ (T4)

East Molesey, Surrey. Palace: ⊙Open daily, 10am–6pm (4.30pm late-Oct–late-Mar). ⊙Closed 24–26 Dec. 🕭Guided tour. ⊙£14.50, child £7.25. Maze only: £3.50, child £2.50. & 🅿 (£3.50 for 3hrs then 50p per hr) ✗. *Chapel Royal: ⊙Open 12.45–1.45pm and Sunday services. Grounds: ⊙Open daily.* ⊙Free (Formal Gardens £4.80), *7am–dusk.* ℘0844 482 7777. www.hrp.org.uk.

This magnificent Tudor palace was begun (1514–29) by **Cardinal Wolsey**. He rose to high office, but he angered King Henry VIII with his great wealth and his failure to obtain papal approval for the king's divorce. He died in disgrace in 1530 and Hampton Court was appropriated by the king, who set about enlarging the palace, including the splendid Great Hall with its hammerbeam roof, and lavishly transformed the chapel. The Astronomical Clock in Clock Court, though made in 1540, was brought here from St James's Palace in the 19C.

In 1688 Wren rebuilt the east and south fronts, the **State Apartments** and the smaller royal apartments. These rooms were decorated with carvings by **Grinling Gibbons** and painted ceilings by **Verrio**. The apartments and rooms contain a superb collection of **paintings** and **furniture**, while the **kitchens** and the **King's Beer Cellars** and the **wine cellars** offer a glimpse of life in Tudor times, all enhanced by costumed actors who interact with visitors. The **gardens**★★★ as seen today are the results of various schemes. The famous triangular **maze** was planted in 1690. In 1768 under George III, Lancelot Capability Brown planted the **Great Vine**★, now a plant of remarkable girth which produces an annual crop of around 500–600 bunches of grapes.

Syon Park★★ (T4)
⊖*Gunnersbury then bus 237 or 267. Brentford.* **Gardens:** ○*Open daily 10.30am–5pm/dusk (winter, Sat–Sun only).* **House:** ○*Open mid-Mar–Oct Wed–Thu, Sun and bank hols 11am–5pm.* ☞*£10; gardens and conservatory only £5.* ♿🅿✕. ✆*020 8560 0882. www.syonpark.co.uk.*
The 1st Earl of Northumberland remodelled this ancient house in 1762, commissioning **Robert Adam**, who richly ornamented and furnished it. A number of notable Stuart portraits by Van Dyck, Lely and others further embellish the interior. **Lancelot Capability Brown** re-designed the gardens and extended them to the river; two of his mulberry trees still survive and a vast rose garden is in bloom from May to August. The **Great Conservatory**, a beautiful semi-circular building with a central cupola and end pavilions, dates from 1827.

Ham House★★ (T4)
NT. ⊖*Richmond then bus. Ham Street.* **House:** ○*Open Apr–Oct Sat–Thu and Good Fri noon–4pm.* **Garden:** ○*Open daily 11am–5pm/dusk (late Dec–mid-Feb 4pm).* ○*Closed 1 Jan, 25–26 Dec.* ☞*£9.90. Gardens only, £3.30* ♿🅿✕. ✆*020 8940 1950. www.nationaltrust.org.uk.*
This is an exquisite three-storey 17C brick house. Much of the original furnishing has survived and is lavish even

by the standards of the age. The house is rich in ornate plasterwork on the ceilings and splendid carved wood panelling on the walls. The Great Staircase of 1637, built of oak around a square well and gilded, has a beautiful balustrade of boldly carved trophies of arms.

Richmond★★ (T3)
Possessing what has been called the most beautiful "urban village" green in England, Richmond grew to importance between the 12C and the 17C as a royal seat. Today private houses stand on the site of Henry VII's Royal Palace in which he died in 1509 (as did his granddaughter, Elizabeth I, in 1603). Among other fine Georgian houses in the "village" note the **Maids of Honour Row**★★ on the Green, built in 1724.

Climb **Richmond Hill**'s steep road, lined by 18C houses with balconied terraces, to enjoy the excellent views immortalised by artists such as Turner and Reynolds. At the top **Richmond Park**★★ (TYZ) is the largest of the Royal Parks and is known for its herds of red and fallow deer. From the top of Henry VIII's Mound, near Pembroke Lodge and the Richmond Gate, on a clear day the **panorama**★★★ extends from Windsor Castle to St Paul's Cathedral in The City.

NORTH
Kenwood House★★ (The Iveagh Bequest) (T2)
EH. ⊖*Archway or Golders Green, then 210 bus. Hampstead Lane.* **House:** ○*Open daily 11.30am–4pm.* ○*Closed 1 Jan, 24–26 Dec.* **Grounds:** ○*Open daily 8am–dusk.* ♿🅿✕, *picnic area.* ✆*020 8348 1286. www.english-heritage.org.uk.*
Set in leafy grounds beside Hampstead Heath, this is one of London's outstanding country houses, remodelled by Robert Adam 1764–79. The richly decorated **library**★★ is one of Adam's great masterpieces. Kenwood also possesses superb paintings including a Rembrandt *(Self Portrait in Old Age).* Its lakeside summer concerts, in a magnificent natural setting, are a highlight of the northwest London social scene.

Windsor★★

Berkshire

Windsor is synonymous with its castle, but there is more to the town than just one building. Windsor Great Park stretches out for miles beyond the castle and is a wonderful place for summer walks and picnics. Windsor town has been a royal borough since being granted the status by Edward I in 1277.

TOWN

The network of old **cobbled streets** bordered by High Street, Castle Hill, Church Lane, Church Street and Albans Street, contains a number of fine 16C–18C timber-framed houses with oversailing upper floors rising to pointed gables. The short High Street is distinguished by St John's parish **church**, rebuilt in 1822, and the **Guildhall**, begun by Sir Thomas Fitch c.1637 and completed by Sir Christopher Wren in 1690.

WINDSOR CASTLE★★★

Open daily 9.45am–5.15pm (4.15pm Nov–Feb); subject to change at short notice, check before visiting; last entry 1hr 15min before closing. St George's Chapel closed Sun. Changing of the Guard on alternate days 11am (exc Sun), weather permitting. Closed 25–26 Dec and various days throughout year (see website). £17, £9.30 during closure of state apartments. Guided precincts tours (30min, free) daily at regular intervals. Ticket to inc Round Tower ("Conquer the

Windsor Castle

© Alamer/Iconotec /Photononstop

- ▶ **Population:** 30,136 (including Eton).
- **Michelin Map:** Michelin Atlas p 20 or Map 504 S 29.
- **Info:** The Old Booking Hall, Windsor Royal Station, Thames Street. ℘01753 743 900. www.windsor.gov.uk.
- ▷ **Location:** Windsor lies 23mi/37km due west of London. There are two stations, Riverside and Central, both centrally located, both with direct London services. The old town comprises one main street, **Thames Street**, intersected by the road leading down from the castle gate, and then continues as High Street and Sheet Street.
- ▲▲ **Kids**: Legoland.

Tower") tour: Aug–Sept only, £23. Tickets to inc.Great Kitchen tour £21. . ℘020 7766 7304. www.royalresidences.com. England's biggest castle is also the largest inhabited stronghold in the world and has been a favourite royal residence, frequently extended and rebuilt, since William the Conqueror first built a motte and bailey on the site c.1080.

A Bit of History

By 1110, the castle had become a royal lodge where Henry I held his first court. Henry II erected the first stone buildings between 1165 and 1179, constructing one range of royal apartments in the Upper Ward (to the east of the Round Tower) and one in the Lower Ward. Faced with rebellion by his sons he modernised the defences, rebuilding the earthen walls and wooden Round Tower in stone. Under Henry III (1216–72) this work was virtually completed. Edward III (1327–77) reconstructed the royal apartments for his newly founded Order of the Garter. Under Charles II the State Apartments were rebuilt in an ambitious renovation project which included the reconstruction of St George's Hall and the King's Chapel, in which the architect Hugh May concentrated on fitting out the interior in a manner fit for a king, insulating the rooms with oak panelling festooned with Grinling Gibbons carvings. However, the principal changes were made in the early-19C when George IV commissioned Sir Jeffry Wyatville as his architect; he built the machicolated walls and several towers, raised the massive Round Tower, giving the castle its famous outline, and remodelled the State Apartments, adding the Waterloo Chamber. This section was badly damaged by fire in 1992. The principal change under Queen Victoria was the addition of a private chapel in memory of Prince Albert, who died here on 14 December 1861. Queen Mary, wife of George V, carried out careful restoration work on the castle at the turn of the 20C century, and it became the childhood home of HRH the Princesses Elizabeth and Margaret during the Second World War, since which it has remained the royal family's principal home. The Court is in official residence throughout April and for Ascot Week in June and the annual Garter Day ceremonies.

The impressive 213-ft/65m-tall tall **Round Tower** stands on the site of William I's original fortress and houses the Royal Archives. In 2011 it was opened to the public for the first time for visitors to enjoy **views**★★ of the castle the Great Park, the Thames Valley and the London skyline. Adjacent, the **North Terrace** (c.1570) affords **views**★★ of Eton College and London.

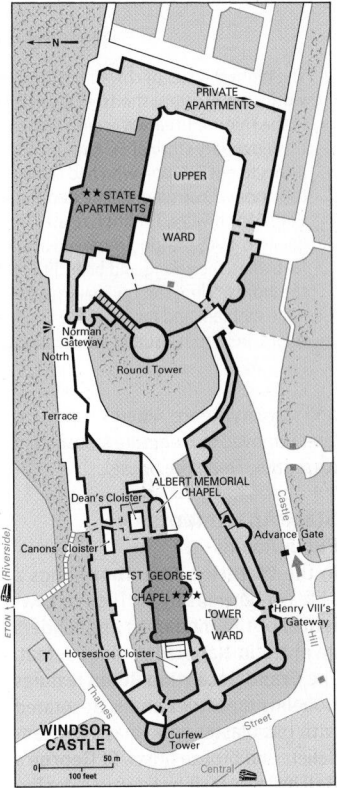

Chapels
St George's Chapel★★★

This great Perpendicular chapel was begun by Edward IV to replace the chapel of Henry III to the east which Edward III had enlarged and dedicated to his **Most Noble Order of the Garter**. The slender clustered piers lead the eye to the crowning glory of the chapel, the **lierne vault**, rich with coloured bosses – completed in 1528. The blank panelling between the tall arcades and the clerestory windows is topped with smiling angels. The aisles are notable for their

fan vaulting. The impressive Perpendicular **west window** depicts 75 figures mainly in early 16C-glass.

The ornate **stalls**★★★, abounding in misericords and other carvings, were built in 1478–85; the top tier, surmounted by a richly carved canopy, is for the Knights of the Garter. Edward III's **battle sword** (6ft 8in/2m) is in the south chancel aisle. The glorious **east window** (30ft/9m high and 29ft/8.8m wide; 52 lights) commemorates Prince Albert (incidents from his life illustrated in the lower tier, below the Resurrection and the *Adoration of the Kings*).

Albert Memorial Chapel

The original chapel (1240) was given its magnificent Victorian embellishment by Sir George Gilbert Scott after the death of Albert and is a supreme example of the 19C revivalist age with Venetian mosaics, inlaid marble panels

The Order of the Garter

The highest order of chivalry in the land is also the oldest to survive in the world. It was established by Edward III in 1348 when England was engaged in the Hundred Years War with France and may have been modelled on the legendary story of 5C King Arthur and his Knights of the Round Table. It was to reward men who had shown valour on the battlefield, and also to honour those who manifested the idealistic and romantic concept of Christian chivalry. Tradition relates how at a ball celebrating the conquest of Calais in 1347, the king retrieved a fallen garter and returned it to its rightful owner, the young and beautiful Joan of Kent, Countess of Salisbury, with the words, "Honi soit qui mal y pense" (Shame on him who thinks evil of it) – the emblem and motto of the Order. A more likely derivation is a strap or sword-belt from a suit of armour to denote the bond of loyalty and concord.

and statuary. Prince Albert's tomb was later removed to Frogmore Mausoleum (*see Box, Frogmore House*).

State Apartments★★
Public Rooms

In the **Waterloo Chamber** hangs a series of portraits by Sir Thomas Lawrence, of the monarchs and leaders involved in Napoleon's final defeat. The **Grand Reception Room** features Gobelins tapestries and is decorated with gilt plasterwork, massive chandeliers and bronze busts. **St George's Hall** hall was built by Edward III for the Knights of the Garter and the Baroque chapel was built for Charles II. The 700 past Garter Knights' escutcheons are set in the panelling of the plaster ceiling. Note the award-winning octagonal **Lantern Lobby**, created after the fire in 1992.

The Queen's Rooms

The **Queen's Guard Chamber** leads into the panelled Queen's Presence Chamber which, with the adjoining **Queen's Audience Chamber**, is essentially unchanged since the time of Charles II. The **Queen's Drawing Room** contains some of the earliest plate glass in England. Eight Van Dyck portraits hang in the ballroom while Holbeins hang in the drawing room.

The King's Rooms

The **King's Drawing Room** contains paintings by Rubens and his followers and Chinese porcelain. The **King's Bed-chamber** has a grandiose "polonaise" bed made for the visit by Emperor Napoleon III and his wife Eugénie in 1855. On the walls of the **King's Dressing Room** are a number of **masterpieces★★** by Dürer, Memling, Clouet, Holbein, Rembrandt, Rubens and Van Dyck. The **King's Dining Room** retains much of the character it had under Charles II.

Queen Mary's Dolls' House

This fascinating miniature masterpiece, designed by Sir Edwin Lutyens, was presented to Queen Mary in 1924. Everything is exactly on a 1:12 scale – not only the furniture, but even the printed leather-bound books in the library, paintings and the cars in the garage.

WINDSOR PARK★

In the mid-18C George II charged his son, William Duke of Cumberland, with the task of organising the vast Windsor Forest, hunting ground of Saxon leaders and medieval knights. 4,800 acres/1,942ha of overgrown woodland were cleared and streams were diverted to drain the marshes into newly dug ponds, which eventually flowed into the especially created 130 acres/53ha of Virginia Water. George III continued this land reclamation work and established two farms.

The park is now divided into **Home Park**, which is private, and **Great Park**, most of which is public. A significant feature of the park is the **Long Walk**, a 3mi/5km avenue running south as far as the **Copper Horse**, an equestrian statue of George III. Under Charles II the avenue was planted with elm trees, in 1685, the year in which he died, but in 1945 the trees, which had fallen victim to Dutch Elm disease, had to be replaced by chestnuts and planes. Two former royal residences are tucked away in the park: Royal Lodge, used as a retreat by George IV and by the late Queen Elizabeth the Queen Mother, and Cumberland Lodge, where William Duke of Cumberland resided while redesigning the park. Smith's Lawn is an area reserved for polo matches, and beyond it stretch the beautiful **Valley Gardens**.

The **Royal Mausoleum**, Frogmore Garden, in Home Park was begun in 1862, the year after Prince Albert's death, specifically so that Queen Victoria and Albert could be buried side by side. The rich interior reflects the Consort's passion for the Italian Renaissance. **Frogmore House** (1684) is furnished largely with possessions accumulated by Queen Mary (black papier mâché furniture, wax and silk flowers).

ETON COLLEGE★★

10min on foot across Windsor Bridge.
Visit by guided tour only, 2pm, 3.15pm on some Wed, Fri, Sat and Sun during term time, and daily during college hols. See website for details.
£6.50. 01753 671 177. www. etoncollege.com/VisitsToEton.aspx.

The most prestigious of all British schools, Eton was founded in 1440 by Henry VI to give free education to 70 poor scholars and choristers.

Henry then founded King's College, Cambridge, so the boys could continue their education and it soon became fashionable for the nobility to send their sons to Eton.

The paved **School Yard**, centre of college life, is dominated by the 16C redbrick **Lupton's Tower** on the east side. To the north is **Lower School**, the 15C brick building originally constructed by Henry VI to house the Scholars. **Upper School** on the west side was built in the 17C to accommodate the increasing number of boys. In the centre of the

yard stands a 1719 bronze statue of the founder.

The **College Chapel**★★, built in 1449–82, is one of the best examples of Perpendicular architecture in England. The 15C **wall paintings**★ are also the finest in the country. The modern stained glass (Evie Holme, John Piper), and the tapestry reredos and panelling by William Morris from designs by Burne-Jones are notable. The brick **Cloister Court** dates back to Henry VI's time. It contains the 15C College Hall where the "collegers" eat; in the undercroft is the **Museum of Eton Life**.

👤🎫 LEGOLAND WINDSOR★★

2mi/3km SW of Windsor on the B 3022. Bus from Windsor town centre, by both railway stations. Open daily from 9.30am/10am mid-Mar/Apr–late Oct; closing times vary (see website). £41.40 ticket at the gate, child £31.20. Book online for 10–25 percent discount; ♿🅿🍴. 0871 2222 001. www.legoland.co.uk.

Millions of Lego building blocks are used to impressive effect in this beautifully landscaped theme park for Lego lovers. Moving models and miniature European towns show the skills of professional Lego-builders and children can have a go at building for themselves but it is the theme park rides, attractions and live shows (geared for children up to the age of 12), that draw the crowds.

Frogmore House

The last resting place of both Victoria and Albert is the Frogmore Mausoleum. It is attached to Frogmore House, set in a very peaceful area of Home Park (the private part of Windsor Park) and renowned for its beautiful landscaped garden and 18C lake. The house also contains works of art by Queen Victoria and her children (open spring and late Aug-bank hol weekends 10am–4pm; £7.50; 020 7766 7305; www.royalcollection.org.uk).

ADDRESSES

🛏 STAY

🔆**Top Tips** – Staying in London can be very expensive. Consider bed and breakfasts (B&Bs) instead: **London Bed and Breakfast Agency Ltd** (*☏020 7586 2768 ; www.londonbb.com)*. Or check out no-frills budget chain hotels such as **Travel Inn** (www.premiertravelinn.com) and **Travelodge** (www.travelodge.co.uk). Beware that breakfast is not included in the room rate for many London hotels. Always check in advance.

MARYLEBONE

⊖⊜⊜**Hart House Hotel** – Plan C2. *51 Gloucester Place*. ⊖Marble Arch, *☏020 7935 2288. www.harthouse.co.uk. 15 rms.* This charming Georgian townhouse was occupied by members of the French nobility during the French Revolution of 1789. For the last 35 years it has been owned and managed by the same family. Good location between Hyde Park and Regent's Park.

⊖⊜⊜**St George Hotel** – Plan C2. *49 Gloucester Place.* ⊖Marble Arch. *☏020 7486 8586. www.stgeorge-hotel.net. 19 rms.* This historic townhouse, a short walk from Oxford Street and Baker Street, offers very comfortable period bedrooms and a warm welcome .

⊖⊜⊜⊜**Durrants** – Plan C2. *26–32 George Street.* ⊖Bond Street. *☏020 7935 8131. www.durrantshotel.co.uk. 92 rms.* A London institution since 1790, Durrants guarantees a very British take on old-fashioned charm. Very pricey, so look for special offers.

COVENT GARDEN

⊖⊜⊜**The Fielding** – Plan D2. *4 Broad Court, Bow Street.* ⊖Covent Garden. *☏020 7836 8305. www.the-fielding-hotel.co.uk.* The main attraction of this comfortable (air-conditioned) period house is its location at the heart of Covent Garden, and free access to the area's premier spa complex.

SOHO

⊖⊜⊜⊜**Hazlitt's** – Plan D2. *6 Frith Street .* ⊖Tottenham Court Road. *☏020 7434 1771. www.hazlitts.co.uk. 22 rms.* This small hotel at the heart of Soho is a Georgian-cum-Victorian gem full of character and luxurious antique fittings. Very expensive.

BLOOMSBURY

⊖⊜**Thanet Hotel** – Plan D2. *8 Bedford Place.* ⊖Russell Square. *☏020 7636 2869. www.thanethotel.co.uk. 16 rms.* Situated on a quiet Georgian terrace, close to the British Museum, this simple but cheerful good-value hotel is run by a friendly husband-and-wife team.

⊖⊜⊜⊜**The Academy** – Plan D2. *21 Gower Street.* ⊖Goodge Street. *☏020 7631 4115. www.theetoncollection.co.uk. 49 rms.* Five Georgian townhouses make up this elegant four-star boutique hotel with private garden.

THE CITY

⊖⊜⊜⊜**The Rookery** – Plan E2 - *12 Peter's Lane - Cowcross Street -* ⊖Barbican - *☏020 7336 0931 - www.rookeryhotel.com - 32 rms.* A sister hotel to Hazlitts (ℓsee above) with the same mix of bohemian luxury and charm, located in trendy Clerkenwell.

SOUTHWARK

⊖⊜⊜⊜**All Seasons Southwark Rose** – Plan E3 – *43–47 Southwark Bridge Road.* ⊖London Bridge. *☏(020) 7015 1480. www.all-seasons-hotels.com. 84 rms.* Impressive stylish modern minimalist newcomer, near the Globe Theatre and Tate Modern. Unlimited internet access.

KNIGHTSBRIDGE

⊖⊜⊜⊜**Knightsbridge Green** – Plan B3. *1159 Knightsbridge.* ⊖Knightsbridge. *☏020 7584 6274. www.thekghotel.com. 16 rms.* Luxury hotel, located in the heart of Knightsbridge, with light spacious, contemporary rooms.

SOUTH KENSINGTON

⊜⊜⊜**Citadines** – Plan A3. *35a Gloucester Road.* ⊖Gloucester Road. *☏0800 376 3898. www.citadines.com. 92 apts.* These beautifully furnished, comprehensively equipped studios *(1–2 persons.)* and apartments *(1–4 persons.)* were completely refitted in 2010.

HYDE PARK

⊖⊜–⊖⊜⊜**Gresham Hotel** – Plan B2. *116 Sussex Gardens.* ⊖Paddington. *☏020 7402 2920. www.the-gresham-london.co.uk - 57 rms* Location (close to the major museums) and value are the selling points for this simple but comfortable central London hotel.

CHELSEA

⊖⊜⊟ – ⊖⊜⊟⊟ **The Rockwell** – Plan A3. *181–183 Cromwell Road.* ⊖*Earl's Court.* ℘*020 7244 2000. www.therockwell.com. 40 rms.* Elegant contemporary and traditional English style mix at this Kensington hotel with a large south-facing landscaped garden. Garden rooms available for a small premium.

BELGRAVIA

⊖⊜⊟ **B&B Belgravia** – Plan C3. *64–66 Ebury Street.* ⊖*Victoria.* ℘*020 7259 8570. www.bb-belgravia.com. 17 rms .* Stylish up-to-the-minute boutique accommodation in a historic Georgian townhouse. Full English organic breakfasts.

♀/ EAT

⊙**Top Tip** – London's cosmopolitan character is typified by its huge range of places to eat and its global range of cuisines. For lunch, you'll have no trouble finding something decent to eat on the run; high-quality sandwiches, bagels, soups, noodles… whatever you fancy!

WESTMINSTER

⊖⊟ – ⊖⊜⊟⊟ **Cinnamon Club** – Plan D3. *The Old Westminster Library, Great Smith Street.* ⊖*St James's.* ℘*020 7222 2555. www.cinnamonclub.com. Closed Sun and hols.* This stylish upmarket Anglo-Indian restaurant is set in the atmospheric surrounds of Old Westminster Library.

⊖⊟ – ⊖⊜⊟⊟ **Shepherd's** – Plan D3. *Marsham Court, Marsham Street.* ⊖*Pimlico.* ℘*020 7834 9552. www.langansrestaurants. co.uk. Closed Sat–Sun.* Classic old-fashioned English restaurant popular with the political fraternity from the nearby Houses of Parliament and other local government officers looking for a discreet dining place.

MAYFAIR

⊖ **Chada Chada** – Plan C2. *16-17 Picton Place.* ⊖*Bond Street.* ℘*020 7935 8212. www.chadathai.com. Closed Sun and hols.* One of the best budget Thai restaurants in town, this elegant little place serves traditional favourites, alongside original recipes.

PICADILLY

⊖ **Ilc Baretto at Alloro** – Plan C2. *19–20 Dover Street.* ⊖*Green Park.* ℘*020 7495 4768. www.atozrestaurants.com. Closed Sun.* Keeping to a simple formula of seasonal Italian favourites – all pastas and breads are made on the premises – this is the informal bar area of one of London's best Italian restaurants

⊖⊟ – ⊖⊜⊟⊟ **Benihana** – Plan C2. *37 Sackville Street.* ⊖*Piccadilly Circus.* ℘*020 7494 2525. www.benihana.co.uk.* The Japanese food is good here but the "show cooking", with ingredients flamboyantly prepared and served in front of diners on a hibachi hot plate, is what most customers come for.

COVENT GARDEN

⊖⊜⊟ **Rules** – Plan D2 - *35 Maiden Lane -* ⊖*Charing Cross/Covent Garden -* ℘*020 7836 5314 - www.rules.co.uk.* London's oldest restaurant (est 1798) specialises in atmosphere and hearty traditional British cooking.

SOHO

⊖ – ⊖⊜⊟ **Dehesa** – Plan C2. *25 Ganton Street,* ⊖*Oxford Circus.* ℘*020 7494 4170. www.dehesa.co.uk. Closed Sun evening.* This calm charcuterie and tapas bar takes inspiration from Spain and Italy, and boasts an impressive wine list.

TEMPLE

⊖⊟ **The White Swan** – Plan E2. *108 Fetter Lane.* ⊖*Temple.* ℘*020 7242 9696. www.thewhiteswanlondon.com. Closed weekends.* Just off Fleet Street this new gastropub serves traditional and modern English dishes, in a very smart dining room above the pub. The Express Lunch menu is handy if you're in a hurry.

REGENT'S PARK

⊖ **The Sea Shell** – Plan C1. *49–51 Lisson Grove.* ⊖*Marylebone.* ℘*020 7224 9000. www.seashellrestaurant.co.uk. Closed Sun.* One of London's best fish and chip "shops" with a smart traditional black-and-white dining room to save your fingers getting messy. Ideal after a day at Regent's Park/London Zoo.

⊖⊟ – ⊖⊜⊟⊟ **Villandry** – Plan C2. *170 Great Portland Street.* ⊖*Regent's Park.* ℘*020 7631 3131. www.villandry.com. Closed Sun evening.* This all-day French restaurant, café, foodshop, bakery and bar (all under one roof) is as good for a quick takeaway as it is for a full-blown elegant classic French dinner.

CITY

◻🍽️🍷 **Le Coq d'Argent** – Plan F2. *1 Poultry –* ⊖*Bank.* ℘*020 7395 5000. www.coqdargent.co.uk. Closed Sat lunch, Sun evening and hols.* At the heart of The City, this vast sixth-floor restaurant features one of the most remarkable roof gardens in London with a wonderful view from its terrace. Classic French menu with contemporary flavours.

TOWER BRIDGE

◻🍽️ **The Blueprint Cafe** – Plan G3. *Design Museum, Shad Thames,* ⊖*Tower Bridge.* ℘*020 7378 7031 - www.dandd london.com - Closed Sun evening.* This long-standing restaurant enjoys a classy location among the converted warehouses of Butler's Wharf. Superb riverside views complement excellent Modern British cuisine.

◻🍽️🍷 **Le Pont de la Tour** – Plan F3 - *Butlers Wharf -* ⊖*Tower Bridge -* ℘*020 7403 8403 - www.lepontdelatour.co.uk -* This elegant establishment, serving fine French cuisine, is a favourite for business and pleasure with a riverside terrace and perfect views of Tower Bridge. Try its Bar & Grill (◻🍽️) for a less formal meal.

◻🍽️–◻🍽️🍷 **Butlers Wharf Chop House** – Plan F3 - *Butlers Wharf. -* ⊖*Tower Bridge -* ℘*020 7403 3403 - www.chophouse.co.uk - Closed Sun evening.* Classic down-to-earth British food, such as chops and steaks and a famous steak and kidney pudding are the signature dishes at this wood-panelled restaurant by the Thames which evokes the style of a boating or cricket pavilion. Great views of Tower Bridge from its riverside terrace.

SOUTHWARK

◻🍽️ **Anchor et Hope** – Plan E3. *36 The Cut.* ⊖*Southwark.* ℘*020 7928 9898. Mon lunch and Sun evening.* One of London's best gastro pubs, serving its own original unfussy take on Modern and traditional British cuisine. No bookings taken so arrive early.

◻🍽️ **Cantina Vinopolis** – Plan F2. *1 Bank End.* ⊖*Southwark.* ℘*020 7940 8333. www.cantinavinopolis.com. Closed Sun.* There's a wide choice of menus in this "shrine to wine" (attached to the visitor attraction, Vinopolis), tucked away under the massive Victorian arches beside the Thames in handsome brick-vaulted dining rooms.

SOUTH BANK

◻🍽️🍷 **Oxo Tower** – Plan E2. *Oxo Tower Wharf, 8th floor. Barge House Street.* ⊖*Southwark.* ℘*020 7803 3888. www.harveynichols.com.* Magnificent views of the capital across the Thames are complemented. by fine pan-Asian and Modern British cuisine. On the same level, the **Oxo Tower Brasserie** is a little cheaper but with equally fine views and excellent cooking.

KNIGHTSBRIDGE

◻ **Le Metro** – Plan B3. *28 Basil Street -* ⊖*Knightsbridge.* ℘*020 7589 6286. www.thelevinhotel.co.uk. Closed Sun evening and hols.* Near Harrods, this modern bistro breaks no new ground with its menu but is ideal for a shoppers' lunch or afternoon tea.

SOUTH KENSINGTON

◻🍽️–◻🍽️🍷 **Racine** – Plan B3. *93 Brompton Road.* ⊖*South Kensington.* ℘*020 7584 4477. www.racine-restaurant.com.* This classic brasserie evokes a typical French neighbourhood restaurant: expect *filet au poivre, lapin à la moutarde, tête de veau, soupe de poisson,* and good-value prix-fixe menus.

CHELSEA

◻🍽️ **Pig's Ear** – Plan B4. *35 Old Church Street.* ⊖*Sloane Square.* ℘*020 7352 2908. www.thepigsear.info.* Tucked away between the King's Road and the Thames, this smart gastropub offers British/French brasserie food, in the bar or in its two formal dining rooms.

◻🍽️🍷–◻🍽️🍷🍷 **Bibendum** – Plan B3. *Michelin House, 81 Fulham Road.* ⊖*South Kensington.* ℘*020 7581 5817. www.bibendum.co.uk.* Housed in London's finest Art Nouveau building and celebrating Michelin's famous "Mr Bibendum", this 20-year-old establishment serves consistently excellent classic French food with a strong British influence. Oyster bar on ground floor.

○○◎–○○◎◎**One-O-One** – Plan C3.
William Street. ⊖*Knightsbridge.* ℘*020 7290
7101. www.oneoonerestaurant.com.* One of
the country's top seafood dining rooms,
located at the Sheraton Park Tower Hotel.
Only sustainable and farmed produce
are used.

🍺 PUBS

Pubs usually open *Mon.–Sat. 11am-11pm,
Sun noon–10.30pm.*

Anglesea Arms – Plan B4. *15 Selwood
Terrace.* ⊖*South Kensington.* ℘*020 8749
1291. www.capitalpubcompany.com.* Set in
a peaceful residential district, this is the
ideal spot for a relaxing drink after a walk,
particularly on the pretty outdoor terrace.
The pub is also known for its excellent
Modern British food, which can also be
served on the terrace (○○◎–○○◎◎).

Dickens Inn – Plan G2. *St Katharine Dock.*
⊖*Tower Hill.* ℘*020 7488 2208.
www.dickensinn.co.uk.* Although it may
look older, this rambling Dickens-themed
pub, looking onto St Katherine Docks,
only opened in 1976. Its restaurant is
famous for its huge "Immenso" pizzas
serving five people at a time; its generous
servings of pasta are also recommended.

George Inn – Plan F3. *77 Borough High
Street.* ⊖*London Bridge.* ℘*020 7407
2056.* London's last galleried inn, dating
from the 17C, is such a treasure that the
National Trust now cares for it, though it
still functions as it has since Shakespeare's
time. The Bard may well have performed
in the original George Inn (which burned
down in 1676) and Dickens mentions the
present inn in *Little Dorrit.*

The Bunch of Grapes – Plan B3.
207 Brompton Road. ⊖*Knightsbridge.
020 7589 4944.* Just a few yards from
Harrods, this classic Victorian pub is
perfect for a relaxing drink after shopping.
Note the remarkable carved wooden
bunch of grapes bar partition.

The Nag's Head – Plan C3. *53 Kinnerton
Street.* ⊖*Knightsbridge.* ℘*020 7235
1135.* Stepping into "the Nag's" is rather
like walking into an old movie, with its
small cosy rooms full of bric-a-brac from
yesteryear. Turn your mobile phone off –
by the way – they are banned!

Ye Grapes – Plan C3. *16 Shepherd Market.*
⊖*Green Park, Hyde Park Corner.* ℘*020 7493
4216. www.ye-grapes.co.uk.* This charming
late-19C pub is tucked away in an alleyway
in village-like Shepherd Market. Upstairs is
a restaurant serving British and Thai food.

🍽 CAFÉS

Café in the Crypt – Plan D2.
⊖*Trafalgar Square.* ⊖*Leicester Square,
Charing Cross.* ℘*020 7766 1158. www2.
stmartin-in-the-fields.org.* Located in
the crypt of St Martin-in-the-Fields
church, this self-service cafe serves good
value snacks and light meals. Live jazz
each Wed *(tickets required after 7pm).*

Fortnum and Mason's – Plan C2.
181 Piccadilly. ⊖*Piccadilly Circus.
www.fortnumandmason.co.uk.* Founded
in 1707, London's world-famous grocery
shop boasts several restaurants. The most
popular are the affordable **Fountain**
(℘*0845 602 5694*), and the more
expensive chic **St James's** (℘*0845 602
5694),* both of which feature a pianist.
Afternoon tea can be taken in both.

Garden Café – Plan C1. *Queen Mary's
Gardens, Inner Circle.* ⊖*Regent's Park, Baker
Street.* ℘*020 7034 0722. www.company
ofcooks.com.* Open 10am–9pm; winter
10am–4pm.* Simple but stylish café in
elegant Regent's Park, serving high-
quality teas, coffees, lunch and evening
meals in summer.

Harrods – Plan B3. *87–135 Brompton Road.*
⊖*Knightsbridge. www.harrods.com.* Open
Mon–Sat 10am–9pm, Sun 11.30am–6pm.*
The most famous shop in town includes
some 30 restaurants and cafés: from sushi
and seafood in their fabulous **Food Hall**,
self-service children's restaurant at **Planet
Harrods** to traditional afternoon tea in
Café Harrods.

Harvey Nichols – Fifth Floor Café –
Plan C3. *109–125 Knightsbridge.*
⊖*Knightsbridge.* ℘*020 7823 1839.
www.harveynichols.com.* Knightsbridge
shopping regulars appreciate this bright,
light spacious café-bar, complete with
open-plan-style kitchen and roof terrace.
There's also a very chic restaurant and a
champagne bar on the same floor.

🛒 SHOPPING

Window shopping is all part of the fun in London, particularly in stores like Harvey Nichols, Harrods and Selfridges which are renowned for their displays. For many people however the famous end of year sales *(late Dec to mid-Jan)* are worth the trip alone.

🔵 **Top Tip**– **Museum shops** are a great source of inspiration when it comes to unusual gifts and souvenirs; try the British Museum, the Science Museum, the Natural History Museum…

Shopping Areas

Around **Covent Garden** *(www.covent gardenlife.com)* you will find all kinds of shops selling unusual gifts, fashion and perfumes (don't miss **Penhaligon's**, at *no. 41 Wellington Street*). In The Market **Peter Rabbit and Friends** (no. 42) delights little ones.

In **St James's**, Jermyn Street is the place for classic gentlemen's fashion. Cheese lovers should follow their noses to no. 93, the home of **Paxton & Whitfield** for their wonderful Stiltons, Cheddars and many more cheeses from Britain (and beyond). In **Mayfair**, Burlington Arcade and Old Bond Street specialise in many of the world's most exclusive fashion brands. Sloane Street in **Knightsbridge** is also synonymous with expensive designer shopping. Sloane Street joins Sloane Square at **Chelsea**, famous for the King's Road and its many one-off fashion shops. In The **City**, the old Royal Exchange building is home to several upmarket shops.

MARKETS

Portobello Road – Plan A2. *Portobello Road.* 🚇*Notting Hill Gate. www.portobello road.co.uk.* On Saturdays the world's largest antique market is held; the rest of the week, antique shops, galleries, and all kinds of specialists and dealers in collectibles flourish here.

Borough Market – Plan F3. *Stoney Street, Borough High Street.* 🚇*London Bridge. www.boroughmarket.org.uk. Thu 11am–5pm, Fri noon–6pm, Sat 8am–5pm.* London's oldest and finest food market opens its doors towards the end of the week to the delight of foodies (including some of the capital's top restaurateurs)

who come here for the gourmet-quality foodstuffs on offer. Many stalls offer free (unresistable!) samples and at some you can sit down to eat.

BOOKS AND READING

Waterstone's Booksellers – Plan D2. *203–206 Piccadilly.* 🚇*Piccadilly Circus.* 📞*0843 290 8549. www.waterstones.com.* Occupying six floors of a lovely 70-year–old building, Waterstone's is the biggest bookshop in Europe. This is also the place to come for a comprehensive selection of foreign newspapers and magazines.

HOME FURNISHING

The Conran Shop, Michelin House – Plan B3 – *81 Fulham Road.* 🚇*South Kensington.* 📞*020 7589 7401. www.conranshop.co.uk.* Housed in the former UK headquarters of Michelin, and still boasting its famous stained-glass Bibendum windows, style-guru Terence Conran presents the very best in contemporary home fashion, for both Londoners and visitors.

TEA

Twinings & Co – Plan E2. *216 Strand.* 🚇*Temple.* 📞*020 7353 3511. www.twinings. co.uk. Closed Sun.* Established in 1717, this is the oldest tea shop in the world, and sells hundreds of varieties of tea in all flavours and packages. There is a small museum at the back of the shop.

TOYS AND GAMES

Hamley's – Plan C2. *188–196 Regent Street.* 🚇*Oxford Circus.* 📞*0871 704 1977. www.hamleys.co.uk.* The world's most famous toyshop is six levels of heaven for children, though beware, it can be unbearably crowded and stressful for parents, particularly at peak periods.

🎭 ENTERTAINMENT

The capital's most famous theatres, cinemas and concert halls tend to congregate around Leicester Square, Piccadilly (particularly Shaftesbury Avenue) and Covent Garden. Some of London's most famous **West End musicals** have been running for over 20 years. Even if you don't really understand all the language it's well worth attending a **Shakespeare play** at the beautifully rebuilt Globe Theatre, just to experience what it was like in those days *(see p109).* London also has great **concert halls** and it's always worth noting what's on at the Barbican, the Royal Albert Hall and the Southbank Centre (Royal Festival Hall, Hayward Gallery, Queen Elizabeth Hall, Purcell Room).

The best listings and reviews of all shows and events in town are in *Time Out* magazine, on sale every Tuesday *(www.timeout.com/london)* and *The London Evening Standard,* *(www.thisislondon.co.uk)*, published daily.

TICKETS

The best way of buying tickets for any show is at the box office. Alternatively you can telephone or buy online, though there is a surcharge (of up to 10 percent). **Ticketmaster** – *48 Leicester Square.* ✆*0844 277 4321; 0044 161 385 3211 (from abroad - www.ticketmaster.co.uk).*

Half-Price Ticket Booth (tkts) – Plan D2. *Leicester Square.* ⊖*Leicester Square.* ✆*020 7557 6700. www.officiallondon theatre.co.uk.* Operated by the Society of London Theatres (SOLT), this kiosk generally offers the best seats in the theatre at **half the normal price**, plus a £3 "booking fee" per ticket. They are only valid for that day and are first come first served. You can pay by cash or credit card (surcharge for the latter); tickets are non-returnable and are limited to four per person.

Beware of half-price tickets imitators also located in Leicester Square! You can also book tickets for the theatre, and for many other events, through the official channels, online at www.visit london.com.

🎭 EVENTS

For more details on any of the events below visit *www.visitlondon.com/ events/calendar*

New Year's Day Parade (1 Jan)
More than 10,000 performers in fancy dress parade through central London. *www.londonparade.co.uk.*

Chinese New Year (late Jan–mid Feb)
The largest Chinese New Year celebrations outside Asia take place in London's Chinatown. *www.chinatownlondon.org.*

Head of the River Race (Mar)
Some 400 eight-man crews from around the globe take to the Thames in one of the capital's longest-running sporting traditions. *www.horr.co.uk.*

The Boat Race (Apr)
The crews of Oxford University and Cambridge University compete, from Putney to Mortlake, in one of the world's oldest sporting events. *www.theboatrace.org.*

Chelsea Flower Show (May)
The world's greatest flower show in the grounds of the Royal Hospital, Chelsea. *www.rhs.org.uk/chelsea.*

Trooping the Colour (2nd/3rd Sat Jun)
Pomp and pageantry at the Queen's official birthday parade on Horse Guards Parade. *www.army.mod.uk/events.*

Wimbledon (last wk Jun– 1st wk Jul)
The world's finest Lawn Tennis Championships. *www.wimbledon.com.*

The BBC Proms (mid-Jul–Sept)
The Royal Albert Hall is the venue for a world-beating series of classical concerts. *www.bbc.co.uk/proms.*

Notting Hill Carnival (last weekend Aug)
Europe's largest carnival celebrations is a blaze of colour and music. *www.nottinghill-carnival.co.uk.*

The Lord Mayor's Show (Nov)
Over 6,000 colourful participants show off London's history and cultural diversity. *www.lordmayorsshow.org.*

Christmas Lights (Dec)
Illuminations and dressed shop windows on Regent Street *(www.regentstreetonline. com)* and Oxford Street *(www.oxfordstreet. co.uk)*; and an enormous Christmas tree in Trafalgar Square.

SURREY, KENT AND SUSSEX

The three counties south of London have been influenced not only by the proximity of the capital, but also by that of the continent. Many of the wealthy inhabitants of the county towns will have commuted at one time or another to London – indeed Brighton is still known as "London-by-the-Sea" – while the remnants of, and deterrents to, foreign invaders can be seen in the Roman villas, medieval castles, famous battlefields, and historic naval dockyards. Christianity also established an early stronghold here, as witnessed by the great cathedrals at Canterbury and Chichester.

Highlights

1 Explore **Leeds Castle** (p135) – the most romantic in England
2 Make your own pilgrimage to **Canterbury Cathedral** (p136)
3 Stroll in the footsteps of smugglers in sleepy historic **Rye** (p143)
4 Marvel at the Oriental-Gothic **Brighton Pavilion** (p146)
5 Be transported back to Tudor and Jacobean times at **Knole** (p151)

Surrey

The capital's southwest commuter belt, Surrey has the busiest road network outside London. Despite this, however, it is also England's most wooded county with many wealthy bucolic havens. The county town of Guildford has no major attractions but is a pleasant base for exploring the region's houses and gardens, and maybe even theme parks

Kent

This southeasternmost part of Britain is famous for the iconic White Cliffs of Dover, defiantly facing France, across the Channel. Kent was formerly the cradle of British sea power, but since Victorian times, places such as Chatham and Rochester have become more famous for their connections with Charles Dickens.

The county is also known as "the Garden of England" for its abundance of orchards and hop gardens so it is no surprise that it boasts many fine gardens. Elsewhere are some of England's best-preserved and most beautiful castles, while Tunbridge Wells is a delightful spa town amid the bucolic Weald.

Sussex

Breezy, bohemian Brighton ("London-by-the-Sea") is the undisputed main attraction of England's south coast with its choice of attractions, and unrivalled dining and nightlife.

Beyond, the glorious South Downs and coastline of Eastbourne – itself a noteworthy resort – make Brighton a touring base too. West Sussex boasts Chichester Cathedral and its water meadows, while time-warped Rye is the jewel of East Sussex.

Leeds Castle

Food Heroes

Kent is known as The Garden Of England, largely on account of its **orchards** and **hop** gardens. Hops are used to flavour beer and were traditionally dried in conical shaped oast houses on farms. Today most hops are dried industrially but the oast houses remain a distinctive part of the Kent landscape. Not surprisingly Kent is famous for its brewing heritage and boasts Britain's oldest brewery, **Shepherd Neame**, located in Faversham. They have been rolling out the barrels since 1698 and are open to visitors for tours (www.shepherdneame. co.uk/brewery/tours).

Also at Faversham is Brogdale Farm (www.brogdalecollections.co.uk), home to the **National Fruit Collection**, including many varieties of apples and pears, plums and cherries, soft fruits, quinces, and more. Orchard tours run daily throughout most of the year and regular food festivals are staged.

Biddenden Vineyard is Kent's oldest commercial vineyard, est. 1969. In addition to still table wines and sparkling wines they also produce traditional Kentish ciders and farm-pressed apple juices (open for tours, www.biddendenvineyards. com). **Chapel Down**, at Tenterden (www.englishwinesgroup.com) is one of England's leading premium wine producers; apparently Chapel Down was served at Buckingham Palace as part of the Royal Wedding celebration. They are open for guided tours, have a very good wine and food store (showcasing local suppliers), and a restaurant, run by Richard Phillips who has a Michelin star to his name.

Whitstable is famous for its oysters. You can get them anywhere in town; the most famous restaurant and oyster bar is Wheelers, est 1856. In late July the town stages its oyster festival www.whitstableoysterfestival.com

In **Canterbury**, the Goods Shed (http://thegoodsshed.co.uk), a beautifully converted Victorian warehouse next to Canterbury West train station, houses a daily Farmers Market (closed Mon), food hall, a small diner and an excellent restaurant. It includes a butcher, bottle shop (featuring the largest number of British bottled beers in the South East, both to take away and to enjoy on the premises), a cheesemaker with around 40 artisanal varieties, and much more.

The county's major regional event of the year is the **Kent Food & Drink Festival**, staged in conjunction with the EuroFair food festival (third weekend Sept, www.canterburyeurofair.co.uk)

Denbies English Vineyard (open for tours, www.denbies.co.uk) in Dorking, Surrey is the UK's largest vineyard and produces sparkling and table wines. In Sussex, Lurgashall Winery (www.lurgashall.co.uk) enjoys a picturesque location and produces English liqueurs, meads and county wines. Its visitor centre and small museum, housed in 17C and 19C century farm buildings, show the many stages of production.

Surrey's largest farmer's market, at **Guildford**, attracts over 60 stallholders (first Tue month except Jan, www.guildford.gov.uk). **Shoreham-by-Sea** (second Sat of month) is home to the largest Farmers' Market in Sussex, also with around 60 stallholders. Based in the heart of the fashionable North Laine district, **Brighton Farm Market** (www.brightonfarmmarket.co.uk) is open daily with around 25 to 30 food stalls each Saturday.

One of Britain's most unusual food festivals, the **West Dean Chilli Fiesta**, is held in West Dean Gardens Sussex, (first weekend Aug, www.westdean.org. uk) showcasing over 300 chillis and their multiple uses, from chilli beer and ice cream to the hottest sauces known to man. Beer and cider tents sooth overheated palates.

Guildford
and the Surrey Downs

Guildford's prosperity can be traced back to the 18C, when it was crowded with coaching inns and travellers breaking their journey between Portsmouth and London. Today it is the quintessential wealthy middle-class southern town, complete with university.

TOWN CENTRE

The elegant cobbled High Street descends towards the River Wey, with the green slopes of the Mount beyond. The High Street is dominated by the **Guildhall** (*open Mon–Sat 9am–5pm; tours Tue and Thu, 2pm, 3pm; 01483 444 035; www.guildford.gov.uk*) with its ornate projecting clock. Nearby, the **Guildford House Gallery** (*155 High Street; open Tue–Sat 10am–4.45pm; 01483 444 751; www.guildford.gov.uk*) is an elegant late-17C town house displaying the borough's art collection. Opposite the landmark **Angel Hotel**, is the fine vaulted-stone **Undercroft** (*open May–Sept Wed 2–4pm, Sat noon–4pm; 01483 444 751; www.guildford.gov.uk*) built by a 13C wool merchant beneath a shop. It may also

Surrey Theme Parks

Close to Guildford lie two of the UK's leading theme parks: **Thorpe Park** (*01871 663 1673; www.thorpepark.com*) and **Chessington World of Adventures** (*01871 663 4477. www.chessington.com*). Both are open all summer long (Thorpe Park is famous for its cooling water rides) and at other times of year; call or see the websites for details. Thorpe Park is a "white-knuckle ride" theme park aimed at teens and adults, while Chessington focuses on younger children. However, there are thrills aplenty at both parks, which get very busy at holiday times. Try to arrive early and book online for big discounts.

- ▶ **Population:** 65,998.
- **Michelin Map:** Michelin Atlas p 19 or Map 504 S 30.
- **Info:** 14 Tunsgate. 01483 444 333. www.guildford.gov.uk.
- **Location:** Guildford lies 31mi/50km southwest of London. Both the train station and the bus station (behind the Friary Centre) are centrally located with regular services to London, Portsmouth and Winchester. A commuter town, Guildford has a fast London rail service.
- **Kids:** Thorpe Park; Chessington World of Adventures.

be visited on the free **guided city tour** (*May–Sept Mon 11am, Wed and Sun 2.30pm, Thu 7pm, meet at Tunsgate Arch; 01483 444 333, no booking required*), which includes the Tudor-style **Abbot's Hospital**, founded by Archbishop Abbot in 1619, and still in use as a home for the elderly. A five-minute walk from here, on Warren Road, is **The Spike**, built in 1906. This housed the forgotten classes of Edwardian England – the poor, the infirm, the ill and destitute. Costumed guides interpret the site (*Tue–Sat 10am–4pm, call in advance to book; 01483 444 333; www.guildford.gov.uk*).

Guildford Castle
Grounds: *Open daily dawn–dusk.* **Keep:** *Open Mar and Oct Sat–Sun 11am–4pm (daily during half-term); Apr–Sept daily 10am–5pm. Keep £2.80. 01483 444 751. www.guildford.gov.uk.* A 12C sandstone keep is virtually all that remains of the castle built by William the Conqueror shortly after the Battle of Hastings in 1066. Inside the grounds is Jeanne Argent's 1990 sculpture *Alice through the Looking Glass* commemorating Lewis Carroll, a frequent visitor to Guildford who rented a nearby house for his sisters. He died while visiting them and is buried in the Mount Cemetery.

WISLEY GARDEN

▶ 6mi/10km NE of Guildford on the A3. ◯ Open Mon–Fri 10am–6pm/dusk, Sat–Sun 9am–6pm/dusk. ◯ Closed 25 Dec. ⊙£9.90. ♿ P ✕. ℘0845 260 9000. www.rhs.org.uk/Gardens.

The flagship gardens of the Royal Horticultural Society are worth a visit in all seasons. Founded in 1903 and boasting many fine trees, there is a great range of different sorts of gardens, including a pinetum, an alpine house, a rock garden, and state-of-the-art new Glasshouse.

BOX HILL★

▶ NT. 5mi/24km E of Guildford via the A 246, 1mi/1.6km N of Dorking via the A24.

This glorious countryside of rolling woodland and chalk downland has been a famous beauty spot for over a century and is now in the care of the National Trust. They have installed an information centre including a Discovery Zone, aimed at children, and a popular café, The Servery (◯ café open daily late Mar–late Oct 9am–5pm, rest of year 10am–4pm, other areas from 11am; ◯ closed 25 Dec; ♿ P (£3); ℘01306 885 502; www.nation altrust.org.uk). If you're feeling energetic, they also hire mountain bikes.

DORKING

▶ 12mi/19 km E of Guildford on A 25. This typical well-to-do southeast English market town nestles in the Surrey Hills. Its main interest is **West Street**, with its fine old houses, 18 antique shops and the **Dorking Museum** (⊙ closed for renovation, due to reopen 2012; www. dorkingmuseum.co.uk).

The area around Dorking comprises some of Surrey's finest countryside, most notably **Leith Hill**, 5mi/8km south. It is crowned by a fortified folly tower which peaks at 1,029ft/314m above sea level, making it the highest point in southeast England (◯ open Jun–Jul and Sept–Oct Tue–Fri 10am–5pm, Aug Tue–Sun 10am–5pm, for rest of year see website; ◯ closed 25 Dec; ⊙£1.30; P; ℘01306 712 711; www.nation altrust.org.uk). You can climb its spiral staircase to enjoy panoramic views.

FARNHAM

▶ EH.10.6mi/17km W of Guildford via the A 31.

This attractive prosperous little market town by the River Wey centres on West Street/The Borough and Castle Hill. The latter is a beautiful wide street crowned by **Farnham Castle**. For 800 years, the Bishops of Winchester used the castle as a home and administrative centre. Only the keep (◯ open daily 9am/10am–dusk; ℘01252 721 194; www.english-heritage. org.uk) is open to visitors.

POLESDEN LACEY★

▶ NT. 5mi/8km) NW of Dorking, 2mi/3km S of Great Bookham off the A 246. ◯ Open Mar–Oct Wed–Sun 11am– 5pm; rest of year Sat–Sun 11am–4pm. ◯ Closed mid–31 Dec. ♿ P (£10.80)✕. ℘01372 458 203. www.nationaltrust.org.uk.

This Edwardian country estate once entertained the very highest people in the land and is set out to re-create its halcyon days. The house is notable for its interiors and collections, with lovely gardens offering superb views across the rolling Surrey Hills.

HATCHLANDS PARK

▶ NT. East Clandon. 5mi/8km E of Guildford ,via the A 246. ◯ Open Apr– Oct Tue–Thu 2–5.30pm; rest of year Sat–Sun 11am–4pm. ♿ P (£6.30)✕. ℘01483 222 482. www.nationaltrust.org.uk.

Hatchlands Park was built in the 1750s and today is a family home, containing a fine collection of paintings and Europe's largest collection of keyboard instruments, associated with J C Bach, Chopin and Elgar.

CLANDON PARK★

▶ NT. West Clandon. 3mi/5km E of Guildford via the A 3/A 247. ◯ Open mid-Mar–Oct Tue–Thu 11am–5pm. ♿ P (£7.70). ℘01483 222 502. www. nationaltrust.org.uk.

Built c.1730 this is one of the country's most complete examples of a Palladian mansion, with a superb collection of 18C furniture, porcelain and textiles.

North Kent Coast

Although this is one of England's least fashionable coastal stretches, the many Dickens connections, magnificent Leeds Castle and the attractions of the Thanet Resorts (including the new Turner Gallery) make North Kent well worth a visit.

◉ **Michelin Map:** Map 504 V 29.
◉ **Don't Miss:** World Naval Base, Chatham; Leeds Castle; any major exhibition at the Turner Gallery.
👥 **Kids:** World Naval Base, Chatham; Dickens World.

ROCHESTER

▶ *35mi/53km E of London. The train station is on the High Street with a frequent London service. Population: 23,971.* 🛈*95 High Street.* ℘*01634 843 666. www.medway.gov.uk.*

The Romans built Durobrivae to dominate the point where Watling Street crossed the River Medway. A 12C Norman castle now stands tall, while the walled town is cut in two by "the silent High Street, full of gables with old beams and timbers" (Charles Dickens). In fact Rochester and the Medway area are the scene of several of Dickens' novels, notably *Pickwick Papers* and *Great Expectations*.

The River Medway cuts Rochester in two. In the centre of town, on the south side of the river near the High Street bridge is the **castle** ★ *(EH;* ⊙*open daily late Mar–Sept 10am–6pm, Oct–late Mar 10am–4pm;* ⊙*closed 1 Jan, 24–26 Dec;* ⊛*£5.50;* ℘*01634 402 276; www.english-heritage. org.uk),* whose early **curtain walls** were built by Gundulf, Bishop of Rochester and architect of Rochester Cathedral and the Tower of London. The present massive **keep** was built in 1127; its ruins

are an outstanding example of Norman military architecture.

Close by, the **cathedral** ★ *(*⊙*open year-round Sun–Fri 7.30am–6pm (Sat 7.30am–5pm);* ⬦*guided tours £4;* ♿✗*;* ℘*01634 843 366; www.rochestercathedral.org)* is where Bishop Gundulf (1024–1108) held England's second episcopal see, from 1077. The cathedral was extended at least twice and is mostly 12C and 13C. Of particular interest is the Norman west front, and its centrepiece, the exuberantly sculptured **west doorway** (1160). Beyond the six Norman **nave bays** the cathedral is essentially Early English. The painting on the choir wall is the *Wheel of Fortune* and dates from the 13C. Note the carvings on the chapter room doorway (c.1350). On the north side between the two transepts is Gundulf's **tower** (c.1100).

Back on the High Street, the **Guildhall** *(*⊙*open year-round Tue–Sun 10am–4.30pm;* ⊙*closed Christmas;* ♿*;* ℘*01634 848 717; www.medway.gov.uk)* is a handsome Renaissance building containing a museum with an actual-size section of a piece of an infamous Medway hulk (Victorian prison ship) alongside displays on more genteel 19C local life.

The Roman Conquest

The Medway area is rich in prehistoric and Roman sites. During Emperor Claudius' invasion of Britain, Roman legions landed near Richborough in Kent and moved westwards. An unhewn stone (15ft/5m high), erected near a ford on the Medway at Snodland, south of Rochester, in 1998, is a belated memorial to a decisive Roman victory in AD 43 over the army of the Celtic king Cunobelinus – Shakespeare's Cymbeline. This event sealed the fate of Britain coming under the Roman Empire. The battle probably took place near a fordable point on the Medway – near Snodland according to modern historians.

▲▲ WORLD NAVAL BASE, CHATHAM★★

▶ *2mi/3km NE of Rochester.* ◐*Open mid-Feb–late Mar daily 10am–4pm; late Mar–late Nov daily 10am–6pm; Dec–Feb Sat–Sun 10am–4pm.* ◉*£15.50, child £10.50.* ♿🅿✗. ✆*01634 823 800; 01634 823 807.*
 www.thedockyard.co.uk.

Established in the reign of Henry VIII, this cradle of British sea power built nearly 500 ships, including *HMS Victory*, before the Royal Navy finally left in 1984. The large complex (80 acres/32ha) of historic maritime buildings and docks now reinterprets the life of the dockyard through exhibits and demonstrations, from the **Sail and Colour Loft** (flags and sails) to the **Ropery**, the award-winning **Wooden Walls** (construction of large wooden ships), **Lifeboat!** and **3 Slip**. The last refers to the immense covered slipway built in 1838, then Europe's largest wide-span timber structure.

▲▲ DICKENS WORLD

▶ *Leviathan Way, Chatham.*
◐*Open year-round daily 10am–4.30pm (Sat–Sun and hols 5.30pm); closed Sept–Easter Tue–Sun); last entry 90min before closing.* ◐*Closed 25 Dec.* ◉*£13, child £8.* ♿🅿✗. ✆*01634 890 421. www.dickensworld.co.uk.*

This highly commercialised theme park is dedicated to the life, works and times of Britain's greatest novelist, and is set on the site where Dickens' father worked as a clerk in the Naval Dockyard. Young Charles lived most of his childhood in Chatham, drawing on it for inspiration in his novels.

LEEDS CASTLE★★

▶ *7mi/11km E of Maidstone, M 20 j 8.*
◐*Open daily Apr–Sept10.30am–6pm; (Oct–Mar 5pm). 10.30am,–5pm; last entry 90min before closing.* ◐*Closed 25 Dec, see website Jul and Nov dates.* ◉*£18.50.* ♿🅿✗. ✆*01622 765 400. www.leeds-castle.com.*

Originally Norman, built on two islands in a lake, Leeds Castle was described by Lord Conway as "the loveliest castle in the world", and is certainly one of the most picturesque in Great Britain. A romantic stone **bridge** links the keep, which rises sheer from the lake, with the turreted and battlemented main building. The interior is graced by splendid **works of art** (14C–19C): statues, carvings and tapestries. The glorious **park** and **gardens** include an aviary, grotto and maze.

WHITSTABLE

▶ *7mi/11km N of Canterbury via the A290.*

Famous for its oysters, and wide choice of fish and seafood eating places, this pleasant little fishing town makes for an ideal stroll along the pebbly seashore after a day in Canterbury.

THANET RESORTS
Broadstairs

▶ *21mi/34km E of Canterbury via the A 256.*

The quietest and prettiest of the Thanet resorts, Broadstairs is also closely associated with Dickens, who made his holiday home here during his most prolific writing years, calling it "Our English Watering Place". It is now home to the **Dickens House Museum** and a tourist information point (◐*open daily Easter–Jun and Oct 2–5pm, Jul–Sept 10am–5pm;* ◉*£3.25;* ✆*01843 861 232/863 453 when museum closed; www.dickensfellowship.org).*

In 2011 the sleepy seaside town of **Margate** (3.6mi/5.8km) northwest became host to the state-of-the-art **Turner Gallery** (◐*open year-round Tue–Sun and bank hol Mon 10am–7pm;* ✆*01843 233 000;* ♿🅿✗; *www.turnercontemporary.org),* dedicated to Britain's greatest landscape artist, J M W Turner, who was a regular visitor. The gallery is the largest art space in the Southeast, outside of London.

Ramsgate

▶ *2.5mi/4km south of Broadstairs.*

The largest of the Thanet Resorts, Ramsgate owes much of its character to its Georgian **Royal Harbour** – now a huge marina – and to its popularity as a bathing resort in Victorian times which has left a rich legacy of Victorian architecture.

Canterbury★★★
and around

The ecclesiastical capital of England, rich in medieval atmosphere, is dominated by its renowned cathedral. The city lies on Watling Street, the great Roman thoroughfare linking London with the port of Dover. It is the terminus of the **Pilgrims' Way**, a trackway of prehistoric origin used by many of the worshippers at the shrine of St Thomas, England's best-known martyr.

A BIT OF HISTORY

Early settlement – Canterbury's recorded history begins with Emperor Claudius' invasion of AD 43 and the foundation of the walled town of Durovernum. After the Roman withdrawal early in the 5C, the city was settled by Jutish invaders and renamed *Cantwarabyrig*, or "Stronghold of the Men of Kent".

A Christian see – In AD 597 **St Augustine** arrived in Kent to convert the pagan population to Christianity. The city became the centre of the English Church and Augustine was consecrated as first archbishop.

In 1170 a later archbishop, **Becket**, was assassinated in the cathedral by four of Henry II's knights who had taken all too literally their ruler's desire to "rid me of this turbulent priest". Thomas was canonised two years later and his shrine immediately attracted count-

- ▶ **Population:** 36,464.
- ⛪ **Michelin Map:** Michelin Atlas p 13 or Map 504 X 30.
- 🛈 **Info:** 12/13 Sun Street. ✆01227 378 100. www.canterbury.co.uk.
- ▶ **Location:** 56mi/90km east of London. The town has two train stations. Canterbury East, just outside the old walls, receives trains from London Victoria and Dover; Canterbury West is five minutes' walking time from the western section of wall, with services from London Charing Cross and Waterloo (East). The bus station is on St George's Lane inside the walls.
- 🔎 **Don't Miss:** Canterbury's stunning cathedral and the Black Prince's tomb.
- ⏱ **Timing:** At least a day.
- 🚶 **Walking Tours:** Canterbury Walking Tours start from the Visitor Information Centre (*daily Apr–Oct 11am, 2pm, Nov–Mar 11am*; ⬮*£6*; ✆*01227 459 779*). They also do many themed tours (see website for details).

less pilgrims, many of whose stories are recounted in **Chaucer's** *Canterbury*

Choir, Canterbury Cathedral

Y. Duhamel/MICHELIN

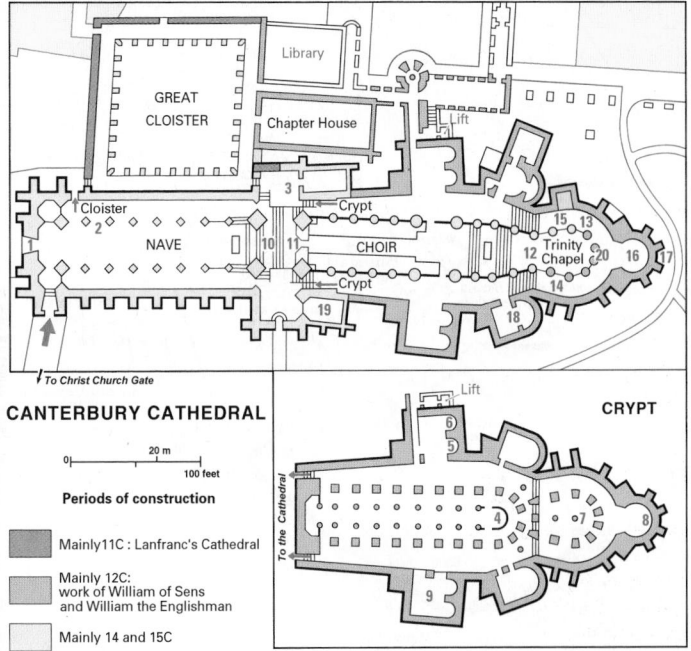

CANTERBURY CATHEDRAL

Periods of construction

Mainly 11C : Lanfranc's Cathedral

Mainly 12C:
work of William of Sens
and William the Englishman

Mainly 14 and 15C

CRYPT

Tales. The cathedral's monastery was the largest in the country and by the 13C Grey Friars and Black Friars were established here as well. This thriving monastic life came to an end with the Dissolution of the Monasteries; the cathedral's treasures were appropriated by Henry VIII, the saint's shrine was destroyed and the pilgrimages ended.

A prosperous city – The post-Reformation saw the arrival of French Huguenot refugees at the invitation of Elizabeth I. These skilled craftsmen contributed to Canterbury's prosperity and in spite of the depredations of the Puritans in the Civil War, the city continued to flourish.

Greater damage was suffered in the "Baedeker" bombing raids of 1942, when part of the historic centre was reduced to rubble though fortunately the cathedral remained untouched.

Today Canterbury is the thriving centre of eastern Kent and the seat of a modern university. The city exerts nearly as strong a pull on the modern tourist as in medieval times and remains a religious centre. The See of Canterbury remains the focal point of the worldwide Anglican Communion.

CANTERBURY CATHEDRAL★★★

🕐*Open (services permitting)*
Mon–Sat summer 9am–5.30pm; winter 9am–5pm. Crypt opens 10am; Sun year-round 12.30–2.30pm; check website for additional hours and closures before visiting. ✆*Guided tour (75min) Mon–Sat £5.* ⊜*£9*&. ✆*01227 762 862. www.canterbury-cathedral.org.*

The original cathedral built by St Augustine was destroyed in 1067 and replaced by the first Norman archbishop, **Lanfranc**. Archbishop **Anselm** replaced his predecessor's choir with an ambitious structure. It too was gutted by fire in 1174, four years after Becket's murder, though the crypt and nave were spared. As the cathedral had become the most important centre of pilgrimage in northern Europe, the opportunity was seized to rebuild in a manner worthy of the martyr, in an early Gothic style which was to be of great subsequent influence in the development of English architec-

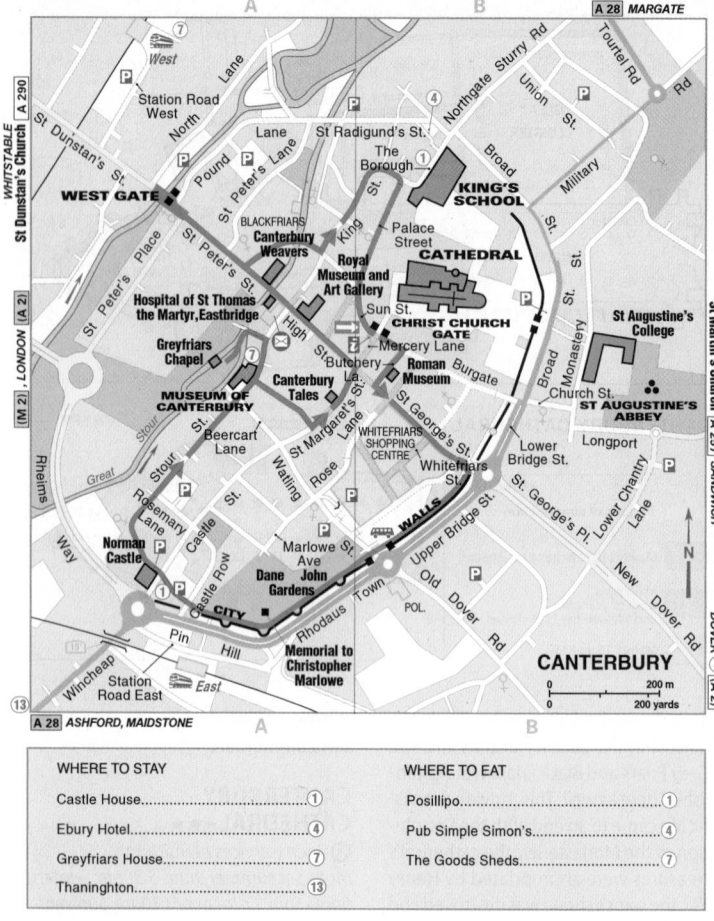

WHERE TO STAY		WHERE TO EAT	
Castle House	①	Posillipo	①
Ebury Hotel	④	Pub Simple Simon's	④
Greyfriars House	⑦	The Goods Sheds	⑦
Thaninghton	⑬		

ture. The work was started by the French architect **William of Sens**, completed by "William the Englishman".

The nave and cloisters were rebuilt in Perpendicular style in the 14C; the transepts and towers, including **Bell Harry Tower**, crowning the entire building, were completed in the 15C. The north-west tower was demolished in 1832 and replaced by a copy of the southwest tower.

Christ Church Gate★ (D), built in the early-16C and decorated with coats of arms, is the main entrance to the cathedral.

Mercery Lane★, a bustling street which has kept its medieval charm, offers an impressive view of Christ Church Gate and the western towers.

Interior

Enter through the SW porch.

In the **nave** built (1392–1404) by Henry Yevele, the slender columns soar majestically to the lofty vault and aisles. The great west window (**1**) contains 12C glass (note Adam delving). Near the north door stands a 17C Classical marble **font** (**2**) depicting the Four Evangelists and the Twelve Apostles. In the north transept the "Altar of the Sword's Point" and a modern cruciform sculpture commemorate the **site of Becket's martyrdom** (**3**). Steps lead down to the 12C vaulted **crypt**. The delicate screens of the **Chapel of Our Lady Undercroft** (**4**) and the capitals are masterpieces of Romanesque carving. The transept houses the altars of St Nicholas (**5**) and

St Mary Magdalene (6). In the eastern extension (post-1174) with its massive columns and pointed vaults is the site (7) where the body of St Thomas Becket was entombed until 1220. Beyond is the Jesus Chapel (8). The south transept was the Black Prince's Chantry (9), subsequently the Huguenots' Church; it is still used for services in French today.

Leave the crypt on the south side to return to the upper level.

Turn right into the crossing to admire the lace-like **fan vaulting underneath the Bell Harry Tower** (10); the bosses are decorated with coats of arms of those responsible for building the tower.

Pass through the iron gates into the choir which contains a mid-15C **screen** (11) with figures of six kings, the High Altar and the 13C marble **St Augustine's Chair** (12) traditionally used for the enthronement of the Archbishop, Primate of All England. From either of the choir aisles the long vistas back to the nave reveal the evolution of Gothic style over three centuries.

The wonderful medieval **stained-glass** windows include one depicting the Miracles (13) wrought by St Thomas in the Trinity Chapel. His shrine, placed here in 1220, has long gone, though the fine Roman mosaic pavement in front of it remains. Among the remarkable tombs is that of the **Black Prince** (14) (d.1376); above hang replicas of his helm, crest, shield, gauntlets and sword; the fragile originals are displayed nearby. Opposite is the alabaster **tomb of Henry IV** (15) (d.1413) and Queen Joan of Navarre. In the **Corona** (16), a circular chapel said to have housed the top of St Thomas' skull, there is an early-13C **Redemption window** (17) behind the altar.

The **Chapel of St Anselm** (18) – *(SW corner of Trinity Chapel)* is mostly Norman and contains a rare 12C wall painting (high up in the apse).

Off the south transept *(main exit)* is the **Chapel of St Michael** (19) with Renaissance and Baroque memorials.

Exterior

The great cathedral with its soaring buttresses, pinnacles and towers above which Bell Harry rises to a height of almost 250ft/76m, is an impressive sight. The elaborate vaulting of the galleried **Great Cloister** (rebuilt c.1400) is ornamented with grotesque faces, religious symbols and scenes of everyday life. Off the east walk is the **Chapter House** with its intricately ribbed oak roof and Perpendicular windows with glass depicting characters in the cathedral's history.

On the eastern side of the cathedral precincts is the **King's School**★(B), an ancient foundation remodelled by Henry VIII in 1541. It occupies buildings of the former cathedral monastery grouped in the main around Green Court.

The immense length of the cathedral is best appreciated from this point. Note the splendid **Norman staircase** (12C).

✿ CITY CENTRE WALK

Start your walk at Christ Church Gate and follow Burgate to the **Canterbury Roman Museum** *(Butchery Lane; ◷open year-round daily 10am–5pm, last entry 4pm); ◷closed 1 Jan, Good Fri, 25–26 Dec; ◷£6; ♿; ℘01227 785 575; www.canterbury-museums.co.uk).* Deep below current street level, part of Canterbury's excavated Roman levels have been transformed into this modern museum, which uses contemporary techniques to bring the Roman city of Durovernum Cantiacorum to life. Authentic reconstructions include a Roman marketplace with stalls and a house with kitchen.

Moving on, follow St George's Street to get to the **city walls**. If you leave the old walled city (and our marked tour) to the east on Church Street, you come to **St Augustine's Abbey**★★ *(EH; ◷open daily Jul–Aug 10am–6pm, Sept–Jun 10am– 5pm; ◷closed 1 Jan, 24–26 Dec; ◷£4.80; ♿; ℘ 01227 767 345; www.english-heritage.org.uk),* founded in AD 597 by St Augustine. Extensive ruins remain of the great Norman abbey church, such as the early-14C Great Gateway.

There are also vestiges of Saxon burial places and of the church of St Pancras (7C); the walls are built of Roman brick.

Continue on Longport to North Holmes Road and take a left for **St Martin's Church**★ (🕐 open Tue, Thu and Sat 11am–3pm; ♿; ✆01233 720 410; www.martinpaul.org) on St Martin's Hill, the oldest functioning church in England. When St.Augustine arrived from Rome in AD597 to convert the English, he set up his mission here. It has Roman brickwork in its walls and a Perpendicular tower. Inside there is a Norman font, a Norman *piscina* and a "Leper Window".

Returning to the tour marked on the map, walk along the top of the well-preserved medieval **city walls**, stoutly built on Roman foundations. Follow them south and you will come to the **Dane John Mound**, which overlooks a charming park and a **memorial** to Christopher Marlowe, born in Canterbury. At the end of this stretch of the wall you will find the 11C **Norman castle** built of flint with bands of stone, of which only the keep remains.

Head north from here along Stour Street and you will come to the **🚶🛈Museum of Canterbury**★ (🕐open year-round Mon–Sat 10am–5pm, (last entry 4pm); 🕐closed 1 Jan, Good Fri, 25–26 Dec; 💷£8, child free (up to 2 per adult); ✆01227 475 202; www.canterbury-museums.co.uk). This modern museum is housed in the Poor Priests' Hospital, founded in the 13C as an almshouse. It presents the history of Canterbury from prehistoric to modern times including lively interactive displays. Oliver Postgate and Peter Firmin created their much-loved children's programmes just outside Canterbury and here you can see the real Bagpuss, original Clangers, Ivor the Engine and Noggin the Nog. Rupert Bear was also created by a local lady and "he" also has a devoted section.

On leaving the museum, continue to no.6 Stour Street and take the little alley to your left, then cross the bridge for **Greyfriar's chapel and garden** (for opening times, see Eastbridge Hospital, below). This was the first English Franciscan friary, built in 1267. The undercroft was originally a pilgrims' dormitory. Upstairs are the refectory and the chapel. The chapel has a fine timber roof. **Greyfriar's House** is the only building now remaining of the first English Franciscan friary, built in 1267 in the lifetime of St Francis of Assisi, 43 years after the first friars settled in Canterbury. An exhibition explores the history of this important settlement.

Return to Stour Street, then take Hawks Lane and St Margaret Street to reach **🚶🛈The Canterbury Tales** (🕐open year-round daily 9.30/10am–4.30/5pm; 🕐closed 1 Jan, 25–26 Dec; 💷£7.95, child £5.90; ♿; ✆01227 454 888; www.canterburytales.org.uk). The converted interior of St Margaret's Church is the setting for this entertaining multimedia attraction, which popularises and brings to life the vivid 14C characters created by Chaucer as they make their pilgrimage from London to Canterbury.

Continue up St Margaret Street and turn left on the High Street to see **The Beaney Institute** (better know simply as "The Beaney"). Formerly home to the **Royal Museum and Art Gallery**, this is scheduled to reopen in Spring 2012 after a three-year closure (see www.futurebeaney.com for more details).

Further up the High Street and across the road is the **Hospital of St Thomas the Martyr, Eastbridge** (🕐hospital open Mon–Sat 10am–5pm; chapel open Easter–Sept 2–4pm; gardens open early morning–5pm/dusk; see Greyfriar's above; ✆01227 471 688; www.eastbridgehospital.org.uk). Founded in 1180, the hospital served as lodgings (in those days hospital meant a place of hospitality) for poor pilgrims to the shrine of St Thomas. After the Dissolution in the 16C, the hospital was re-founded as a boys' school and then as an almshouse, a role it still fulfils today. The building presents a black flint exterior. The 14C door leads into a vaulted hall (11C).

Cross the bridge; on your right you will find the **Canterbury Weavers**. This group of picturesque Tudor houses (by tradition, c.1500) overlooking the River Stour takes its name from the refugee Huguenot weavers who settled in the area. Note the replica of the medieval **ducking stool** that was once located here and which was used to "test" whether or not a woman was a witch. The award-winning **Canterbury Historic River Tours** (*40min tours run every 15–20 mins, daily Mar–early Nov 10am–5pm, and last 40 min; £7.50;* ℘*07790 534 744; www.canterburyrivertours.co.uk*) operate from here.

Continue up St Peter's Street to the **Westgate Towers**★ (*St Peter's Street;* ⏰*open year-round daily 10am–4.30pm;* ⏷*£4;* ℘*01227 789 576; www.canterbury-westgatetowers.com*). This city landmark is the last of the gatehouses that once formed part of the city walls. From 1830 it served as a gaol and the present museum is devoted to this period. From the battlements there are fine **views** of the city and cathedral.

Continue up St Dunstan's Street (leaving our marked tour) and turn left on London Road to see **St Dunstan's Church** (⏰*open year-round, Mon–Sat 9am–4pm, Sun 8am–6pm;* ⏰*closed Good Fri, Christmas week;* ℘*01227 463 654*). The church was founded in the late-1C and used by Henry II in 1174 when he changed into penitential garments for his involvement in the murder of St Thomas Becket. The head of Sir Thomas More is thought to be buried in the Roper family vault. Return back down St Peter's Street; up St Peter's Lane is **Blackfriars Monastery**. All that remains of this 13C Dominican friary are the Great Hall and the Refectory. Back on St Peter's Street, continue towards the West Gate and turn left on The Friars; a statue of **Christopher Marlowe** stands before the theatre that takes his name.

Cross the Stour and turn left on King Street; turn right on Palace Street and continue on Sun Street. The walk takes in beautiful medieval buildings, including **Conquest House** and **Tudor House**.

EXCURSION
👥 Howletts Wild Animal Park

▶ *Bekesbourne Road, Bekesbourne. 3mi/5km S off the A 2.* ⏰*Open daily Apr–Oct 9.30am–6pm; winter (last entry 90min before closing). 10am–5pm (3.30pm last entry).* ⏰*Closed 25 Dec.* ⏷ *£19.95, child £15.95 (book online for discount).* ♿🅿✕. ℘*0844 842 4647. www.howletts.net.*

Set in 90 acres/36ha of beautiful ancient parkland, Howletts is famous as the home of the world's largest family group of gorillas in captivity and the UK's largest group of African elephants. Among the 90 or so other rare and endangered species from around the world are tigers and clouded leopards, black rhinos, tapirs and giant anteaters. A **Treetops Walkways course** (⏷ additional charge) gives adventurous visitors a monkey's-eye view of the park!

Cinque Ports

Traditionally pronounced "sink", even though it refers to the French for five, the Cinque Ports was a maritime league of Kent and Sussex towns established in the 11C by Edward the Confessor to supply ships and men for the defence of the realm. The five were Dover, Hastings, Hythe, New Romney and Sandwich, with Rye and Winchelsea later added, with the title of "ancient towns". This defence, and sometime offence, was against the French, who at the nearest point – from Dover

> ⓖ **Michelin Map:** Map 504;
> ⓓ **Don't Miss:** Dover Castle, Bodiam Castle, Rye;
> 👥 **Kids:** Dover Castle Secret Wartime Tunnels.

to Cap Gris Nez – were (and still are!) just 21mi/34km distant. The towns today have very different functions and characteristics and a large part of modern Dover's remit is to welcome, not repel, foreign visitors: Hasting's most famous moment was almost a millennium ago

DOVER

▶ *84mi/134km southeast of London.*
Dover Priory train station (Approach Road) has a frequent service and shuttle buses to the docks. Bus station: Pencester Road. Both are a 5min walk from the centre. Population: 34,179. ℹ️ *Old Town Gaol, Biggin Street.* ℘ *01304 205 108. www.whitecliffscountry.org.uk.*

Flanked by the famous white cliffs, Dover has been the southeast gateway to England since Roman times, receiving sailing ships, steamships and hovercraft. Despite the opening of the Channel Tunnel the port's cross-Channel ferry traffic remains intense. Dover was badly damaged during the Second World War but retains many historic properties giving the town islands of elegance rarely seen in a working port. German bombs and shells from batteries on the French coast devastated Dover but, together with post-war redevelopment, helped reveal the archaeology of this ancient port. Head east from Dover Priory train station and you come to York Street,then New Street, home to the **Roman Painted House** (○ *open 1st 3 wks Apr and Jun–Sept Tue–Sun 10am–5pm, last wk Apr–May Tue and Sat 10am–5pm;* ○£3; ℘ *01304 203 279; www.theromapaintedhouse.co.uk),* which has the finest Roman wall-decorations to be seen in situ north of the Alps. Just around the corner is the **Dover Museum** (*Market Square;* ○ *open year-round Mon–Sat 10am–5pm (also Apr–Sept Sun until 3pm);* ○*closed 1 Jan, 25–26 Dec;* ○£3; ♿; ℘ *01304 201 066; www.dover museum.co.uk),* whose artefacts include a 50ft/15m section of the world's oldest known seagoing boat, the 3,000-year-old **Dover Bronze Age boat**. Just outside the centre, at Langdon Cliffs, Upper Road is **The Gateway to the White Cliffs Visitor Centre** (*NT;* ○*open daily Mar–Oct 10am–5pm, Nov–Feb 11am–4pm;* ♿ ▣✕; ℘ *01304 202 756; www.nationaltrust.org.uk).* This excellent modern facility offers spectacular views of the iconic chalk cliffs and views across the world's busiest shipping lanes to France. You can also begin dramatic clifftop countryside walks from here.

👥 Dover Castle★★

EH. ○*Open late Mar–Jul and Sept daily 10am–6pm; Aug daily 9.30am–6pm; Oct daily 10am–5pm; reduced hours in winter, see website.* ○*Closed 1 Jan, 24–26 Dec.* ○£16, child £9.60. ▣✕. ℘ *01304 211 067. www.english-heritage.org.uk.*

The high land to the east, commanding town and port, has been fortified since the Iron Age. The Romans built a lighthouse (Pharos) which still stands within the castle walls, and the Saxons a church (St-Mary-in-Castro). The defences were strengthened by William the Conqueror, then by Henry II, who in the 1180s added the splendid **keep**.

The spectacular **Constable's Tower** dates from the early-13C. The warren of tunnels and secret chambers beneath the castle dates from early times but was greatly added to in the Napoleonic period and during the Second World War. Operation Dynamo, the evacuation from Dunkirk in 1940, was planned and directed from here.

A guided tour (timed ticket system) of the 👥 **Secret Wartime Tunnels**★ takes visitors through the dimly lit chambers and passageways of the underground hospital and communications centre for the Combined Headquarters. A dramatic new exhibition vividly re-creates the Dunkirk evacuation, complete with dramatic projections of swooping Spitfires and real film footage.

SANDWICH★

▶ *3mi/21km E via the A 257.*
The road from Canterbury runs through the pretty village of **Wingham**. The fascinating medieval borough of Sandwich was one of the original Cinque Ports, is still largely contained within its earthen ramparts and seems to have changed little since the River Stour began to silt up in the 15C. Its pretty houses of all periods cluster around its three **churches**: St Clement's with a sturdy, arcaded Norman tower; St Peter's with a bulbous cupola reflecting Flemish influence; and St Mary's, much reduced by the collapse of its tower in 1668.

DEAL

▶ *8mi/13km N via the A 258.*

One of the most attractive seaside towns in Kent, Deal is also notable for its two very well-preserved Tudor castles. Deal Castle (*EH; ⏰open Apr–Sept daily 10am–6pm Oct daily 10am–4pm, reduced hours in winter; see website. ⏰closed 1 Jan, 1–3 Jul, 24–26 Dec; ⏰£4.80; ♿🅿 ☎01304 372 762; www.english-heritage.org.uk*) marks the site where Julius Caesar is alleged to have first landed in Britain in 55 BC. It is one of the finest Tudor artillery castles in England, and among the earliest and most elaborate of a chain of coastal forts which included Walmer Castle.

WALMER CASTLE

EH. ▶ *1mi/1.6km S of Deal.* ♿⏰*Open late Mar–Jul and Sept daily 10am–6pm; Aug daily 9.30am–6pm; Oct daily 10am–5pm; reduced hours in winter, see website.* ⏰*Closed 1 Jan, 24–26 Dec.* ⏰*£7.30.* 🅿✕. ☎*01304 364 288. www.english-heritage.org.uk.*

Built by order of Henry VIII, this fine Tudor-rose-shaped castle evolved into the official residence of the Lord Warden of the Cinque Ports (⏰*see Rye, below*). The most notable incumbents were the Duke of Wellington – the armchair in which he died and an original pair of "Wellington boots", worn at Waterloo, are on display – and the late Queen Elizabeth, the Queen Mother, who made regular visits to the castle. Beautiful gardens adjoin the house with fine coastal views.

ROMNEY AND DENGE MARSHES

▶ *31mi/50km southwest via the coast road.*

This area of reclaimed marshland and mile after mile of shingle is a marked contrast to the rest of Kent's green pasturelands. Locally, it is best known for the Dungeness (nuclear) power station. Close by, near Lydd, is the **RSPB Dungeness** bird reserve (⏰*open daily 9am–9pm, or dusk if earlier, visitor centre open Mar–Oct 10am–5pm, Nov–Feb 10am–4pm;* ⏰*closed 24–26 Dec;* ⏰*£3;* ☎*01797 320 588; www.rspb.org.uk*).

The most interesting way to arrive here is aboard the "world's smallest public railway". The **Romney, Hythe and Dymchurch Railway** (⏰*operates year-round, see website for schedule and fares;* ☎*01797 362 353; www.rhdr.org.uk*) is a 15-in gauge line, built in 1927 and operating steam and diesel trains between Hythe and Dungeness via Dymchurch, St Mary's Bay, New Romney and Romney Sands stations. The total journey time is around 65 minutes.

RYE★★

▶ *36mi/58km SW of Dover. Population: 3,708.* 🏛*Heritage Centre, Strand Quay, Rye.* ☎*01797 226 696. www.ryeheriage. co.uk or www.visitrye.co.uk.*

This exquisite little hill town standing at the confluence of three rivers is visible far across the vast expanse of eastward-stretching levels – a multitude of red-roofed houses building up to a massive squat-towered church. Tranquil centuries of decline and its former remoteness have preserved Rye's charming townscape, though much of its medieval fabric wears a Georgian exterior. Many artists and writers, among them Henry James, have lived here.

Rye's early history was one of struggle both on and with the sea. It lies just 40mi/64km northwest of Boulogne and was added to the Cinque Ports; despite this it suffered repeated sackings by the French. It was also battered by storms that changed the course of the River Rother in the 13C and later destroyed many of its buildings. The town is still a minor port, though the sea's retreat has left it 2mi/3km inland.

Old Town★★

With its steep narrow streets, a wealth of different building materials and sudden glimpses of the countryside, the whole of Rye repays exploration on foot. Cobbled **Mermaid Street**★ rises sharply. Its varied buildings include the 15C **Mermaid Inn**, once the haunt of ruthless smuggler gangs. Looking towards Church Square is the handsome Georgian façade of **Lamb House** (*NT;* ⏰*open mid-Mar–late Oct Tue and Sat 2–6pm;*

£4.30; £3; 01580 762 334) ,home of Henry James from 1897 and later of the satirical novelist E F Benson.

South of Cinque Ports Street is **St Mary's Church** (*open daily, except during services, 9am–5.30pm, winter 9am–4.30pm; £2.50 contribution requested to climb tower; 01797 224 935)*, a large impressive building, begun in the 12C. Note the 16C clock, its pendulum (18ft/5m) swinging inside, its elaborate face on the outside of the north transept, flanked by jolly painted quarter boys who strike the quarters (but not the hours). From the tower there is an incomparable **view**★ of Rye's rooftops and its countryside.

BODIAM CASTLE★★

NT. 13mi/21km NW on the A 268. After 11mi/18km turn left at Sandhurst and follow minor roads. Open 1st wk Jan–mid-Feb Sat–Sun 10.30am–4pm; mid-Feb–Oct daily 10.30am–6pm; Nov–Dec Wed–Sun 10.30am–4pm. Closed mid-Dec–1st wk Jan. £6.10. (£2) 01580 830 196. www.nationaltrust.org.uk.

In a pretty landscaped setting among low hills, overlooking the levels of the River Rother, this perfect example of a late medieval castle sits four-square within its protecting moat. It was built in 1385–88 to block movement inland by marauding Frenchmen up the (then navigable) river, and it retains its great gatehouse, curtain walls and drum towers (60ft/18m high) at each corner.

HASTINGS CASTLE AND THE 1066 STORY

Castle Hill Road. 12mi/19km SW on the A 259. Open Feb half-term–Oct daily 11am–5pm; winter daily 11am–4pm. £4.25. 01424 781 111. www.discoverhastings.co.uk.

The ruins of William the Conqueror's first English castle (originally a wooden structure) stand high above the old town and seaside resort below. The history of the castle and the famous battle of 1066 are told in an entertaining audio-visual presentation.

BATTLE★

18mi/29km southwest on the A 259, B 2093 and A 2100.

The momentous victory, on 14 October 1066, of the Normans over King Harold's English army is marked by the remains of the great commemorative **Battle Abbey**★ *(EH; open Apr–Sept daily 10am–6pm, Oct–Mar daily 10am–4pm, reduced hours in winter, see website; closed 1 Jan, 24–26 Dec; £7.30; (charge) 01424 775 705; www. english-heritage.org.uk)* built on its hilltop site by William the Conqueror, and also in the name of the little town which grew up to serve it.

The **1066 Battle of Hastings** exhibition features CGI film and interactive displays to tell the story of the great battle and paints a picture of England at the time of the Conquest. There is also an audio tour of the battlefield.

Over the humble buildings of the town's marketplace rises the imposing 14C **gatehouse**, battlemented and richly decorated. Most of the great Benedictine abbey beyond was dismantled at the Dissolution, though its outlines may be traced. The church altar, erected at William's command, is above the spot where Harold fell.

A **museum** in the gatehouse presents an exhibition on monastic life and the history of the abbey.

Battlefield★

From the **terrace walk** there is a view of the tranquil scene over which this most decisive of English battles was fought. It was on this ridge that Harold deployed his men after their exhausting forced march from York. The day-long battle was fierce and bloody; a pathway with topographical models at intervals follows its course along the fateful slopes.

WINCHELSEA

40mi/65km SW of Dover.

Winchelsea was founded by Edward I to take the place of an older town of the same name, which had been lost to the sea in a series of great storms and now lies beneath the waters of Rye Bay. It rose to become one of the major ports of the religion and was added to the Cinque Ports. Like Rye it was pillaged by the French; the ruined St Thomas Church is a reminder of this period as are its three medieval gates. Unlike Rye, however, the town today is quiet and not on the main tourist trail.

BATEMAN'S

NT. ❍ *Bateman's Lane. 0.5mi/0.8km S of Burwash. 58mi/93km W of Dover via the A 20 and A 259.* ◷ *Open mid-Mar–late Oct Sat–Wed 11am–5pm; 1st fortnight Dec Sat–Sun 11.30am–3.30pm.* ☞*£8.60.* ♿ ▣ ✕. ℘*01435 882 302. www.nationaltrust.org.uk.*

Surrounded by the wooded landscape of the Sussex Weald, this handsome sturdy 17C house, with its mullioned windows and oak beams, was the home of Rudyard Kipling from 1902 until he died here in 1936. When Kipling moved in It had no bathroom, no running water upstairs and no electricity but he still loved it. Today the rooms, described by Kipling as "untouched and unfaked", remain much as he left them, with Oriental rugs and artefacts reflecting his strong association with the East, as immortalised in his poetry such as "Mandalay" and "Gunga Din" and, of course, in his classic stories *The Jungle Book.*

Brighton to Eastbourne

If Brighton is the trendy young star of the south coast, Eastbourne is the reliable old timer, now with a fashionable important gallery of its own, and some stunning coastline. Lewes is a charming inland detour.

BRIGHTON ★★

❍ *55mi/88km due S of London. Trains and buses run here frequently from London; the train station (Queen's Road) is a 5–10-min walk from the centre, while the bus station (Old Steine) is centrally located just back from the seafront. The town is compact and easily explored on foot. To get an overview, jump aboard the City Sightseeing open-top bus (℘01273 886 200; www. city-sightseeing.com), or take the Volks Railway for a 1.2mi/2km ride along the beachfront (℘292 718; www.volkselectricrailway.co.uk). Population: 200,168.* ▯ *Royal Pavilion Shop, Royal Pavilion. ℘01273 290 337. www.visitbrighton.com.*

Brighton is where the English seaside tradition was invented and brought to a pitch of perfection. Within easy reach of the capital, the town has long been a weekend retreat for Londoners. Its south-facing beach is punctuated by piers and backed by a wide promenade

◔ **Michelin Map:** Map 504.

☺ **Don't Miss:** In Brighton: The Royal Pavilion; The Lanes and the North Laine. The Bluebell Railway, running on the East/ West Sussex border.

◷ **Timing:** In summer you'll want to spend at least one night in Brighton to catch some of its famous evening nightlife. The Brighton Festival runs for three weeks every May, and is the biggest mixed arts festival in England. www.brightonfestival.org.

👥 **Kids:** Pier; Sea Life Centre.

and elegant Georgian, Regency and Victorian architecture. The labyrinthine lanes of the old fishing town, with their jewellers and trendy shops, contrast with lavishly planted open spaces and parkways.

Modern Brighton began in the mid-18C with the promotion by Dr Richard Russell of the healthy effect of drinking and bathing in seawater.

The town received a royal seal of approval from the Prince of Wales, following his first visit in 1783. From the 1840s the London, Brighton and South

Coast Railway brought ever-increasing numbers of holidaymakers of all social classes to what had truly become "London-by-the-Sea". Today's mature town has remained young, stage-managing its raffish appeal to attract successive generations of visitors, while acquiring all the ingredients of a miniature metropolis: specialist shops, trendy restaurants, entertainments of all kinds, and on its outskirts, the modern University of Sussex.

Royal Pavilion★★★

🕐 *Open daily Apr–Sept 9.30am–5.45pm (last tickets 5pm); Oct–Mar 10am–5.15pm (last tickets 4.30pm).* 🕐 *Closed from 2.30pm on 24 Dec and all day 25–26 Dec.* £9.80 *(ground floor only).* ☎ *0300 0290 900. www.royalpavilion.org.uk.*

This fantastic Oriental confection in stucco and stone reflects the brilliant personality of George Augustus Frederick, Prince of Wales 1762–1811, Regent 1811–20, finally **King George IV**.

Its exotic gateways and extraordinary silhouette, all bulbous domes, pinnacles, turrets and spikes pricking the skyline, are a free interpretation of "Hindoo" architecture. Within, throughout a series of gorgeously furnished and decorated interiors, Chinoiserie prevails, taken to astonishing lengths in the **Music Room**, lit by lotus-shaped gaseliers, where painted serpents and dragons writhe beneath the gilded scales of a

great dome. Equally sumptuous is the great **Banqueting Room**; from its dome (45ft/14m high) hangs a one-ton crystal lighting device, at its apex a huge winged dragon in silver outlined against enormous *trompe l'œil* plantain leaves. The refurbished **royal apartments** on the first floor are reached by a staircase whose cast-iron bannister is cunningly disguised as bamboo.

All this exuberance is set in restored **gardens**, remodelled and planted as near as possible to its Regency state.

Just northwest of the Royal Pavilion is its former stables on Church Street, home to the splendid **Brighton Museum and Art Gallery**★ (🕐 *open Tue 10am–7pm, Wed–Sat and bank hols 10am–5pm, Sun 2–5pm;* 🕐 *closed 1 Jan, Good Fri, 25–26 Dec;* ☎ *01273 292 882; www. brighton-hove-rpml.org.uk).* In addition to its local history collection, Dutch and English paintings, porcelain and pottery, and its fashion and ethnographical gallery, the intimate interior also houses a well-presented display of 20C decorative arts.

Seafront★★

The meeting of Victorian Brighton and the sea is marked by a broad **promenade**, carried on massive brick vaults and with generous ramps and stairs leading to a roadway at beach level. A wealth of light-hearted detail, from splendid decorative ironwork to jaunty little kiosks and shelters, sets the holiday

Royal Pavilion, Brighton

©diwat26/SXC

mood, and is extended into the sea on the **West Pier** of 1866 and Palace Pier, now ▲▲**Brighton Pier** (🕐*open daily from 10am, 9am school summer hols, until late;* 🕐*closed 25 Dec;* ♿; ✆*01273 609 361; www.brightonpier.co.uk*), a lively place of funfair-style rides and amusements, and refreshments. Close by is the **Sea Life Centre** (▲▲ 🕐 *Marine Parade open daily 10am–5pm; winter daily 10am–4pm;* 🕐*closed 25 Dec;* ✺*£11.20 if booked online, child £9.95;* ♿; ✆*0871 222 6932; www.visitsealife.com*) offering a variety of ways to view marine life at close quarters in the original Victorian vaulted aquarium – the largest in the world when it opened in 1872. The pioneering electric **Volks Railway** of 1883 runs eastwards along the foot of the cliff to the **Marina**.

Within the continuous wall of seafront building is a succession of architectural set-pieces: the most distinguished is **Brunswick Square** (1825–27), with stucco, bow windows, Classical details and elegant ironwork; the earliest is **Royal Crescent** (1798–1807), in black mathematical tiles; the grandest, to the east, is the Victorian panache and elegance of **Lewes Crescent/Sussex Square**, (1823 onwards), exemplified in the many-storeyed and richly decorated Grand and Metropole hotels.

Town Centre

The Lanes★, a maze of animated old town alleyways, lined with countless boutiques and antique shops, focuses on **Brighton Square**. To the east lie the quirky, bohemian boutique, music, clothes and alternative lifestyle shops, not to mention a huge range of places to eat and drink, of the **North Laine**. Tucked away behind the train station to the northeast, **St Bartholomew's**★ (*Ann Street;* 🕐*opening hours vary;* ✆*01273 419 409*) is the most outstanding of Brighton's many Victorian churches. The sublime simplicity of patterned brick walls carrying the nave to the awesome height of 135ft/41m contrasts with rich **furnishings** (Lady Altar, main altarpiece, giant candlesticks), masterworks of the Arts and Crafts Movement.

EASTBOURNE

▶ *22mi/35km E of Brighton.*

This attractive but rather staid resort where Charles Dickens and Lewis Carroll once holidayed is these days known mostly for being a retirement town. Its handsome Victorian seafront, Grand Parade, features most of the usual favourite British seaside icons including a very fine traditional pier.

A couple of blocks inland, the town's main cultural attraction, the ultra-modern **Towner Gallery** (🕐*open year-round Tue–Sun and bank hol Mons 10am–6pm;* ♿✕; *t01323 434 670; www.townereastbourne.org.uk*) stands out like a sore thumb from its surroundings. It hosts major exhibitions of contemporary and historic visual art, alongside changing displays from the Towner Collection. From the windows of the Towner you can see the **South Downs**, Britain's newest national park, and a day walking or cycling through this beautiful landscape, perhaps along the coast to the famous lighthouse at **Beachy Head**★ or a little further to the spectacular **Seven Sisters**★ chalk cliffs, is highly recommended.

LEWES★

▶ *9mi/14km NE of Brighton.*
Population: 15,376. ⬛*Corn Exchange Building, 187 High Street.*
✆*01273 483 448.*

Perched on a hilltop, Lewes was originally a strategic Saxon stronghold on account of its commanding coastal views. The value of the site was also appreciated by William de Warenne, who built his castle here soon after the Conquest. In 1264 Simon de Montfort's rebellion against Henry III led to the defeat of the royal forces at the **Battle of Lewes**, fought on nearby Mount Harry.

The religious conflicts of the 16C were marked by the burning at the stake of 17 Protestant martyrs, commemorated (along with Guy Fawkes and the Gunpowder Plot) on 5 November with torchlit processions, tar-barrel rolling, fireworks and giant bonfires. Today Lewes is one of the few places where the rolling of burning tar barrels on Bonfire

Night still happens and the spectacle draws huge crowds.

For the other 364 days of the year it reverts to being a charming, characterful little county town with a fine architectural heritage.

Town and Castle

The well-preserved **High Street**★ features a delightful variety of traditional building materials: flint, stone, brick, timber, stucco, hung tiles, and the local speciality, "mathematical tiles", which in the 18C were used on older timber buildings to simulate a fashionable brick façade. Cobbled **Keere Street**★ is very pretty, dropping steeply downhill to a fragment of the old town walls and to **Southover Grange**, built of stone taken from the priory.

In Southover High Street is the beautiful Tudor timber-framed **Anne of Cleves' House**, now a local history museum (Ⓞopen Mar–Oct Tue–Thu 10am–5pm, Sun–Mon 11am–5pm; ✆01273 474 610; ☞£4.40; www.sussexpast.co.uk). Entry to **Lewes Castle** is via **Barbican House**, a fine 16C timber-framed building with a late Georgian façade. It too is now home to a local museum (Ⓞopen Tue–Thu 10am–5pm, Sun–Mon 11am–5pm, closed Mon in Jan; ☞£6.40; ✆01273 474 610; www.sussexpast.co.uk). A perfect flint-built 14C **barbican** also guards the castle precinct. From one of its towers there are fine **views**★ of the town and the gracefully sculpted outlines of the chalk hills all around.

SHEFFIELD PARK AND GARDEN★

RHS/NT. ◗ 9.5mi/15km N via the A 275. Ⓞ Open daily mid-Feb–Oct 10.30am–5.30pm; Nov–mid-Feb 10.30am–4pm. ☞£7.80. ♿️🅿️✗. ✆01825 790 231. www.nationaltrust.org.uk.

This large 18C and 19C landscaped park with its four **lakes** linked by cascades was enriched early this century with thousands of trees and shrubs from around the world.

BLUEBELL RAILWAY

Operates year-round, visit website or call for schedule and fares. ♿️🅿️✗. ✆01825 720 825 (24hr infoline); ✆01825 720 800 (general enquiries). www.bluebell-railway.co.uk.

Nostalgically preserved **steam trains** of Britain's first preserved standard gauge passenger railway run along 5mi/8km of the old London Brighton and South Coast Railway company track. This is one of the best known steam railway lines in the South East and at peak holiday times is often very busy.

GLYNDEBOURNE

◗ 3mi/5km E of Lewes.

A picnic on the lawn at the **Glyndebourne Festival** (http://glyndebourne. com) is, for certain people, as indispensable a part of the English summer as strawberries and cream at Wimbledon. Glyndebourne is the only unsubsidised opera house in the country and during the festival presents six productions each year, from mid/late May to August, in a 1,200-seat opera house. Prices and quality are high.

CHARLESTON

◗ 7mi/11km E of Lewes, between Firle and Selmeston. Ⓞ Open Apr–Oct Wed–Sat 1–6pm, Sun and bank hol Mon 1–5.30pm (last entry 1hr before closing). ☞£9. 🅿️✗. ✆01323 811 625; www.charleston.org.uk.

In 1916 this handsome former farmhouse became the country home and meeting place for the writers, painters and intellectuals known as the **Bloomsbury Group**, the most famous of these being Virginia Woolf. The interior was painted by the artists Duncan Grant and Vanessa Bell (Virginia Woolf's lover and sister respectively), and there is a changing programme of exhibitions in the gallery, including works by Renoir, Picasso, Derain, Sickert and Delacroix. There is also a charming walled garden created by Bell and Grant to designs by Roger Fry.

Chichester
and around

On the flatlands between the South Downs and the sea, Chichester and its picturebook cathedral spire present a quintessential English scene.

CHICHESTER★★

⊙ *81mi/130km SW of London on the River Lavant, very close to the south coast. Trains and buses run regularly here from London. The train station is on Stockbridge Road, the bus station close by at South Street; both are a 10 min walk from the centre. Population: 26,050.* 🛈*29a South Street.* ✆*01243 775 888. www.visitchichester.org.* 🅿*Park by the river for the classic view.*

Many English towns grew up around their cathedral, but Chichester was already a thousand years old before the cathedral was considered. The main arteries of North, South, East and West Streets, which run off the ornamental **Market Cross** (1501), still conform to their original Roman plan.

Chichester enjoyed a golden age in the 18C and the harmonious Georgian townscape is best seen in **The Pallants**.

In the heart of Chichester, close to the Market Cross (the centrepoint of the city's main pedestrianised shopping streets), is the **cathedral**★★ *(West Street;* ⊙*open daily Apr–Oct 7.15am–7pm, Nov–Mar 7.15pm–6pm;* 🕮*£5 contribution requested;* ⟡*guided tour (45min) Mon–Sat 11.15am, 2.30pm;* 🕮*£4.50 contribution requested;* ⚹✕*;* ✆*01243 782 595; www. chichestercathedral.org.uk).*

The cathedral took almost 100 years to build, from 1091 to 1184. The interior is Romanesque in style and spirit and its austere nave is Norman, though every architectural movement of the Middle Ages has left its mark. The nave is best viewed looking west, when it appears small, almost intimate. Its splendid screen is Perpendicular Gothic.

The Lady Chapel ceiling paintings are notable but the cathedral's greatest treasures are the 12C **stone panels**★★ in the south choir aisle; they depict scenes from the Raising of Lazarus and

are among the finest examples of Norman sculpture in England.

In the south transept, lit by a Decorated window, are early-16C paintings of the cathedral. In the north transept is the grave of the composer Gustav Holst (1874–1934); east of this is a stained-glass window by the French painter Marc Chagall (1887–1985). Head due east from the cathedral for one block and you will come to North Pallant Street, home to the **Pallant House Gallery**★ *(9 North Pallant;* ⊙*open Tue–Wed and Fri–Sat 10am–5pm, Thu 10am–8pm, Sun and bank hols 11am–5pm;* 🕮*£7.50, Thu 5–8pm free; Tue £3.75* ⚹*;* ✆*01243 774 557; www.pallant.org.uk).* This Queen Anne town house was built in 1712. Today its tastefully furnished period rooms are home to one of the best collections of 20C British art (Henry Moore, John Piper, Ceri Richards, Graham Sutherland…) in the world.

PETWORTH HOUSE★★

NT. ⊙ *14mi/23km NE on the A 27 and A 285.* **House:** ⊙*Open mid-Mar–early Nov Sat–Wed and Good Fri 11am–5pm (Mar 4pm).* **Grounds:** ⊙*Open Feb–Dec.* 🕮*£9.40 (park and grounds only, £3.60).* ⚹🅿*(£2)*✕*.* ✆*01798 342 207; 01798 343 929 (infoline). www.nationaltrust.org.uk.*

This grand 17C mansion (1688) contains the National Trust's finest collection of art. The **grounds**★★, by Lancelot "Capability" Brown, enjoy fine views of the South Downs.

Interior – The rooms contain exquisite carvings, antique statuary and a superb collection of paintings. The most spectacular feature is the **Grand Staircase** with its painted walls and ceiling by Laguerre. The **Turner Room** contains the largest collection of his works outside the Tate Gallery. Other famous artists represented are Reynolds, Van Dyck and Kneller. Lely's *Children of Charles I* hangs in the Oak Hall, Bosch's *Adoration of the Magi* in the Dining Room. **Grinling Gibbons'** carvings adorn the **Carved Room**.

WEALD AND DOWNLAND OPEN AIR MUSEUM★★

◗ *6mi/10km N on the A 286.* ◷*Open 1 Jan, late Feb–late Mar and Nov–late Dec daily 10.30am–4pm; early Jan–mid-Feb Wed and Sat–Sun 10.30am–4pm; Apr–Oct daily 10.30–6pm; last entry 1hr before closing.* ◎*£9.50.* ♿Ⓟ✕. ℘*01243 811 348. www.wealddown.co.uk.*

Over 40 historic buildings have been re-erected on the beautiful Downland slopes. They include a cottage, shop, farmhouse, Tudor market hall, working watermill, toll cottage and school. Many of the interiors have also been re-created and there are demonstrations of typical bygone rural activities.

FISHBOURNE ROMAN PALACE★★

◗ *1.5mi/2.4km W on the A 259.* ◷*Open Mar–Oct daily 10am–5pm; Feb and Nov–mid-Dec 10am–4pm; mid-Dec–Jan Sat–Sun 10am–4pm.* ◄•*Guided tour (1hr) Sat–Sun and bank hols 2.30pm, occasionally also 11pm.* ◎*£7.90.* ♿Ⓟ✕. ℘*01243 785 859. www.sussexpast.co.uk.*

This splendid Roman palace, built c.AD 75, was probably the home of Cogidubnus, an ally of Imperial Rome. The lavish complex, which included guest lodgings and grand colonnades, burned down in the 3C. The rich **mosaics**★ and the tableaux tracing the history of the palace are highlights.

BIGNOR ROMAN VILLA

◗ *Pulborough. 13mi/21km NE on the A 27 and A 29.* ◷*Open daily Mar–May and Sept–Oct 10am–5pm; Jun–Aug 10am–6pm.* ◎*£6.* ♿Ⓟ✕. ℘*01798 869 259. www.bignorromanvilla.co.uk.*

Some of the finest Roman **mosaics**★ in England are preserved here at this Roman farm uncovered in 1811 by a farmer's plough. Also of interest are the Georgian covering buildings that have protected the site so well for nearly 200 years and a modern traditional farm, set in beautiful South Downs countryside.

ARUNDEL

◗ *11mi/18km E on the A 27. www.arundel.org.uk.*

This prosperous hilltop town, picturesquely situated beside the quiet River Arun, is the most attractive small town in West Sussex. Its old characterful streets manage to retain a local feel even though they are also dotted with contemporary art galleries, antique and chichi shops, aimed at London day-trippers, and are a delight to wander, particularly during the August Festival.

The town is dominated by **Arundel Castle**★★ (◷*open Apr–Oct Tue–Sun, bank hol Mon, and Mon in Aug 10am–5pm; last entry 4pm; keep opens 11am, rooms open noon;* ◎*£7.50–£16;* ♿Ⓟ✕; ℘*01903 882 173; www.arundelcastle.org).* This spectacular fortress is the home of the Duke of Norfolk, the premier duke of England. The original Norman **gatehouse and keep** (1138) survive after 750 years of assaults and sieges. Climb up its 131 steps to enjoy panoramic views.

In the castle's Victorian rooms are the **Chapel** and **Barons' Hall** (paintings by Mytens, Kneller, Van Loo and Van Dyck); in the **Drawing Room** hang portraits by Van Dyck, Gainsborough and Reynolds. The Gothic Revival-style **Library** (122ft/37m long) dates from c.1800. On the boundary of the castle grounds stands the Decorated private **Fitzalan Chapel**, crowded with tombs and monuments to the Norfolk dynasty.

The great French Gothic-style hulk of **Arundel Cathedral** (◷*open year-round daily 9am–6pm;* ℘*01903 882 297. www.arundelcathedral.org),* is metaphorically and, at certain times of the day, literally overshadowed by the castle above. Built in 1870, its exterior is arguably more impressive than its interior.

Kent Weald

Weald derives from the German Wald (meaning woods) and although the forest has mostly long gone, the bucolic nature of Kent's rolling hills remains. In harmony with the landscape are some of England's finest gardens, country houses and pretty villages, while the regional centre, Tunbridge Wells is the very epitome of a genteel southern English town.

ROYAL TUNBRIDGE WELLS

42mi/68km SE of London. The train station is at the south end of the High Street. Population: 60,272. Old Fish Market, The Pantiles. *01892 515 675. www.visittunbridgewells.com.*

A graceful combination of Georgiana and Victoriana, amid parks, vistas and a vast semi-wild common, Tunbridge Wells owes its good fortune to the accidental discovery of its mineral springs in 1606 by Lord North.

As a result it soon became a magnet for the fashionable, most famously, Queen Henrietta Maria, who spent six weeks here, in a tent, after the birth of her son, Charles II. Queen Anne provided the tiled paving after which The Pantiles are named and Queen Victoria, who spent holidays here, commented "Dear Tunbridge Wells, I am so fond of it."

The Pantiles★

This perfect pedestrian precinct is on two levels, with an Upper Walk and a Lower Walk.

The **Bath House** (1804) still shows off its spring; the **Corn Exchange** (1802), once a theatre, displays Doric columns and Ceres, Goddess of the Harvest, on the roof; and the **Music Gallery** remains a reminder of the town's past elegance. **Union House** (1969, by Michael Levell) at one end of The Pantiles is an object lesson on how old and new can stand together in dignity. The 17C **Church of King Charles the Martyr** at the other end is also worth a visit.

Calverley Park★ – Not so much a park as a Neoclassical new town by Decimus

Burton. Inspired by Bath, it is best seen around Calverley Park Crescent.

KNOLE★★

NT. Sevenoaks. 15mi/24km north on the A 26, A 21 and A 225. **House:** *Open mid-Mar–Oct Wed–Sun noon–4pm.* **Garden:** *Open Easter–Sept Tue 11am–4pm.* **Park:** *Open daily to pedestrians.* House £10.40, garden only, £5. *01732 462 100; 01732 450 608 (infoline). www.nationaltrust.org.uk.*

This great late medieval, Tudor and Jacobean mansion – the childhood home of **Vita Sackville-West**, English poet, novelist and gardener (1892–1962) – is one of the finest buildings of its kind in England. The present building and its collection reflects the efforts of the Earls of Dorset in the 17C–18C. The **Great Hall** with its exquisite Jacobean screen is impressive. The elaborate grisaille décor of the **Great Staircase** sets off a life-size nude of the beauty Gianetta Baccelli in the lobby; the second-oldest harpsichord case made in England in 1622 is displayed in the **Spangle Dressing Room**. The rooms are ornamented with splendid friezes, ceilings, panelling and chimney-pieces, in particular the **Ballroom**, **Crimson Drawing Room** and **Cartoon Gallery**, where are displayed ornate furnishings and fine paintings (17C–18C family portraits, works by

---

⊘ **Don't Miss:** Knole, Ightam Mote.
Kids: Hever Castle jousting tournaments.

Pick of the Weald

Surrounding Tunbridge Wells are some of southern England's loveliest villages: Beneden, Brenchley and Goudhurst in particular, and the market town of Cranbrook with its picturesque working windmill, are all well worth the detour.

Ightham Mote

Y. Duhamel/MICHELIN

Lely, Reynolds and copies of Raphael's Cartoons). The highlight of Knole is the **King's Room**, with its gaudy grisailles, ostrich feathers, expensive embroidery and silver ornamentation.

IGHTHAM MOTE★★

NT. ▶ *Ivy Hatch. 10mi/16km N on the A 26 and A 227.* ◐*House open early Mar–May and Sept–Oct Thu–Mon 11am–5pm; Jun–Aug Wed–Mon 11am–5pm; Nov–mid/late Dec Thu–Sun 11am–3pm.* ◉*£10.40, winter Sat–Sun £5.20.* ♿️🅿️✕. ☎*01732 810 378.* *www.nationaltrust.org.uk.*
Ightham (pronounced "item"), built of stone and timber in 1340, is the best-preserved moated manor house in England; its survival is probably largely due to its secluded site.

The crenellated gatehouse leads into the courtyard, where the atmosphere is one of calm and privacy. Opposite is the **Great Hall**, built in the 1340s. The carved **frieze** above the fireplace and the **panelling** were designed by Norman Shaw in the 1870s. In the stairwell beyond, the **Jacobean staircase** has a Saracen's head, the Selby family crest, carved on the newel post.

The **New Chapel** has a unique **barrel-vaulted roof**, dating from 1470–80 and with early-16C painted panels.

SISSINGHURST CASTLE GARDEN★

NT. ▶ *Near Cranbrook. 13mi/21km E via the A 264, A 21 and A 262.* ◐*Open mid-Mar–Oct Fri–Tue 11am–5pm.* ◉*£10.* ♿️🅿️✕. ☎*01580 710 700; 01580 710 701 (infoline). www.nationaltrust.org.uk.*
In 1930 **Vita Sackville-West** (◑*see Knole*) and her husband Harold Nicolson took over the Sissinghurst estate. At its heart was (and still is) a garden in the ruin of an Elizabethan house, set in the middle of its own woods, streams and farmland and with long views on all sides across the fields and meadows of the Kentish landscape. "I fell in love… I saw what could be made of it… a castle running away into sordidness and squalor, a garden crying out for rescue." In fact the the **tower** became her study and the **garden** their monument.

PENSHURST PLACE★

▶ *8mi/13km W via the A 26 and B 2176.* **House:** ◐*Open late Mar–Oct daily noon–4pm (last entry).* **Grounds:** ◐*Open daily late Mar–Oct 10.30am–6pm; Nov–Feb 10.30am–4.30pm).* ◉*£9.80, garden only, £7.80.* ♿️🅿️✕. ☎*01892 870 307.* *www.penshurstplace.com.*
This splendid mansion, the home of the Elizabethan poet **Sir Philip Sidney**

(1554–86), is set in a pretty Tudor Revival village, clustering around the 13C church of St John the Baptist, with its Sidney Chapel. The original Great Hall (1346), built of coarse sandstone, has been added to with early Tudor, Jacobean and Gothic Revival wings.

Inside the hall, the chestnut **timber roof** is held up by unusual life-size carvings of humble peasants. The open hearth is a rare feature and the screens are decorated with tracery. The elegant **furnishings** of the formal rooms include rare furniture, tapestries and portraits.

The great terrace is the focus of the formal **gardens** with their clipped hedges. There is a traditional adventure playground, a nature trail, a farm museum and an enchanting **Toy Museum** with puppets, rocking horses and 19C dolls.

CHIDDINGSTONE

▷ *16mi/26km NW on the A 26, B 2176, B 2027 and local roads.*

The delightful 16C–17C dwellings, timber framed, tile hung, pargeted and gabled, clustered around St Mary's Church, present a rare combination of 14C Gothic and Jacobean styles. The village is owned by the National Trust. To the west, near Edenbridge, stands **Chiddingstone Castle** (☉*open Good Fri–last Sun Oct, Sun–Wed 11am–5pm; ☞£7; &❒✕; ☎01892 870 347; www. chiddingstonecastle.org.uk*), a 19C setting for Buddhist, Egyptian, Japanese and English Stuart period works of art amassed by the eccentric Denys Eyre Bower, a bank clerk with a remarkable eye and great enthusiasm.

⚇❖HEVER CASTLE★

▷ *13mi/21km W on the A 264 and B 2026. House:* ☉*Open Feb half-term wk, daily noon–4pm; Mar–Easter Wed–Sun noon–5pm; Apr–Oct daily noon–6pm; Nov–Dec Wed–Sun 11am–4pm.; last entry 1hr before closing. Gardens:* ☉*Open daily 10.30am, close as house. Mazes open and rowing boats for hire Easter–Sept/Oct weather permitting. ☞£14; Gardens only, £11.50. &❒✕. ☎01732 865 224. www.hevercastle.co.uk.*

This fortified manor house, protected by a moat, and the drawbridge and portcullis of its massive gatehouse stand in idyllic countryside. Formerly the childhood home of **Anne Boleyn**, the neglected castle was bought in 1903 by William Waldorf Astor, who lavishly restored both castle and grounds.

Much of the **woodwork** is a re-creation of the finest Renaissance craftsmanship. There are portraits of Anne, and one, by Holbein, of Henry; in her little room is the Book of Hours the young queen took to her execution in 1536. A costumed figure exhibition and tableaux represent the life and times of Anne Boleyn.

Gardens

The lake (38 acres/15ha) is approached via an elaborate loggia and an **Italian garden** with **antique statuary** and **sculpture**. It has recently won a "most romantic garden in the South East" award. However, two mazes, an adventure playground and a lively summer-long programme of activities, including jousting, make this a very good place for children too.

CHARTWELL

NT. ▷ *Mappleton Road. 15mi/24km NW via the A 264 and B 206.* ☉ *House, gardens and studio open mid-Mar–Jun and Sept–Oct Wed–Sun and bank hols 11am–5pm; Jul–Aug Tue–Sun and bank hol 11am–5pm; gardens close winter 4pm. Gardens and studio also open Nov–Dec. ENTRY to house by timed ticket; buy immediately on entry as they can run out. ☞£10.60, garden and studio only, £5.30. &❒✕. ☎01732 868 381; 01732 866 368 (infoline). www.nationaltrust.org.uk.*

This restored Tudor house was the home of **Sir Winston Churchill** (1874–1965). It is packed with Churchilliana, including many of his paintings, and reflects comfortable domestic life.

The **walls** of the fine gardens were partly built by Churchill himself, who loved the splendid prospect over rolling Weald of Kent countryside and was a principal reason why he bought the estate.

ADDRESSES

🏠 STAY

GUILDFORD

Abeille House – *119 Stoke Road.* 𝒞*01483 532 200. www.abeillehouse.co.uk.* 📖*. 4 rms.* A 10-minute walk from the station and town centre, this charming guesthouse offers Victorian- and Edwardian-style bedrooms.

CANTERBURY

Castle House – *28 Castle Street.* 𝒞*01227 761 897. www.castlehousehotel. co.uk.* - 📖*. 7 rms.* The main part of this house was built in the 1730s, incorporating part of the Norman city walls, though the interior lacks historical character. Rooms are spacious and some have a view of the cathedral.

Thanington Hotel – *140 Wincheap.* 𝒞*01227 453 227. www.thanington-hotel. co.uk.* 📖*. 15 rms.* Just outside the city wall, this charming small hotel, originally an 18C farmhouse, is excellent value. On sunny days you can enjoy a hearty breakfast in the walled garden and at any time you can use the indoor swimming pool.

Ebury Hotel – *65–67 New Dover Road.* 𝒞*01227 768 443. www.ebury-hotel. co.uk.* 📖*. 15 rms.* On a pretty street, a 15-minute walk from the centre, this is a lovely peaceful house with a large garden and a heated indoor swimming pool. The bedrooms retain many original Victorian features, and are spacious, light and tastefully decorated. Its elegant restaurant serves fine Anglo-French food *(closed Sun;* 🍴🍴*)*.

DOVER

Castle House – *10 Castle Hill Road.* 𝒞*01304 201 656. www.castle-guesthouse. co.uk.* This attractive Grade-II-listed building guesthouse is ideally situated close to the town centre, port and castle. Rooms are light and mostly spacious and there is a very warm welcome. Good value.

RYE

The Rise – *82 Udimore Road.* 𝒞*01797 222 285. www.therise-rye.co.uk.* 📖*. 3 rms.* This five-star luxury 1920s-built B&B, a 10-minute walk from town, offers large elegant rooms, pleasant gardens and south-facing terraces with superb views over the countryside.

Mermaid Inn – *Mermaid Street.* 𝒞*01797 223 065. www.mermaidinn.com.* 📖. This famous ancient smugglers' haunt has retained some of its 15C atmosphere with exposed beams and period furnishings. Several rooms have four-poster beds. The restaurant serves gourmet Anglo-French cuisine *(*🍴🍴🍴*)*.

Windmill Guest-House – *Mill Lane, off Ferry Road.* 𝒞*01797 240 027. www.ryewindmill.co.uk.* 📖*. 3 rms.* Near the town centre, this unusual B&B has bags of character, with two rooms (a suite and four-poster room) actually in the windmill itself; the other is in the mill building. All are beautifully decorated.

BRIGHTON

🐦Top Tip – Most B&Bs tend to be on the streets running off Marine Parade.

Esteban Hotel – *35 Upper Rock Gardens.* 𝒞*01273 681 161. 12 rms.* Just a few minutes' walk from the centre of town, four-poster beds and a warm welcome are the main attractions of this Victorian boutique hotel.

Paskins – *18–19 Charlotte Street.* 𝒞*01273 601 203. www.paskins.co.uk.* 📖*. 19 rms.* Each bedroom is decorated to a theme in this pleasantly quirky Victorian B&B: Art Deco, Victoriana, Audrey Hepburn, etc. The home-made organic breakfasts are something special!

Nineteen – *19 Broad Street.* 𝒞*01273 675 529. www.hotelnineteen.co.uk. 8 rms.* This luxury B&B is in a tastefully converted Victorian townhouse in the Kemp Town area, just a pebble's throw from the beach. Bright airy contemporary bedrooms.

Hotel du Vin – *Ship Street.* 𝒞*01273 718 588. www.hotelduvin. co.uk. 49 rms.* Situated in The Lanes, near

Mermaid Inn, Rye

© Clive Sawyer/Pictures Colour Library

the seafront, this eccentric Gothic Revival/ mock Tudor building was erected by a wine merchant on the site of an old inn; the original double-height hall now houses a wine bar. The luxurious rooms feature contemporary/traditional styling and there is a classic French bistro.

EASTBOURNE

Grand Parade, Marine Parade and Royal Parade are where you'll find the town's hotels and guesthouses.

Ebor Lodge Hotel – *71 Royal Parade. 01323 640 792. www.eborlodge.co.uk. 6 rms.* Just across the road from the beach. Room 3 in particular has a lovely outlook. Very good value.

Sea Beach House Hotel – *39–40 Marine Parade. www.seabeachhouse.com. 01323 410 458. 10 rms.* Sea Beach House is the only Grade II-listed seafront accommodation in Eastbourne. The friendly owners are a mine of local information.

Albert & Victoria – *19 St Aubyns Road. 01323 730 948. www.albertand victoria.com. 4 rms.* Elegant Victorian house, including a four-poster bedroom, with magnificent sea views.

CHICHESTER

Cherry End – *City centre. 01243) 531 397. www.cherryend.2ya.com. 2 rms.* This Victorian house is a five-minute stroll from the town centre and offers two pretty blue-and-white rooms.

⍩/EAT

GUILDFORD

For a range of cuisines (French, Italian, Asian…) explore around Tunsgate Square.

The Boatman – *Millbrook. 01483 568 024. www.boatman-guildford.co.uk.* This very popular pub has a fine location right on the river, a five-minute walk from the town centre. Extensive food menu from light bites to pub classics.

CANTERBURY

There are numerous restaurants offering cuisines from all around the world in the area just to the northeast of the town centre (Peter Street, The Borough, Palace Street) and also on Dunstan Street.

Simple Simon's – *3–9 Church Lane. 01227 762 355.* Traditional cooking, live music and a good range of beers in one of Canterbury's oldest pubs.

Posillipo – *15–17 The Borough. 01227 761 471. www.posillipo.co.uk.* This acclaimed Italian restaurant serves gour-

met pizzas and rustic pasta dishes but is renowned for its fish.

The Goods Sheds – *Station Road West. 01227 459 153. www.thegoodsshed. net. Closed Sun dinner and Mon.* This smart rustic restaurant is attached to the town's daily farmers' market and serves top-quality seasonal British cuisine.

BRIGHTON

On Saturdays in summer the restaurants of North Laine bring their tables and chairs out onto the street. North Laine and The Lanes account for most of the best restaurants and pubs.

Bill's – *100 North Road. 01273 692 894. www.billsproducestore.co.uk.* Arranged in the style of a farmers' market, this informal but locally famous café-restaurant and shop serves only the best and freshest produce with its mouthwatering all-day dishes made up in the open kitchen.

Sam's of Sevendials – *1–3 Buckingham Place. 01273 885 555. www.seven-dialsrestaurant.co.uk. Closed Sun dinner.* In an old bank building, this award-winning young buzzing place serves superb Modern British bistro food. Great-value prix-fixe at lunchtime.

Terre à Terre – *71 East Street. 01273 729 051. www.terreaterre.co.uk. Closed Mon and bank hols.* This is one of the most acclaimed and most inventive vegetarian restaurants in the country. Great-value prix-fixe menu.

The Gingerman – *21a Norfolk Square. 01273 326 688. www.gingermanrestaurants.com. Closed Mon.* This small intimate stylish modern venue serves excellent Mediterranean cuisine. Bargain prix-fixe lunches.

EASTBOURNE

A large choice of restaurants, including fish and chip shops, are to be found on Terminus Road. Try also the seafront and Sovereign Harbour.

Belgian Cafe – *Burlington Hotel. 11–23 Grand Parade. 01323 729 967. www.thebelgiancafe.co.uk.* If you're in the mood for mussels and chips and a Belgian beer to wash it down, there are over 50 kinds of each to choose from here.

CHICHESTER

Trents Wine Bar – *50 South Street. 01243 773 714. www.trentschichester. co.uk.* This modern restaurant-bar offers a Mediterranean/British menu featuring grills and salads.

HAMPSHIRE, DORSET, WILTSHIRE

These three bucolic counties of southern England were once the heartland of the kingdom of Wessex, ruled, most famously, by King Alfred. During the 10C Wessex unified much of England and was the last English kingdom before it was subdued by the Danes in the 11C. Its romantic appeal was revived during the 19C. Much older historic relics can be found in Wiltshire (Stonehenge and Avebury) and Dorset (the Cerne Abbas Giant, Maiden Castle and prehistoric fossils at Lyme Regis). Hampshire, meanwhile is home to ancient forest land and England's naval heritage. It all makes for a rich mix where the ancient past is never far away.

Highlights

1 Clamber aboard historic ships at **Portsmouth** (p158)
2 Pack a picnic and become part of the scenery at **Stourhead** (p177)
3 Feed the giraffes and see the lions on safari at **Longleat** (p178)
4 Get a spiritual high on the Tower Tour at **Salisbury Cathedral** (p179)
5 Try to solve the puzzle of over five millennia at enigmatic **Stonehenge** (p181)

Hampshire

England's second most wooded county (after Surrey) is a region of both rolling countryside and a coastline with a long naval history. Its best-loved landscape is the New Forest, new in name and national park status only.

Ironically, precious little forest remains, but its atmosphere, traditions and village settlements still go back many centuries.

The county town, Winchester, retains echoes of King Arthur's rule, when it was capital of all England, and its magnificent cathedral and atmospheric college go back to medieval times. It is also a modern lively regional hub, however, and makes a good base.

On the coast, Portsmouth is home to the Royal Navy past and present, from *HMS Victory* to nuclear submarines; it's Historic Dockyard is a sepia-tinted look at how Britannia once ruled the waves, as well as modern naval cutting-edge technology. Neighbouring Southampton has a proud commercial shipping history; every great British ocean liner has sailed from here, including *Titanic*. A short ferry ride away is the Isle of Wight, a favourite resort where Queen Victoria built a magnificent holiday home.

Dorset

For many English visitors Dorset is the transition between the London-influenced southeast and the provincial West Country. It is also the heart of the ancient kingdom of Wessex, which comes most readily to life, particularly around Dorchester, through the late-19C works of its most famous literary figure, Thomas Hardy.

The Dorset coastline is hugely popular, from the typical seaside charm of resorts like Bournemouth, Swanage, Weymouth and Lyme Regis, to uncommercialised natural beauty spots like Durdle Door and Lulworth Cove.

Wiltshire

Landlocked Wiltshire's most famous attraction is Stonehenge. In fact the county is rich in prehistoric remains and the savvy visitor may even prefer visiting Avebury to its world-famous neighbour. The main town is Salisbury, quintessentially English with its cathedral – arguably England's finest – rising above the water meadows, in a scene unchanged over centuries.

In Stourhead and Longleat, Wiltshire possesses two of Britain's finest outdoor attractions, at opposite ends of the cultural spectrum. The former is the apogee of English landscape gardening; the latter is the zenith of how to turn your estate into a commercially successful venture, which in this case has meant transforming swathes of Wiltshire into the plains of Africa, complete with native animals!

Food Heroes

In Hampshire, the delightful Georgian town of **Alresford** ("Arlsford"), together with the beautiful adjacent village of Old Alreford, near Winchester, is known for it **watercress**, with the Watercress Steam Train line *(www.watercressline.co.uk)* passing alongside watercress beds where the green peppery salad plant is grown. There is an Annual Watercress Festival on the middle Sunday in May.

On the south coast between Southampton and Portsmouth, **Wickham Vineyards** *(open for tours, www.wickhamvineyard.co.uk)* produces award-winning wines.

Winchester stages the largest – also recently voted the best – farmers' market in the country *(second and last Sun of month, www.visitwinchester. co.uk)* with around 95 local producers showcasing local Hampshire food and drink.

Dorset is the beginning of the West Country, famous for its **cider** (see Somerset, below). And, while the county does have its share of cider producers it also puts its apples to good use in the delicious and ubiquitous **Dorset Apple Cake** (best served warm with cream). The county is also known for its **Dorset Blue** cheese, and its close relative, **Blue Vinny**. Try the latter in Puddletown, near Dorchester, at The Blue Vinny Restaurant *(www.thebluevinny.co.uk)*.

Hall & Woodhouse (www.hall-woodhouse.co.uk), best known for their Badger beers, offers brewery tours and a visitor centre in Blandford St Mary, near Wimborne. Also at **Wimborne** is the region's top food festival, Feast of Dorset *(late Sept, www.feastofdorset.com)* in the delightful "secret garden" of Dean's Court.

Wiltshire has a long history of pig-keeping and is famous for its high quality, traditionally cured pork and bacon. Above all other things, Wiltshire is known for its ham. The town of Swindon derives its name from 'swine down' or 'pig hill' after the herds of pigs that used to graze there.

The perfect accompaniment to Wiltshire ham is **Wiltshire Tracklements** *(www.tracklements.co.uk)*, arguably the country's finest mustards, chutneys, relishes and meat accompaniments. Wash it down with a pint of the nationally acclaimed 6X Bitter from **Wadworth Brewery** *(www.wadworth. co.uk)* at Devizes. The brewery's giant shire horses still can be seen pulling the dray (traditional delivery wagon) around the streets of the old market town, and brewery tours run daily.

Lardy Cake is a well-known traditional Wiltshire confection, made of lard, dough, sugar and dried fruit. It has an interesting toffee taste and is highly fattening.

Bacon Fraise is a 15C agricultural worker's breakfast dish, consisting of fried bacon, which is then covered with batter and then cooked in the oven. It's worth a try, if you can find it. In the 18C, **Wiltshire cheese** was popular throughout the United Kingdom, but demand for milk in London led Wiltshire's dairy farmers to abandon its production. Thankfully, North Wiltshire Cheese Loaf can now be bought from a few local farmers' markets.

The **Isle of Wight**'s most unusual foodstuffs come from The **Garlic Farm** at Newchurch, *(www.thegarlicfarm.co.uk)*. In addition to fresh bulbs, smoked garlic, garlic bread, pickles and relishes etc, they also do garlic beer and garlic ice cream. You can taste some of them at their own café-restaurant. The Isle of Wight Garlic Festival *(late Aug, (www.thegarlicfarm. co.uk)* attracts around 25,000 visitors.

Portsmouth★
Hampshire

Britain's premier naval base is set between two almost landlocked harbours. The early-15C saw the development of the naval base and in 1495 the first dry dock in the world was built. By the end of the 17C Portsmouth had become the principal naval base in the country. In the 18C when France was Britain's major enemy, the fortifications were strengthened. After heavy bombing in the Second World War the city was rebuilt and expanded onto the mainland.

▶ **Population:** 174,690.

◔ **Michelin Map:** Michelin Atlas p 10 or Map 504 Q 31.

🗓 **Info:** The Hard, Portsmouth – outside Historic Dockyard. ℘023 9282 6722. www.visitportsmouth.co.uk.

◑ **Location:** 81mi/130km south of London. Harbour Station, on The Hard (includes the bus station), is adjacent to the main sights. Portsmouth Station is a 10–15 minute walk from the centre. The Southsea Land Train is a useful way of getting around.

◉ **Don't Miss:** The Historic Dockyard; the view from the Spinnaker Tower.

◔ **Timing:** At least two days minimum.

👥 **Kids:** Historic Dockyard (*HMS Victory* and Action Stations); Blue Reef Aquarium, Southsea; Explosion Museum of Naval Fire Power.

🐾 WALKING TOUR
Historic Dockyard
Victory Gate, Queen Street and The Hard. ◔*Open daily Apr–Oct 10am–6pm; Nov–Mar 10am–5pm; last entry 90min before closing.* ◔*Closed 24–26 Dec.* 🐾*Guided tour HMS Victory (45min) subject to availability, usually only at off-peak visiting times (◉arrive early).* ◉*Passport ticket £19.90 (includes harbour boat tour), child £14.30.* ♿🅿(*charge*) ✕. ℘023 9272 8060. www.historicdockyard.co.uk.*

👥 Action Stations
This exciting hands-on centre is all about today's Royal Navy with high-tech exhibits and simulators which let you take charge of a helicopter, fire ship's guns, control the bridge of a warship, climb the rigging and much more.

HMS Warrior 1860
Once the pride of Queen Victoria's Navy, Britain's first iron-clad battleship was commissioned in the 1860s.
After 100 years of use for various purposes she has been restored and now displays a living exhibition of life in the Victorian Navy.

National Museum of the Royal Navy★★
The museum stands alongside *HMS Victory* and the *Mary Rose*. The galleries are packed with mementoes of those who have served their country at sea through a thousand years of peace and war.

👥 HMS Victory★★★
On 21 October 1805 Admiral Horatio Nelson's splendid three-masted flagship (built Chatham 1759) led the victorious attack on a combined French and Spanish fleet off Cape Trafalgar in Spain – at the cost of her admiral's life. In the 1920s the *Victory* was brought into dry dock after 150 years at sea. Today she continues to serve as the flagship of the Commander in Chief Naval Home Command, still manned by serving Royal Naval and Royal Marines personnel.

The Mary Rose★★
On 19 July 1545, the four-masted *Mary Rose* (built 1509), vice-flagship of Henry VIII's English fleet, keeled over and sank while preparing to meet a French attack. In the 1960s the wreck was found, pre-

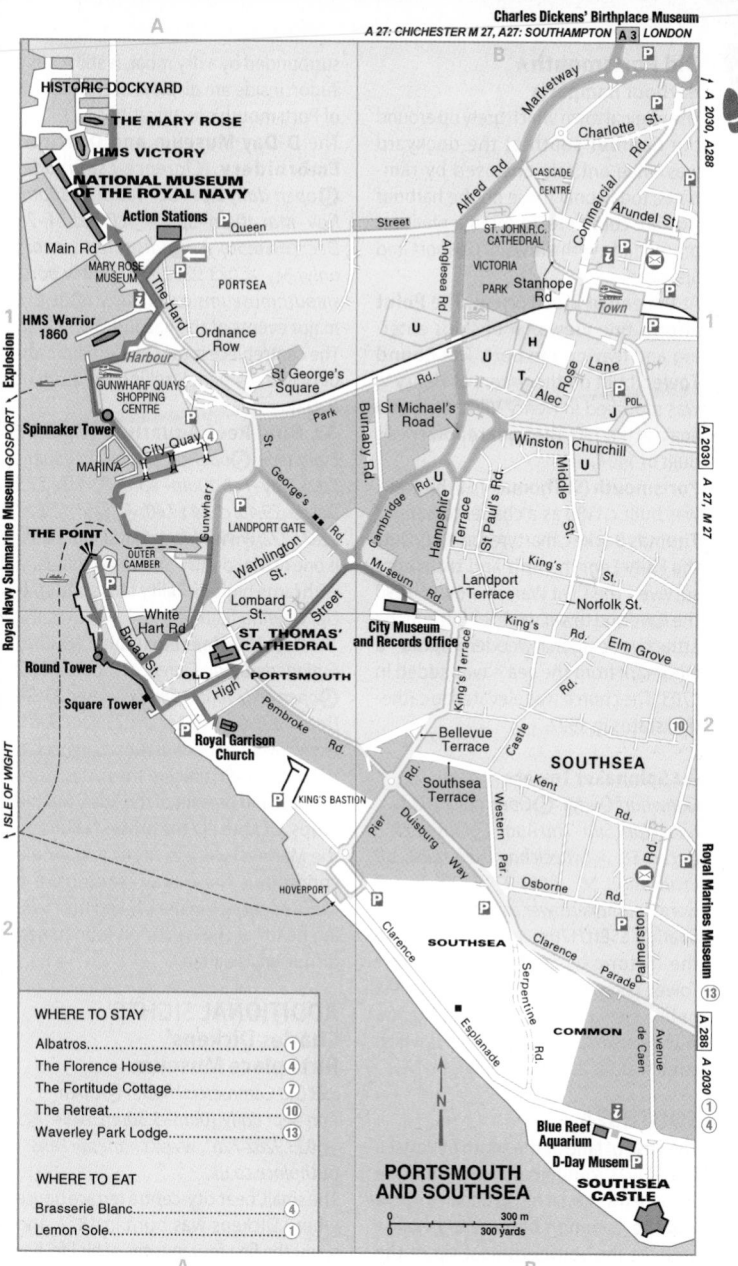

HISTORIC DOCKYARD
THE MARY ROSE
HMS VICTORY
NATIONAL MUSEUM OF THE ROYAL NAVY
Action Stations
Queen
Main Rd
MARY ROSE MUSEUM
PORTSEA
The Hard
HMS Warrior 1860
Explosion
Ordnance Row
Harbour
GUNWHARF QUAYS SHOPPING CENTRE
Spinnaker Tower
MARINA
City Quay
Royal Navy Submarine Museum GOSPORT
St George's Square
Park
THE POINT
OUTER CAMBER
LANDPORT GATE
Warblington St.
Gunwharf
White Hart Rd.
Lombard St.
Broad St.
ISLE OF WIGHT
Round Tower
Square Tower
ST THOMAS' CATHEDRAL
OLD PORTSMOUTH
High
Street
St.
George's
Rd.
Museum
City Museum and Records Office
Royal Garrison Church
Pembroke Rd.
KING'S BASTION
HOVERPORT
Marketway
Charlotte St.
A 2030, A288
CASCADE CENTRE
Alfred Rd
Commercial Rd
Arundel St.
ST. JOHN R.C. CATHEDRAL
VICTORIA PARK
Stanhope Rd
Town
Anglesea Rd.
U
U
U
Rose Lane
Alec
H
T
J
POL.
St Michael's Road
Winston Churchill
Middle St.
St Paul's Rd.
Cambridge Rd.
Burnaby Rd.
Hampshire Terrace
King's St.
Landport Terrace
Norfolk St.
King's Terrace
King's Rd.
Elm Grove
Rd.
Bellevue Terrace
Castle Rd.
SOUTHSEA
Southsea Terrace
Kent Rd.
Western Par.
Pier Rd.
Duisburg Way
Osborne Rd.
Clarence
Clarence Parade
SOUTHSEA
Serpentine Rd.
COMMON
Esplanade Rd.
de Caen Avenue
A 2030 A 27, M 27
Royal Marines Museum
A 288 A 2030
Blue Reef Aquarium
D-Day Museum
SOUTHSEA CASTLE

N

PORTSMOUTH AND SOUTHSEA

0   300 m
0   300 yards

served in the Solent silt; in 1982 the hull was raised and it is now a unique Tudor time-capsule preserved after 437 years on the seabed. The **Mary Rose Museum** exhibiting the many objects recovered – treasures and possessions of her crew – gives an insight into Tudor nautical life.

An audio-visual presentation describes the dramatic salvage operation.

The Mary Rose Ship Hall is currently closed, with the *Mary Rose* withdrawn from view, as construction takes place on a new £35 million museum due to open in 2012.

Old Portsmouth★
Harbour Ramparts

The original town which grew up around the **Camber** south of the dockyard was once entirely enclosed by ramparts; today only those on the harbour side are complete, forming a pleasant promenade with **views** of Gosport and Spithead.

At the end of Broad Street, The **Point** affords fine **views**★★ of ships entering and leaving the port. The **Round Tower**, built on the orders of Henry V, was modified in Henry VIII's reign and again in the 19C. The **Square Tower** was built in 1494.

Portsmouth (St Thomas') Cathedral★ was built c.1180 as a chapel to honour **Thomas Becket**, martyred in 1170. Only the Early English **choir** and **transepts** survived the Civil War; in around 1690 the nave and tower were rebuilt and the attractive octagonal wooden **cupola** – a landmark from the sea – was added in 1703. The church was elevated to cathedral status in 1927.

≗≗ Spinnaker Tower★

Gunwharf Quays. ◷*Open daily 10am–6pm (7pm Sun–Thu Aug).* ◷*Closed 25 Dec.* ◉*£8.* ♿*(wheelchair users must call in advance);* ✕. *℘023 9285 7520. www.spinnakertower.co.uk.*
Soaring 558ft/170m into the sky above the historic harbour, the Spinnaker Tower, completed in 2005, is the tallest public viewing tower in Great Britain, with wonderful panoramic views which stretch as far as the Isle of Wight.

SOUTHSEA

The strip of land at the south of Portsea Island was rough marshland until the 19C when a coastal resort began to grow and the Common became a pleasure area. At the southernmost tip of the island stands the **castle**★ *(Clarence Esplanade;* ◷*open mid-May–Oct Tue–Sun and bank hol Mons 10am–5pm;* ◷*closed 24–26 Dec;* ♿✕; *℘023 9282 7261; www.southseacastle.co.uk),* built by Henry VIII in 1544 as part of the chain of forts protecting the ports along the south and east coast. The central **keep**,

surrounded by a dry moat, is still mainly Tudor; inside are displays of the growth of Portsmouth's fortifications.

The **D-Day Museum and Overlord Embroidery** *(Clarence Esplanade;* ◷*open daily Apr–Oct 10am–5.30pm, Nov–Mar 10am–5pm;* ◷*closed 24–26 Dec;* ◉*£6.50;* ♿ 🅿 *(disabled visitors only)* ✕; *℘023 9282 7261; www.portsmouthmuseums.co.uk)* illustrates the major events of the Second World War. The centrepiece is the Overlord Embroidery with 34 panels telling the story of D-Day.

≗≗ Blue Reef Aquarium *(Clarence Esplanade;* ◷*open daily Mar–Oct 10am–5pm, Nov–Feb 10am–4pm;* ◷*closed 25 Dec;* ◉*£9.40, child £7.40;* ♿✕; *℘023 9287 5222; www.bluereefaquarium.co.uk)* is one of the country's new-wave aquaria with large high-visibility tanks and special viewing features.

The **Royal Marines Museum**★ *(Eastney Esplanade, along Clarence Parade, A 288;* ◷*open daily 10am–5pm;* ◷*closed 23–26 Dec;* ◉*£7.50;* ♿🅿✕; *℘023 9281 9385; www.royalmarinesmuseum.co.uk),* set in the original 19C officers' mess, describes the past and present of the Royal Marine Corps. Of note are the presentations on the Marines' work in Arctic and jungle conditions, the D-Day landings, the Marines' service in the UN and the "talking head" of Hannah Snell, who joined disguised as a man.

ADDITIONAL SIGHTS
Charles Dickens' Birthplace Museum

393 Old Commercial Road. ◷*Open Apr–Sept daily 10am–5.30pm.* ◉*£4.* ♿. *℘023 9282 7261. www.charlesdickens birthplace.co.uk.*
The small, neat city-centre terrace house where Dickens was born in 1812, and spent the first four months of his life, has been restored and furnished in the style of the period. A small exhibition includes the green velvet couch on which he died at Gad's Hill Place in Kent.

Royal Navy Submarine Museum

Gosport: cross harbour by shuttle ferry; alternatively, a Waterbus Service links with Gunwharf Quays and Historic Dockyard. Haslar Jetty Road. ○*Open daily Apr–Oct 10am–5.30pm; Nov–Mar 10am–4.30pm.* ○*Closed 24–25 Dec.* ⊚*£10, online £9.* ▣✕. ℘*023 9252 9217. www.rnsubmus.co.uk.*

Five actual submarines, torpedoes, a Polaris missile and hands-on exhibits of periscopes and diving equipment all help tell the story of submariners and their role in peace and war.

👥 Explosion Museum of Naval Fire Power

Gosport: cross harbour by shuttle ferry alternatively, a Waterbus Service links with Gunwharf Quays and Historic Dockyard. Priddy's Hard. ○*Open Apr–Oct daily 10am–5pm; Nov–Mar Sat–Sun, 10am–4pm.* ○*Closed 1 Jan, 25–26 Dec.* ⊚*£10, child £5.* ⅏▣✕. ℘*012 9250 5600. www.explosion.org.uk.*

The story of naval firepower is traced through audio-visual presentations,

workers' testimonies and exhibits on mines, torpedoes, missiles and more.

EXCURSION
Royal Armouries Fort Nelson

▶*Fort Nelson, Portsdown Hill Road. 9mi/14km NW on the M 27.*

○*Open Apr–Oct Wed 11am–5pm, Thu–Tue 10am–5pm; Nov–Mar Wed 11.30 11.30am–4pm, Thu–Tue 10.30am–4pm.* ○*Closed 25–26 Dec.* ⅏▣✕. ℘*01329 233 734. www.armouries.org.uk.*

This superbly restored Victorian fort is one of a chain built high across Portsdown Hill to defend Portsmouth from French invasion. There are sweeping **views** from the fort walls.

Alongside re-created barracks, the collection of artillery includes ornate medieval bronze cannons from India, China and Turkey, anti-aircraft guns and three sections of the immense "Supergun" impounded in 1990, en route for Iraq in the guise of petro-chemical piping.

Southampton
and around

This important south coast port, naturally favoured with a double tide, began as a Roman coastal garrison, Clausentum, on the east bank of the Itchen. By the 8C it had become the Saxon port of **Hamwic**, serving the royal city of Winchester and it has continued to grow until the present day, becoming one of Britain's major container ports. After severe bombing in the Second World War, the town began a successful recovery in the 1950s and, alongside medieval remains, a modern city has grown up, with a lively university and renewed industry.

🚶 OLD TOWN WALK

A good deal of the medieval defences and town buildings can still be seen today. The impressive northern gate to the town, the **Bargate**★, built c.1180, was given its large towers c.1285 and its forbidding north face in the 15C.

▶ **Population:** 210,138.

✦ **Michelin Map:** Michelin Atlas p 9 or Map 504 P 31.

🛈 **Info:** 9 Civic Centre Road. ℘023 8083 3333. www. visit-southampton.co.uk.

▶ **Location:** South coast, 78mi/125km SW of London; the central train station has a regular direct connection. The bus station is on the other side of the civic centre. Take a tour around the harbour from Ocean Village with Blue Funnel Cruises (℘02380 223 278; www.bluefunnel.co.uk).

👥 **Kids:** Birds at the Hawk Conservancy Trust.

The **west wall** of the early defences rises spectacularly above the **Western Esplanade**, where Southampton Bay once lapped the shore. Note the 15C **Catchcold Tower** and The **Arcade** running from the site of **Biddlesgate** to the **Blue Anchor Postern**. At the top of Blue Anchor Lane the large early-16C **Tudor House and Garden**★ (○open year-round daily 10am–5pm; ⊷call for entry price; ✕; ℰ023 8083 3007; www.tudor-houseandgarden.com) is the city's most important historic building, encompassing over 800 years of history on one site, and incorporating an earlier banqueting hall. It now houses a museum which tells the story of the house and the people who lived and worked there; outside, a lovely 16C **garden** of flowers and herbs and a formal knot garden have been re-created. At the far end steps lead down to the shell of the **Norman House**, a fine example of a 12C merchant's house, which was incorporated into the town wall defences in the 14C. **St Michael's Church** is the oldest building in the medieval town, built soon after the Norman Conquest and enlarged throughout the Middle Ages and in the 19C.

Back on the Western Esplanade is the old Wool House, a fine red 14C stone warehouse. Close by, **God's House** was founded c.1185 as an almshouse and hostel for travellers. To its east stand the early-14C **God's House Gate**, and the early-15C **God's House Tower**.

East of the rail station on Commercial Road is the **Southampton City Art Gallery**★ (○open year-round daily 10am–5pm; ♿🅿(charge) ✕; ℰ023 8083 2277; www.southampton.gov.uk), which has an excellent collection of modern art including works by Spencer, Sutherland and Lowry.

Beside the Civic Hall the Grade-II-listed Old Magistrates' Court building has been transformed into the **Sea City Museum** (○open April 2012; ♿ see www.south hampton.gov.uk for details), Southampton's major new museum and gallery; its permanent exhibitions feature maritime and archaeology collections.

🚗 DRIVING TOUR

TEST VALLEY
▶ *Circular tour approx 75mi/20km. Leave Southampton heading NW on the A 3057.*

The River Test runs swiftly through a fertile valley of often-flooded meadows, passing small market towns and pretty villages with thatched cottages, most notably the Tytherleys, Broughton, the Wallops, the Clatfords, Wherwell and Chilbolton.

Broadlands★
▶ *8mi/13km NW on the A 3057, or 1mi/2km short of Romsey.*

⊷ *Closed for renovation, due to reopen summer 2012.* ♿. *ℰ01794 529 750. www.broadlandsestates. co.uk.*

In 1736 the first Viscount Palmerston bought a small Tudor manor near Romsey and set about transforming its grounds. His son commissioned **Lancelot "Capability" Brown** to continue this work and

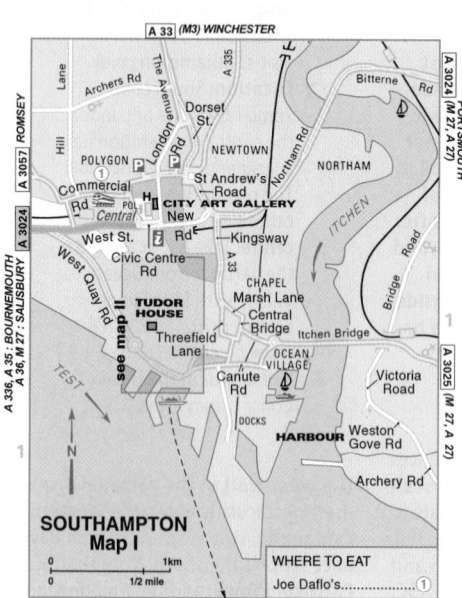

SOUTHAMPTON
Map I

WHERE TO EAT
Joe Daflo's..................①

ISLE OF WIGHT

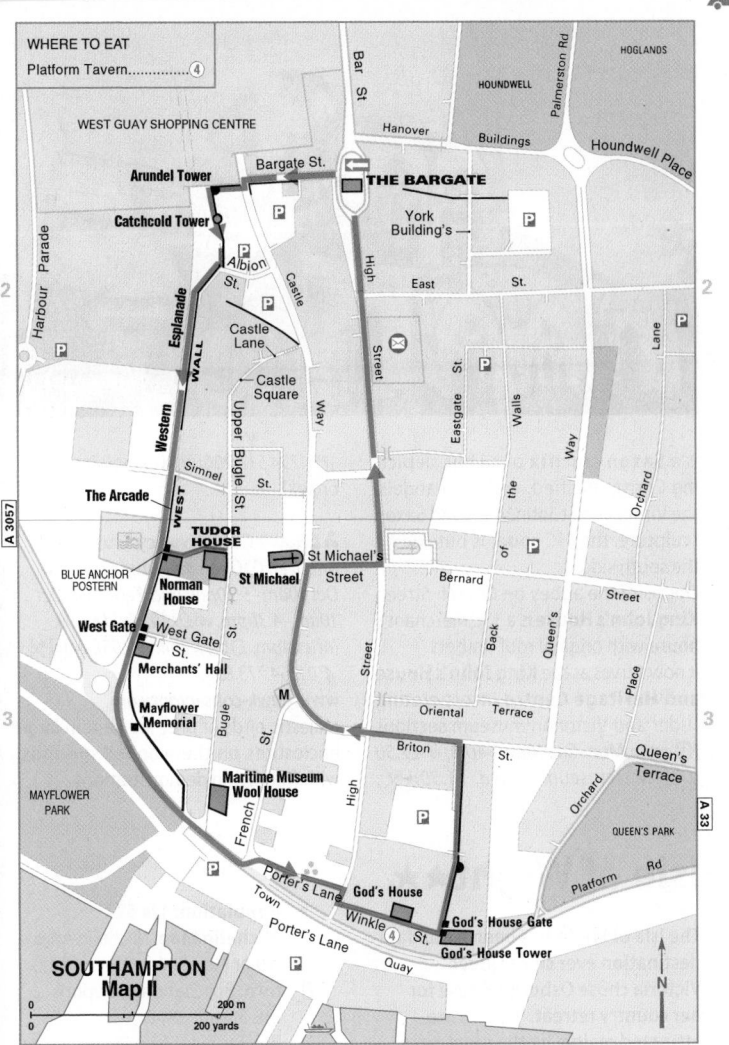

WHERE TO EAT
Platform Tavern..............④

WEST GUAY SHOPPING CENTRE

Bargate St.

THE BARGATE

Arundel Tower

Catchcold Tower

York Building's

Albion St.

Castle Lane

Castle Square

The Arcade

TUDOR HOUSE

St Michael's Street

Bernard

BLUE ANCHOR POSTERN

Norman House

St Michael

West Gate

West Gate St.

Merchants' Hall

Mayflower Memorial

Oriental Terrace

Briton St.

Queen's Terrace

MAYFLOWER PARK

QUEEN'S PARK

Maritime Museum Wool House

Porter's Lane

God's House

God's House Gate

God's House Tower

Porter's Lane

Winkle St.

Quay

SOUTHAMPTON Map II

0   200 m
0   200 yards

N

---

rebuilt the house in the Palladian style. **Henry Holland** created the east entrance front and the elegant dining room – the setting for three splendid **Van Dyck** paintings.

The house is notable for the **Wedgwood Room** with its friezes and mouldings, a fine collection of 18C Wedgwood pieces and four portraits by Sir Peter Lely.

The white-and-gold plasterwork of the **saloon** and the medallions in the drawing room ceiling are exquisite. In the 20C the house was Lord Mountbatten of Burma's (1900–79) residence.

Romsey Abbey★

▶ *9mi/15km NW on the A 3057.* ⏰*Open daily 7.30am–6pm.* ☎*01794 513 125. www.romseyabbey.org.uk.*

The town of Romsey grew up around a nunnery founded by Edward the Elder, son of Alfred the Great, in 907 and rebuilt c.1120–1230. At the Dissolution the buildings were destroyed but the abbey church survived to serve as the parish church. The purity and simplicity of the **interior★★** make this an excellent example of late Norman architecture. In the east chapel of the south choir aisle

Romsey Abbey

©Ian Whatmore/Fotolia.com

is a **Saxon crucifix** of c.1100, depicting Christ crucified, with two angels, the Virgin and St John. A second Saxon sculpture, the 11C **rood**, is outside on the south side.

Opposite the abbey on Church Street, **King John's House** is a 13C merchant's house with original roof timbers.

It now serves as the **King John's House and Heritage Centre** incorporating Tudor and Victorian museum sections (*open Mon–Sat 10am–4pm; £2.50 (Oct–Marmuseum closed, £1.50); ;*

01794 512 200; www.kingjohnshouse. org.uk).

Hawk Conservancy Trust
Andover. Open daily mid–Febmid-Oct 10am–5.30pm; mid-Feb–mid-Oct 10am–4.30pm. £9.10, child £5.95 (after 4pm, £10.77, child £6.05). .
01264 773 850.
www.hawk-conservancy.org.
Majestic birds of prey are kept in large enclosures on the wooded grounds, with free-flying demonstrations.

Isle of Wight★★

The Isle of Wight has been a holiday destination ever since Queen Victoria chose Osborne House for her country retreat. Visitors are attracted mainly by the quiet pace of life, the sandy beaches and the yachting. **It is also increasingly popular for its music festivals.**

 DRIVING TOUR

ISLAND TOUR
Begin your tour of the island here.

Ryde
This is the island's main ferry terminal and an old-fashioned seaside resort. The attractive old village of **Brading★** lies 4mi/6.5km south. **St Mary's Church★**,

▸ **Population:** 124,577.
⟡ **Michelin Map:** Michelin Atlas p 9 or Map 504 P, Q 31 and 32.
⯊ **Info:** Bus Station, Newport; Bus Station, Ryde; Bus Terminal, The Quay, Yarmouth; Seasons, 8–10 High Street, Ventnor: (all) 01983 813 818. www.islandbreaks.co.uk.
▷ **Location:** English Channel, due south of Portsmouth, between 2mi/3km and 5mi/8km from the mainland.
⊗ **Beware:** The island is packed out for the annual Isle of Wight Music Festival (second weekend June).
⊙ **Don't Miss:** Osborne House.
▲▴ **Kids:** Dinosaur Isle.

GETTING AROUND

Three operators service the island. The fastest route takes about 15 minutes, the slowest 40 minutes. **Red Funnel** runs a vehicle ferry and a high-speed passenger-only ferry, both between Southampton and Cowes (*℘0844 844 99 88; www.redfunnel.co.uk*). **Hovertravel** operates a hovercraft service (passenger only) between Southsea and Ryde (*℘01983 811 000; www.hovertravel.co.uk*). **Wight Link** operates vehicle ferries between Portsmouth and Fishbourne, and Lymington and Yarmouth, and a passenger-only catamaran between Portsmouth and Ryde (*℘0871 376 1000; www.wightlink.co.uk*).

built c.1200, boasts impressive 17C family tombs while southwest is the remains of the 3C **Brading Roman Villa**★ (*Oopen year-round daily 9.30am–5pm; Oclosed Christmas hols; ⌂£6.50; ₺ P✕; ℘01983 406 223; www.bradingroman-villa.org.uk*), with some fine 4C **mosaics** and a display of artefacts in the exhibition centre. Close by, **Nunwell House & Gardens**★ (*Coach Lane; 1mi/1.6km W; Oopen Spring Bank Hol Sun–Mon 1–5pm; Jul–early Sept Mon–Wed 1–5pm; ⚲guided tour of house 2pm, 3.30pm; ⌂£5, garden only, £3; P✕; ℘01983 407 240; www.islandbreaks.co.uk*) has been a family home since 1522.

⚇ Dinosaur Isle

▷ *6mi/10km S of Ryde. Culver Parade, Sandown Bay.* *Open daily Apr–Sept 10am–6pm; Oct 10am–5pm; Nov–Mar 10am–4pm. ⌂£5, child £3.50. ₺P✕. ℘01983 404 344. www.dinosaurisle.com.*

Housed in a striking modern building in the shape of a giant pterodactyl, moving models and intelligent interpretations bring to life prehistoric times when dinosaurs ruled the Isle of Wight.

Shanklin

▷ *3mi /5km S of Sandown.*

With its clifftop setting, beach, and pretty Old Village, Shanklin is a favourite stop on the island. A short walk from the Old Village, **Shanklin Chine** (*Chine Hollow or Everton Road; Oopen daily Apr–Oct 10am–5pm, until 10pm late May–mid-Sept when illuminated; ⌂£3.90; ✕; ℘01983 866 432; www.shanklinch-ine.co.uk*) is a lovely leafy gorge that charmed the poet John Keats, who lived nearby. It includes rare plants, a delightful waterfall and a heritage centre.

Ventnor

▷ *3.5mi/5.6km S of Shanklin.*

Another of the island's low-key seaside resorts, Ventnor is known for its tranquil 22-acre/9ha subtropical **Ventnor Botanic Garden** (*Undercliff Drive; Oopen daily Mar–Oct 10am–5pm, until 10pm late May–mid-Sept when illuminated; ⌂£1 to greenhouse, gardens free; ₺P(charge)✕; ℘01983 855 397; www.botanic.co.uk*). East of the town centre, secluded **Bonchurch beach** is where Charles Dickens once stayed. A detour north (*3.5mi/5.6km on the B 3227*) will take you to **Appuldurcombe House**, an 18C country estate, now home to an Owl and Falconry Centre (*Oflying times Apr–Sept daily 11am, 1pm, 3pm, Oct Wed–Sun 11.30am, 1.30pm; house open Apr–Oct Sun–Fri 10am–4pm; ⌂£7.50 (both); ₺P✕; ℘01983 852 484; www.appuldurcombe.co.uk*).

St Catherine's Point

▷ *5mi/8km W of Ventnor.*

The island's southernmost point is marked by **St Catherine's Oratory**, (*www.english-heritage.org.uk*) nicknamed the "Pepper Pot" for its shape. This medieval octagonal tower, allegedly once a lighthouse, dates from 1328.

Alum Bay

▷ *6.5mi/26km W of St Catherine's.*

The westernmost bay of the island, where alum was once mined, is a remarkable geological phenomenon, its sandstone cliffs richly coloured with more than 20 mineral hues. In the afternoon sun, a boat trip to the **Needles**, sea stacks 100ft/30m offshore, gives fine views of the colourful slopes and chalk cliffs.

Carisbrooke Castle★★

EH. ◯ *12mi/9km due E of Alum Bay (1.2mi/2km S of Newport).* ◯*Open daily Apr–Sept 10am–5pm; Oct–Mar 10am–4pm.* ◯*Closed 1–2 Jan, 24–26 Dec,.* ◎*£7.30.* ♿▣☐✕*(summer only).* ℘*01983 522 107. www.english-heritage.org.uk.*

In 1100 Richard de Redvers built the keep and curtain walls on the site of a Roman stronghold. The castle was further fortified against the Spanish in the late-16C. During the imprisonment of King Charles I in 1647–48, prior to his trial in London, the **bowling green** (◯*open to the public*) was created for his entertainment. He is said to have walked daily around the **battlements**, perhaps planning his escape (he made two attempts). The last resident governor, Queen Victoria's daughter, Princess Beatrice, died at Carisbrooke in 1944.

The Norman curtain wall encloses the high motte and 12C **keep** (with **views**★ for miles around). The late-12C **Great Hall** houses a museum of island history. An interactive exhibit in the Old Coach House explores life in the castle and the donkey centre houses the famous Carisbrooke donkeys, who give regular demonstrations in the **well-house** of the unique 1587 treadmill used to draw water from the 161ft-/49m-deep well.

Cowes

◯ *6mi/10km N of Carisbrooke.*

Cowes is the premier yachting centre in Britain, with nautical events throughout the summer, culminating in the world-famous **Cowes Week** regattas in August. Across the River Medina *(1mi/1.6km)* is East Cowes and Osborne House.

Osborne House★★

EH. ◯ *1mi/1.6km SE of East Cowes.* ◯*Open late Mar–Sept daily 10am–6pm; Oct daily 10am–4pm; Nov–Mar see website for days.* ◎*£11.50.* ♿▣✕. ℘*01983 200 022. www.english-heritage.org.uk.*

In a delightful position with views of the sea which reminded him of Naples, Prince Albert worked with Thomas Cubitt to create this enormous Italianate villa with terraced gardens, completed in 1851. For Queen Victoria, Osborne was a favourite home for family holidays with three generations of children.

After Albert's death in 1861 she spent much of her widowhood at Osborne, dying there in 1901. Her insistence that everything should be kept exactly as it had been during Albert's life gives a remarkable picture of royal family life, from richly furnished state rooms to the intimacy of the **Queen's Sitting Room**, where she worked beside her husband at twin desks. The only major addition to the house after Albert's death was the **Durbar Wing**★★ built in 1890; its amazing principal room celebrating Victoria's role as Empress of India.

A carriage ride through the **grounds** takes visitors to the **Swiss Cottage**, imported from Switzerland and erected in 1853, where the royal children learned to cook on small ranges and entertained their parents. Their natural history collections are displayed in a smaller chalet **museum**, near their miniature **fort** with cannon, the queen's bathing hut and a collection of tiny wheelbarrows, each bearing the initials of its royal owner.

Osborne House

Winchester★★
and around

This ancient cathedral city was the capital of King Alfred's **Wessex** and then of England, from the early-9C to about 100 years after the Norman Conquest. Today it is a lively regional shopping, historical and cultural centre.

A BIT OF HISTORY

It was only after the Roman invasion of AD 43 that the city known as **Venta Bulgarum** was founded. After the Romans withdrew, the city declined until the Saxons rebuilt a church and created a bishopric in 662. After 878 **Alfred the Great** consolidated his defence of Wessex against Danish attacks by setting up a series of fortified **burghs**, of which Winchester was the largest.

At the time of the Norman Conquest the city was already of such importance that **William I** was crowned here as well as in London. He built a castle in the southwest angle of the city walls and established a new cathedral in 1070. After the 12C Winchester yielded to London as the preferred royal residence. During the Civil War the Norman castle was largely destroyed, the cathedral damaged and the city looted by Parliamentary troops. After the Restoration the city recovered.

CATHEDRAL★★★

Open year-round. Cathedral Mon–Sat 9.30am–5pm, Sun 12.30–3pm. Visitor centre 9.30am–5.30pm. Guided tours: cathedral (60–90min) Mon–Sat 10am–3pm on the hour; crypt (20min) Mon–Sat 10.30am, 12.30pm, 2.30pm; tower (60–90min) Jun–Aug Mon, Wed and Fri 2.15pm, Sat 11.30am, 2.15pm; Sept–May Wed 2.15pm, Sat 11.30am, 2.15pm. £6.50, £9.50 including tower tour. No children under 12 on tower tour. 01962 857 200. www.winchester-cathedral.org.uk.
The cathedral stands surrounded by lawns on the same site as the 7C Saxon minster, the foundations of which were located in the 1960s. An early bishop of Winchester, **St Swithin**, was buried

▶ **Population:** 36,121.

Michelin Map: Michelin Atlas p 9 or Map 504 P, Q 30.

Info: Guildhall, High Street. 01962 840 500. www.visitwinchester.co.uk.

Location: Winchester is 66mi/106km southwest of London. The train station, with direct London service, is 1mi/1.6km from the centre, on Stockbridge Road. The bus station is right in the centre, on Broadway. Winchester is a small city and can easily be covered on foot.

Don't Miss: The cathedral; St Cross Hospital; Winchester College.

Timing: Allow a full day in Winchester.

Kids: Mid-Hants Watercress Line specials; Marwell Zoo.

outside the west end of the minster in 862. There was torrential rain on the day in 1093 when his grave was transferred inside the new church, though he had expressly asked to be buried in the open air; this gave rise to the legend that if it rains on St Swithin's Day (15 July) it will rain for 40 days.

William Walkelyn, appointed bishop by William I, began building the new cathedral in 1079. In 1202 the east end was reconstructed and in the early-14C the Norman choir was rebuilt in the Perpendicular style and the nave and west front were rebuilt between 1346 and 1404. After further remodellings of the nave, Lady Chapel and chancel in 1486–1528, the longest Gothic church in Europe (556ft/169m) was complete. When, in 1652, Parliament ordered the cathedral (ransacked in the Civil War) to be destroyed, it was saved only by a petition of the citizens. Early in the 20C the east end, built on marshland and supported on a 13C beech tree raft, began to sink, causing the walls to crack and the roof to fall; the cathedral was saved by a diver, William Walker, who worked alone from 1906 to 1912 replacing the rotting rafts with cement.

Exterior

Built largely of stone from the Isle of Wight, the cathedral's exterior, with its squat Norman **tower**, is impressive, though less exciting than the interior.

Interior

Bishop William of Wykeham (1324–1404) rebuilt the Norman pillars in the lofty 12-bay nave, with its bosses and **stone lierne vault**, to support the graceful Perpendicular arches surmounted by balconies with clerestory windows. Of special note are the **west window**, the ornate William of Wykeham's chantry, Jane Austen's tomb, window and brass, the 12C black Tournai marble **font** and the Jacobean pulpit.

The **Holy Sepulchre Chapel** has exquisite 13C wall paintings. In the chancel the **choir stalls** (1308) are ornamented with remarkable **misericords**; the marble tomb of the "ungodly" King William Rufus (d.1100) stands under the tower. The **stone reredos** with statues above the altar is early-16C; the early Tudor **vault** has outstanding **bosses**.

In the Early English retro-choir (13C) the chapels and chantries are dedicated to 15C–16C bishops. The early-13C Lady Chapel lit by seven-light windows is adorned with fine Tudor woodwork and **wall paintings**.

The 12C **Winchester Bible** is the jewel of the rich collection of manuscripts and books in the 12C Library (access from south transept).

In the north aisle of the nave is the grave of the great author **Jane Austen** (1775–1817), who moved to Winchester for treatment in her last illness.

The **Crypt** (guided tours only) open by tour houses the beautiful and critically acclaimed **Sound II** sculpture by Antony Gormley, creator of Angel of the North (see NEWCASTLE-UPON-TYNE).

Cathedral Close

The few remaining monastic buildings south of the cathedral include the **Deanery**, formerly the Prior's Lodging, with a three-arched porch and a 15C hall. The 14C **Pilgrims' Hall** (3 The Close; open daily, call for opening times; 01962 854 189), now part of the choir school, has possibly the oldest **hammerbeam roof** in existence. Beside the sturdy **St Swithin's Gate** stands the 15C timber-framed **Cheyney Court** and early-16C stables, also timber framed and now part of the Pilgrims' School.

CITY

Winchester College★

Guided tours year-round Mon, Wed and Fri–Sat 10.45am, noon, 2.15pm, 3.30pm, Tue and Thu 10.45am, noon, Sun 2.15pm, 3.30pm. The college is sometimes closed for functions (especially Sat afternoon). See website for details. Closed Christmas and New Year. £6. 01962 621 209. www.winchestercollege.org.

The college was founded in 1382 by **Bishop William of Wykeham** (pronounced "wick-um"), to provide an education for poor scholars, as well as "commoners" from wealthy families, to be continued at New College, Oxford, which Wykeham had already founded in 1379. Pupils are still known as "Wyke-hamists" and Winchester has the longest history of any school in the country.

The school is entered by the 14C **Outer Gate** in College Street. Through the Middle Gate is **Chamber Court**, the centre of college life, surrounded by Wykeham's original late-14C buildings. The **hall** on its south side (1st floor) has fine 16C wooden panelling on which hang portraits of former pupils and a 16C portrait of the founder. The **chapel**, with its prominent 15C pinnacled tower, was heavily restored in the 19C, but retains its medieval **wooden vault**, one of the first attempts at fan vaulting in England, and the original 14C **choir stalls** with fine misericords. In the centre of Wykeham's 14C cloister stands the early-15C **Fromond's Chantry**, the only example in England of a chapel so placed. The red-brick and stone **school** (west of cloister), was built in 1683–87 for the increasing number of "commoners". Sir Herbert Baker's simple peaceful **War Cloister**, built in 1924, commemorates Wykehamists who fell in world wars.

Castle Great Hall★

◷Open year-round daily 10am–5pm. ◷Closed 25–26 Dec. See also website for closure days. ◷£2 donation suggested. ℘01962 846 476. www3.hants.gov.uk/greathall.

The hall is the only surviving part of Winchester Castle, built in Norman times and slighted by order of Parliament in the Civil War. The room (110ft x 55ft x 55ft/34m x 17m x 17m) dating from 1222–36, is a splendid example of a medieval hall, with its timber roof supported on columns of Purbeck marble. On the west wall hangs a famous oak **Round Table** (18ft/5m diameter) which dates from the 14C; it is decorated with paintings of the Tudor rose in its centre, King Arthur and a list of his knights around the edge.

High Street

At the east end (The Broadway) stands a statue to Alfred the Great, erected in 1901. Among the buildings in the pedestrian street are the former **Guildhall** (now a bank), built in 1713, opposite the timber-framed **God Begot House**★ dating from 1558 (now a restaurant). Note also the 15C stone-carved **Butter Cross**, where markets were held.

St Cross Hospital★★

◷1mi/1.6km S. ◷Open Apr–Oct Mon–Sat 9.30am–5pm, Sun 1–5pm; Nov–Mar Mon–Sat 10.30am–3.30pm. ◷Closed Good Fri, 25 Dec. ◷£4. ◷⊞✕(Apr–Oct Mon–Sat). ℘01962 851 375. www.stcross.f2s.com.

A lovely walk from the city centre across the water meadows leads to the oldest charitable institution in England. Founded by Bishop Henry de Blois in 1136, its almshouses are still in use today. The **chapel** (late-12C– late-13C) is a fine example of Norman architecture, rich in zigzag stone carving on the arches and chancel vaulting. In the **Lady Chapel** is a

Flemish triptych of c.1530. The **Brethren's Hall** has a minstrels' gallery and an impressive late-15C timbered roof.

EXCURSIONS
▲▲ Mid-Hants Railway Watercress Line

◉Alresford. 8mi/13km NE on the A 31 and B 3046. ◷Station and rolling stock open year-round daily. ◷For train times and fares (standard fare £14, child £7), see website. ◷⊞(charge) ✕. ℘01962 733 810. www.watercressline.co.uk.

Named for the watercress beds which can still be seen in and around the handsome small Georgian town of Alresford (pronounced "Arlsford"), the Watercress Line carries old-fashioned steam engines for 10mi/16km over the hills to the market town of Alton, with special themed services, for adults and children, throughout the year.

Jane Austen's House

◉Chawton. 18mi/29km NE via the A 31 and B 3006. ◷Open Jan–Feb Sat–Sun 10.30am–4.30pm; Mar–May and Sept–Dec daily 10.30am–4.30pm; ◷Closed 25–26 Dec. ◷£7. ◷. ℘01420 83262. www.jane-austens-house-museum. org.uk.

The eight years Jane spent sharing this peaceful red-brick house with her mother, and sister, Cassandra, were some of her happiest and most productive. The tiny table at which she wrote and revised her novels stands in the dining parlour. Early editions are displayed alongside letters, family portraits and pieces of needlework.

▲▲ Marwell Zoo

◉Colden Common. 6mi/10km SE on the B 2177. ◷Open year-round daily 10am–4pm/5pm/6pm, see website for details; last entry 90min before closing. ◷Closed 25 Dec. ◷£12.72–£16.35, child £9.08–£12.72. ◷⊞✕. ℘01962 777 407. www.marwell.org.uk.

The grounds of 16C Marwell Hall are home to over 200 species of animals and birds, including large cats, primates, giraffes and rhinos, with an emphasis on conservation.

New Forest★★

Hampshire

This ancient landscape near the coast has remained more or less unchanged since William the Conqueror named the area his "new hunting forest" in 1079. The ancient system to protect and manage the woodlands and wilderness heaths is still in place and today it is a national park where New Forest ponies, donkeys, deer and cattle roam in England's largest remaining tract of unenclosed pasture.

- ⬡ **Michelin Map:** Michelin Atlas p 9 or Map 503 O, P 31
- ▤ **Info:** Lyndhurst. ℘023 8028 3444. www.thenewforest.co.uk.
- ▷ **Location:** Southern Hampshire.
- ⬡ **Don't Miss:** Beaulieu National Motor Museum; Buckler's Hard.

BEAULIEU★★

This pretty village at the head of the Beaulieu River is famous for the National Motor Museum, one of the world's most comprehensive collections of motor vehicles, set in the grounds of a Cistercian monastery founded in 1204 by King John. After the Dissolution of the Monasteries, the **abbey** fell into ruin, its stone being in demand for Henry VIII's coastal forts; only the footings remain. The cloister has partly survived, notably the lay brothers' quarters, now housing the **Monastic Life Exhibition** (*same ticket as the National Motor Museum, ⬡ see below*) and the 13C refectory, converted into the parish church. **Palace House**, the home of the first Lord Montagu, is a strange mixture of medieval monastic architecture and Victorian comforts.

The ⬡**National Motor Museum**★★ (*⬡ open year-round daily 10am–5pm; ⬡ closed 25 Dec; ⬡£15.50, child £8.25, includes Beaulieu Abbey and Palace House; ⬡▣✕; ℘01590 612 345; www.beaulieu.co.uk*) has a collection of over 250 vehicles and celebrates the story of motoring from 1895 to the present day. The Hall of Fame presents the great motoring pioneers and veteran and vintage cars while racing and record-breaking heroes are also commemorated. You can take a ride through 100 years of motoring with "Wheels" and browse a re-created 1930s country garage before coming bang up to date with a *Top Gear* exhibition and the "Flying" Ford Anglia from *Harry Potter and the Chamber of*

Secrets. Hands-on stations encourage children to explore how vehicles work.

BUCKLER'S HARD★

▷ *2mi/3km SE of Beaulieu.* ⬡*Open daily Mar–Jun and Sept–Oct 10am–5pm; Jul–Aug 10am–5.30pm; Nov–Feb 10am–4.30pm. ⬡£6.20, includes museum.* ▣✕. ℘*01590 616 645. www.bucklershard.co.uk.*

This charming hamlet comprises one very wide street lined with 18C cottages running down to the Beaulieu River. In the 1740s the village became a shipbuilding centre for the Navy. The **Maritime Museum and Buckler's Hard Story**★ illustrates many aspects of life and work in the 18C with the reconstructed interiors of two cottages and the New Inn, furnished in the style of the 1790s. Boat trips run from the wharf (*Easter–Oct; ⬡£4.50*).

LYNDHURST

Capital of the New Forest, this attractive town was where the forest rulers held court in the 17C **Queen's House**. The **New Forest Museum**, housed in the visitor centre (*High Street; ⬡open daily 10am–5pm; ⬡closed 25–26 Dec; ⬡£3.50; ⬡; ℘023 8028 3444; www.newforestmuseum.org.uk*), gives an excellent introduction to the area.

MINSTEAD

This attractive unspoiled village just north of Lyndhurst is home to the 13C **All Saints Church**. North of the church is **Furzey Gardens** (*Garden: ⬡open daily 10am–5pm/dusk; Gallery: ⬡open Mar–Oct daily 10am–5pm; ⬡garden £7,* *gallery free;* &.✕; ✆*023 8081 2464; www. furzey-gardens.org)*, with a 16C thatched cottage showing how New Forest workers lived over 400 years ago.

BROCKENHURST

This may well be your arrival point in the New Forest as it is the main bus and train interchange. The village itself is peaceful with a pretty green often full of grazing ponies and cattle. If you arrive by train, you can **hire cycles**, complete with simple mapped routes, right on the platform, from **Country Lanes** (⏰*open Mar–Oct Tue–Sun 9.30am–5.30pm, Nov– Feb Wed and Sat–Sun;* ✆*01590 622 627; www.countrylanes.co.uk).*

LYMINGTON

Lymington is the liveliest town in the New Forest, full of good shops and places to eat and drink. The High Street leads down to the picturesque small bustling **quayside** and marina area, lined with pretty period cottages, where fishing boats and yachtsmen mingle, fresh fish is sold and people come to enjoy the seaside holiday atmosphere.

FOREST DRIVES
Bolderwood Ornamental Drive★★

2mi/3km from Lyndhurst on the A 35 towards Christchurch, take a right turn for this lovely drive through enclosures created in the 19C with many fine, mature trees. **Walks** enable visitors to see forest deer up close from observation platforms. At the end of the drive is the venerable Knightwood Oak, said to be over 375 years old.

Rhinefield Ornamental Drive★★

2mi/3km from Lyndhurst on the A 35 towards Christchurch, take a left turn for this magnificent drive along an avenue of trees planted in 1859. Today they are Britain's finest collection of mature conifers. Some stand 150ft/46m high.

Bournemouth
and around

The Grand Old Lady of England's south central coast, Bournemouth has been a popular summer and winter resort since the late-19C. It is famous for its two piers and the ever-colourful public gardens. A lively student population ensures a good number of busy pubs and nightclubs.

SIGHTS
Russell-Cotes Art Gallery and Museum★★

East Cliff, Russell-Cotes Road. ⏰*Open year-round Tue–Sun and bank hols 10am–5pm.* ⏰*Closed Good Fri, 26 Dec.* ✎*£3 min donation suggested.* &.✕. ✆*01202 451 858. http://russell-cotes. bournemouth.gov.uk.*
Housed in **East Cliff Hall**, decorated in archetypal ornate High Victorian taste, with inlaid furniture, painted ceilings, decorative windows and coloured wall-

▶ **Population:** 155,488.

🌢 **Michelin Map:** Michelin Atlas p 9 or Map 503 O 31.

🔳 **Info:** Visitor Information Bureau, Westover Road. ✆0845 051 1700. www. bournemouth.co.uk.

◖ **Location:** 105mi/169km southwest of London. The bus station and train station are together, 1mi/1.6km east of the centre. To navigate the seafront jump aboard the land-train which runs for 6mi/10km along the promenade *(Mar–Oct only).*

☺ **Don't Miss:** Russell-Cotes Art Gallery and Museum; Compton Acres; the view of Old Harry Rocks from the Southwest Coast Path.

⏱ **Timing:** In summer allow at least two days.

👥 **Kids:** The beaches.

paper, the collections include numerous paintings (William Frith, Landseer, Leighton, Birket-Foster, Rossetti, Alma-Tadema, Edwin Long), fine English china, gold and silver plate, and souvenirs from abroad (the Orient, Germany, Egypt).

Christchurch★

At the heart of this pretty and prosperous little coastal town is a Norman **priory★** (○open Mon–Sat 9.30am–5pm) and Norman castle grouped around a harbour filled with fishing and pleasure craft.

EXCURSIONS
Compton Acres★★

❯ 164 Canford Cliffs Road. 2mi/3km W by the A 338. ○Open daily Apr–Oct 10am–6pm; Nov–Mar 10am–4pm. ○Closed 25–26 Dec. ⊚£6.95. ♿⃓✕. ℘01202 708 262. www.comptonacres.co.uk.

This series of nine distinct **gardens** (Italian, rock, water and Japanese) spreads over 15 acres/6ha in a rift in the sandstone cliffs; it is famous for having flowers in bloom throughout the year. The **English Garden** lies open to sunsets and a westerly **view★★★** of Poole Harbour, Brownsea Island and the Purbeck Hills.

Poole★

❯ 4mi/6km W on the the A 338.

With its fine sandy beach at Sandbanks and its situation on one of the largest harbours in the world, Poole is a holi-day resort, yachting haven and a major roll-on, roll-off port. By the quay is the recently refurbished **Poole Museum** (High Street; ○open late Mar–Oct Mon–Sat 10am–5pm, Sun noon–5pm; Nov–Mar Tue–Sat 10am–4pm, Sun noon–4pm; ♿; ℘01202 262 600; www.boroughofpoole.com) telling the history of the port and town. Adjacent is **Scaplen's Court** (○open same hours and contact details as Poole Museum), a domestic building from the late medieval period. The attractive 18C **old town** and the 18C Guildhall building are also of note.

Brownsea Island★

NT. ❯ Access by boat from Poole, Sandbanks and Bournemouth. ○Open mid-Feb–late Mar Sat–Sun 10am–4pm; Apr–Oct daily 10am–5pm. ⁎Guided tour of nature reserve. ⊚Landing fee/entry to island £5.80, ferry with Brownsea Island Ferries £9 (includes landing fee). ♿✕. ℘01202 707 744. www.nationaltrust.org.uk; www.brownseaislandferries.com.

This 500-acre/200ha island, covered in heath and woodland and fringed by inviting beaches along its south shore, consists of two nature reserves, either side of **Middle Street** along the central spine of the island. The north reserve is a sanctuary for waterfowl and other birds, and the south reserve, where visitors can wander at will, is likewise home to numerous birds, including peacocks. There is an excellent **view★★** across Poole Bay to the Purbeck Hills from **Baden-Powell Stone**, which commemorates the first Boy Scout camp held here in 1907.

Corfe Castle★

NT. ❯ 18mi/29km SW by the A 35 and A 351. ○Open daily Mar and Oct 10am–5pm; Apr–Sept 10am–6pm; Nov–Feb 10am–4pm. ○Closed 25–26 Dec. ⊚£6.81. ♿⃓✕. ℘01929 481 294. www.nationaltrust.org.uk.

Corfe Castle has dominated the landscape since the 11C, first as a towering stronghold and since 1646 as a dramatic ruin. From the high mound on which it stands, the **views★★** are spectacular. In 987 the 17-year-old King Edward, son

Japanese Garden, Compton Acres
Y. Duhamel/MICHELIN

of Edgar, visiting his half-brother at the castle, was murdered by his stepmother, Queen Aethelfrith; in 1001 he was canonised as **St Edward**, **King and Martyr**. It was the home of Sir John Bankes, Chief Justice to King Charles I. His wife resolutely defended it in 1643–45 and when it fell, owing to the treachery of one of the garrison, it was looted and blown up by the Parliamentarians.

A detour 4mi/6km) northwest will bring you to **Blue Pool**★, a beautiful blue-green lake (3 acres/1.2ha) fringed by silver birch and pine woods, gorse and heather, through which sandy paths meander, giving views of the Purbeck Hills.

Lulworth Cove★

◯ *8mi/13km W of Corfe Castle via the B 3070.*

The circular sweep of Lulworth Cove is almost enclosed by the downland cliffs. From here, the Dorset Coast Path leads to the striking cliff archway of **Durdle Door** to the west, a dramatic climax to the whole of this spectacular area of headlands and bays.

Swanage★

◯ *5mi/8km E of Corfe Castle via the A 351.*

A scenic stretch of road leads to this quarry town and harbour, from which stone and marble were shipped to build Westminster Abbey and the cathedrals of Exeter, Lincoln and Salisbury. Swanage also boasts a good beach and a range of seaside leisure facilities. Take the Southwest Coast Path east of Swanage to discover **Old Harry Rocks**★★, two stacks of gleaming chalk once part of an unbroken shoreline from The Needles but now separated from the mainland and each other (Old Harry is the larger stack, his "wife" is the slimmer!).

Wimborne Minster

◯ *Open Mon–Sat 9.30am–5.30pm, Sun 2.30–5.30pm. Chained Library open Easter Mon–Oct most days 10.30am–12.30pm, 2–4pm.* & *℘01202 884 753. www.wimborneminster.org.uk.*

This huge church dominates the small town of Wimborne. The present struc-

ture is mainly Norman (1120–80) with 15C additions. It has a wealth of detail to enjoy; note the "Quarter Jack" grenadier figure on the west tower striking the time, the astronomical clock, and the splendid stained-glass windows. Ascend the 600-year-old spiral staircase to the old Treasury, which now houses the Library, founded in 1686. This includes the second-largest chained library in the country with manuscripts written on lambskin, dating back to 1343.

Kingston Lacy

NT. ◯ *Open mid-Mar–Oct Wed–Sun and bank hol Mon 11am–5pm.* *£10.50.* & 🅿 ✕. *℘01202 883 402. www.nationaltrust.org.uk.*

Home of the Bankes family for more than 300 years, this striking 17C house is noted for its lavish interiors. The outstanding art collection includes paintings by Rubens, Van Dyck, Titian and Tintoretto, with the largest private collection of Egyptian artefacts in the UK. Outside are beautiful lawns and a restored Japanese tea garden.

🚗 DRIVING TOUR

ISLE OF PURBECK

◯ *30mi/48km. Allow a full day not including visiting time.*

The Isle of Purbeck is in fact a 60sq mi-/155sq km peninsula of unspoiled villages, seaside and castles.

◯ *Begin the tour by crossing the water from Poole, on the Sandbanks Ferry.*

Studland

NT. ◯ *3mi/5km S of the ferry via the A 351.*

This National Trust-owned beach is one of the finest in the West Country and is famous for its (signposted) nudist area.

Swanage★

◯ *3mi/5km S of Studland via B 3351.* 👁 *See above.*

Just over 1mi/1.6km south of Swanage, the road ends at **Durlstone Head** and its Country Park. In the park is **Durl-**

stone Castle, built 1889, as a Victorian folly, complete with its huge stone 40-ton 10ft (3m) diameter "Great Globe" of the world in its grounds. Today the castle houses a visitor centre.

▷ *Return to Swanage and head W on the A 351 5mi/8km S.*

Corfe Castle Village★
Although it is most famous for its spectacular ruined hilltop castle (◔*see above*), this charming little village of low stone houses (and several inns), many dating from the 16C and 17C, is one of the most picturesque spots in Dorset. Visit the quaint model village.

▷ *Head N briefly on the A 351, then turn left to join the B 3070, passing through Church Knowle and Steeple to East Lulworth (total 7.5mi/12km). Follow the signs to the castle.*

Lulworth Castle
◔*Open summer Sun–Fri 10am–5.30pm; call for winter times.* ◈*£5.* ♿ **P** *(£5)*✕. ℘*0845 450 1054; www. lulworth.com)*

Dorchester★
and around

The Romans built the southwest settlement of Durnovaria in the 1C AD on the London–Exeter highway, but Dorchester today is famous for being "Hardy Country", home to the great British novelist, Thomas Hardy and the setting for many of his 19C tales.

VISIT
Dorset County Museum★
High West Street. ◔*Open Jan–Mar Mon–Sat 10am–4pm; Apr–Oct Mon–Sat 10am–5pm; Nov–Dec Tue–Sat 10am–4pm (Mons Jan–Mar).* ◈*£5.90.* ♿. ℘*01305 262 735. www.dorset countymuseum.org.*
A splendid **Victorian gallery**, with painted cast-iron columns and arches supporting a glass roof, houses **Thomas Hardy** memorabilia: furniture and paint-

The castle was built in the early 17C as a hunting lodge, then became the country house of the estate.

▷ *Continue on the same road for 2.5mi/4km; look for the brown signs off the main road to Lulworth Cove car park.*

Lulworth Cove and Durdle Door
◔*See above.*

▷ *Head back to East Lulworth and follow the B30370 N (total 8.5mi/14km).*

Wareham
The centrepiece of this quiet town in summer is its picturesque flower-filled **quay** on the languorous River Frome, plied by colourful pleasure craft. An old granary house (now a restaurant) and the Anglo-Saxon Lady St Mary's Church and Priory complete an idyllic composition.

▸ **Population:** 15,037.
◔ **Michelin Map:** Michelin Atlas p 8 or Map 503 M 31.
▯ **Info:** Antelope Walk. ℘01305 267 992. www.westdorset.com.
▷ **Location:** 126mi/203km southwest of London. London trains arrive at Dorchester South, Bath and Bristol trains at Dorchester West.
◉ **Don't Miss:** Abbotsbury Village and its wwannery, near Chesil Beach.
♟ **Kids:** Abbotsbury Children's Farm and Swannery.

ings and papers from **Max Gate**, the house Hardy built for himself in 1885, as well as a reconstruction of his study.

EXCURSIONS
Bere Regis Church★

▶ *11mi/18km E on the A 35.*

The fine Perpendicular church of **St John the Baptist** is the only building in the village to have survived the last of a series of fires in 1788. Its **roof**★★ is a particular joy.

Maiden Castle★★

EH. ▶ *2mi/3km SW on the A 354.*
Open daily dawn-dusk. **P**.

Britain's finest **earthwork ramparts** were begun c.350 BC on the site of a Neolithic settlement. There were four main building phases before this massive 47-acre/19ha complex was fully equipped with defences c.60 BC.

Chesil Beach/Abbotsbury★★

▶ *10mi/16km SW via Martinstown and Portesham.*

Chesil Beach is a remarkable 8mi/13km shingle bank which forms a lagoon; at one end is the charming thatched golden ironstone village of **Abbotsbury** with its three very popular visitor attractions (money-saving "passport" combination ticket: adult £16, child £10, family £28).

The **Abbotsbury Swannery**★ (*New Barn Road;* open late Mar–Oct daily 10am–5pm/6pm; £9.95, child £6; **P**; ℘01305 871 858; www.abbotsbury-tourism.co.uk) was founded by the monks c.1390 and now accommodates more than 400 mute swans. You can walk right through the middle of the beautifully located nesting grounds and observe the birds at close quarters. A highlight is the mass feeding of up to 600 swans at noon and 4pm daily. A short walk away, the **Children's Farm** (*Church Street;* open as Swannery, Sept–Oct Sat–Sun only; £8.50, child £7; ℘01305 871 817; www.abbotsbury-tourism.co.uk) is housed in and around a splendid **Tithe Barn** built in the 1390s. The lush acclaimed neighbouring **Subtropical Gardens**★ (*Bullers Way;* open year-round daily 10am–dusk; £9.95; **P**; ℘01305 871 387; www.abbotsbury-tourism.co.uk) contrast with the rugged setting of the wind-blown 14C

St Catherine's Chapel★ (*EH;* open any reasonable time) on its 250ft/76m crest.

🚗 DRIVING TOUR

JURASSIC COAST★★

Stretching from Purbeck in the east to Exmouth in the west, this coastline takes its name from the large number of Jurassic-age fossils that have been found in its cliffs. This short route (46mi/74km) along the coast covers the westernmost stretch (distances are from Abbotsbury). Begin at **Abbotsbury**★★ (see above). Follow the coast road west to **Lyme Regis**★ (18.5/30km). This small genteel resort is famous for its Cobb (breakwater) and palaeontology heritage – as explained in the **Lyme Regis Museum** (www.lymeregismuseum.co.uk). **Beer** (28mi/45km) is a classic small Devon fishing village with a broad shingle beach where boats rest overnight. **Sidmouth** (34mi/55km) is another genteel resort, framed between high red cliffs, with its Regency vintage lovingly preserved. The road diverts inland (signposted) to **Bicton Park Botanical Gardens** (40mi/64km). On the broad sandy Exe estuary, **Exmouth** (46mi/74km) is a mix of dignified Georgian houses and "smugglers' alleys". Don't miss **A La Ronde**★ (www.nationaltrust.org.uk), a unique 16-sided, 18C house with an extraordinary interior décor of shells and feathers.

Jurassic Coast towards Lyme Regis

© Martin Kemp/iStockphoto.com

Dorset and Wiltshire Border

The rolling countryside of the Wiltshire/Dorset borders boasts two small picturesque historic towns in Sherborne and Shaftesbury, England's finest landscaped gardens, Britain's most exotic and child-friendly aristocratic estate, and its rudest chalk figure!

SHERBORNE★

With its imposing abbey church, public school and fine warm **Ham Hill stone** buildings, Sherborne has the charm of a miniature cathedral city.

Sherborne Abbey★★

⟳Open daily 8am–6pm; winter 8am–4pm). ⟲Guided tours Apr–Sept Tue 10.30am, Fri 2.30pm (call to confirm). ♿. ☎01935 812 452. www.sherborneabbey.com.

The abbey church, rebuilt during the 15C, contains elements which date back to Saxon times when Sherborne was made the See of the Bishop of Wessex, **St Aldhelm**, in 705. The Norman church extended as far west as the Saxon church, as the late Norman **south porch** proves.

The 15C **crossing tower** on massive Saxon-Norman piers and walls has paired bell openings and 12 pinnacles. Inside, the **chancel** shafts rise directly from the floor up to the earliest large-scale **fan vault** in the country, and the effect is breathtaking. Even more impressive is the late-15C **nave vault**. A splendid, unadorned Norman **tower arch** divides the nave from the chancel. An original **Saxon doorway** can be seen at the end of the north aisle.

Sherborne Castle★

⟳Open Apr–Oct Tue–Thu, Sat–Sun and bank hols 11am (castle Sat 2pm)–4.30pm (last entry). ⊚£9.50, grounds only, £5. ✕. ☎01935 812 072. www.sherbornecastle.com.

ℹ **Info:** www.visitwiltshire.co.uk; www.visit-dorset.com.
⊘ **Don't Miss:** Stourhead; Longleat; Wilton House.
👪 **Kids:** Longleat Safari Park.

The original **Old Castle**, now a ruin, was built in 1107–35. In 1592 it was acquired by **Sir Walter Raleigh**, who decided to build a new Sherborne Castle on the far bank of the River Yeo.

Raleigh created a four-storey house beneath a Dutch gable and balustrade, built of Ham Hill stone. Sir John Digby, who acquired the property following Raleigh's imprisonment, enlarged the castle in 1620–30, keeping to Raleigh's style. The house, set in parkland modelled by Lancelot "Capability" Brown in 1776–79, contains fine collections of paintings, furniture and porcelain. Note the painting (1600) of Queen Elizabeth I, and the 17C plaster ceiling in the Red Drawing Room.

CERNE ABBAS★

➲ 11mi/18km S of Sherborne.

The **village**★ is notable for the beautiful range of timber-fronted 16C houses in Abbey Street, and for **St Mary's Church**, a mix of Early English and Perpendicular, with a spectacular **tower**.

However, it is the spectacular 180ft-/55m-long chalk outline of the naked **Cerne Abbas Giant**, one of the largest hill-figures in Britain, that attracts most visitors. "He" has been connected, for obvious reasons, with local fertility rituals, although his origin and date remain unclear.

SHAFTESBURY

➲ 16.5mi/26km E of Sherborne.

The town is perched on the crest of a 700ft/213m spur, an excellent **vantage point**★, used by King Alfred as a strong-point in his wars against the Danes. And even today Shaftesbury's joy is the steep cobbled picture-book **Gold Hill**★, lined on one side with small 16C–18C houses and on the other by a massive buttressed 13C ochre-coloured wall. It is famous in Britain as the scene of the sepia-tinted nostalgia-laden Hovis bread TV adverts. At the top is the small **Gold Hill Museum** (🕐 open Good Fri/ Apr–Oct daily 10.30am–4pm; 🕾 01747 852 910; www.shaftesburyheritage.org. uk) covering local history.

The **abbey** (🕐 museum open Good Fri/ Apr–Oct, daily 10am–5pm; 🕾 £2.50; 🕾 01747 852 910; www.shaftesburyabbey. org.uk), founded in 888 by King Alfred, became the wealthiest nunnery in England. In the 15C–16C the saying went that if the Abbess of Shaston (Shaftesbury) were to marry the Abbot of Glaston (Glastonbury) their heirs would own more land than the king.

In 1539 Henry VIII dissolved both abbeys and now only the ground plan of Shaston remains visible.

WILTON HOUSE★★

▶ 3mi/5km W of Salisbury.
House: 🕐 Open Good Fri–early Sept Sun–Thu and bank hols 11.30am–4.30pm. **Gardens:** 🕐 Open early/ mid-Apr–early Sept daily 11am–5pm; Sept Sat–Sun, 11am–5pm. 🕐 Closed late Aug bank hol Sat. 🕾 £14, grounds only, £5.50. ♿ 🅿 ✕. 🕾 01722 746 714; 01722 746 729 (info line). www.wiltonhouse.com.

In 1544 the first Earl of Pembroke was given the land of the dissolved Benedictine convent at Wilton by Henry VIII and built a house here. The 4th Earl commissioned Inigo Jones to design the house anew in 1630 and the 11th Earl called in James Wyatt in 1801, who greatly altered the house.

The suite of State Apartments by Inigo Jones has a wealth of Classical detail. The furniture includes pieces by William Kent and the younger Chippendale.

The ceiling of the Colonnade Room boasts fantastical 17C monkey motifs.

In the Great Ante Room are portraits by Rembrandt, Van Dyck and Clouet.

The white-and-gold Double Cube Room, measuring 60ft/18m x 30ft/9m x 30ft/9m, was specially designed by Inigo Jones to house the 4th Earl's unique collection of splendid Van Dyck portraits. It was here that strategic plans were laid

by Eisenhower and Churchill (a frequent visitor) during the Second World War, when Wilton House was the Southern Command headquarters.

The house sits square on a flat lawn which stretches south to the river, marked by the much-photographed **Palladian bridge** (1737). The grounds also include an excellent adventure playground.

STOURHEAD★★★

NT. ▶ Stourton. Nr Warminster, 18.5mi/30km S of Bath. **Garden:** ♿ Open year-round daily 9am–6pm/ dusk. **House:** ♿ 🕐 Open mid-Mar–Oct Fri–Tue 11am–5pm; summer school hols and mid-Oct–early Nov daily 11am–5pm. **Tower:** 🕐 Open mid-Mar–Oct daily 11am–5pm. 🕾 Garden and house £12.10, garden or house £7.30, tower £3.20. 🅿 ✕. 🕾 01747 841 152. www.nationaltrust.org.uk.

One of the most celebrated gardens in the country, Stourhead is a supreme example of English landscape style including a Palladian mansion, delightful garden architecture and rare planting around a tranquil lake.

Garden

This idyllic scenery was created by the banker Henry Hoare II (1705–85), influenced by the landscapes he saw on his travels. Perhaps an even greater influence were the paintings of Claude Lorrain and Nicolas Poussin, in which nature is presented in luminous shades and focal points are provided by statuary or Classical buildings. He first had the great triangular lake formed, then began the planting of trees, "ranged in large masses as the shades in a painting". In collaboration with his architect, Henry Flitcroft, he began to build his garden architecture: the Temple of Flora, the Grotto, the Gothic Cottage, the Pantheon, the Temple of Apollo, and **Palladian bridge**. He also created a quintessential English vista of lake, Turf Bridge, Cross, and, in the background, Stourton church and village. His planting, now wonderfully mature, has been added to by his successors to give a wealth of exotic specimens and of ever-changing seasonal effects.

At the far end of the "outer circuit" stands **Alfred's Tower**, a triangular brick folly built on the spot where Alfred allegedly raised his standard resisting the Danes, but more probably commemorating the succession of George III and peace with France (1762). At the top of the narrow tower is a viewing balcony (205 steps).

House

The original house of 1721 was built for the father of Henry Hoare II. In 1902 a fire destroyed the early-18C interiors, although the contents of the ground floor state rooms were largely saved.

The **hall**, a perfect 30ft/9m cube, is hung with family portraits. The long barrel-vaulted **library**, a particularly fine Regency interior, contains some splendid pieces of **Chippendale** furniture and **Canaletto** drawings of Venice. Further treasures are to be found in the South Wing (furniture) and **Picture Gallery**: landscapes by **Claude** and **Poussin**.

LONGLEAT★★★

◗ Warminster. 19mi/31km S of Bath and well signed from the main roads. ◷ Open mid-Feb–early Nov daily 10am–4pm/5pm/6pm/7.30pm (see website for dates; also for Christmas holidays opening times). ◷ Closed 25 Dec. ☛"Private Chattels" Tours (rooms not normally open to the public), see website (☎£10). Tours of Lord Bath's Murals can usually be booked at the front desk of Longleat House on the day of your visit for a small surcharge. ☎£28 all areas, child £18.50 (15 percent discount online), house only, £12.90. ♿🅿✕. ℘01985 844 400. www.longleat.co.uk.

Set in 900 acres/360ha of Capability Brown-landscaped parkland, the house is one of the best examples of High Elizabethan architecture in Britain. It caused great controversy in 1949, when it became the first stately home to open to the public on a commercial basis, and an even bigger furore in 1966 when it opened the first safari park outside Africa.

House

On the ground floor, the late-16C Great Hall with its fine hammerbeam roof contains a splendid pillared fireplace. The Ante-Library is graced by Italian furniture. The Red Library boasts trompe l'œil ceiling panels, while the gilded coffered ceiling of the Lower Dining Room is modelled on one in the Doge's Palace. In the Breakfast Room family portraits look down on Chippendale-style chairs and japanned gaming tables, while the walls are hung with modern art.

Upstairs, highlights include the State Dining Room with its Cordoba leather walls and a Meissen table centrepiece (c.1760); the 90ft/27m 17C Long Gallery with a massive marble fireplace copied from one in the Doge's Palace; the State Drawing Room paintings and various pieces of 18C French furniture; the Apartments, dress collection and cabinets of porcelain. The Royal Bedrooms comprise an elegant dressing room hung with hand-painted Chinese wallpaper. The outbuildings comprise a butchery and stable block (containing the eclectic "Lord Bath's Bygones"). **Lord Bath's Murals** is a collection famous for its Kama Sutra-type murals.

🚶‍♂️ Safari Park and Other Attractions

The "drive-in zoo" is famous for its lions and monkeys, the latter being notorious for clambering onto cars. There are also enclosures for wallabies, giraffes, zebras, llamas, dromedaries, camels, white rhinos, fallow deer, wolves, tigers, and elephants. Popular new features are **hand-feeding giraffes** at the Watering Hole in the East Africa Reserve and **Jungle Kingdom** feeding lorikeets, walking through the meerkat enclosure and so on… Once out of your car a **safari boat** takes you on a lake among seals and hippos. Another Longleat claim to fame is its **hedge maze**, made up of more than 16,000 English yews; allow between 20–90minutes to complete! There's also a batcave, birds of prey and animals with ranger shows, Pets Corner, a steam railway, motion simulators and various other family activities.

Salisbury★★
and around

Salisbury (pronounced "sauls-bur-ee") is the quintessential English cathedral town. The view, as you approach it, is much as John Constable painted it some two centuries ago, unencumbered by high-rise modernity or sprawling suburbs. The spire, the tallest in England, is the city's focal point.

A BIT OF HISTORY

The earlier city of **Old Sarum**★ *(2mi/3km N)*, originally an Iron Age hilltop fort (28 acres/11ha), had been modified by the Romans and Saxons and became a Norman strongpoint where two successive cathedrals were built. By the beginning of the 13C the citizens and clergy of Old Sarum began to build their third cathedral on the banks of the River Avon. The hilltop buildings fell into ruin and New Sarum, or Salisbury, was born.

MEDIEVAL STREETS

Between the cathedral and the 19C **Market Square** extend medieval streets, lined by gabled half-timbered houses dating from the 14C–17C. At the centre in a small square stands the 15C hexagonal **Poultry Cross**.

At the northeast end of the high street is **Sarum St Thomas Church**★, a Perpendicular church dating from 1220 with a low square tower of 1390. It features a **doom painting** (c.1475), with Christ in Majesty and the New Jerusalem.

CATHEDRAL★★★

Open year-round Mon–Sat 9am–5pm, Sun noon–4pm. £5.50, contribution requested. Guided tours (free). Tower Tour (90min) £8.50, must be booked ahead. &X.
01722 555 156; 01722 555 120.
www.salisburycathedral.org.uk.
For many people, Salisbury Cathedral epitomises the Early English style at its best; Medieval Gothic in its purest, most ascetic form. It is unique among England's older cathedrals, having been built in a single style, in just 38

▶ **Population:** 39,268.
🕭 **Michelin Map:** Michelin Atlas p 9 or Map 503 O 30.
🛈 **Info:** Fish Row. *01722 334956. www.visitwiltshire.co.uk/salisbury.*
🜨 **Location:** Near Southampton and just north of the New Forest, Salisbury is a transport hub with frequent services. The station is on South Western Road 0.5mi/0.8km from the centre. The bus station is central, on Endless Street.

years, with the tallest spire in England (404ft/123m). Outside, the ornate **west screen** extends from the gabled portals up through lines of statue-filled niches, lancet windows and arcading to the pointed gable and corner towers with their miniature angel pinnacles and ribbed spires. The most spectacular feature of the cathedral, the **spire** over the heightened tower, was added almost a century later but harmonises perfectly. Inside, the **nave** (230ft/70m) extends over half the length of the whole building (449ft/137m), its vault towering to a height of 84ft/26m. Note on the south side the tomb chests of **Bishops Roger** (d.1139) and **Joscelin** (d.1184), the shrine of **St Osmund** (d.1099) and the chain-

Salisbury Cathedral

Y. Duhamel/MICHELIN

mailed **William Longespée** (d.1226), half-brother of King John. Giant piers of clustered black marble columns mark the **crossing**, intended to support the original tower, but since the 14C required to bear the additional 6,500 tons of the heightened tower and spire. The piers have in fact buckled a noticeable 3.5in/9cm, despite reinforcing.

A brass plate in the crossing marks the spot where a plumb-line let down from the spire point by Sir Christopher Wren in 1668 reached the floor; 29.5in/75cm off-centre to the southwest. In the north aisle is the oldest working clock in England (c.1386). A **Tower Tour** climbs 332 steps in easy stages by narrow winding spiral staircases to reach the foot of the spire 225ft/69m)above ground level. From here you can see up into the spire through the medieval scaffold, and from the outside you can look over the city and surrounding countryside.

Construction of the Decorated Gothic-style **chapter house** and **cloisters** was begun c.1263, making the latter the earliest in any English cathedral; they are also the longest (181ft/55m). The vault of the octagonal chapter house (58ft/18m across) is supported on a central column, surrounded by eight ringed Purbeck marble shafts which rise from their foliated capitals as ribs to ceiling bosses, before dropping to clusters of slim columns framing the windows. An Old Testament frieze (restored 19C) fills the niches on either side of the canons' seats. The main floor display is dedicated to one of four original copies of the **Magna Carta**.

Cathedral Close★

The Close is spacious and mellow with its 16–18C houses composed of ancient stone and terra-cotta bricks. The Close walls are of stone from the abandoned cathedral and castle of Old Sarum.

The medieval flint-and-brick house **Salisbury and South Wiltshire Museum**★ (*open Jul–Sept Mon–Sat 10am–5pm, Sun noon–5pm, Oct–Jun Mon–Sat 10am–5pm; Closed 24–25 Dec£6; ; 01722 332 151* contains the regimental museum and a

Stonehenge collection, relics from Old Sarum, porcelain and pottery.

The Museum of the Infantry Regiments of Berkshire and Wiltshire is housed in **The Wardrobe**★ (*open Mon–Sat 10am–5pm, Sun noon–4.30pm; ; 01722 419 419; www.thewardrobe.org.uk*), one of the first houses to be built in the Close (1254) as the bishop's document storehouse and wardrobe.

In Chorister's Close, **Mompesson House**★ (*NT; open mid-Mar–Oct Sat–Wed and Good Fri 11am–5pm; £5.20; ; 01722 335 659; 01722 420 980 (infoline); www.nationaltrust.org.uk*) was built in 1701 by Charles Mompesson. It is notable for its ornate Baroque plasterwork and huge collection of some 370 types of English drinking glasses dating from 1700.

EXCURSION
Old Sarum★

EH. 3.5 mi north of Salisbury. Open daily late Mar–Jun and Sept 10am–5pm; Jul–Aug 9am–6pm; Oct and Mar 10am–4pm; rest of year 11am–3pm. Closed 1 Jan, 24–26 Dec. £3.70. . 01722 335 398. www.english-heritage.org.uk.

The mighty ramparts of this great earthwork were raised c.500 BC by Iron Age peoples, then occupied by the Romans, the Saxons and, eventually, the Normans. Here, William the Conqueror paid off his troops in 1070, and in 1086 summoned the great landowners of England to swear an oath of loyalty.

A castle was built, then a royal palace. By the mid-12C a town had arisen complete with a new Norman cathedral, but the lack of water on the scorched hilltop made life almost unbearable.

The answer was a move downhill to the burgeoning New Sarum (Salisbury), where a new cathedral was founded in 1220. Old Sarum went into rapid decline. Its cathedral was demolished and used for building materials and its castle was abandoned.

Today, Old Sarum remains an atmospheric place, the remains of its fortress palace, castle and cathedral still clear, and well interpreted in-situ.

Salisbury Plain
and North Wiltshire

This area is dominated by the enigmatic presence of Stonehenge, though this is but one of many important prehistoric sites on and around the 300sq-mile (780sq-km) Salisbury Plain, much of which is occupied by the Army and is out of bounds. Well-preserved traces of the less distant past are in evidence at Malmesbury, Devizes and Lacock.

- ⚭ **Michelin Map:** Michelin Atlas p 9 or Map 503 O 30.
- ▯ **Info:** www.visitwiltshire. co.uk.
- ⊚ **Don't Miss:** Stonehenge; Avebury; Lacock; Grand Avenue, Savernake Forest; forest; Corsham Court.
- ♣♣ **Kids:** Stonehenge.

♣♣ STONEHENGE★★★

EH. ⭕ *Just N of Salisbury, 84mi/135km SW of London.* ⭘ *Open daily mid-Mar–May and Sept–mid-Oct 9.30am–6pm; Jun–Aug 9am–7pm; mid-Oct–mid-Mar 9.30am–4pm (1 Jan and 26 Dec 10am–4pm). In poor weather, access may be restricted and visitors may not be able to use the walkway around the stone circle.* ⭘ *Closed 24–25 Dec.* ⊶ *£7.* ♿ ▯ ✗. ✆ *0870 333 1181.* www. *english-heritage.org.uk.*

Britain's most celebrated prehistoric monument is between 4,000 and 5,000 years old; radiocarbon dating indicates that its construction was begun in c.2950 BC and completed in three phases by c.1550 BC. For centuries man has speculated upon its purpose but it remains an enigma. Although many of the stones have fallen or disappeared it is still possible, from the centre of the circle, to see the sun rise over the Heel Stone (at the entrance) on midsummer's day; there are suggestions that it was constructed as an astronomical observatory or a sanctuary for a sun-worshipping cult, or even a combination of the two. The main axis has always been aligned with the midsummer sunrise, so Stonehenge must have been linked to the seasons.

A Bit of History

The period – When work began the area was inhabited by nomadic hunters and early farming settlers who had crossed the Channel and North Sea in skin boats. By 2000 BC the Beaker Folk spread into Wessex along the chalk upland tracks, growing into a community of 12–15,000, ruled by the cattle-barons of Salisbury Plain, who also controlled the metal industry. There was a growing priesthood who, at peak periods in the construction of Stonehenge, could call on the population to provide the 600 men needed to haul a sarsen stone up the Vale of Pewsey, or 200 to erect it onsite.

The building design – Like many a medieval cathedral, Stonehenge was much remodelled after its foundation.

Stonehenge

©René Mansi/iStockphoto.com

In the **first phase**, 2950BC–2900 BC, a ditch with an inner bank of chalk rubble (6ft/nearly 2m high) was dug. This, with a ring of 56 holes, known as the Aubrey Holes, after the 17C pioneer of field archaeology John Aubrey (1626–97), encloses an area 300ft/91m in diameter. To the northeast the bank and ditch were cut to make an entrance marked inside by two upright stones and outside by the **Heel Stone** *(near the road)*. Inside the enclosure four **Station Sarsens** were set up at the cardinal points of the compass.

In the **second phase**, c.2100 BC, a double ring of undressed **bluestones** was set up towards the centre; these stones, weighing up to 4 tons each, were transported 240mi/386km from the Presely Hills in southwest Wales, mainly by water, and finally along the wide **Avenue**, which was built from the River Avon to the entrance of the henge.

In the **third phase**, c.2000 BC, the structure was transformed. The bluestone rings were replaced by a circle of tall trilithons. These standing stones were tapered at one end and tenoned at the top to secure the curving mortised lintels, which were linked to each other by tongues and grooves, having been levered gradually into position. Inside the circle five separate giant trilithons rose in a horseshoe, opening towards the Heel Stone. The entrance was marked by new uprights, one of which, the Slaughter Stone, now fallen, remains. By the end of this **final phase**, c.1550 BC, the dressed bluestones were reintroduced in their present horseshoe formation, within the sarsen horseshoe.

DEVIZES

⊙ *24mi/39km E of Bath and 90mi/145km W of London.*
Population: 13,205. ⓘ *Market Place.*
℘01380 734 669. www.devizes.org.uk.
Devizes flourished as a cloth market from medieval times to the 19C; from the 17C it profited from tobacco, which was then grown widely in the area and it is now probably best known for its local brewery, Wadworths, whose shire

horses make daily deliveries in town. All this accounts for the number of handsome 18C town houses, pubs and not one but two town halls.

St John's Church★★

39 Long Street. Ⓛ*Open year-round daily during daylight hours.* ℘*01380 723 705. www.sjbnet.org.uk.*
This important Norman parish church has a mighty oblong **crossing tower** with, on the inside, round arches towards the nave and chancel and an early example of pointed arches towards the transepts. Inside, the vaulted east end is typically Norman, decorated with interlaced arches articulated with chevron and zigzag mouldings. The side chapels (1483) are separated from the chancel and sanctuary by decorative stone screens and have fine lacunar roofs resting on carved corbels.

Wiltshire Heritage Museum★

41 Long Street. Ⓛ*Open year-round Mon–Sat 10am–5pm, Sun noon–4pm.*
🎫*£4, Sun free.* ♿. ℘*01380 727 369. www.wiltshireheritage.org.uk.*
In addition to geology and natural history collections and an art gallery, the museum has a renowned archaeological department. Models of nearby Stonehenge and Avebury are displayed among a collection of local finds including those from Bush Barrow, described as "the Crown Jewels of the King of Stonehenge"

AVEBURY★★

NT/EH. ⊙ *7mi/11km NE of Devizes on the A 361. Gallery and museum:*
Ⓛ*Open daily Apr–Oct 10am–6pm; Nov–Mar 10am–4pm.* Ⓛ*Closed 24–26 Dec.* 🎫*£4.40. Manor Garden:*
Ⓛ*Same hours as gallery and museum.*
🎫*£3.50. Stones:* Ⓛ*Open access.*
🎫*Free.* ♿ Ⓟ*(charge)*✕. ℘*01672 539 250. www.nationaltrust.org.uk; www.english-heritage.org.uk*
Though less famous than Stonehenge, for many visitors Avebury is more rewarding. The surrounding district is extremely rich in prehistoric monuments and earthworks, the earliest dat-

White Horses

Within a 30mi/50km radius of Marlborough are no fewer than seven white horse figures carved into the chalky landscape. The oldest, largest and most famous is the **Uffington White Horse**, 20mi/32km northeast of Marlborough on White Horse Hill, Berkshire Downs. It is visible from the A 420 or B 4508 or B 4507 east of Swindon. This is one of England's oldest chalk hill figures.

It is 365ft/111m long, though it can only be seen fully from the air, so leading to the theory that perhaps it was a sign to ancient gods. It was once thought that it might be from the Iron Age, as its shape is similar to those found on coins from the period; or perhaps Anglo-Saxon, constructed to celebrate King Alfred's victories over the Danes in AD 871. However, new testing methods on soil samples have revealed that the horse is in fact about 3,000 years old (late Bronze Age). But who carved it and why remains a mystery.

ing from c.3700BC–3500 BC. The site is all the more fascinating as the village lies inside the circle of 30-ton–40-ton sarsen stones within the earth "ramparts".

The Stones★

It is difficult to make out the plan of the stones, since the only vantage points are on the earth banks, reinforced by an inner ditch, around the 28 acre/11ha site. These are broken at the cardinal points of the compass to allow access to the centre (now used by modern roads) and enclose a circle of 100 sarsens from the Marlborough Downs and two inner rings. From the south exit, an avenue of about 100 pairs of stones (only some of which can still be seen) once led to

the burial site known as the Sanctuary on Overton Hill (excavated in 1930). The **Barn Gallery and Alexander Keiller Museum** gives a valuable insight into this and neighbouring sites.

SILBURY HILL★
◗ *2mi/3km S of Avebury.*
A 130ft/40m high man-made chalk mound, one of the largest of its kind in Europe. The reasons for its construction remain a mystery.
The **West Kennet Long Barrow**★ *(3mi/5km S)* is England's finest burial barrow (340ft/104m long x 75ft/23m wide), dating from 3500–3000 BC. The entrance (⚬ *closed to the public*) at the east end is flanked by giant sarsens, and the passage, lateral vaults and chamber at the far end are roofed with massive capstones supported on upright sarsens and drystone walling. Some 50 skeletons from the early Neolithic period were discovered in the vaults.

THE RIDGEWAY PATH★★
◗ *Overton Hill is around 1mi/1.6km S of Avebury. www.nationaltrail.co.uk.*
This ancient trade route was already in use by the nomadic peoples of the Palaeolithic and Mesolithic ages, who followed the line of the chalk ridge, as it was easier going than the lower slopes covered in forest or scrub. The modern path, opened in 1973, runs from Overton Hill, via the Uffington White Horse, to the Ivinghoe Beacon near Tring in Hertfordshire (85mi/137km).

Stones of Avebury
© Eurasia Press/Photononstop

Kennet and Avon Canal

In 1794 a scheme to build a canal between navigable sections of the River Avon and River Kennet, thereby linking Bristol and Bath with Newbury and Reading, began. In 1810 it was completed with its most spectacular section being the flight of locks up Caen Hill. However, just three decades later the advent of the Great Western Railway meant canal traffic had declined to the point where the waterway was abandoned.

Recently restored, southern England's most picturesque canal is once more open to navigation, threading its way through the Avon Valley, the Vale of Pewsey and on into Berkshire. To see how the canal was built and for details of **boat trips** (*Wed, Sat–Sun and bank hols*) visit the **Kennet and Avon Canal Trust Museum** (*Canal Centre, Couch Lane, Devizes;* ⏱*open, daily 10am–5pm, winter 10am–4pm;* ⏴*£3.30;* ☎*01380 729 489; www.katrust.org*).

MARLBOROUGH★

▶ *6mi/10km E of Avebury.*

This former market town, strategically placed on the London–Bath road (A 4), has been home to the famous exclusive public school of **Marlborough College** since the 19C. To the north of the town stretch the **Marlborough Downs**, crossed by the Ridgeway Path and home to flocks of sheep (every town in Wiltshire was originally a wool town). The attractive **High Street** leads from The Green to Marlborough College. **St Mary's Church**, also at the east end, was rebuilt after a fire during the Commonwealth, hence its Puritan austerity. The High Street boasts a couple of interesting 17C **coaching inns** (Castle and Ball, Sun Inn). At the west end, the **Church of St Peter and St Paul** (now an arts and crafts centre) is Norman in origin, but was rebuilt in the 15C and extensively restored in the mid-19C.

A couple of miles southeast of Marlborough lies **Savernake Forest★★**, a privately owned but publicly accessible forest. Its 4,000 acres/1,619ha is a wonderful place to explore on foot or by bicycle. Cutting through the forest northwest to southeast is the **Grand Avenue★★★**, lined with superb beeches laid by Lancelot "Capability" Brown.

LACOCK★★

NT. ▶ *5.5mi/25km W of Avebury.*
🚩*Town Hall, Market Lane, Malmesbury.* ☎*01666 823 748. www.visitwiltshire. co.uk; www.nationaltrust.org.uk.*

This peaceful picturesque stone-and-brick village is owned by the National Trust. It comprises little more than four streets laid out in a square but has provided the film set for numerous period TV dramas and movies, including brief appearances in two *Harry Potter* films. The wide **High Street★** leading to the abbey is lined with cottage-shops and houses of various heights, sizes and designs, some of which date from as long ago as the 14C and 16C. **West Street** and **East Street** are enclosed by interesting old houses and inns (the **George Inn** is the oldest inn in the village, built 1361). **Church Street** (note the 14C Cruck House and 15C Sign of the Angel Inn) runs parallel to the High Street, leading into the village's original Market Place on the right.

The church of **St Cyriac★** (⏱*open year-round daily 10am–5pm;* ☎*01249 730 272*) is a superb example of a Perpendicular "wool church" reflecting the village's prosperity from the 14C to the 17C.

Lacock Abbey and Fox Talbot Museum of Photography★

NT. **Museum, cloisters and grounds:** ⏱*Open daily mid-Feb–Oct 11am–5.30pm; Nov–mid-Feb 11am–4pm.* **Abbey:** ⏱*Open mid-Feb–Oct Wed–Mon 11am–5pm; Nov–mid-Feb Sat–Sun noon–4pm.* ⏱*Closed 1 Jan, 25–26 Dec.* ⏴*£10.40.* ♿*.* ☎*01249 730 459. www.nationaltrust.org.uk.*

To the east of the village lies the abbey, founded in the 13C and converted into a stately home following the Dissolution (the cloisters, sacristy and chapter house survive) in 1539. Successive generations of the **Talbot family** added decorative features following the tastes of their day. The pioneer photographer, **William Henry Fox Talbot** (1800–77), added three oriels to the south front in 1827–30, the central one of which was the subject of his historic first successful photograph (1835). The **Fox Talbot Museum**, housed in a 16C barn at the abbey gate, is devoted to Talbot and his contemporary photographers.

CORSHAM COURT★★

▶ *5mi/8km N of Lacock.* ◑*Open late Mar–Sept Tue–Thu, Sat–Sun and bank hols 2–5.30pm; Oct–Nov and Jan–late Mar Sat–Sun 2–4.30pm.* ◉*£7, gardens only, £2.50.* ⌖ 🅿. *℘01249 701 610. www.corsham-court.co.uk.*

This Elizabethan mansion built in 1582 was bought by Paul Methuen in the mid-18C. Corsham was altered and enlarged on several occasions, by architects such as Lancelot "Capability" Brown in the 1760s, John Nash in 1800 and Thomas Bellamy in 1845–49, to house the extensive Methuen Collection of Master **paintings** (16C and 17C Italian and 17C Flemish), **statuary**, **bronzes** and **furniture**. It includes works by Caravaggio, Tintoretto, Veronese, Rubens and Van Dyck, as well as pieces by the Adam brothers and Chippendale. The **Cabinet Room** contains Fra Filippo Lippi's Annunciation (1463), while the highlight of the **Octagon Room**, designed by Nash, is Michelangelo's *Sleeping Cupid*.

MALMESBURY★

▶ *12.5mi/20km N of Lacock.*
The centre of this small south Cotswold market town is graced by a **market cross**★★, one of England's finest, built of local stone in 1490, when the town was known for its tanning, wool weaving and other textile industries. Malmesbury is a hilltop town shaped by the course of two rivers, the Bristol and Tetbury Avons.

Malmesbury Abbey★

◑*Open daily 10am–5pm; winter 10am–4pm.* ◉*£2 contribution requested.* ◉*£7.* ⌖. *℘01666 826 666. www.malmesburyabbey.com; www.abbeyhousegardens.co.uk.*

The present church was begun in the 12C and by the 14C extended 320ft/98m from east to west. However, a storm in the late-15C and the collapse of its tower (with subsequent damage) a century later means that the existing structure is about one-third the size of the building at its largest. The ruins are a dramatic backdrop to the present church.

The masterpiece of the abbey is the **south porch**, an outstanding example of Norman sculpture and decoration featuring geometrical patterning and magnificent carved figures in a style reminiscent of that found in the churches of southwest France. The massive Norman pillars inside have scalloped capitals. On the south side is the **watching loft** from where the abbot or a monk could follow the service beyond the chancel screen.

Abbey House Gardens★★

◑*Open late Mar–Oct 11am–5.30pm.* ◉*£7.* ⌖✕. *℘01666 822 212. www.abbeyhousegardens.co.uk.*

Planted on neglected land in 1994, these gardens have become one of the best loved in the south of England. A large part of their appeal is their location, adjacent to and in sympathy with the beautiful 16C abbey house and abbey ruins. Keeping the historical link are ancient stones from the abbey complex, a herb garden, arcading (reminiscent of cloisters), statues of monks and a monk's stone coffin. The formal part of the gardens are divided into a series of delightful rooms and lawns with knot gardens. Tens of thousands of bulbs are planted each year to create a real splash of colour including the county's largest private collection of roses. The wilder part of the gardens tumble down to the river and monastic fish ponds.

Channel Islands★★

The Channel Islands lie west of the Cherbourg peninsula of the Normandy coast. Blessed by better weather than mainland Britain and unspoiled rural countryside, the islands have developed tourist facilities to attract sailors, surfers and swimmers, birdwatchers, walkers and cyclists. Life in general is lived in the slow lane and a characteristic feature of the islands is the "honesty boxes" along the road, advertising fresh, home-grown produce.

- ▶ **Population:** 146,314.
- **Michelin Map:** Michelin Atlas p 5 or Map 503 P, Q 33.
- **Info:** Jersey: Liberation Place, St Helier. ℘01534 44 88 00. www.jersey.com. Guernsey: North Plantation, St Peter Port. ℘01481 723 552. www.visitguernsey.com.
- ▶ **Location:** Stay on either Jersey or Guernsey and use it as a base from which to visit the other main island and the smaller islands.
- **Don't Miss:** Durrell Wildlife Park; Jersey War Tunnels; St Peter Port, Guernsey; if you seek peace and quiet, Sark and Herm.
- **Timing:** Allow a few days to relax here.
- **Kids:** Durrell Wildlife Park. Both Guernsey and Jersey have good sandy beaches.

A BIT OF HISTORY

The islands are rich in prehistoric tombs and monuments indicating human habitation in 7500BC–2500 BC. They were annexed by the Normans in 933 and later attached to the English Crown by William the Conqueror. Some customs and traditions and the Norman–French dialect heard on these islands, which have only been universally English-speaking since the early-20C, date back to this period. In 1204 King John was forced to cede Normandy to the French, but the Channel Islanders chose to remain loyal to the English Crown in return for certain privileges, one of which was an independent parliament.

Despite this, the French tried repeatedly to capture the islands. Threats of invasion by Napoleon account for the many Martello defence towers built along the coasts. The islands were occupied by the Germans from 1940 to 1945, the only British territory to fall to the enemy during the Second World War.

The Channel Islands are divided into the **Bailiwick of Jersey** and the **Bailiwick of Guernsey**. The original Norman laws and systems have been renewed and modified by subsequent monarchs, though in matters of defence and international relations the islands are subject to decisions made by the Home Office in London. The Channel Islanders benefit from a **VAT-exempt** economy and lower rates of income tax. Coins, bank notes, and postage stamps are issued locally and are not legal tender elsewhere. The islands have therefore become a tax haven for wealthy British citizens and have developed a buoyant industry in **financial services**. **Farming** still plays an important part in the local economy and maintains a supply to mainland Britain of early vegetables (potatoes, tomatoes, grapes), cut flowers and rich Channel Island milk, produced by the famously pretty local cattle.

JERSEY★★

The largest and southernmost of the group, only 12mi/19km from the coast of France, Jersey possesses a charming combination of English and Norman–French traditions and local features echo both Normandy and Cornwall. Being so close to the Gulf Stream, it is thick with flowers in spring and summer. The sandy bays which characterise the coastline occur even among the steep pink granite cliffs of the sparsely populated north.

GETTING THERE

BY AIR – Direct to Jersey, Guernsey and Alderney from the UK by: Aurigny Air Services Ltd (✆01481 822 886; www.aurigny.com); British Airways (✆0844 493 0787; www.britishairways.com); bmi baby (✆0905 828 282, cost 65p/min; www.bmibaby.com); Blue Islands (✆08456 20 21 22; www.blueislands.com). Aurigny also operates flights to Guernsey from Grenoble and Dinard.

Jersey Airport ✆01534 446 247. www.jerseyairport.com.
Guernsey Airport ✆01481 237 766. www.guernsey-airport.gov.gg.
Alderney Airport ✆01481 822 551. www.alderney.gov.gg.

BY SEA – Condor Ferries from Weymouth, Poole and Portsmouth (also St Malo). ✆01202 207 216. www.condorferries.com.

St Helier

The capital is named after the 6C hermit saint who brought Christianity to the island. On an islet *(access on foot via causeway at low tide, at other times DUKW vehicle)* stands **Elizabeth Castle** (◕*open early Apr–early Nov daily 10am–5.30pm;* ⊜£9 (including ferry £11.50); ✆01534 633 376; www.jerseyheritagetrust.org), begun in the mid-16C. In the Civil War it was adapted to resist attacks by the Parliamentarians and during the Second World War the occupying German forces made their own additions. West of the **Militia Museum** (mementoes of the Royal Jersey Regiment) the Upper Ward encloses the Mount (keep) affording **views**★ across St Aubin's Bay. Today a breakwater leads south to the 12C hermitage chapel on the rock on which St Helier lived *(procession on or about 16 Jul, St Helier's Day)*. The centre of the town is marked by the charming **Royal Square** with a statue of George II dressed as a Roman emperor. St Helier's two main collections are the **Jersey Museum and Art Gallery**★ *(The Weighbridge;* ◕*open daily early Apr–early Nov 10am–5pm, Nov–Dec 10am–4pm;* ◕*closed 24–26, 31 Dec;* ⊜£8; ♿; ✆01534 633 300; www.jerseyheritagetrust.org) containing award-winning displays of maritime exhibits and the story of Jersey; and the **Maritime Museum** (◕*open early Apr–Oct daily 10am–5pm;* ⊜£8; ♿; ✆01534 811 043.;www.jerseyheritagetrust.org), installed in converted 19C warehouses, celebrating the importance to Jersey of the sea and displaying a 12-panel tapestry (6ft x 3ft/2m x 1m) illustrating the Occupation of Jersey during the Second World War (based on archive photos).

♨♨ Durrell Wildlife Park★★

❯ *Trinity. 4mi/6km N of St Helier.* ◕*Open daily 9.30am–6pm; (last Sun Oct–last Sun Mar 5pm;* ◕*Closed 25 Dec.* ⊜£12.90, child £9.40. ♿🅿✕. ✆01534 860 000. www.durrell.org.

The remit of this famous wildlife park – the word zoo is never used – named after its founder, the naturalist **Gerald Durrell**, is to preserve and breed rare and endangered species that live in an environment as similar as possible to their natural habitat. Its success has led to exchanges with other leading UK wildlife parks and zoos and the re-introduction of a number of threatened species to the wild.

Eric Young Orchid Foundation★

Victoria Village, Trinity. ◕*Open early Feb–late Dec Wed–Sat 10am–4pm.* ⊜£4. ♿. ✆01534 861 963. www.ericyoungorchidfoundation.co.uk.

A fabulous show of prize plants appealing to amateurs and professionals.

La Hougue Bie★

❯ *Grouville. 2.5mi/4km NE of St Helier.* ◕*Open early Apr–Oct daily 10am–5pm.* ⊜£7. ♿🅿. ✆01534 633 373. www.jerseyheritagetrust.org.

La Hougue Bie is a cruciform **Neolithic tomb**★ dating from 3000 BC, a 33ft/10m passage grave, roofed with granite slabs leading to a 10ft/3m x 30ft/9m funeral chamber and three side chambers. On top of the mound stand the 12C **Chapel of Our Lady of the Dawn** and the 1520 **Jerusalem Chapel** containing early-16C frescoes of archangels.

Hamptonne Country Life Museum★

▶ *La Rue de la Patente, St Lawrence. 3mi/5km from St Helier.* ◐*Open daily 10am–5pm; mid-Apr–Oct during school hols only.* ✆£7. &. ✆01534 633 300. *www.jerseyheritagetrust.org.*
Part-thatched and with bags of atmosphere, Hamptonne House is thought to have been completed in 1637. It provides an insight into family lifestyle during the 17C and early-18C with staff dressed in period costume.

Jersey War Tunnels★

Meadowbank, Les Charrieres Malorey. ◐*Open mid-Feb/Mar–late Nov daily 10am–6pm; (last entry 4.30pm.* ✆£10.90. & ▣✕. ✆01534 860 808. *www.jerseywartunnels.com.*
This large complex of tunnels is kept as a memorial to the forced labourers who worked on its construction for three and a half years under the harshest conditions. Wartime films, archive photographs, newspaper cuttings, letters and memorabilia document the personal suffering and trauma of those caught up in the events.

Mont Orgueil Castle★

The charming old port of **Gorey** is dominated by Mont Orgueil Castle (◐*open Apr–Oct daily 10am–6pm, Nov–Mar Fri–Mon 10am–4pm;* ✆£10.50; ✆01534 633 375; www.jerseyheritagetrust.org), which dates back to the 13C. Set on a rocky promontory, its position and defensive strength account for the name (Mount Pride). A spiral network of steps and passages between separate defence systems leads up to excellent **views**★★ at the top.
Other sights in the port include the **Jersey Pottery**★ (*Gorey Village;* ◐*open Mon–Sat 9am–5.30pm, Sun 10am–5.30pm;* ◐*closed 25 Dec–1 Jan;* & ✕; ✆01534 850 850; www.jerseypottery. com), set in a magnificent garden, and

Mont Orgueil Castle

©AJ/Fotolia.com

the 49ft/15m **Faldouet Dolmen**, dating from 2500 BC, with a 20ft-/6m- wide funeral chamber.

St Matthew's Church

Millbrook. ◐*Open Apr–Sept Mon–Fri 9am–6pm, Sat–Sun for services only; Oct–Mar Mon–Fri 9am–4.30pm, Sat–Sun for services only.* & ▣✕ (*Thu only*). ✆01534 502 864. www.glasschurch.org. The "Glass Church", built in 1840, is remarkable for **René Lalique**'s rich **glasswork**★ interior executed in 1934.

Fishermen's Chapel

St Brelade. ◐*Open year-round daily 7am–7pm. www.stbreladeschurch.com.* Built in the 11–12C the chapel is decorated with delicate medieval **frescoes**★.

GUERNSEY★

The second principal Channel Island features wild, dramatic **southern cliffs**, while the sandy beaches and rocky promontories of the west and north coasts are excellent for bathing, surfing and rock-pool exploring.

St Peter Port★★

The island capital, attractively situated on a hillside on the east coast, overlooks a sheltered harbour. A late-18C building boom produced a delightful Regency town built in local granite. **Castle Cornet**★ (◐*open Apr–Oct daily 10am–5pm;* ✆£9, from 4pm £1); ▣✕; ✆01481 706 961; www.museums.gov.

gg), dating back to c.1206 and reinforced under Elizabeth I, remained loyal to the king in the Civil War, being the last of the royal strongholds to surrender, after eight years of siege.

In 1672 an explosion destroyed much of the structure and the castle was subsequently rebuilt.Today it also includes four small museums, dedicated to the Royal Guernsey Militia, the Guernsey Maritime History, Royal Guernsey Light Infantry and 201 Squadron RAF respectively. The Ceremony of the **Noonday Gun** is performed by two Guernsey Militia men daily. St Peter Port **Town Church**★ dates back as far as 1048, when it also served as a fort, and was completed around 1475. It now contains several memorials to famous Guernseymen. **Victor Hugo** lived on Guernsey in political exile at **Hauteville House**★ *(*🕐*open Apr–Sept Mon except bank hols–Sat 10am–4pm; 🎫£6; ✆01481 723 552; www.victorhugo. gg)*, which he decorated in a highly individual way.

Set in Candie Gardens the **Guernsey Museum and Art Gallery** *(*🕐*open daily Feb–24 Dec 10am–5pm, winter 10am–4pm; 🎫£5.50; ♿✗; ✆01481 726 518; www.museums.gov.gg)* contains art and archaeological collections.

Around the Island

At **St Martin** is the elegant Queen Anne period **Sausmarez Manor** *(Sausmarez Road; 🏠house by guided tour only, late Mar–May and Oct Mon–Thu 11.30am. Jun–Sept open daily, for more details of extra tours see website, subtropical gardens and art park open daily 10am–5pm; 🏠house £6.90, garden £5, art park £5; ♿Pℹ✗; ✆01481 235 571; www. sausmarezmanor.co.uk)*, also home to a subtropical garden and an art park with 150–250 pieces of sculpture.

Coppersmiths may be seen at work; other attractions include golf and train rides. Not to be confused with the manor, **Saumarez Park**★, at Castel, is the venue for the annual **Battle of Flowers**, a famous parade held on the fourth Thursday in August, originally started in 1902 for the coronation of Edward VII. Afterwards the floats are broken up and the crowd pelt each other with flowers. The **Guernsey Folk & Costume Museum**★ *(NT; 🕐open mid- Mar–Oct daily 10am–5pm; 🎫£5; P; ✆01481 255 384; www.nationaltrust-gsy. org.gg)* is housed in the park.

Between St Peter Port and Guernsey Airport is the **German Military Underground Museum** *(Les Eperons, La Vassalerie; 🕐open mid Mar–mid-Nov daily 10am–5pm; 🎫£3.50; ✆01481 239 100)*. The largest construction in the Channel Islands, yet almost invisible from the surface, this tunnel complex covers 1.7acres/0.7ha. It was hewn out of solid rock by slave workers of many nationalities.

The island's most notable **prehistoric remains** are the burial chambers **Déhus Dolmen** *(N)*, **le Trépied Dolmen** *(W)* and **La Gran'mère du Chimquièra**, a Stone Age figure at the gate to St Martin's churchyard. A similar female figure stands outside the 12C church of **Ste Marie du Câtel**, which also contains 13C frescoes.

Guernsey's satellite islands, **Alderney, Herm** and **Sark**★★ are well worth a visit. Sark has stayed remarkably remote from modern society, and is totally free of cars.

Sons and Daughters

The most famous name connected with Jersey is **Lillie Langtry** (1853–1929), the "Jersey Lily" who became an actress and captivated British high society with her beauty and who was also a close friend of Edward VII – she is buried in St Saviour's churchyard.

The fashionable 19C painter **Sir John Everett Millais** (1829–96), who won acclaim with his painting entitled *Bubbles*, grew up in Jersey and belonged to an old island family. So too did **Elinor Glyn** (1864–1943), who became a novelist and Hollywood scriptwriter.

The well-known French firm which makes Martell brandy was founded by **Jean Martell** from St Brelade.

ADDRESSES

🛏 STAY

PORTSMOUTH/SOUTHSEA

🛏 **Albatross** – *51 Waverley Road, Southsea. ℘02392 828 325. www.albatrossguesthouse. co.uk. 7 rms.* Simple centrally located guesthouse.

🛏 **Waverley Park Lodge** – *99 Waverley Road, Southsea. ℘02392 730 402. www.waverleyparklodge.com. 12 rms.* Simple rooms a 10-minute stroll from the seafront.

🛏–🛏🛏 **Fortitude Cottage** – *51 Broad Street . ℘02392 823 748. www.fortitudecottage.co.uk. 6 rms.* This smart B&B is right in the heart of Old Portsmouth, with a view of the fishing boats and ferries. Ask about their splendid penthouse room (🛏🛏–🛏🛏🛏).

🛏🛏 **The Retreat** – *35 Grove Road South, Southsea. ℘02392 353 701. www.the retreatguesthouse.co.uk. 4 rms.* Set in a leafy quiet residential area this fine Victorian home has been carefully restored and sensitively refurbished with light, airy elegant rooms. No children.

🛏🛏–🛏🛏🛏 **Florence House Hotel** – *2 Malvern Road, Southsea. ℘02392 751 666. www.florencehousehotel.co.uk. 7 rms.* Set just off the seafront, this small Edwardian boutique hotel is a lively combination of contemporary and period styles. The owners take great care of their guests.

ISLE OF WIGHT

🛏🛏 **The Lawns Hotel** – *72 Broadway, Sandown. ℘01983 402 549. www.lawns hotelisleofwight.co.uk. 15 rms.* This lovely Victorian house, a short stroll from the beach in a pleasant area of Sandown, has been tastefully refurbished in contemporary and traditional style.

WINCHESTER

🛏🛏🛏–🛏🛏🛏🛏 **Hotel du Vin** – *14 Southgate Street. ℘01962 841 414. www.hotelduvin.com. 24 rms.* This handsome early-18C red brick house is located in a quiet part of the city centre. its elegant décor reflects the wine theme with very stylish contemporary/traditional bedrooms. Its acclaimed restaurant (🛏🛏🛏–🛏🛏🛏🛏) features a walled garden and champagne bar.

NEW FOREST

🛏🛏🛏🛏 **The Montagu Arms Hotel** – *Beaulieu. ℘01590 612 324. www.montagu armshotel.co.uk. 23 rms.* This luxury 17C country house hotel, complete with its Michelin-star restaurant and free spa membership, is an oasis of calm.

BOURNEMOUTH

🛏 It's not hard to find relatively cheap lodgings in Bournemouth as long as you don't want a sea view and you stay away from the seafront. Try the streets running off here, and also Tregonwell Road (in the Westcliff area). You'll also find guesthouses and B&Bs aplenty on the Isle of Purbeck, particularly in Swanage.

🛏 **Mount Stuart** – *31 Tregonwell Road. ℘08450 554 639. www.mountstuartho.tel. co.uk. 18 rms·* This large Victorian villa has been run by the same family for over 20 years. Rooms are small but pleasant and you're a short walk from town.

🛏🛏🛏–🛏🛏🛏🛏 **Highcliff Marriott** – *St Michael's Road, West Cliff. ℘01202 557 702. www.bournemouthhighcliff marriott.co.uk. 157 rms·* Perched on the clifftop with a pool and magnificent sea views, this is one of the town's top hotels with contemporary design rooms and every comfort. Look for last-minute deals.

DORCHESTER

🛏🛏🛏 **(Best Western) Kings Arms Hotel** – *30 High East Street. ℘01305 263 353. www.kingsarmsdorchester.com. 37 rms.* Victorian elegance is the hallmark of this historic recently refurbished 18C hotel. Four-poster beds and luxury bathrooms.

SALISBURY

🛏🛏–🛏🛏🛏 **Milford Hall** – *106 Castle Street. ℘01722 417 411. www.milfordhallhotel.com. 35 rms.* This beautiful 19C building is a five-minute walk from the centre of town. The formal Georgian-style interior and rooms won't suit everyone's taste. Breakfast extra.

JERSEY

🛏 **Au Caprice** – *Route de la Haule, St Brelade. ℘01534 722 083. www.aucapricejersey.com.* Next to a large sandy beach this guesthouse offers pretty, comfy rooms; the small seaview surcharge is very good value.

GUERNSEY

🍽🛏 **La Michele** – *Les Hubits, St Martin.*
📞*01481 238 065. www.lamichelehotel.com.*
This 16-room hotel enjoys a quiet country
location, a short walk from picturesque
Fermain Bay. Conservatory lounge,
beautiful secluded garden and small pool.
Tariff includes breakfast and dinner. No
children under 10. B&B tariff may also be
available.

⅋/ EAT

PORTSMOUTH

🍴 Gunwharf Quays and Port Solent are
bursting with cafés and restaurants.
🍽 **Brasserie Blanc** – *1 Gunwharf Quays.*
📞*02392 891 320. www.brasserieblanc.com.* Part of the empire of masterchef
Raymond Blanc, this lively brasserie
adheres to his general cooking principles
and applies them to classic brasserie
dishes; large outdoor terrace.

SOUTHAMPTON

🍴The town boasts a good choice of
independent (non-chain) restaurants.
🍽 **Platform Tavern** – *Town Quay.* 📞*02380
337 232. www.platformtavern.com.*
Standard pub grub is served up in a lively
bar in the old dockyard area. Live blues
music most nights.
🍽 **Joe Daflo's** – *61 Commercial Road.*
📞*02380 231 101. www.joedaflos.co.uk.
Closed Sun.* This is a very smart conversion
of a church to an all-day restaurant,
serving snacks and standard bistro fayre.
Saturday night dinner dances.

ISLE OF WIGHT

🍽 **Liberty's** – *12 Union Street, Ryde.*
📞*01983 811 007. www.libertyscafebar.co.uk.*
This stylish, stripped down contemporary
dining venue appeals to a wide range of
diners, serving light bites at lunch, cocktails
and elegant dinners in the evenings.

WINCHESTER

🍽 **Café Monde** – *22 The Square.* 📞*01962
877 177. Closed 8pm.* In a very busy pretty
little square by the cathedral, this is a
good place for breakfast, a light lunch or a
snack, tea or coffee at any time of the day.
🍽–🍽🛏 **Wykeham Arms** –
75 Kingsgate Street. 📞*01962 853 834.
www.fullers.co.uk.* This famous 18C inn
is tucked away on a cobbled street
and packed with Winchester College
memorabilia. Dishes range from simple
soups and pies (try their signature Wyk Pie

at lunchtime) to full traditional roasts and
continental cuisine. Bar meals are best for
value and atmosphere.

BOURNEMOUTH

🍽 **Beau Monde** – *Exeter Park Road.*
📞*01202 311 181. www.beaumondebistro.co.uk.* Tables in the restaurant overlook
Bournemouth's beautiful Lower Gardens,
while the bistro opens onto the terrace
allowing seasonal al fresco dining. Both
traditional English and contemporary
European dishes feature.

DORCHESTER

🍽🛏 **Sienna** – *36 High West Street.*
📞*01305 250 022. www.siennarestaurant.co.uk. Closed Sun–Mon, fortnight in spring
and fortnight in autumn.* Awarded a
Michelin star in January 2010, this is
probably the best food in Dorset – Italian
influenced as it's name suggests – albeit
served in a tiny and surprisingly basic
setting. Friendly owners.

SHAFTESBURY

🍽 **The Mitre Inn** – *22 High Street.*
📞*01747 853 002. www.youngs.co.uk.* Tasty
home-cooked traditional pub food in a
nicely old-fashioned inn with great views
over the Dorset countryside from the
outside terrace.

SALISBURY

🍽 **The Victoria & Albert Inn** –
*Netherhampton. Take the A 36 to Warminster
then two left turns, or a 40-min walk from
town.* 📞*01722 743 174.* The village pub: a
warm welcome, log fires in winter and
a good variety of local dishes expertly
cooked by the pub chef. Excellent choice
of both beers and wines.

JERSEY

🍽–🍽🛏 **Old Court House Inn** –
St Aubin's Harbour. 📞*01534 746 433.
www.oldcourthousejersey.com.* This
atmospheric rustic (in parts) 15C inn, right
on the picturesque harbourfront, offers a
choice of bars, bistro or formal "white-linen dining" Their cosmopolitan menus
have, unsurprisingly, a seafood emphasis.

GUERNSEY

🍽 **Fleur du Jardin** – *Kings Mills, Castel.*
📞*01481 257 996. www.fleurdujardin.com.*
Set in the heart of the island, the beamed
pub-like restaurant of this smart 15C hotel
offers fresh, seasonal, locally sourced
gastro-pub food cooked simply. Outdoor
dining in the summer.

CHILTERNS, OXFORDSHIRE, COTSWOLDS

Within easy day-tripping distance of the capital, the Cotswolds are a magnet for visitors who only have a short time to discover idyllic English villages and rural scenery. They are a must-see, but at peak times of the year can become almost unbearably busy. Oxford also justifies its reputation as one of Britain's top attractions and although better equipped to handle the crowds, is still much more comfortable out of season. The Chiltern Hills, like the Cotswolds, are designated an Area of Outstanding Natural Beauty: situated close to London, they have much less appeal in terms of visitor attractions or quaintness; however, for walkers and seekers of solitude, they may be a better bet.

Highlights

1 Stroll among some of Europe's finest landscaping at **Stowe Gardens** (p195)

2 Be awestruck at **Christ Church College, Oxford** (p204)

3 See where Churchill lived like a king at **Blenheim Palace** (p205)

4 Find the medieval Cotswolds at **Chipping Campden** (p212)

5 Feel like Alice in Wonderland at **Hidcote Garden** (p212)

Chiltern Hills

Providing a breath of fresh air, pastoral scenery and good walking territory within easy commuting distance of London, the Chilterns are a very desirable part of southeast England. There are few set piece visitor attractions or even obvious places to stay for more than a night or two so you'll probably want to keep moving between their small towns and villages.

Oxford

The glittering spires of Oxford are deservedly world famous. Easily covered on foot, the town is, as you would expect from an internationally renowned University, young, lively and cosmopolitan. However the university is also the oldest in Britain and imparts a very British sense of history and tradition, matched elsewhere in the UK only by Cambridge. The peaceful tiny college "quads" (quadrangles/squares) and cloisters have a real sense of history and old-world atmosphere, but a walk around the old alleyways of the city cen-

tre, particularly by night, admiring the city's stunning architecture at almost every turn, is to take a step back several centuries in time. Just outside Oxford, Blenheim Palace is one of England's greatest treasures.

Cotswolds

If you want to find the England you've seen on old-fashioned jigsaws, chocolate boxes and picture calendars, then you won't be disappointed by the Cotswolds. Wool brought it untold riches in medieval times, as celebrated by the number of "wool churches" erected in gratitude by wealthy merchants, but the Industrial Revolution simply passed it by. This meant that the glorious golden-stone Cotswold villages were preserved until they were popularised for the birth of modern tourism in the 1920s and 30s. Some places may have sold their souls to tourism and wealthy out-of-towners, but it's done in the best possible rural taste with cream teas on manicured lawns beside thatched cottages in summer, and roaring log fires and foaming pints of ale in winter. Fast food chains and shopping malls are a century away. There are some very atmospheric time-capsule houses (Chastleton and Snowshill Manor) and wonderful gardens here too, notably the Alice-in-Wonderland-like Hidcote.

Gloucester

The glory of Gloucester is undoubtedly its cathedral. Its docks make an interesting diversion while in autumn, Westonbirt Arboretum is a splash of New England colour in the heart of old England. Spend the night out of town, at posh Regency neighbour, Cheltenham.

Food Heroes

Oxford's **Victorian Covered Market**, trading since 1774, is foodie heaven, chock-a-block with butchers, fresh fruit and vegetable stalls, fishmongers, cookie makers, chocolatiers and bakers, all mixed with retail shops and small cafés under one roof. Pick up a jar of Frank Cooper's **Oxford marmalade** from here; made in Oxford between 1874 and 1967, it is supposedly a favourite of HM the Queen. Captain Scott even took a jar to the Arctic. It was found, perfectly preserved by the cold, with the remains of the expedition in 1980. Frank Cooper was a grocer and you can see the building where he came up with the recipe on the High Street in Oxford at number 83, although it has long since changed hands.

Oxford sauasages, sometimes know as Oxford Skate, are skinless, semi-circular and made of a combination of veal and pork. Oxford's covered market is a good place to find them, as well as **Oxford Blue Cheese**, which was created in the 1990s and has won many awards since. **Oxford sauce** would be a perfect accompaniment to Oxford sausages, being similar to Cumberland sauce, but sadly it is no longer widely used. Oxford's butchers have long been associated with its colleges, and so there are some unique cuts of meat hewn here, including **Oxford John**, a lamb steak from the leg, and Oxford brawn, which is made from the meat of a pig's head. Head to the market to find some of these.

Lovers of traditional desserts should try a **Banbury Cake**, which is made from puff pastry, currants and rosewater. Oxford has a number of other stodgy puddings to its name. **Oxford Pudding** is made of apricots, cream, eggs and puff pastry; **New College Pudding** is similar to a steamed pudding and is made of suet and currants; **Spiced Oxford Cake** is a type of fruitcake; while **Hollygog Pudding** is a warming mess of treacle and crumbly dough, best served with plenty of custard.

Hook Norton brewery has been operating from the small village of Hook Norton (between Chipping Norton and Banbury) for over 150 years (*tours Mon-Sat; www.hooknortonbrewery.co.uk*). The brewery's shire horses can be seen delivering around the streets of Hook Norton village.

Brakspear beers have been brewed in Oxfordshire since the early-18C. When the original Henley Brewery closed in 2002 (*now occupied by the Hotel du Vin*), the **Wychwood** Brewery in Witney took over brewing the beers, and moved several large pieces of historic brewing kit to their home in Witney (*tours Sat–Sun; www.brakspear-beers.co.uk*).

Brightwell vineyard, beside the Thames, near Wallingford is the region's largest wine producer (*sales and tastings; Fri–Sun pm, tours by appointment; brightwellvineyard.co.uk*).

Gloucestershire is known for its semi-hard **Gloucester cheese**, made from the milk of Gloucestershire breed cows farmed within the county. It always comes in rounds – with Double Gloucester allowed to age for a longer period. It can be found all over, but for a wide choice of traditional cheeses – both local and beyond – from an expert cheesemonger, visit the House of Cheese, Tetbury (*www.houseofcheese.co.uk*).

Gloucestershire Old Spots Pork, which comes from a black-spotted pedigree breed of pigs, has recently become a protected name under EU regulations and is prized for its tenderness and juiciness. Aylesbury has a long history of "ducking" and the free-range **Aylesbury duck** is famous for its taste.

Chiltern Hills★

The chalk downs known as the Chiltern Hills run some 60mi/97km on a southwest to northeast axis bordered by the River Thames and Luton respectively. They rise gently to their highest point at Coombe Hill (852ft/260m). Two of Britain's ancient roads, the **Icknield Way** and the **Ridgeway**, follow the line of the hills.

◆ WALK

The gentle rolling Chilterns are ideal for walkers. The **Ridgeway National Trail** was one of Iron Age Britain's main highways; today it is a waymarked long-distance footpath.

Another easy route is the Thames Path, which follows the river and crosses the Ridgeway. Tourist offices will be able to provide detailed walking maps, and *www.chilternsaonb.org* can also be useful for planning your trip.

AYLESBURY AREA

Aylesbury, Buckinghamshire's county town, was a major market town in Anglo-Saxon times and played a large part in the English Civil War.

The **Buckinghamshire County Museum** on Church Street (○ open mid-Feb–Sept Tue–Sat 10am–5pm (open bank hol Mons and during school hols), Oct–Feb Tue–Sat 10am–4pm; Dahl Gallery open year-round Mon–Sat, times vary, call or see website; ○ museum free; ▲▲ Dahl Gallery £6, child £4; entry by timed ticket); visits last an hour and entry is on

Roald Dahl

Roald Dahl lived and wrote for 36 years in Great Missenden village; it is now home to the award-winning **Roald Dahl Museum and Story Centre** (▲▲○ open year-round Tue–Fri 10am–5pm, Sat–Sun and bank hol/half-term Mons 11am-5pm; ○£6, child £4; ♿P 𝒫 01494 892 192; www.roalddahlmuseum.org; book ahead if possible).

○ **Michelin Map:** Michelin Atlas pp 18, 19 and 28 or Map 503 Q R 27 and 28.

▤ **Info:** Kings Head, Market Square, Aylesbury. 𝒫 01296 330 559. The Old Gaol, Market Hill, Buckingham. 𝒫 01280 823 020. www.visitbuckinghamshire.org.

◐ **Location:** Main tourist centres are Buckingham, Aylesbury, Marlow and Henley-on-Thames.

◈ **Don't Miss:** Waddesdon Manor; Stowe Gardens.

○ **Timing:** At least two days.

▲▲ **Kids:** Roald Dahl Gallery; Roald Dahl Museum.

the hour, booking (○£1 fee) is advised; ✕; 𝒫 01296 331 441; www.buckscc.gov.uk) traces local history but many visitors head straight for the **Roald Dahl Children's Gallery** – a delight for fans of the great author.

South of Aylesbury in the village of Hartwell is **Hartwell House**, now a hotel, first mentioned in the Domesday Book and once the home of an illegitimate son of William the Conqueror.

5mi/8km northwest of Aylesbury via the A 41 is **Waddesdon Manor**★★ (NT; ○ open Apr–Oct Wed–Fri and bank hol Mons, noon–4pm, Sat–Sun 11am–4pm; House also open between Christmas and New Year Wed–Sun, see website for details; ○£13.63–£15.45 (gardens only, £5.90–£7.27; in peak periods booking for house tickets recommended (free online); ♿P✕; 𝒫 01296 653 226; www.waddesdon.org.uk), built in 1874–89 in French Renaissance style, for Baron Ferdinand de Rothschild, set in 150 acres/61ha of landscaped grounds. It contains the acclaimed **Rothschild collection** of Dutch, French and English paintings, French furniture, porcelain, carpets and many other works of art. Twenty rooms are furnished with French 18C royal furniture, Sèvres porcelain and Savonnerie carpets. Works by Gainsborough, Reynolds and Romney, plus pictures by Rubens, Cuyp, Van der Heyden and Dutch masters grace the walls.

Some 10mi/16km northwest of Aylesbury, off the A 41 to Waddesdon, is **Claydon House**★ *(NT; Middle Claydon; ○open early Mar–Oct Sat–Wed 11am–5pm; ⊕£6.65; ⚂☐✕; ☏01296 730 349, 01494 755 561; www.nationaltrust.org. uk),* famous for its extravagant Rococo work, the parquetry staircase and the "Gothic Chinoiserie" woodwork of the Chinese Room. There are mementoes of Florence Nightingale, who was a frequent visitor.

BUCKINGHAM AREA
Buckingham was Buckinghamshire's county town until Aylesbury took over in the 16C. Today it is best used as a base for walks in the surrounding area and for visiting **Stowe Landscape Gardens**★★ *(NT; 3mi/5km NW, off the A 422; gardens: ○open: Mar–Oct Wed–Sun bank hol Mons, and daily during half-terms 10.30am–5.30pm; Nov–Feb Sat–Sun 10.30am–4pm, last entry 1hr 30mins before closing; house: ○times vary, visit www.shpt.org for information; ○closed Christmas hols, last Sat May; ⊕gardens £7.30; ☐✕; ☏01280 822 850 (weekdays), 01494 755 568 (weekends); www. nationaltrust.org.uk).* These magnificent landscaped gardens, some of the finest in Europe, were created over a period of 200 years starting in 1700.

In 1733 **William Kent** began work and in 1741 **Lancelot "Capability" Brown** was appointed head gardener. The long, straight approach up the **Grand Avenue** (1.5mi/2.5km) gives glimpses through the trees of the temples, columns and arches and also a full view of the north front of **Stowe House**.

Part of the exclusive Stowe School, this is open to the public at certain times; see their website *(www.stowe.co.uk)* for details. A full tour of the gardens would take several hours but a shorter walk close to the house provides a visit or a view of the major features. Nearby, the **parish church** is the sole survivor of the medieval village of Stowe.

VALE OF WHITE HORSE
This shallow valley lying between the Ridgeway and the River Thames, and bounded by Wantage and Farringdon, stretches from the edge of Oxford to the threshold of the Cotswolds. Its name comes from the oldest chalk figure in Britain dating back to around 1000 BC.

Wantage
In the centre of this small market town stands a statue of its most famous son, King Alfred the Great. You can learn more about him and the region in the **Vale & Downland Museum** *(Church St ○open year-round Mon–Sat excbank hols, 10am–4pm; ⚂✕; ☏01235 771 447; www.wantage.com).* One of the most rewarding short stretches of the famous **Ridgeway** footpath is 2mi/1.2km south of here, so the town makes a good base for walkers.

White Horse Hill
This stylised, almost modern-art figure of a 374ft-/114m-long horse (or perhaps a dragon) has perplexed scholars for centuries. It was carved out of the chalk hillside some 3,000 years ago but by whom, and for why, remains a mystery. One school of thought says that the figure represents a horse goddess connected with the local Belgae tribe.

Woolstone and Uffington
Just below the White Horse, **Woolstone** is possibly the prettiest of the region's many attractive villages. It has a beautiful 12C church and a pretty thatched pub – The White Horse Inn (naturally…). Neighbouring **Uffington** also has a fine church, known locally as "The Cathedral of the Vale". Thomas Hughes (1822–96), author of *Tom Brown's School Days*, was born here. Hughes' books are based on local people and places; and the 17C schoolhouse featured in his most famous work is now **Tom Brown's School Museum** *(○open Mar–Oct Sat–Sun 2–5pm; www.museum.uffington.net).* It includes mementoes of the late poet laureate Sir John Betjeman (1906–84), who also lived for many years in Uffington.

St Albans★

and around

The Romans built the first real settlement here on the south bank of the River Ver and named it Verulamium. Around AD 250, so the legend goes, Alban, a pagan living in the town, was converted to Christianity when he sheltered a Christian priest. Facing imminent discovery, Alban switched cloaks with the priest, was arrested in his place by Roman soldiers and executed, thus becoming England's first Christian martyr. Following the Romans' departure the town's building blocks were transferred to the other bank of the river to build an abbey, beside which the town of St Alban's developed.

VERULAMIUM★

❯ *Western outskirts of St Albans just off the A 4147/Bluehouse Hill.*

Verulamium, the third-largest city in Roman Britain, was established in AD 49 on Watling Street and rebuilt at least twice – once after being sacked by Boadicea in AD 61 then again c.155 after a major fire. When the Romans withdrew, Verulamium fell into ruins, was lost and not uncovered until the 20C. **Verulamium Park**, beside the river, includes town wall remains, the hypocaust of a large villa in situ (*open during museum opening hours, see below, free entry*). and the remains of the **Roman Theatre of Verulamium** (*open daily 10am–5pm; 4pm Nov–Mar; £2; 01727 835 035; www.romantheatre.co.uk*). Also in the park, the **Verulamium Museum**★ (*St Michael's Street. open year-round daily 10am (2pm Sun)–5.30pm. £3.80. (Charge). 01727 751 810. www.stalbansmuseums.org.uk*) displays some of the most impressive Roman works to be unearthed in Britain – ironwork, jewellery, coins, glass, pottery and **exceptional mosaics**.

CATHEDRAL★

Open daily 8.30am–5.45pm. £3 contribution requested. Guided tours Mon–Sat 11.30am, also Sat 2pm,

▶ **Population:** 80,376.
Michelin Map: Michelin Atlas p 19 or Map 504 T 28.
Info: Town Hall, Market Place. 01727 864 511. www.stalbans.gov.uk.
▶ **Location:** 27mi/43km northwest of London. Train station (direct link to London) is a 10-min walk from the centre. Most buses stop at the central clock tower.
Don't Miss: Verulamium Museum; cathedral; Woburn Abbey; Hatfield House.
Timing: Allow half a day.
Kids: Woburn Safari Park; Whipsnade Wild Animal Park; Hatfield Park Farm and Adventure Playground.

Sun–Fri 2pm. Tower tours (£6) Sat–Sun, see website for dates. . 01727 860 780. www.stalbanscathedral.org.uk. The original abbey was a Saxon shrine to St Alban. The present building, dominated by its Norman tower, began in 1077. The impressive Norman nave was lengthened in the Early English style; the Victorian west front dates from 1879, the chapter house from 1982.

The beauty of the interior lies in the furnishings – the exquisite medieval wall paintings and ceiling panels, the nave screen (1350), the reredos (1484), the Lady Chapel (1320) and the **shrine** of St Alban.

EXCURSIONS
Hatfield House★★

❯ *6mi/10km E of St Albans on the A 414.* **House:** *Open Easter Sat–Sept Wed–Sun and bank hols noon–5pm.* **Park and gardens:** *Open Easter Sat–Sept Wed–Sun and bank hols (Jul–Aug daily) 11am–5.30pm. East Garden open Wed only (additional £3.50 charge). House, and park £9. East Garden (open Wed only) £4. Park and West garden only, £6. Park only, £3.* **Farm and Adventure Playground:** *Open*

Elizabeth I at Hatfield

It was at Hatfield under an oak tree in what is now **Hatfield Park** that Elizabeth I heard of her succession – "It is the Lord's doing and it is marvellous in our eyes." All that remains of her childhood home, a palace built by Cardinal Morton, is the old Tudor Palace **Hall** – "one of the foremost monuments to medieval brickwork in the country" according to the acclaimed architectural historian, Pevsner. The adjacent **knot garden** is said to be where Elizabeth I spent much of her childhood and in November 1558, she held her first Council of State here. Sadly, it is only open today as a venue for social and corporate functions. The **long gallery** holds the queen's silk stockings, hat and gloves.

year round Tue–Sun and bank hol Mons. ◐closed 1 Jan, 25–6 Dec ✍£6, child £3. ♿🄿✕. ✆01707 287 010. www.hatfield-house.co.uk.
This is one of the finest and largest Jacobean houses in England, the home of the Cecil family since the time of Henry VIII. The **interior** is notable for its hall, staircase and long gallery. In the **Marble Hall** the magnificently carved screen, minstrels' gallery and panels are Jacobean;, the gigantic 17C allegorical tapestry is from Brussels. The **Ermine Portrait** of Elizabeth I is attributed to Nicholas Hilliard while the one of her cousin Mary Queen of Scots is said to be by Rowland Lockey. The **grand oak staircase** is Jacobean carving at its best. Note the relief of the horticulturalist John Tradescant, gardener to Charles I, who was employed at Hatfield, on one of the newels at the top of the stairs, and the *Rainbow Portrait* of Elizabeth I. In the library is displayed a letter

from Mary Queen of Scots and her execution warrant.
The extensive **gardens** include a scented garden and fountains, and a famous knot garden (*see Box above*). The **West Garden** includes a scented garden and herb garden and features a major annual summer **sculptural exhibition** (✍extra charge).
The estate also includes the 12C **St Etheldreda's Church** and the **Hatfield Real Tennis Court**. For children there's the 👪**Hatfield Park Farm**, featuring traditional breeds, and the **Bloody Hollow Adventure Playground**.

Knebworth House★

▶ *5mi/8km N by the A 1 junction 7.*
◐*Open Easter Sat–last weekend Sept noon–5pm. Easter–mid-Apr and most of May, Jun and Sept Sat–Sun only. Open daily school holidays inc. all Aug and Jul except during music festival. See website for exact dates.* ✍*Entry by guided*

Hatfield House

tours only, except on busy weekends. £10.50. 🅿️✕. 📞01438 812 661. www. knebworthhouse.com.

The great hall with its richly carved screen and minstrels' gallery has hardly changed since the house was built in the 15C. The Gothic style was introduced by **Edward Bulwer-Lytton**, Victorian novelist, playwright and politician; it is best seen in the **State Drawing Room** with its turreted fireplace, painted panels and stained-glass windows, used as a film set many times in Hollywood movies, including *Batman* (1989). Knebworth is also famous for its rock concerts.

👪 Whipsnade Wild Animal Park★

▶ *Dunstable. 13mi/21km NW via the A 5183.* 🕐*Open daily ate Mar–Oct 10am–5.30pm/6pm, Nov–late Mar 4pm.* 🕐*Closed 25 Dec.* ⬥, 🅿️ *£4,* ✕. £16.70 or £17.70, child £12.70 or £13.20. 📞0844 225 1826. www.zsl.org.

Part of London Zoo, Whipsnade plays a major role in animal conservation and welfare. Star attractions are baby elephants, sea lions, bears, lions, tigers, zebras, rhinos, penguins, chimpanzees and a walk-through lemur area.

Woburn Abbey★★

▶ *22mi/35km N via the M 10, then M 1 to junction 12 and minor road W.* **Abbey:** 🕐*Open mid-Apr–first weekend Oct daily 11am–4pm (last entry).* **Deer park, gardens and grounds:** 🕐*Open daily 10am–5pm (last entry).* £12.95. *Combined tickets with safari park (* ℹ️ *see below) £24.95, child £17.95.* 🔊 *Guided tours.* 🅿️✕. 📞01525 290 333. www. woburnabbey.co.uk.

Woburn was a Cistercian abbey for 400 years before becoming a private mansion. The north range was refurbished in 1630 but the more significant changes date from the 18C.

The **interior** contains sumptuously furnished apartments including the **Mortlake Tapestries**, based on Raphael's *Acts of the Apostles.*

The **State Rooms** include **Queen Victoria's Bedroom** with etchings by Victoria and Albert; **Queen Victoria's Dressing**

Room with walls adorned by superb 17C Dutch and Flemish paintings including works by Aelbert Cuyp, and Van Dyck; the **Blue Drawing Room** with its ceiling (1756) and its fireplace by Duval and Rysbrack; the **State Saloon** with its ornamental ceiling and Rysbrack chimneypiece; the **State Dining Room** graced by a Meissen dinner service and a portrait by Van Dyck; the **Reynolds Room** displaying 10 of his portraits; and the **Canaletto Room** hung with 21 Venetian views.

The **Library**, the finest room in the Holland range, is divided into three parts by Corinthian columns; on the walls hang *Self-Portrait* and *Old Rabbi* by **Rembrandt**. The **Long Gallery**, also divided by columns, by Flitcroft, is hung with 16C paintings including the *Armada Portrait* of Elizabeth I.

The **Deer Park** (3,000 acres/1,200ha) was landscaped by Humphry Repton and is home to some one thousand deer from nine different species.

👪 Woburn Safari Park

▶ *Entrance 1mi/1km from the house.* 🕐*Open late Mar–Oct daily 10am–5pm (last entry). late Oct–early Mar (weather permitting) Sat–Sun 11am–3pm/dusk.* £19.95, child £14.95. *Reduced prices in winter (see website).Combined tickets with abbey (* ℹ️ *see above) £24.95, child £17.95.* ⬥🅿️✕. 📞01525 290 407. www.woburnsafari.co.uk.

This is the largest drive-through safari park in Great Britain and includes white rhino, elephant, tiger, lion, giraffe, bear, wolves, monkeys, eland, oryx, gemsbok, zebra, camel, bison and many more animals. You can **drive your own vehicle** through the reserves as often as you wish before parking in the Wild World Leisure Area. From here you can make another trip on the off-road **Safari Lorry**, take a short foot safari to see the smaller (less dangerous!) animals, attend feeding and ranger talks, or allow the kids to let off steam in the several play areas.

The park is also home to the excellent **Go Ape** high-wire forest adventure course.

Upper Thames Valley★★

The Thames gently winds between Kew and its source in the Cotswolds, offering many varied pleasures as it passes through an often idyllic English countryside of low hills, woods, meadows, country houses, pretty villages and small towns.

Church of Mapledurham
© Peter Clark/Dreamstime.com

- **Michelin Map:** Michelin Atlas p 18 or Map 504 Q, R 28 and 29.
- **Info:** Town Hall, Henley-on-Thames. ℘0149 578 034. www.visithenley-on-thames.co.uk.

SIGHTS

Cookham

This pretty village has been immortalised by the artist **Sir Stanley Spencer** (1891–1959). The chapel which Spencer attended as a boy is now the **Stanley Spencer Gallery**★ (◯ open Apr–Oct daily 10.30am–5pm. Nov–Easter Thu–Sun (Christmas hols daily) 11am–4.30pm; ◎£5; ♿; ℘01628 471 885; http://stanleyspencer.org.uk). Cookham features in many of his paintings.

Henley-on-Thames

In the first week of July some of the world's best oarsmen visit this charming town for the **Henley Royal Regatta**, England's premier rowing event. The **River and Rowing Museum** (Mill Meadows; ◯open daily 10am–5pm, May–Aug 5.30pm; ◯Closed 1 Jan, 24–25 & 31 Dec; ◎£8, child £6; ♿ 🅿 ✕; ℘01491 415 600; www.rrm.co.uk) illustrates the evolution of rowing; the River Thames as a habitat for wildlife, a means of trade and source of pleasure; the history of Henley-on-Thames; and the Royal Regatta. The **Wind in the Willows** gallery celebrates the famous story set on the Thames, by Kenneth Grahame, who lived in neigbouring **Pangbourne** (1922–32).

Mapledurham★

◯Open Good Fri–Sept Sat–Sun and bank hols 2–5,30pm; Oct Sun only, 2–5.30pm. ◎House £8. ♿🅿✕. ℘0118 972 3350. www.mapledurham.co.uk. An Elizabethan **manor house** beside a 14C church and a fully operational **watermill** dating back to the 15C form an almost perfect riverside picture.

Basildon Park★

NT. ◯House main rooms open early Mar–mid-Dec Wed–Mon 11–5pm (House and grounds open 10am). Nov–Dec closes 4pm. Entry Mon by guided tour only. ◎£9. ♿🅿✕. ℘0118 984 3040. www.nationaltrust.org.uk. The splendid Palladian villa overlooking a lush part of the Thames Valley was built by John Carr in 1776. It is rich in exquisite **plasterwork** and boasts a fine collection of 18C paintings.

Goring and Streatley

These two villages, with the weir and Goring Lock, are set in one of the most beautiful parts of the Thames, offering enjoyable riverside walks.

Oxford★★★

Blenheim Palace and around

The city of Oxford is famous as the home of England's oldest university. Its romantic townscape of "dreaming spires", mellow golden stone walls and students in black gowns on bicycles has been the setting for any number of works of fiction, from *Harry Potter* to *Inspector Morse* and *Jude the Obscure*.

A BIT OF HISTORY

Oxford developed in Saxon times around the 8C nunnery of St Frideswide, now Christ Church, and still maintains its original street plan and parts of its city walls. Religious foundations sprang up and in about 1200 the university emerged as a federation of monastic halls; it is still a federation of autonomous colleges today. Oxford was the headquarters of the Royalists during the Civil War (Charles I staying at Christ Church and Henrietta Maria at Merton College). Reform came in the 19C, with the Anglo-Catholic Oxford Movement – which revived the Catholic tradition within the Anglican Church – and the growth of scientific research. In the 20C women were admitted and most of the colleges are now co-educational. However, the essence of Oxford remains unchanged.

The bicycle shop opened in Longwall Street by **William Morris** in 1902, where he began to make motorcycles, has since developed into a vast motor manufacturing enterprise in the suburb of Cowley, where BMW now produces Minis.

MUSEUMS AND TRINITY COLLEGE

Oxford's finest collections can be found in the **Ashmolean Museum**★★ (M[1]; *Beaumont Street;* ⏱ *open Tue–Sun & bank hol Mon 10am–6pm;* ♿,✕; ✆ *01865 278 002; www.ashmolean.org).* Built in 1845, this museum houses the university's archaeology and art collections. Greek and Roman sculptures, Egyptian antiquities, and the decorative and fine arts of China, Japan, Tibet, India and

▶ **Population:** 118,795.
🚗 **Michelin Map:** Michelin Atlas p 18 or Map 504 Q 28.
📋 **Info:** 15–16 Broad Street. ✆01865 252 200. www.visitoxfordand oxfordshire.com.
▷ **Location:** 58mi/93km northwest of London. The train station is west of the bus station, a 10-minute walk from the centre. The bus station is in the centre at Gloucester Green. Oxford is compact and can be covered on foot, or from an open-top bus (✆*01865 790 522; www.citysightseeing oxford.com).*
👁 **Don't Miss:** Punting on the river; Christ Church; Bodleian Library; Ashmolean Museum; University Museum of Natural History/Pitt Rivers Museum.
🕐 **Timing:** At least three days. Many of the colleges are open only in the afternoon; visiting times are usually displayed at the porter's lodge. Opening times at www.ox.ac.uk.
👥 **Kids:** Oxford Castle Unlocked.
🗣 **Walking Tours:** Contact the tourist office. The **tour** marked on the map (*p202*) shows the city's highlights.

Persia are well represented. The outstanding object here is the exquisite late-9C Alfred Jewel, probably made for Alfred the Great. The principal art collections are: Italian paintings, with masterpieces by Uccello and Piero di Cosimo; Renaissance works by Bellini, Veronese, Tintoretto and Giorgione; outstanding Pre-Raphaelite paintings including works by Hunt and Charles Collins; a good selection of French Impressionists; and 20C British works from the Camden Town school.

From the Ashmolean, head east on Beaumont Street, past the **Martyr's Memorial** (**D¹**) and enter **Balliol College** (note the scorch marks on the inner and outer quad doors from the 16C burning of two Protestant bishops in Broad Street) to access **Trinity College** (*Broad Street;* ⏰*open Mon–Fri 10am–noon, 2–4pm, Sat–Sun (term time) 2–4pm, Sat–Sun (hols) 10am–noon, 2–4pm;* ⏰*closed Christmas hols;* ✆*£2;* ✆*01865 279 900; www.trinity.ox.ac.uk).* Trinity was founded 1555. Standing well back from Broad Street behind gardens in the Front Quad is the **chapel**★, with Grinling Gibbons' exquisite carvings. Note in the Durham Quad the 17C Library and in the Garden Quad, facing **Trinity Gardens**★, the north range by Sir Christopher Wren.

Head north from Trinity up Parks Road to visit the **University Museum of Natural History**★ (*Parks Road, off Broad Street;* ⏰*open year-round daily 10am–5pm;* ⏰*closed Easter and over Christmas;* ♿*;* ✆*01865 272 950; www.oum.ox.ac.uk).* Founded in 1860, the museum's natural history contents (including the famous Oxford Dodo) arguably tell us more about the Victorians than the natural world, though both sink into insignificance beside the extraordinary building: a cast-iron neo-Gothic Revival cathedral designed like a railway station, with 19C decorated stone carvings of animals and plants by the Irish sculptor-mason family, the O'Sheas. A doorway at the end leads to the **Pitt Rivers Museum**★ (⏰*open year-round Tue–Sun & bank hol Mons 10am–4.30pm, Mon noon–4.30pm;* ⏰*closed Easter and over Christmas;* ♿*;* ✆*01865 270 927; www.prm.ox.ac.uk),* Oxford's splendidly bizarre anthropological collection of masks, musical instruments, jewellery, skulls, totem poles and armour.

CITY CENTRE

Oxford's heart is Radcliffe Square and the landmark Baroque **Radcliffe Camera**★, which contains two reading rooms, mainly used by undergraduates (**P**; ⊶*closed to the public).* This rotunda,

Punting on the river

©Lulla Bi/Bigstockphoto.com

designed by James Gibbs, is a useful reference point when exploring the many colleges that branch off it. The route marked on the map offers a tour of all of the colleges, but you may prefer simply to wander and admire the architecture.

North of the Quadrangle

On the north side of the quadrangle you will find one of the world's great libraries, the **Bodleian Library**★★ (**A**; *Broad Street;* ⏰*Divinity School, Old Schools Quadrangle and Exhibition Room open year-round Mon–Fri 9am–5pm/ later in summer, Sat 9am–4.30pm, Sun 11am–5pm;* ✆*Divinity School £1, Exhibition Rooms free;* ✆*tours see website for times.* ✆*tours Divinity School and Library £4.50–£6.50;* ♿*;* ✆*01865 277 224; www.bodley.ox.ac.uk),* which contains a copy of every book printed in Britain. Established in the 14C and rebuilt in the 17C, the Bodleian contains more than 6 million books, manuscripts and maps. The main entrance leads to th Old Schools Quadrangle, built in 1439 in the Jacobean-Gothic style. On the right is the Tower of the Five Orders, richly decorated with the five classical orders of architecture. Opposite is the 15C Divinity School – *Harry Potter* fans may recognise it from the first two films – famous for the bosses and pendants of its **lierne vaulting**★. Above is Duke

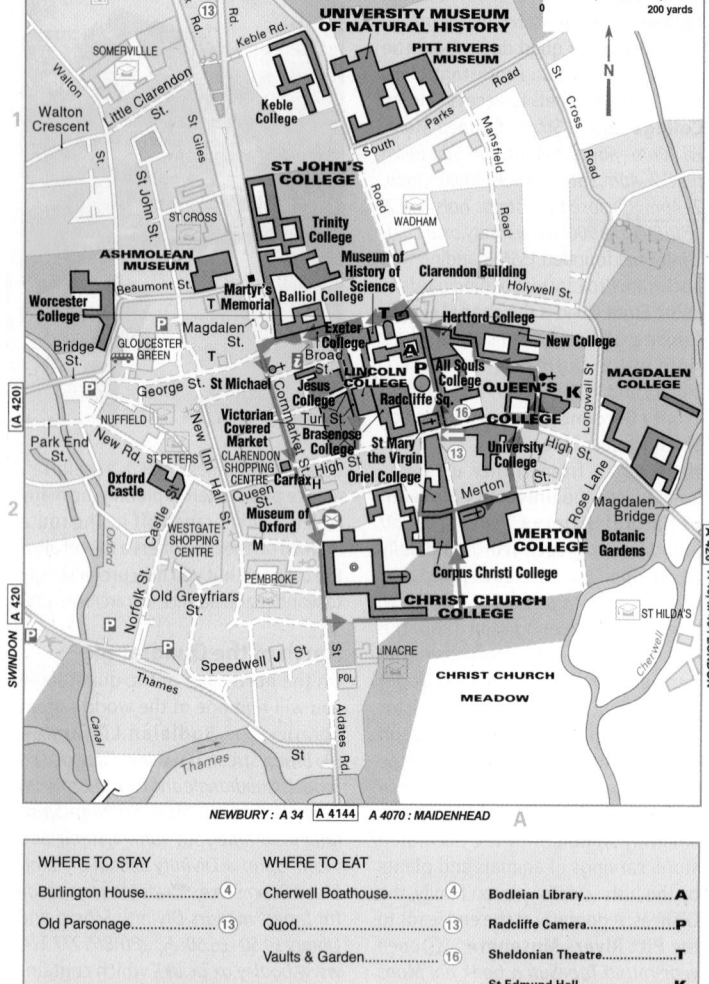

A 40 : CHELTENHAM
A 44 : STRAFORD-
UPON-AVON A 4144 ④ A 4165 ④   A 34 : NORTHAMPTON
A 4260 : BANBURY   A

OXFORD

0   200 m
0   200 yards

NEWBURY : A 34 A 4144   A 4070 : MAIDENHEAD   A

WHERE TO STAY	WHERE TO EAT	
Burlington House...........④	Cherwell Boathouse...........④	Bodleian Library.......................**A**
Old Parsonage...............⑬	Quod.................................⑬	Radcliffe Camera.....................**P**
	Vaults & Garden................⑯	Sheldonian Theatre................**T**
		St Edmund Hall.......................**K**

Humphrey's Library (1610–12), with its decorated **ceiling**★★.

Just north of the Bodleian you will find the **Clarendon Building** and, next door, the **Sheldonian Theatre**★ (*Broad Street;* 🕐*open (university functions permitting) Mon–Sat 10am–12.30pm, 2–4.30pm (3.30pm Nov–Feb);* 🕐*closed Easter and Christmas;* ⊜*£2.50;* &; ✆*01865 277 299; www.sheldon.ox.ac.uk).* Built 1664–69,

Oxford's first Classical building and Sir Christoper Wren's first work of architecture was designed to accommodate formal university ceremonies, a function it fulfils today, alongside its role as a recital room for small music concerts. Next door is Hawksmoor's 1713 Palladian **Clarendon Building (BZ),** now part of the Bodleian Library.

View from Sheldonian Theatre

D. Chapuis/MICHELIN

East of the Quadrangle

On the east side of the quadrangle you first come to **All Souls College** (*High Street;* open year-round Mon–Fri 2pm–4pm; *closed Easter, Aug and 3 Jan–22 Dec;* 01865 279 379; *www.all-souls.ox.ac.uk*). Founded in 1438 as a memorial to those killed in the Hundred Years War, the Front Quadrangle is mid-15C and the larger North Quad, by Nicholas Hawksmoor, is 18C. Between them is the 1442 Perpendicular **chapel**★, with 15C glass in the antechapel, and a magnificent medieval reredos.

Further east are **Hertford College** and **New College** (*New College Lane gate summer, Holywell Street gate winter;* open daily Easter–Oct 11am–5pm Oct–Easter 2–4pm; £2 (winter, free); 01865 279 555; *www.new.ox.ac.uk*). Founded by William of Wykeham in 1379, New College still maintains some of its original buildings. The Great Quad is quintessential English Perpendicular; the hall is the oldest in Oxford. The 15C **chapel**★ is vast, complete with 14C glass. The cloister is a place of calm, offering a view of the 1400 Bell Tower. In the gardens is Oxford's finest section of city walls, including five bastions.

Across Longwall Street from New College is **Magdalen College**★★ (open year-round daily 1pm (noon Jul–Sept)–dusk/7pm; closed Christmas; £4.50; (summer only); 01865 276 000; *www.magd.ox.ac.uk*). Founded in 1458 Magdalen (pronounced "mordlin") was

originally the Hospital of St John the Baptist; the wall running along the High Street is even earlier, dating from the 13C. The chapel, bell tower and cloisters are sumptuous late Perpendicular. The chapel is adorned with gargoyles and pinnacled buttresses.

The 150ft/46m bell tower is still "the most absolute building in Oxford" (James I). The gargoyles on the cloister buttresses are a familiar feature of the Great Quadrangle.

Beside Magdalen Bridge is a boat house and punting station (you will also find these at Folly Bridge and Bardwell Road). A relaxing trip on a flat-bottomed **punt** along the Cherwell or the Thames is almost de rigueur for many visitors, and self-hire and chauffered punts are available by the hour (for more details visit *www.oxfordpunting.co.uk*).

West of the Quadrangle

Just west of the quadrangle is **Brasenose College** (*Radcliffe Square;* open year-round daily, usually 2–4.30pm/5pm summer; closed 25–26 Dec; £1; 01865 277 830; *www.bnc.ox.ac.uk*). Founded 1509, the Gatehouse, Front Quad and Hall are early-16C, the Library and Chapel mid-17C and the old kitchen a 14C relic of Brasenose Hall (the name refers to a doorknocker from the hall). Adjacent to Brasenose is **Lincoln College**★ (*Turl Street;* open year-round Mon–Fri 2–5pm, Sat–Sun 11am–5pm; closed 1 Jan, 25–26 Dec; 01865 279

800; www.linc.ox.ac.uk). Founded 1427, the Front Quad and Hall were built in 1436 and provide a rare glimpse of medieval Oxford. The 1610–31 chapel in the Back Quad contains original 17C Flemish stained glass. Between the two quads are the rooms of **John Wesley**.

Christ Church and South

The **Botanic Gardens** (Rose Lane; ⏰ open daily 9am–5pm Mar–Apr and Sept–Oct, May–Aug 9am–6pm, Nov–Feb 9am–4.30pm; ⏰ closed Good Fri, 25 Dec; ⊚£3.80, winter Mon–Fri contribution requested; ♿; ☎01865 286 690; www.botanic-garden.ox.ac.uk) to the southeast were established in 1621; these are the oldest botanic gardens in England. They provide a view of both the college towers and spires and the River Cherwell.

West of here is **Merton College**★★ (⏰ open year-round Sat–Sun 10am–4pm; ⏰ closed Easter wk and Christmas; ☎01865 276 310; www.merton.ox.ac.uk). Founded in 1264, Merton has the oldest and most picturesque college buildings in Oxford. The oldest square is **Mob Quad**, a complete 14C quadrangle with the **Library** (1371–78) – the first medieval library to put books on shelves – on two sides. Adjacent is the **Decorated Chapel** (1294–97) with 14C transepts, and stained glass.

Leaving the chapel you immediately see **Corpus Christi College** (⏰ open daily 1.30pm–4.30pm; ⏰ closed Easter and Christmas; ☎01865 276 700; www.ccc.ox.ac.uk). Founded in 1517, the gateway and Front Quad are early Tudor. The Pelican Sundial in the centre of the quad was designed in 1581, the 16C Hall has a splendid hammerbeam roof and the 16C chapel contains an altarpiece attributed to the studio of Rubens.

Just beyond Corpus Christi is **Christ Church**★★ *(college, cathedral and hall:* ⏰ open year-round Mon–Sat 9am–5.30pm, Sun 2–5.30pm; Cathedral closes 4.30pm; *picture gallery:* ⏰ open May–Sept Mon–Sat 10.30am–5pm, Sun 2–5pm; Oct–Apr Mon–Sat 10.30am–1pm & 2–5pm, Sun 2–4.30pm; ⏰ closed 25 Dec; ⊚see website for details; ♿; www.chch.ox.ac.uk). Founded in 1525 by Cardinal Wolsey "The House" is Oxford's biggest and grandest Renaissance college. Oxford's largest quadrangle is **Tom Quad**★. Above the gatehouse is Wren's synthesis of Baroque and Gothic, **Tom Tower**★, a fine domed gateway. The **Tudor Hall**★★, by James Wyatt, boasts a magnificent fan-vaulted entrance stairway, hammerbeam roof and portraits by Kneller, Romney, Gainsborough, Lawrence and Millais. The **Picture Gallery** at Christ Church holds one of the most important private collections of Old Master drawings in the country and includes work by Leonardo, Michelangelo, Dürer, Raphael and Rubens. Picturesque Christ Church Meadow stretches from St Aldate's to the River Thames. **Christ Church Cathedral**★, originally the church of St Frideswide's Priory, is late Norman with a 16C roof. Its glory is its 15C stellar vaulted **choir roof**★. Nearby, up Cornmarket Street is the **Museum of Oxford** (⏰ open year-round Tue–Thu & Sat 10am–5pm; ♿; ☎01865 252 761; www.museumofoxford.org.uk). Here you will discover the story of the city including its earliest residents' medieval crafts, Civil War, famous literary connections and the growth of the modern city.

A little further up Cornmarket Street is **Carfax** (⏰ open daily Apr–Sept 10am–5pm, rest of year 10am–4pm; ☎01865 790 522; ⊚£2.10; ⊘No children under five admitted), the centre of the Saxon and medieval city. This 14C tower is all that remains of St Martin's Church.

There are good views of the High Street ("the High") from the top of the tower. There are four entrances from the High Street to the delightful **Victorian Covered Market**★, which dates back to 1774. It is home to all kinds of speciality shops, not exclusive to, but with the emphasis on food, and includes traditional butchers, greengrocers, fishmongers and cheesemongers. It is very lively, well worth browsing and also includes several places for snacking and stocking up on picnics.

West of Carfax, along Queen Street and Castle Street is ♦♦**Oxford Castle**★

(🕐 *open year-round daily 10am–5.30pm (last tour 4.20pm;* 🕐 *closed 25 Dec;* ☞*£7.95, child £5.65;* ♿✕; *℘01865 260 666; www.oxfordcastleunlocked.co.uk).* The city's most recent visitor attraction, this is a brilliant restoration of the former castle/prison complex, including a hotel and restaurants, and is worth a visit whether or not you go inside. George's Tower is a striking survival from Oxford Castle, built 1071. Since then the site has been used as a place of incarceration until its closure in 1996. The more colourful events – violence, executions, escapes, betrayal, romance – which shaped its grim history are explored with relish.

WOODSTOCK

📍 *8hmi/13km N of Oxford.*
Effectively the lobby to Blenheim Palace, the elegant little mellow Cotswold-stone town of **Woodstock** is well worth a visit in its own right. Old coaching inns and antique shops cluster round the Classical town hall. Across the street, the **Oxfordshire Museum** (🕐*open daily year-round Tue–Sat 10am–5pm, Sun 2–5pm;* ♿✕; *℘01865 811456; www. oxfordshire.gov.uk)* tells the story of both town and county. Kids will enjoy its Dinosaur Garden and Gallery.

BLENHEIM PALACE★★★

📍 *Woodstock.* 🕐 *Park: Open daily (except 25 Dec) 9am–4.45pm (last entry).* 🕐 *Closed 25 Dec. House and*

grounds: 🕐*Open mid-Feb–Oct daily; Nov–mid-Dec Wed–Sun 10.30am– 5.30pm.* ☞*Palace and park £19, child £10.50).* 👣*Guided tour (1hr) except Sun, bank hols and busy periods).* ♿🅿✕. *℘0800 849 6500. www.blenheimpalace.com.*
The greatest building of the English Baroque, residence of the Dukes of Marlborough, is matched in splendour by the sublime landscaping of its vast park.

A Bit of History

The Royal Manor of Woodstock once the hunting ground of Saxon kings, was the birthplace of Edward the Black Prince (b.1330). In the 18C the royal manor was given to **John Churchill, Duke of Marlborough** (1650–1722), to mark his victory in 1704 over the armies of Louis XIV at Blenheim in Bavaria. Seemingly limitless funds from the national purse were made available for a *"Royall and National Monument"* to be erected in celebration of this decisive check to France's pan-European ambitions. Leading architects and craftsmen were employed, foremost among them **Sir John Vanbrugh**, one of England's most original architects, whose inventiveness and sense of drama found full expression here. The grandiose project, a monument rather than a home, was completed in 1722. A century and a half later, on 30 November 1874, his direct descendant, **Winston Churchill**, grandson of the 7th

Blenheim Palace viewed from the Italian Garden
© Eurasia Press/Photononstop

Duke, was born here. (This most illustrious of Englishmen is buried in the churchyard at Bladon, 3mi/5km south). On the first floor "Blenheim Palace: The Untold Story" is a good introduction to the estate's 300-year history.

Palace★★★

The palace's huge scale and fortress-like character are relieved by almost theatrical composition and exuberant detail. Its silhouette has a romantic, even medieval air, with an array of turrets, pinnacles and disguised chimney-pots, and the Great Court (450ft/137m long) is like a stage set, a succession of colonnades, towers and arcades leading the eye inexorably to the main façade with its imposing portico. Symbols of military prowess and patriotism abound; over the courtyard gateway the cockerel of France is mauled by the English lion.

Interior

A series of splendidly decorated rooms continues the monumental theme. In the **Great Hall** (67ft/20m high) the ceiling is painted with an allegory of Marlborough's victory. Sir Winston Churchill's life is celebrated in a suite of rooms, including the one in which he was born. State apartments are furnished with original pieces. There are portraits by Reynolds, Romney, Van Dyck and one, by Sargent, of the 9th Duke with his family and American-born wife Consuelo. The vast **Saloon** has a great painted colonnade, apparently open to the sky. The **Long Library**, with a magnificent stucco ceiling, runs the entire length (180ft/55m) of the west front. In the chapel is the bombastic **tomb** of the 1st Duke.

Grounds★★★

The ancient hunting park, with its venerable trees and deer-proof wall, was worked upon in the early-18C by the royal gardeners. The **Italian Garden** to the east of the palace and the spectacular **Water Garden** to the west are modern, as is the symbolic maze of trophies, cannon and trumpets in the walled garden, but they capture something of the spirit of the formal avenues and geometrical parterres which were mostly swept away by **Lancelot "Capability" Brown**, the greatest of English landscape architects. The redesigned park is his masterpiece, offering from the Woodstock Gate what has been described as "the finest view in England". Sweeping grassy slopes, noble groves of trees and the curving outline of the great lake, crossed by Vanbrugh's **Grand Bridge**, provide a more than worthy setting for the palace.

The huge **Doric column** (134ft/41m high) is topped by a statue of the 1st Duke with Victory in his grasp. Downstream, Brown's water engineering terminates in his **Grand Cascade**, over which the little River Glyme foams to rejoin its former bed.

In the ▲♿**Pleasure Grounds** (the area nearest the house) are various attractions including Blenheim Bygones, a lavender garden, a maze, a butterfly house (🕐*closed winter*) and an adventure play area. A land train (🚌*free*) saves weary feet. You are also free to wander the 2100 acres/850ha of beautiful parkland.

DORCHESTER★

◗ *10mi/16km S of Oxford.*

This historic village dates back to the Bronze Age and boasts a fine Norman **abbey church** (🕐*open daily 8am–6pm/ dusk, abbey museum open early Apr–Sept daily 2–5pm;* 🅿✕; 🕿*01865 340 007; www.dorchester-abbey.org.uk*).

ABINGDON★

◗ *11mi/17km S of Oxford.*

The town grew up around an abbey founded in the 7C, though the only remaining abbey buildings are the 13C **Chequer** with its tall chimney, the c.1500 **Long Gallery** with an oak-beamed roof and the 15C **gateway** beside the medieval church of St Nicholas. Abingdon's skyline is characterised by the 15C spire of the wide five-aisled **St Helen's Church**. Delightful 15C **almshouses**★ border the churchyard.

Cotswolds★★★

Cirencester to Chipping Campden

Rising gently from the Upper Thames Valley in the southeast to a dramatic escarpment overlooking the Severn Vale in the west, the Cotswolds cover around 770sq mi/2,000sq km), encapsulating rural England in concentrated form. Airy open uplands, sheltered in places by stately belts of beech trees, alternate with deep valleys enfolding venerable golden limestone villages and small county towns.

A BIT OF HISTORY

The region has long been favoured for settlement. The commanding heights in the west are crowned more often than not by the hill forts of prehistoric man, whose burial places also abound, from the chambered tombs of the Neolithic to the round barrows of the Bronze Age. Great estates were farmed from the Roman villas lying just off Ermin Street and the Fosse Way. In the Middle Ages it was the wool from countless sheep grazing on the fine pasture of the wolds which gave rise to a trade of European importance and to a class of prosperous merchants, whose monuments are the great "wool" churches which they built from the underlying oolitic limestone. Ranging in colour from silver or cream to deepest gold, this loveliest of building stone is synonymous with "Cotswold character". Yielding the sophisticated

- **Michelin Map:** Michelin Atlas pp 17 and 27 or Map 503 O 27 and 28.
- **Info:** 1 Cotswold Court, Broadway. ℘01386 852 937 (summer only). The Old Police Station, High Street, Chipping Campden. ℘01386 841 206. Corinium Museum, Park Street, Cirencester. ℘01285 655 611. Victoria Street, Bourton-on-the-Water. ℘01451 820 211. www.visitcotswolds.co.uk.
- **Location:** Most of the central villages make a good base. Alternatively, stay in Oxford, Stratford, Cheltenham or Bath. Regular Cotswolds bus tours depart from all of these in summer.
- **Don't Miss:** The villages of Bibury and Chipping Campden; Chastleton House; Snowshill Manor; Hidcote Manor Garden; the view from Broadway Tower.
- **Beware:** Busy roads and crowds during school summer holidays.
- **Timing:** At least three days.
- **Kids:** Cotswold Wildlife Park and Bourton-on-the-Water's many child-friendly attractions.

Arlington Row, Bibury

© Taylor Richard/Sime/Photononstop

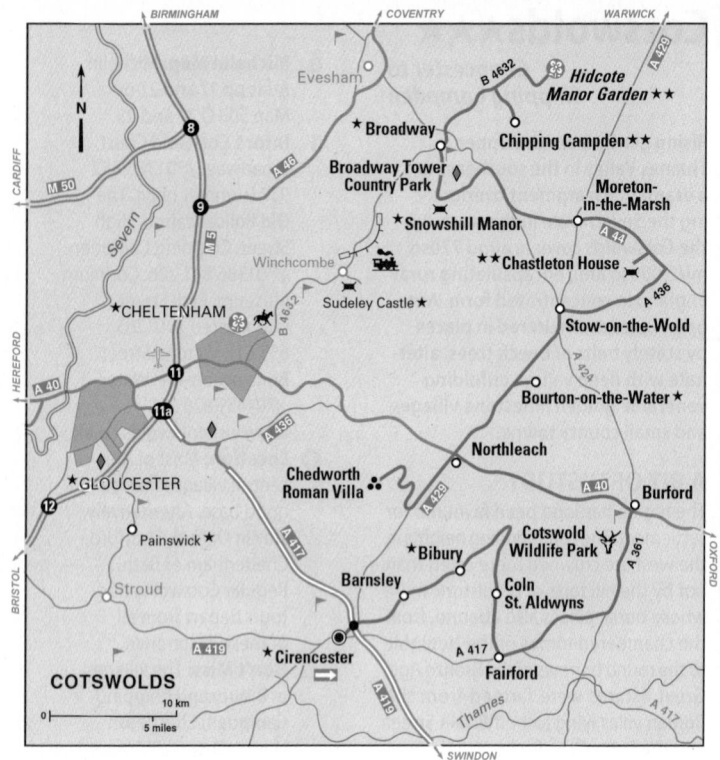

masonry of manor houses, the "tiles" of cottage roofs, rough-dressed walls of barns and even the drystone boundaries of fields, it creates a rare harmony of building and landscape. Far removed from coalfields and big cities, the area escaped the effects of industrialisation; its rural pattern is intact, an idyllic setting for quiet exploration of the past.

🚗 DRIVING TOUR

CIRENCESTER TO CHIPPING CAMPDEN
⟩ *40mi/64km; Allow a day.*

This tour runs north through some of the region's most delightful small towns and villages towards the escarpment above Broadway with its spectacular views.

Cirencester★
The "Capital of the Cotswolds" is still the market town for a prosperous rural region. It was founded as a Roman fort, Corinium, established early in the Roman occupation at the junction of three major roads – Ermin Street, Akeman Street and the Fosse Way; by the 2C AD it had become a walled city, second only to London in size, the centre of a flourishing countryside of great villa estates. The old town is compact and has kept a traditional townscape, little marred by incongruous intrusions. It is hemmed in by the green spaces of two ancient estates: the gardens of the abbey sloping down to the pretty River Churn (the abbey buildings were demolished at the Dissolution) and the grandiose formal landscape of **Cirencester Park**, which contains the magnificent length of the **Broad Avenue** (5mi/8km) and the great house, concealed from the town by a high wall and an even higher yew hedge.

On Coxwell Street, the **Church of St John the Baptist**★ (⟩*open year-round daily 9.30am–5pm , except during ser-*

vices; ⏱closed 25–Dec except for services; ☎01285 659 317; www.cirenparish.co.uk) is one of the largest parish churches in the country, and an important example of a Cotswold "wool church". The lofty tower of 1400–20, supported by powerful spur buttresses, rises grandly above the town. The unusual three-storey porch opening into the marketplace once served as the town hall.

The nave is exceptionally high and spacious; its immensely tall piers carry angels bearing the coats of arms of those pious townsfolk responsible for the ambitious rebuilding of 1516–30. Throughout the interior there is a wealth of detail: an unusual pre-Reformation pulpit; the **Boleyn Cup**, a gilt cup made for Anne Boleyn; memorial brasses grouped in the Chapel of the Holy Trinity; and, in the Lady Chapel, the charming effigies of Humfry Bridges (d.1598), his wife and their numerous children. On Park Street, the **Corinium Museum**★ (⏱ open year-round daily Mon–Sat 10am–5pm, Sun 2pm–5pm; closes 4pm daily Nov–Mar; ⏱closed 1 Jan; 23–26 Dec; ⏴£4.80; ♿✖; ☎01285 655 611; http://coriniummuseum.cotswold.gov.uk) is a modern well-arranged museum explaining Cotswold history from geological to recent times. It holds one of the finest and most extensive Roman collections in the country, including a series of superb **mosaic pavements**★. The building also houses the local tourist information office.

▷ *From Cirencester take the A 429 and the B 4425 E.*

Bibury★

William Morris' epithet of "the most beautiful village in England" is justified by the combined prospect of the friendly River Coln, stone bridges, weavers' cottages and the gables of Bibury Court against a wooded background. Dating from the 17C, **Arlington Mill** is a particularly attractive property.

▷ *From Bibury return SW by the B 4425; at the crossroads turn left; in Poulton turn left on to the A 417.*

Fairford

This old coaching village is famous for the **Church of St Mary**★, (⏱open year-round daily 10am–5pm/3.30pm in winter; ☎01285 712611; www.stmaryschurchfairford.org.uk), harmoniously re-built in the late-15C. Sculptures, some humorously grotesque, enrich the exterior. Inside, the screens, stalls and misericords of the choir are of exceptional quality. But the church's glory is its wonderful set of **stained-glass windows**★★ (c.1500), tracing in colour the Bible's story from Adam and Eve to the Last Judgement.

▷ *From Fairford take the A 417 E and the A 361 N.*

👥👤Cotswold Wildlife Park

⏱Open year-round daily 10am–6pm (winter 5pm). Last entry 90mins before closing. ⏴£12.50, child £8.50 (narrow-gauge railway ⏴£1). ♿🅿✖. ☎01993 823 006. www.cotswoldwildlifepark.co.uk. The peaceful natural habitat of the park and gardens (160 acres/65ha), set around a listed Victorian manor house, is home to a wide variety of wildlife – rhinos, zebras and ostriches protected by unobtrusive moats; tigers and leopards in grassed enclosures; monkeys and otters in the old walled garden and tropical birds and plants in the tropical house; there is also a reptile house, aquarium and insect house. Additional attractions include an adventure playground, brass rubbing centre, children's farmyard and narrow-gauge railway.

▷ *Continue N on the A 361.*

Burford

One of the focal points of the wool trade, later an important coaching town, Burford's growth stopped when the turnpike road (A 40) bypassed it in 1812. With its wealth of beautifully preserved buildings, nearly all of Cotswold limestone, it is one of the region's "show villages". The single main street descends to cross the pretty River Windrush. About halfway down, the black-and-white timber

-fronted building on stone pillars is the 16C **Tolsey**, once the courthouse, and toll collecting point, now the local museum (open Easter–Oct daily 2–5pm; 01993 823 196).

Slightly apart from the town is the large **Church of St John the Baptist★**, its tall spire rising gracefully above the water-meadows. Norman in origin, the church exhibits a rich variety of work from many periods; the pinnacled three-storey 15C porch is outstanding. Note the exuberant monument to Edward Harman (d.1569), decorated with American Indians, and rows of kneeling children.

 Take the A 40 W to Northleach.

Northleach

This small market town is graced with many fine historic buildings but its "wool church" takes pride of place. It boasts Britain's finest collection of memorial brasses, dedicated (unsurprisingly) to the merchants whose money built the church. Note the huge brass dedicated to John Fortey (d.1458), over 5ft /1.5m long, beneath the North Arcade. On the High Street is **Keith Harding's World of Mechanical Music Museum**, (open year-round daily 10am–5pm; closed 25–26 Dec; £8; ; 01451 860 181, www.mechanicalmusic.co.uk), a showcase of ingenious self-playing musical instruments and automata introduced and played by expert guides.

 Take the A 429 S and turn right to Chedworth.

Chedworth Roman Villa

NT. Yanworth, nr Cheltenham. Open Mar–Oct Wed–Sun and bank hols 10am –5pm (most of Mar 4pm). £7. . 01242 890 256. www.nationaltrust.org.uk.

This large and rich villa stood at the head of a small valley beside its own spring. It was undoubtedly one of the grandest buildings of the Roman Cotswolds. The remains, including good mosaic floors, have been carefully excavated and are well presented. The museum displays items found on the site.

 Return to Northleach and continue N on the A 429.

Bourton-on-the-Water★

The village owes its special charm to the clear waters of the Windrush, which run between well-tended grass banks beside the main street and under elegant stone bridges. It is the most commercialised of the Cotswolds villages, due in no small part to three very popular family attractions: The **Model Village** (Rissington Road, behind Old New Inn; open year-round daily 10am–6pm/winter 4pm; £3.60, child £3.80; ; 01451 820 467; www.theoldnewinn.co.uk; the excellent **Cotswold Motoring Museum & Toy Collection** (The Old Mill; open 10am–6pm Feb half-term hols–first Sun Dec; £4.35, child £2.90; ; 01451 821 255; www.cotswold-motor-museum.co.uk) and **Birdland Park and Gardens** (Rissington Road; open year-round daily 10am–6pm/Nov–Mar 4pm; £7.25, child £5; ; 01451 820 480; www.birdland.co.uk).

 Make a detour W of the A 429 by a minor road to the Slaughters.

The Slaughters

Frequently cited as two of the prettiest villages in the Cotswolds, both **Lower** and **Upper Slaughter** are picturesquely sited by the River Eye. The word "Slaughter" is in fact derived from the Old English word "Slohtre" meaning muddy place.

The **Old Mill** (open Apr–Oct daily 10am-5pm; charge; 01451 820 052, www.oldmill-lowerslaughter.com) at Lower Slaughter is worth a stop, not just for its local history but also for its riverside tearooms and (organic) ice cream parlour.

 Take the minor road NE into Stow-on-the-Wold.

Stow-on-the-Wold

This is the highest settlement in Gloucestershire and probably originated as a Roman lookout post on the Fosse Way. It is a regular stop for visitors on the traditional Cotswold circuit, to browse in the antique shops, admire the 14C cross in the marketplace or the Crucifixion by Caspar de Crayer (1610) in the church.

▷ *Take the A 436 NE; at the crossroads turn right onto the A 44.*

Chipping Norton

This is one of the Cotswold's liveliest towns with a good number of pubs, restaurants and shops and an acclaimed theatre *(www.chippingnortontheatre. co.uk)*. It has a fine wool church but the only visitor attraction is the modest local museum.

Take a detour 2.6mi/4.2km north via the B 4026 to Little Rollright, where you will see signs to the **Rollright Stones**, (Ⓞ*open daily sunrise–sunset;* ⊛*£1; www. rollrightstones.co.uk*). Set in a field is an ancient small stone circle – 70 stones, 104ft/31m in diameter – which according to the local legend represents a future king of England and his knights, turned to stone by a witch. The circle, some 4,000–4,500 years old, is known as The Kings Men. There is the (separate) King Stone, and the remains of a 5,000-year-old megalithic tomb, known as The Whispering Knights.

▷ *Return along the A 44.*

Chastleton House★★

NT. Chastleton, nr Moreton-in-Marsh. Ⓞ*Open mid-Mar–Oct Wed–Sat 1pm–5pm (Oct & Mar 4pm). Entry by timed ticket, issued at reception on first-come, first-served basis from 12.30pm.* ⊛*£8.25.* ℗. ☎*01608 674 981. www.nationaltrust.org.uk.*

This rare gem of a Jacobean country house was built in the early-17C by a wool merchant and is a near-perfect time capsule. The absence of shop, tearoom and other modern accretions adds to the atmosphere.

The **Great Hall**, one of the last of its kind to be built, the richly decorated **Great Chamber** and the tunnel-vaulted Long Gallery, running the whole length of the top floor, evoke the atmosphere of domestic life in the 17C.

On the forecourt are the 17C stables and the little **Church of St Mary**. To the east of the house is a great rarity, a small formal **garden** surviving from about 1700.

▷ *Continue W on the A 44.*

The route passes through **Moreton-in-Marsh**, an attractive little market town, where the Fosse Way broadens out to form the main street.

▷ *After 6mi/10km turn left onto the B 4081.*

Snowshill Manor★

NT. Snowshill, nr Broadway. **House:** Ⓞ*Open Jul–Aug Wed–Mon 11am–4.30pm. Apr–Jul & Aug–Oct Wed–Sun & bank hols 11am–5pm.* ⊛*House and garden £8.50; Entry to house by timed ticket only, issued at reception on first-come, first-served basis. On busy days (particularly bank hols and Sun) tickets often run out so arrive early to avoid disappointment.* ♿℗✕. ☎*01386 852 410. www.nationaltrust.org.uk.*

This typical Cotswold manor house (c. 1500) is snugly sited below the rim of the escarpment. The low-lit house is very atmospheric and crammed with a fascinating jackdaw's nest of objects, acquired by the eccentric owner Charles Wade (1883–1956), the most striking of which is the **Samurai armour** collection displayed to its full menacing effect on brooding warrior mannequins in the gloom of the Green Room. Stepping out into the light, Wade also laid out the enchanting **terraced garden**★.

▷ *Return NE on the B 4081; turn left onto a minor road.*

Broadway Tower Country Park

Ⓞ*Open year-round daily 10.30am–5pm (may vary in poor weather).* ⊛*£4.50.* ♿℗✕. ☎*01386 852 390. www.broadwaytower.co.uk.*

Broadway Tower, a battlemented folly (1800), marks one of the highest points (1,024ft/312m) in the Cotswolds.

It houses exhibitions on three floors about the history of its occupants. On a clear day the **panorama**★★★ extends to the Welsh borders. The country park includes a red deer enclosure and beautiful nature walks.

▷ *Continue on the minor road; turn left into the A 44, down a long hill.*

Broadway★

This handsome village, more formal than its neighbours, is famous for its variety of genteel upmarket antique and craft shops, cafés and restaurants, hotels and guesthouses.

The long, partly tree-lined "broad way" rises gently from the village green at the western end to the foot of the escarpment, flanked by mellow stone buildings, from picturesque thatched cottages to the stately Lygon Arms hotel.

▷ *Take the B 4632 and B 4035 N and E to Chipping Campden.*

Chipping Campden★★

The long curving High Street, lined with buildings of all periods in the mellowest of limestone, makes Chipping Campden the embodiment of the Cotswold townscape. The town has been quietly prosperous since the great days of the medieval wool trade and something of its present state of preservation is due to the care and skill of the artists and craftspeople who were attracted to Chipping Campden in the early-20C.

Many of the houses in the **High Street** are substantial but, more than individual distinction, it is the overall harmony of the street scene which impresses. The centre of the town is marked by the arched and gabled **Market Hall** of 1627. Further north, distinguished by its two-storeyed bay window, is the **house of William Grevel**, "the flower of the wool merchants of all England", who died in 1401 and is commemorated by a fine brass in the splendid **St James's Church** (⏱*open daily;* ⊙*£1 donation requested;* ℘*01386 841 927; www.stjames churchcampden.co.uk*). In Church Street stand the almshouses built in 1617 by Sir

Baptist Hicks. His own mansion *(opposite)* was destroyed but two pavilions survive, together with pepperpot lodges and the gateway, near the entrance to the church.

▷ *Take the B 4081 N (signposted).*

Hidcote ★★

NT. Hidcote Bartrim. ⏱*Open Jul–Aug daily 10am–6pm. Sept & Mid-Mar–Jun Sat–Wed 10am–6pm. Oct-early Nov Sat–Wed 10am–5pm. Early Nov–3rd week Dec Sat–Wed 11am–4pm.* ⊙*£9.05.* 🅿✕. ℘*01386 438 333. www.nationaltrust.org.uk.*

The horticulturalist Lawrence Johnstone has managed an enchanting variety of effects in such a small space (10 acres/4ha) and created one of the greatest English gardens of the 20C, an Arts and Crafts masterpiece. Calm expanses of lawns (one of which is open for croquet), vistas down avenues or into the countryside contrast with luxuriant but carefully controlled wildness. A labyrinth of "garden rooms" encloses an arrangement of herbs, plants entirely in white, and a mysterious pool.

CHELTENHAM★

▷*55mi/88km N of Bath and 96mi/155km W of London. Population: 91,301.* 🚇*77 Promenade.* ℘*01242 522 878. www.visitcheltenham.com.*

The benefits of the waters of this elegant English spa town were discovered early in the 18C, but it was at its most fashionable in the Regency period, when it developed the Classical architecture, squares, terraces and crescents, all in a delightful setting of trees and gardens, which are still its pride today. Despite its older residents and retirement-home status, it has an animated cultural life, with internationally important musical and literary festivals.

Town Centre★

Of pre-spa Cheltenham there remains little but the secluded Church of St Mary and the line of the much rebuilt High Street. At right angles is the **Pro-**

menade; its spacious lower part is lined on one side by the **Municipal Offices**, an imposing terrace of 1823; its upper part, twice as broad, rises gently to the stately stuccoed façade of the **Queen's Hotel** of 1838. To the east are the **Imperial Gardens**, a floral cocktail in summer; to the west, behind an avenue of trees, are some of the refined **Regency houses** with classical details and exquisite balcony ironwork which characterise the town. Farther south is **Montpellier Walk**, whose mid-19C shopfronts are divided up by Grecian caryatids; it terminates in the colonnade and dome of the old **Montpellier Spa** (now a bank).

Cheltenham Art Gallery & Museum

Closed to the public, scheduled to reopen late 2012 /early 2013. See website for latest news. www.cheltenham museum.org.uk.

The highlight of the town gallery is its **collection of applied art** illustrating the importance of the Cotswolds in the Arts and Crafts movement. The thoroughly modern new redeveloped building will include a rooftop terrace with views over the church and the surrounding conservation area.

Pittville

This distinguished district of Classical terraces and villas (1mi/1.6km N of the High Street) was laid out in the early-19C by Joseph Pitt. In romantic Pittville Park great trees and sweeping lawns surround a picturesque lake.

Pittville Pump Room★

Open year-round (events permitting) Wed–Mon 10am–4pm. Closed bank hol Mons, 25–26 Dec. 🅿. ℘01242 521 621. www.pittvillepumproom.org.uk.
During the Regency this was the most magnificent of several buildings where the spa waters were taken. This outstanding Grecian building (1825–30), with its Ionic colonnade and domed interior, was designed by Joseph Pitt. You may enter as long as there is not a function on, and sample a glass of water.

Holst Birthplace Museum

4 Clarence Road, Pittville. Open early Feb–mid-Dec Tue–Sat (and some bank hols) 10am–4pm. £4.50 (cash/cheques only). ℘01242 524 846. www.holstmuseum.org.uk.
Near the park entrance is the Regency house where Gustav Host, composer of The Planets, was born in 1874.

DEERHURST★

▶ 7mi/11km N of Cheltenham via the A 4019, A 38 and a minor road W.
This tiny village possesses two important Anglo-Saxon buildings. Once part of a flourishing monastery, vestiges of **St Mary's Church**★ (open daily 8.30am–dusk; ℘01684 292 562) date from the 8C, and it is typically Saxon.
Odda's Chapel (EH; open year-round daily Apr–Sept 10am–6pm, Nov–Mar 4pm; closed 1 Jan, 25–26 Dec; 🅿; www.english-heritage.org.uk) was dedicated by Earl Odda in 1056 and consists of a nave and chancel, both of touching simplicity. It was rediscovered in the 19C, having served as the kitchen of the adjoining farmhouse.

TEWKESBURY★

▶ 8mi/13km N of Cheltenham on the A 4019 and A 38.
This little Saxon town is dominated by the great Norman abbey church. Tewkesbury grew little in the 19C and has conserved its historic character almost intact.

Tewkesbury Abbey★★

Church Street. Open year-round Mon-Sat 8.30am (Sun, Wed, Fri 7.30am)–5.30pm. Guided tours Easter–Oct (£4). Tower tours (£3), most summer Sun afternoons and bank hol Mons. ℘01684 850 959. www.tewkesburyabbey.org.uk.
Once part of a wealthy and important Benedictine abbey, the church combines a noble simplicity of structure with great richness of detail, and many of the abbey's important benefactors are buried here. There are two survivals from monastic days – the **Abbey House** and the **Gatehouse**, just outside the

precinct. At the Dissolution it was saved from demolition by the townsfolk.

The most impressive elements are the huge 12C **tower** and the grandeur of the **west front**, with its recessed arch (65ft/20m high).

The Norman **nave**★★ is covered by a beautiful 14C vault which replaced an earlier timber roof. The church's many monuments are grouped around the choir. Bishop Wakeman is grotesquely commemorated by the *memento mori*, of a decomposing cadaver crawling with vermin. The 14C **stained-glass windows** of the choir depict local notables. The choir **vault**★ is a glorious web of ribs and bosses.

SUDELEY CASTLE★

▶ *Castle Street, Winchcombe. 7mi/ 11km NE of Cheltenham via the B 4632. Castle Street, Winchcombe.* ○*Open daily Apr–Oct 10.30am–5pm.* ▨*£7.20.* ⓹▣✖. ☎*01242 602 308. www.sudeleycastle.co.uk.*

The house is surrounded by the dramatic scenery of the Cotswold escarpment. Once a medieval stronghold, it became the home of **Katherine Parr**, widow of Henry VIII. During the Civil War it was besieged and largely destroyed. In the 19C the house was restored, although some parts were left ruined. The collection includes Turner, Van Dyck and Rubens. The **gardens** are glorious, with the centrepiece Queens' Garden billowing with hundreds of varieties of old-fashioned roses. The grounds also include St Mary's Church, a rare breeds Pheasantry and adventure playground.

STROUD

The most westerly and least typical of the major Cotswold settlements, Stroud is the only one to have been affected significantly by the Industrial Revolution. Its interesting history can be traced in the **Museum in the Park** (*Stratford Park;* ○*open Apr–Sept Tue–Fri (also Mon in May)10am–5pm, Sat–Sun and bank hol Mon 11am–5pm, Oct–Mar Tue–Fri 10am–4pm, Sat–Sun 11am–4pm, Dec call for details;* ○*closed Good Fri;* ⓹▣✖; ☎*01453 763 394, www.museu-*

minthepark.org.uk) housed in a 17C wool merchant's mansion.

The Wildfowl and Wetlands Trust, Slimbridge★

▶ *15mi/24km SW of Gloucester.* ○*Open daily 9.30am–5.30pm (5pm Nov–Mar).* ▨*£9.41.* ⟶*Canoe Safari daily Easter–Sept 11am–4pm;* ▨*£5 per adult, child free.* ⓹▣✖. ☎*01453 891 900. www.wwt.org.uk.*

Bordering the extensive wetlands of the tidal Severn, this pioneering waterbird sanctuary, created by the late Sir Peter Scott, has acquired an international reputation for research and conservation and as a place where a great variety of native and exotic wildfowl can be observed from hides, observatories and a canoe safari at close quarters. Visitors can also enjoy the spectacular winter arrival of thousands of wild ducks, geese and swans.

Berkeley Castle★★

▶ *20mi/32km SW of Gloucester.* ○*Open early Apr–Oct and all school hols and bank hols Sun–Thu, 11am–5.30pm. Butterfly House open Good Fri–Sept.* ▨*£9.50.* ▣✖. ☎*01453 810 332. www.berkeley-castle.com.*

This archetypal medieval stronghold commanded the narrow strip of lowland between the Cotswolds and the Severn; its defences could be strengthened by flooding the surrounding water meadows. The inner courtyard is dominated by the great drum of the **keep** of 1153. The **interior** is a confusion of twisting passages and stairways, vaulted cellars, ancient kitchens and deep dungeons.

In the King's Gallery can be seen the chamber where the deposed **Edward II** was kept prisoner and then horribly murdered, possibly by agents of his former queen. Other rooms are richly furnished with reminders of the castle's continuous occupation since the 12C.

In the **Butterfly House** hundreds of exotic and rare freeflying butterflies represent over 40 species.

Gloucester★

and around

Gloucester (pronounced "Gloster") is a busy centre of administration, manufacturing and commerce, dominated by its glorious cathedral.

CITY
City Centre
The point where the Roman streets intersect is marked by **St Michael's Tower**. The late-medieval timber **Bishop Hooper's Lodging**★ in Westgate Street houses **Gloucester Folk Museum** (ⓘ *open year-round Tue–Sat 10am–5pm; ⬤£3 (inc.entry to City Museum);* ✕; ☎*01452 396 396, www.gloucester.gov.uk),* where the lively exhibits include fishing on the Severn, toys, games and agricultural bygones. Nearby, on Brunswick Road, just off Eastgate Street, is the recently renovated **Gloucester City Museum and Art Gallery** (ⓘ*opening times and details as Folk Museum);* highlights include an Interactive Roman Kitchen exhibition, a toys and games gallery, and a garden gallery.

Gloucester Docks★
The fine 19C inland port and warehouses have been conserved. The **Gloucester Waterways Museum** (Llanthony Warehouse; ⓘ *open year-round daily 11am–4pm (Jul–Aug 10.30am–5pm);* ⓘ*closed 1 Jan, 25–26 Dec;* ⬤*£4.75; boat trip (Easter–Oct) £4.95;* ♿ 🅿*(charge)* ✕; ☎*01452 318 200; www.gloucesterwaterwaysmuseum.org.uk)* explores the long history of river and canal navigation in Britain through models, displays, text panels, video simulations and a variety of historic vessels moored by the quay. Take a 45-minute boat trip on the Gloucester and Sharpness Canal, complete with commentary by the captain.

👫 House of the Tailor of Gloucester (Beatrix Potter Museum)
9 College Court, just off Westgate Street. ⓘOpen daily 10am–5pm, Sun noon. ☎01452 422 856. www.tailor-of-gloucester.org.uk.

▶ **Population:** 114,003.

⚲ **Michelin Map:** Michelin Atlas p 17 or Map 503 N 28.

🛈 **Info:** 28 Southgate Street. ☎01452 396 572. www.thecityofgloucester.co.uk.

▶ **Location:** 104mi/167km west of London and 47mi/76km north of Bath. The train and bus stations face each other on Way, a five-minute walk from the compact city centre. The docks are a short walk further on.

⊘ **Don't Miss:** Gloucester Cathedral; excursions to Berkeley Castle, Painswick and the Wildfowl and Wetlands Trust (⚲*see Hampshire, Dorset, wiltshire)*

🕐 **Timing:** Allow 3–4 hours.

👫 **Kids:** The House of the Tailor of Gloucester.

The Tailor of Gloucester, published 1903, was Beatrix Potter's personal favourite among her Peter Rabbit Books. In 1897, when on holiday here, she became fascinated by a local folk tale about John Pritchard, a tailor who had been commissioned to make a fine suit of clothes for the Mayor of Gloucester, and so the story was born. The shop, set in a lovely little alley, still exists today, selling a full range of Beatrix Potter merchandise alongside a small museum.

CATHEDRAL★★
Cathedral: ⓘ*Open year-round Mon–Sat 7.30am–6pm in term time (closed Mon–Fri 8.45– 9.15am for school assembly). Sun 11.45am–2.45pm.* ⬤*£5 minimum contribution requested.*
Exhibition, Whispering Gallery, Treasury: ⓘ*Open Mon–Fri 10.30am–4pm (Sat 3.30pm).* ⬤*£2 (Treasury free).* ✎*Guided tours Mon–Sat 10.45 am–3.15pm, Sun noon–2.30pm. Tower tours (269 steps) Apr–Oct Wed–Fri and Mon–Tue during school hols 2.30pm. Also 1.30pm tour Sat and bank hols.*

Severn Bore

The village of Minsterworth *(4mi/ 6.5km W of Gloucester by the the A 40 and A 48)* is a good place from which to observe the phenomenon known as the Severn Bore, a roaring wall of water (up to 6ft/2m high) advancing up the Severn estuary, which occurs most vigorously at the time of the equinoxes.

Tickets sold on the day of the tour on a first-come – first -served basis – arrive early as there are only 25 spaces. ⊛*£3.* ⟨*⟩ ⟨*. ℘*01452 528 095.* *www.gloucestercathedral.org.uk.*

The present structure is essentially the creation of the Norman Benedictine abbot, Serlo, and of his 14C successors, who pioneered the Perpendicular style and adorned the transepts and choir using funds provided by royal patronage, or by pilgrims visiting the tomb of Edward II, who was murdered in 1327 at nearby Berkeley Castle (⟨*see Cotswolds*). The building was extended in the 15C by the addition of the Lady Chapel.

Massive Norman columns, reddened at the base by a fire in 1122, give an impression of enormous strength, while Perpendicular elegance prevails in the exquisite tracery of the high **vault** (92ft/28m), the **east window** – the largest of its kind in medieval glass, commemorating the Battle of Crécy – and in the wonderfully light **Lady Chapel** c.1500.

Edward's effigy, north of the choir, is protected by a 14C stonework canopy of rare delicacy. The **Cloisters** (which have featured in three *Harry Potter* films) contain the **lavatorium** where the monks washed their hands at the entrance to the refectory; the 14C fan vaulting, the earliest of its kind, is exceptionally rich.

The mid-15C **tower** (225ft/69m), with its unmistakable crown of parapet and pinnacles, rises gracefully above **College Green**, a pleasant combination of mainly 18C houses, replacements of ear-

lier monastic buildings. **St Mary's Gate** is an impressive medieval survival.

EXCURSIONS
Tetbury/Westonbirt (The National Arboretum)★

▶ *Tetbury. 22mi/35km S of Gloucester via the A 38 and A 4135. www.forestry. gov.uk/westonbirt.*

The road passes through **Tetbury**, an elegant Cotswold town built of silvergrey stone round a quaint Market House (1655) and **St Mary's Church**, a refined 18C interpretation of medieval motifs. On Church Street the tourist information centre also houses a Police Bygones Museum.

Take the A 433 3mi/5km southwest to reach the **Westonbirt (The National Arboretum)**, first planted in 1829 (◷*open Apr–Nov Mon–Fri 9am–8pm/ dusk, Sat–Sun 8am–8pm/dusk; Dec– Mar Mon–Fri 9am–5pm/dusk, Sat–Sun 8am–5pm/dusk.* ↝*guided walks Easter–Oct Sat–Sun 2pm, midweek walks details posted on site;* ◷*visitor centre closed Christmas week;* ⊛*£6–£9.* ⟨*(£5).* ⟨*; ℘01666 880 220).* This important plant collection has grown steadily over the last 180 years to comprise some 14,000 trees and shrubs from all over the world. There are many miles of signed walks and an attractive visitor centre. Some trees here are the largest of their kind in Britain. The many types of maple guarantee a spectacular show in **autumn**.

Painswick★

The streets of this beautiful little hilltop village contain many old buildings of golden Cotswold stone. The elaborate Baroque tombstones in the parish churchyard are accompanied by 99 clipped yew trees.

On the outskirts of the village *(take the B 4073)* is the **Painswick Rococo Garden** (◷*open second wk Jan–Oct daily 11am– 5pm;* ⊛*£6;* ⬚*; ℘01452 813 204, www. rococogarden.org.uk).* Originally laid out in the early-18C, and set in a hidden valley, it boasts magnificent views of the surrounding countryside.

ADDRESSES

🏠 STAY

CHILTERN HILLS

⊜🍽–⊜🍽🍽 **The Nag's Head** – *London Road, Great Missenden.* ✆*01494 862 200. www.nagsheadbucks.com. 7 rms.* This delightful characterful award-winning 15C contemporary-styled pub serves excellent Anglo-French food (⊜🍽–⊜🍽🍽).

OXFORD

🏠 A large number of B&Bs can be found on Banbury Road, Iffley Road and Abingdon Road.

⊜🍽–⊜🍽🍽 **Burlington House** – *374 Banbury Road.* ✆*01865 513 513. 12 rms.* This Victorian merchant's house, dating from 1889, a 10-minute ride from town, has been beautifully renovated into a luxurious boutique-style B&B.

⊜🍽🍽🍽 **Old Parsonage** – *1 Banbury Road.* ✆*01865 310 210. www.oldparsonage-hotel.co.uk. 30 rms.* This small luxurious 17C boutique hotel is just a five-minute walk from town. The atmosphere is calm, almost fun, but also chic and clubby. Live jazz and summer barbecues in the beautiful garden.

COTSWOLDS

⊜🍽–⊜🍽🍽 **The Old Manse Hotel** – *Victoria Street, Bourton-on-the-Water.* ✆*01451 820 082. www.oldmansehotel.com. 15 rms.* Dating from 1748, the Old Manse encompasses traditional Cotswold charm and has a lovely riverside location.

⊜🍽🍽🍽 **Lamb Inn** – *Sheep Street, Burford.* ✆*01993 823 155. 15 rms.* This charming quintessential (14C) Cotswold inn with antique furnished bedrooms, gourmet restaurant (⊜🍽🍽🍽) and pub bar (⊜🍽🍽🍽) with summer terrace and log fires is one of the nicest and most prestigious places to stay in the region.

CHELTENHAM

⊜🍽–⊜🍽🍽 **Mercure Queen's Hotel** – *The Promenade.* ✆*01242 514 754. www.mercure.com/cheltenham-queens. 79 rms.* Set behind large white Neoclassical colonnades, this beautiful Regency four-star hotel has the perfect location in the heart of the city, overlooking the Imperial Gardens and Promenade. Contemporary British cuisine and grills in the hotel's Napier restaurant (⊜🍽🍽).

🍽 EAT

OXFORD

⊜ **Vaults & Garden** – *Radcliff Square.* ✆*01865 279 112. www.vaultsandgarden.com. Open 8.30am–6.30pm.* On Radcliffe Square, adjoined to the University Church, dine either in the vaults of the university's Old Congregation House, or alfresco surrounded by architectural treasures, flowers and aromatic herbs. Breakfasts, light lunches, salads, afternoon teas using seasonal produce from local organic producers. Excellent value.

⊜🍽 **Quod** – *Old Bank Hotel, 91–94 High Street.* ✆*01865 799 599. www.oldbank-hotel.co.uk.* This Modern British and European bistro is the trendiest place in Oxford, serving fine food alongside fun food such as giant pizzas and gourmet burgers. Dine alfresco in good weather. It is set in the beautiful boutique-style Old Bank Hotel (⊜🍽🍽🍽), voted "UK city hotel of the year" in 2011.

⊜🍽🍽 **Cherwell Boathouse** – *Bardwell Road.* ✆*01865 552 746. www.cherwellboathouse.co.uk.* Dine on inventive English dishes (desserts a speciality) at this charming riverside restaurant in a perfect location while watching the punts go by. Lovely summer terrace.

COTSWOLDS

⊜🍽 **Eagle & Child** – *Digbeth Street, Park Street, Stow-on-the-Wold.* ✆*01451 830 670. www.theroyalisthotel.com.* Part of **The Royalist Hotel** *(12 rms.* ⊜🍽🍽*)* – thought to be the oldest inn in England – this equally historic pub serves comforting locally sourced British food at very reasonable prices.

⊜🍽 **Rose Tree** – *Riverside, Bourton-on-the-Water.* ✆*01451 820 635.* Classic British dishes and simple continental favourites, all cooked well, have made this a favourite with visitors.

⊜🍽–⊜🍽🍽 **Eight Bells Inn** – *Church Street, Chipping Campden.* ✆*01386 840 371.* This 14C inn features exposed beams, log fires, secret passages, a summer terrace and serves Modern British cuisine.

BRISTOL, BATH AND SOMERSET

Gateway to the West Country, this region includes two of Britain's finest cities. Cultured Bath, with its eponymous Roman springs and glorious architecture, is probably the finest 18C city in the world, and is the only World Heritage city in the UK. By contrast, neighbouring Bristol has a more raw energy, built upon maritime and engineering trade. However, while it exploits this rich heritage with many superb waterside attractions, and a Georgian beauty of its own, Bristol also has a vibrant contemporary scene. Somerset, famous for its cider apples, is very rural, with the UK's most popular caves, a gem of a tiny cathedral city, and mythical Glastonbury.

Highlights

1 Board Brunel's *SS Great Britain* in **Bristol docks** (p221)

2 The magnificent architecture of the Royal Crescent in **Bath** (p228)

3 Fashion spotting at the Fashion Museum in **Bath** (p228)

4 The magnificent 13C front of the cathedral in **Wells** (p230)

5 Go underground in the caves of **Cheddar Gorge** (p232)

The revitalised dockside and magnificent churches of **Bristol** are the main attractions in the city centre, while the beautiful suburb of Clifton and its breathtaking bridge sit amid bucolic splendour. **Bath** is admired as much for its natural springs as is architecture. Just outside town the American Museum and Bradford-on-Avon are well worth a visit. In **Somerset**, Cheddar Caves and Wookey draw underground explorers, while Glastonbury is the focus of both Christian and Arthurian legends, and a New Age shrine. Wells, England's smallest city, is almost a time capsule.

Food Heroes

Bristol's association with chocolate goes back to 1847 when Joseph Fry invented eating **chocolate** as we know it today, moulding solid chocolate in his Bristol shop (until then chocolate was just a drink). The last remaining chocolate maker in the city is Guilbert's (www.guilberts.com), hand-making chocolates here since 1910. In 2012 a major new attraction, the Chocolate Harbour complex, is planned to celebrate the city's heritage.

The Victorian market buildings on **Corn Street** are the daily home of St Nicholas Market, a bastion of both local and global cuisine. The emphasis is on local food every Wednesday for the Central Bristol Farmer's Market, and on the first Sunday of the month for the Slow Food Market (www.slowfoodbristol.org).

Bath is famous for the **Bath Bun**, a rich egg-and-sugar brioche invented by Dr William Oliver (1695–1764) of Bath. Try one at Sally Lunn's (www.sallylunns. co.uk). Dr Oliver also invented the less fattening **Bath Oliver** biscuit, usually eaten with cheese. In 1997 Bath hosted Britain first modern day farmers' market. It is still held at Green Park Station (Sat, www.bathfarmers market.co.uk).

Someset is "where the cider apples grow". Good places to see and taste are Sheppy's Cider Farm, Shop and Museum (www.sheppyscider.com); Perry's Cider (www.perryscider.co.uk); The Somerset Distillery (www.ciderbrandy. co.uk) and Avalon Vineyard (www.avalonvineyard.co.uk). The term "scrumpy", refers to the still (non-sparkling) stronger/more alcoholic types of cider.

Somerset is also the birthplace of **Cheddar cheese**. The Cheddar Gorge Cheese Company (www.cheddargorgecheeseco.co.uk) are the only cheese makers left in Cheddar. Visit them to see how traditional cheddar is still made.

Bristol★★

and around

In the 10C Bristol was a settlement at the western limit of Saxon influence, trading with Ireland. Its port, on the site of today's Harbourside, flourished and by the Middle Ages Bristol was England's second city. By the 17C its trade had expanded to the Canaries, South and North America, Africa and the West Indies. In the 18C and 19C new industries developed locally: iron, brass, copper, porcelain, glass, chocolate and tobacco. To overcome the problems caused in the port by the exceptionally high tidal range (the second highest in the world), an elaborate system of locks was constructed in 1804–09 to maintain a constant water level along the city's extensive quaysides, so creating the **Floating Harbour★★★**. The Industrial Revolution drew interests north, however, and the city declined. Modern docks on the estuary of the Severn now enable commercial shipping to avoid the difficult Avon Gorge passage.

▶ **Population:** 407,992.

● **Michelin Map:** Michelin Atlas p17 or Map 503 M 29.

▤ **Info:** E Shed, 1 Canons Road, Harbourside. ℘0906 711 2191 (50p/min). http://visitbristol.co.uk.

▶ **Location:** 118mi/190km west of London and 13mi/21km northwest of Bath. Bristol has two mainline stations, Parkway (out of town) and Temple Meads, a 20-minute walk from the centre. The bus station is in Marlborough Street, a 5–10-minute walk from the centre. Try the open-top hop-on hop-off bus (*www.bristolvisitor.co.uk*).

◉ **Don't Miss:** *SS Great Britain*; Clifton.

○ **Timing:** At least two days.

👥 **Kids:** Bristol Zoo; At-Bristol; *SS Great Britain*.

⛴ **Boat Trips:** The Bristol Packet Ltd operates a city docks tour and river trips.

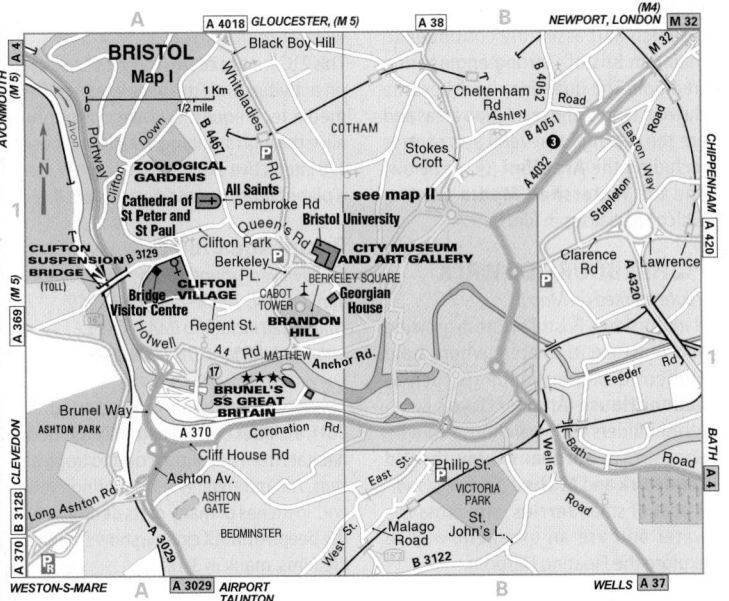

Bristol Harbour and the spire of St Mary Redcliffe in the background

©Asher Welstead/iStockphoto.com

MODERN BRISTOL

Bristol is strongly linked with the visionary engineer **Isambard Kingdom Brunel** (1806–59), designer of the Clifton Suspension Bridge, the *SS Great Britain* and architect of the Great Western Railway, which reached its terminus here, at the Station Building, in 1841. In 1940–42 the city was heavily bombed and much of today's centre is the result of post-war rebuilding. Bristol's present affluence and regeneration is underpinned by the electronic age: high-technology research and assembly continues to maintain Bristol's strong engineering tradition. The quaysides have become thriving leisure and recreation areas and are the setting for several arts centres including the **Arnolfini** (♿ *see below*) and the **Watershed Media Centre**, which specialises in films.

🐾 HARBOURSIDE WALK
Route marked on Map II.
Harbourside is Bristol's fastest-growing and most exciting area, where bold modern designer buildings such as **Canons House** (Arup for Lloyd's Bank) rub shoulders with warehouse conversions such as **Bordeaux Quay**, the **Old Leadwork** and **M Shed** (♿ *see below*). A host of small **ferries** criss-cross the water and are an excellent way to explore the Floating Harbour.

Millennium Square features sculptures of famous locals, fountains and lights, and lots of places to eat and drink.

👨‍👧 At-Bristol★
Harbourside. ⏰*Open year-round Mon–Fri during school term 10am–5pm; daily during school hols 10am–6pm.* ⏰*Closed 24–25 Dec.* 🎫*£11.35, child £7.25. "Toddler time" tickets Mon during Bristol schools term time, from 1.30pm, adult with child under 5 yrs old £5.67.* ♿🅿️✕. ☎0845 345 1235. *www.at-bristol.org.uk.*
This 21C science centre combines hands-on activities with the very latest multimedia techniques. Science is brought alive through stunning visuals and over 170 interactive experiences. There is also a planetarium (🎫*additional 50p/£1*).

Bristol Aquarium
⏰*Open year-round 10am–5pm, Sat–Sun and hols 10am–6pm.* 🎫*£13.50, child £9.20 including IMAX (less £2 online).* ♿🅿️✕. ☎0117 929 8929. *www.bristolaquarium.co.uk.*
The city's new aquarium, opened in 2011, includes over 40 naturally themed habitats from the British coast to tropical seas. An underwater tunnel brings you within inches of many of its denizens of the deep. An IMAX cinema shows marine life films, many in 3-D.

Pero's Bridge

The distinctive feature of this pedestrian bascule bridge is its pair of horn-shaped sculptures which act as counterweights for the lifting section. "Pero" was the slave of wealthy merchant John Pinney (♿ *see below Georgian House, below*).

Arnolfini

🕐 *Galleries open Tue–Sun 11am–6pm.* ♿✕. ☎0117 917 2300. *www.arnolfini.org.uk.* Est 1961, this is the oldest and most acclaimed arts centre in Bristol, staging live music, films, contemporary live art, performance and dance.

M Shed

Princes Wharf, Wapping Road. 🕐*Open Tue–Fri 10am–5pm, Sat–Sun and bank hols 10am–6pm.* ♿✕. ☎0117 352 6600. http://mshed.org. Bristol's latest museum is a busy modern interactive place where visitors explore over 2,000 years of city history. Topics include Bristol's inglorious role in the transatlantic slave trade, the city's wartime experiences, industrial and engineering history, its present-day successes in technology, music and art.

▲▲ SS GREAT BRITAIN★★★

Map I. 🕐*Open daily Apr–Oct 10am–5.30pm; Nov–Mar 10am–4.30pm.* ☞£12.50, child £6.25. ♿🅿✕. ☎0117 926 0680. *www.ssgreatbritain.org.* Launched in 1843, Brunel's revolutionary steamship (*ss*) *Great Britain* was the very first iron-built, propeller-driven Atlantic liner. She sailed until 1886, travelling 32 times around the world covering nearly one million miles. She was finally abandoned and scuttled in the Falkland Islands, in 1937, after more than 40 years' use as a floating warehouse. In 1970 the most ambitious salvage project ever attempted finally brought her home to Bristol, where she is now conserved. Sitting in her original dry dock, above the waterline the ship has been meticulously restored to her halcyon days, when she transported both freight and passengers around the world. Below the waterline, glass plates, covered in a thin layer of water, form a sealed space, which is dehumidified to inhibit the rusting process of the ship's fragile hull. The ingenious facilities allow visitors to walk around the bottom of this leviathan (322ft/98m long and 51ft/16m across) viewing the giant propellor and anchor, with water high above.

Back on the dockside is a superb **museum** that tells the fascinating story of the ship, the many colourful characters who sailed in her, the epic salvage operation and the emotional homecoming to Bristol. The ship itself has been meticulously restored, right down to the dirty plates and the ship's cat chasing rats in the galley. Audio guides relate the story of what it was like to travel both steerage (3rd class) and Upper Saloon (1st class) in colourful detail.

❧ OLD TOWN WALK

Map II. Occupying a peninsula formed by St Augustine's Reach and the port of Bristol, the old town area is set around Queen Square, a large grassy area with a few early-18C houses and an impressive equestrian statue of King William III.

King Street

This historic cobbled street contains 18C and 19C warehouses, 17C almshouses and pubs, notably the **Llandoger Trow**,

---

"Shipshape and Bristol Fashion"

This expression was coined to describe the many and varied preparations required before a ship sailed up the river. Given the dramatic rise and fall of the tide, ships were often left askew when stranded on the mudflats; if cargo was not properly stowed it was liable to fall or spill. Appropriately enough, it was a Bristol-born man, **Samuel Plimsoll**, who came up with the idea of limiting cargo weight and checking whether it was correctly loaded by means of the elementary concept known as the Plimsoll line.

and the 18C **Theatre Royal**★★. The latter opened in 1766 and is the oldest playhouse in the country still in use. The **Merchant Venturer's Almshouses**★ was built in 1544 and enlarged in 1696.

St Stephen's Church★

St Stephen's Street. ⏰*Open year-round daily 8.45am–4pm.* ✕. ☎*0117 927 7977. www.saint-stephens.com.*

The 15C tower of the city parish church rises 130ft/40m to a distinctive crown. The interior houses memorials to local merchants, 17C wrought-iron gates and a medieval eagle lectern.

Corn Street

The imposing **Exchange** was built in 1741–43 by John Wood the Elder. Its original function was a corn and general trade exchange, recalled by the four bronze-topped pedestals dating from the 16C and 17C, where deals were concluded (these were known as "nails", hence the expression to pay on the nail, meaning instant cash payment).

The Exchange and its precincts is now home to the home to the largest collection of independent retailers in Bristol, the lively **St Nicholas Market**.

To the left of the 19C Council Hall is the exuberant façade of Lloyd's Bank (1854–1858). Note also the Coffee Shop, built in the 18C, where Georgian merchants would once have met to trade.

Church of St John the Baptist★

Tower Lane. ⏰*Open Tue–Thu 10am–1pm.* ☎*0117 929 1766. www.visitchurches.org.uk.*

This 14C church with its battlemented tower and spire stands over one of the six medieval gateways in the city walls. It contains a vaulted crypt and some interesting 17C woodwork (lectern, communion table, hour-glass).

Lord Mayor's Chapel★

⏰*Open Wed–Sat 10am–noon and 1pm–4pm. Sun, services only.* ⊜*Donation requested.* ☎*0117 929 4350. www.bristol.gov.uk.*

St Mark's Chapel was once part of a medieval hospital. The impressive Perpendicular chapel beside the narrow nave contains 15–17C **tombs**. Note the 16C continental **glass**, the mayors' hatchments, the gilded sword rest (1702) and the fine wrought-iron gates.

Bristol Cathedral★

College Green. ⏰*Open year-round daily 8am–after Evensong.* ⌐⌐*Guided tours most Sats 11.30am (see website).* ⊜*Contribution requested.* ✕. ☎*0117 926 4879. www.bristol-cathedral.co.uk.*

A church has stood here for over a thousand years. The cathedral is a 14C–15C Perpendicular Gothic church; the nave and twin west towers are 19C. Note the screen, the choir stalls (lively **15C misericords**), the 19C reredos and, over the nave, the early-14C vault, unique in English cathedrals. The **East Lady Chapel** (added 1298–1330) has a riot of medieval colour highlighting the elaborately carved stone. The **Harrowing of Hell**, a remarkable 1,000-year-old Saxon carved stone coffin-lid, stands in the south transept. Note too the late Norman ribvaulted **chapter house** and columned vestibule.

REDCLIFFE

Map II.

Separated from the old town by an arm of the port, Redcliffe can be reached by Bristol Bridge, via Baldwin Street or by Redcliffe Way, off Queen Square.

St Mary Redcliffe★★

Redcliffe Hill. ⏰*Open year-round Mon–Fri 9am–5pm, Sun 8am–7.30pm.* ☎*0117 929 1487. www.stmaryredcliffe.co.uk.*

"The fairest, goodliest, and most famous parish church in England" according to Queen Elizabeth I, St Mary represents the perfect expression of the Gothic style, and has stood for over 800 years. The **spire** (1872) rises 292ft/89m above the city. The Decorated hexagonal **north porch** (1290) is the antechamber to the shrine of Our Lady, in an inner, more modest Early English porch (1185). The church contains a number of interesting furnishings, most notably the late-16C wooden statue of Queen

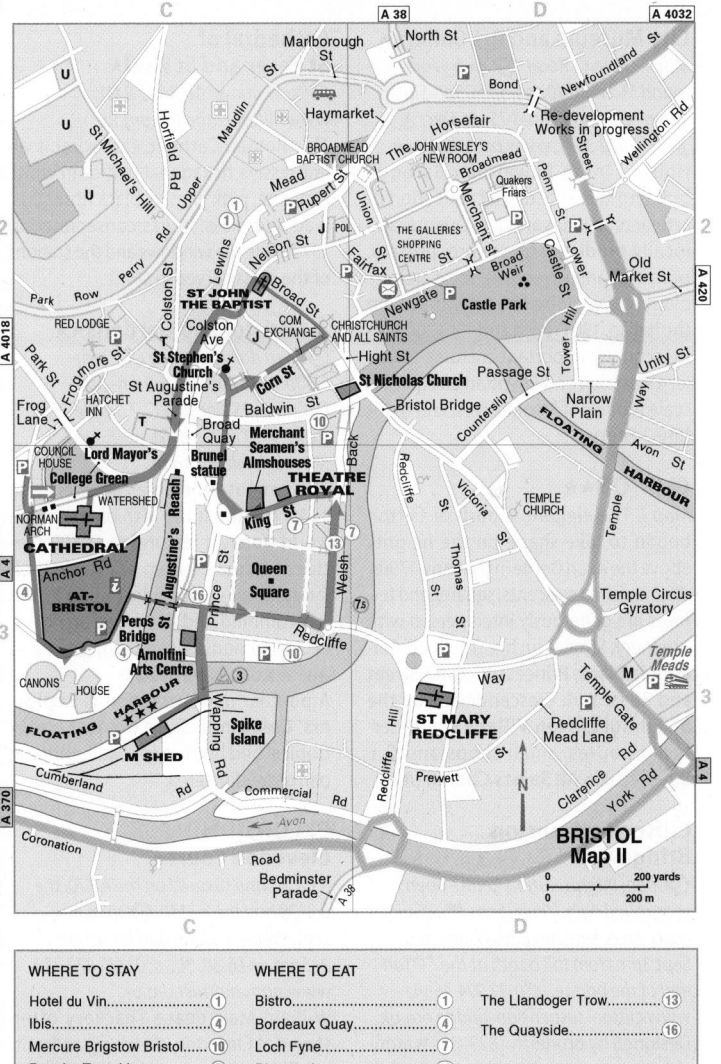

BRISTOL Map II

0   200 yards
0   200 m

WHERE TO STAY		WHERE TO EAT			
Hotel du Vin	①	Bistro	①	The Llandoger Trow	⑬
Ibis	④	Bordeaux Quay	④	The Quayside	⑯
Mercure Brigstow Bristol	⑩	Loch Fyne	⑦		
Premier Travel Inn	⑦	Riverstation	⑩		

Elizabeth I, and armour of Admiral Sir William Penn, in the **American chapel**.

BRANDON HILL
Georgian House★★
Map I.
🕐*Open Jul–Aug Tue–Sun and bank hol Mon 10.30am–4pm; Oct–Easter Wed–Thu, Sat–Sun and bank hol Mon 10.30–4pm.* 🕐*Closed Good Fri, 24–28 Dec.* 📞*0117 921 1362. www.bristol-city.gov.uk/museums.*

This handsome, typical Bath stone house was built c.1790 for the merchant and sugar planter John Pinney. Among the fine furniture note the mid-18C **bureau-bookcase**, the **desk** and the **long-case clock** (c.1740) in the hall; the elaborate gilded **girandoles** in the first-floor drawing room; the **double secretaire bookcase** (c.1800) and his collector's cabinet. Note the **cold-water plunge bath** which Pinney used daily.

City Museum and Art Gallery★
Map I. Queen's Road. ⏱*Open year-round Mon–Fri 10am–5pm, Sat–Sun 10am–6pm.* ⏱*Closed 25–26 Dec.* ♿✕. ☎*0117 922 3571. www.bristol.gov.uk.*
Housed in an Edwardian Baroque building this substantial collection of artefacts includes antique, Oriental and locally produced glassware, pottery, porcelain and silverware, local archaeology and geology, fine art (works from the Italian, 19C French and 19C–20C British schools), important costume jewellery, Assyrian and Egyptian antiquities, scale models of locomotives, and maritime history…

CLIFTON★★
Map I. The elegant suburb of Clifton began to take shape on the heights above the Avon Gorge in the early-1790s; distinguished crescents, squares and terraces are generously interspersed with greenery. Streets such as The Mall, Caledonia Place, Princess Victoria Street and Royal York Crescent make up the delightful **Clifton Village**★ with terraced houses, small shops and G E Street's 1868 **All Saints Church (AX)**.

Clifton Suspension Bridge★★
⏱*Open: Interpretation Centre open year-round daily 10am–5pm.* ↝*Guided tours (free) Sat–Sun Easter Sun–mid-Sept 3pm from toll booth at the Clifton end of the bridge.* ☎*0117 974 4664. www.clifton-suspension-bridge.org.uk.*
Designed by Brunel in 1829, this is arguably the most beautiful of early English suspension bridges. Unfortunately funds ran out and Brunel never saw his 702ft-/214m-long bridge completed; he died five years earlier, in 1859.
An **Interpretation Centre** at the Leigh Woods end relates the history of its construction. Close by, on the cliff, stands the 1729 **Observatory Tower** (*Litfield Place;* ⏱*open year-round, weather permitting, Easter–Oct daily 10am–5pm, Oct–Easter Sat–Sun only;* ✑£2; ☎*0117 974 1242*), at the top of which is an 18C **camera obscura**.

Cathedral of St Peter and St Paul★
Clifton Park. ☎*0117 973 8411. www.cliftoncathedral.org.uk.*
This Roman Catholic cathedral is an impressive hexagonal edifice in white concrete, pink granite, black fibreglass, lead and glass; it was consecrated in 1973. Note the windows and the stations of the cross carved in stone.

♟♟ Bristol Zoo Gardens★★
⏱*Open daily Jun–late Oct 9am–5.30pm late Oct–May 9am–5pm.* ⏱*Closed 25 Dec.* ✑£12.72, child £7.72. ♿✕. ☎*0117 973 8951. www.bristolzoo.org.uk.*
This famous venerable zoo opened in 1836, making it the fifth oldest in the world. Today it features over 400 species of animals – from gorillas in their landscaped compound to Bug World – accommodated in various architect-designed houses; see the Reptile and Ape Houses in particular.
A popular new attraction is **Explorers' Creek** including a wet play area, a tropical bird house and a walk-through parrot-feeding area.

EXCURSION
Clevedon Court★
NT. ▶ *11mi/18km W on the A 370, the B 3128 and the B 3130.* ⏱*Open Apr–Sept, Wed–Thu, Sun and bank hols 2–5pm.* ✑£6.30. ✕. ☎*01275 872 257. www.nationaltrust.org.uk.*
William Makepeace Thackery often stayed at Clevedon, sketching and writing. This well-preserved early-14C house features a 12C tower and 13C Great Hall. The exterior dates to 1570, but inside you will find evidence of earlier centuries. The **Great Hall** has Tudor windows and fireplaces; the remarkable Hanging Chapel, with its unusual reticulated window tracery, contains 17C prayer desks and 15C and 16C biblical carvings. The contents of the 14C State Bedroom reflect 10 generations of family taste, while the Justice Room displays local Nailsea glass made between 1788 and 1873. Georgian terraced gardens.

Bath★★★

and around

Set in rolling Somerset countryside, Bath's hot springs, Roman Baths, splendid abbey and Georgian stone crescents have attracted visitors for centuries. The city combines the grace and elegance of the 18C with a long and varied past.

A BIT OF HISTORY

In 500 BC, according to legend, **Prince Bladud** (the father of King Lear) was cured of his leprosy by wallowing in the mud here. The **Romans**, in the 1C AD, made Bath England's first spa resort with baths and a temple.

In the 11C the Bishop of Wells bought Bath for £500. He began a vast Benedictine cathedral priory, and built a palace, new baths and a school. Bath became a prosperous wool town, but at the Dissolution the monks were forced to sell off parts of the abbey. In 1574 Queen Elizabeth I set up a fund to restore the abbey and enhance the town.

In the following centuries **Ralph Allen** (1694–1764) and John Wood (1700–54) transformed its architecture and urban plan. Inspired by Bath's Roman past they built in the Palladian style with the local honey-coloured stone, now known as **Bath-stone**. But it was in the early 18C that Bath saw its golden age.

In 1704 **Beau Nash** (1673–1762) came to Bath, opened the first Pump Room for taking the waters and organised concerts, balls and gambling. Bath prospered – as did Nash – and, for a while at least, became England's most fashionable city.

CITY WALK
Roman Baths★★

Pump Room, Stall Street. ○Open Jan–Feb and Nov–Dec 9.30am–5.30pm; Mar–Jun and Sept–Oct 9am–5pm; Jul–Aug 9am–9pm; last entry 1hr before closing. ○Closed 25–26 Dec. ☜£12, Jul–Aug £12.50 (combined ticket with Fashion Museum £15.50). Combined ticket with Thermae Bath Spa also

▶ **Population:** 85,202.

⌖ **Michelin Map:** Michelin Atlas p17 or Map 503 M 29.

▣ **Info:** Abbey ChurchYard. ℰ0906 711 2000/ ℰ0906 711 2000 (50p/min) Email: tourism@bathtourism.co.uk From overseas ℰ0844 847 5257. www.visitbath.co.uk.

◗ **Location:** 107mi/172km southwest of London. Bath Spa train station and Bath bus station are on Manvers Street in the centre. The city centre is compact and most major sights are within walking distance. Bath Bus Company/City Sightseeing operate a hop-on hop-off bus tour (○*daily £12; t01225 330 444; www.bathbuscompany.com*).

◈ **Don't Miss:** The baths; Royal Crescent; American Museum.

○ **Timing:** Allow at least two full days.

✦ **Walking Tours:** The Mayor's Guides free walking tours depart (○*summer daily Sun–Fri 10.30am, 2pm, Sat 10.30am; May–Sept also Tue and Fri 7pm*) from outside the Roman Baths entrance. There are many other different themed walking tours; for details visit www.visitbath.co.uk.

Ⓟ **Parking:** A park and ride system is in operation (follow the signs).

available. &.✕. ℰ01225 477 785. www.romanbaths.co.uk.

One of the best-preserved Roman spas in the world, the baths are fed by a spring which pours out 250,000 gallons/1,136,000 litres of water per day at a temperature of 116°F/46°C.

The Roman complex consisted of the Great Bath, a large warm swimming pool, now open to the sky (sadly, bath-

Roman Baths, Bath Abbey in the background

© Mauritius/Photononstop

ing is not allowed), and two baths of decreasing heat; later a *frigidarium* was built on the west side with openings at the north, overlooking the sacred spring, and two more heated chambers (*tepidarium* and *caldarium*).

The east end was enlarged, the baths were elaborated and the *frigidarium* transformed into a cold-plunge circular bath.

After the Romans had left, the drains soon clogged through lack of attention and mud covered the site. In the early Middle Ages the Normans constructed the King's Bath around the tank which the Romans had lined with Mendip lead. Modern excavations have revealed the temple and baths complex and a wide variety of artefacts.

Pump Room★

⊙*Open daily for lunch and light refreshments.* ⊙*Closed 25–26 Dec.* &. *℘01225 444 477 (table reservations). www.romanbaths.co.uk.*

The present Pump Room was built in 1789–99. The interiors are elegantly furnished with ornamental pilasters, gilded capitals, a coffered ceiling, antiques and a glass chandelier. The bay overlooking the King's Bath contains the drinking fountain, from which visitors can still "take the waters".

Thermae Bath Spa

The Hetling Pump Room, Hot Bath Street. ⊙*Open year-round daily – New Royal Bath: 9am–10pm; last entry 7.30pm. Cross Bath: 10am–8pm; last entry 6.30pm. Visitor centre: Open Apr–Oct Mon–Sat 10am–5pm, Sun 11am–4pm.* ⊙*Closed 25–26, 31 Dec.* ⊜*Spa session from £15 for 1hr 30min, visitor centre free.* ℘*01225 331 234. www.thermaebathspa.com.*

Opened in 2006 Britain's only natural thermal spa is a combination of the best of the original Georgian spa, housed partly in an 18C building and partly in a glass-sided ultra-modern building, offering 21C comforts and facilities, including four thermal baths and the latest therapies. The open-air rooftop pool of the **New Royal Bath** looks directly onto the abbey and also offers romantic twilight sessions.

Bath Abbey★

13 Kingston Buildings. Abbey: ⊙*Open Mon–Sat 9am–6pm (Nov–Mar 4.30pm), Sun 1–2.30pm, 4.30–5.30pm.* ⊜*£3 contribution requested. Tower:* ⊸ *Tours Apr–Oct Mon–Sat (hourly)10am–4pm/5pm; Nov–Mar 11am, noon, 2pm.* ⊜*£6.* &. ℘*01225 422 462. www.bathabbey.org.*

The present sanctuary, on the site of an abbey founded early in the reign of King Offa (757–96), was begun in 1499

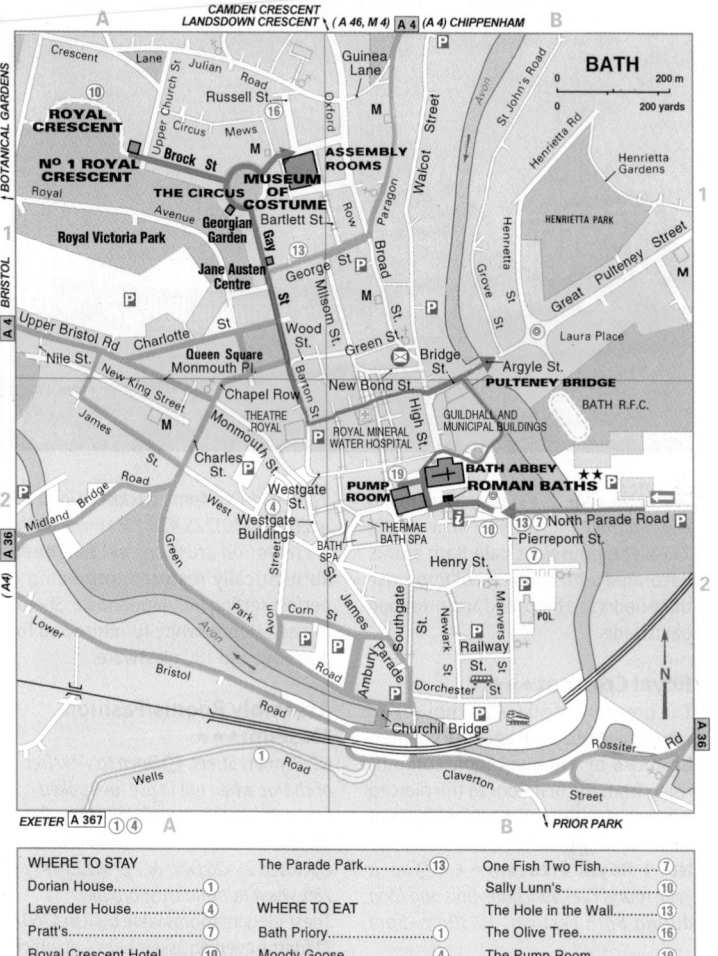

CAMDEN CRESCENT
LANDSDOWN CRESCENT \ (A 46, M 4) A 4 (A 4) CHIPPENHAM

BATH

WHERE TO STAY		The Parade Park...............⑬		One Fish Two Fish..............⑦
Dorian House.....................①				Sally Lunn's.......................⑩
Lavender House................④		WHERE TO EAT		The Hole in the Wall...........⑬
Pratt's..............................⑦		Bath Priory.......................①		The Olive Tree..................⑯
Royal Crescent Hotel.........⑩		Moody Goose....................④		The Pump Room................⑲

by Bishop Oliver King. From the pillars of the Norman church arose the pure late Perpendicular abbey. At the Dissolution, the incomplete building fell into disrepair, but restoration was begun in the late-16C. Inside, the nave, chancel and narrow transepts soar to **fan vaulting** by Robert and William Vertue (of Westminster Abbey fame).

Pulteney Bridge★

This magnificent bridge, built in 1769–74 to Robert Adam's design, has small shops on both sides, domed end pavilions and a central Venetian window. It is best viewed from Parade Gardens by the crescent weir.

Jane Austen Centre

40 Gay Street, Queen Square. ◑*Open mid-Mar–Oct daily 9.45am–5.30pm (Jul–Aug Thu–Sat 7pm); Nov–mid-Mar Sat 9.45am–5.30pm, Sun–Fri 11am–4.30pm.* ◑*Closed 1 Jan, 24–26 Dec* ◉£7.45. ℘01225 443 000. *www.janeausten.co.uk.*
Jane Austen knew Bath (◔ *see above*), as a visitor and a resident, and this exhibition is devoted to every place in Bath associated with Jane or her novels.

The Circus★★★

The King's Circus is a tight circle of identical houses, pierced by three equidistant access roads. Although one of John

227

Royal Crescent

©trentham/Dreamstime.com

Wood the Elder's earliest concepts, it was not built until the year of his death, 1754. The houses of pale Bath stone, decorated with coupled columns, rise three floors to a frieze and acorn-topped balustrade.

Royal Crescent★★★

The great arc of 30 terrace houses, in which the horizontal lines are counter-balanced by 114 giant Ionic columns rising from the first floor to the pierced parapet, was the great achievement of John Wood II, built 1767–74.

No. 1 Royal Crescent★★ (⏲ *open year-round Tue–Sun, bank hols and Mon during Bath Festival, 10.30am–5pm*

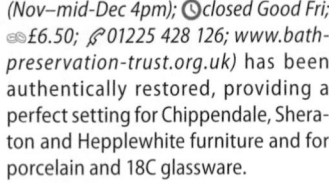

Jane Austen (1775–1817)

Jane visited Bath when staying with her aunt and uncle, the Leigh Perrots, at no. 1 The Paragon, and it was in Bath that she set much of *Northanger Abbey*. In May 1799 the Austen family took lodgings at 13 Queen Square; later, they resided at 4 Sydney Place; it was during their time at 27 Green Park Buildings that Jane's father died in January 1805; on two further occasions, the remaining ladies of the family lived both at 25 Gay Street and in Trim Street.

(Nov–mid-Dec 4pm); ⏲*closed Good Fri;* 💷*£6.50;* 📞*01225 428 126; www.bath-preservation-trust.org.uk)* has been authentically restored, providing a perfect setting for Chippendale, Shera-ton and Hepplewhite furniture and for porcelain and 18C glassware.

Assembly Rooms/Fashion Museum★★★

NT. Bennett Street. ⏲*Open to view free of charge when not in use for booked functions (check ahead) daily Mar–Oct 10.30am–6pm; Nov–Feb 10.30–5pm.* ⏲*Closed 25–26 Dec.* ♿. 📞*01225 477 789. www.nationaltrust.org.uk.*

These elegant rooms were built in 1769–71 for the evening assemblies – at which high society met to dance, play cards, drink tea and to gossip. The **Octagon** was intended as a small card room. The **Tea Room** has a rich interior with a splen-did two-tiered screen of columns at its west end. Within the Assembly Rooms, the fascinating **Fashion Museum** (⏲*open daily Mar–Oct 10.30am–5pm, Nov–Feb 10.30–4pm;* ⏲*closed 25–26 Dec;* 💷*£7.25, combined ticket with Roman Baths £15.50;* ♿; 📞*01225 477 173; www.fashionmuseum.co.uk)* presents a colourful and elegant display of every sort of garment from the Stu-art period to a 2008 ensemble by Karl Lagerfeld for Chanel. Note the museum's oldest complete attire, the **Silver Tis-sue Dress** (1660s), and its selection of superb gloves.

EXCURSIONS
The American Museum in Britain★★

▶ Claverton. 3mi/5km E on the A 36. ◷Open mid-Mar–Oct and late Nov–mid-Dec Tue–Sun, bank hol Mon and Mon in Aug noon–5pm (Nov–Dec noon–4.30pm). ⊗£8, free 4 Jul. ♿🅿✕. ℘01225 460 503. www.american museum.org.

Housed in historic Claverton Manor, located in an area of outstanding natural beauty, with spectacular views over the valley of the River Avon, this is the only museum of Americana outside the United States. Its remarkable collection of folk arts and decorative arts shows the diverse and complex nature of American culture over 200 years. The collection is shown off to great effect in a series of furnished rooms dating from the late-17C to the middle of the 19C. A major annual exhibition on a popular theme is also staged (for example, 2011 was on Marilyn Monroe)

Bradford-on-Avon★★

▶8mi/13km via the A 4 and A 363.

The old houses picturesquely rising up the hillside from the River Avon give Bradford-on-Avon its charm and character. The nine-arched **bridge**★, built in 1610 with a small square, domed chapel topped by a weather-vane, is the best starting point for the walk to the top of this attractive town.

The American Museum in Britain

Y. Duhamel/MICHELIN

It's thought that the Saxon **Church of St Laurence**★★ (*◷open daily 10am–7pm, winter 10am–4pm; ♿; ℘01225 865 797*) may date from the 7C–8C when St Aldhelm built a church here. Having served as a school, cottage and charnel house, the church was rediscovered in 1856. A short walk along the River Avon lies a vast early-14C stone **tithe barn**★ *(EH; ◷ open year-round daily 10.30am– 4pm; ♿🅿 (charge); www.english-heritage.org.uk)* with gabled doorways and a superbly constructed wooden cruck roof.

Bradford-on-Avon

Y. Duhamel/MICHELIN

Mendips and Quantocks

This quiet rural part of North Somerset features England's smallest cathedral city in Wells and its two most visited show caves in Wookey Hole and Cheddar Gorge. Meanwhile, Glastonbury continues its centuries-old tradition as a place of pilgrimage, these days for music festival lovers and New Agers.

WELLS

▶ *23mi/37km SW of Bath.*
Population: 9,763. ⬛*Wells Museum.*
℘01749 671 770.
www.wellssomerset.com.
The calm of the cathedral within its precinct contrasts with the bustle of the Market Square. In the Middle Ages Wells prospered as a wool centre.

Wells Cathedral★★★

⊙*Open daily Apr–Sept 7am–7pm;*
Oct–Mar 7am–6pm. ⬥*Guided tours*
(⊜free) Mon–Sat hourly. ⊜*£6 contribution requested, photo permit £3.* ♿✕.
℘01749 674 483.
www.wellscathedral.org.uk.
Wells was the first cathedral church in the Early English style; it took more than three centuries to plan and build, from c.1175 to 1508.

- ⬢ **Michelin Map:** Michelin Atlas p16 or Map 503 M 30.
- ⬡ **Don't Miss:** Wells Cathedral; Cheddar Gorge; the view from Glastonbury Tor.
- 👥 **Kids:** Wookey Hole; Cheddar Gorge and Caves.

Despite weathering and much destruction by the Puritans, the **west front** is one of England's richest displays of 13C sculpture – with its figures coloured and gilded, it would have once resembled an illuminated manuscript or sumptuous tapestry. Although now monochrome, it is tinted at sunset and gilded by floodlights at night. The screen front is nearly 150ft/46m across, twice as wide as it is tall, with some 300 statues rising to a climax in the centre gable.

Inside the cathedral, set into the west wall of the north transept is a **quarterjack** – 15C knights who strike the bells with their pikes at the quarters. The most striking feature of the **nave** is the **scissor arch**, constructed in 1338–48, when the west piers of the crossing tower began to subside.

The nave was completed in 1239. There are interesting carvings in the **south transept**: men's heads, animal masks and everyday scenes such as a man with

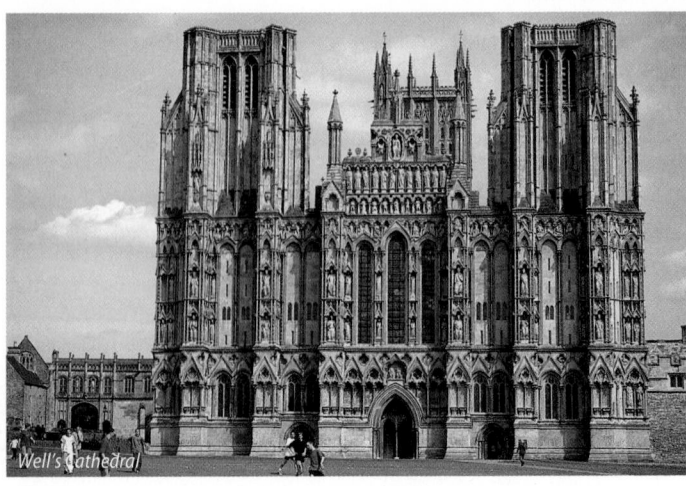
Well's Cathedral

toothache and two men caught in the act of stealing apples from an orchard. The medieval **misericords** show a man killing a wyvern and Alexander the Great being lifted to heaven by two griffins. In the north transept is an **astronomical clock** of 1390, with the sun and a star revolving round the 24-hour dial and, above, a **knights' tournament** in which one knight is struck down each quarter-hour. A wide curving flight of steps, laid c.1290, leads to the splendid octagonal **chapter house**, completed 1306.

Cathedral Precinct

Three 15C **gates** lead from the city streets to the calm of the Green and the spectacular view of the cathedral exterior. The **Chain Gate** gives access to **Vicars' Close**, a street of identical cottages built c.1348.

On the south side of the cathedral stands the 800-year-old **Bishop's Palace**★ (⊙ *open last wk Feb daily 10.30am–4.30pm, Apr–Oct daily 10.30am–6pm; ⊙ closed several days Jul–Sept for private functions, see website; ⊛£5.45; ♿✕; ✆01749 988 111; www.bishops palacewells.co.uk), stoutly walled and encircled by a moat. Inside are walled gardens and the well springs from which the city gets its name – belching out 3,400,000 gallons a day, or 40 gallons a second (over 15 million litres a day, or 180 litres a second). There are also the ruins of the old banqueting hall, the present palace and an excellent **view**★★ of the cathedral.

THE MENDIP HILLS

Immediately north of Wells and some 8mi/13km south of Bristol, the Mendip Hills is a triangular-shaped Area of Outstanding Natural Beauty, reaching a modest height of 1,066 ft/325m. It is composed of porous limestone and is most famous for its outstanding caves at Wookey Hole and Cheddar Gorge.

🚶🚶 Wookey Hole★

▷ *2mi/3km NW.* ⊙*Open Apr–Oct daily 10am–5pm; Nov and Feb–Mar 10am–4pm; Dec–Jan Sat–Sun and school hols only.* ⊙*Closed 25–26 Dec.* ⊛*£16, child*

West Country Cheese

According to one fanciful legend, the history of West Country cheese began when monks on a pilgrimage to Glastonbury took shelter from a terrible storm in the Cheddar caves and found that the milk they were carrying in leather pouches had turned into a delicious cheese: Cheddar has since become synonymous with English cheese, notably abroad. In fact Cheddar caves was inaccessible to all but climbers until the 19C. The truth is that itinerant holy men, especially early Celtic monks from Ireland, developed the art of cheese-making not only as a means of saving what otherwise might be wasted milk, but also for eating on days of fasting when meat was forbidden.

£11 (15 percent discount online). 🅿✕. ✆*01749 672 243. www.wookey.co.uk.* Spectacular **caves** have been formed by the River Axe, which gushes in a torrent through a hole in a 200ft-/61m-high cliffside, then descends into a series of six chambers. The river is always present, in echoing cascades and deep blue-green pools. The tour leads through some 350yds/320m of extravagantly lit caverns featuring **stalactites**, **stalagmites**, petrified waterfalls and translucent pools. These were inhabited by Iron Age man in 300 BC and later by Romano-British and Celtic peoples.

However, the caves mix history and legends fairly liberally, and with each passing tourist season, they more and more resemble a theme park, with the "mistress of ceremonies" being the Witch of Wookey.

Family attractions in the caves and its gardens include circus shows, a Fairy Garden, life-size dinosaur replicas, a mirror maze, a Victorian games arcade and adventure golf.

The most interesting "add-on" is the **papermill**★– paper was first made at Wookey Hole c.1600.

♣♣ Cheddar Gorge and Caves★★

⬤ *9mi/14km NW.* ⬤ *Open daily Jul–Aug, Easter and school half-term hols 10am–5.30pm; Sept–Jun 10.30am–5pm.* ⬤ *Closed 24–25 Dec.* ⬤ *£17.80, child £11.50 (10 percent discount online).* 🅿✕. ℘*01934 742 343.* *www.cheddarcaves.co.uk.*

Evidence of human settlement at Cheddar Gorge dates back to the Upper Late Palaeolithic era. The gorge is 2mi/3km long with a one in six gradient, twisting and turning in its descent from the Mendips, and the cliffs rise vertically 350ft–400ft (107m–122m).

The caves are near the gorge bottom on the south side *(left, going down).* **Cox's Cave** was discovered in 1837 and **Gough's Cave** in 1890. The series of chambers follows the course of underground streams through the porous limestone, past stalagmites, stalactites and petrified falls.

As with neighbouring Wookey Hole, the caves have become heavily commercialised. Also included in the ticket price is the **Museum of Prehistory**; the **Crystal Quest** (a dark-walk fantasy adventure); **The Lookout Tower**, a staircase of 274 steps which leads up to a panoramic **view**★; and an open-top bus tour *(Mar–Oct only).*

If you prefer your own company, there is a 3mi-/5km- walk which starts at The Lookout Tower, offering more stunning views. Also on offer is rock climbing and caving, both suitable for beginners (⬤*£19 each, see website for details).*

This is, of course, also the home of the famous **cheese** (♿ *see above*), on sale in the shop, and in **Cheddar** village, which lies at the foot of the gorge.

GLASTONBURY★★

⬤ *29mi/47km SW of Bath.* *Allow half a day minimum to see the abbey and explore the town.* *Population: 7,747.* 🈳*High Street.* ℘*01458 832 954.* *www.glastonburytic.co.uk.*

Glastonbury Abbey, a ruin since it was dissolved in 1539, was once one of the richest abbeys in the land and renowned as a centre of learning. The town, which grew up around the abbey, has become an important centre of spiritualism and is now synonymous with an alternative lifestyle which finds its most public expression in the hugely successful annual open-air Glastonbury music festival attended by over 130,000 people (there is no festival, however, in 2012).

A Bit of History

According to the Holy Grail legends, an abbey was founded by Joseph of Arimathea, who donated his own prepared tomb for the burial of Jesus and caught the blood of the crucified Christ in the cup of the Last Supper.

When he planted his staff in the ground here, it sprouted and became the famous **Glastonbury Thorn**, a tree whose descendant still flowers here at Christmas and in May. The dual flowering was once considered miraculous.

Another legend links **King Arthur** with Glastonbury: mortally wounded by his stepson Mordred, Arthur sailed to the the Isle of Avalon, held to be near Glastonbury. He and Guinevere were supposedly buried in Glastonbury, and in

Cheddar Gorge

A. Taverner/MICHELIN

Abbey Ruins, Glastonbury

Y. Duhamel/MICHELIN

1191 their bodies were "discovered" in the abbey cemetery (a plaque marks the spot).

Abbey Ruins★★

○Open year-round daily 9am/10am–4.30pm/6pm, see website for details. &. Guided tours by costumed guides Mar–Oct. ○Closed 25 Dec. £6. 01458 832 267. www.glastonburyabbey.com.

The ruins extend far across the lawns, standing tall amid majestic trees. The Lady Chapel in Doulting stone has a corner turret, decorated walls, and rounded doorways, the one to the north enriched by carved figures.

On the impressive Gothic transept piers remain the chancel walls and beyond them the site of the Edgar Chapel, a mausoleum for the Saxon kings.

The 14C **Abbot's Kitchen**★, the sole building to survive intact, features an eight-sided roof with lanterns, which served to draw the smoke from the corner fires in the kitchen up the flues in the roof. North of the abbey stands the **Glastonbury Thorn Tree** (see above).

Town

Glastonbury's two main streets are **Magdalene Street**, lined with attractive little 17C–19C houses, and **High Street**, overlooked by the 15C **George and Pilgrims Hotel** and the 14C **Tribunal**. The latter houses the tourist information centre and **Lake Village Museum** (EH; ○open year-round Fri–Sat 10am–4.30pm, Sun–Thu 10am–4pm; £2.50; 01458 832 954; www.english-heritage.org.uk), featuring excavated artefacts from an **Iron Age Lake Village** northwest of town.

Looming above the High Street is the 134ft/41m tower of the 15C **church of St John the Baptist**★★ (○open Mon–Sat 10.30am–12.30pm, also Easter–Sept Mon–Fri 2–4pm; 01458 830 060; www.stjohns-glastonbury.org.uk), one of the finest churches in Somerset. Inside, its St Katherine's Chapel survives from the 12C building.

A 10-minute walk away, the **Somerset Rural Life Museum**★ (Chilkwell Street; ○open Tue–Sat and bank hol Mon 10am–5pm; ○closed Good Fri; (summer only); 01458 831 197; www.somerset.gov.uk/museums), illustrates daily life on a Somerset farm in the 19C. The outstanding exhibit is the splendid 14C **barn** of Glastonbury Abbey.

Glastonbury Tor★

The tor, 521ft/159m high, is a landmark for miles around. The tower at its summit is the last remnant of a Church to St Michael, built in the 14C. On a fine day, the **view**★★★ embraces the Quantocks, Bristol Channel and the Mendips.

BRIDGWATER

▶ *41mi/66km SW of Bath.*

Bridgwater's place in history was secured in 1685 at the **Battle of Sedgemoor** (3mi/5km outside town), when the Duke of Monmouth, an illegitimate son of Charles II, proclaimed himself king and fought the superior forces of James II. Monmouth was routed, and the bloody reprisals that followed (💧 *see below*) left a historic stain on the area. The **Blake Museum** (Blake Street; ⏱*open year-round Tue–Sat 10am–4pm;* ♿; ℘01278 456 127; www.bridgwater museum.org.uk) relates the story of the battle. Today Bridgwater is famous for its **Guy Fawkes Carnival**, Europe's largest illuminated procession.

TAUNTON★

▶ *53mi/85km SW of Bath. Population: 55,855.* 🏛*Library, Paul Street.* ℘01823 336 344. www.heartofsomerset.com.

The county town of Taunton, gateway to the West Country, is an agricultural and commercial centre at the heart of the fertile Vale of Taunton (Taunton Deane), famous for its cider apples.

Taunton Castle

The castle, dating from the 11C–12C, has been owned by successive Bishops of Winchester. The Civil War put Taunton, and the castle in particular, under siege three times. In 1685 the **Duke of Monmouth** and many of his followers were tried in the castle's Great Hall; 508 of them were condemned to death in what came to be known as the notorious **Bloody Assizes** and another thousand or so were transported to the West Indies. Monmouth was executed on Tower Hill a month later. Part of the castle houses the **Museum of Somerset**★ (⏱*closed until 2012;* ℘01823 278 805; www.somerset.gov.uk/museums).

St Mary Magdalene Church★

⏱*Open Mon–Fri 8.30am–5.15pm, Sat 9am–4pm.* ℘01823 272 441. www.stmarymagdalenetaunton.org.uk.

In the Somerset tradition, this splendid medieval church culminates in a soaring tower (1488–1514) built of lovely red and tawny-gold Ham Hill stone. Inside, the roof carvings are also typical of Somerset craftsmanship.

St James's Church★

⏱*Opening times, call* ℘01823 333 194. www.stjamestaunton.co.uk.

St James's dates mostly from the 14C–15C and features a 120ft/37m tower of Quantock red sandstone with Ham Hill stone decoration.

ILMINSTER★

▶ *45mi/72km SW of Bath.*

This Ham stone market town, which flourished from the wool trade in the 15C–16C, was listed as having a **minster**★★ in the Domesday Book. The most impressive feature is its 90ft/27m crossing tower, modelled on that of Wells Cathedral.

The 15C Perpendicular building with nave, transepts, chancel and tower was extended with aisles in the 16C. Note the fan vaults inserted at the crossing and **Wadham Chapel**, built in 1452 to house the tomb chest of Sir William Wadham, founder of Wadham College, Oxford.

QUANTOCK HILLS

Rising to a peak of 1,261ft/384m and extending for around 12mi/19km, the Quantock Hills are a peaceful Area of Outstanding Natural Beauty where pretty villages, such as Combe Florey and Crowcombe, nestle in wooded valleys known as combes. The hills start just west of Bridgwater and run northwest to the Bristol Channel. A good way to see the landscape is to either drive along the A 358 or hop aboard one of the historic **West Somerset Railway** (⏱*see website for timetable and fares; www.west-somerset-railway.co.uk)* steam locomotives. The line runs for around 20mi/32km) between the pleasant village of **Bishops Lydeard** and the commercialised seaside resort of Minehead.

Yeovil

and around

Yeovil was an important leather and glove centre from the 14C onwards, and was later known for its flax. The opening of the railway link with Taunton in 1853 broadened the town's horizons. The population increased and the buildings we now see are mainly 19C–20C, albeit with a few scattered 18C–19C Georgian houses and older inns on the likes of Princess Street, High Street and Silver Street.

- **Population:** 28,317.
- **Michelin Map:** Michelin Atlas p8 or Map 503 M 31.
- **Info:** Hendford. ℘01935 845 946. www.visit southsomerset.com.
- **Location:** Yeovil lies 41mi/66km south of Bristol.
- **Kids:** Fleet Air Arm Museum.

EXCURSIONS

▲ Fleet Air Arm Museum★★

Yeovilton. 6mi/10km N. Open *Apr–Oct daily 10am–5.30pm; Nov–Mar Wed–Sun (daily during school hols) 10am–4.30pm; last entry 90min before closing.* Closed *24–26 Dec.* £13, child £9. (half price last 90min before closing). ℘01935 840 565. www.fleetairarm.com.

Europe's largest naval aviation collection is set within aircraft hangars next to the Royal Naval Air Station, where helicopters are daily put through their paces. The display includes over 90 aircraft including the second prototype of **Concorde**, the famous Anglo-French jet airliner. A highlight is the **Aircraft Carrier Experience**, where visitors feel the noise and rush of jets around them.

Montacute House★★

NT. Montacute. 5m/8km W. **House:** Open *mid-Mar–Jul and Sept–Oct Wed–Mon 11am–5pm; Aug daily 11am–5pm.* **Garden:** Open *Jan–mid-Mar and Nov–Dec Wed–Sun 11am–4pm; mid-Mar–Oct Wed–Mon 11am–5.30pm.* £9.30, garden and park only, £5.70 (winter £4). ℘01935 823 289. www.nationaltrust.org.uk.

This handsome Elizabethan three-storey mansion was built 1597–1601 for Sir Edward Phelips, a successful lawyer, Speaker of the House of Commons (1604) and Master of the Rolls (1611). Entrance to the house is through the original east doorway into the screens passage. At the far end of the **Great Hall**, the charming **Skimmington Frieze** is a 17C plaster relief depicting the ordeals of a hen-pecked husband. The **Parlour**, with its original Ham Hill stone fireplace, Elizabethan panelling and frieze of nursery animals contains some fine 18C furniture (beautiful centre table by Thomas Chippendale the Younger), as does the **Drawing Room**. **Lord Curzon's Room** (*first floor*) contains his lordship's bath stowed in a "Jacobean" cupboard, a 17C overmantel of King David at Prayer, an 18C bed, a Dutch oak drop-leaf table and an 18C japanned skeleton mirror. The **Crimson Room**, so-called since the 19C when red flock wallpaper replaced the tapestries below the plaster frieze, contains a sumptuous oak four-poster bed carved with the arms of James I. The **Library**, once the formal dining room and destination of the dishes brought from the distant kitchens, features some remarkable heraldic glass. Other interesting features in this former state room are the Portland stone mantelpiece, plaster frieze, Jacobean inner porch, 19C moulded plaster ceiling and bookcases.

The Long Gallery (172ft/52m), lit with oriels at either end, occupies the entire top floor; it is the longest in existence. It now provides the perfect setting for a panoply of Tudor and early Jacobean England through 90 portraits (on loan from the National Portrait Gallery). The formal layout of the gardens is designed to enhance that of the house, with lawns and yews providing a fine foreground to the warm hues of Ham Hill stone.

ADDRESSES

🍽 STAY

BRISTOL

🛏 **Ibis** – *Explore Lane, Harbourside.* ☎*0117 989 7200. www. ibishotel.com. 182 rms.* Modern comfortable rooms with clean lines are on offer at this low-price chain hotel just off Millennium Square.

🍽🍽 **Premier Travel Inn** – *King Street.* ☎*0871 527 8158. www.premiertravelinn. co.uk. 60 rms.* This budget chain hotel enjoys a great dockside location in one of Bristol's oldest streets. Next door, and part of the same company, is the hotel's "dining room", the famous Llandoger Trow pub.

🍽🍽–🍽🍽🛏 **Mercure Brigstow Bristol** – *5–7 Welsh Back.* ☎*0117 929 1030. www.mercure.com. 115 rms.* This four-star contemporary boutique hotel is in the heart of old Bristol, ideally situated at the water's edge.

🍽🍽🛏–🍽🍽🛏🛏 **Hotel du Vin** – *The Sugar House, Narrow Lewins Mead.* ☎*0117 925 5577. www.hotelduvin.com/ bristo. 40 rms.* Bristol's finest hotel is a five-minute walk from the waterfront. It occupies a magnificently restored 18C sugar refinery and warehouse complex, with wine-themed, post-industrial chic loft-style rooms (including stunning double-height suites) with every comfort, including walk-in showers and large freestanding baths. The atmospheric public areas include a beautiful bar with courtyard and a superb bistro (🍽🍽🛏 ♨*see opposite*). Staff are exemplary.

BATH

⊕Hotels in Bath are often very expensive, so you may like to consider a B&B instead.

🍽🍽 **Parade Park** – *8–10 North Parade.* ☎*01225 463 384. www.nilviphotelsgroup. com. 35 rms.* Good-value, no-frills accommodation with crisp white linen, in a Georgian townhouse built by John Wood in the 1740s. Four-posters available. A few steps to the Roman Baths and just three minutes to bus and railway stations.

🍽🍽–🍽🍽🛏🛏 **Lavender House** – *17 Blooming Park.* ☎*01225 314 500. www.lavenderhouse-bath.com. 5 rms.* This elegant spacious Edwardian house just outside the town centre has delightful gardens and a family atmosphere.

🍽🍽🛏 **Dorian House** – *1 Upper Oldfield Park.* ☎*01225 426 336. www.dorianhouse. co.uk. 11 rms.* Beautifully furnished Victorian-meets-contemporary styled rooms with bags of period charm in an 1880 Bath-stone house. Extensively refurbished in 2009 with marble bathrooms and high-pressure showers, a breakfast orangery and lovely garden. Four-posters available.

🍽🍽🛏 **Pratt's** – *South Parade.* ☎*01225 460 441. www.prattshotel.co.uk. 46 rms.* This genteel Georgian hotel in the centre of town was originally built as five townhouses by John Wood.

🍽🍽🛏🛏 **Royal Crescent Hotel** – *16 Royal Crescent.* ☎*01225 823 333. 35 rms.* The best address in Bath, this 18C townhouse is now an exclusive de-luxe hotel with one of the UK's most acclaimed hotel spas and a gourmet restaurant overlooking leafy secluded gardens.

WELLS

🍽🍽 **The Crown** – *Market Place.* ☎*01749 673 457. www.crownatwells.co.uk. 15 rms.* This 15C coaching inn in the centre of town provides a mix of sympathetic contemporary and traditional styles. In 1685 William Penn visited the pub and preached to a crowd below. Four-posters available. Anton's Bistrot (🍽🍽) is recommended (♨*see opposite*).

🍽🍽 **The White Hart Hotel (The Ancient Gate House)** – *Sadler Street.* ☎*01749 672 029. www.ancientgatehouse.co.uk. 15 rms.* This family-run hotel and restaurant has a wonderful aspect facing the famous west front of Wells Cathedral and the Cathedral Green. Bedrooms are Laura Ashley designed and furnished in 2011. Four-posters available Try the excellent Rugantino restaurant (🍽🍽🛏); al fresco dining, weather permitting, with views of the cathedral.

🍽🍽🛏🛏 **The Swan Hotel** – *Sadler Street.* ☎*01749 836 300. www.swanhotelwells. co.uk. 50 rms.* The bedrooms at this former coaching inn feature period antique furniture and some boast original four-poster beds. Several have spectacular views of the cathedral. Good restaurant (🍽🍽🛏🛏).

GLASTONBURY

⊕There are few hotels in town but plenty of B&Bs; many of them are run by vegetarians and breakfasts are meat-free.

♀/ EAT

BRISTOL

The Llandoger Trow – *King Street.* *℘0870 990 6424.* Bristol's most famous inn, once frequented by Daniel Defoe, now with wine bar and restaurant serving standard pub food.

Bordeaux Quay – *First Floor, V Shed, Canons Way. ℘0117 943 1200 . www.bordeaux-quay.co.uk.* This large multi-award-winning complex of restaurant *(closed Mon)*, brasserie, bar, deli, bakery and cookery school ticks all the boxes, serving acclaimed organic European-style dishes by the waterside.

Loch Fyne – *King Street. ℘0117 930 7160. www.lochfyne.com.* Situated in the Old Granary – a beautiful listed building on the waterfront – this branch of a nationwide chain specialises in fish and seafood.

Riverstation – *The Grove. ℘0117 914 4434. www.riverstation.co.uk. Closed Sun dinner.* This stylish modern restaurant and bar on the harbourside has al fresco terraces overlooking the water. Excellent Modern European cuisine using fresh, local carefully sourced ingredients.

Hotel du Vin Bistro – *The Sugar House, Narrow Lewins Mead. ℘0117 925 5577. www.hotelduvin.com/bristol.* This beautifully decorated though unfussy incarnation of a fin-de-siècle French bistro shimmers romantically at night as candlelight reflects off its myriad wine glasses, bottles and gleaming wooden surfaces. Excellent cooking, faultless friendly informal service. Highly recommended.

The River Grille – *Bristol Hotel, Prince Street. ℘0117 923 0333. www.doyle collection.com.* This light, airy, quayside restaurant uses fresh local food in its Modern British dishes.

BATH

The Pump Room – *℘01225 444 477. www.romanbaths.co.uk.* Take morning coffee, lunch or afternoon tea in the style of Bath's Georgian High Society in the very place where the original spa waters bubbled up.

Sally Lunn's – *4 North Parade Passage. ℘01225 461 634 - www.sallylunns. co.uk.* Bath's oldest and most famous eating house dates from 1482. In cosy small rooms try the signature Bath Bun with a tea or coffee, or a traditional Trencher Bread meal.

The Hole in the Wall – *16 George Street. ℘01225 425 242. www.theholein thewall.co.uk.* This charming long-established place nestles in the vaults of two Georgian town houses. Accomplished Modern British cooking.

Bath Priory – *Weston Road, 1.2mi/2km Won the A 4. ℘01225 448 267. www.thebathpriory.co.uk.* Set in a beautiful Georgian country house and presided over by Michelin two-star chef, Michael Caines, this is probably the finest food in the area.

Moody Goose – *7a The Old Priory House, Kingsmead Square, Midsomer Norton, 11mi/18km SW. ℘01761 416 784. www.moodygoose.co.uk.* Acclaimed modern gourmet dining in the setting of a perfect English country house hotel.

The Olive Tree – *Queensberry Hotel, Russell Street. ℘01225 447 928. www.thequeensberry.co.uk.* Stylish contemporary dining room serving expertly produced Modern European cuisine. Good-value prix-fixe lunch menu and an acclaimed wine list.

WELLS

Anton's Bistrot – *The Crown, Market Place. ℘01749 673 457. www.crown atwells.co.uk.* Satirical cartoons decorate the walls. Good-value prix-fixe lunch menu. Modern British dishes at dinner.

The City Arms – *High Street. ℘01749 673 916. www.thecityarmsatwells.com.* Set in a historic 17C beamed inn, now a mix of contemporary and traditional, this approach is also used in the cooking, which specialises in Aberdeen Angus beef but also throws up some unusual takes on classic British dishes.

CHEDDAR

There are several types of restaurants between the village and the gorge

TAUNTON

Brazz@The Castle – *Castle Green. ℘01823 272 671. www.the-castle-hotel. com.* Modern and traditional British dishes, with some unusual choices, are on offer at this modern brasserie-style restaurant, housed within the luxury hotel, part of beautiful Taunton Castle.

DEVON AND CORNWALL

With two very distinct coastlines, historic towns and cities, picture-postcard villages and fishing harbours, unspoiled moors and national parks, stately homes and even statelier gardens, and a fascinating and unexpected industrial heritage, Devon and Cornwall pack a lot of interest into a small geographical area. This is England's main holiday playground and whatever the weather it is not simply a cliché to say that there is always plenty to see and do. The north coast is generally rugged and windblown (Newquay, for example, is a world-class surfing centre) while the south is characterised by sheltered coves and creeks reaching far inland, though both coasts have sheltered resorts enjoying beautiful golden beaches. While the coast is commercialised in parts and farming is still strong inland, much of the region and many of its inhabitants, locals and particularly newcomers, have a bohemian and arty character; from the hippy culture of Totnes to the modern art of St Ives. It is 284mi/454km from London to Penzance and this relative remoteness leads some locals to think of it an independent state. If you have more time, you can leave the English mainland altogether, to explore the quiet unspoiled Scilly Isles.

Highlights

1 Sail along the glorious RiverDart at **Dartmouth** (p245)

2 Pretend you're in a Mediterranean village at **Clovelly** (p256)

3 Leave the 21C behind by sailing to **Lundy Island** (p256)

4 Go green in gardener's heaven at the **Eden Project** (p260)

5 The giant children's sandcastle that is **St Michael's Mount** (p267)

Coast and Country

Devon's county town, **Exeter** is a thriving university city with a famous cathedral, old quarter, and historic quayside. Due south, "the **English Riviera**" comprises Torquay, Paignton and Brixham. This is archetypal British seaside holiday territory; from donkey rides at Paignton to bracing clifftop walks at Berry Head; a working fishing fleet at Brixham to Torquay marina's glamorous Sunseeker powerboats; from sunbathing on golden sands to exploring caves on rainy days. A short distance from the glitziest part of the English Riviera, **Dartmoor** is the largest remaining wilderness in southern England. It has two distinct faces: crowded cream-tea show villages, and paths less trodden, leading to prehistoric remains and mighty tors (rock outcrops). Devon's southernmost tip is the

South Hams. For many visitors this quiet understated area is the most beautiful and charming part of the whole West Country. You can explore the River Dart and Kingsbridge estuary by rail, road or boat. Totnes and Dartmouth are two of southern England's most attractive small towns. **Plymouth** is Devon's second city, the place from where Sir Francis Drake famously sailed to repel the Spanish Armada. It still has a salty maritime air, particularly around the cobbled Barbican from where the Pilgrim Fathers set sail. West of Plymouth begins the **south Cornish coast**. Some of England's loveliest seaside villages and scenery can be found along this heavily indented coastline, where magnificent gardens frequently tumble down to picture-postcard bays. The meandering seashore continues west via the beautiful creeks and inlets around Falmouth, the dramatic rocky Lizard Peninsula, via Penzance, to spectacular Land's End. The **north Cornish coast** is blessed with some of Britain's finest beaches. St Ives is for families and art lovers, the crashing surf at Newquay is for surf dudes and party people, and in between there's something for most tastes. Dramatic rocky shores characterise the **North Devon coast** with low-key resorts and pleasant market towns inland. East of Ilfracombe lies **Exmoor** National Park, comprising sparse uplands, rolling verdant pastures, and streams and ravines meeting in dramatic beauty spots.

Food Heroes

Cornwall's most famous food is the ubiquitous **Cornish pasty**, a D-shaped shortcrust pastry case, traditionally enclosing potato, swede, onion and steak/beef. It is said that the top edge was crimped into a "handle" (which would be thrown away) so that tin miners could safely eat the pasty without touching it with their arsenic-tainted fingers. Highly rated traditional pasty shops include Ann's Pasties *(www.annspasties.co.uk)* at Helston.

The **pilchard** (an adult sardine) was once the mainstay of the Cornish fishing industry, In 1871 nearly 16,000 ton were caught, but by the end of the 20C it had declined to a mere 6 ton per annum, and the image of pilchards was that of a tinned food of last resort. In 2003, however, the humble pilchard was reborn as the fashionable "Cornish sardine" and sales have come on recently in leaps and bounds. Cornwall's fish champion is TV chef Rick Stein, who has elevated Padstow *(www.rickstein.com, see North Cornish Coast)* into a shrine for fish and seafood gourmets. **Mackerel** is the main catch of St Ives (you can hire a boat and line and catch your own, at several places, with no experience) but is widespread throughout Cornwall, and is also sold potted.

Clotted cream is associated with both Devon and Cornwall. Rich and thick, it is made by indirectly heating full-cream cow's milk (using steam or a water bath) and then leaving it to cool slowly. It is an indispensable part of a "cream tea" (scones, jam and cream, served with tea). Another sweet Cornish treat is the saffron cake or bun. Although traditionally associated with Easter, it is widely available all year.

Devon's rich milk is still being used to create a variety of Devon cheeses. **Devon Blue** comes from Totnes, while **Beenleigh Blue** is made from ewes milk from the River Dart area and **Harbourne Blue** is made from the milk of goats that graze on Dartmoor. Other Devon cheeses of note include Curworthy, Sharpham, Tyning and Belstone. The Victorian market in Barnstaple is a good place to pick up all of the above. Devon's pear orchards used to supply the fair in Barnstaple, which reveals the origins of the **Barnstaple Fair Pears** dessert.

Laverbread is a traditional Welsh baked good that has long been popular in North Devon; its key ingredient is seaweed, *laver*, collected from the beach.

The traditional drink of Devon and Cornwall is **cider** *(see Somerset)*. You can see how it is made at Healey's Cornish Cyder Farm, *(www.thecornishcyderfarm. co.uk)* near Truro. Wine making also takes place in the Southwest. **Vineyards** open for tours include Yearlstone *(www.yearlstone.co.uk)* at Bickleigh Devon, Sharpham *(www.sharpham.com)* at Totnes, Devon (who also boast a creamery producing superb cheeses), and Camel Valley, near Bodmin, Cornwall *(www. camelvalley.com)*, whose sparkling wines have won top international prizes in recent years.

South Devon is one of the best places in the West Country both for eating out in general and for local produce; **South Devon crab** is said to be one of the finest varieties of crab in the world. In a beautiful setting, the **Dartmouth Food Festival** *(late Oct; www.dartmouthfoodfestival.com)* is a very high-quality major annual event.

The largest food festival in the region is **Flavourfest**, held in Plymouth, with 100 stalls attracting around 150,000 people *(late Aug; www.plymouth.gov.uk)*. Plymouth is also famous for gin; its **Black Friars Distillery** is the oldest working gin distillery in England, making **Plymouth Gin** since 1793.

Exeter★★

and around

A visit to Exeter, the regional centre of this part of the Southwest, is rewarding for the charm of its crescents and terraces and in particular for its cathedral, standing out in elephant grey against the red sandstone of the city churches and city wall, and red brick Georgian houses.

A BIT OF HISTORY

The Saxon town which succeeded the ancient Roman stronghold was devastated by the Danes in the 9C and 10C, but was rebuilt for the bishop's see to be transferred from Crediton to Exeter in 1050. Medieval trade prospered thanks to the city's position at the head of the navigable waters of the River Exe and it became one of the chief markets of country woollens. With steam power and machinery, however, Exeter's woollen trade declined and the city settled down to the calm life of a county town. Heavy bombing in 1942 destroyed much of the city's medieval fabric.

CATHEDRAL★★

⊙ Open year-round Mon–Sat 9am–4.45pm. ⊚ £5. ☞ Guided tours (⊜ free) Mon–Sat 11am, 12.30pm, 2.30pm (no 2.30pm tour Sat). Roof tours (75min) Apr–Sept Tue and Thu 2pm, Sat

▶ **Population:** 94,717.
⚲ **Michelin Map:** Michelin Atlas p 4 or Map 503 J 31.
🛈 **Info:** Dix's Field. ℘01392 665 700. Quay House (Quayside). ℘01392 271 611. www.exeter.gov.uk.
◖ **Location:** 84mi/135km SW of Bath and 171mi/275km SW of London. There are two train stations, Central (in the heart of town and St David's, around 0.5mi/0.8km northwest of the centre. Both are serviced by London trains. The bus station is on Paris Street in the centre. The city is can be covered on foot.
☺ **Don't Miss:** The cathedral nave vaulting and misericords; the Devon Gallery and ethnography collection in the Royal Albert Memorial Museum.
⊙ **Timing:** Allow a day.
👪 **Kids:** Have fun at the play areas at Bicton Gardens.
💬 **Walking Tours:** The route marked on the map offers a pleasant stroll. Free "Redcoat" walking tours operate daily. ℘01392 265 203.

Terrace in the Cathedral Close

© AGE/Photononstop

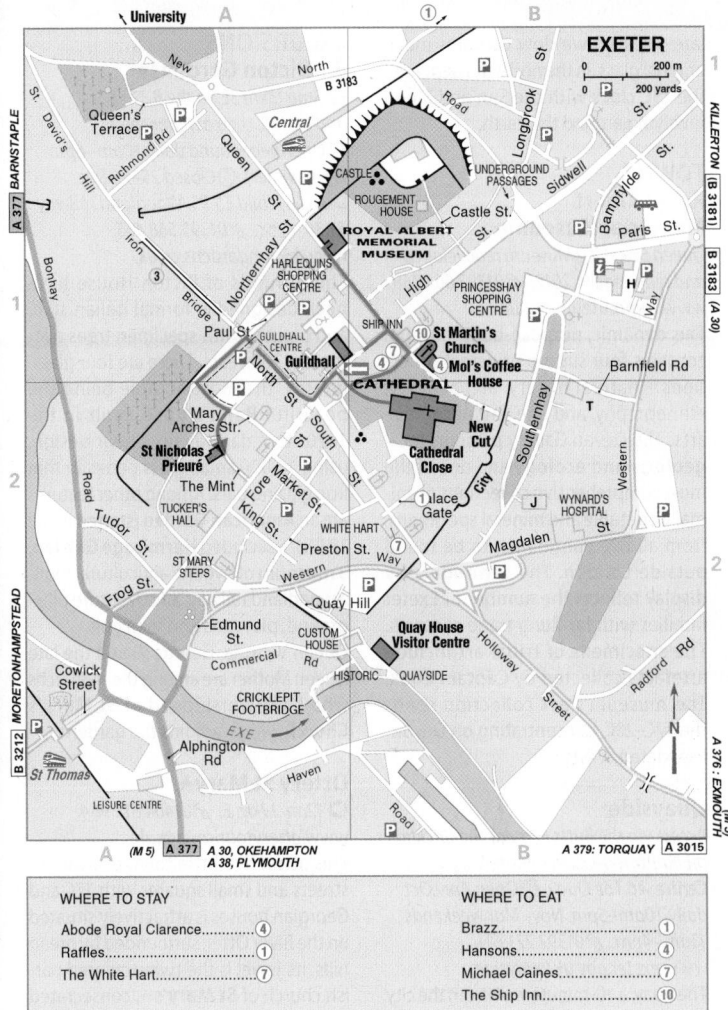

Exeter

WHERE TO STAY

Abode Royal Clarence	④
Raffles	①
The White Hart	⑦

WHERE TO EAT

Brazz	①
Hansons	④
Michael Caines	⑦
The Ship Inn	⑩

11pm. Booking (by phone) essential. ✆From £8.50. ♿✕. ✆01392 285 983. www.exeter-cathedral.org.uk.

The cathedral is set in its **Close**, an island of calm amid the city's traffic and surrounded by buildings from many periods. The west front rises through tier upon tier of carved angels, bishops and monarchs, through decorated tracery to castellated parapets. The **Norman transept towers** are the earliest part of the building, since the majority of the building was remodelled and improved in the 13C. Inside the cathedral, the most striking feature is the **nave vault-**

ing, extending 300ft/91m from west to east. Also impressive are the 14C **corbels** between the pointed arches of the arcade. Note the 14C **minstrels' gallery** (north side) with 14 angels playing instruments and the west rose window with reticulated tracery (20C glass).

Behind the high altar stands the **Exeter Pillar**, the prototype of all the others in the cathedral. Sir Gilbert Scott's canopied choir stalls (1870–77) incorporate the oldest complete set of **misericords** in the country, carved in 1260–80. The exquisite bishop's throne was carved in oak in 1312. Above the high altar the late-14C east window contains much original glass. In the north transept note the 15C clock with the Sun and Moon revolving around the Earth.

TOWN
Royal Albert Memorial Museum★

Queen Street. ⏱Museum redeveloped and reopened in 2012. ✆01392 665 858. www.rammuseum.org.uk.

This dynamic, purpose-built museum contains four superb principal collections – natural history, archaeology, ethnography, and fine and decorative arts. The Devon Gallery presents local **geology and ecology** and one of the most comprehensive collections of animal, vegetable and mineral specimens, from all five continents, to be found outside London. The **ethnography** display reflects the number of Exeter families with far-flung trade contacts. The specimens of tribal art include artefacts collected by Captain Cook. The museum's **art** collection spans the 17C–20C, concentrating on Devon-associated artists.

Quayside

Access via the Butts Ferry or the Cricklepit Footbridge. Quay House Visitor Centre, 46 The Quay. ⏱Open Apr–Oct daily 10am–5pm. Nov–Mar weekends 11am–4pm. ✆01392 271 611. www.exeter.gov.uk/quayside.

The quay, a 10-minute walk from the city centre, dates from the days when Exeter was a tidal river port, during a period of prosperity which was brought to an abrupt end in the 13C, when Isabella, Countess of Devon, built a weir across the river and successfully diverted all trade from Exeter to Topsham.

The visitor centre presents models, paintings and artefacts and an audio-visual history of Exeter. There is a regular programme of music and events throughout the summer months including spectacular dragonboat racing and other regattas. More sedate river cruises (✆07984 368 442; www. exetercruises.com) operate in summer from the quayside.

EXCURSIONS
▲▲Bicton Gardens★

▶ *8mi/13km SE on the B 3182 and B 3179, then a minor road.*
⏱*Open year-round daily 10am–6pm (5pm winter).* ⏱*Closed 25–26 Dec.* ⬤*£6.95, child £5.95. Woodland railway £1.30.* ♿✕. ✆*01395 568 465. www.bictongardens.co.uk.*

The grounds of Bicton House have been designed in formal Italian style and planted with specimen trees over the last 200 years. There are four glass-houses, the most notable being the beautiful **Palm House**, built in the 1820s to a daring curvilinear design, using 18,000 small glass panes in thin iron glazing bars. Among other features are an **American Garden** (started in the 1830s), a secluded **Hermitage Garden**, a **museum** of bygone agricultural tools, a woodland railway, an adventure playground, play area and mini golf.

Queen Victoria, George VI and the late Queen Mother are among the monarchs who have worshipped at **St Mary's Church**, which adjoins the gardens.

Ottery St Mary★

▶ *12mi/19km E.* ✆*01404 813 964. www.otterytourism.org.uk.*

This attractive little town of winding streets and small squares with 17C and Georgian houses is attractively situated on the River Otter, surrounded by green hills. Its jewel is the twin-towered parish church of **St Mary's★**, consecrated in 1260 and converted into a collegiate foundation in 1336: the chancel, nave, aisle and Lady Chapel were remodelled in the Decorated style and many of the furnishings belong to this period, including **Grandisson's clock** in the south transept and the gilded wooden **eagle lectern**, one of the oldest and grandest in England. A special feature of the church is its varied **vaulting**, superb coloured **bosses** and **corbels**.

Ottery St Mary is famous for its flaming **Tar Barrels** and Tar Barrel rolling on 5 November, and its **carnival**, held on the Saturday before, with its parade of spectacular floats and marchers from many towns and villages in the area.

English Riviera
South Hams and Plymouth

The English Riviera is a marketing term coined in the 1980s to evoke images of sophisticated French coastlines, and encompasses the resorts of Torquay, Paignton and Brixham, also known collectively as Torbay. Originally fishing villages, the three towns have capitalised on natural advantages which include a mild climate, exotic palm-tree vegetation, sea views and wide sandy beaches by adding hotels, promenades, piers, pavilions and public gardens to become fully fledged holiday resorts.

- **Michelin Map:** Michelin Atlas p 4 or Map 503 J 32.
- **Info:** 5 Vaughan Parade Torquay. www.english riviera.co.uk.
- **Don't Miss:** Dartmouth Steam Railway & River Boat.
- **Kids:** Paignton Zoo; Kents Cavern; Plymouth – National Marine Aquarium; Dockyards and Warships trip.
- **Sailing:** The English Riviera and South Hams offer some of the UK's best sailing waters. Marina at Torquay and a smaller one at Brixham.

TORQUAY

This is the most popular resort in Devon and of the three Torbay towns, the one that most lives up to its glamorous "English Riviera" billing.

Houses extend up the hill behind the shore; large pale Victorian and Edwardian hotels and villas set in lush gardens are being replaced by modern apartment blocks and high-rise hotels.

Most activity takes place around the bustling harbour/marina and beaches.

Kents Cavern★

(Wellswood, Ilsham Road.
Entry by guided tour only, year-round daily 10.30am–4 pm all year, see website for details; ghost tours Jul–Aug Wed–Fri 6.30pm, call to book.
Closed 1st week in Jan, 25–26 Dec.
£8.95, child £7.95 (online discount 15 percent) ghost tours. £8.50, child same (online discount 10 percent).
£2. 01803 215 136.
www.kents-cavern.co.uk.

Excavations have shown that this group of limestone caves were inhabited by prehistoric animals and by men for long periods from the Paleolithic era, 100,000 years ago, until Roman times.

The tour *(0.5mi/0.8km)* leads through contrasting chambers with petrified "waterfalls" beautiful white, red-brown and green crystals and many **stalactites** and **stalagmites** all beautifully lit. There are lots of activities for children in and around the caves.

Torre Abbey

Torbay Road. Open daily 10am–6pm (Nov–Feb 5pm). £5.85. 01803 293 593. www.torre-abbey.org.uk.

Set in luxuriant gardens, Torre Abbey consists of an 18C house, the so-called Spanish Barn and the ruins of the medieval abbey. The house is home to Torbay's art collection including about 600 oils and watercolours from the 18C to the mid-20C. They include Pre-Raphaelite works, with paintings by artists such as Holman Hunt and Burne-Jones.

PAIGNTON

2.5mi/4km S of Torquay.
The Esplanade. 0844 474 2233. www.theenglishriviera.co.uk.

Despite the Riviera tag, Paignton remains the poor relation to upwardly mobile Torquay. It has a good beach, however, and one of England's best zoos.

Paignton Zoo★★

A 3022 Totnes Road, 1mi/1.6km from Paignton town centre. Open 10am–6pm (5pm Nov–Feb). Closed 25 Dec. £11.90, child £8.40. 0844 474 2222. www.paigntonzoo.org.uk.

Dame Agatha Christie (1890–1976)

Agatha Christie was born and brought up in Torquay. At the outbreak of the First World War she worked in the own hall while it doubled as a Red Cross Hospital. This inspired her to create Hercule Poirot, distilled from the many Belgian refugees stranded in Torquay at that time. After nursing she trained in a pharmacy – perfect inside information on the poisons which feature in her novels. In 1938 she bought **Greenway House** on the River Dart as a holiday home and lived here until 1959. Today it belongs to the National Trust and, in 2009, the beautiful 30-acre/12ha gardens and house were opened to the public (NT; ⏰ *open early Mar–Oct Wed–Sun 10.30am–5pm, also Tue Easter school hols and late Jul–Aug; house visit by timed ticket only, allocated upon arrival, on busy days there may be a wait;* ⬤£8.75; 🅿*(must book ahead)*✕; ✆01803 842 382; www.nationaltrust.org.uk).

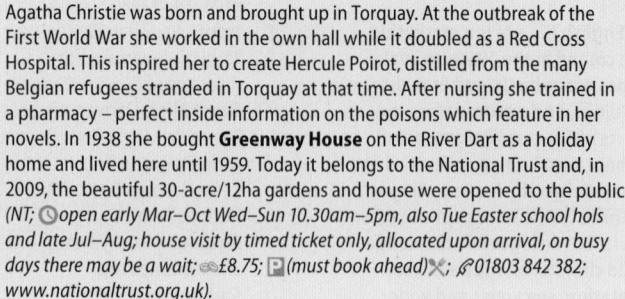

This is one of Britain's largest zoos, home to over 3,000 animals, set in 80 acres/32ha of luxuriant botanical gardens. The animals are kept as part of a far-reaching conservation programme.

BRIXHAM

▶ *8 mi /13km S of Torquay.*
🮰*Hob Nobs Gift Shop, 19–20 The Quay.* ✆*0844 474 2233. www.theenglish riviera.co.uk.*

Unlike its sister resorts, Brixham has a life aside from tourism, as a major fishing port which lands the highest-value catch in England.

It has no major visitor attractions as such; most people are happy to look around its compact picturesque harbour, perhaps board the replica 🮰🯊**Golden Hind** (⏰*open Feb–Oct 10am–4pm, until 9pm Aug;* ⬤*£4, child £3;* ✆*01803 856 223, www.goldenhind.co.uk*), take a boat trip around the bay and, of course, enjoy a fish supper.

The short excursion, 2mi/3km)west, to the unspoiled clifftop nature reserve of **Berry Head**, for its **sea views** is very worthwhile.

SOUTH HAMS★★

A different world to the English Riviera, the South Hams, lying immediately to the south and west, is mostly agricultural, studded with small villages. The countryside is beautiful, particularly around the River Dart and Kingsbridge estuary. Totnes, Dartmouth and Salcombe are the three jewels in its crown.

Dartmouth★★

▶ *10mi/16km S of Torquay.*
🮰*The Engine House, Mayor's Avenue.* ✆*01803 834 224. www.discover dartmouth.com.*

Dartmouth enjoys one of the most beautiful and unspoiled settings in southwest England, occupying a deepwater haven in a tidal inlet encircled by verdant hills. It grew wealthy on maritime trade and the quay was constructed in 1548, when it served as the centre of the town's activities. In appearance little has changed since, still lined with elegant merchants' houses, built in the early–mid-17C. In the late-17C trade moved to Bristol and London, and Dartmouth became purely a naval port.

The Town

The **Butterwalk**★ *(Duke Street)* is a terrace of four shops with oversailing upper floors supported on 11 granite pillars (built 1635–40). Just off here is **St Saviour's Church** *(Anzac Street)*. The tall square pinnacled tower has been a landmark for those sailing upriver since it was constructed in 1372. Note especially the south door with its two ironwork lions and rooted Tree of Life, and the medieval altar with legs carved like ships' figureheads. Farther along Duke Street is the old cobbled market square and building (1829), at its liveliest on a Friday when the pannier market takes place. **The Shambles**, the main street of the medieval town, is still lined with houses of that period – the early-17C

Dartmouth Harbour
Y. Duhamel/MICHELIN

four-storey **Tudor House** and the **Carved Angel**, a late-14C half-timbered merchant's house, now an inn.

Britannia Royal Naval College

🕐 *Open only by guided tour Easter–Oct Wed, Sat and Sun, enquire at Dartmouth Tourist Information Centre ℘01803 834 224 to book/confirm times and charges.*
On the hill above town, this huge, majestic building (1905) is a naval school where many members of the Royal Family received their training, most recently Prince Charles and Prince Andrew.

Dartmouth Castle

EH. 🔘 *1mi/1.6km SE by Newcomen Road, South Town and Castle Road.*
🕐 *Open daily 10am–5pm (6 pm Jul–Aug, 4pm Oct–Mar); Nov–Mar check website for days.* 🕐 *Closed 1 Jan, 24–26 Dec.* 🎫*£4.70.* 🅿 *(charge).* ℘*01803 833 588. www.english-heritage.org.uk.*
The fort was begun in 1481 by the merchants of Dartmouth to protect their homes and deepwater anchorage, and modified in the 16C and 18C. It commands excellent **views**★★★ out to sea and across and up the estuary.

Salcombe★

🔘 *20mi/32km SW of Dartmouth.*
🚹*Market Street.* ℘*01548 843 927. www.salcombeinformation.co.uk.*
Brilliant blue Salcombe Bay, aflutter with white triangular sails, fringed by golden pocket-handkerchief-sized beaches and perfectly framed by rolling green hills, is one of the finest sights in Devon. Salcombe is one of the largest yachting

centres in England and several old wharf houses are workshops for boat makers and marine engineers. Other old properties have been converted to fashionable places to eat and drink.

Totnes★

🔘 *13 mi /21km NW of Dartmouth.*
🚹*Town Mill, Coronation Road.* ℘*01803 863 168. www.totnesinformation.co.uk.*
Ancient Totnes is one of the most rewarding small towns in England, standing at the highest navigable and lowest bridging point on the River Dart on the south Devon coast. The narrow main street runs steeply between 16C–17C wealthy merchants' houses built of brick and stone or colour-washed. Totnes is unusual for a town of its size, eschewing chain stores, devoted almost entirely to small individual shops and cafés, many catering for the bohemian-chic lifestyle for which the town is famous.

Rail and River

The **Dartmouth Steam Railway & River Boat Company** synchronises river and rail trips between Lower Street Dartmouth (river) and Queen's Park Station, Paignton (rail) *(Apr–Oct and Christmas; see website for timetable and prices).* They also run standalone river boat trips and coastal cruises daily in summer *(see website for out-of-season times and prices.* ℘*01803 555 872; www.dartmouth railriver.co.uk).*

View over Totnes town

©Ann Taylor-Hughes/iStockphoto.com

Fore Street

The half-timbered **Elizabethan Museum**★ *(70 Fore Street; ⏱open mid-Mar–Oct and two weeks Dec Mon–Fri 10.30am–5pm; ≋£2; ℘01803 863 821. www.devonmuseums.net/totnes),* the dark red-brick **mansion** (now a community education centre), a late-18C Gothic house (in Bank Lane), and other attractive buildings (nos. 48 and 52) testify to Totnes' former prosperity.

High Street

Interesting features include the mid-16C **Guildhall** *(⏱ open Apr–Sept, Mon–Fri, some bank hols,10.30am–4.30pm, check website for Oct times; ≋£1.50; ℘01803 862 147; www.totnes information.co.uk),* which occupies the site of an earlier Benedictine priory; the house at no. 16, now a bank built in 1585 by a local pilchard merchant; and the granite pillared **Butterwalk**★, which has protected shoppers from the rain since the 17C.

St Mary's★

The 15C parish and priory church with its red sandstone tower adorned with gruesome gargoyles contains a beautiful late-15C rood screen.

Castle

EH. ⏱Open daily Easter/late Mar–Oct 10am–5pm (6pm Jul–Aug, 4pm Oct). ≋£3.40. 🅿. ℘01803 864 406.

www.english-heritage.org.uk/totnes. High on a mound sits the castle, encircled by 14C ramparts built to strengthen the late-11C motte and bailey earthworks. The castle walls command excellent **views**★★★ of the Dart River Valley.

PLYMOUTH★★

▶ *Plymouth is on the border between Devon and Cornwall, delineated by the River Tamar. 🚇Plymouth Mayflower, 3–5 The Barbican. ℘01752 306 330. www.visitplymouth.co.uk.*

Plymouth is the principal town of the southwest with nearly 250,000 inhabitants. It is arranged in three distinct areas: the Hoe and its environs, adorned with the splendour of Victorian and Edwardian buildings; the older, bustling Barbican district by the harbour with its narrow streets; the commercial post-war centre, with wide shop-lined avenues.

A Bit of History

The Plantagenet period brought trade with France and by the Elizabethan period trade had spread worldwide, so that for a time Plymouth was the fourth-largest town in England after London, Bristol and York. From the 13C Plymouth also played a prime role as a naval and military port, from which warriors and explorers such as Drake, Raleigh, Hawkins and Grenville (all Devonians), Cook and the Pilgrim Fathers set sail. The Royal Naval Dockyard was founded by William III in 1691 at Devonport and today employs some 4,800 workers. In the Second World War the city suffered terrible bomb damage.

WALKING TOUR

👥 National Marine Aquarium★
Rope Walk, Coxside. 🕐*Open year-round daily 10am–6pm (5pm Nov–Mar); last entry 1hr before closing.* 🕐*Closed 25 Dec.* 👛*£11.50, child £7 (4-D film extra £2.50).* ♿🄿✕. ✆*01752 600 301. www.national-aquarium.co.uk.*
Opened in 2001 this was the first aquarium in the UK to be set up solely for the purpose of education, conservation and research, and remains Britain's largest aquarium. The tanks represent different environments, such as a fresh stream, shallow sea and coral reef; with an array of fish, from delicate sea horses to mighty sharks. An extra treat for the kids is a 15-minute fishy 4-D film.

Barbican
Old Plymouth survives in the Barbican, an area extending a quarter of a mile inland from Sutton Harbour, combining modern amenities with medieval houses, Jacobean doorways and cobbled alleys. The **Mayflower Stone** on the pier commemorates the voyage of the **Pilgrim Fathers**, who set sail in 1620 in their 90ft/27m ship, the *Mayflower*. Many other famous voyages are commemorated in the numerous stones and plaques on the pier.

Mayflower Exhibition
3–5 The Barbican. 🕐*Open Apr–Oct Mon–Sat 9am–5pm, Sun 10am–4pm; Nov–Mar Mon–Fri 9am–5pm, Sat 10am–4pm.* 👛*£2.* ✆*01752 306 330. www.visitplymouth.co.uk.*
In the same building as the tourist office, this traces the voyage of the *Mayflower* (👉*see above*) and contemporary events.

Elizabethan House
32 New Street. 🕐*Open Apr–Sept Tue–Sat and bank hols 10am–noon, 1–5pm.* 👛*£2.50.* ✆*01752 304 774. www.plymouth.gov.uk.*

This house and its neighbour were built in the late-16C as part of a development for wealthy merchants and sea-captains.

Plymouth Gin Distillery
60 South Side Street. 👁*Visit by guided tour only (50min) Mon–Sat 10.30am–4.30pm, Sun 11.30am–3.30pm.* ♿✕. 👛*£6.* ✆*01752 665 292. http://plymouthgin.com.*
The distillery is housed in what was once a Dominican Friary founded in 1425. You can take a guided tour to see how gin is made and enjoy a drink and bite to eat in The Barbican Kitchen.

Merchant's House
33 St Andrew's Street. 🕐*Open Apr–Sept Tue–Sat and bank hols 10am–noon, 1–5pm.* 👛*£2.50.* ✆*01752 304 774. www.plymouth.gov.uk.*
This mid-16C timbered house, its upper floors supported on stone corbels, houses the **Museum of Old Plymouth** including a reconstruction of an old city Edwardian **pharmacy★**.

St Andrew's Church
🕐*Open daily 9am–4pm.* ♿. ✆*01752 661 414. www.standrewschurch.org.uk.*
Founded in 1050 and rebuilt in the 15C, the church was firebombed in 1941, leaving only the walls, granite piers, chancel arches and the 136ft/41m tower standing. The rebuilt church features six vividly coloured **windows** by John Piper (1904–92). On a window ledge is the so-called **Drake crest scratching** showing the *Golden Hinde*. It is thought to have been carved by a mason working in the church at the time of Drake's return from circumnavigating the world (3 November 1580). Among the **memorials** are tablets to Frobisher and Drake.
Just south of the church stands **Prysten House** (*Finewell Street;* 🕐*open subject to functions, enquire while you're at St Andrew's, or* ✆*01752 661 414*), dating from 1490 and thought to be the oldest house in Plymouth. It is a fine three-storeyed building around an inner courtyard with open timber galleries.

City Museum and Art Gallery★

Drake Circus. ○Open Tue–Fri 10am–5.30pm, Sat and bank hols 10am–5pm. ₤₳✕. ℘01752 304 774. www.plymouth-museum.gov.uk.

The spacious Victorian building displays a fraction of its splendid collections relating to the city's **maritime history**. Plymouth was also the home of **William Cookworthy**, discoverer of the Cornish kaolin which made the production of **hard paste porcelain** a reality in this country from 1768; an excellent display relates this story.

Plymouth Hoe

On "that loftie place at Plimmouth call'd the Hoe", **Sir Francis Drake** (1540–96) is said to have seen the "invincible" Spanish Armada arriving one day in 1588 and decided to finish his game of bowls (perhaps waiting for the tide to turn) before going to battle. It remains an ideal point to **view** maritime traffic on the Sound, the natural harbour at the mouth of the Tamar and Plym rivers.

Smeaton's Tower (○open Apr–Sept Tue–Sat and bank hols 10am–noon, 1–4.30pm, check Fri and Sat openings; ₪£2.50; ℘01752 304 774; www.visitplymouth.co.uk), a red-and-white-painted lighthouse, was erected on the Hoe in 1884 after 123 storm-battered years on Eddystone Rocks, some 14mi/23km southwest of Plymouth. The present **Eddystone Lighthouse**, built in 1878–82, can be seen from the Hoe and even better from the top of Smeaton's Tower, from where there is a splendid **view**★★. Other monuments testifying to Plymouth's role in history include Boehm's 1884 **Drake Statue**, the **Armada Memorial** and the **Naval War Memorial**. Also on the Hoe is **Tinside Lido**, a restored Art Deco outdoor pool.

Royal Citadel

EH. ○☜Guided tour May–Sept Tue and Thu 2.30pm. ₪£5. ℘01752 304 849. www.english-heritage.org.uk.

In 1590–91 Drake began a fort intended to protect the Sound against marauding Spaniards and it was in this place that Charles II had the present castle built in 1666–71. The **ramparts** command **views**★★ of the Sound, the Barbican and the Tamar.

EXCURSIONS

Buckland Abbey★★

NT. ❯ 9mi/14km N of Plymouth. ○Open mid-Feb–23 Dec : mid-Mar–Oct daily 10.30am–5.30pm, Feb & Dec daily 11am–4.30pm, rest of year Fri–Sun 11am–4.30pm. ₪£8.05. ₤▣✕. ℘01822 853 607. www.nationaltrust. org.uk/buckland.

Buckland was founded in 1278. At the Dissolution, the property was sold to the Grenvilles and converted into an Elizabethan mansion before their famous cousin, **Sir Francis Drake**, purchased the estate in 1581. The property has since been transformed from Tudor mansion to Georgian family home. The garden is largely 20C with the striking exception of the 14C **Great Barn**, buttressed and gabled, built to store the abbey's tithes and dues.

The house accommodates elements of the original church in its domestic context in a fascinating way, outlined in the **Four Lives Gallery**. The **Drake Gallery**, which dominates the first floor, was added in the 1570s and houses an exhibition on the great seaman explorer.

The panelled **Drake Chamber** is hung with a series of 16C–17C portraits and contains English and continental furniture of the same period. The **Great Hall**, at the heart of the old abbey, is paved in pink-and-white tiles, lined with oak panelling, and features striking original plasterwork. The furniture is predominantly 16C–17C. The kitchen, with French-style brick charcoal ovens and a range of old-fashioned kitchen utensils, was added in the 17C.

Saltram★★

*NT. ❯ 3.5mi/5.5km E on the A 374 then S on the A 38 to Plympton. **House:** ○Open mid-Mar–Oct Sat–Thu and Good Fri noon–4.30pm. **Garden and gallery:** ○Open daily mid-Mar–Dec 11am–5pm (Winter 4pm, Jan-mid-Mar closed Fri). ₪£9.10. ₤▣✕. ℘01752 333 503. www.nationaltrust.org.uk.*

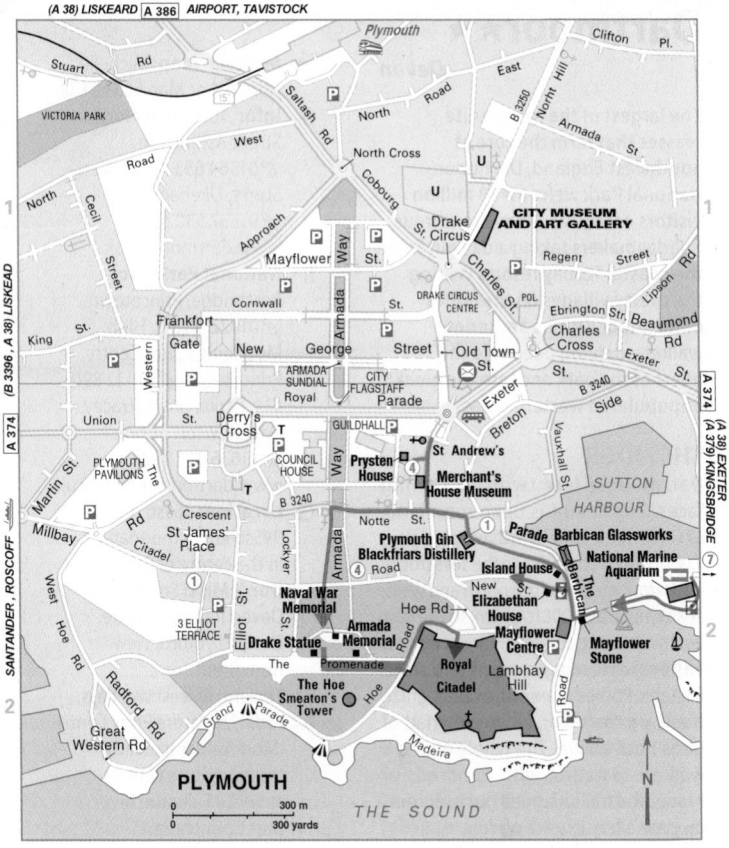

Map of Plymouth showing: (A 38) LISKEARD, A 386 AIRPORT, TAVISTOCK, VICTORIA PARK, CITY MUSEUM AND ART GALLERY, DRAKE CIRCUS CENTRE, ARMADA SUNDIAL, CITY FLAGSTAFF, GUILDHALL, COUNCIL HOUSE, PLYMOUTH PAVILIONS, Prysten House, St Andrew's, Merchant's House Museum, Plymouth Gin Blackfriars Distillery, Island House, Parade, Barbican Glassworks, National Marine Aquarium, Naval War Memorial, Armada Memorial, Elizabethan House, Mayflower Centre, Mayflower Stone, Drake Statue, The Hoe Smeaton's Tower, Royal Citadel, Lambhay Hill, PLYMOUTH, THE SOUND. Scale 300 m / 300 yards.

WHERE TO STAY		WHERE TO EAT	
Ashgrove House	①	Barbican Kitchen	①
Holiday Inn Plymouth	④	Tanners	④
Premier Travel Inn	⑦		

This is a magnificent Georgian house with some of the finest 18C rooms in the country, with opulent Robert Adam interiors, gardens, follies and landscaped parkland. To complete Adams' interior design, Chippendale contributed furniture, Reynolds portraits and Angelica Kauffmann paintings.

Mount Edgcumbe

⚫ *Mount Edgcumbe Country Park, Cremyll. 25mi/40km by road; best visited by Tamar River cruise, departing from Mayflower Steps, or via Cremyll Ferry.* **Park:** ⏱*Open year-round daily 8am–dusk.* **House:** ⏱*Open: Apr–Sept Sun–*

Thu and bank hol Mon 11am–4.30pm. ⊚*£7.20, river cruise and entry £10 (park free).* ♿🅿✕. ✆*01752 822 236. www. plymouth.gov.uk/mountedgcumbe.*

Built in the 1500s, and now restored to its 18C appearance, the house include paintings by Sir Joshua Reynolds and William van der Velde, Irish Bronze Age horns, 16C tapestries and 18C Chinese and Plymouth porcelain.

However, for many people, the best reason to visit is its large **country park**, looking out to sea. This includes the National Camellia Collection, the majority of the formal gardens and the Orangery Restaurant.

Dartmoor★★

Devon

The largest of the five granite masses that form the core of Southwest England, Dartmoor National Park welcomes 8 million visitors each year. Many are curious holidaymakers taking a day out from the coastal Torbay resorts visiting the pretty villages on the edges of the moor. Others are serious walkers, delving deep into the heart of the park and into the bleak unpopulated western areas.

THE MOOR

Dartmoor offers two contrasting faces. The centre is open moorland, often bleak and windswept rising 1,000ft/300m high, while the **tors** (rocky outcrops), mainly to the north and west, are as much as 2,000ft/600m. To the east and southeast, however, are **wooded valleys**, cascading streams and small villages. Ponies, sheep and cattle graze freely on the moor, while a myriad of birds flock above. The whole area is a walker's paradise with hundreds of routes and trails mapped out to accommodate every level of walker.

You can join one of the many Dartmoor National Park Authority walks led by a guide with a wealth of local knowledge or simply blaze your own trail, using one of the eight walks compiled on their website, but do take the usual precautions.

- **Michelin Map:** Michelin Atlas p 4 or Map 503 H, I 32.
- **Info:** Town Hall, North Street Ashburton. ☏01364 653 426. 3 West Street, Okehampton. ☏01837 53020. www.dartmoor.co.uk.
- **National Park Info:** Postbridge, Princetown. ☏01822 88272. High Moorland Visitor Centre, Princetown. ☏01822 890 414. Parke, Bovey Tracey, near Newton Abbot. ☏01626 832 093. www.dartmoor-npa.gov.uk.
- **Location:** 365sq mi/ 945sq km of moorland in the centre of Devon.
- **Don't Miss:** South Devon Railway; Castle Drogo; Lydford; view from Brent Tor.
- **Timing:** At least two days.
- **Kids:** Miniature Pony Centre (Moretonhampstead); the adventure centres at Becky Falls and River Dart Country Park.
- **Warning:** On enclosed land, access is by public footpaths and bridleways only and it is an offence to drive or park more than 15yds/15m off a road.

Haytor Rocks, Dartmoor

©Black Beck Photographic/iStockphoto.com

🚗 DRIVING TOUR

▷ Leave Plymouth E on the A 398.

Buckfastleigh
This small market town is the terminus of the steam-driven **South Devon Railway** (🕐operates Apr–late Oct daily, rest of year see website; ➳Buckfastleigh–Totnes £10; ♿🅿✕; ☎0845 345 1466; www.south-devonrailway.co.uk/what-to-see-and-do), one of the most picturesque railway lines in England.

Buckfast Abbey
Abbey and grounds: 🕐Open Mon–Sat 9am (Fri 10am)–6pm. Sun noon–6pm. *visitor centre:* 🕐Open daily 9am–5.30pm (10am–4pm winter). ♿🅿✕. ☎01364 645 550. www.buckfast.org.uk. The present abbey church was consecrated in 1932, some 900 years after the original foundation under King Canute. Norman in style, it follows the plan of the Cistercian house dissolved by Henry VIII. The interior of white Bath stone rises to a plainly vaulted roof, 49ft/15m above the nave floor. Note the ornate **high altar** and the modern **Blessed Sacrament Chapel** (1966) with walls of stained glass. An exhibition in the **crypt** traces the abbey history.

▷ Return to the A 38.

Ashburton
This former stannary (coinage) town stands on a tributary of the River Dart at the beginning of the old road (B 3357) across the moor to Tavistock. The church was built in the 15C when the town was a significant wool centre. Slate-hung houses indicate its importance as a slate mining centre from the 16C to the 18C. Signposted from town is the 🧍**River Dart Country Park** (🕐River Dart Adventures operate Easter/Apr–Sept daily, rest of year weekends only; ➳£7.50, 3–4 year-olds £3.75; ☎01364 652 511; www.riverdart.co.uk), a popular country park with a range of outdoor facilities and amusement for all the family.

▷ Take the road to Buckland.

Buckland in the Moor
Thatched stone cottages set in a wooded dell and the medieval moorstone church form this characteristic Devon village.

▷ Go back to the B 3357; turn right.

At **Dartmeet** the West and East Dart rivers converge from the uplands to flow through a gorge-like valley lively with bird- and animal-life.

▷ Turn right on the B 3387.

Widecombe-in-the-Moor
A cluster of white-walled thatched cottages, grouped around the church, stands in the shallow valley (wide combe) surrounded by granite ridges which rise to 1,500ft/460m. The vast Perpendicular **Church of St Pancras**, with its imposing pinnacled 135ft-/41m-tall tower, is known as the Cathedral of the Moor. The church house dates back to 1537, when it was an alehouse.
The road to Bovey Tracey runs close by **Haytor Rocks** (1,490ft/454m), from where there is a fine **view**★.

Bovey Tracey
This small town is a gateway to Dartmoor. Many of its cottages are built of moor granite, mellowed by thatch. The 15C **Church of St Peter, St Paul and St Thomas of Canterbury**★ was founded in 1170 by Sir William de Tracey, possibly in atonement for his part in St Thomas Becket's murder. The church contains interesting Jacobean tombs, a 15C-lectern, carved pulpit, and rood screen.
The **Riverside Mill** is home to the **Devon Guild of Craftsmen** (🕐open daily 10am–5.30pm, Jun–early Sept Fri until 9pm; ♿🅿✕; ☎01626 832 223; www.crafts.org.uk), founded in 1954. This is the largest contemporary crafts centre in Southwest England, and exhibits a variety of top-quality local work.

▷ Retrace your steps and turn right towards Manaton.

The Becka Brook tumbles some 70ft/20m from the moor into the beautiful wooded glade occupied by ♟♟**Becky Falls Woodland Park** (○*open late Feb–Oct daily 10am–5pm/dusk; ∞£7.25, child £6.25; Jul/Aug plus 50p;* 🅿🍴*;* ☎*01647 221 259, www.beckyfalls-dartmoor.com).* Children's activities include animal shows and feeding. The estate is criss-crossed by nature trails.

Moretonhampstead

The old market town of "Moreton" was a coaching stage on the Exeter–Bodmin road. The 14C–15C granite **church** has a commanding west tower; note the unusual row of thatched, colonnaded granite **almshouses**, dating from 1637. About 2mi/3km west, in 20 acres/8ha of beautiful parkland, the ♟♟**Miniature Pony Centre** (○*open daily Apr–Jun and Sept–Oct 10.30am–4.30pm, Jul–Aug 10am–5pm; ∞£7.75, child £6.75;* ♿🅿🍴*;* ☎*01647 432 400; www.miniature ponycentre.com)* is a great favourite with young children and also features a daily birds of prey display.

◑ *B 3212 towards Exeter, turn off for Dunsford and continue, passing the triple-arched 16C Fingle Bridge, to Drewsteignton.*

Castle Drogo★

NT. ○*Open mid-Mar–Oct daily 11am–5pm, visit website for winter opening times/days.* ∞*£8.20.* ♿🅿🍴*.* ☎*01647 433 306. www.nationaltrust.org.uk.*
On discovering his descent from the 12C Norman nobleman Dru/Drogo, the grocery magnate, Julius Drewe, commissioned **Edwin Lutyens** (1869–1944) to create an extravagant castle to the glory of his name. The castle was built in 1911–30 of granite partly from Drewe's own quarry; the exterior shows Norman and Tudor influences while the interior is very much Lutyens at his best, including superb oak fittings.

Sticklepath

This attractive rural village is home to the **Finch Foundry** (*NT.* ○*open mid-Mar–Oct Wed–Mon 11am–5pm; ∞£4.60;* 🅿🍴*.* ☎*01837 840 046; www.nationaltrust.org.uk),* a restored 19C edge-tool factory and water-powered forge, offering demonstrations of tools and waterwheels.

Okehampton

This market town was a Norman strongpoint and prospered during the great

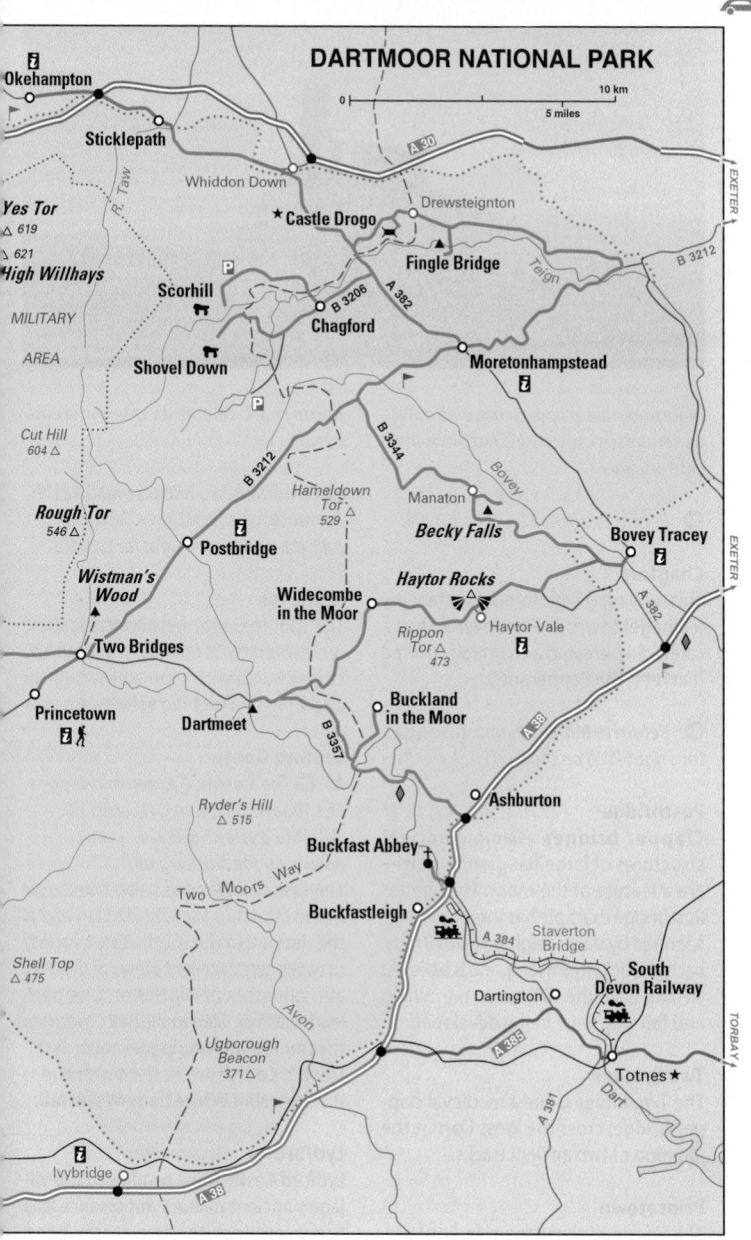

DARTMOOR NATIONAL PARK

wool period. The ruins of **Okehampton Castle** *(EH; ♿ ⏰ open Apr–Sept daily 10am–5pm (6pm Jul–Aug);* ⌖*£3.70;* 🅿*;* ☎*01837 52844; www.english-heritage. org.uk),* enjoy a picturesque setting. Initially a Norman motte and bailey, rebuilt in the 13C, it includes the gatehouses,

barbican, outer and inner baileys, keep and stair turret. In town, an 18C mill is home to the **Museum of Dartmoor Life** *(3 West Street; open Easter/Apr Mon–Oct Mon–Sat 10.15am–4.30pm, for Sun and winter times call;* ⌖*£3.50;* ♿✕*;* ☎*01837 52295; www.museum*

13C church on Brent Tor

© Anthony Collins/age fotostock

ofdartmoorlife.eclipse.co.uk), with exhibits reminiscing on rural Dartmoor life a century ago.

▶ *Return to the A382; left on B 3206.*

Chagford

This thriving village, formerly a stannary (coinage) town, boasts several shops, cafés, old pubs and a charming covered market ("The Pepperpot").

▶ *Return to Moretonhampstead and turn right (SW) on the B3212.*

Postbridge

Clapper bridges – simple ancient structures of large flat granite slabs – are a feature of the moor. The famous Postbridge example has three openings spanned by slabs weighing up to 8 tons, each about 15ft/5m long, and is believed to date from the 13C, when tin-mining and farming were being developed.

Two Bridges

The Two Bridges, one a medieval clapper bridge, cross the West Dart at the junction of two ancient tracks.

Princetown

This is the highest town in England, dominated by a famous prison. Built 1806–08 to hold Napoleonic prisoners of war, it became one of the most feared prisons in the country.

It is still in use, and the adjacent **Dartmoor Prison Museum** (*⏱ open year-round daily 9.30am–12.30pm & 1.30–4pm/4.30pm; ⌖£3; www.dartmoor-prison.co.uk)* relates its often grim history.

▶ *Return to Two Bridges and take the Tavistock road (B 3357). In Tavistock, take the minor road right for Lydford.*

Brent Tor

The 1,130ft-/344m-hill of volcanic stone is crowned by St Michael's, a small 13C stone church with a low stalwart tower affording far-reaching **views**★★.

Lydford Gorge

NT. ▶ *The Stables.* ⏱ *Open mid-Mar–Oct 10am–5pm (4pm Oct).* ⌖£5.80. ♿ ℗ ✗. ℘ *01822 820 320. www.nationaltrust.org.uk.*

This lush oak-wooded steep-sided river gorge stretches for 1.5mi/2.5km and is the deepest in the southwest. A variety of walks give excellent **views** of the river and glimpses of Dartmoor. One path leads via Pixie Glen to the Bell Cavern via the thundering whirlpool known as the **Devil's Cauldron**. At the south end is the 90ft/30m **White Lady Waterfall**.

Lydford★★

Lydford Castle ruins testifies to the village's ancient military importance as a Saxon outpost; the two-storey **keep** dates from 1195. Alongside is the 16C oak-timbered Tudor **Castle Inn**, which at one time served as the rector's house. **St Petroc's Church**, founded in the 6C, was rebuilt and enlarged on Norman foundations in the 13C, the south aisle and tower in the 15C, and further changes were made in the 19C.

North Devon

North Devon changes in character from east to west. The long sandy beaches of traditional resorts such as Ilfracombe end at Westward Ho!, with dramatic rocky foreshores at Clovelly and Hartland Point. Inland are relaxed market towns, such as Barnstaple and Bideford.

ILFRACOMBE

The most popular resort on the North Devon coast, pretty coves and cliff scenery are set against a backdrop of attractive wooded hills and valleys.

The hills around the town provide good vantage points for surveying the area: **Capstone Hill** (156ft/47m) offers a good **view**★ of the town, the harbour mouth, the rock-enclosed bays and beaches; **Hillsborough**, at the centre of the pleasure ground, rises to 447ft/136m and affords an extensive **view**★★ along the coast.

Holy Trinity

The parish church dates from the Norman period (enlarged in the 14C) and has an ancient, elaborately carved **wagon roof**★★.

St Nicholas' Chapel

Lantern Hill. ○*Open late May–mid Oct daily 10am–1pm, 2.30pm–5pm (May–Aug until dusk).*

In the early 14C the beacon set as a marker on Lantern Hill was replaced by this mariners' chapel, which still shines a red light to guide shipping. From the rock platform on which the chapel stands there is a good **view**★ over the almost land-locked harbour and out to sea.

👪 Tunnels Beaches

Granville Road. ○*Open (subject to tide) Easter school hols–Sept daily 10am–6pm, summer school hols 10am–7pm, Oct, closed Mon & Fri, except half term week, 10am–5pm.* ✆*£2.25, child £1.75* ⌖✕. *www.tunnelsbeaches.co.uk.*

In the 19C the hill between the road and the sea was tunnelled and the rock

▶ **Population:** 10,941.
🖈 **Michelin Map:** Michelin Atlas p 6 or Map 503 H 30.
�ℹ **Info:** Landmark Theatre, Seafront. ✆01271 863 001. www.visitilfracombe.co.uk. The Square, Barnstaple. ✆01271 375 000. www.staynorthdevon.co.uk.
▶ **Location:** Ilfracombe lies on the coast, just west of Exmoor National Park.
🔎 **Don't Miss:** Arlington Court; Clovelly; Lundy Island.
👪 **Kids:** Tunnels Beaches; Watermouth Castle.

cove, on the far side, made accessible. The cove was then equipped with a sea wall to prevent the tide running out and so provide all-day bathing.

👪 Watermouth Castle

○ *1mi/1.6km SE on the A 399.*
○*Open late Mar/Easter–Oct Sun–Fri, peak 10am–5pm (last ride), off-peak 10.30am–4.30pm (last ride).* ✆*£13, child £11, under 36in/92cm free.*
🅿✕. ✆*01271 867 474.*
www.watermouthcastle.com.
Overlooking picturesque Watermouth Cove, this Victorian folly castle is a handsome sight. Its landscaped gardens host a lively theme park for young children.

BARNSTAPLE★

○ *13mi/21km S of Ilfracombe.*
Barnstaple is the regional centre and its 19C cast-iron-and-glass **Pannier Market** (○ *open year-round Mon–Sat 9am–4pm; www.barnstaplepanniermarket.co.uk*), adjoining **Butchers' Row**, is busy selling local produce (*Tue, Fri & Sat*) arts and crafts (*Mon Apr–Xmas & Thu year-round*) and antiques and collectables (*Wed*).
Long Bridge★ (520ft/158m) was first built c.1273; three of its 16 stone arches were replaced c.1539.
The 13C **parish church** (○*open Mon–Fri 9am–3pm, Sunday services;* ✆*01271 344*

589) is notable for its memorial monuments and its 17C lead-covered spire. The 17C **Horwood Almshouses** and **Alice Horwood School** *(Church Lane)* have attractive wooden mullioned windows. The 19C **Guildhall** *(High Street;* ⏰*open Apr–Oct Sat 10am–2pm, to visit at other times call* ☎*01237 373 003)* contains the Dodderidge Parlour, panelled in 17C oak, in which the town's collection of corporation plate is displayed. The **Museum of North Devon** *(The Square;* ⏰*open year-round Mon–Sat 9.30am–5pm;* ⏰*closed bank hols and Christmas wk;* ♿*;* ☎*01271 346 747; www.devonmuseums.net/barnsta ple)* traces regional history.

Downriver from the bridge is the colonnaded **Queen Anne's Walk** (1609), built as a merchants' exchange and crowned by a statue of Queen Anne. Amid the colonnades a former 19C bathhouse is home to **Barnstaple Heritage Centre** *(*⏰*open Apr–Oct Tue–Sat 10am–5pm, Nov–Mar Tue–Fri 10am–4.30pm, Sat 10am–3.30pm;* ♿*;* ☎*01271 373 003; www.barnstapletowncouncil.co.uk)* with more displays on local history.

ARLINGTON COURT★★

NT. ➤ *8mi/13km NE of Barnstaple on the A 39.* ⏰*Open late-Feb–week before Christmas: mid-Mar–Oct daily 11am (10.30am gardens)–5pm; Feb daily 11am–3pm; rest of year Sat–Sun only 11am–3pm.* 🎫*£8.05 (gardens and carriage collection only, £5.90).* ☎*01271 850 296. www.nationaltrust.org.uk.*
This Classically styled house (1820–23) contains the varied collections of *objets d'art* accumulated by its former owner, Miss Rosalie Chichester (1865–1949), the most remarkable of which is her collection of **model ships** including 36 made by Napoleonic prisoners of war. The house is also home to the National Trust **Carriage Museum**.

CLOVELLY★★

30mi/48km SW of Ilfracombe. ⏰*Entry via visitor centre Jul–Sept daily, 9am (9.30am Oct–Jun) to 6pm/dusk.* ⏰*Closed 25 Dec.* 🎫*£5.95. Landrover shuttle (Easter–Oct) £1–£2.* 🅿🍽.

☎*01237 431 781. www.clovelly.co.uk.*
This charming picture-postcard village, mentioned in the Domesday Book, is now privately owned. The **visitor centre** outlines its history as a fishermen's community and its preservation. The steep, stepped and cobbled **High Street**, known as **Down-a-long** or **Up-a-long** (depending on the direction being faced), is lined with small, white-washed 18C and 19C houses decked with bright flowers. Donkeys and mules are still the only form of transport up and down the High Street. At the bottom of the High Street lies **Quay Pool**, the small, restored 14C harbour protected from the open sea by a curving breakwater which offers a **view** extending from Lundy to Baggy Point. The pebble beach is backed by stone-built cottages and balconied houses, the old harbour lime-kiln, the inn and the lifeboat store.

Just west (4.5mi/7km) is the village of Hartland, the gateway to **Hartland Point** (3mi/5km north), the spectacular rocky apex of North Devon, comparable to Land's End for its drama and a shipping graveyard over the centuries.

LUNDY ISLAND★★

➤ *2hrs by MS Oldenburg (267 passengers) operates from Bideford Quay all year, also from Ilfracombe Pier (summer only).* 🎫*£33.50 day return, also private launches from Clovelly and helicopter (£99).* ☎*01271 863 636 (sailing); 01237 470 422 (Lundy Island Manager). www.lundyisland.co.uk.*
The island derives its name from the Icelandic word for puffin, *Lunde*. The attraction is its fascinating bird- and marine-life, in a peaceful setting free of many of the trappings of modern life including cars. Despite the name, however, there are reportedly only 30 breeding pairs of puffins here *(May–Jul)*. Other residents include razorbills, guillemots, fulmars, Manx shearwaters, shags, kittiwakes and various gulls. Lundy has been designated a **Marine Nature Reserve** since 1986, with grey seals, basking sharks and porpoises. Clear waters and several wrecks mean excellent diving. A complete circuit of

the island is 11mi/18km *(4hrs on foot)*, with a pub and various points of historical interest en route.

THE TORRIDGE ESTUARY

◯ *Bideford is 10mi/16km W of Barnstaple.*

🔲 *www.destinationbideford.co.uk.*

The principal settlement along the Torridge is the small market town of Bideford; its 17C quay is from where fishing boats and the Lundy ferry sail.

Don't miss the views from the new bridge over the River Torridge, which take in its 24-arch 16C stone bridge. Bideford hosts a lively pannier market *(Tue and Sat)*.

Appledore (3mi/5km north) is a charming old-fashioned fishing village with narrow cobbled streets, pastel-washed cottages and the small **North Devon Maritime Museum** (◯*open Easter–Oct, see website for details; www.devon museums.net).*

Exmoor★★
and around

This great southwest moor (267sq mi/692sq km) on the boundary between North Devon and Somerset is one of Britain's national parks. Red deer, wild Exmoor ponies, sheep and cattle still roam the moor, which is vividly described in R D Blackmore's classic novel *Lorna Doone* (1869). Exmoor's coastline is in places rugged and wild but also home to popular seaside resorts, such as Minehead.

DULVERTON★

◯ *Southern Exmoor off A 396.*

The southern gateway to Exmoor National Park, Dulverton sits amid beautiful scenery and boasts a solid church (rebuilt in the 19C) with a 13C west tower and pretty cottages.

Set in a National Nature Reserve, **Tarr Steps★★**, the finest **clapper bridge** *(T see Dartmoor)* in the country, dating back to the Middle Ages or earlier, crosses the River Barle near Liscombe, 6mi/10km north of Dulverton,.

DUNSTER★★

◯ *16mi north of Duverton, near the coast.*

The beautiful old town of Dunster, right on the northeast edge of Exmoor, enjoyed a flourishing coastal and continental trade until the sea retreated in the 15C–16C, whereupon it became a wool market and weaving centre. It is now a popular tourist destination in sea-

- ⚜ **Michelin Map:** Michelin Atlas pp 6, 7 or Map 503 8 I, J 30.
- 🔲 **Info:** There are several tourist information centres: www.visit-exmoor.co.uk; www.visitsomerset.co.uk.
- ◯ **Location:** On the Bristol Channel coast of Southwest England.
- ⬡ **Don't Miss:** The views from Dunkery Beacon; Dunster Castle; Watersmeet; Tarr Steps.
- ◯ **Timing:** Allow 2–3 days excluding activities. Visitor centres give information on paths, cycle routes, bridleways, guided walks and nature trails.

son. The red sandstone **castle★★** *(NT; castle:* ◯*open mid-Apr–Oct Fri–Wed, daily school hols, 11am–5pm, garden and park:* ◯*open daily 10am–5pm, winter 11am–4pm;* ☜*£8.50 (garden and park only £4.70);* ✆*01643 821 314,* ✆*01643 823 004; www.nationaltrust.org. uk),* dominates the town from the tor on which a fortification has stood since Saxon times. The castle was begun by the Norman baron William de Mohun and in 1867 transformed to its present fortified Jacobean mansion.

Dunster Working Water Mill★ *(NT; Mill Lane;* ◯*open Apr–Oct daily 11am–4.30pm;* ☜*£3.50 inc NT members;* ✗;

Literary Associations

The 14C thatched pub, the **Rising Sun Inn** Lynmouth, is said to have sheltered **R D Blackmore** while he wrote *Lorna Doone*. In 1797 the poets **Wordsworth** and **Coleridge** arrived here, having walked 30mi/48km from Nether Stowey. While staying at Culbone nearby (now called Ash Farm), Coleridge began his poem *Kubla Khan*. In 1812 the disowned young poet **Shelley** came to Lynmouth with his 16-year-old "bride" Harriet Westbrook and attendants. During his stay, Shelley distributed his revolutionary pamphlet, the *Declaration of Rights*: some he sealed inside bottles wrapped in oiled cloth and packed into crates fitted with a sail before being launched from the beach; others he despatched in miniature balloons.

01643 821 759; www.nationaltrust. org.uk) on the River Avill, rebuilt and improved since Domesday, ground corn until the late-19C, came back into use during the Second World War and was rebuilt and restored to working order in 1979–80.

The long, wide **High Street** lined by 17C–19C houses is graced by the unique 1812 octagonal, dormered **Yarn Market**. Many of the buildings along **Church Street** are related to the priory founded in 1090, including the 14C nunnery and Priest's House (restored 19C) and 20ft-/6m-high early medieval **dovecote**★ (beyond the gate in the end wall of the Priory Garden). **St George's Church**★ was originally built by the Normans in the 12C then rebuilt by the monks in the 14C. Its 110ft-/34m-**tower**, dating from 1443, houses a carillon. Inside are **wagon roofs**, a splendid 54ft/16m carved **screen**, a 16C Perpendicular **font** and the **Luttrell tombs**.

WINSFORD★
◗ *8mi/13km N of Dulverton.*

Tucked away in a valley Winsford is often cited as Exmoor's most attractive village and is notable for its series of eight bridges crossing its many small streams in quick succession, the oldest being the **packhorse bridge**, possibly from the 17C.

EXFORD
◗ *Central Exmoor, 10mi northwest of Dulverton.*

On the River Exe, at the very heart of Exmoor National Park, lies Exford with its attractive village green surrounded

by shops, restaurants and hotels. It is a busy walking, fishing and equestrian centre.

Some 6mi/10km north east is **Dunkery Beacon**, at 1,705ft/520m, the highest point on the moor, visible for miles around, with commanding **view**★★★.

MINEHEAD
◗ *19mi north of Dulverton, on the coast.* ◨ *Warren Road.* *01643 702 624. www.minehead.co.uk.*

Lying just outside the northeastern boundary of Exmoor, Minehead is the region's only real "bucket-and-spade" resort, boasting a large sandy beach. It is dominated by Butlins holiday camp, the largest in the UK, and aside from its beach has little to offer. It is the northern terminus of the **West Somerset Railway** (◗*see Mendips and Quantocks*).

LYNTON AND LYNMOUTH★
◨ *Town Hall, Lee Road, Lynton.* *01598 752 755. www.lynton-lynmouth-tourism.co.uk.*

These complementary towns sit in a hollow at the top and at the foot of 500ft/152m North Devon cliffs and enjoy glorious **views**★ across the Bristol Channel to the distant Welsh coast.

Lynmouth, at the foot of the cliffs, remains a traditional fishing village with small stone cottages and houses.

Directly above, Lynton is predominantly Victorian–Edwardian in character.

Linking the two is the unusual (for Britain) small funicular **Cliff Railway** (◷*open early/mid-Feb–early Nov daily 10am–dusk;* ◧*£2 single, £3 return;* *01549 753 486;* &; *www.cliffrail*

waylynton.co.uk), which operates at a gradient of 1:1.75 ascending approx 500ft /152m. There are two cars, each of which has a huge water tank which is filled at the top and emptied at the bottom, thus causing the lower car to be pulled up to Lynton, while the heavier car from the top descends to Lynmouth. The railway was officially opened in 1890 and offers spectacular **views**.

Most visitors make the ascent to visit the **Valley of the Rocks**★ *(1mi/1.6km W of the railway)*, great jagged formations spectacularly carved by the wind rising from a wide grass-covered valley. Housed in Lynton's oldest surviving domestic dwelling, the **Lyn & Exmoor Museum** (◎ *open Easter–Oct Mon–Fri 10am–4pm, Sun 2–4pm;* ◉ *£2; www. devonmuseums.net)* includes the story of the tragic Lynmouth flood of 1952 that killed 34 people.

OARE
◗ *6mi/10km E of Lynmouth.*
This tiny village owes its fame entirely to **Lorna Doone**. The Doone family is said to have lived here and it was in the restored 14C–15C church that Lorna was married to John Ridd. A path leads to **Doone Valley**★ *(6mi/10km)*, made famous by Blackmore's novel, based on tales of a group of outlaws and cut-throats in the 1620s.

PORLOCK★
◗ *11.5mi/18.5km E of Lynmouth.*
🛈 *High Street.* ✆ *01643 843 150.*
This is an attractive much-visited village with old thatched cottages and a good selection of shops, cafés, restaurants and places to stay. It was made famous by "the man from Porlock", who interrupted Coleridge as he was writing *Kubla Khan* (◔ *see Box opposite).* The 13C **St Dubricius Church**★ with its truncated shingle-covered spire is dedicated to a legendary figure who lived until he was 120 and is said to have been a friend of King Arthur. Inside is a remarkable canopied tomb with alabaster effigies.
Motorists should beware that **Porlock Hill**, part of the A39, is the UK's steepest A-road, with a gradient that reaches 1

in 4/25 percent. It can, however' be by-passed by a toll road.

WATERSMEET★
NT. ◗ *1.5mi/2.4km E of Lynmouth.*
◎ *Open: site freely accessible. Tearoom open mid-Mar–Oct daily 10.30am– 4.30pm/5pm). www.nationaltrust.org. uk/watersmeet.*
This very popular beauty spot is where the rivers East Lyn and Hoaroak meet in a deep wooded valley, the riverbed picturesquely strewn with boulders around which the water swirls endlessly. It is worth a visit alone for its charming **Edwardian tearoom and gardens**.

COMBE MARTIN★
◗ *12.8mi west of Lynmouth.*
🛈 *Cross Street.* ✆ *01271 883 319. www.visitcombemartin.com.*
Immediately west of the Exmoor boundary in Devon, the sprawling village of Combe Martin is situated in a beautiful and fertile valley and its two headlands – Great Hangman and Little Hangman – funnel visitors into the village, then down to the pretty, sheltered harbour and beach.
Just outside the village (1mi/1.6km south), set in over 30 acres/12ha of spectacular gardens within the North Devon Area of Outstanding Natural Beauty, is ♣♣**The Wildlife & Dinosaur Adventure Park** (◎ *open school half-term Feb–1st wk Nov daily 10am–5pm, see website for winter opening;* ◉ *£13.50 on the day, £9.50 online min. 7 days ahead; child £11.50/£8.50 online;* ✗; ✆ *01271 882 486; www.devonthemepark.co.uk).* This features lions, sea lions, meerkats, lemurs, birds of prey shows, a tropical house, Earthquake Canyon, Tomb of the Phaor07ahs, NASA Space & Light show and animatronic dinosaurs.
On the same road heading further south (7.5mi/12km south of Combe Martin), also on the Exmoor border, you can find more animals at ♣♣**Exmoor Zoo** (◎ *open year-round daily 10am– 5pm/6pm/dusk;* ◎ *closed 24-26 Dec;* ◉ *£10/£9 in winter, child £7.50/£6.50;* ♿✗; ✆ *01598 763 352; www.exmoorzoo. co.uk)* including cheetahs and leopards.

South Cornish Coast★★★

Immediately west of the bustling historic city of Plymouth (☉see *English Riviera*) the picture-postcard villages and beaches of holidaymakers' Cornwall begin. The relatively sheltered conditions make this a yachtsman's paradise. Inland the climate is benevolent, encouraging some of England's finest gardens.

🚗 DRIVING TOUR

1 PLYMOUTH – MORWENSTOW

❍ *Leave Plymouth on A 38. After Landrake, take the left to St Germans.*

St Germans

In the centre of this delightful old village are a group of Tudor **almshouses** (1583) and a beautiful **church**★ with a carved-stone **Norman arch** at the west front and a **window** by Burne-Jones and William Morris.

❍ *Take the A387 towards Looe. At Polperro you must park at the entrance to the village and take the horse-drawn cart or electric bus to the centre.*

Polperro★

The closely packed cottages and winding alleys of this attractive old fishing village lie at the bottom of the steep road which follows the stream down to the double harbour in the creek.

A converted pilchard factory on the waterfront houses the small **Heritage Museum** (☉*open Mar–Oct daily 10am–6pm;* ∞*£1.75;* ✆*01503 272 423; www.polperro.org/museum.html*), mostly devoted to fishing and smuggling.

❍ *Follow the coast road to Polruan, where a ferry crosses the Fowey Estuary.*

☉ **Michelin Map:** Michelin Atlas pp 2, 3 or Map 503 D to H 32, 33.
☺ **Don't Miss:** The Eden Project; Trewithen Garden; Fowey.
☉ **Timing:** Allow four days.
👪 **Kids:** National Seal Sanctuary; Kynance Cove; Mullion Cove.
🅿 **Parking:** Park on the edge of towns and villages as the streets can be narrow.

Fowey★★

🛈 *5 South Street.* ✆*01726 833 616. www.fowey.co.uk.*

This small town (pronounced "foy"), which dates back to the 11C, and was once one of England's busiest ports, is set on the hillside above a superb natural harbour at the mouth of the River Fowey. Walk out to **Gribbin Head**, from where there are **views**★★ for miles around, and also take a **boat trip** round the harbour and coast, where the cliffs rise dark and sheer from the water, or up river between wooded hillsides.

In town, **Fore Street** is lined with picturesque old houses. The 14C–15C **church of St Nicholas** (on the site of a Norman church dedicated to St Fimbarrus) boasts a tall, pinnacled tower, a two-storey porch in Decorated style, a fine wagon roof and a Norman font.

❍ *Take the road towards St Austell and at the town entrance go right at the roundabout on the A391, then follow the signs to the Eden Project.*

Eden Project★★★

Bodelva. ☉*Open daily 9.30am–6pm; peak times until 8pm/9pm, late Oct– 23 Dec until 3pm. Last entry 90 mins before closing.* ☉*Closed 24–25 Dec.* ∞*£20 walk in, online discount up to 15 percent.* ♿🅿✕. ✆*01726 811 911. www.edenproject.com.*

As one of the Landmark Millennium Projects in the UK, an abandoned china-clay pit (197ft/60m deep) was converted

into an extraordinary gigantic botanical "green theme park" project. Happily, and unusually for such schemes, it has been both critically acclaimed and a huge commercial success. Here the plant world, the conservation of natural habitats and indigenous species and man's dependence on plants for food and medicine can be studied by visitors in the context of global biodiversity. The star features are the two **biomes**, vast multi-faceted glasshouses, the larger of the two measuring 200ft /60m high with a 329ft/100m span. The smaller biome (around half this size) recreates the climate of the Mediterranean, South Africa and southwestern USA; the larger is devoted to the tropics. The latest addition to this stunning architectural ensemble is **The Core**, which takes its inspiration from the tree, incorporating a central trunk and canopy roof that shades the ground and harvests the sun. The design is based on the Fibonacci code, nature's fundamental growth blueprint.

▶ *Return to St Austell, take the A 390, then almost immediately turn left onto the B 3273.*

Mevagissey★★

This picturesque old fishing village, with its old quayside boathouses and sail lofts, maze of twisting backstreets and nets of all shapes and colours drying on walls, attracts crowds of visitors all summer. It boasts an unusual double harbour with a 1770s pier.

Coastal Paths

Remoteness and wildness are the charms of the Cornwall peninsula with its long rugged coastline. The Cornwall Coast Path – part of the larger Southwest Coast Path – winds a sinuous course (268mi/431km) above the sheer cliffs and indented coves and is the ideal way to discover the scenic splendours of the peninsula. The footpath is clearly waymarked and there is a wide choice of inland paths as shortcuts.

▶ *Follow the St Ewe road for 1mi/1.6km.*

Lost Gardens of Heligan★

Pentewan. ⏱*Open daily 10am–6pm (5pm Oct–Mar). Last entry 90 mins before closing.* ⬤£10. ♿🅿✕. ☏*01726 845 100. www.heligan.com.*
These 57acre/23ha gardens, originally laid out in the 18C by Thomas Gray but left to grow wild by the 20C, have been painstakingly recovered from dereliction since 1991. They include Flora's Garden (rhododendrons), a walled vegetable garden, fruit orchards, "The Jungle" (exotic trees planted in the 19C) and "The Lost Valley" (indigenous species and a water-meadow).

Roseland Peninsula

Veryan★ – This village's unique charm comes from four curious little white-

Mevagissey Harbour

E. Zane/MICHELIN

walled **round houses** with Gothic windows and conical thatched roofs, surmounted by a cross.

St Just-in-Roseland★★ – The **church** here, built on a 6C Celtic site in the 13C and restored in the 19C, has a remarkable setting in an enchanting churchyard garden. It stands so close to the creek and little harbour that at high tide it is reflected in the water.

St Mawes Castle★ – In 1539–43 Henry VIII constructed this cloverleaf-shaped **castle**★ *(EH; ⏱open Jul–Aug Sun–Fri 10am–6pm, Apr–Jun and Sept Sun–Fri 10am–5pm, Oct 10am–4pm, Nov–late Mar see website; ⏱closed 1 Jan, 24–26 Dec; ⊜£4.30; ☎01326 270 52; www.english-heritage.org.uk),* with motte and bailey, as a pair with Pendennis Castle (on the opposite bank of the River Fal) to safeguard the 1mi/1.6km entrance to the estuary. Situated in lovely gardens, it affords excellent **views**★ right out to Manacle Point (10mi/16km).

▷ *Take the B 289 towards Truro and the ferry across the broad waterway of the Carrick Roads.*

Trelissick Garden★★

NT. ▷Feock. ⏱Open mid-Feb–late Oct daily 10.30am–5.30pm. Rest of year daily 11am–4pm. ⏱Closed 1 Jan, 24–26 Dec. ⊜£7. ♿✗. ☎01872 862 090. www.nationaltrust.org.uk.
From the gardens beyond the Classical, porticoed house (built 1750, remodelled 1825), there are superb **views**★★ over the park, Falmouth and out to sea.
The woodland dropping down to the river has a variety of trees, shrubs, exotics and perennials. Spacious areas of lawn feature hydrangeas (over 130 varieties), azaleas and rhododendrons. The Cornish Apple Orchard has been created to preserve traditional varieties.

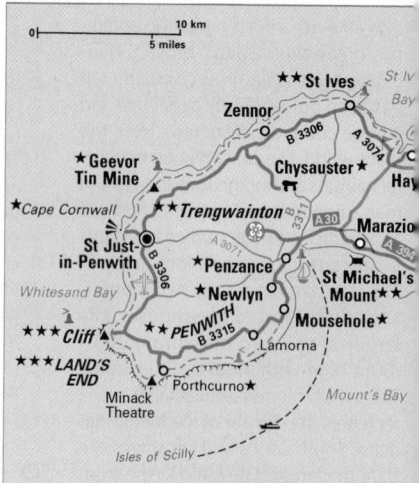

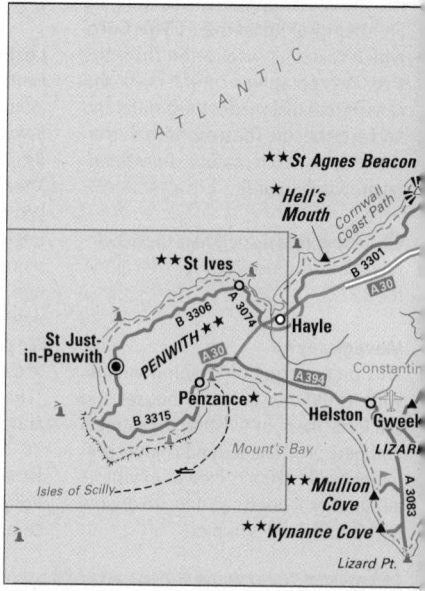

▷ *Turn right onto the A 390.*

Truro

🛈 *Boscawen Street. ☎01872 274 555. http://tourism.truro.gov.uk.*
Once a river port and mining centre, Truro is the finest Georgian town west of Bath, with a host of 18C houses. Just south of St Clement Street is **Truro Cathedral** *(⏱open year-round Mon–Sat 7.30am–6pm, Sun 9am–7pm.Bank hols 9.30am–6pm; ⊜£5 suggested*

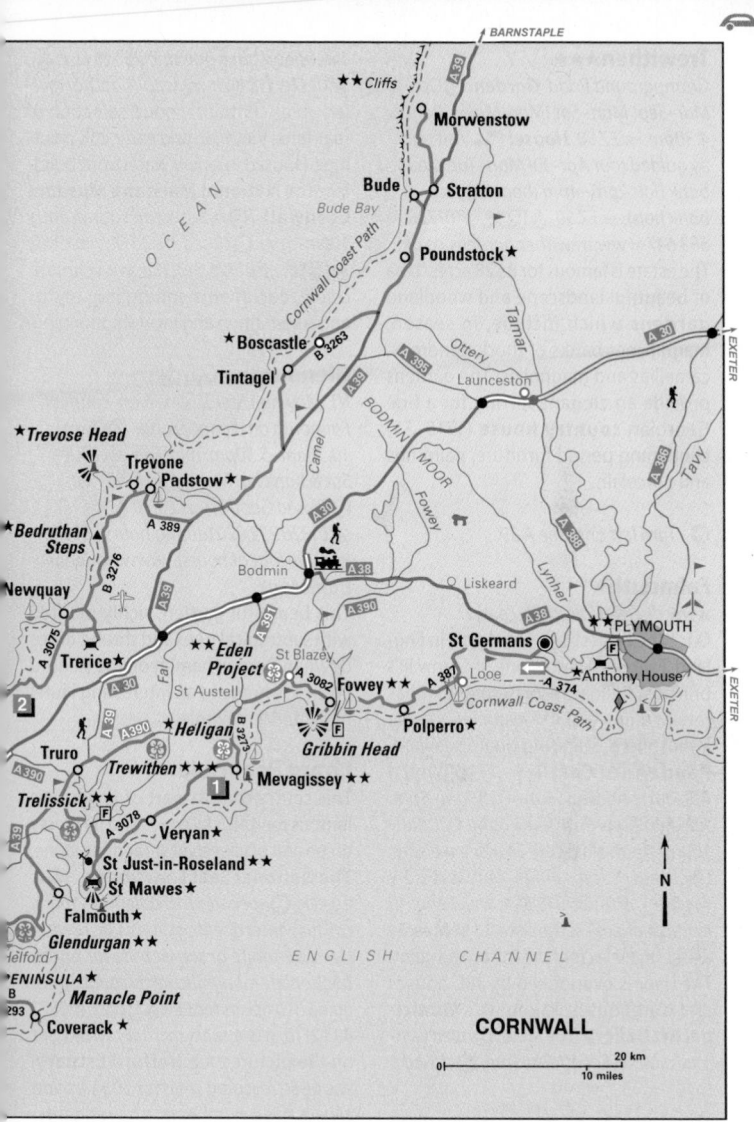

CORNWALL

20 km

10 miles

donation; Guided tours Apr–Oct Mon–Thu and Sat 11am, Fri noon, Aug Mon–Fri 2pm; ; 01872 276 782; www.trurocathedral.org.uk).
Completed 1910, this Gothic Revival building features upswept vaulting, vistas through tall arcades and, outside, three steeple towers which give the building its characteristic outline. A short walk west, via Boscawen Street, is the **Royal Cornwall Museum**★★ *(River Street; open year-round Tue–*

Sat 10am–4.45pm; ; 01872 272 205; www.royalcornwallmuseum.org.uk). Cornwall's oldest and most prestigious museum is the repository for a variety of artefacts relating to the geology, archaeology and social history of Cornwall as well as a collection of fine and decorative arts.

▶ *Rejoin the A 390; E for 6mi/10km.*

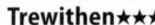

Trewithen★★★

Grampground Road. Garden: ⏱*Open Mar–Sept Mon–Sat (Mar–May), 10am–4.30pm.* ⬦*£7.50. House:* 🚶*Visit only by guided tour Apr–Jul Mon–Tue & Aug bank hols 2pm–4pm (booking recc. bank hols).* ⬦*£7.50.* ♿🅿✕. *℘01726 883 647, www.trewithengardens.co.uk.* The estate is famous for its 28 acres/11ha of beautiful landscape and woodland **gardens** which include, in season, magnificent banks of rhododendrons, camellias and magnolias. The gardens provide an elegant setting for a fine Georgian **country house** (1715–55) containing period furniture, paintings and porcelain.

▶ *Turn left onto the A 39.*

Falmouth★

www.discoverfalmouth.co.uk.
Once the busiest provincial port in England, Falmouth is now one of Cornwall's principal holiday resorts, though it has retained much of its unspoiled marine atmosphere. Standing guard seaward, **Pendennis Castle**★ (*EH;* ⏱ *open Apr–Jun and Sept Sun–Fri 10am–5pm, Jul–Aug Sun–Fri 10am–6pm; Oct daily 10am–4pm, Nov–late Mar see website;* ⏱ *closed 1 Jan, 24–26 Dec;* ⬦*£6.30;* ♿🅿✕; *℘01326 316 594; www.english heritage.org.uk),* is the sister to **St Mawes** (🍃*see above*) across the Fal, on the point. The river is overlooked by 18C houses and warehouses. Falmouth's **Municipal Art Gallery** (*The Moor;* ⏱*open year-round Mon–Sat 10am–5pm;* ⏱*closed 1*

Jan, winter bank hols and 25–26 Dec; ♿; *℘01326 313 863; www.falmouthartgallery.com),* contains a good selection of maritime, Victorian and early-20C paintings. Housed in a new waterfront building, the **National Maritime Museum Cornwall** (⏱ *open year-round daily 10am–5pm;* ⏱*closed 25–26 Dec;* ⬦*£9.50;* ♿🅿✕; *℘01326 313 388; www.nmmc.co.uk),* documents smuggling, myths and superstition and local shipbuilding.

Glendurgan Garden★★

NT. Mawnan Smith. 4mi/6km) south of Falmouth on a minor road. ⏱*Open 10.30am–5.30pm: mid-Feb–Oct Tue–Sat & bank hol Mons; Aug Mon–Sat* ⏱*Closed Good Fri.* ⬦*£6.30* ♿✕. *℘01326 252 020 (during hours), 01872 862 090 (out of hours). www.national-trust.org.uk.*
This beautiful garden, richly planted with subtropical trees and shrubs, drops down to Durgan hamlet on the Helford River. It is home to an interesting laurel maze and a maypole.

Lizard Peninsula★

This southernmost part of England is famous for its rocky coves and its glossy green and black-velvet serpentine stone. **The National Seal Sanctuary**★ (👥; *Gweek;* ⏱*open summer daily from 10am, call for winter opening times;* ⏱*closed 25 Dec;* ⬦*enquire or see website for prices, book online for significant discounts, price guide two tickets for £15;* ♿🅿 ✕; *℘0871 423 2110; www.sealsanctuary.co.uk),* set on the picturesque **Helford Estuary**, has been rescuing seals for 50 years and always has a number of cute residents. On the south side of the estuary is the **Manacles** (an underwater reef responsible for many a shipwreck); the famous old fishing and smuggling village of **Coverack**★; **Landewednack**★ with its thatched roofs and **church**★ decorated with serpentine stone; the Lizard and its 1751 lighthouse (altered in 1903) on the southernmost tip of England; and the popular picture-postcard **beaches** of 👥**Kynance Cove**★★ and 👥**Mullion Cove**★★. **Helston** is the peninsulas market town.

Dancing Furries

On 8 May (or the previous Saturday if this falls on a Sunday or Monday), Helston town is closed to traffic for the famous **Flora Day Furry Dance**★★. Five processional dances are performed along a 1.8–2.4mi/3–4km route (beginning and ending at the Guildhall), including the children's procession at 10am and the Invitation Dance for couples at noon.

North Cornish Coast★★★

This is probably the most dramatic stretch of the Cornish peninsula, in places harsh and forbidding, formerly feared by mariners for its wrecking potential. Yet it is also home to beautiful golden sand beaches, the most popular of which are at **Newquay**, Britain's premier surf resort.

🚗 DRIVING TOUR

② MORWENSTOW TO ST AGNES BEACON

▷ *North–south on the A 39 and coastal B roads.*

Morwenstow
Cornwall's northernmost parish boasts a fine **church**★ with a Norman door and spectacular **cliffs**★★ (450ft/137m high) reaching out to offshore rocks.

Bude
This cliffside harbour town is a popular resort with golden sandy beaches and breakers ideal for surfing. The **breakwater**★★ has a good sea view.

- ⚅ **Michelin Map:** Michelin Atlas pp 2, 3 or Map 503 D to H 32, 33.
- ⊚ **Don't Miss:** Tate St Ives; Land's End cliff scenery; Minack Open-Air Theatre; St Michael's Mount.
- ⊙ **Timing:** Allow a day in St Ives, at least two days for excursions.
- 👥 **Kids:** Newquay Zoo; the Southwest's sand beaches, Land's End; Geevor Tin Mine.
- 🄿 **Parking:** Park on the edge of towns and villages as the streets can be narrow.

Poundstock★
The 13C–15C **church**★, with its square unbuttressed tower and square 14C font, the lychgate and the unique, sturdily built 14C **guildhouse**★ form a secluded group in a wooded dell.

Boscastle★
Off the B 3263. 🄸*The Harbour.* ☎*01840 250 010. www.visitboscastle andtintagel.com.*
The pretty village straggles downhill to a picturesque natural harbour inlet between 300ft/91m headlands.

View of the coast from Tintagel Castle

© Geoff Pickering/Bigstockphoto.com

Tintagel

17mi/27km SW of Bude.
▌Bossiney Road. ℘01840 779 084.
www.visitboscastleandtintagel.com.

Tintagel in particular and the West Country in general are associated with the elusive legend of **Arthur**, "the once and future king". The story lives on, perpetuated by tourism and the New Age movement.

Tintagel Castle *(EH; ◔open daily late Mar–Sept 10am–6pm, Oct 10am–5pm, Nov–Mar 10am–4pm; ◔closed 1 Jan, 24–26 Dec; ✏£5.50; ✕; ℘01840 770 328; www.english-heritage.org.uk)* occupies a dramatic **site**★★★, which overlooks the sea from precipitous rocks. The site is more impressive than the fragmentary castle ruin, which includes walls from the 1145 chapel and great hall, built on the site of a 6C Celtic monastery, and other walls dating from the 13C – all centuries after Arthur's time.

On Fore Street, which leads from the B 3263 to the castle, is the **Old Post Office**★ *(NT; ◔open daily: Apr–Sept 10.30am–5.30pm; mid-Feb–Apr and Oct–early Nov 11am–4pm; ✏£3.80; ℘0840 770 024; www.nationaltrust. org.uk)* a small manor house with thick walls and undulating slate roofs dating from the 14C.

The atmospheric, compact house has simple country furniture and a delightful cottage garden.

Padstow★

The harbour is enclosed by quays lined with attractive old houses. A network of narrow streets behind the quay ends at **St Petroc's Church** and **Prideaux Place**★ *(◔open Easter week and mid-May–early Oct, Sun–Thu 1.30pm–4pm (last tour); grounds open Sun–Thu 12.30pm–5pm; ✏£7.50, grounds only £2; ℘01841 532 411; www.prideauxplace. co.uk)*, an Elizabethan house with 18C battlements, set in gardens and land-scaped parkland.

In recent years Padstow has become something of a shrine to lovers of **seafood**, thanks to chef, restaurateur and television presenter **Rick Stein**. He first opened a seafood restaurant here in 1974 and now operates four restaurants, three shops and a cookery school.

Trevone

The **Cornwall Coast Path**★★ *(5mi/8km on foot)* is a spectacular way of reaching Trevone from Padstow, circling the 242ft/74m Stepper Point and passing the natural rock arches of Porthmissen Bridge. The village and chapel (with a slate spire) stand in a small, sandy cove guarded by fierce offshore rocks. A large blowhole leading directly down to the sea can be found in one of the cliffs.

Trevose Head★

6mi/10km W on the B 3276 and by-roads; last 0.5mi/0.8km on foot.

From the lighthouse on the 243ft/74m head, it is possible to see that of Hartland Point, 40mi/64km northeast, and that of Pendeen on West Penwith. The **views**★★ take in bay after sandy cove after rocky island.

Bedruthan Steps★

NT. ◔cliff staircase open Mar–Oct. ✕.

A much-photographed long arc of sand (1mi/1.5km), spectacularly scattered with giant rocks worn to the same angle by waves and wind, is visible over the cliff edge. Legend has it that the rocks were the stepping stones of the giant Bedruthan.

Newquay

This popular, sometimes rowdy resort, with its sandy beaches, lies at the foot of cliffs in a sheltered, north-facing bay.

By the 18C Newquay was a pilchard port, exporting salted fish to Italy and Spain. The **Huar's House** on the headland, from which the huar summoned the fishermen when he saw shoals of fish enter the bay, dates from this period. Newquay has recently enjoyed a surfing-led revival and hosts world-class competitions.

In Trenance Gardens in the centre of Newquay, east of Edgcumbe Avenue, is **Newquay Zoo**★ *(▲▲; ◔open daily Apr–Sept 9.30am–6pm, Oct 10am–5pm; ✏£9.95, child £7.45; ♿P; ℘0844 474 2244; www.newquayzoo.co.uk)*. This is one of the UK's best medium-sized wildlife parks, at the forefront of conservation, education and innovative enclosure design. Set in beautiful gardens, it specialises in breeding many endangered smaller species.

Trerice★

NT. Kestle Mill. ◐Open early Mar–early Nov daily 11am (garden 10.30am)–5pm. ✆£7. ♿♨❌. ℘01637 875 404. www.nationaltrust.org.uk/trerice.

This small, silver-grey stone Elizabethan **manor house** was rebuilt 1572–73. The east front has a highly ornate exterior and interior notable for the quality of its 16C **plasterwork** and fine furniture.

St Agnes Beacon★★

The beacon, at 628ft/191m, affords a **panorama**★★ from Trevose Head to St Michael's Mount, with the typical north Cornish landscape, windswept and speared by old mine stacks.

Penwith★★

Penwith is the most westerly headland in England, famous for Land's End with its spectacular cliffs and coastal scenery staring out to America. Much of the area is a semi-bare plateau standing around 430ft/130m above sea level. This sparsely populated region has its own bleak beauty deriving from its granite foundation, the wind, the blue of the ocean and its small granite churches and Celtic wayside crosses. The principal settlements of this largely rural district are Penzance and Newlyn, both continuing the age-old Cornish fishing tradition, and St Ives, one of the West Country's favourite resorts. Leave the coast road for clifftop views and to enjoy Penwith's many beautiful golden sandy beaches.

 **DRIVING TOUR**

Penwith Coast (◐map p 262)

St Michael's Mount★★

NT. Causeway from Marazion. Access at high tide by ferry; at low water on foot across the sands and causeway. Castle: ◐open late Mar–Oct Mon–Fri & Sun 10.30am–5pm, Jul & Aug 5.30pm. Winter (subject to weather conditions) Tue and Fri, entry by guided tour only, 11am, 2pm, call ahead. Garden: ◐open

> ☺ **Don't Miss:** Land's End and St Michael's Mount views.
> ◐ **Timing:** Allow two days.

May–Jun Mon–Fri 10am–5.30pm. Jul–Oct open Thu–Fri only. ✆£7 castle £8.75 inc garden. ♿♨. ℘01736 710 507; 01736 710 265. www.stmichaelsmount. co.uk. www.nationaltrust.org.uk.
According to Cornish legend, in AD 495 fishermen saw the archangel Michael on the granite rock rising out of the sea. The island became a place of pilgrimage and a Celtic monastery is said to have stood on the rock from the 8C to the 11C. In c.1150 Abbot Bernard of Mont-St-Michel, off the coast of Normandy, built a Benedictine monastery here. It was appropriated by the crown in 1425 and dissolved in 1539. The rock frequently served as a strongpoint from the Middle Ages to 1647, when its last military commander, Colonel John St Aubyn, bought the **castle** as a family residence. It is now a hybrid of 14C–19C styles, with a Tudor doorway bearing the St Aubyn arms, a 14C entrance hall, a restored 14C church with 15C windows, and an 18C Rococo-Gothic drawing room.

Trengwainton Garden★★

NT. 2mi/3km NW of Penzance. ◐Open early Feb–Oct Sun–Thu and Good Fri, 10.30am–5pm. ✆£5.90. ♿♨❌. ℘01736 363 148. www.nationaltrust.org.uk.

The garden's splendid rhododendron and azalea collection stems from the late-1920s when specimens were brought back from Burma, Assam and China. From here is a **view**★★ of Mount's Bay. A series of walled gardens contains magnolias and other flowering trees.

Penzance★

 www.visit-westcornwall.com.
This busy market town, built largely post-1800, has been a popular holiday resort for over 150 years (since the arrival of the Great Western Railway). The 0.5mi-/0.8km-long **Western Promenade** reflects 19C Penzance's importance as a resort. The harbour area has a wonderful **outlook**★★★ over Mount's Bay and St Michael's Mount. It is from here that the *MV* **Scillonian III** sails to the **Isles of Scilly**.

The town centre, particularly **Market Jew Street** and **Chapel Street**★, boasts some attractive 17C, 18C and 19C buildings including Market House, the surprising Egyptian House (1835), Abbey House and The Admiral Benbow. Close by, the **Penlee House Gallery and Museum**★ *(Morrab Road; open Good Fri–Sept Mon–Sat 10am–5pm, Oct–Good Fri 10.30am–4.30pm; £4.50, Sat free;   ; 01736 363 625; www.penleehouse.org.uk)* is a centre of art and heritage for West Cornwall including a fine collection of art from 1750 to the present with works by the Newlyn school. Modern and contemporary works of art can be found in the **Exchange Gallery** *(Princes Street; entry details as Newlyn Art Gallery, see below;   ; 01736 363 715).*

Newlyn★

Newlyn is the major fishing village in the Southwest with a large fleet that brings in mackerel, whitefish, lobster, crab and – its signature fish – pilchards (large sardines), now also called Cornish sardines. The beautiful light and the charm of the cottages clustered round the harbour and on the hillside attracted a group of painters who founded the famous **Newlyn school** in the 1880s. Their works are on display

in the **Newlyn Art Gallery** *(open Easter–Oct Mon–Sat 10am–5pm, bank hols 11am–4pm, Nov–Easter Tue–Sat 10am–5pm; closed 1 Jan, 25–26 Dec, ; 01736 363 715; www.newlyn artgallery.co.uk).*

Mousehole★

Mousehole ("Mowzel") is an attractive little village. Its **harbour** is protected by a quay of Lamorna granite and a **breakwater** dating from 1393. Set back from the low granite fishermen's cottages at the water's edge is the half-timbered Keigwin Arms, the only house left standing after a Spanish raid in 1595.

Porthcurno★

This idyllic sheltered cove is famous for the **Minack Open-Air Theatre**★ *(performances May–late Sept, Mon–Fri at 8pm; also Wed and Fri at 2pm. £8/£9.50;   01736 810 181. www.minack. com),* founded in 1929 with its stunning ocean backdrop and views over Lamorna. The theatre's fascinating history is recounted in the **visitor centre** *(open Apr–Oct 9.30am/10am–5pm/5.30pm; Nov–mid-Mar, 10am–4pm; closed Wed and Fri afternoons during theatre season May–late Sept; £4;   ; 01736 810 181; www.minack. com)* which gives access to the theatre; *(plays £8.50).*

Land's End

The attraction of Land's End is less its physical beauty (and much less its visitor attractions) than its position at the western most point of England, overlooking **cliff scenery**★★★ perpetually assailed by the surging swell of the Atlantic. For a peaceful view, come early and walk along the coastal path, or come at sunset and wait for the beams from the lighthouses to add a magical touch. Ramblers and walkers can approach along the Cornwall Coastal Path.

The tip of Land's End is occupied by a mini theme park, also known as **Land's End** *(site: open daily 10am–dusk; attractions: open Easter–Oct 10am–4pm/5pm, later at peak times, Nov–Easter 10.30am–3.30pm; late open-*

© David Noble/Pictures Colour Library

St Michael's Mount

ing every Tue and Thu Aug for 'Magic in the Skies' Fireworks; ⏲ *closed 2 Jan– 1 Feb, 24–25 Dec;* 🎫*inclusive ticket £10, child £7, or pay per attraction £3–£4, child £2–£3;* ♿ 🅿 *(£4)* ✕; 📞*0870 4580 044; www.landsend-landmark.co.uk).* This comprises two **4-D films**, the **Air Sea Rescue** motion theatre experience, the **End to End Story** (🎫free), devoted to the select band who have completed the length of Britain from Land's End to John O'Groats, and the child-friendly **Greeb Farm** collection of small animals.

St Just-in-Penwith

The prosperity enjoyed by this 19C mining town is reflected in the substantial buildings lining the triangular square, the fine terraces of cottages and the large Methodist chapel. The **church**★ features a 15C pinnacled tower, dressed granite walls, an elaborate 16C porch, wall paintings and a 5C tomb in the north aisle.

About 1mi/1.6km west, the hillock of **Cape Cornwall**★ rises 230ft/70m, giving **views**★★ of Brisons Rocks, Land's End and the Longships Lighthouse. Just before reaching Land's End, the road passes through the little village of Sennen, home to the most westerly church in England (walk down to **Sennen Cove**★, 20 minute there and back,

for a good **view**★ of Whitesand Bay, Brisons Rocks and Cape Cornwall).

👥 Geevor Tin Mine★

Near Pendeen lighthouse. Pendeen. ⏲*Open Apr–Oct Sun–Fri 9am–5pm. Nov–Mar 9am–4pm.* ⏲*Closed 1 Jan, Christmas week.* 🎫*£9.75, child £5.* 🅿✕. 📞*01736 788 662. www.geevor.com.*

Until its closure in 1990 Geevor was a working tin mine, with almost 300 years of history. The miners searched for tin not only deep underground but also in shafts which went far below the sea. Today it is the largest preserved mining site in the UK with many surface buildings open to the public and a guided underground tour through 18C and 19C workings, often with former employees who worked the mine. It also features a museum, which explains how tin was extracted and processed, as well as a mineral gallery.

Chysauster Ancient Village★

EH. ⏲*Open Apr–Oct daily 10am– 5pm (6pm Jul–Aug, 4pm Oct).* 🎫*£3.40.* 🅿. 📞*07831 757 934. www.english-heritage.org.uk.*

This well-preserved prehistoric Cornish village was inhabited c.100 BC–AD 250. It consists of at least eight circular stone houses, which would originally have been roofed with turf or thatch, in two lines of four just below the crest of the hill.

Zennor

The outdoor **Wayside Folk Museum** (①*open Apr–Oct Sun–Fri 11am–5pm, also Sat during summer school and bank hols.* ☜*£3.25;* 🅿️; ✆*01736 796 945*), set in an old miller's house, shows the evolution of implements from stone to iron. The 12C–13C granite **church**★, on a 6C site, was enlarged in the 15C and restored in the 19C. Inside are a tithe measure, now serving as a holy water stoup, two fonts of Hayle limestone and, on a bench-end, the 16C carving of the pretty **Mermaid of Zennor**.

ST IVES★★

▶ *17mi/27km NE of Land's End.*
🄸 *www.visit-westcornwall.com.*
This picturesque fishing harbour on the North Cornish coast is a much-visited summer resort and has been a favourite with artists since the 1880s when Whistler and Sickert followed Turner.

Today its network of stepped winding alleys and hillside terraces, lined by shoulder-to-shoulder colour-washed fishermen's houses, is still home to an artists' community.

Tate St Ives★★

Porthmeor Beach. ①*Open Mar–Oct daily 10am–5.20pm. Nov–Feb Tue–Sun 10am–4.20pm. Last Fri of month. Free entry to the galleries 6pm–9pm. Music, food and bar in the café until 10pm.* ①*Closed 24–26 Dec.* ☜*£6.25, joint entry to Barbara Hepworth Museum £9.75.* ♿☒. ✆*01736 796 226. www.tate.org.uk/stives.*
This splendid building (1973) enjoys a **view**★★ over the sands of Porthmeor Beach. The asymmetrical gallery consists of swirling forms spiralling upwards while inside, stairways climb through airy space for access to the changing exhibitions of post-war modern works from the London Tate collection. These concentrate particularly on artists associated with St Ives including Alfred Wal-

lis, Ben Nicholson, Barbara Hepworth, John Wells, Terry Frost and Patrick Heron (who designed the stained-glass window on the ground floor). A number of ceramics works by Bernard Leach are also on display.

Barbara Hepworth Museum★★

Barnoon Hill. ①*Entry details as Tate St Ives (©see above). Entry at peak times may be restricted.*
Barbara Hepworth (1903–75) came to St Ives with Ben Nicholson in 1943, decided to settle, and stayed here until her death. The house she lived in, filled with sleek, polished wood and stone abstract **sculptures** spanning a life's work, and workshops with unfinished blocks of stone, left pretty much as they were at the artist's death, contrast with the small white-walled garden, which provides a serene setting for some twenty abstract compositions in bronze and stone.

Parish Church★

The church dates mostly from the 15C and is dedicated to the fishermen-Apostles St Peter and St Andrew, and St Ia, the early missionary who arrived in the area from across the sea on a leaf and after whom the town is named. It stands by the harbour, distinguished by its pinnacled 85ft/26m tower of Zennor granite. Note the **wagon roof**, carved **bench ends** and stone **font**. The **Lady Chapel** contains the tender *Mother and Child* (1953) by Barbara Hepworth.

Smeaton Pier

The pier and its octagonal domed lookout were constructed 1767–70 by the builder of the third Eddystone lighthouse, John Smeaton. At its shore end is the small St Leonard's sailors' chapel.

St Nicholas Chapel

This small ancient chapel, surrounded on three sides by the sea, is also a traditional seamen's chapel, built as a beacon. It commands a wide **view**★★ across the bay.

Isles of Scilly★

Cornwall

This wind-battered archipelago off England's southwesterly tip is designated an Area of Outstanding Natural Beauty, a Heritage Coast, and its waters have been granted Marine Park status. The approach by sea or air gives a partial view★★★ of the 5 inhabited islands, 40 uninhabited islands, and 150 or so named rocks in a close group in the clear blue-green ocean.

▶ **Population:** 2,048.
🜨 **Michelin Map:** Michelin Atlas p 2 or Map 503 A, B
◑ **Location:** 34 – 28mi/45km southwest of Land's End
🛈 **Info:** Hugh Street, St Mary's. ✆01720 424 031. www.simplyscilly.co.uk.

VISIT

St Mary's

3mi/5km across at its widest, with a coastline of 9mi/15km, St Mary's is the largest and principal island on which all but a few hundred Scillonians live. The main settlement is **Hugh Town**, formerly home to the **Garrison**. The mid-18C **Guard Gate** gives access to **Star Castle**★ *(now a hotel, freely accessible to the public)* built in 1594 at the time of Elizabeth I's feud with Spain. From the rampart walls are excellent **views**★★.

Tresco★

On being appointed Lord Proprietor in 1834, Augustus Smith built a Victorian medieval castle mansion near the ruins of a priory. Around these ruins he created the subtropical **Abbey Gardens**★★ *(⊙open daily 10am–4pm; ☜£10; ♿▣✕; ✆01720 424 108; www.tresco.co.uk)*, from seeds and plants brought back by Scillonian sailors and plant collectors. The garden is home to species from 80 countries, ranging from Brazil to New Zealand and Burma to South Africa, and due to the micro-climate, even at the winter equinox more than 300 plants will be in flower. From the terraces, there are fine **views**★★ over the gardens. On the edge of the gardens is **Valhalla**, an extraordinary collection of figureheads.

GETTING THERE

The *Scillonian III* operates a summer boat service from Penzance to St Mary's. Fixed-wing aircraft services operate from Southampton, Bristol, Exeter, Newquay and Land's End (✆0845 710 555; www.islesof scilly-travel.co.uk). Helicopter flights take 20 minutes from Penzance to St Mary's and operate daily in summer with regular flights throughout the day (✆01736 363 871; www.islesofscilly helicopter.com).

Old Town beach, St Mary's

© Sharpshot/Dreamstime.com

ADDRESSES

🛏 STAY

DEVON

Exeter

🛏🛏 **Raffles** – B1. *1 Blackall Road. ℘01392 270 200. www.raffles-exeter.co.uk. 7 rms.* This sympathetically restored Victorian townhouse is furnished with antiques.

🛏🛏 **The White Hart** – B2. *66 South Street. ℘01392 279 897. www.whitehartpubexeter.co.uk. 55 rms.* Historic pub on the way from the Quayside, with recently refurbished rooms; small supplemente for four-posters.

🛏🛏🛏–🛏🛏🛏🛏 **Abode Royal Clarence Hotel** – B1. *Cathedral Yard. ℘01392 319 955. www.abodehotels.co.uk/ exeter. 52 rms.* Behind a Georgian façade and opposite the cathedral, this classy contemporary hotel offers excellent rooms and dining (⌚*see opposite*). Look out for bargain rooms online.

Torquay

🛏 Guesthouses and hotels can be found on King's Drive. Book well ahead for anywhere on the English Riviera in summer.

Dartmouth

🛏🛏🛏–🛏🛏🛏🛏 **The Royal Castle** – *The Quay. ℘01803 833 033. www.royalcastle.co.uk. 25 rms.* Superb location with many of its traditionally furnished bedrooms enjoying river views. Four-poster beds and spa baths available.

North Devon

🛏 **Ilfracombe** is well stocked with B&Bs. Stay in an unusual historic property on **Lundy Island** courtesy of the Landmark Trust *(www.landmarktrust.co.uk)*.

Plymouth

🛏 There are a series of small Victorian hotels and B&Bs behind the Hoe on Citadel Road. **Dartmoor National Park** has a wide selection of both hotels and campsite. You can even camp "wild" on the moor as long as you observe certain park regulations *(www.dartmoor-npa. gov.uk)*.

🛏 **Ashgrove House** – *2. 218 Citadel Road. ℘01752 664 046. www.ashgrovehotel-plymouth.co.uk. 9 rms.* Simple well-kept traditionally furnished Victorian house with a warm welcome, a good location and the right price.

CORNWALL

🛏 For high-quality B&Bs, and self-catering farm and cottage holidays try www.cornishfarmholidays.co.uk.

Polperro

🛏🛏 **Claremont** – *The Coombes. ℘01503 272 241. www.theclaremonthotel.co.uk. 12 rms.* Set on the main street going down to the port, but free of passing traffic noise, this large fisherman's cottage, parts of which date back to the 17C is ideally placed to enjoy Polperro.

Fowey

🛏🛏🛏🛏 **Fowey Hall** – *Hanson Drive. ℘01726 833 866. www.foweyhallhotel. co.uk. 23 rms.* This beautiful historic luxury landmark property occupies a spectacular location overlooking Fowey and the bay. It boasts a splendid spa and gourmet restaurant but is also very family-friendly.

Truro

🛏🛏🛏 **Mannings** – *Lemon Street. ℘01872 270 345. www.manningshotels. co.uk. 26 rms.* In 1876 Prince Albert stayed here but not in the well-equipped, stylish, bright airy contemporary rooms we see today. Smart bar and restaurant.

Falmouth

🛏🛏🛏🛏 **Greenbank** – *Harbourside. ℘01326 312 440. www.greenbank-hotel. co.uk. 57 rms.* The restaurant and many of the contemporary-styled bedrooms here enjoy a magnificent view (small supplement) over the River Fal.

Padstow

🛏🛏🛏 **Cross House** – *Church Street. ℘08717 168 148. www.crosshouse.co.uk. 11 rms.* This charming Georgian house right in the centre of Padstow has a lovely front garden where afternoon teas are served. Traditional Victorian furnishings within.

Penzance

🛏🛏 **Chy-An-Mor** – *15 Regent Terrace. ℘01736 363 441. www.chyanmor.co.uk. Closed Dec–Jan. 10 rms.* This elegant Regency house sits in an elevated position on Penzance's finest street and some of its prettily decorated rooms have sea views.

St Ives

🛏🛏🛏🛏 **The Garrack** – *Burtwallan Lane. ℘01736 796 199. www.garrack.com. 18 rms.* Just five minutes from the centre, overlooking the main beach, but in an elevated country setting with lawns and an indoor pool, this is the perfect St Ives location. Rooms are very stylish and the award-winning restaurant serves Modern British cuisine.

ST MARY'S (SCILLY ISLES)
⊖–⊖⊜ **Evergreen Cottage** – *The Parade, Hugh Town.* ℘*01720 422 711. www.evergreencottageguesthouse.co.uk. 5 rms.* This pretty 300-year-old cottage offers simple rooms, just a few steps away from the port.

ST MARTIN'S (SCILLY ISLES)
⊖⊜⊜⊜ **St Martin's-on-the-Isle** – ℘*01720 422 090. www.stmartinshotel. co.uk. Closed Oct–Mar. 28 rms.* One of the finest hotels in the UK, this superb hotel enjoys an idyllic location above a white-sand beach. Its restaurant Teän (⊜⊜⊜), a former recent holder of a Michelin star, uses local ingredients, including from its own garden, in its Modern British dishes.

ⵎ/ EAT

DEVON

Exeter
⊛On **Quayside**, good places for a snack or lunch include The Riverside Café, in the Antiques Centre and The Prospect Inn, in the **city centre**; try Tea on the Green, beside the Cathedral Green.
⊜⊜ **Brazz** – B2. *10–12 Palace Gate.* ℘*01392 252 525.* Lively modern brasserie with a varied international menu.
⊜⊜ **The Ship Inn** – B1. *6 Martin's Lane.* ℘*01392 272 040.* Historic pub with a restaurant on the first floor.
⊜⊜–⊖⊜⊜⊜ **Michael Caines** – B1 - *Cathedral Yard, via St Martin's Lane.* ℘*01392 319 955. www.michaelcaines.com. Closed Sun evening.* The **Abode Royal Clarence Hotel**'s restaurant is presided over by one of the UK's top chefs, Michael Caines. Contemporary food in a contemporary setting to suit most budgets, from superb-value prix-fixe to lavish tasting menus.

Dartmouth
⊖⊜⊜⊜ **Angelique** – *2 South Embankment.* ℘*01803 839 425. www.thenewangel.co.uk.* Dartmouth's most famous gastronomic address has recently changed hands but has lost none of its quality with a Michelin-starred chef at the helm. Reservations essential. It also includes a stylish coffee bar.

Plymouth
⊜⊜ **Barbican Kitchen** – 2. *Plymouth Gin Distillery, 60 Southside Street.* ℘*01752 604 448. www.barbicankitchen.com.* Top-quality wine bar/brasserie food served up by Plymouth's two young star celebrity chefs – the Tanner Brothers (⚭*see below*) – in the funky atmospheric award-winning setting of a 16C distillery.
⊜⊜⊜⊜ **Tanners** – 2. *The Prysten House, Finewell Street.* ℘*01752 252 001. www.tannersrestaurant.com. Closed Sun–Mon.* The oldest house in town is now home to the city's most innovative contemporary cooking (⚭*see above*).

CORNWALL

Polperro
⊜⊜ **Nelsons** – *The Saxon Bridge.* ℘*01503 272 366. Closed Mon.* This long-established village centre restaurant has the feel of a nautical-themed Victorian pub and serves a wide range of classic local dishes in its upstairs restaurant, and as bar meals.

Padstow
⊜⊜⊜⊜ **Margot's** – *1 Duke Street.* ℘*01841 533 441. http://margotspadstow. blogspot.com. Closed Sun–Mon.* Excellent informal Modern British cooking with an emphasis on fish and vegetarian dishes in a cosy little café setting with just eight tables.
⊜⊜⊜–⊖⊜⊜⊜ **The Seafood Restaurant** – *Riverside.* ℘*01841 532 700. www.rickstein.com.* Probably the most famous seafood restaurant in the country, thanks to its celebrity chef owner (Rick Stein), and undoubtedly also one of its best. Reservations essential.

Penzance
⊜⊜⊜ **Harris's** – *46 New Street.* ℘*01736 364 408. www.harrissrestaurant.co.uk.* This small elegant long-established town centre restaurant serves classic traditional local dishes using the finest and freshest ingredients.

St Ives
⊜⊜–⊖⊜⊜ **Alba** – *Old Lifeboat House, The Wharf.* ℘*01736 797 222. www.thealbarestaurant.com.* Housed in the old lifeboat house on the harbourfront, this smart seafood restaurant is renowned for its contemporary menu produced from local produce. Daily lunch specials.

EAST ANGLIA

In the popular imagination, East Anglia is a flatland, devoid of interest, fringed by a handful of old-fashioned seaside resorts, and chilled even in summer by the winds from Europe. Its climate and soils mean that much of its gently undulating farmland is in arable cultivation supplying much of England's food crop, and as a result fields are large with many trees and hedges removed. However, this aside, England's largest area of low relief is also a region of surprising individuality. Densely populated and wealthy in medieval times, it boasts a rich legacy of ancient villages and small towns. In the early-19C Constable painted it as a rural idyll and pockets of such countryside still remain.

Many visitors make their only regional stop in **Cambridge** and while this is the jewel in the crown a tour of the **Stour Valley** and an excursion to **Bury St Edmunds** are very rewarding. The **Suffolk Coast** has an unspoiled beauty while only geographical isolation prevents the regional capital, **Norwich**, from being nationally renowned.

West of here, great cathedrals arise from **Ely** and **Peterborough** to cast their gaze over the marshy Fenlands, the watery playground of the **Norfolk Broads**, and the **North Norfolk** coast including **King's Lynn** and many fine historic houses.

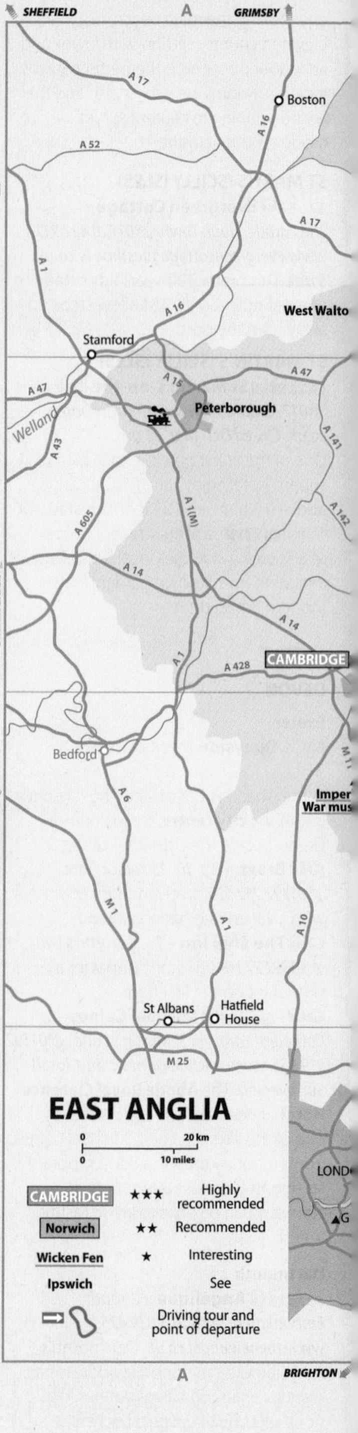

Highlights

1 Take a tour of St John's College, **Cambridge** (p276)
2 Put yourself in the picture in **Constable Country** (p281)
3 Go boating on the **Norfolk Broads** (p288)
4 The **Holkham** estate with its palatial Palladian **Hall** and magnificent **beach** (p289)
5 The magnificent medieval cathedral at **Ely** (p292)

EAST ANGLIA

CAMBRIDGE	★★★	Highly recommended
Norwich	★★	Recommended
Wicken Fen	★	Interesting
Ipswich		See
⟿		Driving tour and point of departure

274

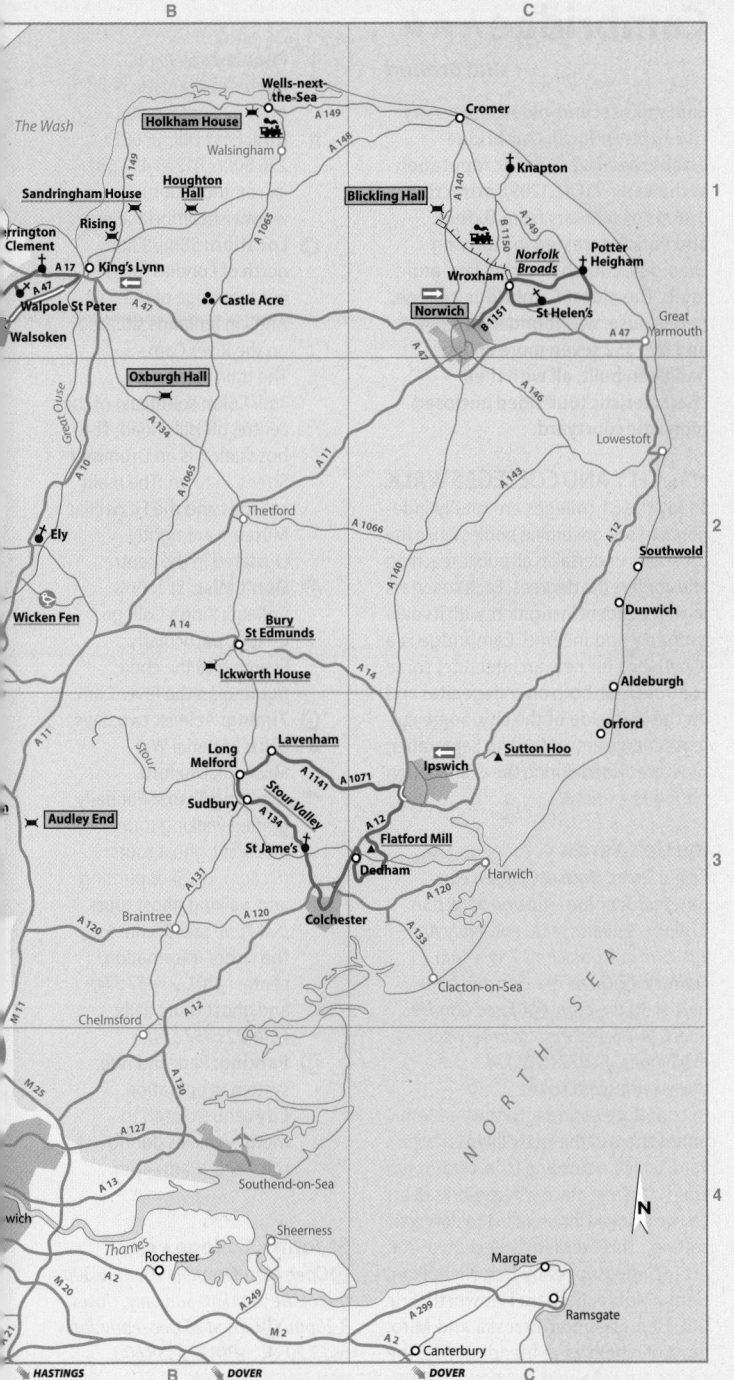

Cambridge★★★
and around

England's second-oldest university city (after Oxford), Cambridge established its academic reputation in the early-13C (c.1209), attracting groups of scholars from Oxford and Paris interested in studying theology, church and civil law, and logic. The oldest Cambridge college, Peterhouse, was founded in 1284 and by 1352 seven more colleges had been built, all with their characteristic four-sided enclosed monastic courtyard.

ꙮ CITY AND COLLEGES WALK

Today the 31 colleges are totally independent self-governing bodies while the university undertakes all public teaching and confers the degrees. Each college is an independent institution, with its own property and income. Cambridge is a showpiece for new architecture, some controversial, both on college sites and on the west side of the city. Some colleges charge entry March to September; most are closed during the examination period May–June.

Kettle's Yard★

Castle Street. **House:** ◷*Open early Apr–mid Sept Tue–Sun and bank hols 1.30pm–4.30pm; mid-Sept–early Apr Tue–Sun and bank hols 2pm–4pm.* **Gallery:** ◷*Open Tue–Sun and bank hols 11.30am–5pm.* ◷*Closed Good Fri, 1 Jan, 24–26, 29 Dec; also in between exhibitions.* ℘*01223 352 124. www.kettlesyard.co.uk.*
In complete contrast to the academic atmosphere of the Fitzwilliam is Kettle's Yard, which, according to its creator Jim Ede, is "a living place where works of art can be enjoyed inherent in the domestic setting". This excellent collection of 20C art includes works by Ben Nicholson, Henry Moore, Barbara Hepworth, Eric Gill, Henri Gaudier-Brzeska and Miró, most of whom were friends of Ede; the pieces are set about the house among the furniture so that visitors may sit to admire the exhibits or read the books.

▶ **Population:** 95,682.
◔ **Michelin Map:** Michelin Atlas p29 or Map 504 U 27.
▯ **Info:** Peas Hill. ℘0871 226 8006; 01223 457 581. (accommodation) www.visitcambridge.org.
▷ **Location:** 58mi/93km north of London on the western edge of the East Anglian fenlands situated on the River Cam. The train station is 1mi/1.6km southeast of the centre, off Hills Road. The bus station is on Drummer Street, in town. The main colleges and the Fitzwilliam Museum are tightly clustered in the centre.
◉ **Don't Miss:** St John's College; King's College Chapel, particularly listening to the choir; punting on the River Cam.
◔ **Timing:** At least two days.
▲▲ **Kids:** Imperial War Museum, Duxford.
ꙮ **Walking Tours:** For daily guided walking tours (☞£8/£9), ghost tours (Fri 6pm; ☞£5) or punting and walking ghost tours (Sat 7pm; ☞£15) contact the visitor information centre (℘01223 457 574) and ghost tours daily (℘01223 457 574).
▯ **Parking:** Park and ride system in operation. City centre closed to motor vehicles during the week 10am–4pm.

St John's College★★★

◷*Open Mar–Oct daily 10am–5.30pm; rest of the year Sat–Sun only, closes 3.30pm.* ◷*Closed 25 Dec–early Jan.* ☞*£3.20.* ◔. ℘*01223 338 600. www.joh.cam.ac.uk.*
St John's (founded 1511) is the second-largest college in Cambridge; its tur-

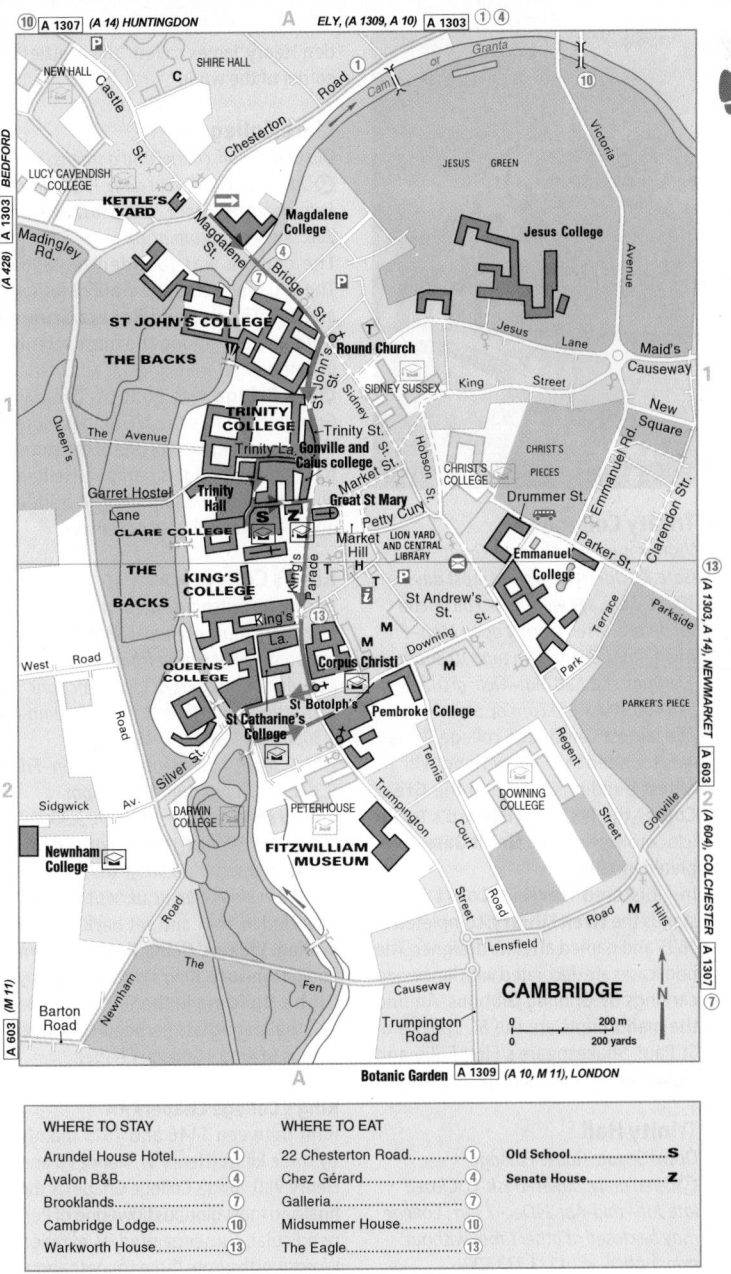

CAMBRIDGE

WHERE TO STAY		WHERE TO EAT	
Arundel House Hotel.............①		22 Chesterton Road..............①	Old School........................**S**
Avalon B&B.........................④		Chez Gérard.........................④	Senate House.....................**Z**
Brooklands.........................⑦		Galleria..............................⑦	
Cambridge Lodge...............⑩		Midsummer House...............⑩	
Warkworth House...............⑬		The Eagle...........................⑬	

reted gatehouse is one of the most beautiful.

First, **Second** and **Third Courts** are predominantly Tudor; Ruskin called the Second the most perfect in Cambridge.

Behind Third Court is the 18C Kitchen Bridge, with its view of Hutchinson's exquisite **Bridge of Sighs**. The 13C **School of Pythagoras** is the oldest medieval stone house in Cambridge.

Bridge of Sighs, St John's College

© Eurasia Press/Photononstop

den Henry James called "the prettiest corner of the world".

Clare College★

Old Court, Hall, chapel and gardens.
⏰*Open usually all year daily 10.30am–5pm.* 🎫*Easter–Sept £2.50.* 📞*01223 333 200. www.clare.cam.ac.uk.*

The college was founded in 1326. The 17C ranges are the work of father and son **Thomas** and **Robert Grumbold** and are among the most serene in Cambridge.

Clare Bridge was built by Thomas Grumbold, before the 17C ranges. Note the missing segment of one of the stone balls on the bridge's parapet. He had vowed never to complete the bridge unless he was paid. He never was.

King's College★★

Entrance: Gatehouse at front (Oct–Mar); north gate of chapel (Mar–Sept); temporary walkway at front of college (Jul–Aug). College: ⏰*Open (functions permitting) term-time Mon–Fri 9.30am–3.30pm, Sat 9.30am–3.15pm, Sun 1.15–2.30pm; out of term-time, Mon–Fri 9.30am–4.30pm, Sun, 10am–5pm. Choral services: Sun 10.30am, 3.30pm. Mon–Sat 5.30pm,* ⏰*Closed Easter term (except chapel).* 🎫*£6.50.* 📞*01223 331 212. www.kings.cam.ac.uk/visitors.*

Founded in 1441 and set back behind **William Wilkins'** Gothic Revival **screen** and **gatehouse**, King's is dominated by **Gibb's Building** in the Classical style and the soaring late Perpendicular buttresses of King's College Chapel.

King's College Chapel★★★

Built between 1446 and 1515 mainly by three kings (Henry VI, Henry VII and Henry VIII), King's College Chapel is the final and most glorious flowering of Perpendicular. Turner painted its exterior, Wordsworth wrote three sonnets about it, and Wren, marvelling at the largest single-span vaulted roof in existence, offered to make one himself, if only someone would tell him where to lay the first stone.

The dimensions (289ft/88m long, 94ft/29m high, 40ft/12m wide) suggest

Trinity College★★

Visitors must enter via the Great Gate. ⏰*Open year-round most days 10am–5pm, see website or call ahead for details. Wren Library open Mon–Fri noon–2pm, Sat in term time 10.30am–12.30pm.* 🎫*£2.80 Mar–Oct.* 📞*01223 338 400. www.trin.cam.ac.uk.*

The largest Cambridge college, Trinity, was founded in 1546 by Henry VIII; its oldest buildings surround the **Great Court** – the 1432 **King Edward's Tower** (clock tower) and the **Great Gate**, completed in 1535.

In cloistered **Nevile's Court** (1612) stands the **Wren Library**, completed in 1695 and named after its designer. The bookcases are decorated with limewood carvings by Grinling Gibbons. Among the manuscripts are the 8C Epistles of St Paul, Shakespeare's First Folio and illuminated 15C French Books of Hours.

Trinity Hall

Down Senate House Passage.
⏰*Open daily, dawn–dusk.* ⏰*Closed late Jun–mid-Apr 24Dec–2 Jan. College may be closed at other times without prior notice.* 📞*01223 332 500. www.trinhall.cam.ac.uk.*

Trinity Hall was founded by Bishop Bateman of Norwich in 1350. Behind the 18C ashlar of **Principal Court** are three ranges (best viewed from North Court) which date from 1350, and beyond the delightful Elizabethan Library is the gara cathedral choir rather than a college chapel; the 18 side chapels and door emphasise the height of the 22 buttresses which take the weight of the roof. The 12-bay nave rises upwards on stonework so slender that it forms a mere frame to the 25 stained-glass windows (16C) illustrating episodes from the Old Testament (above) and from the New Testament (below). The vaulting (nearly 2,000 tons) appears weightless. The architect was **John Wastell**.

Note the splendid early Renaissance **screen** and **stalls** by foreign craftsmen and **Rubens'** Adoration of the Magi. Above the screen is the organ in its 17C case used for services broadcast live on Christmas Eve across the world featuring the famous King's College Choir.

Queens' College★

Visitors' Gate, Queens' Lane. ○*Open year-round most days 10am–4.30pm or 2–4pm, see website for details.* ○*Closed 3rd week May–3rd week Jun (exams).* ◉*£2.50 Nov–Mar free).* ☎*01223 335 511. www.quns.cam.ac.uk.*

Named after the patronage bestowed by two successive queens, Margaret of Anjou, wife of Henry VI, and Elizabeth Woodville, wife of Edward IV, the college was granted its first charter in 1446.

Old Court, completed in 1449, shows late medieval brickwork; in charming **Cloister Court** the half-timbered building is the **President's Lodge**. The Dutch philosopher **Desiderius Erasmus** taught Greek at Queens' but his rooms (Erasmus' Tower) cannot be definitely identified; his name, however, lives on in the brick Erasmus Building (1960) by Basil Spence. Another recent addition is the glass, and, concrete Cripps' Court (1981) by Powell, Moya and Partners. The famous wooden **Mathematical Bridge** over the river is a 20C copy (1904), the second, of the original one (1749) designed by James Essex.

The Backs★★

The "Backs" (of the colleges) along the River Cam are as fine as the fronts; they form a wonderful combination of buildings and lawns in a riverside setting and are best viewed from a punt (on hire at Silver Street Bridge).

Fitzwilliam Museum★★

Trumpington Street. ○*Open year-round Tue–Sat 10am–5pm. Sun and bank hols noon–5pm,* ○*Closed Good Fri, 1 Jan, 24–26, 31 Dec,.* ✦*Guided tour Sat 2.30pm (*◉*£4).* ♿✕. ☎*01223 332 900. www.fitzmuseum.cam.ac.uk.*

Interior of King's College Chapel

© Adrian Zenz/Dreamstime.com

Founded in 1816, the Fitzwilliam Museum houses world-class collections of art and antiquities from Egypt, Sudan, the Ancient Near East, Greece, Rome (look for the marble **Pashley sarcophagus**, AD 130–150), English and European pottery and glass, sculpture, furniture, armour, illuminated manuscripts, Oriental art, Korean ceramics, coins and medals.

The art collection includes 25 watercolours by J M W Turner (donated by John Ruskin) and a selection of some of William Blake's best works in addition to works by Gainsborough, Reynolds, Stubbs and Constable and an outstanding collection of prints by Rembrandt.

The paintings include **Old Masters** of exceptional quality with works by Domenico Veneziano, Leonardo da Vinci, Titian, Rubens and Van Dyck. The collection of French Impressionists includes landscapes by Monet, Seurat and Cézanne as well as studies by Renoir and Degas. Representing the 20C are pieces by Picasso, Nicholson and Sutherland.

Cambridge & County Folk Museum

Castle Street. ○*Open Tue–Sat 10.30am –5pm, Sun & bank hol Mons 2–5pm.* ○*£3.50.* ⌂. ✕. ☏*01223 355 159. www.folkmuseum.org.uk.*

This charming friendly small museum is set in a higgledy-piggledy 17C building which served as the White Horse Inn for 300 years. It now features nine themed rooms (kitchen, bar, Fens and folklore, childhood…), which explore the lives of ordinary Cambridgeshire people as far back as the 1660s, using original memorabilia and exhibits.

EXCURSIONS
▲▲ Imperial War Museum, Duxford★

○*9mi/14km S on the M 11.* ○*Open daily 10am–6pm (4pm late-Oct–mid-Mar).* ○*Closed 24–26 Dec.* ○*£14.95, child free.* ⌂✕. ☏*01223 835 000. http://duxford.iwm.org.uk.*

Duxford is Europe's premier aviation museum as well as having one of the finest collections of tanks, military vehicles and naval exhibits in the country. It began as an airfield in the First World War and also played a vital role in the Second World War. Today its vast hangars, and notably **AirSpace**, its stunning main exhibition space, house dozens of civil and fighter aircraft, several of which, including Concorde, you can climb aboard. To celebrate the Second World War associations of this former Battle of Britain base with the USAAF it is also home to the **American Air Museum in Britain**.

Audley End★★

EH. ○ *13mi/21km S.* ○*Open year-round Wed–Sun. House: Apr–Sept noon–5pm, Oct noon–4pm. Gardens and Service Wing: Apr–Sept 10am–6pm. Oct 10am–5pm. Nov–late Dec 10am–4pm.* ○*£12.50.* ⌂□✕. ☏*01799 522 842; www.english-heritage.org.uk.*

When this estate came into the possession of Thomas Howard, Earl of Suffolk and Lord High Treasurer in the early-17C, it was one of the greatest Jacobean houses in England. "Too large for a king, but might do for a Lord Treasurer" said James I, who unintentionally helped to finance it at a cost of £200,000, and later imprisoned the earl for embezzlement. It was partially demolished in 1721 when the interior was redesigned by **Robert Adam** and the grounds by **Lancelot "Capability" Brown**. The present house, vast enough, is but a shadow of its former glory. The interior is laden with the possessions of the 3rd Baron Braybrooke, who inherited Audley End in 1825, filling it with paintings by Masters such as Holbein and Canaletto. The restored historic **stables**, complete with resident horses and a Victorian groom, includes an exhibition where you can find out about the workers who lived on the estate in the 1880s.

Stour Valley

and Ipswich

The valley of the River Stour is the southernmost part of East Anglia, where Essex, on the fringe of London, meets rural Suffolk. It is best known for its association with John Constable (1776–1837), whose landscapes of this area are among the most popular and valuable in British art. However, while the Lower Stour is **Constable Country**, the Upper Stour is **Gainsborough Country**, named after another great 18C English painter, Thomas Gainsborough (1727–88).

IPSWICH

St Stephen's Church. *℘01473 258 070. www.visit-ipswich.com.*

This bustling county town is mostly Victorian and modern in character. All that remains of the distant past is its Anglo-Saxon street layout and about a dozen medieval churches, some just towers, built when the town was a rich port and trading centre. The **Victorian Wet Dock**, once the largest in the world, with its recently converted warehouses, merchants' houses and maltings, makes an interesting walk.

In the centre of town, within Christchurch Park is **Christchurch Mansion** (*open Tue–Sun 10am–5pm; closed 1 Jan, 24–26, 31 Dec; ℘01473 433 554; www.ipswich.gov.uk*), a much-restored Tudor manor house, set in pleasant parkland and full of treasures from Ipswich and the surrounding countryside. It holds a good collection of paintings by Suffolk-born artists, including works by Thomas Gainsborough and the largest collection of art by John Constable outside London.

Head due south on Northgate Street and take a right onto Buttermarket to see the **Ancient House** (*open Mon–Sat 9am–5.30pm*). The exterior of this 15C house abounds in Restoration plasterwork, pargeting (ornamental plastering) and stucco reliefs of nymphs, pelicans and the four (then-known) continents. The coat of arms is that of Charles II who

- **Michelin Map:** Michelin Atlas p23 or Map 504 X 27.
- **Location:** Ipswich is at the head of the Orwell estuary on the southeast Anglian coast

visited the building in 1668. Now a shop, visitors can view several panelled rooms (c.1603) with wall pargeting – a form of exterior decorative stucco work which is a speciality of Suffolk – ornamental ceilings and 18C ceramic tilework.

🚗 DRIVING TOUR

STOUR VALLEY★

This tour is quite literally a drive through England's artistic heritage.

▷ *Take the A 12 S for 8mi/13km, turn left on the B 1070 and follow signs.*

Flatford Mill★

The mill (1773) at East Bergholt was the home of Constable (his father was the miller) and inspired some of his best-loved landscapes – *The Haywain*, *Boatbuilding* and *Flatford Mill*. It is now home to a field studies centre and there is no entry for individuals though group tours may be arranged (*℘01206 297 110*). Adjacent is the picturesque thatched **Bridge Cottage**, formerly known as Willy Lott's Cottage, (*NT; open May–Sept daily 10.30am–5.30pm, Oct daily 11am–4.30pm, Mar Wed–Sun 11am–4pm, Apr daily 11am–5pm, Nov–Dec Wed–Sun 11am–3.30pm, Jan–Feb Sat–Sun 11am–3.30pm; closed 1 Jan, 25 Dec; (charge); ℘01206 298 260; www.nationaltrust.org.uk*), which has an exhibition on Constable and the valley, plus a lovely riverside tearoom.

▷ *Take the A 12 S (3.7mi/6km) or walk along the riverbank path.*

Dedham

This lovely quintessential English village, its main street lined with timber-framed houses, was often painted by Constable and is still recognisable from his works.

▷ *Return to the A 12 and head S.*

Colchester

Once the capital of all England, Colchester is well worth a visit for its castle and collection of Roman antiquities. Built with 12ft-/4m-thick walls on the vaults of the Roman Temple of Claudius, **Colchester Castle**★ *(Castle Park; ○ open Mon–Sat 10am–5pm, Sun 11am–5pm; ○ closed 1 Jan, 25 Dec; ⊜£6; ⌁ guided tour of castle vaults, roof and chapel daily, additional £2.50; ₲ ✕; ℰ 01206 282 939; www.colchestermuseums.org.uk)* is the largest keep ever built by the Normans (151ft/46m by 110ft/34m), half as big again as the White Tower at the Tower of London. it now houses one of the largest collections in Britain of **Roman antiquities** gathered from one site.

▷ *Take the A 134 N and turn right on the B 1087 to Nayland ,where the 15C parish church contains The Last Supper by Constable. Continue on the B 1087.*

Stoke by Nayland

With its many traditional cottages and timber-framed houses this picturesque village is often cited as the prettiest in the region. The Church of St Mary was a favourite painting subject of Constable.

▷ *Return to the A 134, continue N.*

Sudbury

The regional centre of the Upper Stour Valley, Sudbury is best known as the birthplace of Thomas Gainsborough, the leading English portrait painter of the 18C. His birthplace, **Gainsborough's House**★ *(46 Gainsborough Street; ○ open Mon–Sat 10am–5pm; ⊜£4.50; ℰ 01787 372 958; www.gainsborough.org)* is a medieval building set behind an elegant 18C façade. It houses a large collection of Gainsborough's paintings, drawings and prints. There is also a walled garden with a 400-year-old mulberry tree and used for exhibitions of sculpture during the summer months.

▷ *Take the A 134 N for 3mi/5km.*

Long Melford

The long main street (2mi/3km) is lined with 16C, 17C and 18C timbered and pink-plastered houses. It terminates in a spacious triangular **green**, overlooked by **Trinity Hospital** (1573), **Holy Trinity Church** (late-15C) – one of the great "wool churches" of East Anglia – and **Melford Hall**★ *(NT; ○ open Easter–Sept Wed–Sun and bank hols 1.30–5pm, Apr and Oct Sat–Sun and bank hols 1.30–5pm; ⊜£6. ₲ ▣ ✕. ℰ 01787 376 395. www.nationaltrust.org.uk).*

The house is early Elizabethan, built around three sides of a courtyard, but only the **Main Hall** has preserved its Elizabethan features. The Drawing Room is splendidly Rococo. The West Bedroom contains the original Jemima Puddle-Duck watercolours by **Beatrix Potter**, who was a frequent visitor.

Lavenham★

This is a superbly preserved medieval wool town crowded with timber-framed houses. These are zealously preserved and the town is also renowned for its pargeting *(₲ see above, Ipswich).*

The late-15C **Church of St Peter and St Paul**★ *(○ open year-round 8.30am–5.30pm/3.30pm; ₲,),* is one of the great "wool" churches with a noble tower and porch and enchanting misericords.

The impressive **Guildhall of Corpus Christi** facing the Market Place dates from c.1520. It stages exhibitions and houses a **museum** *(NT; ○ open Easter–Oct daily 11am–5pm, Mar Wed–Sun 11am–4pm, Nov Sat–Sun 11am–4pm; ⊜£4; ₲ ▣ ✕; ℰ 01787 247 646; www.nationaltrust.org.uk)* on the East Anglian wool trade and local history.

Bury St Edmunds★

The historic market town of Bury St Edmunds boasts the ruins of what was once one of the richest abbeys in Christendom, as well as a perfect late Perpendicular cathedral and a wide range of English architectural styles, from secular medieval (**The Guidhall**) to Georgian (**Athenaeum**), and Regency (**Theatre Royal**) to grand Victorian.

▶ **Population:** 31,237.

◔ **Michelin Map:** Michelin Atlas p22 or Map 504 W 27.

▣ **Info:** Angel Hill. ℘01284 764 667. www.visit-bury stedmunds.co.uk.

◖ **Location:** 28mi/45km east of Cambridge. The train station is a 10-minute walk north of the centre; the bus station is central, on St Andrew Street North. Bury's medieval grid layout makes orientation easy. Take a guided walking tour from the tourist office.

◒ **Don't Miss:** The cathedral.

◔ **Timing:** Allow a half-day. Market days are Wednesday and Saturday.

TOWN

On Angel Hill in eastern Bury St Edmunds is the parish church, **St Edmundsbury Cathedral**★(◷*open year-round daily 8.30am–6pm; ⊛suggested donation £3 per adult, 50p per child; ⚊ guided tours Apr–Sept Mon–Sat 11.30am; ⚇; ℘01284 748 726; www.stedscathedral. co.uk*), which dates from 1530 and was originally dedicated to St Denys. It changed its name when it was granted cathedral status in 1914. A composition of nine bays leads the eye to the chancel and transepts (1960) by Stephen Dykes Bower. Note the Flemish stained-glass Susanna window (c.1480) and hammerbeam roof (19C) with angels. Until recently, however, it has remained unfinished. In 2005 the skyline of Bury St Edmunds changed with the completion of the Millennium Tower, a 150ft/46m Gothic **lantern tower**. This and other recent works – the North Transept, the Chapel of the Transfiguration, a crypt and East Cloisters – were all added employing traditional materials and methods. The Chapel of the Transfiguration was consecrated by the Archbishop of Canterbury in June 2009 and in 2010 a colourful painted and gilded vault was unveiled under the tower. Another popular recent addition is the **Edmund Gallery** art and exhibition space.

In the grounds behind the cathedral lie the **Abbey Ruins**★ (◷*open year-round Mon–Sat, 7.30am–30min before dusk, Sun and bank hols 9am–30min before dusk; ℘01284 757 490; www.stedmunds bury.gov.uk*). Founded in 633 and later renamed in honour of the Saxon king and martyr Edmund (d.870), it was rebuilt by Benedictine monks in the 11C. Today only two of its monumental crossing towers still stand upright. Remnants of nave, chancel and transepts, together with the **Abbey Gate**, give some idea of its vastness (505ft/154m long). The **Norman Tower**'s richly decorated gateway frames a bronze of St Edmund by Elisabeth Frink and the cathedral precinct houses, built into the abbey's west end.

Moyse's Hall Museum

Cornhill. ◷Open Mon–Sat 10am–5pm, Sun noon-4pm. ⊛£5. ⚇. ℘01284 757 076. www.moyseshall.org.

A rare and important example of Norman domestic architecture, Moyse's Hall dates from the second half of the 12C. It comprises a medieval gallery, exhibitions on social history, a regimntal gallery and museum, and a permanent exhibition. "Faces of Time", which showcases the museum's very fine horological collection.

Under ornate plasterwork ceilings the collection concentrates on clocks but also includes costumes, textiles, portraits and *objets d'art* bequeathed by local families.

Suffolk Coast★

North of Ipswich is a delightful stretch of unspoiled coastline known in modern times as the Suffolk Heritage Coast, which includes Aldeburgh, home of a famous classical music and arts festival, and fashionable Southwold, a fine, old, unspoiled and uncommercialised genteel resort.

ℹ **Info**: www.visit-suffolk coast.co.uk

ORFORD AND ORFORD NESS

One of the prettiest villages on the Suffolk Heritage Coast, in the Middle Ages Orford was a thriving seaport from where Eleanor of Aquitaine set off to ransom her son King Richard I (the Lionheart). The gradual silting up of the river has left it a quiet village of brick and timber houses. The 12C castle (*⊙open Apr–Sept daily 10am–5pm, Jul–Aug 6pm, Oct Thu–Mon 4pm, winter see website. ⊜£5.60; ℘01394 450 472, www.english-heritage.org.uk/orford*), built by Henry II and the fine medieval church dominate the skyline. The castle looks across the water to the largest spit in Europe (some 10mi/16km long), home to **Orford Ness National Nature Reserve** (*NT; ⊙access by NT ferry only 10am–2pm: Easter–late Jun & Oct Sat only, late Jun–Sept Tue–Sat; ⊜£7.50; ℘01394 450 900 or (infoline)01728 648 024).* This mysterious place, closed to the public for many decades, was formerly administered by the Ministry of Defence, which until 1971 conducted secret military tests here during both world wars and the Cold War. What makes a visit here unique is the fact that the general public can actually access some of these dramatic, once potentially deadly, buildings (albeit they are now empty shells) and get so close to several others.

ALDEBURGH AND AROUND

In the 16C Aldeburgh was a thriving port and shipbuilding area. By Victorian times it had become a seaside resort. Notable town landmarks include the **Moot Hall**, the meeting place of the Town Council for the last 400 years, and the **Church of St Peter and St Paul**, its memorial window designed by John Piper, dedicated to the memory of Benjamin Britten (1913–76). Britten, acclaimed as one of England's finest ever composers, co-founded the Aldeburgh Festival in 1948 (*www.aldeburgh.co.uk*) for which the village is famous. It takes place every June and is centred on the concert hall at nearby Snape Maltings.

DUNWICH

The "Lost City of Dunwich" sparks the imagination of most visitors. It may have possessed as many as 18 churches at the height of its fortune when it was the main port of East Anglia during the 12C and 13C. However, the lost city was swept away in a great storm in 1286 and today continues to be eroded by the sea at the rate of around a metre each year. Nowadays it's a tiny village (*pop. c.120*) with a few fishing boats, a 17C pub, a beach café and Dunwich Museum (*⊙open Mar Sat–Sun 2–4.30pm, Apr–Sept daily 11.30am–4.30pm, Oct daily noon–4pm. ℘01728 648; www.dunwichmuseum.org.uk*) devoted to its fascinating history.

SOUTHWOLD★

Favoured by well-heeled weekenders, Southwold is one of England's most attractive little seaside resorts, retaining vestiges of its maritime history, but embracing none of the crassness of modern-day resorts. It is much loved for its pastel-hued beach huts, its greens, an award-winning pier, a 100ft-/30m-tall lighthouse and its seaside walks. On the attractive, mainly Georgian, High Street, the **Sailors Reading Room** (*⊙open year-round daily 9am-5pm, Apr–Sept 3.30pm*) contains pictures, ship models and other items of seafaring interest. The **Church of St Edmund, King and Martyr** has an imposing flint tower, while the screens, the 15C pulpit, the vast font cover and the richly wrought choir stalls are all notable.

Norwich ★★

and around

In 1066 Norwich was the fourth most populous city in England, and later grew rich as the centre of the East Anglian wool trade. Today it is one of the country's best-preserved medieval cities and the surviving towers and spires of over 30 flint churches, many now redundant, etch the skyline. The city is dominated by the hill-top castle; below is the centre of old Norwich, where cobbled streets, lined with half-timbered houses, lead through stone gateways to the cathedral. It is famous for its Norman cathedral, castle and Sainsbury Centre for Visual Arts (part of the University of East Anglia).

▶ **Population:** 171,304.
Michelin Map: Michelin Atlas p31 or Map 504 Y 26.
Info: Millennium Plain. ℘01603 213 999. www.visitnorwich.co.uk.
▶ **Location:** 62mi/100km northeast of Cambridge. Train station 10 minutes from centre. Buses – Surrey Street Station (10 minutes from centre), or Castle Meadow (central). Tourist buses (t01263 587 005; www.city-sightseeing.com).
Don't Miss: Cathedral; Blickling Hall.
Walking Tours: The tour marked on the map offers a pleasant stroll.

NORWICH CATHEDRAL ★★

Palace Street. ⏲*Open daily 7.30am–6.30pm; Hostry (visitor centre) open Mon–Sat 9.30am–4.30, Sun noon–3pm.* ⟲*Contribution requested.* ⟶*Guided tour Mon–Sat 11am, noon, 1pm, 2pm, 3pm.* ⚒ ℘*01603 218 300. www.cathedral.org.uk.*

The Norman cathedral was begun in 1096 and consecrated in 1278. Its choir clerestory was rebuilt in Early English style in the 14C and Perpendicular vaults added in the 15C and early-16C. The 15C **spire** (315ft/96m) is the second-tallest in England after Salisbury.

Inside, above the steadfast Norman nave and transepts the 400 carved and painted bosses on the vaults portray "a strip cartoon of the whole story of God's involvement with man from creation to last judgement". Note the **misericords** of the choir stalls, the ambulatory, St Luke's Chapel (displaying the famous 14C five-panelled Despenser Reredos) and Jesus Chapel (displaying Martin Schwarz's *Adoration of the Magi* (1480). The **Prior's Door**, leading from the nave to the cloisters, with its sculptured figures of Christ flanked by two angels, two bishops and two monks, is one of the most beautiful doors of the early Decorated style. The unusual two-storeyed cloisters, the largest in England, were rebuilt (c.1297–1430).

CITY CENTRE

⚎ Norwich Castle Museum and Art Gallery ★ (Z)

Castle Meadow. ⏲*Open Mon–Sat 10am–4.30pm, Sun 1–4.30pm (peak season daily 5pm).* ⟲*£6.60. £1 one hour before closing, also noon–1pm weekdays during school term.* ⏲*Closed 1 Jan, 24-27 Dec.* ⚒ ⟶ *Guided tours.* ℘*01603 493 625. www.museums.norfolk.gov.uk.*

The castle was begun in 1160, built on a commanding hilltop. The high-walled stone **keep** has retained many of its original features – Norman arches, windows, chapel niche and the well (110ft/34m deep) and makes for an atmospheric display. Its **battlements** and **dungeons** can also be visited by guided tours (⟲*£2.40 each*).

The art gallery *(ground floor)* displays an outstanding collection of works by the **Norwich school** of painters, greatly influenced by Dutch landscape artists. Also on display are works by 20C **East Anglian** artists – Alfred Munnings, Edward Seago – as well as Victorian and Dutch works.

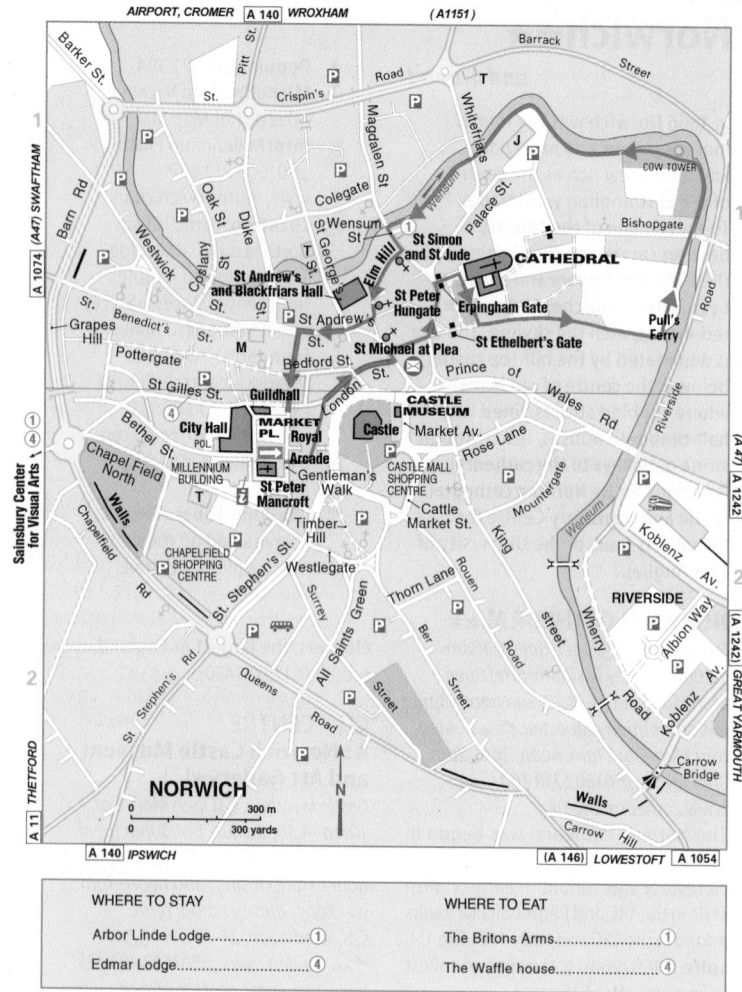

WHERE TO STAY		WHERE TO EAT	
Arbor Linde Lodge	①	The Britons Arms	①
Edmar Lodge	④	The Waffle house	④

History galleries are devoted to **Queen Bouadicea**; **Anglo-Saxon and Viking life** in East Anglia, including a remarkable reconstruction of a grave site, and an Egyptian tomb with mummies. Two new **decorative arts** galleries trace 600 years of style and design in "The Arts of Living", while "Trade and the Exotic" exhibits objects brought back from the east.

Market Place★

The square, which is 900 years old and the largest in East Anglia, is occupied six days a week by market stalls mostly selling local produce. To the north is the chequered flint **Guildhall**, begun in 1407. To the west is the modern **City Hall**, considered by Pevsner to be "probably the foremost English public building of between the wars".

The Forum

2 Millennium Plain, Bethel Street. ⏱*Open year-round daily 7am–midnight.* ♿🅿️✕. ✆*01603 727 920. www.theforumnorwich.co.uk.*
This spectacular new glass building, the landmark Millennium project for the East of England, houses the tourist office. To the south is Norwich's grandest parish church, **St Peter Mancroft**, Perpendicular par excellence, with a fine

hammerbeam roof, a great east window with medieval glass, and a 15C font. To the east is the Art Nouveau **Royal Arcade**, famously home to **Colman's Mustard Shop** (◷ *open normal shop hours;* ℰ*01603 627 889, www.colmansmustardshop.com*) a careful replica of a Victorian trade premises, combining shop and museum, covering all aspects of the history and production of Britain's most famous mustard, which has been made locally since 1823.

Another colourful museum, the **South Asian Decorative Arts & Crafts Collection** (◷*open year-round Mon–Sat 10am–5pm, Sat 5.30pm* ; &; ℰ*01603 663 890, www.southasiandecorativeartsandcrafts. co.uk*) lies on adjacent Bethel Street in an intriguing restored building which was originally a Victorian skating rink, then a vaudeville theatre. It exhibits pictures and prints, architectural items, vernacular furniture and objects which illustrate the everyday arts and crafts of the region.

Elm Hill

This quaint cobbled street, formerly the centre of the weaving industry, is lined with medieval brick and timber houses. At the Tombland end stands the church of **St Simon and St Jude**, now put to commercial use. Farther along sits the thatched 15C restaurant, **Britons Arms** *(right)*, and **Hungate Medieval Art**, an interpretation centre occupying the church of St Peter Hungate, re-built 1460 (◷*open Apr–Sept Mon–Sat, 10am–5pm;* &.). Across the street can be seen the east window of **Blackfriars Hall**, which together with **St Andrew's Hall** once formed the choir and nave of the Convent Church of the Blackfriars. Both halls, with fine hammerbeam roofs, are now used for public, private and civic functions.

Sainsbury Centre for Visual Arts★

University of East Anglia. 3mi/5km W of the city centre. ◷*Open Tue–Sun 10am–5pm.* &✕. ℰ*01603 593 199. www.scva.org.uk.*

This important regional gallery is housed in one of the most exciting buildings of the 1970s, designed by Norman Foster. The 19C and 20C European works by Degas, Seurat, Picasso, Epstein, Bacon, Modigliani, Moore and Giacometti are delightfully juxtaposed with African, Pacific, Oriental and American-Indian art and high-quality artefacts.

EXCURSION
Blickling Hall★★

NT. ➲ *15mi/24km N on the A 140.* ◷*Open late Feb–Oct Wed–Sun and bank hols 11am–5pm; late-Jul–early Sept also open Mon.* ✎*Guided tours Mon–Tue 1pm, 2pm, 3pm, other days 10.45am.* ➾*£9.75.* &▣✕. ℰ*01263 738 030. www.nationaltrust.org.uk.*

This splendid turreted and gabled brick mansion was built 1619–25 by Robert Lyminge, the architect of Hatfield House, and is one of the most intact of great Jacobean houses, famed for its long gallery, fine tapestries, paintings and the National Trust's most important collection of books. There is a magnificent staircase; a plastered ceiling (120ft/36m) portraying the *Five Senses* and *Learning* in the Long Gallery; a splendid tapestry of Peter the Great defeating the Swedes; and paintings by Reynolds, Gainsborough and Canaletto. The present parterre and gardens date from the late-19C.

Blickling Hall

© VIEW Pictures/Photononstop

Norfolk Broads★

One of Britain's premier wildlife habitats, the Broads – 14 large lakes formed out of medieval peat diggings – are the home of Chinese water deer, kingfishers, bitterns, herons and great crested grebes which are found nowhere else in Britain. Peaceful waterways wind their way through misty fens, cutting between lush woods and open marshes beneath a seemingly endless sky. Over 125mi/200km of these are navigable by boat. The villages are famous for their churches, some of which have hammerbeam and thatched roofs.

WROXHAM

The "capital of the Broads", on the River Bure, is usually the first port of call for the widest choice of boat hire.

HOW HILL

▶ *6mi/10km E of Wroxham.*
Toad Hole Cottage (◐ *open daily summer 9.30am–6pm, reduced hours winter; ✆01603 756 096, www.waterscape.com*), built 1780–1820, was once home to Broads "marshmen". Now a museum, it shows their basic living conditions and tells the story of how they maintained and harvested the watery landscape.

> ℹ **Info: Norwich:** Millennium Plain. ✆01603 213 999. www.visitnorwich.co.uk/norfolk-broads.aspx.
> **Hoveton:** ✆01603 756 907.
> **How Hill** (Toad Hole Cottage): ✆01603 756 096.
> **Whitlingham:** ✆01603 756 094. www.enjoythebroads.com; www.visitnorfolk.co.uk; www.visitnorthnorfolk.com.
> ⊛ **Don't Miss:** Norfolk Broads boating in the summer.

POTTER HEIGHAM

▶ *9mi/14km E of Wroxham.*
This is a popular boating centre on the River Thurne. **St Nicholas' Church** has a Norman tower and a hammerbeam and thatched roof.

RANWORTH

▶ *6mi/10km SE of Wroxham.*
The Perpendicular tower and Decorated south porch of **St Helen's Church** (◐ *open daily, 9am–6pm; 4pm winter;* ♿✗ *)* give no hint of the splendour inside "the cathedral of the Broads". It is home to the finest rood screen (15C) in East Anglia, a brightly painted array of saints, apostles and martyrs. For a wonderful panorama, climb the winding stone staircase to the top of the tower.

River Ant near How Hill

© Laurence Gough/Fotolia.com

North Norfolk Coast

Norfolk has more to offer than just the Broads (see opposite). Away from the busy boating centres is a land of peace and quiet and empty skies, excellent for nature-watching.

CROMER

24mi/39km north of Norwich.
Cromer reached its height as a fashionable resort with the coming of the railway in the 1880s. It has failed to keep up with the times though still has a loyal following thanks to its fine beach, exhilarating clifftop walks and a charming pier, unspoiled by seaside amusements. Don't miss the **view** from the tower *(172 steps)* of the medieval **Church of St Peter and St Paul** or the local delicacy of **crab**, with which Cromer is indelibly associated.

CLEY NEXT THE SEA AND BLAKENEY POINT

Cley is 12mi/19km W of Cromer.
Cley (pronounced "cly") is renowned for its birdwatching with a recently opened **Norfolk Wildlife Trust** visitor centre (open year-round daily 10am–5pm; 4pm Nov–Feb; £5; 01263 740 008, www.norfolkwildlifetrust.org.uk) offering superb views across Cley Marshes.
Some 4mi/6.5km west Blakeney Point is one of the best places in Britain to see **seals**. The 500-strong colony is made up of common and grey seals. The common seals pup between June and August. Local ferry operators run seal watching trips from Moston Quay.

WELLS-NEXT-THE-SEA

9mi/14km) W of Cromer.
Despite the name you'll find this attractive little town a mile inland from the sea. Largely unaffected by 20C commercialisation, it retains many of its fine Georgian houses and is also the area's only working port. In summer a narrow-gauge railway runs out to the beach.

HOLKHAM★★

11mi/18km west of Cromer.
The seat of the Earls of Leicester and of Coke of Norfolk (1754–1842) – the inventor of modern agriculture – the Holkham (pronounced "hokum") Estate is the grandest in the region. **Holkham Hall★★** (open Apr–Oct Sun, Mon, Thu noon–4pm £9, combined ticket with Bygones Museum £11; £2.50; 01328 710 227. www.holkham.co.uk) was designed in the palatial Palladian style by **William Kent**. Most monumental of the interiors is the Marble Hall. The Grand Drawing Room has works by Claude and Poussin and the Saloon boasts Rubens and Van Dyck. In the South Sitting Room hang works by Titian, Guido Reni, Gainsborough and Battoni; the Landscape Room is devoted to Poussin and Claude.

Housed in the stable block is the **Bygones Museum** (open Apr–Oct daily 10am–5pm. £4) ranging from mechanical toys, household implements and agricultural tools, to vintage cars and massive steam engine. Adjacent is a (free) **History of Farming Exhibition**. The sweeping **park** that surrounds the hall is home to fallow deer and a small herd of red deer.

The estate is also blessed with **Holkham Beach★**, voted the best beach in Britain 2009, 2010 and 2011 by the authoritative *Coast* magazine. With 4mi/6.4km) of golden sand and pine woods to explore, it has changed little in centuries and was famously used for the final scene in the movie *Shakespeare in Love*.

King's Lynn

North Norfolk Coast

Set amid the marshes, in what is known locally as the Fenlands, King's Lynn dates from the Norman Conquest (1066). In the Middle Ages it was a bustling port and member of the Hanseatic League, exporting cloth and wool. Today's fine townscape is especially rich in medieval merchants' houses; many with their own well-constructed warehouses line the River Ouse. Within a short distance are some outstanding country houses, including a royals' retreat, and some superb churches.

TOWN CENTRE WALK

Begin at **Tuesday Market Place**, a large open space at the top of King Street, surrounded by well-preserved Georgian and Victorian buildings. **King Street** presents a delightful succession of houses of varied dates and materials including **St George's Guildhall**, the largest surviving medieval guildhall in England, where Shakespeare is supposed to have acted.

On the right is the Dutch-inspired **Custom House** (17C), on the corner of Purfleet Quay, leading to the River Ouse, part home to the tourist information centre and part home to elegant rooms (*open year-round daily Mon–Sat 10am/10.30am–3.30pm/4.30pm, Sun noon–3.30pm/4.30pm; £1; 01553 763 044; www.west-norfolk.gov.uk) housing displays on the merchants, customsmen and smugglers of Lynn.

King's Staithe Lane, which is the next lane south, contains 16C and 17C warehouses; in cobbled King's Staithe Square stands a grand double-fronted red brick house, with a statue of King Charles I.

In **Queen Street**, which is mainly Georgian in character, stands **Thorseby College**, founded in 1502 for training priests but later converted into a merchant's house with a 17C courtyard.

This leads to Saturday Market Place and **Tales of the Old Gaol House** (*open mid-Apr–Oct Wed–Sat 10am–*

<table>
<tr><td>▶</td><td>Population: 41,281.</td></tr>
<tr><td>⚲</td><td>Michelin Map: Michelin Atlas p30 or Map 504 V 25.</td></tr>
<tr><td>ℹ</td><td>Info: The Custom House, Purfleet Quay. 01553 763 044. www.west-norfolk.gov.uk.</td></tr>
<tr><td>▶</td><td>Location: On the River Ouse 44mi/71km north of Cambridge. The train station is a five-minute walk east.</td></tr>
<tr><td>⊘</td><td>Don't Miss: At least one of the area's stately homes.</td></tr>
<tr><td>🕐</td><td>Timing: Allow 4–6 hours; more for excursions.</td></tr>
<tr><td></td><td>Walking Tours: May–Oct Tue, Fri Sat 2pm. Jun & Jul also 7pm. £4. 01553 763 044. www.west-norfolk.gov.uk.</td></tr>
</table>

4pm; £3.20; 01553 774 297; www.west-norfolk.gov.uk). Occupying the chequered flint **Guildhall** (1421), visitors pass through the old police station with its tiny cells and bleak history.The **Regalia Room** features civic silver and the **King John Cup** (1340).

Turn right onto Church Street to see **St Margaret's Church** (*open year-round daily, 7.45am–5.45pm (7.45pm Sun); 01553 772 858; www.stmargarets kingslynn.org.uk),* a twin-towered church originally built in the 13C. Surviving glories include 14C screens, a Georgian pulpit and a 17C moon clock.

Walk back towards Saturday Market Place and turn right onto St James Street, then left onto Tower Street, left into Blackfriar's Street, fork right onto Paradise Parade, which will lead you to Market Street and the **Lynn Museum** (*open year-round Tue-Sat 10am–5pm £3.50, free Oct-Mar; 01553 775 001; www.west-norfolk.gov.uk).* This is the town's main collection and pride of place goes to **Seahenge**, a remarkable meticulously crafted c.4,000-year-old timber circle found on the beach.

Return to Paradise Parade, turn right onto New Conduit Street, then walk straight ahead via Broad Street, Chapel Street and St Anne's Street. Turn right onto North Street, home to **True's Yard** (◷ *open year-round Tue–Sat 10am–4pm, Mon Jun & Jul;* ◷ *closed 25 Dec–3 Jan;* ✍*£3;* ✗*;* ☏*01553 770 479; www.trues yard.co.uk*) where two cottages house a small museum illustrating the hardships of the former fishing community.

EXCURSIONS
Houghton Hall★★

▷ *13mi/21km E via the A1 076 and the A 148.* ◷ *Open Easter Sun–Sept, Wed, Thu, Sun, bank hols 1.30pm–5pm (grounds 11am–5.30pm).* ✍*£8.80 grounds and park only, £6.* ♿🅿✗. ☏*01485 528 569.*
www.houghtonhall.com.
Houghton Hall, which is transitional between Baroque and Palladian, was built (1722–35) for Sir Robert Walpole, Britain's first prime minister. Its main rooms by William Kent are dedicated to "taste, expense, state and parade". Its joys are its ceilings and Kent furniture, Sèvres porcelain, thrones by Pugin and 17C Mortlake tapestries.

Oxburgh Hall★★

NT. ▷ *18mi/29km SE. House:*
◷*Open late Feb–Oct Sat–Wed 11am–5pm (late Feb–early Mar & Oct 4pm); last 3 wks Apr & Aug daily. Garden:*
◷*Open as house except Nov–Feb (Sat–Sun only).* ✍*£7.45.* ♿🅿✗. ☏*01366 328 528. www.nationaltrust.org.uk.*
This romantic moated manor house was built as a status symbol in 1482. Its **gatehouse** and flanking ranges are 15C; the hall range is 19C. The interior presents elaborate **embroideries** depicting mammals; letters from Henry VIII, Queen Mary and Queen Elizabeth I; woodcarvings by Grinling Gibbons and a secret priest's hole.

Sandringham★

▷*8mi/13km NE.* ◷*Open Easter Sat–late Jul and Aug–late-Oct/early-Nov, daily 11am–5pm (4pm Oct).* ✍*£11 (grounds and museum only, £7.50).* ♿🅿✗. ☏*01485 545 408. www.sandringham-estate.co.uk.*

Oxburgh Hall

© Cyril Privezentzev/Dreamstime.com

"Dear old Sandringham, the place I love better than anywhere else in the world", wrote George V of the Royal Family's country home, a Revival Jacobean house acquired in 1862. The large Saloon is hung with family portraits and 17C tapestries. The corridor is adorned with intricately wrought Oriental arms and armour. In the main Drawing Room is Russian silver and Chinese jade.

FENLAND CHURCHES★
The glories of the Fens are its sunsets and churches, admirably complemented by the flat and featureless landscape.
St Clement's Church (*Terrington St Clement;* ☏*01553 828 430*) boasts a splendid west window and northwest tower. The interior has exquisite Georgian panelling and a 17C **font cover**.
St Peter's Church (*Walpole St Peter*). Huge plain-glass windows illuminate the magnificent interior of the 14C "Cathedral of the Fens".
St Mary's Church (*West Walton,* ☏*01945 780 252; www.ely.anglican.org/parishes/ westwalton*) is mid-13C Early English at its most profuse and extravagant.
All Saints' Church (*Walsoken;* ☏*01945 583 740; www.allsaintswalsoken.co.uk*). Dating from 1146, "the grandest Norman parish church in Norfolk" presents a hammerbeam tie-beam roof, an eight-sided **font** portraying the Seven Sacraments and Crucifixion, and a 16C wall painting, the *Judgement of Solomon*.

Ely

Cambridgeshire

Once called Elig or Eel Island because of the abundance of eels, Ely lies on the River Ouse. It has been a place of worship since St Etheldreda, a Saxon queen, founded a religious community and built an abbey here in the 7C. The small town is still dominated by the cathedral and monastic buildings and retains many medieval houses. In 1066 the legendary rebel, Hereward the Wake, made his last stand against the Normans in Ely, and Oliver Cromwell lived here in the mid-17C.

▶ **Population:** 10,329.

Michelin Map: Michelin Atlas p29 or Map 504 U 26.

Info: Oliver Cromwell's House, 29 St Mary's Street. ℘01353 662 062. http://visitely.eastcambs.gov.uk.

Location: 16mi/26km north of Cambridge. Ely railway station is a 1-minute walk from the centre, on The Gallery. Regional buses stop by the cathedral.

CATHEDRAL★★

◷*Open year-round daily 7am–6.30pm. (5.30pm Sun in winter).* ◉*£6.50 (free Sun). Additional charges: Octagon and West Tower (£5.50 each, £8 on Sun). Stained Glass Museum £4. combined ticket to all areas and tea/coffee £15.20;* ◗*Guided tours (*◉*free) daily.* ♿✕. *℘01353 660 344. www.cathedral.ely.anglican.org; www.stainedglassmuseum.com.*

The superb Norman nave and transepts contrast with the surprises beyond: the wonderful Decorated east end and Lady Chapel, and that 14C masterpiece, the Octagon. The present church was begun in 1083; in 1250 the east end of the original Norman building was reconstructed. In 1321 work started on the Lady Chapel. The following year the great Norman crossing tower fell down. The solution, cutting off the four Norman corners of the crossing and building an octagonal space (three times the size of the Norman tower) on the eight points, was a triumph of medieval engineering.

The cathedral is best viewed from the northwest to appreciate its length (537ft/164m), castellated west tower (215ft/66m), Early English Galilee Porch, the Decorated Octagon (170ft/52m) and the wooden lantern above it.

The richness of the colours emanating from ceilings, stained-glass windows and stone pillars is awe-inspiring. The **southwest transept** (c.1200) is an outstanding example of the Romanesque period. Above all else, the eye is led to the **Octagon**. Its eight pillars support 200tons of glass, lead and timber; below its high windows are panels decorated with angels. The Octagon is separated by a 19C **screen** (by George Gilbert Scott) from the beautifully vaulted Early English choir, with its splendid 14C **choir stalls**. In front of the High Altar lies the shrine of St Etheldreda. The light and spacious **Lady Chapel** was the largest single span of vaulting in its time; most of its treasures were lost during the Dissolution.

The **Stained Glass Museum** in the triforium *(via a steep winding staircase)* shows stained-glass and lead-cutting processes by means of diorama models. The group of medieval domestic buildings, together with the ruined cloisters, is the largest of its kind in England; some form part of the King's School.

OLIVER CROMWELL'S HOUSE★

29 St Mary's Street. ◷*Open Apr–Oct daily 10am–5pm. Nov–Mar Sun–Fri 11am–4pm, Sat 10am–5pm.* ◉*£4.50.* ♿. *℘01353 662 062. www.oliver-cromwellshouse.co.uk.*

Born and bred in East Anglia, for 10 years Oliver Cromwell, Lord Protector of England, lived in this 13C house in Ely. The furnished rooms are few – kitchen, bedroom, study – but the flavour of the age and the history of its most illustrious resident is superbly evoked.

Peterborough
and around

Peterborough began life as a village around a monastery. It became a town around a cathedral and then a city dominated by brickworks. It is now a high-tech centre for financial institutions but ancient survivals include the cathedral, the 17C arcaded guildhall, the church of St John the Baptist in Cowgate and some Georgian houses in Priestgate. A pedestrian zone has replaced the ancient city centre.

CATHEDRAL★★

○*Open year-round Mon–Fri 9am–5.15pm, Sat 9am–3pm, Sun noon–3.15pm.* ⊜*£3.50 donation requested.* ♿🅿 *(wheelchair users only)*✕. 👞*Guided tours (*⊜*£7) Apr–Sept Mon–Sat 2pm (Wed 11.30am); Tower tours Apr–Oct most Sats & Weds, see website for dates, (*⊜*£10), must be booked*✆*01733 343 342.* ✆*01733 343 342. www.peterborough-cathedral.org.uk.*

Peterborough, together with Ely (♿*see opposite*), was one of the two great monasteries of the Fens. The present building was started in 1118 and consecrated in 1238. In 1643 Cromwell's men destroyed the stained glass, the high altar, the cloisters and statues.

The Early English **west front** is fascinating with its three giant arches and its rich early Perpendicular (14C) porch. The interior is a superb example of Norman architecture. The nave has an uninterrupted vista towards the altar. The transepts and choir with their **Norman elevations** are a robust expression of faith. The 13C **nave ceiling** is a wonderful example of medieval art with figures of bishops, saints and mythical beasts. The 15C wooden ceiling in the sanctuary is decorated with bosses and the superb **fan vaulting** at the east end (in the New or Eastern Building) is late -15C Perpendicular. In the north choir aisle Catherine of Aragon is buried and in the south choir aisle Mary Queen of Scots was temporarily laid to rest (1587–1612).

▶ **Population:** 134,788.
♿ **Michelin Map:** Michelin Atlas p29 or Map 504 T 26.
🅸 **Info:** 9 Bridge Street. ✆01733 452 336. www.visitpeterborough.com.
▶ **Location:** 25mi/40km north of Cambridge. Direct rail link to London (45 minutes), the train station is a short walk from the centre. Queensgate Bus Station is close by.
👁 **Don't Miss:** The cathedral's west front, 13C nave ceiling and fan vaulting.
○ **Timing:** Allow half a day in Peterborough.
👥 **Kids:** One of the Specials Days at Nene Valley Railway.

EXCURSIONS

Flag Fen Archaeology Park★★

▶ *The Droveway, Northey Road. 3mi/5km E via the A 47 and A 1130 (signposted).* ○*Open Apr–Sept daily 10am–5pm, call or see website for winter hours.*⊜*£5.* ♿🅿✕. ✆*01733 313 414. www.flagfen.org.*

Flag Fen is one of the most important prehistoric sites in Britain, home to the country's oldest wheel and a 0.6km-/1km-long wooden causeway and platform that's been perfectly preserved in the wetland for 3,300 years.

👥 Nene Valley Railway★

▶ *8mi/13km W on the A 47 and S on the A 1.* ○*Operating season Mar–Oct plus specials, call or visit website for times and dates.* ⊜*From £10.50, child £5.* ♿🅿✕. ✆*01780 784 4404 (timetable), 01780 784 444 (enquiries); www.nvr.org.uk.*

Steam locomotives with shiny wooden fascias puff between Wansford and Peterborough *(15mi/24km – 90min return)* in a scene from yesteryear. At Wansford are displays of railway memorabilia and old rolling stock, some from abroad.

ADDRESSES

🛏 STAY

CAMBRIDGE

🛏 **Avalon B & B** – A1. *62 Gilbert Road. ☎01223 353 071. www.avaloncambridge. co.uk.* 🚭. 🅿. *2 rms.* A pleasant 20-minute walk or 5-minute bus ride from the centre, this 1930s detached house offers pleasant unfussy bedrooms, a warm welcome and hearty breakfasts.

🛏 **Brooklands** – A2. *95 Cherry Hinton Road. ☎01223 242 035. www.brooklands guesthouse.co.uk.* 🅿. *7 rms.* One mile from the city centre, and five minutes from the train station this simple guesthouse has lovely boutique-style bedrooms (one of which has a jacuzzi and four-poster bed).

🛏 **Warkworth House** – A2. *Warkworth Terrace. ☎01223 363 682. www.warkworth house.co.uk.* 🚭. 🅿. *3 rms.* In the city centre, this small Victorian B&B offers a handsome spacious double room, and simple family and single rooms.

🛏🛏🛏 **Arundel House Hotel** – A1. *53 Chesterton Road. ☎01223 367 701. www.arundelhousehotels.co.uk.* 🅿. *103 rms.* Arundel House occupies one of the finest hotel sites in town, a few minutes' walk from the centre, overlooking the River Cam and open parkland. It has a beautiful garden and conservatory. Chintzy bedrooms.

🛏🛏🛏 **Cambridge Lodge** – A1. *139 Huntington Road. ☎01223 352 833.* 🅿. *15 rms.* This mock-Tudor mansion, 1mi/1.6km from the city centre, has a calm setting with a garden and patio. Rooms are well equipped and chintzy.

IPSWICH

🛏🛏 **Sidegate Guest House** – *121 Sidegate Lane. ☎01473 728 714. www.sidegateguesthouse.co.uk.* 🅿. *6 rms.* In a residential area, 2mi/3km from the city centre, this attractively decorated and furnished guesthouse has modern and light but cosy rooms.

🛏🛏🛏–🛏🛏🛏🛏 **Salthouse Harbour Hotel** – *1st Neptune Quay. ☎01473 226 789. www.salthouseharbour.co.uk.* 🅿. *30 rms.* On the marina, this rejuvenated warehouse has been converted into a striking contemporary space containing an eclectic blend of urban and country, vintage chic and cutting-edge design.

EAST BERGHOLT

🛏 **The Granary Flatford** – *Flatford Mill. ☎01206 298 111. www.granaryflatford.co.uk.* 🅿. *2 rms.* Next door to a thatched granary once owned by John Constable's father, an 18C wool store has been tastefully converted into a characterful B&B accommodation with exposed beams and leaded windows. It opens onto a beautiful garden bordered by the River Stour.

🛏 **Edmar Lodge** – 2. *64 Earlham Road. ☎01603 615 599. www.edmarlodge.co.uk .* 🅿. *5 rms.* Traditional cosy rooms in a family-run B&B a 10-minute walk from the city centre. DVD library for bedroom DVD player.

COLCHESTER

🛏🛏 **The Red Lion** – *High Street. ☎0800 435 165. www.brook-hotels.co.uk.* 🅿. *24 rms.* This 15C inn has been furnished and decorated sympathetically in period style with modern touches. Four-posters available.

BURY ST EDMUNDS

🛏🛏🛏 **The Angel Hotel** – *3 Angel Hill. ☎01284 714 000. www.theangel.co.uk.* 🅿. *70 rms.* Opposite the abbey gardens this fashionable hotel, behind a classic Georgian façade, offers contemporary-traditional styling, some rooms with shabby chic. The restaurant serves fine Modern British cuisine (🍴🍴🍴).

NORWICH

🛏 **Arbor Linden Lodge** – 2. *557 Earlham Road. ☎01603 462 308. www.guesthouse norwich.com. 6 rms.* Very close to the university, this family-owned guesthouse provides pleasant well-equipped bedrooms at a very good price.

KING'S LYNN

🛏🛏🛏🛏 **The Victoria** – *Holkham. ☎01328 711 008. www.holkham.co.uk/ victoria. 10 rms.* This beautiful Colonial-themed hotel, formerly a pub, lies on the glorious Holkham Estate a few minutes' walk from Holkham Beach (🏖see *North Norfolk Coast*) Minmum two-night stay at weekends. Look for special offers off season. The award-winning restaurant (🍴🍴🍴) serves excellent local dishes.

ELY

🛏🛏 **Cathedral House** – *17 Mary's Street. ☎01353 662 124. www.cathedralhouse. co.uk.* 🚭. 🅿. *3rms.* Set almost in the shadow of the cathedral this lovely cosy quiet Georgian house offers simple pleasant white bedrooms. Minimum two-night stay at weekends.

⚶ EAT

CAMBRIDGE

🅐 Look on Regent Street, Bridge Street and along Quayside. There are also over 100 pubs and bars throughout the town.

🍽 **The Eagle** – A2. *Benet Street.* ☏01223 505 020. This is the best-known pub in Cambridge, famous among older visitors for its USAF wartime links. Good bistro-style pub food and an alfresco terrace.

🍽🍽 **22 Chesterton Road** – A. *22 Chesterton Road.* ☏01223 351 880. *www.restaurant22co.uk. Closed Sun –Mon.* Critically acclaimed high-quality dining from a prix-fixe dinner menu (though beware hefty supplements on certain dishes!) which changes monthly.

🍽🍽 **Galleria** – A1.*3 Bridge Street.* ☏01223 362 054. *www.galleriacambridge.co.uk* This light airy brasserie serves excellent Modern European dishes (and snacks at lunchtime) on a pretty riverside terrace.

🍽🍽🍽🍽 **Midsummer House** – *Midsummer Common.* ☏01223 369 299. The only Michelin two-star establishment in East Anglia, Cambridge's finest enjoys an idyllic location beside the Cam, with conservatory dining. The French-Mediterranean cuisine offers inventive detailed cooking.

NEAR CAMBRIDGE

🍽🍽🍽 **The Three Horseshoes** – *High Street, Madingley.* ☏01954 210 221. *www.huntsbridge.com.* A picture-perfect thatched pub five mi/8km west of Cambridge, with a stylish airy interior. The menu is an inventive fusion of Modern Mediterranean, British and Asian styles.

IPSWICH

🍽🍽–🍽🍽🍽 **Mariners** – *Neptune Quay.* ☏01473 289 748. *www.mariners ipswich.co.uk.* High-quality French Brasserie cuisine is served aboard a much-travelled late-19C wooden sailing ship (formerly a gunboat, then a hospital ship), with polished beams and gleaming brass.

COLCHESTER

🍽🍽 **The Lemon Tree** – *8 St Johns Street.* ☏01206 767 337. *www.the-lemon-tree. com.* The exposed brickwork in this atmospheric restaurant is the town's historic city wall, though everything else is very contemporary, including the popular British and European dishes.

NORWICH

🅐 Look on St Giles Street, Upper St Giles Street, Elm Hill and St George Street.

🍽 **The Britons Arms** – 1. *Elm Hill.* ☏01603 623 367. *Open Mon–Sat 9.30am–5pm.* ⚶. Tihs long-established cosy place serves quiches, waffles, cakes and more with a delightfully secluded terraced garden and an open fire for winter days.

🍽 **The Waffle House** – 2. *39 St Giles Street.* ☏01603 612 790. This buzzing café bar specialises in sweet and savoury Belgian waffles individually cooked to order using organic and free-range ingredients. They also do other light lunches.

KING'S LYNN

🍽🍽 **Bankhouse** – *King's Staithe Square.* ☏01553 660 492. *www.thebankhouse.co.uk.* The restaurant of this beautiful Georgian hotel serves modern brasserie food, from burgers, steaks, pastas and salads, to the more exotic, and may be enjoyed in any of three dining areas, or in the summer, outside on a lovely riverside terrace.

SIGHTSEEING

City Sightseeing Tours operate hop-on hop-off open-top bus tours of the city, with buses running every 10–20 minutes. Tickets (☞*£10*) can be purchased directly from the driver, or in advance from the Cambridge Tourist Information Centre. No trip to Cambridge would be complete without a **punting** trip. **Scudamores** offers both chauffeured and self-punting hire (☏*01223 359 750; www.scudamores. com*). Motorcycle tours and ghost tours also available. For riverboat cruises: contact Cambridge Passenger Cruises (☏*01223 307 694; www.georgina.co.uk*).

🎭 ENTERTAINMENT

The Cambridge Folk Festival (*late Jul/early Aug*), is Britain's best music festival of its kind (☏*01223 357 851; www.cambridgefolkfestival.co.uk*).

🛒 SHOPPING

Most high-street and department stores can be found in **Petty Cury**, **Market Square**, **Lion Yard**, **St Andrew's Street** and the **Grafton Centre**. Shoppers looking for something slightly different or quirky should try the shops in **King's Parade**, **Rose Crescent**, **Trinity Street**, **Bridge Street**, **Magdalene Street**, **St John's Street** and **Green Street**. In **Market Square** there is a general market (Mon–Sat).

EAST MIDLANDS

Comprising Nottinghamshire, Leicestershire, Northamptonshire and Lincolnshire, the East Midlands has never been a region that has figured too highly on the itineraries of too many visitors, foreign or domestic. Nottingham's Robin Hood is the star name – though there is precious little tangible evidence of the outlaw – and Lincoln's cathedral is the star attraction, but who can even place Lincoln on a map?! The latter is certainly worth the detour and Nottingham has more than just a legend to sustain visitor interest. Cosmopolitan Leicester, and its shire, is possibly the most pleasant surprise package while Stamford is the hidden gem of this underrated region. Between the 9C and 10C the East (and North) Midlands was controlled by Danish conquerors, whose kingdom was known as the Five Boroughs of the Danelaw. Its five principal towns are still the region's centres: Nottingham, Leicester, Lincoln, Stamford and Derby.

Highlights

1 Explore **Nottingham Castle** and its caves (p298)

2 National Space Centre, **Leicester** (p300)

3 Marvel at **Lincoln Cathedral** both within and without (p303)

4 Be taken in by the Gothic fantasy of **Belvoir Castle** (p307)

5 Wander around the 600 listed buildings of **Stamford** town centre (p309)

Nottingham

The town and shire is best known for its connections with Robin Hood and Sherwood Forest. This 12C gentleman robber poached from the lands of the hated Sheriff of Nottingham, installed to enforce the law by the equally unpopular Prince John, who was the de facto ruler while King Richard (the Lionheart) was fighting the Crusades. Robin Hood, or Robyn Hode, therefore became the symbol of English resistance to Norman rule and it is unlikely that a single character like him ever existed at all. More likely "he" was an amalgam of different people around this period. Robin would recognise nothing of modern Nottingham. Even D H Lawrence, the region's early-20C literary giant, would struggle, though the Lacemarket and castle would be familiar to him.

Leicestershire

Pronounced "lester-sheer", this was once the seat of the 8C East Mercian bishops and the capital of King Lear's kingdom. In recent times Leicester was a centre for the hosiery trade, and this was a major factor in attracting Asian emigrants. Today over a third of its population is Asian. Despite this accommodating nature the city is a relative newcomer to welcoming tourists. The National Space Centre put Leicester on the day-visitor map and its new Curve Theatre has added to its cultural appeal.

Northamptonshire

Northants (as it is often abbreviated) is a pleasant county with ancient stone villages and some fine country houses. If you like shoes, you'll love the city museum.

Lincolnshire

A county of old-fashioned seaside resorts and industrial fishing ports on the windy east coast, Lincolnshire is never to going to attract much passing trade from visitors.

The town of Lincoln, however, is well worth the dedicated journey. With a wonderful natural location, its magnificent cathedral is one of the finest in England, and the old town spreading around its feet is a delight.

To the south of Lincoln are some fine country houses and Belvoir Castle while in the far southwest of the county Stamford has more in character with Northants or Leicestershire than Lincolnshire, and is the finest "town built all of stone" in England. To the east of Lincoln is the haunting waterlogged landscape of the Fens.

Food Heroes

The small market town of **Melton Mowbray** boasts the title of "UK Rural Capital of Food" and is synonymous with Melton Mowbray Pork Pies. These hand-made pies are encased in a rich hot-water crust pastry, then traditionally baked without using a supporting tin or hoop, which gives the pie its classic bow-sided shape. Natural bone-stock jelly is added to the pie after baking to enhance the natural uncured (and slightly spiced) pork flavour. They are generally eaten cold as a snack. The oldest pork pie bakery in the country, Dickinson & Morris (*www.porkpie.co.uk*) have been baking at Ye Olde Pork Pie Shoppe in the centre of the town since 1851 (production has recently moved to an out-of-town factory).

Melton Mowbray is also home to one of the six producers of **Stilton** cheese (*www.stiltoncheese.com*), which by law can only be produced in the three counties of Derbyshire, Nottinghamshire and Leicestershire. Colston Bassett is another of the six accredited places, and its creamery has a small shop selling Colston Bassett Stilton, though it is not open to the public for tours. Still, in the village you can taste and buy some different 40 cheeses, including Stilton, from the Colston Basset Store (*www.colstonbassettstore.com*); you can also eat at their delightful Garden Café Restaurant. Another well known local cheese is **Red Leicester**, a hard cows' milk cheese made in a similar way as Cheddar, but with a moister, crumblier texture and a milder flavour. It is coloured with a vegetable dye called annatto, which gives the cheese its distinctive orange appearance.

Melton Mowbray is the venue for the annual **East Midlands Food Festival** (*first weekend Oct, www.eastmidlandsfoodfestival.co.uk*).

Near Melton Mowbray, at Old Dalby, is the Belvoir (pronounced "beaver") Brewery (*tours daily, www.belvoirbrewery.co.uk*). Lincolnshire is historically associated with the **Lincolnshire sausage** (available nationwide) which has a distinctive sage flavour. The area's best artisan cheese is Lincolnshire Poacher (*www.lincolnshirepoachercheese.com*). You can find it in The Cheese Society Shop & Café (*www.thecheesesociety.co.uk*), in the city centre, and at The Cheese Shop, at Louth (*www.thecheeseshoplouth.co.uk*), east of Lincoln, which in 2011, won the Daily Telegraph "Best Small Food Shop in Britain" award.

Salt pork filled with herbs, otherwise known as **stuffed chine**, is a speciality of Lincolnshire. A chine is a square cut of meat cut from between the shoulder-blades. The county is also a producer of **haslet**, (pronounced 'hacelet'). This traditional pork meat loaf is seasoned with sage.

Lincolnshire plum bread is made with dried fruit (sultanas and currants rather than plums) - it's worth finding a good baker for a better version than that sold in supermarkets.

Samphire is relatively widely available in Lincolnshire, where it grows on the marshland. **Grantham Gingerbread** is also well-known here, which has a hard crust, slightly gooey interior and strong ginger flavour.

Lincolnshire's best known brewery is **Bateman**'s, which has been in business since 1874. IPA and Nut Brown are a couple of its well-known beers.

Held during the first week of October, **Nottingham Goose Fair** dates back to the 13C, making it perhaps the oldest in the country. Today it is just a funfair, but nevertheless, roast goose remains a popular dish in Nottingham. Bramley cooking apples originate in Nottingham and what better way to have them than baked in a **Nottingham Batter Pudding**?

Nottinghamshire

This is the famous home of Sherwood Forest, home to Robin Hood and his band of medieval merry men. Later, literary giants such as D H Lawrence would paint a much grittier local picture, while Lord Byron also has local associations.

- **Michelin Map:** Michelin Atlas p36 or Map 504 Q 25.
- **Info:** 1–4 Smithy Row, Nottingham. ℘08444 775 678.
- **Kids:** Galleries of Justice Museum.

NOTTINGHAM

Although this is the city that has adopted Robin Hood as its own, it is the outlaw's arch enemy, and chief villain, the Sheriff of Nottingham, who lures our hero into town from the safety of the forest. On safer historical ground, Nottingham made its early name from lace.

Nottingham Castle★

Castle Road. ⏰*Open Tue–Sun Mar–Sept 10am–5pm; Oct–Feb 10am–4pm.* ⏰*Closed 1 Jan–2, 25–26 Dec.* ⏶*£5.50, includes entry to the Museum of Nottingham Life at Brewhouse Yard.* ♿✕. ℘*0115 915 3700. www.nottinghamcity.gov.uk.*

Of the original Norman castle, only the subterranean passage, **Mortimer's Hole**, from the castle to the **Brewhouse Yard** (now part of the Nottingham Castle Caves tour), and **Ye Olde Trip to Jerusalem** survive. The latter is one of the oldest inns in England, built into the foot of the castle walls, accessed separately. The "new" castle, a 17C ducal mansion, is home to a lively museum and art gallery, housing a large collection of silver, glass, decorative items, visual arts and paintings. Don't miss the fine examples of medieval Nottingham **alabasters★**. Beneath lie **Nottingham Castle Caves** (*tours Easter–Oct Tue–Sat 11am, 2pm, 3pm, Sun noon, 1pm, 2pm, 3pm; Nov–Easter Sun 2pm only; tour places on first-come first-served basis, and subject to availability and weather conditions;* ⏶*£2.50),* a labyrinth dating, to medieval times. with over 300 steep and strenuous steps alleviated by colourful tales.

If you want to get into the **Robin Hood** spirit of things, take a tour of the city centre (⏤*tours depart from the castle gatehouse every Sat during summer, see website for dates and times;* ⏶*£10 including castle entry) with the man "himself" (or at least a lookalike!).*

Just outside the gatehouse, next to Ye Olde Trip pub, is the **Museum of Nottingham Life at Brewhouse Yard** (⏰*open year-round Fri–Sun 10am–5pm; other details as castle)* housed within five charming red-brick 17C cottages. Once a thriving small community of 20 houses, the surviving buildings contain a mixture of reconstructed room and shop settings depicitng social history.

Galleries of Justice Museum

Shire Hall, The Lace Market. ⏰*Open year-round 9am–5pm, Mon and school hols 10.30am–5pm.* ⏰*Closed 24–28 Dec, 31 Dec–1 Jan.* ⏤*Self-guided audio tours only, Mon–Tue excluding school and bank hols.* ⏶*Performance tours £8.95, child £6.95 (self-guided audio tours, £5.95. child £4.50)* ℘*0115 952 0555; www.galleriesofjustice.org.uk.* Behind the elegant 18C façade the turnkey takes visitors on a guesomely entertaining actors-led "performance" tour of caves, dungeons and prison cells featuring highwaymen (and women), convict ships, Great Train Robbers, Robin Hood (inevitably) and executions that took place just outside the cramped and squalid prison on this site that dates back to the 15C.

It is worth wandering around the narrow streets of the surrounding **Lace Market** area, particularly Stoney Street, to soak up its Victorian atmosphere. By night this is one of the city's buzzing hubs.

Off Stoney Street, High Pavement leads into Weekday Cross and the new, strikingly modern, boxy **Nottingham Contemporary** (⏰*open year-round, galle-*

ries Tue–Fri 10am–7pm, Sat and bank hols 10am–6pm, Sun 11am–5pm; ℘0115 948 9750; www.nottinghamcontemporary. org), one of the largest contemporary art centres in the UK.

EXCURSIONS
D.H. Lawrence Birthplace Museum

▷ 8a Victoria Street, Eastwood. 10mi/ 16km NW on the A 610. 8A Victoria Street. ☞ year-round Tue–Sun, guided tour only, 10.15am, 11.15am, 12.25pm, 1.45pm, 2.45pm (family tour), 3.45pm; it is advisable to book ahead. ☜£5. ℘01773 717 353. www.dhlawrenceheritage.org.

This tiny terraced cottage, where Lawrence was born in 1885, was the first of four Lawrence family homes in Eastwood. The tour gives an insight into the writer's early life and influences in this small mining town.

Newstead Abbey★

▷ 12mi/19km N of Nottingham off the A 60. **House:** ☞ guided tour only Apr–Sept Sun 1pm, 2pm, 3pm. **Gardens:** ◷Open daily 9am–6pm/dusk. ◷Closed last Fri Nov, 25 Dec. ☜£10, gardens only, £4. ▣✗. ℘01623 455 900. www.newsteadabbey.org.uk.

The medieval priory of the abbey was converted in the 16C into a house that became the ancestral seat of Lord Byron. The 19C rooms include the apartments of Byron and a selection of his manuscripts, memorabilia and portraits. Lakes, gardens and parkland.

Sherwood Forest

▷ 21mi/34km N of Nottingham.
Once one of the 65 Royal Forests which covered much of England, Sherwood was protected from agriculture and development by royal hunting laws: in this perfect environment for poaching, the outlaw bands became legends, and by the 15C **Robyn Hode** had become a composite folk-tale character embracing all their exploits. The **Sherwood Forest Visitor Centre and Country Park** (1mi/1.6km N of Edwinstowe; ◷open daily dawn–dusk, visitor centre open daily 10am–5pm, winter 10–4.30pm; ◷closed 25 Dec; ♿▣ (charge) ✗; ℘01623 823 202; www.nottingham shire.gov.uk) marks the area that was the legendary haunt of Robin Hood. From the visitor centre paths lead to the **Major Oak**, beneath which the outlaw is supposed to have sheltered. The tree is between 800 and 1,000 years old, and around 33ft/10m in diameter.

Southwell Minster★★

▷ 14mi/23km NE. ◷Open daily 7am–7pm/dusk. ☜£3 donation requested. ♿▣✗. ℘01636 812 649. www.southwellminster.org.uk.

Southwell – pronounced "su'thel" – is dominated by the Norman Minster, well known for the foliage carving of its late-13C master masons. It is the only cathedral in England to boast a complete set of three Norman towers and dates from c.1108. Smooth lawns and well-spaced graves frame the **west front**, pierced by a Perpendicular seven-light window. The intimate **interior** combines Norman severity with the glory of the mid-14C **screen**, depicting 286 images of men, gods and devils, and the even more glorious Early English **choir** and **chapter house** (1288). The latter is the first single-span stone-vaulted chapter house in Christendom, decorated with some of the finest medieval naturalism (late-13C) carved in stone.

Rufford Abbey Country Park

▷ Ollerton. 18mi/29km N.
◷Open daily summer 10am–5pm; winter 10.30am–4.30pm. ◷Closed 25 Dec. ♿▣ (charge summer weekends and bank hols).✗. ℘01623 821 338. www.nottinghamshire.gov.uk/ ruffordcp.

The present-day park once formed part of a 12C Cistercian abbey estate. Today's abbey is a mixture of Cistercian remains and one wing of a country house from the early-1600s. The Stable Block, which houses the Craft Centre (◷closed most Mons), dates from the 1660s with Victorian renovations. The grounds of the Abbey retain some fascinating features, such as its Ice Houses.

Leicestershire

Once the capital of King Lear's kingdom, and the seat of the 8C East Mercian bishops, the wealth of Leicester was based on the manufacture of hosiery, and to a lesser degree, coal mining, from the medieval period until the mid-20C. Today it is a cosmopolitan and increasingly fashionable town with the new £60 million Curve Theatre at the heart of its cultural regeneration.

LEICESTER

In the city centre, between the River Soar and St Martin's Square, is the **Guildhall**★ *(Guildhall Lane; ⓒOpen Feb–Nov Mon–Wed and Sat 11am–4.30pm, Sun1–4.30pm; ℘0116 253 2569; www.leicestermuseums.ac.uk)*, one of the best-preserved timber-framed halls in the country, dating back six hundred years. Note the robust timber roof and uprights in the Hall, the early-16C glass in the mayor's parlour, and one of the earliest public libraries in England.

It is now mainly a performance venue but also holds a small museum, including Victorian cells with a couple of "inmates" that amuse children.

Head southwest from the Guildhall to St Nicholas Circle, then turn down Castle Street for **St Mary de Castro Church**★ *(ⓒopen Easter–Oct Sat and bank hols 2–5pm; ⓖ; ℘0116 270 9995)*. The shadowy and attractive interior goes back to 1107. The best Norman work is the sedilia.

Southeast of the Guildhall, along Gallowtree Gate and Granby Street on New Walk *(ⓖsee map I)* at no. 53 is the town's major collection, the **New Walk Museum and Art Gallery**★ *(ⓒopen year-round Mon–Sat 10am–5pm, Sun 11am–5pm; ⓖ✕; ℘0116 255 4900; www.leicestermuseums.ac.uk)* The art galleries showcase changing displays of Modern and Old Masters including works by Hogarth and Francis Bacon and a permanent display of Picasso ceramics. There are also galleries on biodiversity, World Arts, and the ever-popular dinosaur and Egyptian mummies.

- ⚙ **Michelin Map:** Michelin Atlas p28 or Map 504 Q 26.
- ⬛ **Info:** 7–9 Every Street, Town Hall Square, Leicester. ℘0844 888 5181. www.goleicestershire.com.
- ⚇ **Kids:** National Space Centre; Snibston.
- ⚐ **Tours:** The route marked on the map offers a pleasant stroll.

EXCURSIONS

⚇ National Space Centre★

▷ *2mi/3km N, just off the A6.*
ⓒ*Open Tue–Sun and Mon during school hols 10am–5pm/4pm (last entry 90min before closing). ⊜£13, child £11. ▣(£2). ✕. ℘0116 261 0261. www.spacecentre.co.uk.*

Themed galleries include actual space hardware (a Russian Soyuz capsule, the British Blue Streak rocket…), hundreds of interactive hands-on activities and an exploration of the universe through the latest in audio-visual technology. The 138ft-/42m-high landmark **Rocket Tower** includes the only lunar lander simulator outside of America. Another highlight for many visitors is the 360-degree **Space Theatre** show, with laser and animation techniques, inside the UK's largest planetarium.

⚇ Snibston★

▷ *Ashby Road, Coalville. 16mi/26km NW on the A 50. ⓒOpen Apr–Oct. ⊜ Museum 6.95, child £4.75. ⓖ▣✕. ℘01530 278 444. www.leics.gov.uk/snibston.*

Coalville was a mining town from 1832 until the closure of its colliery in 1986. The pit and ancient colliery buildings have been transformed into landscaped grounds and a country park. Activities *(ⓒSat–Sun and school hols only)* include an above-ground **colliery tour** with an underground simulator *(⊜£1.95, child £1.20)*, and a short ride aboard a full-size 1960s **train** *(⊜£1.50, child 95p)*. An impressive exhibition hall and museum contains over 90 hands-on sta-

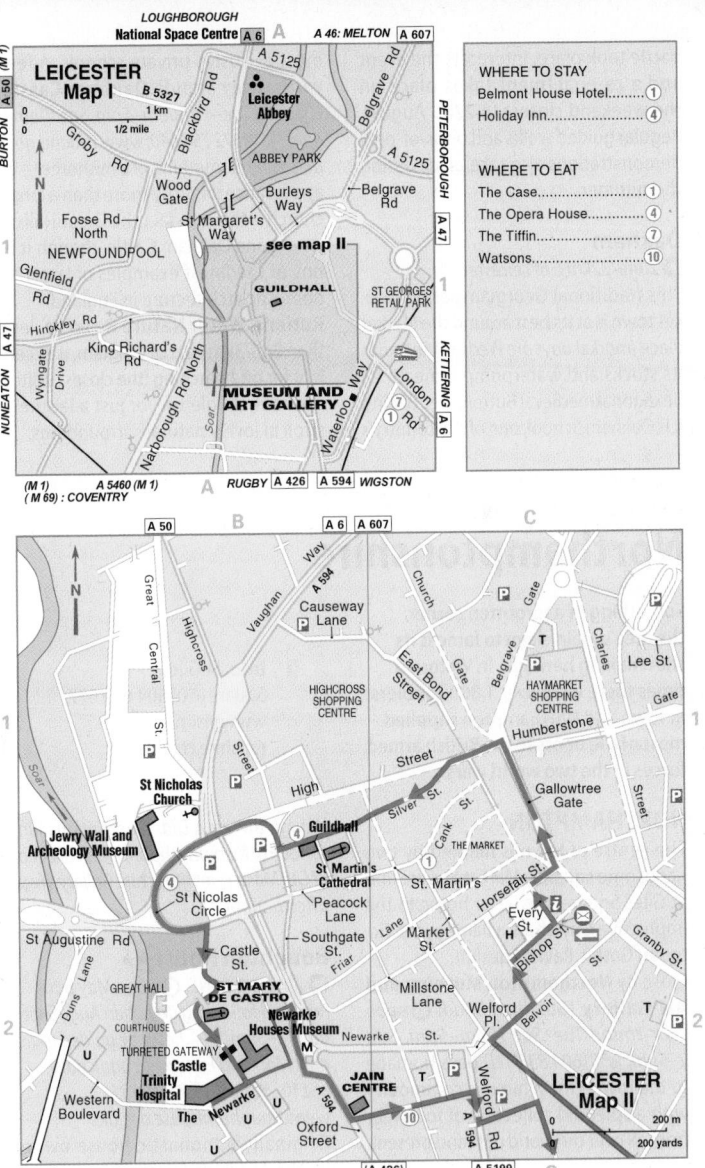

LEICESTER
Map I

National Space Centre

LEICESTER Abbey

ABBEY PARK

Wood Gate

Burleys Way

Belgrave Rd

St Margaret's Way

see map II

NEWFOUNDPOOL

Fosse Rd North

Glenfield Rd

Hinckley Rd

King Richard's Rd

GUILDHALL

ST GEORGES RETAIL PARK

MUSEUM AND ART GALLERY

(M 1)   A 5460 (M 1)   RUGBY   A 426   A 594   WIGSTON
(M 69) : COVENTRY

WHERE TO STAY

Belmont House Hotel.........①

Holiday Inn.....................④

WHERE TO EAT

The Case.........................①

The Opera House.............④

The Tiffin.......................⑦

Watsons.........................⑩

LEICESTER Map II

HIGHCROSS SHOPPING CENTRE

HAYMARKET SHOPPING CENTRE

St Nicholas Church

Jewry Wall and Archeology Museum

Guildhall

St Martin's Cathedral

St Nicolas Circle

Gallowtree Gate

THE MARKET

St Augustine Rd

Castle St.

GREAT HALL

ST MARY DE CASTRO

COURTHOUSE

TURRETED GATEWAY

Newarke Houses Museum

Castle

Trinity Hospital

Western Boulevard

The Newarke

JAIN CENTRE

Oxford Street

tions telling the story of local technology and design. It includes an impressive working steam engine, a prototype jet engine, and an extensive range of clothing created by some of the UK's biggest names in fashion.

Bosworth Battlefield

▶ *Sutton Cheney, Market Bosworth. 14mi/23km W.* ⏱ *Heritage centre open daily Feb–Mar and Nov–Dec 10am –4pm; Apr–Oct 10am–5pm.* ⊗£7. 🅿 *(£2.50).* ✕. ☎*01455 290 429. www.bosworthbattlefield.com.*

In 1485 Richard III was killed at the Battle of Bosworth and the first Tudor monarch, Henry VII, took the throne, ending years of dynastic war. An excellent new state-of-the-art visitor centre, on the edge of the rolling fields where the battle took place, interprets the event and a re-enactment takes place on the weekend closest to 22nd August. Regular guided walks and birds-of-prey demonstrations also take place during the summer.

Oakham

▶ *20mi/32km E of Leicester.*

This traditional Georgian-period market town is at its best around the Market Place *(market days are Wed and Sat)* with its stocks and waterpump beneath its hexagonal medieval Buttercross. Behind it is Oakham School, one of the country's most exclusive private schools. A few yards away stands **Oakham Castle** (◷ open Tue–Fri 10am–5pm, Sat 10am–4pm; ☏ *01572 758 440; www.rutland.gov. uk/castle).* Something of a misnomer – in appearance it is little more than a large church – this is in fact the Great Hall of long-gone Oakham Castle, though it is one of the finest examples of late-12C domestic architecture in England.

Rutland Water Nature Reserve, less than 2mi/3km east of Oakham, is excellent for birdwatching (the closest visitor centre is at Egleton), or just a leisurely stroll in lovely natural surroundings.

Northamptonshire

Something of a forgotten corner, the area's main claim to fame is its shoemaking heritage. In Victorian times there were over 1,800 cobblers in town and Northampton supplied most of the boots to the British armed forces in the two world wars.

> **Info:** St Giles Square ☏ 01604 622 677. www.visitnortham-tonshire.co.uk

NORTHAMPTON

The centre of town is marked by two handsome squares, Market Square and St Giles Square, the latter home to the impressive **Guildhall**, a flamboyant Victorian Gothic Revival design.

Close by **Northampton Museum and Art Gallery** (*Guildhall Road;* ◷ *open year-round Tue–Sat 10am–5pm, Sun 2–5pm;* ☏ *01604 838 111)* pays homage to the town's most famous commodity with a splendid collection of footwear from all over the world past and present.

EXCURSIONS
Althorp

▶ *6mi/10km NW.* ◷ *Open Jul–Aug daily 11am–5pm.* ✆ *£13.* ☏ *01607 770 107. www.althorp.com.*

Althorp is the seat of the Spencer family and is best known as being the final resting place of **Diana, Princess of Wales**. *Her grave is on an island in a lake and is not accessible to the public,* though there is a Diana exhibition filling six rooms; for many the priceless collection of Old Masters in the Picture Gallery are an afterthought.

Boughton House★★

▶ *21mi/34km NE.* ◷ *Open May bank hols and following day, then Aug–Sept daily 2–5pm.* ⟜ *Entry by guided tours only Mon and Fri (except bank hols).* ✆ *£10 .* ✕ *.* ☏ *01536 515 731. www.boughtonhouse.org.uk.*

Originally a monastic house owned by the Abbey of Edmundsbury, it was bought by Edward Montagu in 1528 and extended. More were made by the first Duke of Montagu, ambassador to Louis XIV, who built the north front and embellished the interior turning it into "the English Versailles". Among its paintings are masterpieces by El Greco, Murillo, Teniers the Younger, Gainsborough, Van Dyck, Lely and Kneller.

Lincolnshire

The city of Lincoln and its cathedral rises physically and metaphorically above the wolds, marshes and north East Anglian seaside resorts like a beacon. Only Stamford is comparable in terms of metropolitan interest though there are also many fine country houses to visit.

LINCOLN★★

Set high on a limestone plateau beside the River Witham and dominated by the triple towers of the cathedral, Lincoln is visible for miles around the eastern English countryside. Much of the lower part of the town is a pedestrianised shopping area dotted with the occasional medieval church; steep narrow streets lead to the upper town with its imposing cathedral, castle and Roman remains.

A Bit of History

Lindum Colonia, a settlement established since the Bronze Age and occupied by the Ninth Legion in about AD 60, was turned into a *colonia* (colonial settlement) in about AD 96 and confined to the plateau-top (42 acres/17ha) surrounded by a wooden palisade. In the 3C Lincoln, now one of the four provincial capitals of Roman Britain, doubled in size. The city spread down the southern slopes to the river and was encased in a gated stone wall (4.5ft/1.5m thick) – offering a

▶ **Population:** 80,281.

⚙ **Michelin Map:** Michelin Atlas p36 or Map 502 S 24.

🛈 **Info:** 9 Castle Hill, Cathedral Quarter. ✆01522 545 458. www.lincoln.gov.uk; www.visitlincolnshire.com.

▶ **Location:** Northeast Midlands, 88mi/142km from Birmingham and 39mi/63km from Nottingham. The train station and bus station are almost opposite each other in the lower part of the city centre. It's easy to cover the centre on foot, albeit a steep walk from "downhill" to "uphill".

👁 **Don't Miss:** The cathedral, especially the roof tour (Saturday only) on a clear day; the High Bridge; Belvoir Castle.

🕐 **Timing:** Allow a full day to see the cathedral and town.

🚶 **Walking Tours:** The Lincoln Guild of Guides operates several city centre tours on a daily basis. Ask at the tourist office.

Lincoln Cathedral

A. Williams/MICHELIN

good view from the Bishop's Old Palace. The surviving **Newport Arch**, the only Roman arch in England through which traffic still passes, was the city's north gate.

Lincoln survived the Roman decline, emerging as the capital of the Anglo-Saxon kingdom of Lindsey, and converted to Christianity in c.630. After the Conquest, it gained in importance, with the building of the castle and cathedral, and became one of the most prosperous cities in medieval England, shipping its wool direct to Flanders. Many half-timbered buildings survive from this time

CITY WALK

Cathedral★★★

⊙ *Open summer Mon–Fri 7.15am–8pm, Sat–Sun 7.15am–6pm; winter Mon–Sat. 7.15am–6pm, Sun 7.15–5pm.* *Guided tours Mon–Sat 11am onwards (free), cathedral floor, tower (Apr–Oct) and roof (Apr–Oct), see website for details.* £6. . . ℘ 01522 561 600. www.lincolncathedral.com.

The first cathedral, built by Remigius, was early Norman, the result of a short and decisive programme between 1072 and 1092. Alexander, Lincoln's third bishop, builder of Newark Castle, re-roofed the cathedral following a fire in 1141. Hugh of Avalon, a French monk, built the present Early English cathedral following the earthquake of 1185, which virtually destroyed the original Norman building.

Few cathedrals have achieved such even proportions: the chancel is as long as the nave, the west towers almost as high as the crossing tower. The **west front**, the most famous view, consists of early Norman central sections, surrounded by a cliff-face of Early English blind arcading. The south side is graced by the intricate carving inside the **Galilee Porch** and **Judgement Porch** and the north side provides a splendid and varied view of the buttressed Decorated **east end**, the north transept and the flying-buttressed chapter house.

Interior – Lincoln limestone and Purbeck marble shafts combine to create piers of contrasted texture which support the tri-forium, clerestory and vaults, showing Early English architecture at its best.

The **nave** is composed of seven bays; an exceptional font of Tournai marble stands in the second south bay; the windows are filled with Victorian stained glass. The crossing is flooded with light from the windows of the **Dean's Eye** (13C glass) in the north transept and the **Bishop's Eye** (14C leaf-patterned tracery, filled with fragments of medieval stained glass) in the south.

East of the magnificent 14C stone screen is **St Hugh's Choir**, furnished with 14C oak **misericords** and covered with the so-called "crazy vault of Lincoln", the first rib-vault of purely decorative intentions in Europe, curiously asymmetrical yet "easier to criticise than improve" (Pevsner). The **Angel Choir** is geometrical (late Early English), rich, light and spacious, so called after the 28 carved stone angels in the spandrels beneath the upper windows.

The soaring **East Window** of Victorian glass depicts biblical scenes in the earliest Gothic eight-light window (1275). High on the first pier from the east end on the north side, the **Lincoln Imp**, the grotesque little character that has become the city's emblem, looks down on the shrine of St Hugh.

The 13C **cloister** is vaulted in wood (note the bosses: a man pulling a face, a man sticking out his tongue). Forming the north range is Christopher Wren's **Library**, above a Classical loggia. East of the cloister is the **Chapter House** (early-13C) – the vaulting springing from a central shaft and externally supported by flying buttresses – where Edward I and II held some of the early English parliaments.

Precincts – Amid the mostly Georgian and Victorian houses the **Vicar's Court** dates from 1300–1400; the four ranges and mid-15C barn behind are a rare survival and among the prettiest examples of their kind in England.

The **Bishop's Palace**, *(EH;* ⊙ *open Apr–Oct Thu–Mon 10am–5pm, Nov–Mar Sat–Sun 10am–4pm;* ⊙ *closed 1 Jan, 24–26 Dec;* £4.40; ; ℘ 01522 527 468; www.english-heritage.org.uk)* is ruined but redolent of its former grandeur and gives an idea of the richness of Lincoln's medieval prelates. According to a description before its destruction in the Civil War, "the great hall is very fair, lightsome and strong… one large middle alley and two out alleys on either side with eight grey marble pillars bearing up the arches and free-stone windows very full of stories in painting glass of the Kings of this land."

Castle Hill

This street, which is lined by houses dating from the 16C to the 19C, links the 14C **Exchequer Gate** and the East Gate leading to the castle.

Castle★

🕐 Open daily Apr and Sept 10am–5pm; May–Aug 10am–6pm; Oct–Mar 10am–4pm. 🚶 Guided tour Apr–Sept daily 11am, 2pm; for winter times, see website. 🕐 Closed 1 Jan and 24–26 Dec. May–Aug 10am–6pm, May and Sept 10am–5pm; Oct–Apr 10am–4pm. 🎫£6. ✕. ☏01522 511 068.
www.lincolnshire.gov.uk.

The construction of the Norman cast was begun by William the Conqueror in 1068, though nothing remains of the original. The keep's mound is now crowned by the late-12C **Lucy Tower**, once surrounded by a ditch (20ft/6m deep) and a drawbridge. At the top is a circular Victorian burial ground for prisoners, marked by rows of small gravestones. The **East Gate** was added in the 12C, **Cobb Hall** in the 13C. This was a defensive tower and in the 19C the roof was the scene of public hangings. Iron rings, still fixed to the walls, were used to attach prisoners' chains.

A Norman tower was enlarged in the 14C and added to in the 19C when it became known as the Observatory Tower, from which there is a splendid **view** of the cathedral and the surrounding countryside. It is possible to walk round the walls along the east, north and west sides (not recommended for vertigo sufferers). Although besieged in the wars of 1135–54 and 1216–17, the castle gradually lost its military significance but became a centre for the administration of justice which continues to this day; it is home to the Crown Court.

The Georgian **Prison Building**, constructed between 1787 and 1791, is now used to display one of the four surviving copies of **Magna Carta** (1215) in a darkened room accompanied by a voice intoning its contents in medieval Latin. The vellum document is preceded by a small exhibition explaining the document's history and importance to democracy.

In the **Victorian Prison Building** (1845/46), where prisoners were kept in solitary confinement, is a tableau showing oakum picking and the tiered **Prison Chapel** where a preacher addressed prisoners in their separate pews.

Jew's House★

The house and its beautifully designed Norman windows and doorway and original chimney buttress date from c.1170; the adjoining **Jew's Court** was once used as a synagogue.

The Collection and Usher Gallery★

Danes Terrace. 🕐 Open year-round daily 10am–4pm. 🕐 Closed 24–26, 31 Dec. ♿✕. ☏01522 550 990.
www.thecollection.lincoln.museum.

This is a new space devoted to art and archaeology in Lincoln. The latter comprises artefacts from the Stone, Bronze and Iron Ages, Roman, Saxon, Viking and medieval eras as well as fine, decorative and contemporary visual arts. Usher Gallery treasures are 16C–19C **miniatures**, 17C and 18C French and English clocks, Chinese, Sèvres, Meissen and English **porcelain** and English and continental glass. A room is devoted to the watercolours of **Peter de Wint** (1784–1849), who painted views of the Lincolnshire countryside and of Lincoln Cathedral. In the **Tennyson** room are many of the poet's personal items including hats, pens, the warrant appointing him Poet Laureate, and photos of his funeral. Other treasures include paintings by Turner, Stubbs and Lowry, and clocks with wooden movements by Robert Sutton.

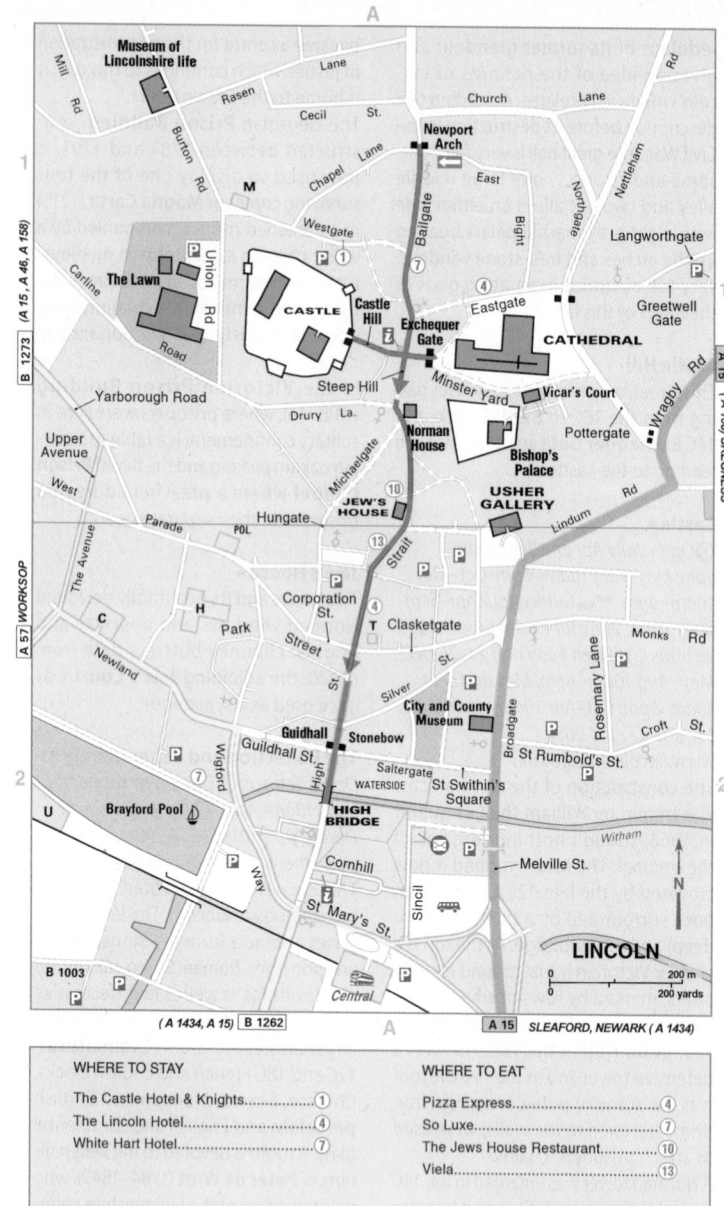

LINCOLN

WHERE TO STAY	
The Castle Hotel & Knights	①
The Lincoln Hotel	④
White Hart Hotel	⑦

WHERE TO EAT	
Pizza Express	④
So Luxe	⑦
The Jews House Restaurant	⑩
Viela	⑬

High Bridge★★

Medieval (though much restored), with the River Witham flowing through its Norman vaults (the Glory Hole), its timber-framed houses are a unique reminder of what Old London Bridge must have looked like. Upstream is **Brayford Pool**, Lincoln's medieval port,

while downstream are two historic inns, the 14C Green Dragon and the 15C Witch and Wardrobe.

Museum of Lincolnshire Life

Burton Road. ⊙Open; Apr–Sept daily 10am–4pm; Oct–Mar Mon–Sat 10am–4pm. Ellis Mill open; Apr–Sept Sat–Sun

2–5pm; Oct–Apr. Sun 2pm–dusk. ⏰Closed 1 Jan, 24–26, 31 Dec. ✕. ☎01522 528 448. www.lincolnshire.gov.uk.
Housed in the former barracks of the Royal North Lincoln Militia is a display on local domestic, social and industrial life over the last two centuries, with recreations of traditional life.
Behind the museum, the **Ellis Mill** is a restored late-18C working windmill.

EXCURSIONS
Belvoir Castle★★
▶ 35mi/56km SW on the A 607 via Grantham; in Denton turn right (signs).
🔦Guided tour only May–Aug most Suns–Mons 11.15am, 1.15pm, 3.15pm, see website for dates. Gardens open 11am–5pm. ⏱£12. ♿🅿(charge)✕. ☎01476 871 002.
www.belvoircastle.com.
Built by John Webb, a pupil of Inigo Jones, in 1654–68, Belvoir (pronounced "beaver") was romanticised by James Wyatt into an early-19C "castle on a hill." The interior is part Gothic fantasy, part Baroque fantasy; the Ballroom contains Thomas Becket's illuminated breviary. The ceiling of the Elizabeth Saloon depicts Jupiter, Juno, Mercury and Venus. In the picture gallery are miniatures (Hilliard and Oliver) and paintings by Jan Steen, Cornelius Janssen, David Teniers II, Poussin and Gainsborough. The Regent's Gallery (131ft/40m long) is hung with vast Gobelins tapestries.

Belton House★
NT. ▶ 26mi/42km S on the A 607.
⏰Open 1st2 Sats–Suns Mar, mid-Mar–Oct Wed–Sun, Good Fri and bank hols 12.30am–5pm. ⏱£9.95. ♿🅿✕. ☎01476 566 116.
www.nationaltrust.org.uk.
Belton is the fulfilment of the golden age of English domestic architecture from Wren to Adam. The Classical simplicity of the Marble Hall provides the setting for paintings by Reynolds, Hoppner and Romney; the woodcarvings in the Salon are possibly the work of Grinling Gibbons; and in the Red Drawing Room is Fra Bartolomeo's Madonna and Child.

Doddington Hall★
▶ 5mi/8km SW. ⏰Open Easter Sun–Sept Wed, Sun and bank hols. Garden also open mid-Feb–Apr and Oct Sun only. House 1pm–5pm. Gardens 11am–5pm. ⏱£8.50, gardens only, £5. ♿🅿✕. ☎01522 694 308.
www.doddingtonhall.com.
Doddington Hall is late Elizabethan and outward-looking, abandoning the traditional internal courtyard. With the exception of the parlour, all the interior was refurbished in 1764 by Thomas Lumby, a local builder. The **parlour** itself is in Queen Anne style, its walls graced with paintings, including works by Sir Thomas Lawrence, Sir Peter Lely and Ghaerardt. The stairs are a masterpiece. The superb **Long Gallery** has displays of paintings and porcelain.
The **West Garden** is a riot of colour from April through to September, with luxuriant, wide borders.

Belvoir Castle

© Ian Bracegirdle/Dreamstime.com

Gainsborough Old Hall★

EH. ◐ *18mi/29km W on the A 57 (Z) and N on the A 156.* ◑*Open Mar–Oct Mon–Fri 10am–5pm, Sat–Sun 11am–5pm; Nov–Feb Mon–Fri 10am–4pm, Sat 11am–4pm.* ◑*Closed 2wks over Christmas and March 2012.* £5. ♿⃝🅿✕. ℰ*01427 612 669.*
www.gainsborougholdhall.co.uk; www.english-heritage.org.uk.

One of the best-preserved late-medieval manor houses in England, this striking timber-framed hall was built between 1460 and 1480. Richard III visited it in 1483. It was originally all timber framed, except for the brick kitchen, brick tower and stone bay window, but Elizabethan features were added to the two ranges. The Hall itself has a sturdy single-arched braced roof; the **kitchen** gives an excellent impression of medieval life in the servants' quarters. The east wing contains great chambers, while the west wing is a unique example of 15C lodgings. The tower is furnished as a late-15C bedchamber. There is a permanent exhibition about the Old Hall and the Mayflower Pilgrims.

WOLDS AND COAST

ℹ*www.visittheseaside.com.*
Unless you have children in tow or you are a fan of the old-fashioned English seaside resort, you'll probably want to give a wide berth to Skegness/Ingoldmells, Mablethorpe and Cleethorpes. However, the rest of Lincolnshire's 50mi/80km of coastline is a wild and unspoiled haven for nature with a rich variety of reserves, sanctuaries and long sandy beaches to enjoy.
The Wolds, low rolling hills and valleys, are at their most attractive around Louth.

Louth

◐*27mi/43km NE of Lincoln.* ℹ*Town hall.* ℰ*01507 609 289. www.louth.org.*
The "historic capital of the Wolds", Louth is its most attractive town. Dating mostly from the 17C and 18C its skyline is dominated by the Church of St James, with a 295ft-/90m-tall spire. It gained historical fame as the centre for an uprising

against the religious reforms of Henry VIII, for which its vicar paid the ultimate price. The town champions independent shops and local produce best seen on market days *(Wed, Fri, Sat).*

Skegness

◐*43mi/69km east of Lincoln.*
ℹ *Embassy Theatre.* ℰ*0845 674 0505. www.visitskegness.co.uk.*
With its broad golden sands, seaside pier, souvenir shops, amusement arcades/parks, caravan sites and boarding houses, Skegness is the quintessential English seaside resort of yesteryear. It reached its peak in the 1960s and in essence hasn't changed much since then. Its most worthwhile visitor attraction is the **Natureland Seal Sanctuary** *(North Parade;* ◑*open daily from 10am, see website for closing times;* £7.20, child £4.70; ℰ*01754 764 345; www.skegness natureland.co.uk),* which has been tending to abandoned baby seals since 1965.
If you prefer nature in the raw, head south to **Gibralter Point National Nature Reserve** *(*◑*visitor centre open Apr–Oct daily 10am–4pm, Nov–Mar Mon–Fri 11am–3pm, Sat–Sun 11am–4pm;* ♿🅿 (charge)✕; ℰ*01754 898 057; www.lincstrust.org.uk/reserves),* home to a great variety of birdlife including wildfowl, waders and gulls.

LINCOLNSHIRE FENS

ℹ *www.visitlincolnshire.com.*
By turns, fascinating and monotonous, this pancake-flat, almost treeless territory, criss-crossed by narrow waterways, has been reclaimed from the sea to provide some of England's finest arable land.

Boston

◐*32mi/51km SE of Lincoln.*
ℹ *Guildhall Museum, South Street.*
This attractive market town is dominated by the vast bulk of its 14C **St Botolph's Church** *(*◑*open daily 8.30am–4.30pm;* £2.50 to ascend tower Mon–Sat; ℰ*01205 354 670; www.parish-of-boston. org.uk),* whose 271ft-/83m-16C tower is a landmark for miles around.

The **Guildhall** (South Street; ⏰ open Wed–Sat 10.30am–3.30pm; ☎ 01205 365 954; www.bostonguildhall.co.uk) is the best place to learn how the town developed from its Hanseatic League port and wool-trading origins, how Boston, Massachusetts was named after Boston Lincolnshire, and more.

A 10-minute walk (1mi/1.6km) from the High Street, is the spectacular **Maud Foster Windmill** (⏰ open year-round Wed and Sat 10am–5pm, summer school hols Wed–Sat 10am–5pm; £2.50; ☎ 01205 352 188; www.maudfoster.co.uk), one of the tallest windmills in the country. Climb its seven floors to see flour being made.

Stamford★★

▶ 45mi/72km S of Lincoln.
🛈 Arts Centre, 27 St Mary's Street.
☎ 01780 755 611.
www.southwestlincs.com.

Stamford has a long history, being one of the five Danelaw towns. Sir Walter Scott called it "the finest stone town in England" and it has maintained its elegance. In 1967 it was the first town in England to be designated a Conservation Area, boasting over **600 listed buildings** of mellow limestone in the town centre alone, and including five medieval churches.

St Martin's Church★

High Street St Martin's. ⏰ Open daily 10am–4pm. Contribution requested.
The church was rebuilt c.1480 in the Perpendicular style. The north chapel is dominated by the alabaster monument to **William Cecil**, **Lord Burghley** (1520–98). In the nearby churchyard is the grave of **Daniel Lambert** (1770–1809, 52st 11lb/335kg when he died), reputed to be the fattest man in England.

Lord Burghley's Hospital★

Station Road and High Street St Martin's. These charming late Elizabethan almshouses were built on the site of the medieval hospital of St John the Baptist and St Thomas the Martyr in 1597.

Browne's Hospital★

Broad Street. ⏰ Open May–Sept Sat and bank hols 11am–4pm, Sun 2–4.30pm. £2.50. ☎ 01780 763 153. www.stamfordcivicsociety.org.uk.
One of the best-preserved medieval hospitals in England, Browne's was built c.1475, with cubicles for "ten poor men". The chapel and the audit room are lit by late-15C stained glass.

Stamford Library

High Street. ☎ 01780 482 518. www.lincolnshire.gov.uk.
The library is due to host a new museum of Stamford history (⏰ scheduled to open Dec 2011) which will tell the story of Stamford from its Saxon origins onwards. One of its favourite exhibits will be a life-size model of **Daniel Lambert** (👆 see above), with his original clothes.

Burghley★★

▶ 2mi/3km E of Stamford.
⏰ Open mid-Mar–Oct daily 11am–4.30pm. House open Sat–Thu and Good Fri. Guided tour daily 3pm. £12.20, gardens only, £7. ☎ 01780 752 451. www.burghley.co.uk.

This is one of the country's finest Elizabethan mansions, built by **William Cecil**, **Lord Burghley**. The extensive late-17C redecorations include Baroque ceilings painted by **Laguerre** and **Verrio**, at their most exuberant in the **Heaven and Hell Rooms**.

The distinguished collection of **paintings** includes works by Veronese, Bassano, Gainsborough, Kneller and Lawrence and Brueghel the Younger. Capability Brown (by Nathaniel Dance) looks out over the grounds he created. A fascinating recent addition to the grounds is **The Gardens of Surprise**, including a moss house, swivelling Caesar busts, jets of water, a mirrored maze and more. There is also a contemporary **Sculpture Garden**.

ADDRESSES

🏨 STAY

NOTTINGHAM

⬤ **Best Western Westminster Hotel** – *312 Mansfield Road.* ℘*0115 955 5000. www.bw-westminsterhotelnottingham. co.uk.* 🅿. *75rms.* £⬤. Adjoining Victorian houses converted to a hotel, the Westminster is a family-friendly place 1mi/1.6km from the city centre.

⬤ **Park Hotel** – *5–7 Waverley Street.* ℘*0115 978 6299. www.parkhotel nottingham.co.uk.* 🅿. *27 rms.* This recently refurbished premium budget hotel combines original turn-of-the-20th-century features with a modern design and soft tones. A short walk from town, with a view of the arboretum, it enjoys both a quiet and a central location.

⬤⬤⬤ **Nottingham Belfry Hotel** – *Mellers Way, Off Woodhouse Way.* ℘*0115 973 9393. www.qhotels.co.uk.* 🅿. *120 rms.* Some 3mi/5km out of town, this luxury business-oriented hotel, in contemporary steel-and-glass boxy style, is superbly equipped including a top-class spa and indoor pool.

LEICESTER

🏨 The city centre has plenty of hotels but B&Bs are mostly on the outskirts.

⬤⬤–⬤⬤⬤ **Belmont House Hotel** – *De Montfort Street.* ℘*0116 254 4773. www.belmonthotel.co.uk.* 🅿. *77 rms.* Ideally situated in a pleasant part of the town centre this handsome family-owned and run characterful Victorian terrace hotel features recently refurbished sumptuous décor alongside contemporary furniture.

⬤⬤⬤⬤ **Holiday Inn** – *129 St Nicholas Circle.* ℘*0871 942 9048.* . *www.holidayinn. com.* 🅿. *188 rms.* Modern city-centre high-rise chain hotel with swimming pool, sauna and jacuzzi.

LINCOLN

⬤⬤⬤ **The Castle Hotel** – *Westgate.* ℘*01522 538 801. www.castle hotel.net.* 🅿. *20 rms.* The bedrooms at this smart modern city-centre hotel feature timeless, classic styling, and most have excellent views of the castle walls or the cathedral.

⬤⬤⬤ **The Lincoln Hotel** – *Eastgate.* ℘*01522 520 348. www.thelincolnhotel.com.* 🅿. *72 rms.* This light airy very modern hotel features rooms stepping out to a garden or balcony with cathedral views. There are also fabulous views from the restaurant, lounge and terrace lawn bar.

⬤⬤⬤ **White Hart Hotel** – *Bailgate.* ℘*01522 526 222. www.whitehart-lincoln. co.uk.* *59 rms.* Elegant very British luxury hotel with traditional furnishings, antiques and modern comforts. Many of the rooms have views of the cathedral or castle. Good grill restaurant (⬤⬤⬤).

STAMFORD

⬤⬤ **Garden House** – *42 High Street, St Martin's.* ℘*01780 763 359. www.garden househotel.com.* 🅿. *20 rms.* Near Burghley Park, a few minutes' stroll from the centre of town, and dating in part from the late-17C, the Garden House has retained much of its original charm to provide a haven of calm. It features 1 acre/0.4ha of walled gardens, and a charming conservatory restaurant serving classic English dishes. The rooms are elegant (superior rooms include four-posters) and offer superb value.

⬤⬤⬤⬤ **The George of Stamford** – *71 St Martin's.* ℘*01780 750 750. www.georgehotelofstamford.com. 47 rms.* The town's premier address, this 900-year-old inn, once used by the Knights Crusaders, then a coaching inn (its current incarnation), has a walled garden and courtyard, oak-paneled dining rooms and exudes old-fashioned English luxury.

🍽/EAT

NOTTINGHAM

🏨 Nottingham is famous for the number of bars and pubs in the city centre. The most traditional are **Ye Olde Trip to Jerusalem** – the oldest inn in England (*Brewhouse Yard;* ℘*0115 947 3171; www.triptojerusalem.com);* **The Salutation Inn** (*73–75 Maid Marian Way;* ℘*0115 988 1948);* **The Bell Inn** (*18 Angel Row;* ℘*0115 947 5241).*

⊖–⊖⊜ **Cock & Hoop** – *25 High Pavement. ℘0115 852 3231. www. thefinessecollection. com.* Set in the heart of the buzzing Lace Market, this traditional Victorian alehouse has been tastefully restored into a gastropub with cosy corners, comfy armchairs, well-chosen antiques and beautiful artwork. The food is a modern take on pub classics and British "nursery puddings".

LEICESTER

⊛ Leicester has a large Asian population and many excellent authentic Indian restaurants – try Belgrave Road/Melton Road ("Little India").

⊜ **The Tiffin** – *1 De Montfort Street. ℘0116 247 0420. www.the-tiffin.co.uk.* This very popular place with a gentle Eastern theme to its décor serves northern Indian cuisine.

⊜⊜ **The Case** – *4-6 Hotel Street. ℘0116 251 7675. www.thecase.co.uk. Closed Sun and bank hols.* This stylish modern restaurant is set on the first floor of a light airy Victorian luggage factory with lots of gleaming wood. Robust Modern British cooking (comfort food favourites also always on the menu) served in a lively atmosphere. Book a window seat for fine views down onto the city centre. Also includes a champagne bar, tasting rooms and shop.

LINCOLN

⊜⊜ **Straits Brasserie** – *8–9 The Strait. ℘01522 576 765. www.viela.co.uk. Closed Sun–Mon.* An odd, but winning combination of Brazilian classics and Lincolnshire favourites, combined with Modern British cooking.

⊜⊜⊜ **The Jews House Restaurant** – *15 The Strait. ℘01522 524 851. www.jews houserestaurant.co.uk.* Set in a beautiful 12C stone house (one of the oldest in all England) in the city centre, the Jew's House serves Modern European cuisine.

STAMFORD

⊜ **The Tobie Norris** – *12 St Paul's Street. ℘01780 753 800. www.tobienorris.com.* This is not only the best pub in town, it is one of the finest of its kind in the country. Set in a very rustic 13C building, on three floors each of its seven spacious atmospheric rooms are decorated with country-style antiques, large wooden

settles and comfy settees; outside is a large enclosed patio. It serves a superb range of real ales and excellent home-made food specialising in stone-baked pizzas.

CALENDAR OF EVENTS

NOTTINGHAM

Goose Fair – *www.nottinghamgoosefair. co.uk.* One of Europe's largest travelling fairs, held in early October.

Robin Hood Festival – *www.nottinghamshire.gov.uk/ robinhoodfestival. End Oct.* medieval-themed celebrations in Sherwood Forest on the life and times of the famous outlaw.

LEICESTER

Indian festivals: Navaratri *(Oct)*, music and dance; **Diwali** *(Nov)*, the festival of light, culminating in a huge fireworks display.

Leicester Caribbean Carnival – *℘0116 273 6649. www.leicestercarnival.com. Aug.* The Afro-Caribbean community celebrates its culture with colourful floats and vibrant music in the second-largest carnival (after Notting Hill) in Britain.

TOURS

NOTTINGHAM

Take a Nottingham Ghost Walk or a Nottingham Heroes and Villains walking tour *(www.experience nottinghamshire.com).*

LINCOLN

BY BOAT – On the River Witham departing from Brayford Pool:

Lincoln Boat Trips – *℘01522 881 200. www.lincolnboattrips.com. Easter–Sept daily 11am–3.45pm; Oct Sat–Sun 11am–3.45pm.* ⊜⊜⊜*£6.50.*

Walking tours – *℘01522 874 056. www.lincolnhistorywalks.co.uk. Wed– Sat 7pm, depart from the tourist office.* ⊜⊜⊜*£4.* Medieval Walks and Ghost Walks.

BOSTON

BY BOAT – Sailings from The Jolly Sailor Cafe, The Sluice Bridge, Witham Bank East, with Maritime Leisure Cruises *(℘07776 251 878. www.maritimecruises.co.uk).*

WEST MIDLANDS AND PEAKS

The Industrial Revolution began in the Midlands, its raw material hammered out in the forges of Ironbridge and refined in the world's first industrialised conurbation. The region is still a major industrial centre, though increasingly tourism and retail are coming to the fore. Its industrial heritage is second to none, while unspoiled shires and countryside, magnificent country houses and some of England's best walking trails are only ever a short distance away. Shakespeare's Stratford-on-Avon is a world famous cultural pilgrimage.

Highlights

1 A midsummer's night at the theatre in **Stratford-on-Avon** (p316)

2 Storm the castle during summer festivities at **Warwick** (p318)

3 Explore Britain's industrial heritage at **Ironbridge Gorge** (p324)

4 A summer's day out in the glorious gardens and house at **Chatsworth** (p336)

5 Hold on for dear life at **Alton Towers** theme park (p341)

Stratford-on-Avon may be inextricably linked with The Bard, but you don't have to be a fan of his works to appreciate its many beautiful timber-framed buildings or the picture-perfect thatch of Anne Hathaway's Cottage. There are more medieval properties to enjoy in neighbouring **Warwick**, which is even more compact than Stratford. Warwick Castle however is the big attraction, famous nationwide as England's finest castle. By contrast, the city of **Coventry**, relentlessly bombed during World War II, is a late-20C city, renowned for its striking 1960s cathedral. Its recovery was based on being Britain's "Motown" and it has a superb car museum to prove it. At the very centre of England **Birmingham** was formerly "the city of 1001 trades" and is often described as England's "second city" (in importance after London). Recently this former powerhouse of the Industrial Revolution has made huge strides from manufacturing centre to cultural hub.

To the south west, **Worcestershire** is the birthplace of a spicy sauce, the home of Royal Worcester Porcelain, and the site of the final battle of the English Civil War; but walkers know the county for the beautiful rolling landscapes of the quintessentially English Malvern Hills. Adjacent, **Herefordshire and the Wye Valley** butt up to the marches, or borderlands, of Wales. This is also perfect walking territory, with romantic ruined abbeys and castles recalling the area's rich history. Now returned to its beautiful natural state, you would never guess that Shropshire, to the north, was the birthplace of the Industrial Revolution. Evoking the days of dark satanic mills, the living history museums of Ironbridge comprise probably the finest industrial heritage complex in the world.

Elsewhere, **Shropshire** is quiet and unexplored, with the exception of charming historic Ludlow, now England's most important provincial food-lovers' town .

The **Peak District National Park** is another walkers' paradise, where, appropriately, the "right to roam" was born. Below rambling feet are a network of caves rejoicing in names such as the Devil's Arse, typical of the straight-talking qualities of the local folk. By contrast, magnificent halls and country houses also abound; Haddon Hall and Hardwick Hall are perfect showcases for the lives of 16C and 17C country nobility but finest of all is Chatsworth, probably the finest country estate in Britain.

Just outside the Park are the towns of **Derby** and **Stoke**. The latter's famous Potteries date back to the 14C but it was Josiah Wedgwood who really put Stoke on the map in the 18C. Today's visitors are more likely to be in search of white-knuckle thrills at Alton Towers, Britain's top theme park. Derby's porcelain also gained fame in the 18C and many splendid country houses are a short drive away.

Food Heroes

The charming market town of **Ludlow**, in Shropshire, is known as the provincial food and drink capital of England, thanks to its abundance of high quality independent food specialists in all sectors of the market. There are too many good local food shops to mention here but Wall's butchers (www.wallsbutchers.co.uk), Price's bakery (www.pricesthebakers.co.uk); and the Mousetrap (see below) are particularly worth a visit.

Just out of town the award-winning **Ludlow Food Centre** (www.ludlow foodcentre.co.uk) brings together local farming, food production and retailing: it butchery sources meat from the Centre's own estate; its bakery uses local flour; it has a deli, and a kitchen whose signature dish is Shropshire Fidget Pie, made with gammon, cooking apples, onions and potatoes), plus a jam and pickle kitchen. They make their own pasta and pastries and there is a café too.

The highlight of the food year is the **Ludlow Food Festival** (first weekend Sept, www.foodfestival.co.uk) featuring over 130 producers from Ludlow and the Marches (England–Wales border country). The Ludlow Spring Festival (Sat–Sun mid-May www.springevent.org.uk) is a beery celebration including over 140 draught real ales. A weekly Farmers' Market (www.localtoludlow.org.uk) takes place the second and fourth Thursday of each month.

Herefordshire has a proud, near 200-year old reputation for the quality of its **beef**, and the Hereford bull is a symbol of the town. The county is also renowned for **cider** making (www.ciderroute.co.uk) and Weston's Cider (www.westons-cider.co.uk), in Much Marcle, offer tours. Much less traditional is the county's newest success story, a premium vodka, made from potato and apple, at Chase Distillery (www.chasedistillery.co.uk), near Ledbury. Voted best vodka in the world 2010, it is on sale nationwide; stockists include the Ludlow Food Centre (see above). Chase also produce liqueurs, gin, marmalade vodka and an apple vodka.

You can watch **Little Herefordshire Cheese** being made at Pleck Farm, Monkland, just west of Leominster (www.mousetrapcheese.co.uk); the farm shop also stocks a range of other British farm cheeses, and there's a rustic café too. The company also has three Mousetrap Cheese Shops, (www.mousetrapcheese.co.uk), in Leominster, Ludlow and Hereford.

Bakewell, in Derbyshire, has given its name to the now ubiquitous commercially produced shortcrust pastry, jam and almond Bakewell Tart. However two shops in Bakewell offer what they both claim is the original recipe. The Bakewell Tart Shop & Coffee House (www.bakewelltartshop.co.uk) sells a Bakewell Tart while the (more historic) Old Original Bakewell Pudding Shop (www.bakewellpuddingshop.co.uk), which has a café/restaurant attached, bakes and sells a Bakewell Pudding.

Pork scratchings are perhaps the most popular snack in this region. These salted, crisp pieces of cooked pig skin are sold in small plastic bags. In the Birmingham area, scratchings is sometimes used as a term for diced, fried lard, which is eaten with pepper and salt.

Pikelets are the diminutive cousin of the crumpet, best served hot from the griddle (or the toaster if you buy them pre-prepared) with plenty of butter. In Warwickshire, Coventry is well-known for its **Coventry Godcakes**, which have a triangular shape in reference to the Holy Trinity.

In modern times Birmingham has become famous for its Balti cusiine, which originates from Pakistani Kashmir. There are over a hundred restaurants serving the cuisine in the city.

Stratford-upon-Avon★★

and around

Stratford is not only Shakespeare country but Forest of Arden country too. Its timber frames were hewn from the surrounding woods and its favourite son's mother was called Mary Arden. **William Shakespeare** (1564–1616) forsook his home town and his wife, Anne Hathaway, for London, where success came to him as a jobbing playwright, who was able to distil sex and violence, farce and philosophy into the most potent lines in the English language. He returned to Stratford in 1611, rich and famous enough to acquire a coat of arms, and lived at New Place until his death. Today Stratford is one of England's most popular tourist destinations.

▶ **Population:** 22,231.

Michelin Map: Michelin Atlas p27 or Map 503 P 27.

Info: 62 Henley Street. ℘01789 264 293. www.discover-stratford.com.

Location: 24mi/39km south of Birmingham. Its train station is on the edge of town, a 10-min walk away, the regional Riverside bus station is a 5 minute walk from the centre. Stratford is small enough to be able to comfortably cover most attractions on foot. A hop-on, hop-off City Sightseeing Bus covers the rest (℘£11.75; ℘01789 412 680; www.city-sighseeing.co.uk).

Don't Miss: Hall's Croft; a night at the theatre; Mary Arden's Farm.

Warning: The town can be very congested during the summer months.

Timing: Allow two days; more for excursions.

●TOWN WALK

Shakespeare's Birthplace★

Open daily Apr–May and Sept–Oct 9am–5pm; Jun–Aug 9am–6pm; Nov–Mar 10am–4pm. ℘£12.50 including entry to Hall's Croft and Nash's House joint ticket to all five houses £19.50 (buy online for 10 percent discount and free return). ℘01789 204 016. www.shakespeare.org.uk.

The half-timbered house where the dramatist was born is part museum (including a First Folio), part shrine. Note the graffiti on the upstairs windows (Scott, Carlyle, Ellen Terry and Henry Irving). In the same complex is an exhibition illustrating Shakespeare's life and times.

Harvard House

Closed until at least late-2012. For further information, call; ℘01789 204 016. www.shakespeare.org.uk.

This ornately carved half-timbered house bears the date 1596, when it was home to Katharine Rogers. The American flag flies in honour of her son, **John Harvard** (b.1607), founder of Harvard University, which owns the building today.

Tudor World (at the Falstaff Experience)

Open year-round daily 10am–5.30pm (winter may vary, see website. ℘£5. ℘01789 298 070. www.falstaffexperience.co.uk.

Two huge oak gates open onto the oldest remaining cobblestones in Stratford, where you will find the cavernous 16C Shrieve's House Barn, formerly the site of The Three Tunn's Tavern, run by William Rogers, the model for Shakespeare's Falstaff. The barn holds exhibits relating to crime and punishment, the plague, medicine, alchemy, school (and more) and re-creates part of a Tudor Street. Actors add a touch of drama to the proceedings. The property is internationally famous in paranormal circles –said to be one of the most haunted properties in the world – and **ghost tours** depart daily and nightly.

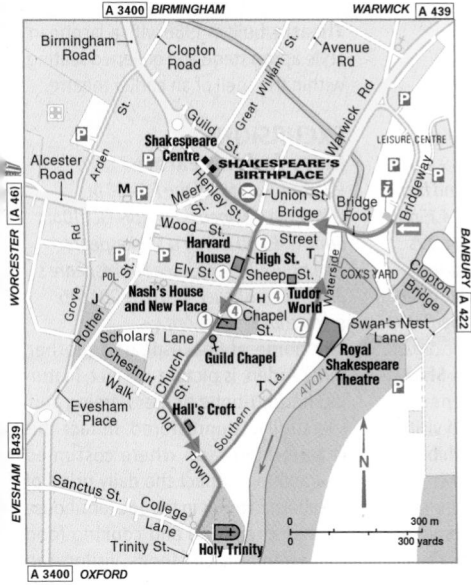

**STRATFORD-
UPON-AVON**

WHERE TO STAY

Mercure Shakespeare
Hotel..........................④

The Arden Hotel................⑦

The Legacy Falcon Hotel....①

WHERE TO EAT

Garrick Inn.......................①

Lambs..............................④

The Marlowe's
Restaurant.......................⑦

Nash's House and New Place★

🕐*entry details as Shakespeare's
Birthplace, but opens one hour later.*
Of New Place, Shakespeare's retirement
home, built in 1483, only the foundations remain marked by a picturesque
garden space. However, next door,
Nash's House, home of Shakespeare's
granddaughter, has been beautifully
restored and houses exhibitions.

Guild Chapel

🕐*Open daily 10am–4.30pm.*
📞*01789 204 671. www.stratfordguild
chapel-friends.org.uk.*
The Chapel of the Guild of the Holy
Cross (founded 1269), the ruling body
of Stratford before the Reformation,
is predominantly Perpendicular, with
wall-paintings of Christ, Mary, St John,
St Peter and the Last Judgement.

King Edward VI Grammar School

Exterior only.
Built c.1417 as the Holy Cross Hall and
turned into a school after the Reformation, it listed among its pupils a certain
William Shakespeare.

Hall's Croft★

🕐*Open daily Apr–Oct 10am–5pm;
Nov–Mar 11am–4pm. All other details as
Shakespeare's Birthplace.*
Shakespeare's eldest daughter, Susanna,
married physician John Hall and the cou-
ple lived here until some time after 1616.
The restored house, part 16C, part 17C,
contains furniture and paintings from
Hall's time, notes about his patients and
a small exhibition on medicine in his day.

Holy Trinity Church

🕐*Open (special services permitting)
Apr–Sept Mon–Sat 8.30am–6pm, Sun
12.30–5pm; Oct–Mar Sun 12.30–5pm;
Oct–Mar Mon–Sat 9am–4pm/5pm,
Sun 12.30–5pm; last entry 20min before
closing.* 🕐*Closed 1 Jan, Good Fri, 24–
26 Dec.* 💳*Church free, £2 donation
requested to view Shakespeare's grave.*
📞*01789 266 316. www.stratford-
upon-avon.org.*
With an Early English tower and transepts and early Perpendicular nave and
aisle, Holy Trinity would be notable even
without **Shakespeare's grave** on the
north side of the chancel. "Blessed be
the man who spares these stones / And
cursed be he that moves my bones."

Royal Shakespeare Company★

Royal Shakespeare Theatre (RST) and Swan Theatre open Mon–Sat from 9am, from 10am Sun and bank hols. Guided tours RST Mon–Sat 9.15am, 11.15am, 1.15pm, 5.15pm, Sun and bank hols 10.15am, 12.15pm, 2.15pm, 4.15pm. Closed 24–25 Dec. Guided tours £6.50, tower £2.50 (timed tickets for tours and the tower are available online, advance booking is recommended). 0844 800 1110. www.rsc.org.uk.

The long-awaited new **Royal Shakespeare Theatre** (RST) opened for business in 2011 and is open to visitors throughout the day with free exhibitions and galleries, talks, children's activities and eating and drinking places enjoying wonderful riverside views. A highlight in every sense is ascending the theatre **tower**, which rises 118ft(36m) above the River Avon, providing fantastic views of the town.

The 1,000-seat **Courtyard Theatre**, which served as a temporary home for the RSC between 2006 and 2011, closed until 2012 for the World Shakespeare Festival as part of the Cultural Olympiad.

Sharing front of house space with the Royal Shakespeare Theatre is the **Swan Theatre**, built in 1986 with a Jacobean-style apron stage and galleried seating, within the shell of an earlier theatre.

EXCURSIONS
Mary Arden's Farm★

3mi/5km N, off the A 3400 in Wilmcote. Open daily Apr–Oct 10am–5pm. £9.50 or buy a Shakespeare Five House Ticket (see Shakespeare's Birthplace, above). 01789 204 016. www.shakespeare.org.uk.

The home of Shakespeare's mother, Mary Arden, is picture-perfect, featuring herring-bone timber framing and, mercifully, is unrestored. In fact this is a working farm where costumed characters re-enact the daily grind of Elizabethan times in the 16C farmhouse kitchen preparing and cooking food using traditional methods. Visitors can even help if they wish!

Between the house and neighbouring Glebe Farm (preserved as a c.1900 farmhouse) are dovecotes, cowsheds, barns and outbuildings.

Anne Hathaway's Cottage★

1mi/1.6km W via Shottery Road. Open daily Apr–Oct 9am–5pm; Nov–Mar 10am–4pm. Guided garden tours summer. £7.50 or buy a

Mary Arden's House

A. Williams/MICHELIN

Shakespeare Five House Ticket (☞see Shakespeare's Birthplace, above). ☏*01789 204 016. www.shakespeare.org.uk.*

This much-loved romantic picture-postcard building, where young William wooed his beloved Anne, is more a farmhouse than a cottage, and the rear was rebuilt after a fire in 1969. Upstairs are some dramatic tie-beams and the Hathaway bed. The award-winning **grounds** are equally picturesque featuring a herb-scented garden, orchard and Shakespeare tree garden. From late June to August the annual **Sweet Pea Festival** provides a wonderful display of colour and scent.

Ragley Hall★

▶ *10mi/16km W off the A 46, 2mi/3km beyond Alcester.* ⏰*Open late Feb–Oct Sat–Sun and school hols, see website for dates. House: Sun–Fri noon–4pm. Park and Gardens: 10am–5pm; (last entry 3.30pm.* ☞*£6.50.* ♿🅿✕. ☏*0800 093 0290, 01789 762 090; www.ragley-hall.com.*

This noble hall was designed and built by Robert Hooke in Palladian style, 1679–83. James Gibbs added some of the most perfect plasterwork **ceilings** he ever conceived around 1750, and 30 years later Wyatt built the gigantic portico. The walls are hung with paintings by Wootton, Van Loo, Reynolds, Hoppner, Lely and Cornelius Schut. The surprise is the **South Staircase Hall** decorated by Graham Rust between 1969 and 1983, with its ceiling of *The Temptation* and murals portraying Classical gods, monkeys, birds and contemporary members of the Seymour family.

The grounds include **The Jerwood Collection Sculpture Garden**, an adventure playground, woodland walks and an attractive lakeside picnic area.

Upton House★

NT. ▶ *Nr Banbury. 14mi/23km SE on the A 422. Garden:* ⏰*Open Mar Sat–Wed 11am–5pm; Apr–Oct daily 11am–5pm; Nov–Dec Sat–Wed noon–4pm. House:* ⏰*Open Apr–Aug daily 1–5pm; Nov–Dec Sat–Sun 1pm–4pm.* ☞*Guided*

tours house Apr and late Jul–Aug 11am–1pm. ☞*House and garden Mar–Oct £8.09, Nov–Feb £4.77; garden only, £4.77/£3.36.* ♿🅿✕. ☏*01295 670 266. www.nationaltrust.org.uk.*

This late-17C house was bought by Viscount Bearsted, son of the founder of the Shell company, and exhibits his spectacular collection of porcelain and paintings in the setting of a 1930s millionaire's mansion. In the **Hall** is a view of Venice by Canaletto and a landscape by Wootton. In the **Long Gallery** are Dutch paintings – note Jan Steen's *Four Senses* as well as the Chelsea and Bow porcelain. The **Boudoir** is reserved exclusively for French 18C and 19C works, including Boucher's *Venus and Vulcan*.

The **Porcelain Lobby** is packed with Sèvres, Chinese, Chelsea and Derby china and porcelain. In the Games Room are Hogarth's *Morning* and *Night*. The pride of the collection is in the **Picture Gallery**, where among works by Holbein, Hogarth, Guardi, Tintoretto, Bruegel the Elder and Bosch hangs El Greco's *Christ Taken in Captivity*.

Of more general interest is an exhibition of Shell Oil publicity posters and – you'll either love it or hate it – Lady Bearsted's red-and-silver Art Deco bathroom.

Heritage Motor Centre

▶ *Nr Gaydon. 13mi/21km W.* ⏰*Open year-round daily 10am–5pm.* ⏰*Closed 1 Jan, 24 Dec.* ☞*£11.* ♿🅿✕. ☏*01926 641 188. www.heritage-motor-centre.co.uk.*

In the 1960s the West Midlands was the centre of the thriving UK car industry and, fittingly, this motor museum is the repository for the world's largest collection of historic British cars.

The centre traces the story of the British motor industry with entertaining and educational interactive exhibitions and events. Optional extras include a hair-raising 4 x 4 **Land Rover Experience** (☞*£7*) and a mini-roadway driving track for children (⏰*Sat–Sun and school hols;* ☞*£3*).

Warwick★
and around

Much loved by visitors and locals alike – Pevsner called it "this perfect county town" – Warwick is built mostly in the Queen Anne style. This both contrasts and complements its dominant 14C castle – "the most perfect piece of castellated antiquity in the kingdom".

TOWN
♦♦Warwick Castle★★

◔Open daily May–Sept 10am–6pm; Oct–Apr 10am–5pm. ◔Closed 25 Dec. ⊜Castle only, £21, child £15; plus Dungeon £26.40, child £21; all areas £29.40, child £24.40 (save 20 percent online). ♿⊓✗. ℘0870 442 2000 (information). www.warwick-castle.co.uk.

Britain's finest medieval castle occupies a picturesque location beside the River Avon. The curtain walls and gatehouse are 14C; the Bear Tower and Clarence Tower date from the 15C. The castle was begun by Thomas de Beauchamp, 11th Earl of Warwick (1329–69). Paintings and furniture are displayed in the 17C and 18C **State Rooms** including works by Lely, Van Dyck and furniture by Boulle. Now part of the Tussauds Group, the castle is brought dramatically to life by both historically accurate and fantasy characters. The highlight of the year is the summer season when the magnificent riverside **grounds** come alive with jousting knights, medieval character

- ▶ **Population:** 22,476.
- ⚲ **Michelin Map:** Michelin Atlas p27 or Map 503.
- ℹ **Info:** Jewry Street. ℘01926 492 212. www.warwick-uk.co.uk.
- ◔ **Location:** 22mi/35km southeast of Birmingham. The train station is a 10-minute walk from town; the bus station is in the centre on Market Street
- ♦♦ **Kids:** Warwick Castle.

actors of every persuasion, a spectacular **siege machine** which fires twice daily, falconry and lots more. Almost forgotten amid the razzmatazz is the Mill and Engine House (◔open to visitors), the Conservatory and Peacock Gardens and the Victorian Rose Gardens.

The latest addition to the castle is the adventure experience **Merlin: The Dragon Tower**, based on the hit BBC TV series. Ascend the tower to meet "The Great Dragon". Braver souls meanwhile can descend to the gory **Castle Dungeons** horror house (by the company responsible for the London Dungeon).

Lord Leycester Hospital★

High Street. ◔Open Tue–Sun and bank hols Apr–Sept 10am–5pm; Oct–Mar 10am–4.30pm. ◔Closed Good Fri, 25 Dec. ⊜£4.90. ℘01926 491 422. www.lordleycester.com.

Warwick Castle and the River Avon

©Martin Lovatt/iStockphoto.com

This picturesque black-and-white timber-framed ensemble was founded in 1571 by Queen Elizabeth's favourite, Lord Leicester. The oldest parts of the building, which surrounds a charming partly cloistered courtyard, are the chapel (1383) and the guildhall (1450).

Collegiate Church of St Mary★

Church Street. ○*Open daily Apr–Oct 10am–6pm; Nov–Mar 10am–4.30pm.* ⊜*£2 suggested donation, plus charge for tower.* ㅤ*. ℘01926 403 940. www.saintmaryschurch.co.uk.*
Rebuilt after a fire in 1694, though it originally dates from 1123. Its glory is the 15C Beauchamp (pronounced "beechum") Chapel containing the **tomb**★ and gilded bronze effigy of Richard de Beauchamp, Earl of Warwick. The church tower offers spectacular views.

EXCURSIONS
Coventry
◐ *12mi/19km N of Warwick via the A 46.*
🏛 *Cathedral ruins. ℘024 76225616. www.visitcoventryandwarwickshire.co.uk.*
Coventry is known for terrible devastation during the Second World War, its magnificent modern cathedral and the legend of **Lady Godiva** ("guh-die-ver"). In 1043 the city was so heavily taxed by Leofric, Earl of Mercia that his wife, Lady Godiva, repeatedly begged him to repeal the taxes. In the end he agreed to do so if she rode naked through the streets. The people of Coventry cleared the route in order not to embarrass the Lady, everyone, that is, with the exception of a tailor, named Tom. On seeing Godiva he was struck blind and so the name Peeping Tom was coined. A statue of Godiva graces Broadgate in the centre of town and behind, her ride is "re-enacted" by a small horse appearing from a clock each hour.

On 14 November 1940 the biggest bombing raid of its time destroyed most of the city, including the 13C church, which in 1918 had become a cathedral. The only remains of medieval Coventry are the timber-framed properties in **Spon Street (Y)**.

Cathedral★★

Fairfax Street. ○*Open year-round Mon–Sat 9am–5pm, Sun noon–5pm. Old cathedral tower open daily except during bell-ringing sessions.* ⊜*New cathedral £3.50 contribution requested, old cathedral tower £2.50. ℘024 7652 1200. www.coventrycathedral.org.uk.*
The **new cathedral**, by Sir Basil Spence, was one of the few post-war buildings to meet with the approval of the general public. The tower and spire, with restored bells, dominate the city centre of Coventry, which is known as the city of the three spires. Flanking the entrance steps is *St Michael Defeating the Devil* by **Jacob Epstein**. The majestic porch links the new cathedral with the ruins of the old as a symbol of resurrection. The overwhelming impression of the **interior** is of height, light and

Coventry Cathedral

©John Cave/iStockphoto.com

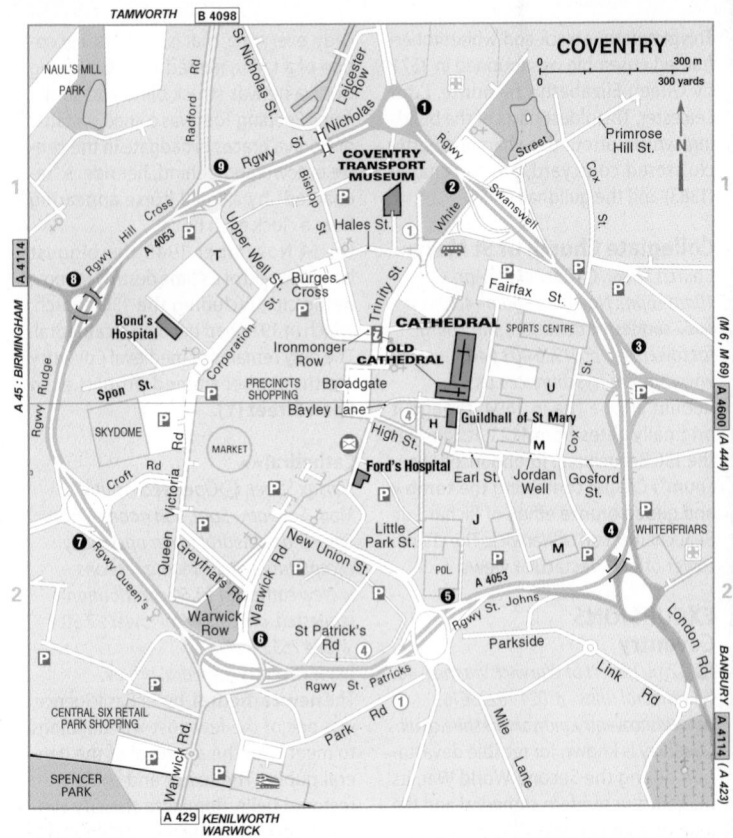

WHERE TO STAY		WHERE TO EAT	
Abbrymar	①	Nando's	①
Spire View	④	Pizza Express	④

colour: height from the soaring slender nave pillars supporting the canopied roof; light from the great west screen, a wall of glass engraved with patriarchs, prophets, saints and angels by John Hutton; colour from the Baptistery window by John Piper.

The font is a great rough boulder from the hillside at Bethlehem. The whole is dominated by the huge tapestry, *Christ in Glory* designed by **Graham Sutherland**.

The ruined **old cathedral**★ is late-13C with large-scale Decorated and Perpendicular additions. All that remains are the walls, the crypt and the tower (294ft/90m), and the spire, one of the architectural glories of England,

exceeded in height only by Norwich and Salisbury. The east end is marked by a simple cross of charred timbers.

♣♦ Coventry Transport Museum★
Millennium Place, Hales Street. ⏰*Open year-round daily 10am–5pm.* ⏰*Closed 24–26 Dec.* ♿✕. ☎*024 7623 4270. www.transport-museum.com.*

This museum, featuring the world's largest road transport collection, is wholly appropriate for the city that was the birthplace of the British car industry and had nearly 600 companies making cycles, motorcars, commercial vehicles and motorcycles. Walk through time, from 19C boneshakers, via a land speed record simulator and into the future.

Worcestershire★

Best known for the tangy sauce which originated here, once away from the busy northern parts, Worcestershire is a mostly green and pleasant rural county, watered by the mighty rivers Severn and Avon.

WORCESTER

The great red sandstone cathedral rising above the bend in the River Severn, the wealth of timber-framed buildings and the Georgian mansions make Worcester among the most English of cities. The city name is also synonymous with its Royal Worcester porcelain and Worcester(shire) sauce. Worcester was the site of the final battle of the Civil War, where Cromwell's "New Model Army" defeated Charles I's Cavaliers.

Cathedral★★

◷Open year-round daily 7.30am–6pm. Tower open Easter–Sept Sat, and Mon–Sat during school hols, 11am–5pm (⚌£4). ⚓Guided tours (⚌£3) Apr–Nov Mon–Sat 11am, 2.30pm; Dec–Mar Sat only. ⚌£3 contribution requested. ☕✕. ℘01905 732 900. www.worcester-cathedral.co.uk.

In the late-11C an earlier church was rebuilt by Wulstan, the Saxon Bishop of Worcester, who thrived under his new Norman masters and was later canonised. His superb **crypt** survives but the greater part of his building, including the tower, was reconstructed in the 14C. The **choir** is an outstanding example of the Early English style. Monuments include **King John's tomb** in the choir, the **Beauchamp tomb** (14C) in the nave, and the alabaster effigy (c.1470) of the Virgin and Child in the southeast transept. **Prince Arthur's Chantry** and its delicate tracery are late Perpendicular work. The Cloisters were rebuilt in 1374 with wonderful medieval bosses. The east walk leads to the **chapter house** (c.1150), with its shaft vaulting. The **Edgar Tower**, once the main entrance to the medieval monastery and fortified against anti-clerical rioters, now opens into the serene cathedral precincts.

▶ **Population:** 82,661.
◔ **Michelin Map:** Michelin Atlas p27 or Map 503 N 27.
🛈 **Info:** High Street. ℘01905 726 311. www.visitworcester.com.
▶ **Location:** 28mi/45km southwest of Birmingham. Foregate Street Station is 0.5mi/0.8km north of the centre. The bus station, to the rear of Crowngate shopping centre, is a little closer.

Worcester Porcelain Museum

Severn Street. ◷*Open Easter–Oct. Mon –Sat 10am–5pm; Nov–Easter Tue–Sat 10.30am–4pm.* ⚌*£6.* ☕🄿✕. ℘*01905 21247. www.royal-worcester.co.uk.*
Founded in 1751, Royal Worcester's historical success was due to the use of Cornish soaprock to simulate Chinese porcelain and the ability to adapt to changing fashions (Chinoiserie, Classicism, Romanticism), all of which are displayed here. However, in 2006 tableware production ceased in Worcester and only a few talented artists continued to hand paint and gild bespoke items. The Worcester factory site closed in 2009.

MALVERN HILLS

🛈 *21 Church Street, Malvern.* ℘*01684 892 289. www.visitthemalverns.org.*
The Malverns boast some of the most spectacular views in the region, crisscrossed with 100mi/160km of bridleways and footpaths, with routes for both short strolls and long-distance hikes. The highest of the hills is **Worcestershire Beacon** (1,395ft/425m), from which there is claimed to be a **view** of 15 counties and three cathedrals.
Sir Edward Elgar (1857–1934), that most "English" of composers, helped put the area on the map and his music evokes this countryside of broad, tranquil vales and soaring hills. A 40mi/64km circular tour, known as the **Elgar Route★**, signposted with "violins", includes the **Elgar Birthplace Museum** (*Crown East Lane, Lower Broadheath; 3mi/5km*

W of Worcester; ⏱*open daily 11am–5pm;* ⮢*£7;* ♿*;* ✆*01905 333 224; www.elgar foundation.org).*

Great Malvern
◐ *8mi/13km S on the A 449.*
In the late-18C this small settlement, which had grown up round a priory, became fashionable owing to the medicinal properties of the local water.

A Greek Revival-style **Pump Room** and Baths were built in 1819 and its popularity as a spa town grew in the Victorian era. You can no longer "take the waters" here, but many of the impressive old spa buildings remain in public use. George Bernard Shaw and Edward Elgar brought Great Malvern into the 20C with their music and theatre festivals held in the Winter Gardens.

Herefordshire

This quiet unspoiled sparsely populated agricultural county borders Powys and Monmouthshire in Wales and shares towns with both. It is notable for its "black-and-white villages" (of half-timbered houses). Wye Valley is particularly beautiful.

HEREFORD★
Seat of a bishop in AD 676, Hereford was a flourishing city and became capital of Saxon Mercia, with its own mint. In 1070, however, a new market was created where the roads converged north of the town. Today Hereford is the prosperous centre for a rich agricultural region on the border with Wales. There are many outstanding half-timbered buildings preserved in the city. In the heart of the city, just north of the River Wye, is the **cathedral**★★ *(Cathedral:* ⏱*open year-round Mon–Sat 9.15am–5.30pm, Sun 9.15am–3.30pm;* ◐*guided tour cathedral floor spring half-term and Easter–Oct Mon–Sat 11.15am, 2.15pm, tower tours*

> ▸ **Population:** 48,277.
> ⛑ **Michelin Map:** Michelin Atlas p26 or Map 503 L 27.
> ▯ **Info:** 1 King Street. ✆01432 268 430. www. visitherefordshire.co.uk.
> ◐ **Location:** Hereford is 56mi/90km southwest of Birmingham and 57mi/ 92km northeast of Cardiff.

Easter–mid-Sept Wed–Thu ⮢*suggested entry donation £5, brass rubbing £1.50;* ♿✗*;* ✆*01432 374 200; Mappa Mundi Exhibition and Chained Library:* ⏱*open year-round Mon–Sat 10am–5pm, last Sun in May and Aug noon–4pm;* ⮢*£6;* ✗*;* ✆*01432 374 209; www.herefordcathedral. org),* a mainly 12C red sandstone building. The massive tower was added in the 14C. The chantry to John Stanbury, bishop in 1453–74, is a fine example of Perpendicular architecture.

Among the treasures is the **Mappa Mundi**★, a map of the world with Jerusalem at its centre, made by Richard of Haldingham in Lincolnshire, c.1300. The **Chained Library**, one of the finest in the country, contains 1,400 books and over 200 manuscripts, dating from the 8C to the 15C, including the "Cider Bible" in which the "strong drink" of the authorised version has been translated as "cidir". There is a small 13C Limoges enamel reliquary, which used to contain a relic of St Thomas Becket, whose murder is depicted on the side.

Head west from here towards Eign Street and turn left down Ryelands

South Door, Kilpeck Church
A. F. Kersting/MICHELIN

Street until you arrive at no. 21 and the **Cider Museum** (*open Tue–Sat, bank hol Sats–Suns and cider festival mid-Oct Sat–Sun Apr–Oct 10am–5pm, Nov–Mar 11am–3pm;* £5; ⓖⓟ✕; ✆01432 354 207; www.cidermuseum.co.uk). An old cider factory houses this museum, which tells the story of cider-making through the ages, particularly during its heyday in the 17C.

EXCURSIONS
Kilpeck Church★★
8mi/13km southwest of Hereford via the A 465 and a minor road (right). Open year-round daily dawn–dusk. Contribution requested. ⓟ. ✆01981 570 315.

The Church of St Mary and St David was built in 1135. Nowhere else in Britain has such rich Norman **carving** decoration survived. Only two of the 70 grotesques around the corbel have any religious significance. The gargoyle heads on the west wall are pure Viking. and there is a notorious sheela-na-gig.

Hay-on-Wye
20mi west of Hereford. Oxford Road. ✆01497 820 144. www.hay-on-wye.co.uk.

Set on the Welsh–English border in Powys, though also claimed by Hereford, this likeable little town is Britain's most famous literary centre, world famous for its secondhand and antiquarian **book-shops**. It is also renowned for its numerous festivals, of which the biggest is the **Hay Festival of Literature** when for 10 days *(late May/early Jun)* around 85,000 people from all over the UK and abroad descend on Hay-on-Wye.

Ross-on-Wye
15mi southeast of Hereford. Market House. ✆01432 260 675. www.herefordshire.gov.uk.

This pretty little market town owes its fame to the spectacular stretches of the **Wye Valley**★ close by. In fact it claims to be the birthplace of the British tourist industry, when in 1745, the local rector started taking friends on boat trips down the valley from Ross-on-Wye.

The valley's chief man-made attraction are the mighty remains of **Goodrich Castle** (*EH. Goodrich; open Apr–Jun and Sept–Oct daily 10am–5pm, Jul–Aug daily 10am–6pm, Nov–Feb Sat–Sun 10am–4pm;* £5.80; ⓟ (£1); ✆01600 890 538;. www.english-heritage.org.uk) standing majestically on a wooded hill above the river in the picturesque valley known as **Symonds Yat**. Built in the 11C, the castle was destroyed in the English Civil War. **Symonds Yat Rock**★, a viewpoint towering some 40ft/120m above the river on the Gloucestershire side, provides a panoramic much-photographed viewpoint of the River Wye.

Shropshire

Despite its proximity to the industrial heartlands of the West Midlands, Shropshire is largely untouched by 20C industry, or major roads, and its patchwork fields hark back to days of pre-mechanised agriculture. Ironically this was the birthplace of the Industrial Revolution and Ironbridge Gorge, now a UNESCO World Heritage Site, is Britain's greatest industrial heritage site, with intelligent award-winning visitor attractions set in beautiful surroundings. The county town of

- **Info:** www.shropshiretourism.co.uk
- **Location:** Shropshire borders Wales to the west.
- **Don't Miss:** A full day at Ironbridge Gorge; Weston Park; Ludlow.
- **Timing:** Allow at least two days to see Ironbridge Gorge alone.
- **Kids:** Blists Hill and Enginuity at Ironbridge Gorge.

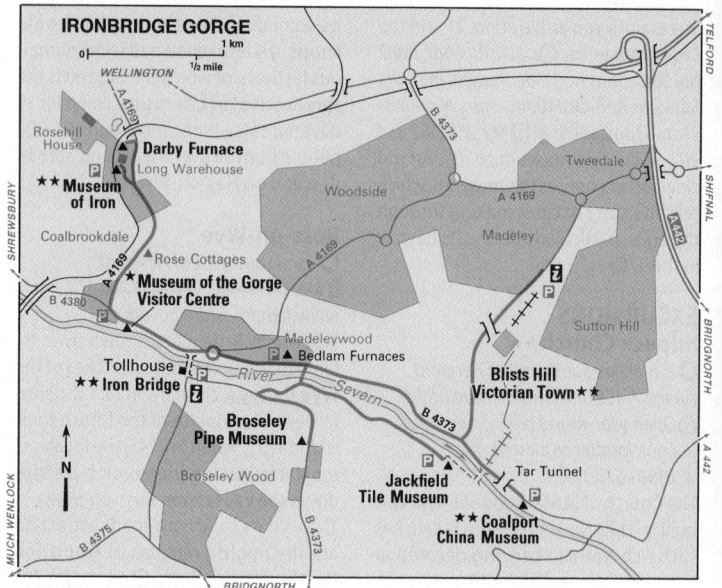

IRONBRIDGE GORGE

Shrewsbury and smaller market towns also have much to offer while Shropshire's "blue-remembered hills" are renowned for being wonderful walking territory.

IRONBRIDGE GORGE★★

The Gorge is on the River Severn, 5 mi 5mi/8km S Telford. 📍 ℘01952 884 391. www.ironbridge.org.uk.

The densely wooded, mineral-rich Severn Gorge was the birthplace of the Industrial Revolution. In 1708 Abraham Darby (1678–1717) came to Coalbrookdale and revolutionised the industry by using coke as a fuel for smelting iron, replacing traditional charcoal.

His experiments made it possible to use iron in transport, engineering and construction (including the world's first iron bridge. A number of sites along the gorge now form the UK's most important, and most interesting, industrial heritage complex. The Iron Bridge itself

Iron Bridge at Coalbrookdale

©David Bailey/Dreamstime.com

is one of the great symbols of the Industrial Revolution.

Ironbridge Gorge Museums★★★

Coalbrookdale. ⏰*Open year-round daily 10am–5pm (10am–6pm bank hol Mons and preceding Suns).* ⏰*Closed 1 Jan, 24–25 Dec.* 🎫*Passport ticket for all sites £22.50, child £14.75 (prices for individual museum entry below). The Gorge Connect shuttle bus connects most sites Easter–Oct Sats–Suns and bank hol Mons (free to Passport ticket holders.* ♿🅿. ✕ *at all sites.* 📞*01952 433 424. www.ironbridge.org.uk.*

Ironbridge Area

The **Iron Bridge**★★ is the iconic landmark bridge across the Severn Gorge at Coalbrookdale, erected to replace the hazardous ferry crossing. It was designed by Shrewsbury architect Thomas Pritchard, and built over three years by Abraham Darby III, opening on New Year's Day 1781. The bridge's single graceful span was a triumph of the application of new technology to the solution of a difficult problem. The ironwork weighs over 378tons. In the old Tollhouse (🎫*entry fee*) is an information centre with a display illustrating the history of the bridge.

The **Museum of the Gorge**★ (🎫*£8.75*) houses an exhibition and audio-visual introduction to Ironbridge Gorge.

The **Jackfield Tile Museum** (🎫*£7.60*) is housed in an original gas-lit trade showroom, where galleries and period room settings show off the often magnificent colourful wall and floor tiles once manufactured here in immense quantities.

Broseley Pipeworks (⏰*open late May–late Sept daily 1–5pm;* 🎫*£4.75*) was once the biggest clay tobacco pipe-maker in Britain, exporting all over the world. It closed in the 1950s but remains preserved, as if in a time capsule.

Coalbrookdale Area

The **Museum of Iron & The Old Furnace**★★ (🎫 *£7.60*) illustrates the history of iron-making and the story of the Coalbrookdale Company. It is housed in

a huge warehouse, built in 1838, with cast-iron windows, sills and lintels. By the time of the Great Exhibition in 1851, the Coalbrookdale Company employed 4,000 men and boys and produced 2,000 tons of cast iron a week, for railway stations, bridges, fireplaces and a multitude of other uses.

👥**Enginuity** (🎫*£7.85, child £6.75*) is a hands-on interactive exhibition designed to explain the principles of the manufacturing processes at Ironbridge in simple and fun terms.

The **Darby Houses** (🎫*£4.75, combined ticket with Museum of Iron £8.75*) are where the Ironmasters lived; the rooms are packed with original furniture, costumes and mementoes.

Blists Hill area

The **Coalport China Museum**★★ (🎫*£7.60*) dates from 1792, and manufacturing continued here until 1926. The old works, including the interior kiln of a bottle oven, have been restored as a museum of china, showing techniques of manufacture and particularly the products of Coalport.

Nearby, you can walk through the **Tar Tunnel** (⏰*closed winter;* 🎫*£2.60*), cut in 1786 to aid drainage from the Blists Hill Mine. It was found to ooze bitumen through the mortar of the brick lining (it still does) and this was turned into pitch, lamp-black and rheumatics remedies.

Many visitors' favourite part of the whole Ironbridge area is 👥**Blists Hill Victorian Town**★★ (⏰*closes winter 4pm;* 🎫*£14.95, child £11.95; www.blistshill.org*), a delightful reconstruction of a Victorian community of the 1890s, including a bank, pub, butcher's shop, school, mason's yard, mine, miner's railway and candle factory, as well as the inclined plane which carried boats from Blists Hill to the Severn and Coalport. Many of the buildings have been brought from elsewhere and rebuilt on site.

SHREWSBURY

▶ *14mi/22km northwest of Ironbridge. Population: 64,219.* ℹ*Roweleys House, Barker Street.* 📞*01743 281 200. www.visitshrewsbury.com.*

Set at the very heart of Shropshire, the medieval border settlement of Shrewsbury grew up around its Norman castle, which commanded the loop in the Severn. The modern county town has elegant Queen Anne and Georgian buildings, a wealth of black-and-white houses and "shuts" – medieval shortcuts and alleyways.

Shrewsbury Abbey★

Open Mon–Sat 10.30am–3pm, Sun 11.30am–2.30pm. & *01743 232 723. www.shrewsburyabbey.com.*
The Benedictine Abbey, founded in 1083, stands just outside the town, across the landmark **English Bridge**. The 14C tower has a statue of Edward III, in whose reign it was built, and there are Norman pillars in the nave dating from the 11C.

WESTON PARK★★

22mi/36km E of Shrewsbury via the A 5. **House:** *Open late May– early Sept Sun–Fri (Jun–Aug daily); by guided tours only, Tue–Thu 1–5pm. Closed part of Aug. £8 house and gardens.* **Park and gardens:** *Open 10.30am– 6pm. £5.* & P X. *01952 852 100. www.weston-park.com.*
This 17C house is unusual in having been built by a woman, Lady Elizabeth Wilbraham. The splendidly furnished interior is remarkable for the quality of the portraits – from Holbein to Lely's likeness of Lady Wilbraham and a rare portrait by Constable.

Beyond the formal gardens is the park, designed by Capability Brown, grazed by deer and rare breeds of sheep. It contains many family attractions – a miniature railway (£2), pets corner and adventure playground. The recently converted **Granary**, built 1767, is now the beautiful new home to an art gallery, farm shop and restaurant.

MUCH WENLOCK

12mi/20km SE via the A 458. **The Museum, High Street.** *01952 727 679.*
This pretty little market town boasts a wealth of historic buildings and its

colourful small **museum** (*open daily Easter–Oct 10.30am–1pm & 1.30–5pm, Oct–Easter Tue and Fri 10.30am–1pm, 1.30–4pm, Sat 10am–noon; 01952 727 679*) tells the fascinating little-known story of the **Much Wenlock Olympic Games**, initiated in 1850 by a local doctor. They inspired the modern Olympic movement and are still held in the village today.

A short walk away are the tranquil ruins of **Wenlock Priory**★ (*EH; open Apr– Aug 10am–5pm, Sept–Oct Wed–Sun 10am–5pm, Nov–Mar Sat–Sun 10am– 4pm; Feb half-term hol daily 10am–4pm. £4; 01952 727 466; www.english-heritage.org.uk*), set in beautiful landscaped grounds. The Cluniac priory was founded c.690, pillaged by the Danes and later refounded. The church, one of the longest monastic churches in England (the nave is 350ft/106m long), was built in the 1220s by Prior Humbert. The delicate interlaced arcading of the chapter house is the work of the Normans. So too is the magnificent **lavatorium** (1180), where the monks washed before meals.

Just southwest on the B 4378 is **Wenlock Edge**★, a massive limestone escarpment providing magnificent **views**.

CHURCH STRETTON

13.5mi/22km S via the A 49. **Library, Church Street.** *01694 723 133. www.churchstretton.co.uk.*
This is the probably the most popular part of the whole county for **walking**, with the favourite starting point being the National Trust-owned Chalet Pavilion at **Carding Valley** (just outside Church Stretton), which dispenses information alongside tea and coffee. There are walking trails for all comers and NT rangers also lead guided walks. A popular route is **The Port Way**, an ancient track which was used in prehistoric times by drovers and axe traders. It follows the crest of the **Long Mynd** (mynd is Welsh for mountain), which comprises some 4–5sq mi/10–13sq km of wild moorland plateau, its higher slopes covered with gorse and bracken, and its eastern side intersected by many steep valleys. As

well as walking it is renowned for gliding, hang gliding and paragliding.

The **village** of Church Stretton was a thriving health resort in Victorian times. Its fine church is part Norman, part 17C.

Nearby at **Acton Scott Farm** (🕐 *open early Apr–Oct Tue–Fri 10am–4.30pm, Sat, Sun and bank hols 10.30am–5pm; £6.40; ♿✕; 📞01694 781 307; www. actonscott.com), a star of several recent BBC TV programmes, you can watch traditional 19C farm life unfold daily.*

STOKESAY CASTLE★

EH. ▶ *21mi/34km S.* 🕐*Open Apr–Sept daily 10am–5pm; Oct Wed–Sun 10am–5pm; Nov–Mar Sat–Sun 10am–4pm (Feb half-term hol daily).* 🕐*Closed 1 Jan, 24–26 Dec. £5.80. ♿🅿.* 📞*01588 672 544. www.english-heritage.org.uk.*

Set alongside a picture-postcard yellow pastel-washed 16C gatehouse and a 17C church Stokesay Castle is part of a much-photographed grouping. Something of a misnomer, the "castle" is the best-preserved example in England of a 13C fortified manor house. The hall has a fine roof of shaped and tapered tree trunks. The solar is furnished with a notable stone fireplace, peepholes into the hall below and 17C fittings.

LUDLOW★

▶ *28mi/45km S. Population: 9,040.* 🏛 *Castle Square.* 📞*01584 875 053. www.ludlow.org.uk.*

Set in the south of the rolling Shropshire Hills, close to the Welsh border, Ludlow is a Norman "planned town". One-time seat of the powerful Mortimer family, the castle passed into royal ownership with the accession of Edward IV. The town prospered in the 16C and 17C in its role as seat of the Council for Wales and the Marches.

The centrepiece of the **Ludlow Festival** (*last wk Jun–first wk Jul*) is a Shakespeare play performed in the inner bailey of the castle. In recent years the town has also become one of Britain's **gastronomic capitals** with a famous **food and drink festival** each September.

Town

The picturesque ruin of **Ludlow Castle**★ (*Castle Square;* 🕐 *open Feb–Nov daily from 10am, Feb–Mar and Oct–Nov closes 4pm, Apr–Jul and Sept closes 5pm, Aug closes 7pm, Dec–Jan Sat–Sun 10am–4pm;* 🕐 *closed 25 Dec, see website for other days; £5; ♿✕; 📞01584 874 465; www. ludlowcastle.com*) stands on a fine defensive site protected by the River Teme and low limestone cliffs and dominates the view of the town. It was begun by Roger de Lacy shortly after the Domesday survey and built of locally quarried stone. It was from here that Roger Mortimer, the most powerful and perhaps the richest man in all England, virtually ruled the country, after using his power to topple Edward II in 1326. He completed the block of buildings containing the **Great Hall** and Solar, one of the leading palaces of the day. **Arthur, Prince of Wales** brought his young bride **Catherine of Aragon** to honeymoon in Ludlow in the winter of 1501 and it was here that Arthur died early the following year (to be succeeded by his brother and future king Henry VIII). The chapel with its richly ornamented west door is one of only five round chapel naves still standing in Britain.

Heading east from the castle towards Bull Ring/Old Street, take a left onto College Street to find **St Laurence's Church**★ (🕐*open daily Apr–Oct 10am–5.30pm, Nov–Mar 11am–4pm; £3 contribution requested; ♿; 📞01584 872 073; www.stlaurences.org.uk*). The tower dominates the surrounding countryside and is mentioned in the locally famous collection of poems, *A Shropshire Lad* by **A E Housman** (1859–1936), whose ashes are buried in the churchyard. Twenty eight **misericords**★ in the choir stalls date from 1447.

On Bull Ring is the **Feathers Hotel**★ (*www.feathersatludlow.co.uk*). The existing building was enlarged and re-fronted in 1619 to produce what Pevsner described as "the prodigy of timber-framed houses".

Birmingham★
and around

The "Second City of the Kingdom" and one of the centres of the Industrial Revolution, Birmingham still produces a high proportion of Britain's manufactured exports. Tourism is also very much a priority of the city these days, however.

A BIT OF HISTORY

Industry – Industrialisation began in the mid-16C, the city "swarming with inhabitants and echoing with the noise of anvils" (William Camden). Its 18C growth, marked by the miles of canals radiating from the centre (Birmingham has more miles of canal than Venice), attracted **James Watt** (1736–1819), inventor of the double-action steam engine, **William Murdock** (1754–1839), inventor of coal-gas lighting, and **Matthew Boulton** (1728–1809), whose Soho factory was the first to be lit by gas.

The grim conditions caused by the city's phenomenal growth in the 19C stirred the philanthropic cocoa manufacturer, George Cadbury (1839–1922), to create one of the world's first garden suburbs, **Bournville**.

Modern city – Though much crass post-war development was demolished in the course of enthusiastic redevelopment, enough fine late-19C/early 20C-buildings remain to evoke the atmosphere of the city's civic heyday. The **Bull Ring**, a symbol of insensitive mid-20C architecture, became Europe's largest retail-led regeneration project, representing an investment of over £1billion into a new shopping centre boasting spectacular designer buildings – most notably the astonishing landmark **Selfridges** department store, clad in 15,000 shiny aluminium discs, supposedly inspired by a sequinned dress.

Today Britain's second city is determined to acquire a new image as a **European business and cultural centre**. A superb symphony hall in the **International Convention Centre** is home to the internationally acclaimed City of Bir-

▶ **Population:** 965,928.
◔ **Michelin Map:** Michelin Atlas p27 or Maps 503 or 504 O 26.
▯ **Info:** 150 New Street (junction with Corporation Street). Central Library, Chamberlain Square. Birmingham Airport Information Desk. ℘0844 888 3883 (all offices). www.visitbirmingham.com.
▶ **Location:** Birmingham lies very close to the geographical centre of England, 117mi/188km northwest of London. New Street Station ("Birmingham Gateway"), in the heart of the city, is where most train travellers arrive. The Digbeth bus station is a 10-minutes walk from the centre.
◑ **Don't Miss:** Birmingham Museum and Art Gallery, especially its Pre-Raphaelite collection; Barber Institute of Fine Arts; Black Country Living Museum; Dudley.
◔ **Timing:** Allow two days.
▯ **Parking:** Avoid driving in the city centre.
👥 **Kids:** Cadbury World, Bournville; Thinktank; National Sea Life Centre; Black Country Living Museum.
🖝 **Tours:** The route marked on the map offers a pleasant stroll.

mingham Symphony Orchestra (CBSO), while the refurbished Birmingham Hippodrome Theatre is the new headquarters for the equally renowned Birmingham Royal Ballet, formerly Sadler's Wells. In the heart of town the **National Indoor Arena** (NIA), and, 14mi/23km west, the **National Exhibiton Centre** (NEC) host important exhibitions, concerts, shows and sporting events.

CITY CENTRE
Birmingham Museum and Art Gallery★★

Chamberlain Square. ◷*Open year-round Mon–Thu and Sat 10am–5pm, Fri 10.30am–5pm, Sun 12.30–5pm.* ◗*Guided tours (£2) Thu 1pm, Sat–Sun 2.30pm.* ⚹✕. ℘*0121 303 1966.* *www.bmag.org.uk.*

Birmingham's municipal gallery is famed for its outstanding collection of **Pre-Raphaelite paintings**. The elaborate ironwork of the two-tiered Industrial Gallery is a late Victorian marvel, a fascinating setting for its ceramics and stained glass. Beyond is the spectacular **Edwardian Tea Room**.

Among the extensive holding of European paintings are outstanding works, like the *Madonna and Child* by Bellini, Claude's *Landscape near Rome* and a *Roman Beggar Woman* by Degas. At the heart of the collection are the Pre-Raphaelites: mostly key works like *The Last of England* by Ford Madox Brown, *The Blind Girl* by Millais, *Beata Beatrix* by Rossetti and *Two Gentlemen of Verona* by Hunt.

Even this collection, however, has recently been eclipsed by the **Staffordshire Hoard**; comprising over 3,500 items of gold and silver with precious stone decorations it is the largest hoard of Anglo-Saxon gold ever found. It was discovered in 2009, in a farmer's field near Lichfield, and part of it is now on permanent display here.

Other rooms are devoted to local history, archaeology and natural history; there is a spectacular **fossilised skull** of a triceratops. The Pinto Gallery holds an amazing array of wooden objects.

▲▲Thinktank Birmingham Science Museum

Millennium Point, Curzon Street. ◷*Open year-round 10am–5pm; (last entry 4pm).* ◗*Closed 24–26 Dec.* ◉*£12.25, child £8.40; IMAX £9.60, child £7.60 (combined ticket £20.50, child £14.50).* ⚹. ℙ*(charge)*✕. ℘*0121 202 2222. www.thinktank.ac.*

Four floors of interactive galleries (the past, the present, the city, the future) chart both local and global scientific and technological invention. Testimonies from people involved in the various activities which account for Birmingham's industrial progress give a historical perspective while the IMAX cinema and a state-of-the-art planetarium (◉free with museum entry) add a wow factor.

Gas Street Basin Canal Walk

▶ *1mi/1.6km.*

The walk between Gas Street Basin and Newhall Street passes the canals, locks, bridges and buildings spawned by the city's 19C expansion.

The **Gas Street Basin** is surrounded by both new and restored 18C and 19C buildings. The painted narrowboats moored along the quay are typical of the craft that once plied the Midlands' canal network. Nearby, the **Water's Edge** and **Brindle Place** (Oozells Square) developments are full of lively wine bars, cafés, restaurants and traditional canalside pubs. The latter is also home to the **Ikon Gallery of Contemporary Art**.

BEYOND THE CITY CENTRE
Barber Institute of Fine Arts★★

University of Birmingham, Edgbaston. ▶ *2.5mi/4km S of the centre on the A 38. From the Bristol Road turn right up Edgbaston Park Road to the university south car park.* ◷*Open year-round Mon–Sat 10am–5pm, Sun noon–5pm.* ◷*Closed 1 Jan, Good Fri, 25–26 Dec.* ⚹ℙ. ℘*0121 472 0962 (24hr info); 0121 414 7333 (enquiries).* *www.barber.org.uk.*

This small but lovingly chosen collection was built up with the bequest of Lady M C H Barber (d.1933) and is displayed together with furniture and other *objets d'art*. Among the Italian Old Masters are several Venetians including Bellini, Cima and Guardi. Flemish painters include Brueghel the Younger and Rubens.

The French school is well represented, with works by Poussin, Watteau, Delacroix, Ingres, Corot and Courbet and an outstanding group of Impressionists and post-impressionists, including Bonnard,

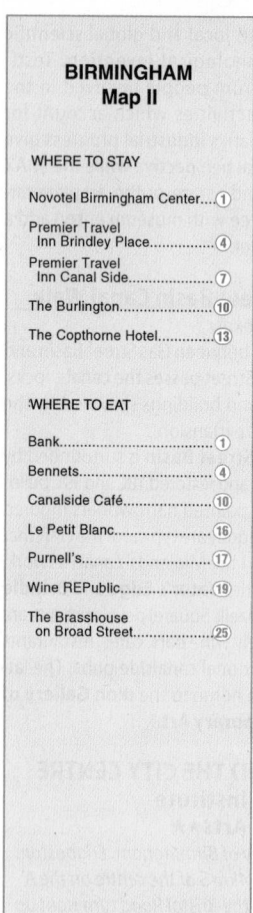

BIRMINGHAM
Map II

WHERE TO STAY

Novotel Birmingham Center....①

Premier Travel
Inn Brindley Place..............④

Premier Travel
Inn Canal Side...................⑦

The Burlington.......................⑩

The Copthorne Hotel.............⑬

WHERE TO EAT

Bank...①

Bennets....................................④

Canalside Café.....................⑩

Le Petit Blanc........................⑯

Purnell's...................................⑰

Wine REPublic.......................⑲

The Brasshouse
on Broad Street...................㉕

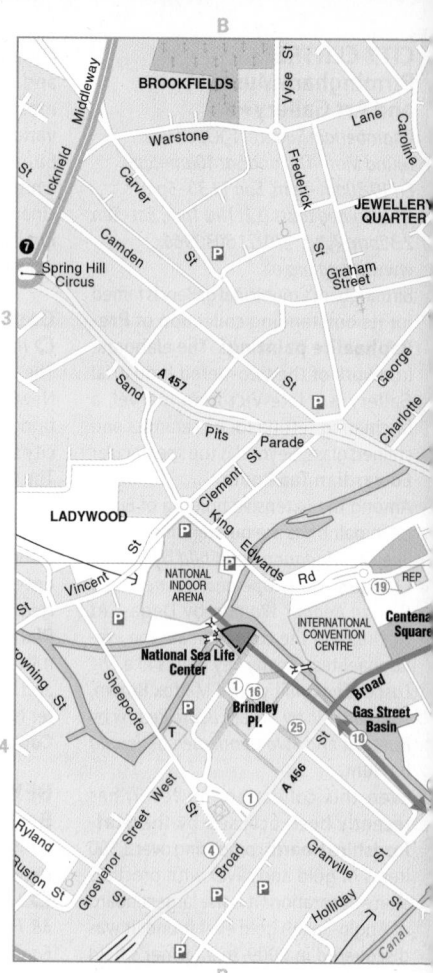

Degas, Gauguin, Manet, Monet, Renoir, Vuillard and Van Gogh. English painters include Gainsborough, Turner and Whistler.

Aston Hall★★

◗ *2mi/3km N of the city centre on the A 38 (M).* ◗*Open Easter–Oct Tue-Sun and bank hols noon–4pm.* ◗*ClosedSat–Sun Aston Villa FC home matchdays.* ◗£4, *free first Sun of month.* ◻✕. ✆*0121 675 4722. www.bmag.org.uk.*

The "noble fabric which for beauty and state much exceedeth anything in these parts" was built 1618–35 by John Thorpe. The Jacobean **interior** is characterised by splendidly ornate ceilings and fire-

places. Its most gorgeous rooms are the Long Gallery, with its strapwork ceiling, arcaded oak panelling and de la Planche tapestries of the *Acts of the Apostles*, and the Great Dining Room, with more extravagant strapwork and paintings by Romney and Gainsborough.

Jewellery Quarter

◗ *Hockley. 1mi/1.6km NW.*

Something of the atmosphere of early industrial Birmingham, with its countless workshops and specialist craftspeople, survives in this densely built-up area just outside the city centre. The **Museum of the Jewellery Quarter** (*75–79 Vyse Street;* ◗*open year-round Tue–Sat and*

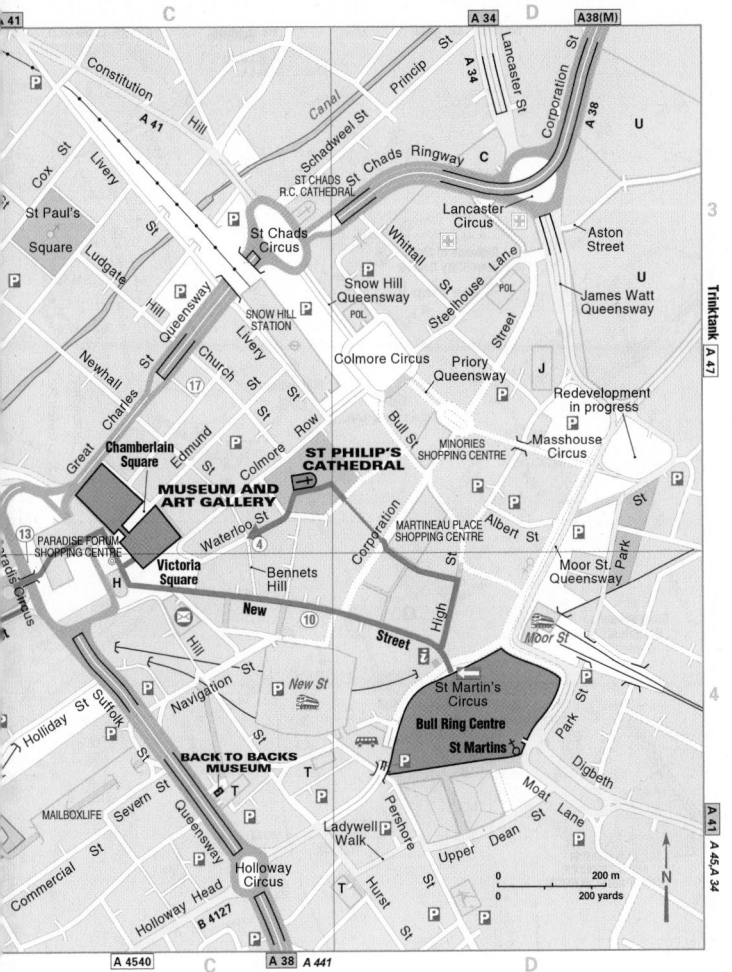

bank hols 10.30am–4pm; ⊙ closed 1 Jan, 25–27 Dec; ♿ ✕; ⊚ £4; ☎ 0121 554 3598; www.bmag.org.uk), set up in the former premises of a jewellery business, tells the story of the area as well as demonstrating traditional skills and techniques. A 10-minute walk away via Spencer Street and Caroline Street, the splendid Georgian **St Paul's Church** forms the centrepiece of St Paul's Square, the only remaining 18C square in Birmingham.

👥 National Sea Life Centre

Brindley Place. ⊙ Open year-round Mon–Fri 10am–5pm Sat–Sun and bank hols 10am–6pm. ⊙ Closed 25 Dec. ⊚ £18, child £14.40 (buy online for significant savings). ♿ ✕. ☎ 0121 643 6777. www.sealife.co.uk.

While boasting the usual features of this nationwide group of marine life centres, this new-wave aquarium also concentrates on the specific story of the River Severn. A pathway climbs up through the displays of sea and freshwater fish as the landscape changes from the oceans to the estuary and upriver to its source. From the top, with a view over the canals below, a lift takes visitors down to the "seabed" and an impressive transparent tunnel, to walk beneath rays and sharks. Also included in the ticket price is a **4-D movie** with special effects including wind, rain and snow supplementing

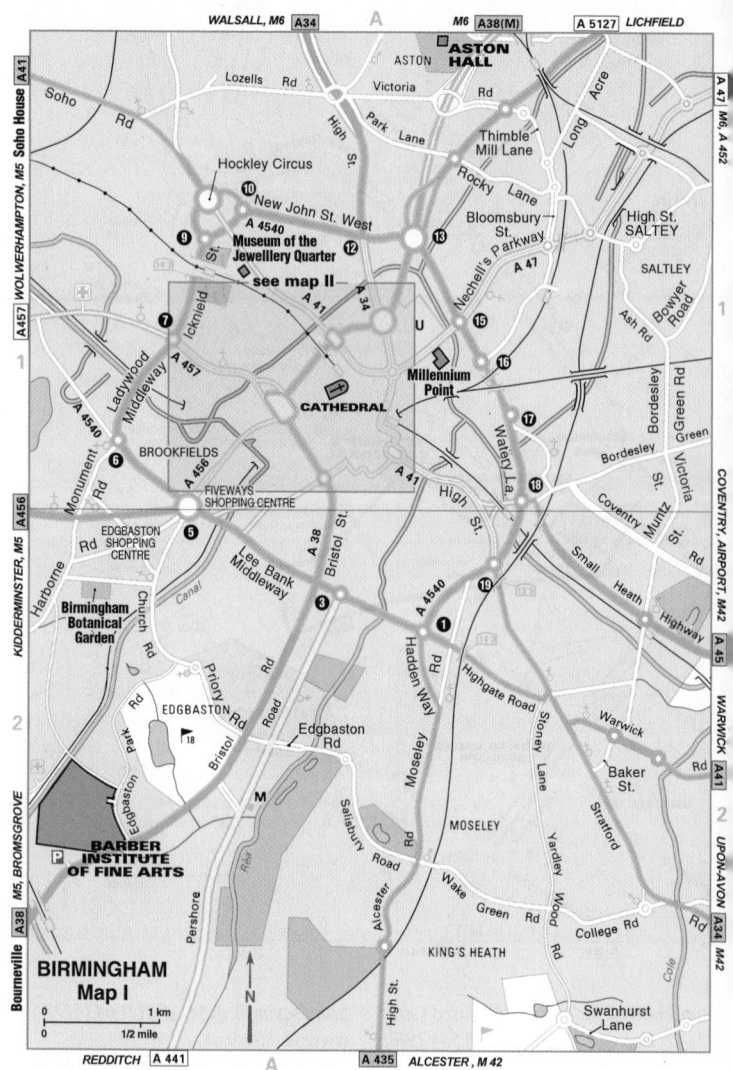

BIRMINGHAM Map I

the 3-D screen images. Dolphins, sea lions and other sea creatures leap from the screen as you feel the wind and salt spray on your face.

Bournville★

▶ *4mi/6km SW of the city centre on the A 38 and A 441.*

In 1879 the Quaker Cadbury brothers moved their cocoa factory from the cramped conditions of the city centre to the rural surroundings of the Bournbrook estate. Cottages and community facilities for their workers were built around the Village Green, where the stone Rest House, presented to Mr and Mrs George Cadbury in 1914 as a silver wedding anniversary gift from Cadbury employees worldwide, is now an information centre. To one side the Bournville School tower houses the **Bournville Carillon**, which rings out every Saturday at noon and 3pm (*open Feb–Dec Mon–Sat 11.30am–4.30pm; www.bournville-web.net).

Selly Manor

Maple Road, NW of the green. ○*Open Apr–Sept Tue–Fri 10am–5pm, Sat–Sun and bank hols 2–5pm; Oct–Mar Tue–Fri 10am–5pm.* ∞*£3.50.* ℘*0121 472 0199. www.bvt.org.uk/sellymanor.*

Selly Manor and Minworth Greaves are two of the city's oldest houses, rescued by George and Laurence Cadbury. Relocated and restored, they are now home to a fine collection of 13C–18C vernacular furniture. A Tudor-style garden has been re-created featuring plants that would have been planted in home gardens.

♣♦ Cadbury World

○ *S of the green.* ○*Open mid-Jan–Dec 9am/10am–3pm/5pm. Call or see website for details; reservations advised.* ○*Closed early Jan, late Nov–Dec Mon and Fri.* ∞*£14.30, children £10.40 (5 percent discount online).* ♿🅿✕. ℘*0845 450 3599. www.cadburyworld.co.uk.*

This is the visitor centre of the famous chocolate company, and it should be emphasised that the factory itself is *not* open to visitors. Instead this chocolate-flavoured mini theme-park (with animatronics, video presentations, multi-sensory cinema, interactive displays and activities) tells the story of the product, of the company, gives an insight into production and marketing, past and present, and (of course) tasting opportunities.

EXCURSIONS
♣♦ The Black Country Living Museum★

○ *Tipton Road, Dudley. 10mi/16km NW of Birmingham on the A 4123 or 3mi/5km from junction 2 on the M 5.* ○*Open Mar–Oct daily 10am–5pm; Nov–Feb reduced hours/days, see website.* ○*Closed 25 Dec.* ∞*£13.60, child £7.10.* ♿🅿(£2). ✕. ℘*0121 557 9643. www.bclm.co.uk.*

The sprawling landscape of the South Staffordshire coalfield may have given rise to the name Black Country, which comprises Wolverhampton, Walsall, Dudley and Sandwell. Over 50 historic buildings from all around the area have been moved and authentically rebuilt to form this museum-village, which covers 26 acres/11ha. Costumed actors present the rich industrial heritage and everyday life of the region. Coal mining is represented by a reconstructed pit-head and an impressive underground display of the conditions in a "Thick Coal" mine in the 1850s. Nearby is a working replica of the world's first steam engine (1712). The heart of the display, reached by an electric tramway and flanked by two canal arms, is the village: houses, a grocery, hardware shop, baker's, chemist's, sweet shop, glasscutter's, chainmaker's, nail shop, rolling mill, anchor forge, boatdock, Methodist chapel and pub. Spectacular limestone caverns beneath the adjacent Castle Hill can be visited by canal boat.

Lichfield★

○ *17mi/27km north.* 🄸 *Litchfield Garrick, Castle Dyke.* ℘*01543 412 112. www.visitlichfield.co.uk.*

This predominantly Georgian town lies just north of the Midlands industrial conurbation and is graced by its **cathedral★★** (○*open year-round Mon–Fri 7.30am–6.15pm, Sat 8am–6.15pm, Sun 7.30–5pm;* ∞*contribution requested;* ♿✕. ℘*01543 306 100. www.lichfield-cathedral.org.uk).* the smallest in the country but also one of the most beautiful and most picturesquely sited. The present building, which replaced an earlier Norman church, was begun in 1195 and is a fine synthesis of the Early English and Decorated styles. During the Civil War the cathedral was bombarded and the central spire collapsed in 1646. Repairs were made during the 1660s and the interior of the building was changed substantially by Wyatt in the 18C, but its medieval grandeur was restored by the sensitive work carried out by Sir George Gilbert Scott (1857–1901).

The three spires – unique among English cathedrals – are known as the **three sisters** of the vale. On the west front the red sandstone is carved with saints. The perfectly proportioned nave, adorned with wooden roof **bosses** and decorated capitals, leads the eye past the Transitional crossing and western choir to the Lady Chapel and the fine 16C Flemish glass at the east end. Among the many fine monuments are those to Samuel Johnson and David Garrick.

Samuel Johnson Birthplace Museum
Breadmarket Street. ○Open daily Apr–Sept 10.30am–4.30pm; Oct–Mar 11am–3.30pm. ○Closed 1 Jan, 25–26 Dec. ℘01543 264 972. www.samuel johnsonbirthplace.org.uk.
Samuel Johnson (1709–84), the famous **lexicographer**, was born in this house, built by his father. The exhibits illustrate his life from childhood to marriage, his move to London, the English dictionary and his friendship with Boswell

ADDRESSES

🛒 SHOPPING

Birmingham is the principal shopping centre for the Midlands with branches of famous London stores, such as Selfridges, in the Bull Ring Centre, and Harvey Nichols, in the designer mall, The Mailbox. Explore the Jewellery Quarter for shops selling handmade gold and silver jewellery.

🎭 ENTERTAINMENT

The City of Birmingham Symphony Orchestra (CBSO) and Birmingham Royal Ballet are internationally renowned. Pop and rock concerts and other events are staged in the National Indoor Area (NIA), part of the National Exhibition Centre (NEC). After dark, Broad Street, The Mailbox and the Water's Edge are hot-spots for drinking, dining and dancing.

Peak District★★
South Yorkshire, Derbyshire, Staffordshire

Bordering the teeming northern industrial areas of Sheffield, Manchester, the Potteries and West Yorkshire, is the unspoiled landscape of the Peak District National Park. To the north, the sombre moorlands and precipitous outcrops of the Dark Peak culminate in Kinder Scout (2 087ft/636m), while to the south is more pastoral White Peak, a plateau divided up by drystone walls and by spectacular steep-sided dales. It was on Kinder Scout, in 1932, that a mass trespass by ramblers, anxious to establish a permanent right of access to these wild spots, was organised. It resulted in the imprisonment of five of their number. In the end, however, it helped lead to the establishment of the national parks.

◐ *Sights from N to S*

DERWENT RESERVOIRS
◐ *10mi/16 km W of Sheffield.*

- 🦽 **Michelin Map:** Atlas p35 or Map 502 O, P 23 and 24.
- ⓘ **Info:** Ashbourne, Bakewell, Buxton, Castleton, Derby, Edale, Matlock and Matlock Bath; visit www.visitpeakdistrict.com for details. The Peak District National Park Moorland Centre at Edale (℘01433 670 207; www.peakdistrict.gov.uk.) is the place for walking information.
- ◐ **Location:** The park (555sqmi/1,437sq km) is bounded by Holmfirth (north), Ashbourne (south), Sheffield (east) and Macclesfield (west).
- 👪 **Kids:** A cave visit; the Heights of Abraham; Abrahamarmyard and Adventure Playground.

Created to supply water to the nearby cities, **Derwent**, **Howden** and **Ladybower reservoirs** are today a mini-"Lake District" enjoyed by yachtsmen, cyclists and walkers alike.

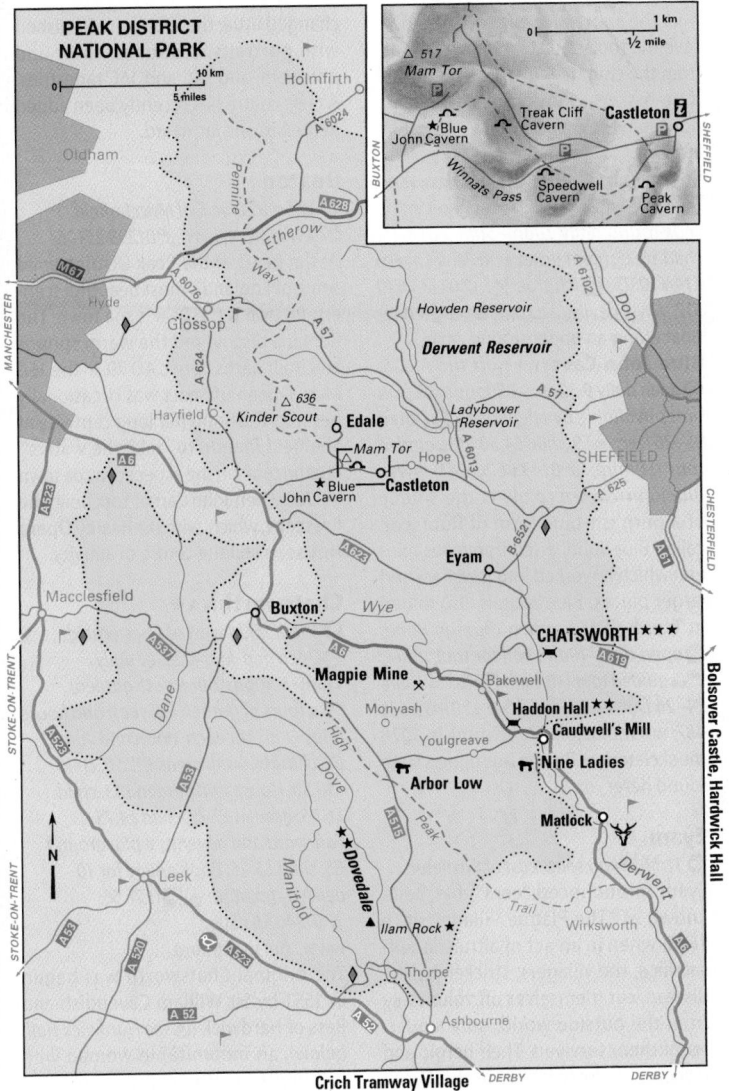

CASTLETON AND CAVES

17mi/27km W of Sheffield.

Buxton Road. ℘01629 816 558.

The village of Castleton is dominated by the ruined 12C keep of **Peveril Castle** (EH. ☉*open daily Apr–Oct 10am–5pm, Nov–Mar Sat–Sun (daily during Feb half-term hols) 10am–4pm;* ☉*closed 1 Jan, 4–26 Dec;* ☎*£4.30;* ℘*01433 620 613; www.english-heritage.org.uk)*, built soon after the Norman Conquest. From the top are wonderful views over the Hope Valley.

The local caves – lofty chambers with attractive mineral colourings and limestone formations – are natural cavities and/or lead-mining workings.

Peak Cavern/"Devil's Arse" (*off Goosehill;* ⟿*guided tour only (1hr), Apr–Oct daily 10am–5pm, Nov–Mar Sat–Sun 10am–5pm;* ☎*£8.25, child £6.25, (joint ticket with Speedwell Cavern £14/£10.25);* P *(charge)* ✕; ℘*01433 620 285; www.devilsarse.com)* is entered at the foot of the hill below the castle.

Near the impressive entrance of the cave the roof is still blackened by soot from the chimneys of a community of rope-makers, who occupied and built houses in the cave for 300 years until 1974.

Speedwell Cavern (Winnat's Pass, W on the B 6061; ↝guided tour only (45min), year-round daily 10am–5pm; ∞£8.75, child £6.75; (joint ticket with Peak Cavern £14/£10.25) P (charge)✕; ℘01433 620 512; www.devilsarse.com) is reached by boat along an underground canal.

Blue John Cavern★ (off the A 625; ⊙open daily 9.30am–5.30pm/dusk (Jan times available by telephone); ⊙closed 25–26 Dec; ∞£9, child £4.50; ↝guided tour (50min); ℘01433 620 642; www. bluejohn-cavern.co.uk) is the source of a purplish-blue form of fluorspar, called Blue John, a semi-precious mineral which is worked into jewellery and larger pieces. Blue John is also mined in **Treak Cliff Cavern** (Buxton Road; ⊙open daily 10am, call for tour times; ↝guided tour (40min); ⊙closed 1 Jan, 24–26 Dec; ∞£7.95; P ✕; ℘01433 621 487; www.bluejohnstone.com). In 1926 the skeletons of Bronze Age miners were found here.

Eyam

❱ 11mi/18km) southeast of Castleton.
Eyam (pronounced "eem") has been known as "The Plague Village" since 1665, when in an act of altruistic self-sacrifice, the villagers, stricken by the disease, cut themselves off voluntarily from the outside world; only a quarter of them survived. Their heroic and fascinating story is told in the **Eyam Museum** (Hawkhill Road; ⊙open late Mar–early Nov Tue–Sun and bank hols 10am–4.30pm; ∞£2; ℘01433 631 371; www.eyammuseum.demon.co.uk).

Eyam Hall (Hope Valley; ⊙house open early Apr–early May and Aug Wed–Thu, Sun and bank hols noon–4pm; gardens open Jul–Aug, same days as house, noon–4.45pm; Craft Centre open year-round Tue–Sun 10.30am–5pm; ∞£6.25, gardens only, £2; ᵹ✕; ℘01433 631 976; www.eyamhall.com) is still owned by the Wright family, who built it in 1671. It has changed little: the rooms are furnished with portraits, costumes, silver and porcelain, and 15C and 16C tapestries. A craft centre has recently been added in the historic farmyard.

Buxton

❱ 12.5mi/20km E of Macclesfield.
🛈 Pavilion Gardens. ℘01298 25106.
At the heart of the Peak District, amid some of England's most beautiful scenery, Buxton is the Peak's spa town. The Romans discovered the warm springs and built baths here c.AD 79. In the 16C Mary Queen of Scots was occasionally permitted, during her long captivity at Sheffield Manor, to "take the waters". Buxton took on the aspect of a spa town in 1780 when John Carr of York built **The Crescent**, which, with the nearby **Opera House**, is still the centre of activity.

Chatsworth★★★

❱ 10mi/16km west of Chesterfield.
⊙Open mid-Mar–23 Dec daily 11am–5.30pm (6pm/dusk garden).
↝Tours of garden (all year) and house (May–Jun) 1hr each, noon and 2pm (∞charge). ∞All areas £17.50, child £10.50. House and garden £13, child £6.25; garden £7.75, child £4.75. Farmyard and adventure playground £5, child £5.25. Book online for 10 percent discount. ᵹP (£2). ✕.
℘01246 565 300.
www.chatsworth.org.
The original Chatsworth was begun in 1551 by Sir William Cavendish and Bess of Hardwick (ᵹsee Hardwick Hall, below), an indomitable woman who married four times and multiplied her wealth with each marriage. It was transformed 1686–1707 by the first Duke of Devonshire into a Baroque palace, and extended 1820–27 into "the second Versailles".
Today, set amid magnificent countryside, not only is it one of the finest stately homes in the country with one of Europe's outstanding private art collections, but it consistently wins national awards for its excellence as a visitor attraction. The glorious verdant grounds are a delight.

House

The Painted Hall, by Laguerre, is unashamedly Baroque; the ceilings and walls are a soaring profusion of colours. Beneath the Great Stairs is the **grotto**, with superb stone carvings. The two coronation chairs in the lobby were used by William IV and Queen Adelaide in 1830. The long landscape by Gaspard Poussin is "among the finest landscapes in the world" (Gustave Waagen).

The State Rooms are characterised by unrestrained ceilings by Laguerre and Verrio and Louis XIV furniture; the gilt side tables in the Dining Room are by Kent; the Drawing Room tapestries (c.1635), based on Raphael, were woven at Mortlake; the violin on the inner door of the Music Room is a remarkable *trompe l'œil* by Jan van der Vaart.

The wrought-iron panels on the landings of the West Stairs are by Jean Tijou. The ceiling depicting the Fall of Phaeton is an early work by Sir James Thornhill (1675–1734) and the painting of Samson and Delilah is by Tintoretto (1518–94). In the corridor are two Egyptian memorial tablets which are 3,800 years old. The chapel is unaltered since 1694 and includes a fine work by Verrio and a gloriously Baroque altarpiece by Cibber. A Veronese hangs in the passage.

The Library (90ft/28m) has some 17,000 books and a splendid gilded stucco ceiling by Edward Goudge (Wren's best pupil) framing Verrio's paintings.

The **Sculpture Gallery** houses an incomparable collection, including works by Antonio Canova. Hanging amid these is *King Uzziah* by Rembrandt.

👥 Park and Garden★★★

The genius of Capability Brown made this one of the grandest of 18C parks. The garden's most majestic feature is the Cascade, designed in 1696, each step a different height that varies the sound of the falling water that disappears into pipes, to reappear out of the Seahorse Fountain on the south lawn. The garden as we see it today is mostly the creation of Joseph Paxton (1803–65).

Modern family-friendly additions include a waterworks in which children

---

Well Dressing

The annual Well Dressing is a unique Peak District tradition. Pagan thanksgivings to local water spirits have been transformed into Christian ceremonies, in some 20 Peak District villages. Eyam, Youlgreave, Wirksworth and Monyash are just some of the villages where the dressing takes place from early May to August each year. A large board is covered in clay, a design pricked out on it and then flowers, seeds, bark, lichens and grasses are used to fill out the design in colours. The board is then placed by the well or spring and blessed at a special open-air church service.

---

can freely splash around, a maze, the **farmyard**, which features milking demonstrations and daily animal-handling sessions, and a huge woodland adventure playground for children. There is also a sculpture garden.

Bolsover Castle★

EH. ⏺ *16mi/26km E of Matlock.* 🕐*Open May–Oct daily 10am–5pm; Nov–Apr Sat–Sun (daily during Feb half-term hols) 10am–4pm.*🕐*Closed 1 Jan, 24–26 Dec.* ⌨£7.80. ♿ 🅿 ✕. ✆01246 822 844. www.english-heritage.org.uk.

This Gothic folly castle is perched on a hill above the coal mines and pit-heads. Completed in 1633, its interior is rich in carved Jacobean fireplaces, panelling, strapwork and ceiling paintings.

Hardwick Hall★★

NT. ⏺ *20mi/32km east of Matlock.* **Hall:** 🕐*Open late Feb–Oct Wed–Sun, Good Fri and bank hols noon–4.30pm; 1st 3 Sats–Suns weekends Dec. 11am–3pm* ·📷Hall tours Feb–Oct 11am–noon (book ahead). **Gardens:** 🕐*Open same days as house (daily during summer school hols) 11am–5pm; Dec 11a–3pm.* ⌨£9.98. 🅿 ✕. ✆01246 850 430. www.nationaltrust.org.uk.

Directly after building Chatsworth and abandoning her husband, the Earl of Shrewsbury, **Bess of Hardwick** returned to the modest manor house where she was born, and rebuilt it. However, her descendants preferred to live at Chatsworth so the Old Hall fell into ruins and the New Hall was left unoccupied, frozen in time, one of the purest examples of 16C design and décor in the country. The **interior** is famous for its Elizabethan fireplaces, friezes, tapestries and **embroideries**; one of these is by Mary Queen of Scots and three are by Bess. The house appeared in the last two *Harry Potter* films as Malfoy Manor.

Haddon Hall★★

◯ *2mi/3km S of Bakewell.*
◯ *Open noon–5pm; Easter weekend Good Fri–Tue; early Apr and Oct Sat–Mon; May–Sept daily: early–mid-Dec daily 10.30am–4pm.* ◯*£9.50.* ◯ *(charge)* ✕. ◯ *01629 812 855. www.haddonhall.co.uk.*

Overlooking the River Wye since the 12C, Haddon Hall is one of the finest fortified medieval manor houses in the country, continually enlarged until the early -17C. The rambling **interior**, like the exterior, is in a multitude of styles; the Hall (1370) is medieval, the Dining Room and Great Chamber are Tudor and the Long Gallery is Elizabethan. The rooms are matched in splendour by their Mortlake **tapestries**. The chapel boasts splendid **murals**. The terraced **gardens** date from the 17C or earlier. Lavishly planted with roses they tumble prettily to the river with its venerable stone packhorse bridge.

Arbor Low

◯ *3mi/5km W of Youlgreave, 11mi/8km W of Matlock.*

The best known of the Peak's prehistoric monuments, this circle of stones lies within a surrounding bank and ditch.

Matlock Bath and Matlock

◯ *Matlock Bath is 17mi/27km N of Derby.* ◯ *Mining Museum, Matlock Bath; Crown Square, Matlock. Both* ◯ *01629 583 388.*

The cliffs and woods of the deep gorge carved by the River Derwent formed a picturesque setting for the Victorians to develop spa facilities at Matlock Bath; with its riverside cliff setting, it resembles an inland seaside resort. The former Matlock Bath Hydro now houses a **freshwater aquarium** (*110 North Parade;* ◯*open Easter–Oct daily 10am–5.30pm, Nov–Easter Sat–Sun and Christmas hols 10am–5pm;* ◯*£2.40;* ◯*01629 583 624; www.matlockbathaquarium.co.uk*). A far older Peak District industry, lead mining, is celebrated in the fascinating **Peak District Mining Museum** (◯*museum open year-round daily: summer 10am–5pm, winter 11am–3pm; mine visits noon, 2pm: summer daily, winter Sat–Sun;* ◯*museum or mine £3.50, both £6;* ◯*charge;* ◯*museum only;* ✕; ◯*01629 583 388; www.peakmines.co.uk*), housed in the grand turn-of-the-20C Pavilion, once the centre of the town's social life.

A ◯◯**cable car** runs from Matlock, 2mi/3km north of Matlock Bath, over the river gorge to the **Heights of Abraham**, where you can take **cave tours**, see exhibitions on the area, enjoy views from the Victorian Prospect Tower, and explore hilltop trails (◯*open mid-/late Feb–late Mar Sat–Sun/daily school hols 10am–4.30pm, late Mar–late Oct daily 10am–4.30pm, later at peak times;* ◯*£12.50, child £8.80;* ◯◯✕; ◯*01629 582 365; www.heightsofabraham.com*).

Dovedale★★

NT. ◯ *Ilam Park Visitor Centre is 4.6mi/7.4km NW of Ashbourn.*
◯*visitor centre open year-round 9am–5pm.* ✕. ◯*01335 350 503. www.nationaltrust.org.uk.*

This dramatic gorge in the Derbyshire hills has been formed by the River Dove washing away the soft limestone, exposing cliffs, caves and crags. From its entrance between Thorpe Cloud (942ft/287m) and Bunster Hill (1,000ft/305m), it meanders for 2mi/3km below the rocky outcrops of Lovers' Leap, The Twelve Apostles and **Ilam Rock**★.

Derby★

and around

Derby is not one of England's most attractive county towns but it does provide a base for the Peak District and is surrounded by outstanding country houses. In 1756 the Derby porcelain industry began here, and in the early-20C it was the birthplace of Rolls-Royce.

▶ **Population:** 223,836.

Michelin Map: Michelin Atlas p35 or Map 502 P 25.

Info: Market Place. ✆01332 255 802. www.visitderby.co.uk.

Location: 41mi/66km northeast of Birmingham. The train station is 1mi/1.6km southeast of the centre; the bus station is a five minutes walk from town.

CITY

At the heart of the city, west of the River Derwent on Queen Street is **Derby Cathedral** (○open year-round Mon–Wed and Fri 8am–6pm, Thu 8am–7.30pm, Sat 9am–6pm, Sun 7.30am–7.30pm; ⤳guided tours 10.30am 2nd Mon of each month, entrance to tower on certain days; ⤳cathedral £5 contribution suggested, tower tour £3; ♿; ✆01332 341 201; www.derbycathedral.org), a sublime blending of three eras – early-16C (the high tower), early-18C (James Gibbs' nave) and late 20C (retrochoir). The highlight is the magnificent Bakewell wrought-iron **screen and gates**, and the baldachin over the high altar. South of the chancel rests Bess of Hardwick (⤳see Peak District, Hardwick Hall).

Close by, on The Strand, is the **Derby Museum and Art Gallery**★ (○open Mon 11am–5pm, Tue–Sat 10am–5pm, Sun and bank hols 1–4pm; ○closed Christmas and New Year; ♿; ✆01332 716 659; www.derby.gov.uk/museums), home to two superb collections. The **Gallery of Ceramics** contains the world's largest collection of **Derby Porcelain**★, while the **Wright Gallery** holds many of the finest paintings and drawings of Joseph Wright of Derby (1734–97).

A 20-minute walk south of here, near the Derbyshire Royal Infirmary, is **Royal Crown Derby Porcelain**★ (194 Osmaston Road; ○open Mon–Sat 10am–5pm; ⤳factory tours (booking essential) Tue–Fri 11am, 1.30pm; ⤳museum and studio only, £3, factory tour £5; ♿ ▣ ✖; ✆01332 712 833; www.royal-crown-derby.co.uk). A collection dating from 1756 to the present day is on display in the museum. In the

Raven Room a priceless mint collection of Royal Crown Derby is displayed as it would have been in a Victorian house.

EXCURSIONS

Kedleston Hall★★

NT. ▶4mi/6km NW of Derby on Kedleston Road. **House:** ○Open late Feb–Oct Sat–Wed noon–5pm. **Pleasure grounds and park:** ○Open year-round daily late Feb–Oct 10am–6pm; Nov–late Feb 10am–4pm. ⤳£8.90, park and pleasure grounds only, £3.95. ♿▣✖. ✆01332 842 191. www.nationaltrust.org.uk.

This Palladian mansion is the work of three architects: Matthew Brettingham, James Paine and Robert Adam; together they created one of the grandest 18C houses in England. The Curzon family have lived here since the 12C. The **rooms** centre on the **Marble Hall**. The **State Drawing Room** shows Adam at his most colourful; note the Cuyp landscape and the Veronese Achilles. The **Saloon** or **Rotunda** reaches to the coffered dome (62ft/19m). Adam's **Ante Room** and **Dressing Room** is graced by a Neoclassical screen with a segmental arch above the entablature, in a room hung with 17C and 18C Masters.

Sudbury Hall and the National Trust Museum of Childhood★★

NT. ▶15mi/24km W of Derby via the A 516 and A 50. **Hall:** ○Open mid-late Feb–Oct Wed–Sun, Good Fri and bank hols 1pm–6pm. **Museum:** ◐Open 11am–5pm: mid–late Feb–Mar Wed–Sun; Apr–Oct daily; Nov–mid-Dec Sat–Sun. **Grounds:** ◐Open mid-Feb–Oct 10am–6pm. ☞Hall £7.80, museum £8.40 (child £4.80). Both £14.50. ♿🅿✕. ℘01283 585 337. www.nationaltrust.org.uk.

Although the **Jacobean exterior** (1660–1702) of this fine mansion is conservative, the **interior**, a radical combination of late Renaissance Classicism and Baroque, is exuberant. The hall, which is densely hung with 18C paintings, is beautified by the work of Grinling Gibbons, Edward Pierce and James Pettifer (all craftsmen who had worked with Wren on many of his London churches) and capped by Louis Laguerre's ceiling paintings. The **Staircase** was built by Pierce and the exquisite plasterwork above it is by Pettifer; note the superb **Long Gallery** ceiling.

The 👥 **Museum of Childhood** covers a variety of childhood experiences from the 19C to the present day, in eight new interactive galleries including outdoor adventures, stories and imagination, and archive films.

Denby Pottery Visitor Centre

▶ Derby Road, Denby. 8mi/13km N of Derby. **Visitor centre:** ◐Open year-round daily Mon–Sat 9.30–5pm, Sun 10am–5pm. ☞Tours Feb–Oct: factory (90min) Mon–Thu 10.30am, 1pm; craftroom (60min) daily 11am, noon, 2pm, 3pm. ◐Closed 25–26 Dec. ☞Factory tour £6.95, craftroom tour £5.25 (child £4.25). ♿🅿✕. ℘01773 740 799. www.denbyvisitorcentre.co.uk.

All aspects of the production of the famous Denby earthenware are demonstrated to visitors with opportunities to try making and decorating pieces, plus food demonstrations and glassmaking.

Stoke-on-Trent
and around

The potteries that this area is world famous for (and for which it is nicknamed) existed long before the time of England's most distinguished potter, **Josiah Wedgwood** (1730–95). Kilns date back to the early-14C but it was the opening of Wedgwood's Etruria factory in 1769, the exploitation of Staffordshire's coalfields and the digging of the Trent–Mersey Canal that turned a local industry into a national one and an industry into an art. Most of the great brick kilns have now disappeared but a few monumental survivors remain, particularly in Longton.

CITY MUSEUMS
Gladstone Pottery Museum★

▶ Uttoxeter Road, Longton. ◐Open year-round daily 10am–5pm. ☞£6.95. ♿🅿✕. ℘01782 237 7076. www.stoke.gov.uk/museums.

▶ **Population:** 266,543.
⚲ **Michelin Map:** Michelin Atlas p35 or Map 503 N 24.
🛈 **Info:** Victoria Hall. ℘01782 236 000. www.visitstoke.co.uk.
▶ **Location:** 43mi/69km north of Birmingham. A car is best for getting around the "Five Towns" that make up Stoke-on-Trent.
🎡 **Don't Miss:** Wedgwood; Little Moreton Hall.
◐ **Timing:** Allow 1–2 days including an excursion.
👥 **Kids:** Alton Towers; Trentham.

This unique surviving pottery factory or "potbank" retains its original workshops, cobbled yard and distinctive bottle ovens. It produced bone china from 1850 until the 1960s when it was converted into a museum of British pottery. The potters' traditional skills are demonstrated in the workshops.

The Potteries Museum and Art Gallery★

Bethesda Street, Hanley. ◐*Open year-round Mon–Sat 10am–5pm, Sun 2–5pm.* &✕. *℘01782 23 23 23. www.stoke.gov.uk/museums.*

The main city museum houses a superb ceramics collection from 14C English pottery right through to the modern studio movement, and current industrial production.

There is a Second World War Spitfire, and major art exhibitions are regularly held. All have been upstaged recently, however, by the **Staffordshire Hoard**; comprising over 3,500 items of gold and silver with precious stone decorations it is the largest hoard of Anglo-Saxon gold ever found. It was discovered near Lichfield in 2009, and part of it is now on permanent display here.

EXCURSIONS
♟♟ Alton Towers★★

▶ *12mi/19km E via the A 50, A 521 and B 5032.* ◐*Open late Mar–early Nov daily, gates open 9.30am. Rides start 10am, closing times vary.* ✆*Theme park from £31.68 (online), child from £24.48. Waterpark (online) £15, child £10.50.* &🅿(£4)✕. *℘0871 222 3330. www.alton-towers.co.uk.*

Britain's most famous theme park still offers more thrills than the rest with a huge variety of spectacular rides, a waterpark, and a spa as well as tranquil gardens. It is set in the beautiful grounds of Alton Towers, a 19C Gothic Revival mansion, now in ruins.

Biddulph Grange Garden★

NT. ▶ *Grange Road, Biddulph. 7mi/11km N.* ◐*Open last wk Feb daily 10.30am–3.30pm; Mar Thu–Mon 10.30am–5.30pm; Apr–Oct daily 10.30am–5.30pm; Nov–late Dec Fri–Mon 10.30am–3.30pm.* ✆*Mid-March–Oct £6.68, rest of year £3 (joint ticket with Little Moreton Hall (&see below) £12.75).* 🅿✕. *℘01782 517 999. www.nationaltrust.org.uk.*

This unusual and exciting garden with themed sections devoted to different parts of the world was designed in the mid-19C by James Bateman to display specimens from his extensive plant collection.

Little Moreton Hall★★

NT. ▶ *Congleton 10mi/16km N.* ◐*Open late Feb–mid Mar and Nov–late Dec Sat–Sun 11am–4pm; Mar–mid-Oct Wed–Sun 11am–5pm. Open bank hol Mons.* ✆*Guided tour (free) most days main season.* ✆*£6.70 (joint ticket with Biddulph Grange (&see above) £12.75).* &🅿✕. *℘01260 272 018. www.nationaltrust.org.uk.*

This beautiful moated half-timbered manor house is characterised by rich and intricate patterns on square panels, elaborate joinery and window tracery and 16C glass.

It was begun in the 1440s with the building of the Great Hall and completed some 140 years later with the addition of John Moreton's Long Gallery.

Wedgwood Visitor Centre★

▶ *7mi/11km S on the A 500, A 34 and a minor road (left) to Barlaston.* ◐*Open year-round Mon–Fri 9am–4pm/5pm, Sat–Sun 10am–4pm/5pm.* ✆*£10.* &🅿✕. *℘01782 204 218. www.wedgwoodvisitorcentre.com.*

Established in 1938 the Wedgwood Factory offers the perfect overview of the pottery-making process, with a suitably excellent collection of Wedgwood ware, and Wedgwood portraits by Stubbs, Reynolds, Lawrence and Wright of Derby.

♟♟ Trentham★

▶ *5mi/8km south of Hanley.* ◐*Open Easter–Sept 10am–6pm/dusk.* *℘01782 646 646. www.trenthamleisure.co.uk. www.trentham-monkey-forest.com.*

Britain's most spectacular Italian garden, designed by Capability Brown, covers 750 acres/300ha. It has recently become the region's second-largest leisure centre, featuring a monkey forest, treetops walk, big wheel, garden centre, shopping and restaurants.

ADDRESSES

🛏 STAY

STRATFORD-UPON-AVON

👄🛏🛎 **Mercure Shakespeare Hotel** – Chapel Street. ☏01789 294 997. www.mercure.com . 73 rms. Housed in a charming 17C half-timbered building, this smart hotel stylishly combines old and new all at keen prices.

👄🛏🛎 **The Arden Hotel** – 44 Waterside. ☏01789 298 682. www.theardenhotel stratford.co.uk. 63 rms. Opposite the Royal Shakespeare Theatre, the Arden is the smartest address in town. It boasts the chic new Waterside Brasserie, a champagne bar, and rooms with river views.

👄🛏🛎 **The Legacy Falcon Hotel** – Chapel Street. ☏0844 411 9005. www.legacy-hotels.co.uk. 84 rms. In the centre of town, behind a half-timbered façade, this stylish hotel combines ancient and modern to good effect. Lovely courtyard garden in summer, log fires in winter. Very good value.

COVENTRY

👄🛏 **Spireview** – 36 Park Road. ☏01926 492 799. www.spireviewguesthouse.co.uk. Simple B&B accommodation.

WARWICK

👄🛏 **The Aylesford Hotel** – 1 High Street. ☏01926 492 799. www.aylesfordhotel. co.uk. 8 rms. This charming Georgian townhouse, just a five-minute walk from the castle, offers not only comfortable stylish rooms, some with four-poster beds, but a café-brasserie.

WORCESTER

👄🛏🛎 **Diglis House Hotel** – Severn Street. ☏01905 353 518. www.diglishousehotel. co.uk. 30 rms. This gracious 18C house enjoys a wonderful position on the banks of the Severn, just a short walk from the city centre. Accommodation is in a modern annex.

LUDLOW

👄🛏🛎 **The Feathers Hotel** – Bull Ring. ☏01584 875 261. www.feathersatludlow. co.uk. 40 rms. Set in a magnificent timber -framed building, and centrally located, the famous Feathers features spacious, elegantly decorated bedrooms, an award -winning restaurant, and can be surprisingly good value.

BIRMINGHAM

👄–👄🛏 **Premier Inn – Brindley Place**, 80 Broad Street. ☏0871 527 8076 and **Canal Side** 20 Bridge Street. ☏0871 527 8078. www.premiertravelinn.com. These cheerful budget chain hotel branches offer simple comfortable modern accommodation in two excellent locations in and around Birmingham's buzzing canal area.

👄🛏🛎 **Hotel du Vin** – Church Street. ☏0121 200 0600. www.hotelduvin.com. 🅿. 66 rms. Set in the revitalised Jewellery Quarter, the large ornate Victorian red-brick Birmingham Eye Hospital has been sympathetically converted to timelessly styled bedrooms and suites, set around a courtyard. There is also a spa, gym, billiards room, a bistro and pub.

👄🛏🛎 **Novotel Birmingham Centre** – 70 Broad Street. ☏0121 643 2000. www. novotel.com. 🅿. 148 rms. Set in the centre of town there may be few surprises in this modern international-style chain hotel but it provides a very comfortable base.

👄🛏🛎🛎 **The Burlington** – Burlington Arcade, off New Street. ☏0121 633 1716. www.macdonaldhotels.co.uk/burlington. 110 rms. Polychrome marble, plush carpets and elegant décor give an inimitable Victorian atmosphere in this historic hotel, strong on design and modern art. VIPs visiting the city stay here.

PEAK DISTRICT

👄 **Fountain Villa** – 86 North Matlock Bath. ☏01629 56 195. www.fountainvilla. co.uk. 🅿. 4 rms. This elegant classic Georgian house is something of an Aladdin's cave inside with fussy but characterful rooms. Good value.

👄🛏 **Buxton's Victorian House** – 3a Broad Walk, Buxton. ☏01298 78759. www.buxtonvictorian.co.uk. 🅿. 8 rms This welcoming 1860-built guesthouse, opposite the pavilion gardens, puts you right into the refined heart of Buxton.

👄🛏🛎 **Cavendish Hotel** – Chatsworth Estate, Baslow. ☏01246 582 311. www. cavendish-hotel.net. 🅿. 23 rms. Located on the Chatsworth House Estate, and originally the local inn, the building is steeped in history, with perfect views and peaceful surroundings. Throughout are open fires, oak beams, antique furnishings.

DERBY

👄🛏🛎–👄🛏🛎🛎 **Marriott Breadsall Priory Hotel** – Moor Road, Morley. ☏01332

832 235. www.marriott.co.uk/emags. 112 rms.
Set in a beautiful 162-acre/62ha estate,
this wonderful golden-stone house,
dating back to the 13C, is now a
four-star country club with spa.

♈️ EAT

STRATFORD-UPON-AVON

🐇 **Sheep Street** is good for eating out.

⊜ 🍽️ **Garrick Inn** – *High St. 𝄐01789 292
186. www.garrick-inn-stratford-upon-
avon.co.uk.* You wouldn't be surprised
to find The Bard himself quaffing a pint
of ale in this venerable Olde English
pub (est 1595), now also a restaurant.

⊜ 🍽️ **Lambs** – *12 Sheep Street. 𝄐01789 292
554. www.lambsrestaurant.co.uk. Closed
Mon lunch.* Hidden behind a 16C façade,
this fashionable, stylish restaurant serves
brasserie favourites in a modern way.

⊜ 🍽️🍽️ **Marlowes Restaurant** – *18 High
Street. 𝄐01789 204 999. www.marlowes.biz.*
This classic Elizabethan house (built
1595), all oak panelling and ancient oak
beams, has been a favourite over the
years with many famous RSC actors.

WORCESTER

🐇 Try **Friars Street** for European
and ethnic cuisines.

⊜ – ⊜ **Brown's** – *The Old Cornmill.
South Quay. 𝄐01905 26263. www.browns
restaurant.co.uk.* A trendily coverted
old mill by the river is the setting for
this "all-day, all-kinds-of-eating" (and
drinking) venture by Brown's, who made
their name in the city with fine dining.

HEREFORD

⊜ 🍽️ **The Stewing Pot** – *17 Church Street.
𝄐01432 265 233. www.stewingpot.co.uk -
Closed Sun–Mon.* This casual restaurant
in minimalist surroundings serves
award-winning Modern British cuisine.

LUDLOW

⊜ – ⊜ 🍽️ **Green Cafe** – *Mill on the
Green, Dinham Bridge. 𝄐01584 879 872.
www. ludlowmillonthegreen.co.uk. Open
10am–4pm. Closed Mon and Jan.* Part of a
restored watermill complex, overlooking
Dinham Weir, the café features seasonal
cooking using local organic products.
Its pricing proves you can eat very well
in Ludlow without breaking the bank.

⊜ 🍽️🍽️🍽️ **La Bécasse** – *17 Corve Street.
𝄐01584 872 325. www.labecasse.co.uk.*
The characterful dining room of this

Michelin-starred 17C former coaching
inn is split into three intimate areas, with
linen-laid tables and wood panelling.

BIRMINGHAM

🐇 Visit the **Water's Edge** and **Brindley
Place** developments in the Gas Street
Basin area for lively wine bars, cafés,
restaurants and traditional English
pubs. Birmingham is most famous for
its Indian and Chinese restaurants and
its Balti curry houses are renowned.

⊜ **Canalside Café** – *35 Regency Wharf,
Gas Street Basin. 𝄐0121 248 7979.* This
tiny former cottage, built 1770, at the
side of Gas Street Basin, is now a pub
serving real ales which wash down its
home-cooked, good-quality food.

⊜ 🍽️ **Bank** – *4 Brindley Place. 𝄐0121
633 4466. www.bankrestaurants.
com.* This spacious airy modern
brasserie has large glass walls which
look onto its canalside terrace. Grills
and shellfish are the specialities.

⊜ 🍽️ **Celebrity Indian Restaurant** –
*44 Broad Street. 𝄐0121 643 8969.
www.celebrityrestaurant.co.uk.* Popular
upmarket stylish Indian restaurant in a
canalside location, serving contemporary
dishes alongside old favourites.

⊜ 🍽️🍽️ **Purnell's** – *55 Cornwall Street.
𝄐0121 212 9799 . www.purnellsrestaurant.
com. Closed Sun–Mon, and 1st fortnight
Aug.* This contemporary fine-dining
restaurant was set up by a Michelin-star
local chef in July 2007, and occupies
a Victorian red-brick building.

PEAK DISTRICT

⊜ 🍽️ **Rowley's** – *Church Lane, Baslow.
𝄐01246 583 880. www.rowleysrestaurant.
co.uk.* On the edge of the Chatsworth
Estate, and under the same ownership
as the one-star Michelin restaurant at
Baslow Hall Hotel, this sturdy old stone-
built pub offers Modern British cuisine.

DERBY

🐇 **The Brunswick Inn** *(Railway Terrace)*,
near the station, and **Ye Olde Dolphin**
(Queen Street), by the cathedral, are
two of Derby's best traditional pubs.

⊜ 🍽️🍽️ **Tonic** – *6 Chapel Quarter. 𝄐0115
941 4770. www.tonic-online.co.uk. The* place
to be seen eating out in Derby, Tonic is
sophisticated, very modern and beautifully
lit. It serves Modern British cuisine.

NORTHWEST

Although the classic North-South divide has long gone, the Northwest still retains a fiercely independent spirit, not only regionally but in its own city loyalties. There is little love lost between Mancunians and Liverpudlians, with the rivalry, at its fiercest on the football pitch. For visitors, the good news is that there's a rivalry too, to offer the finest visitor attractions (drawing on a rich working-class heritage), and the finest shopping, eating, drinking and nightlife. As a result this region is one of the most exciting in the country.

Highlights

1 Get hands on with the industrial past at MOSI, **Manchester** (p346)

2 The architecture and collections at the Imperial War Museum and The Lowry, **Salford Quays** (p349)

3 Take a shopping stroll back in time at The Rows, **Chester** (p350)

4 Enjoy all things Liverpudlian at Albert Dock, **Liverpool** (p353)

5 Take in the view from the top of the Tower at **Blackpool** (p361)

Manchester

Today's visitors will find little trace of "Cottonopolis" (the world's first industrial city) as Manchester was known in its first flush of fame. The present face of the city reflects both its Victorian wealth and its recent modern urban redesign. Salford Quays is the most stunning example of the latter but there are also many iconic new buildings popping up in the city centre. Manchester also hosts some superb visitor attractions, but what makes the city special is its buzz: from its shops to its nightclubs; a dynamic art and student scene; a thriving gay community; great live music, from some of the finest rock bands to world-beating classical orchestras; and of course, the world's most famous football club.

Chester

By contrast with the two major cities of the Northwest, Chester is quiet and provincial, but for visitors more easily accessible in terms of size and layout. Its centre is a perfect little black-and-white half-timbered walled town which is the repository of some of Britain's most important Roman heritage.

Liverpool

Liverpool is famous for its music, which dominated the world (thanks largely to The Beatles) in the 1960s, and its football team, which did the same in the 1980s. The wry, often black humour of its (Scouse) inhabitants – their regional accent instantly recognisable – reflects the long vibrant history of living and working in a major port which has had its many ups and downs, particularly over the last half-century or so. At present, however, Liverpool is very much on the up, reinventing itself to the extent of being named European Capital of Culture 2008, and most noticeably, as far as visitors are concerned, revitalising its docks to house the best museums in the north of England. Like Manchester, it also boasts a vibrant restaurant, nightlife and shopping scene.

Blackpool

England's most famous seaside town enjoyed its heyday in the 1950s and 60s before the advent of cheap foreign travel. Today it tends to polarise opinion, and while it is deeply unfashionable to many, the resort still attracts well over one million overnight visitors per annum. They come for the donkey rides, the long golden beaches, the famous promenade, the white-knuckle rides of Pleasure Beach theme park, the shows at the recently revitalised iconic Blackpool Tower, and seaside culture. Out of summer (Sept–Oct) they visit again to enjoy the town's famous Illuminations.

Isle of Man

To escape the crowds, though probably not the damp of the Pennines, and experience a slower way of life (and some unusual antique transport), the Isle of Man can make a rewarding short break. Pack your hiking boots.

Food Heroes

Liverpudlians are traditionally known as "Scousers", a term that is thought to come from the food, **scouse** (derived from the German *Lebskaus*, or Scandinavian *lapskaus/lobscouse*), which was originally a thrifty leftovers stew of mutton/lamb and vegetables, sometimes served with a sharp vinegary beetroot or red cabbage. It's increasingly hard to find; try local pubs, Maggie May's Café on Bold Street, or the Malmaison Hotel.

The best restaurants to find local specialities on the menu in **Liverpool** are The London Carriage Works (*www.thelondoncarriageworks.co.uk*) and Delifonseca (*www.delifonseca.co.uk*). The former is not only one of the city's finest places to eat, but a fierce champion of local producers. Delifonseca is more casual, with two city branches; its Dockside restaurant includes a butchery and food hall under the same roof.

On the cheeseboard, look out for **Lancashire** (Mrs Kirkham's is a popular make) and **Cheshire** cheeses. Both offer blue mould varieties; Garstang Blue from Lancashire, and Blue Cheshire. Two of the best regional cheese shops are The Cheese Shop (*116 Northgate Street; Chester: www.chestercheeseshop.co.uk*) who stock over 150 different British cheeses, and the Liverpool Cheese Company Ltd (*www.liverpoolcheesecompany.co.uk*), based in an old Grade-II-listed-dairy in picturesque Woolton Village, Liverpool.

On the **Wirral Peninsula**, Claremont Farm (*www.claremontfarm.co.uk*) is famous for its asparagus (in season from late May to August) and is regarded as "the good food hub of the Wirral" with a farm shop, and food events staged year-round including the annual Wirral Food and Drink Festival (*last Sun and bank hol Mon Aug; www.wirralfoodfestival.co.uk*).

Liverpool city centre hosts five **farmers' markets** each month, (*http://liverpool.gov.uk*). The Wirral Farmers' Market in New Brighton is always popular with over 30 stalls. The biggest city event of the year is the week-long Food and Drink Festival (*early Sept; www.liverpoolfood anddrinkfestival.co.uk*).

Manchester hosts the biggest food festival in the Northwest, lasting 10 days (*early–mid-Oct; http://foodanddrinkfestival.com*), mixing local producers with celebrity chefs, live music and a real ale festival. The city's best retail showcase for local produce is the splendid deli-grocery of Unicorn (*www.unicorn-grocery.co.uk*) at Chorlton, which is run on a co-operative basis. For a brewery tour visit Hydes (*Mon–Thu 7.30pm; www.hydesbrewery.co.uk*), who have been brewing in the city since 1863.

Just outside Manchester is **Eccles**, birthplace of the famous raisin-filled puff pastry Eccles cake, delicious eaten warm. The nearest version of the long-gone original is probably the Real Lancashire brand (*www.lancashire ecclescakes.co.uk*).

Other **regional specialities** to look out for are: Lancashire hotpot, lamb/mutton, vegetables and onions, topped with sliced potatoes and slow-cooked in the oven; potted shrimps from Southport; Goosnargh corn-fed chicken and duck, from Goosenargh, near Preston, recently championed by top chefs including Gordon Ramsay.

The **Hollies Farm Shop** (*www.theholliesfarmshop.co.uk*) at Tarporley, near Chester, and at Warrington (halfway between Chester and Manchester) has been described as the "Harrods Food Hall of the North", albeit one crammed with locally sourced, traditionally produced foods. Both shops have café/restaurants which feature local produce.

Manchester★

and around

Though the smoking chimneys of the cotton mills in this Northwest metropolis have long gone, Manchester retains many fine historic buildings erected by the Victorian successors to the city's hard-headed Georgian merchants. Today, it has developed into a major provincial centre of finance, and has recently added a number of high-profile visitor attractions. It has long been renowned for its nightlife, the local music scene and the most famous football club in the world.

A BIT OF HISTORY

Thanks to trade with the American colonies, Manchester became the centre of the rapidly expanding cotton industry. However, its principles of free trade led to tragedy on 16 August in 1819 when a crowd assembled on St Peter's Fields to demand Parliamentary reform and repeal of the Corn Laws; the cavalry were sent in to disperse them and in what came to be known as the **Peterloo Massacre**, 11 died and many were injured. The **Free Trade Hall** was constructed on the site of this outrage.

CASTLEFIELD★

South end of Deansgate.
Castlefield is the perfect place to trace the development of Manchester, from Roman times to the present day. In fact the remains of the **Roman fort** – "the castle in the field" – and the north gate and part of the west wall have been reconstructed on their original site.
In 1761 Castlefield became the centre of Manchester's famous canal system, which started with the Duke of Bridgewater's canal. The towpath is open to pedestrians and a walkway (*1mi/1.6km*) beside the River Irwell links Castlefield with the Ship Canal and Salford Quays. Cruises are now offered along the waterways that once carried goods across the Pennines by **Manchester Ship Canal Cruises** (*☎0151 330 1444; www.merseyferries.*

▶ **Population:** 402,889.
◔ **Michelin Map:** Michelin Atlas p39 or Map 502 N 23.
▤ **Info:** Piccadilly Plaza, Portland Street. *☎0871 222 8223. www.visit manchester.com.*
◖ **Location:** Manchester has three main stations; Piccadilly, a ten minute walk east of the city centre. The two coach stations, Chorlton Street and Piccadilly Gardens, are close to each other, a five-minute walk east. The city centre is compact. The **Metrolink tram** system (*www.metrolink.co.uk*), runs fast frequent services in the city and beyond. The **free Metroshuttle bus** service (*www.tfgm. com*) links to all main sights in the city centre.
◉ **Don't Miss:** MOSI; The Lowry; The Imperial War Museum North.
◷ **Timing:** Allow at least two days to visit Manchester.
⚏ **Kids:** Get hands-on at MOSI; for football-mad kids, the National Football Museum and Manchester United's stadium tours.

co.uk), between Salford Quays and Liverpool (approx *6hrs*), and the **Irwell and Mersey Packetboat Company** (*☎0161 736 2108*), along the Irwell and Ship Canal to Salford Quays (*50min*).
In 1830 the world's first passenger railway station was opened by the Liverpool and Manchester Railway and on its Liverpool Road site stands the city's largest museum.

⚏ Museum of Science and Industry (MOSI)★★

◷*Open daily 10am–5pm.* ◷*Closed 1 Jan, 24–26 Dec.* ⊜*Galleries free, charge for temporary exhibitions, 4-D theatre*

Museum of Science and Industry

© Carassale Matteo/Sime/Photononstop

(£4, child £3), simulator ride (£2.50, child £1.50) and planetarium (£2) ♿ 🅿 *(£5).* ✕. ℘*0161 832 2244. www.mosi.org.uk.*
Manchester's industrial heritage is presented in a series of lively exhibition galleries devoted to textiles, cameras, gas and electricity, working engines, locomotives, "discoveries, inventions and innovations", the history of flight, a science centre, a walk-through Victorian sewer, an 1830s warehouse, and more. All have interactive features.

CITY CENTRE
National Football Museum
🕐*Scheduled to open early-2012. Cathedral Gardens.* ℘*0161 870 9275. www.nationalfootballmuseum.com.*
Housed in a stunning glass building, the national museum of the national game features exhibits such as the 1966 World Cup Final ball and Maradona's 1986 Argentina ("Hand of God") shirt.

Manchester Cathedral★
🕐*Open daily Mon Fri 8.30am–6.30pm, Sat 8.30am–5pm, Sun 8.30am–7pm* ♿✕. ℘*0161 833 2220. www.manchestercathedral.org.*
The parish church of Manchester, built 1215, was refounded as a chantry college in 1421 and became the cathedral in 1847. Six bays form the nave – the widest of any church in England – and six the **choir**, famed for its medieval carving. The **choir screen** is unique and in the choir itself, note the workmanship on the **stalls and canopies★**. The **misericords** (c.1500) are a comic depiction of medieval life.

Royal Exchange
Manchester owes its prosperity to "King Cotton". Raw cotton imported via Liverpool and the canal network, pure water from the Pennines, a high degree of humidity, and a large available working population were the factors responsible for the rapid growth of the cotton and ancillary industries. English cotton was sold throughout the world and the Manchester cotton exchange was the nerve centre of this trade. Inside the exchange, the prices of cotton on the day the market last traded are still shown (on the board near the roof). Today this immense hall is occupied by the 700-seat **Royal Exchange Theatre**, a spectacular seven-sided, glass-walled capsule, suspended from huge marble pillars, providing theatre in the round. A striking recent addition to Exchange Square is **The Wheel of Manchester** (🕐*Open Fri–Sat 10am–11pm, Sun–Thu 10am–9m;*⊜*£7.50, online £6.38;* ♿; ℘*0161 831 9918, www.greatcityattractions.com*), a 196ft /60m observation wheel. An even bigger wheel is planned for Piccadilly Gardens, a 10-minute walk west.

People's History Museum
Left Bank, Spinningfields. 🕐*Open Mon– Sat 10am–5pm.* ♿✕. ℘*0161 838 9190. www.phm.org.uk.*
Occupying its current striking premises since 2010, this is the national museum of the history of working people in Britain. Much of its content deals with social justice, and the exhibition starts with the **Peterloo Massacre** of 1819 (🕐*see above*) and ends in the present day.

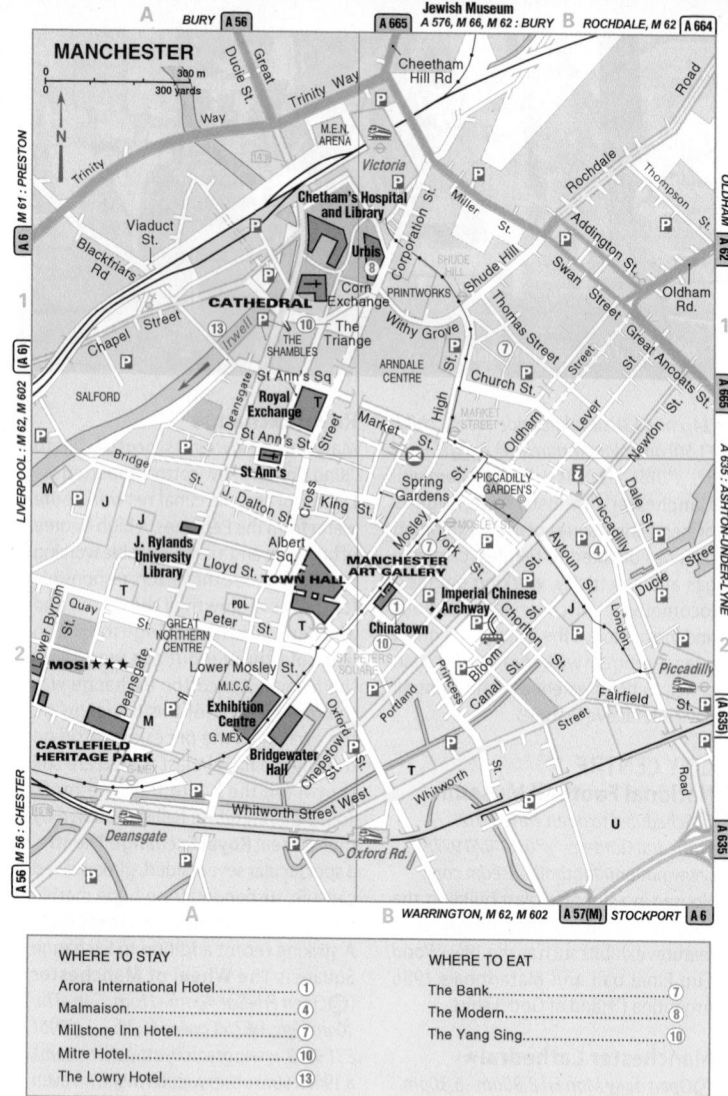

WHERE TO STAY		WHERE TO EAT	
Arora International Hotel	①	The Bank	⑦
Malmaison	④	The Modern	⑧
Millstone Inn Hotel	⑦	The Yang Sing	⑩
Mitre Hotel	⑩		
The Lowry Hotel	⑬		

John Rylands University Library

⏱ *Open Sun–Mon noon–5pm, Tue–Sat 10am–5pm.* ♿✕. ✆*0161 306 0555. www.library.manchester.ac.uk/ deansgate.*

This beautiful library is one of the finest examples of modern Gothic architecture in Europe, designed by Basil Champneys, opened in 1900 and founded in memory of a successful textile manufacturer. The library possesses many early printed books, and rare and valuable manuscripts. Exhibitions, events and tours showcase many of these.

Town Hall★

Designed in Gothic style by Alfred Waterhouse and built in 1868–77, the town hall is one of the greatest civic buildings of the Victorian era. Its tower with octagonal top stage rises 286ft/87m above the pedestrian area of Albert Square. Two staircases lead from the low vaulted entrance hall to the **Great Hall**, with its hammerbeam roof and 12 Pre-Raphaelite-style murals by Ford Madox Brown 1876–88.

Manchester Art Gallery★

Mosley Street. ○*Open Tue–Sun and bank hols, 10am–5pm.* ○*Closed 1 Jan, Good Fri, 24–26, 31 Dec.* ☂✕. ℘*0161 235 8888.*
www.manchestergalleries.org.uk.
Recently restored to its 19C glory, this acclaimed gallery boasts a fine Pre-Raphaelite collection, with works by Millais, Hunt and Rossetti, and Ford Madox Brown's *Work* (1852) illustrating the various classes of a developing industrial society. Note the works of Stubbs, Turner and Constable and the industrial landscapes of the North, captured by L S Lowry (☂*see below*).

SOUTHWEST CITY CENTRE
♠♦The Lowry★

○*2.5mi/4km southwest of city centre. Pier 8, Salford Quays.* ○*Galleries open daily 11am (Sat 10am)–5pm.* ☂✕. ℘*0843 208 6000. www.thelowry.com.*
This visually stunning arts and entertainment complex, opened in 2000 as one of Britain's flagship Millennium projects, gracing the regenerated docks of **Salford Quays**. It houses two theatres and studio space for performing arts, presenting drama, opera, ballet, dance, musicals, children's shows, popular music, jazz, folk and comedy. Its gallery space showcases the works of **L S Lowry** (1887–1976), a locally born painter, nationally famous for his childlike "matchstick" figures and northern England street scenes, alongside contemporary exhibitions.

Imperial War Museum North★

○*2.7mi/4.3km SW of city centre. Salford Quays, Trafford Wharf.* ○*Open daily 10am–5pm.* ○*Closed 24–26 Dec.* ☂☐*(£4).* ✕. ℘*0161 836 4000.*
http://north.iwm.org.uk.
Located in an astonishing award-winning building, by international architect Daniel Libeskind, on the city's ship canal, this museum, like its London counterpart, takes a sober look at how 20C conflicts have affected both ordinary combatants and the people at home. A highlight is the **Big Picture Show**, a 360° audio-visual show which immerses visitors into the IWM's world-renowned collections of war-related images and sound.

Continually changing images are projected onto the gallery walls, floor and visitors themselves, accompanied by music, sounds and reminiscences from the oral history archives. Visit the **Air Shard viewing platform** (☞*£1.20*) for spectacular views over The Quays.

♠♦Manchester United Museum & Stadium Tour

○*2.5mi/4km SW of city centre. Old Trafford, North Stand.* ○*Open non-weekend match days only and closes 3hrs before kick-off on midweek match days: museum 9am–5pm, tours (must be pre-booked) 9.40am–4.30pm.* ☞*museum and tour £15, child £10 (museum only, £10.50, child £8.50)* ☐✕. ℘*0161 868 8000. www.manutd.com.*
Take a look behind-the-scenes to see what makes the world's most famous football club so successful.

Whitworth Art Gallery★

○*1.5mi/2.5km S. Whitworth Park, Denmark Road.* ○*Open Mon–Sat 10am–5pm, Sun noon–4pm.* ℘*0161 275 7450. www.whitworth. manchester.ac.uk.*
Internationally famous for its collections of art and design, the gallery is home to an impressive range of watercolours, prints, drawings, modern art and sculpture by Barbara Hepworth and Henry Moore. The Whitworth also features the largest collections of textiles and wallpapers outside London.

EXCURSIONS
Quarry Bank Mill★

NT. ○*10mi/16km S. Quarry Bank Road, Styal.* ○*Open mid-Mar–Oct daily 11am–5pm. Jan–mid-Mar & Nov–Dec, Wed–Sun (daily school hols) 11am–3.30pm.* ☞*Mill and house £10.40 (mill only, £7.25).* ☂☐✕. ℘*01625*

527 468, 01625 445 896. (Infoline). www.nationaltrust.org.uk.

In a wooded country park (284 acres/ 115ha) beside the fast-flowing River Bollin, stands a five-storey cotton mill, built in 1784, powered by the most powerful working waterwheel in Europe (50tons), with two mill engines which help to bring the past to life. The production of cloth, from the cotton plant to the bolt of calico on sale in the mill shop, is traced in a fascinating exhibition including live demonstrations of hand-spinning and loom weaving.

The Apprentice House shows the spartan lifestyle of the pauper children that worked here.

Jodrell Bank Discovery Centre

21mi/34km S Bomish Lane. Open daily 10am–5pm. £5.50–£6.50, child £4–£4.50. 01477 571 766. www.jodrellbank.net.

Discover how the giant landmark Lovell Telescope works and explore the Universe with interactive exhibits at this small complex attached to Britain's most famous radio telescope.

Chester★★

Cheshire

Set on the northeast border of Wales in green and prosperous Cheshire, Chester has been an important city since Roman times and retains many tangible reminders of this period. The lasting impression on most visitors, is, however, its classic black-and-white half-timbered buildings, which feature prominently in this well-preserved historic walled city.

A BIT OF HISTORY

Deva (or Dewa), the Roman legionary fortress and naval base built on a loop of the River Dee, was one of the largest in Britain and home to the XX Valeria Victrix Legion for 200 years. The legionary headquarters stood at the junction on the site now occupied by St Peter's Church.

The port of Chester is known to have been used by seagoing vessels during the Roman occupation. The period of greatest prosperity was the 12C–14C; even until the end of the 16C, Chester regarded Liverpool as a "creek of the Port of Chester".

But by the 15C the Dee estuary was silting up and ships had to anchor some 12mi/19km downstream.

The **Roodee** (Anglo-Saxon for "Island of the Cross") is a tract of land between

- ▶ **Population:** 80,110.
- **Michelin Map:** Michelin Atlas p34 or Map 403 L 24.
- **Info:** Town Hall, Northgate Street. 0845 647 7868. www.visitchester.com.
- **Location:** Almost everything of interest is inside the old city walls. Take a walking tour (daily, from the information centre), or open-top bus tour: either hop-on hop-off with City Sightseeing (01244 381 461; www.city-sightseeing.com), or a 40-min tour on a 1924 vintage bus with Chester Heritage Tours (t0844 585 4144; www.chesterheritagetours.co.uk).
- **Don't Miss:** The Rows; the horse racing at Chester's historic racecourse (www.chester-races.co.uk).
- **Timing:** At least a day, more if you visit the zoo.
- **Kids:** Chester Zoo; Dewa Roman Experience.

the river and the city wall now occupied by Chester Racecourse. Horse races have been held here since 1540.

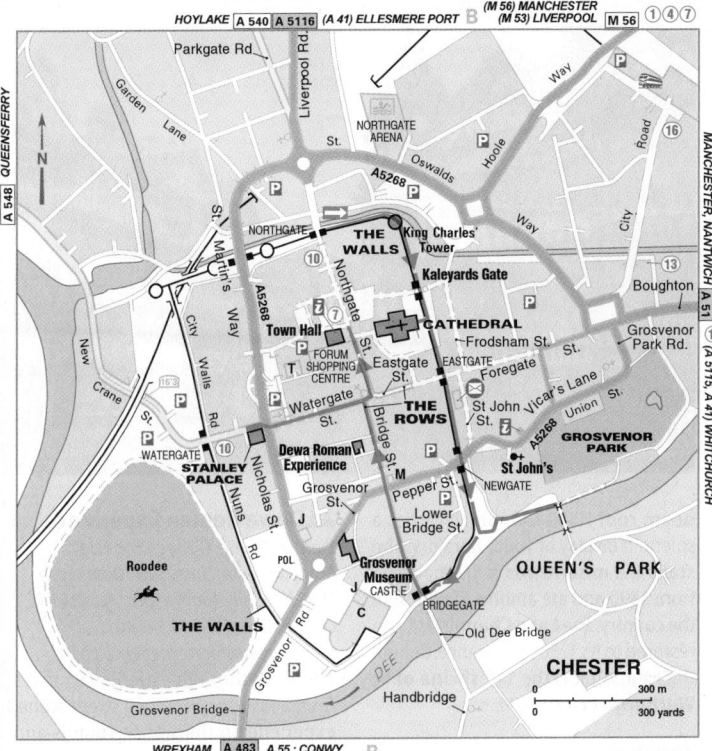

WHERE TO STAY		WHERE TO EAT	
Chester Court Hotel	①	The Coach and Horses	⑦
Chester House Bed & Breakfast	④	The Fat Cat	⑩
Comfort Inn	⑦	The Old Harkers Arms	⑬
Pied Bull	⑩		
Ramada Chester	⑬		
The Queen Hotel	⑯		

✾✾ WALKING TOUR
City Walls★

No other city in Britain has preserved a continuous circuit of walls. From the Eastgate, by the Clock Tower, looking west to the spire of Holy Trinity Church (now the Guildhall) you can see the width of the Roman fortress.

Parts of the Roman wall are visible between the Northgate and **King Charles' Tower**.

Chester Cathedral★

🕐Open year-round Mon–Sat 9am (bank hols 10am)– 5pm, Sun 1–4pm. ⊜£5 (inc.audio tour). ⛓✗. ℘01244 324 756. www.chestercathedral.com.

The 14C gateway leads into Abbey Square, once the outer courtyard of the abbey; ahead are the cloisters. The Norman abbey church was replaced between 1250 and 1540 by the present magnificent red sandstone building.

Many of the original abbey buildings stand round the 16C **cloisters**. The hammerbeam roof of the refectory has been superbly re-created. The Dean and Chapter still meet in the 13C **Chapter House** and the clergy and choir assemble in the vestibule before services. The north transept contains the oldest part of the cathedral fabric, an 11C round-headed arch and arcade, and the oldest wooden ceiling, the **camber**

The Rows

© Olaf Protze/age fotostock

beam roof (1518–24), which carries a splendid display of Tudor heraldry. The **stalls** and **misericords** in the choir date from 1390 and are among the finest in the country. The **Lady Chapel** has been restored to its 1250 appearance. Behind the High Altar is the 14C **shrine of St Werburgh** (d. c.AD 700).

The Rows★★

The Rows are continuous half-timbered galleries, reached by steps, which form a second row of shops above those at street level. Unique in Britain, they probably originated in the 14C when merchants erected shops at street level against the lower courses of the Roman buildings that had lined the streets, or on top of the stone rubble, and made steps and walkways to link them. Upper storeys provided accommodation for the traders and their families.

Grosvenor Museum

27 Grosvenor Street. ○*Open year-round Mon–Sat 10.30am–5pm, Sun 1–4pm.* ℘*0300 123 8123. www.grosvenormuseum.co.uk.*
This lively Chester history museum is particularly strong on the Roman period but all ages are covered. To the rear of the museum is a townhouse which re-creates domestic life from the 17C to the 1920s including a Victorian kitchen, Georgian drawing room, a nursery and a fully fitted Edwardian bathroom.

♁♁Dewa Roman Experience

Pierpoint Lane. ○*Open Feb–Nov Mon–Sat 9am–5pm, Sun 10am–5pm, Dec–Jan daily 10am–4pm.* ♿. ☞*£4.95, child £3.25.* ℘*01244 343 407. www.dewaromanexperience.co.uk.*
This walk-through experience moves from a Roman galley to a street scene, experiencing the sights, sounds and smells of Dewa (Roman Chester). There is an audio-visual presentation, archaeological excavations and lots of hands-on exhibits where you can try on Roman armour, fire a catapult, handle Roman-style artefacts and more.

EXCURSION
♁♁Chester Zoo★

▶ *3mi/5km N on the A 5116. Upton-by-Chester.* ○*Open daily mid-Apr–Oct 10am–5pm (6pm weekends, bank hols and school hols), Nov–mid-Apr 10am–4pm/4.30pm.* ☞*£12.50–£15.40, child £9–£11.50. Book online to avoid queueing). Monorail and waterbus £2 each, child £1.50.* ♿🅿✕. ℘*01244 380 280. www.chesterzoo.org.*
A splendid zoo where the 7,000 or so animals are housed in spacious enclosures, amid ward-winning gardens, separated from the public by moats and flower borders, rather than cages.

Liverpool★
and around

Though its days of mercantile splendour are long over, Liverpool remains an eminently handsome city, with some glorious architecture and fine civic buildings, reflecting the energy, taste and philanthropy of the Victorian age. The city's most famous sons, The Beatles, gave the city a new reputation in the 1960s, and the Liverpool sound they helped create, their lives and their career are still celebrated throughout the city. During the 1980s Liverpool Football Club dominated the football world and are still a major force today. In the 21C leisure developments have led the way in the revival of the city's fortunes, now including more museums and galleries than anywhere outside London. In 1999 the first **Liverpool Biennial** was held and has since grown to be the largest as well as one of the most exciting contemporary visual arts events in the UK; with around 1 million visits, it is one of the best-attended events of its kind in the world. The next one takes place in 2012 *(3rd week Sept–end Nov)*. In 2008 the city received the accolade of European Capital of Culture.

A BIT OF HISTORY
On 28 August 1207 King John granted a charter for settlers to establish a port on the Mersey. Gradual silting up of the Dee estuary and the attendant abandonment of Chester, a port since Roman times, turned the new village of Liverpool into England's second port. It centred around seven streets, which still exist today – Castle and Old Hall, Water and Dale, Chapel and Tithebarn, up to Hatton Garden – and the "Pool", an inlet following today's Canning and Paradise Streets and Whitechapel.

Liverpool started to expand when trade with the West Indies – sugar, rum, cotton and, until 1807, slaves – brought such prosperity that by 1800 there were more

▶ **Population:** 481,786.
Michelin Map: Michelin Atlas p34 or Map 502 L 23.
Info: The 08 Place, Whitechapel. Anchor Courtyard, Albert Dock. ℘0151 233 2459. www.visitliverpool.com.
Location: Liverpool is in northwest England, around 75mi/120km due south of the Lake District and 34mi/55km west of Manchester. Lime Street Station links to a small underground network; the bus station is just around the corner on Norton Street. Get to know the city's streets and the River Mersey in one tour with **Liverpool Duck Tours** *(Gower Street, Albert Dock; operate year-round daily 10.30am/11am–6pm; peak £12.95, off-peak £9.95 (child £7.95/£9.95); t0151 708 7799; www.theyellowduckmarine.co.uk).* City Sightseeing hop-on hop-off open-top bus tours run every hour *(www.city-sightseeing.com).*
Don't Miss: Walker Gallery; Liverpool Anglican Cathedral; Albert Dock museums.
Timing: Allow at least two days (to include one excursion).
Kids: Liverpool Duck Tours; hands-on fun at World Museum; sharks at Blue Planet Aquarium; animals at Knowsley Safari Park; World of Glass.
Walking Tours: Daily in summer from the tourist office and Albert Dock.

than 80,000 "Liverpudlians". In the 19C Liverpool, home to the Cunard and

White Star liners, was Britain's gateway to the Empire and the world. The Mersey Docks and Harbour Company handled the cargo traffic, employing some 20,000 men in the immediate post-war period. Today, with container ships and mechanical handling, only just over 2,500 men now work in the docks.

⚓ WATERFRONT WALK

Pier Head

The spirit of Liverpool and the Mersey is best appreciated by standing on the corner of Water Street and the Strand. The ferries on the Mersey have been part of the scene since the monks of Birkenhead Priory began rowing travellers across in about 1150. The green-domed **Port of Liverpool Building** (1907) and its neighbour, the **Cunard Building** (1913), reflect the city's maritime connections but the **Royal Liver Building** (1908), with its "Liver Birds" (pronounced "lie-ver") on the cupolas, is probably the best-known symbol of Liverpool. This ensemble is known locally as "The Three Graces".

Museum of Liverpool★

Pier Head. ⓘ*Open daily 10am–5pm.* ⓘ*Closed 1 Jan, 24–26 Dec,* ♿ ℙ ✕. *𝄞0151 478 4545. www.liverpool museums.org.uk.*

Opened in 2011 as the largest newly built national museum in Britain for more than a century, this stunning new city flagship covers 800 years from medieval "Lyverpoole" to 21C "Livercool". It includes the following galleries: Wondrous Place, featuring Liverpool's sporting and cultural history with particular emphasis on the Beatles, and Liverpool and Everton football clubs; East Meets West, the relationship between Liverpool and Shanghai; The People's Republic, about the experience of living in the city and what it means to be Liverpudlian; Little Liverpool, a children's hands-on space; the Skylight Gallery, a dramatic space featuring changing art exhibitions.

Albert Dock★ (CZ)

Massive brick warehouses enclose a dock basin (7 acres/3ha). Completed in 1846, finally closed in 1972, the complex has now been revitalised with shops, cafés and apartments, museums and the northern arm of the Tate Gallery.

Merseyside Maritime Museum★

ⓘ*Open daily, 10am–5pm.* ⓘ*Closed 1 Jan, 24–26 Dec.* ♿ ℙ ✕. *𝄞0151 478 4499. www.liverpoolmuseums.org.uk.*

Liverpool's rich seafaring heritage is presented through displays on the history of shipbuilding; the evolution of the port; Liverpool and the American Civil War; Emigration, the poignant story of the 9 million emigrants to the New World who passed through Liverpool between 1830 and 1930; Hello Sailor! gay life on the ocean wave; Battle of the Atlantic, ship models and paintings; and much more… The museum's largest exhibit is the *Edmund Gardner* (⚓ *Aug–Sept only by free guided tour, book ahead; 𝄞0151 478 4788*), a former pilot cutter now in dry dock. Visitors can also step aboard the *Brocklebank* tugboat. In the basement is Seized! Border and Customs Uncovered, which charts the fight against smuggling over the centuries as well as modern detection methods.

International Slavery Museum★

ⓘ*All entry details as Merseyside Maritime Museum.*

Sharing the same building as the Maritime Museum is the moving and unsettling International Slavery Museum, just yards away from the dry docks where 18C slave trading ships were repaired and fitted out. Its main permanent galleries and exhibitions are: History of the Slave Trade; Slaves' Stories; Campaign Zone; Life in West Africa; Enslavement and the Middle Passage – the latter being the second leg of the triangular slave trade route; Legacies of Slavery; as well as temporary exhibitions.

Tate Liverpool★

Open daily 10am–5.50pm (closed Mon Oct–Apr). Closed Good Fri, 24–26 Dec. Charge for touring exhibitions only. Guided free tour daily at 12.30pm. ♿ 🅿 ✕. *0151 702 7400. www.tate.org.uk/liverpool.*

The Tate family, who made their fortune from sugar before becoming synonymous with modern art in Britain, originated from Liverpool, so the choice of Liverpool to house part of their national collection of 20C art in this transformed warehouse was wholly appropriate.

The gallery is best known for hosting major touring exhibitions but it also boasts semi-permanent exhibitions from the Tate's primary collections of 20C art (presently the DLA Piper Series: This is Sculpture). These are displayed alongside Liverpool Biennial exhibits (*see above*).

The Beatles Story

Britannia Vaults, Albert Dock, and Mersey Ferries Terminal Building, Pier Head. Open Apr–Oct daily 9am–7pm. Nov–Mar 10am–6pm. Last entry 5pm. Closed 25–26 Dec. £12.95. ♿ 🅿 *(charge). 0151 709 1963. www.beatlesstory.com.*

Relive or discover the decade of the Beatles, the 1960s, the new phenomena of rock'n'roll, teenagers, the Merseybeat and, of course, Beatlemania.

The Beatles group consisted of **John Lennon** (1940–1980), **Paul McCartney** (b.1942), **George Harrison** (1943–2001) and **Ringo Starr** (b.1940); their manager was Brian Epstein, "the Fifth Beatle" (1934–67). The places (The Cavern, Strawberry Fields, Penny Lane, Hamburg) and the hits are presented in a lively and entertaining manner by a walk-through presentation.

The Pier Head part of the exhibition (*5 min by free shuttle bus or 10 min on foot*) is housed in the striking new Mersey Ferries Terminal Building and hosts special exhibitions and the "Fab4D" cinema experience.

The **childhood homes** of two of The Beatles, Paul McCartney and John Lennon, are now owned by the National Trust and are open to the public via a minibus tour (*operates late Feb–Nov Wed–Sun and bank hols, see website for details, advance booking advisable; £20, NT members £8.30; 0151 427 7231 or 0151 707 0729 if calling on day of tour; www.nationaltrust.org.uk/beatles*). **20 Forthlin Road** was the home of McCartney and where the Beatles composed and rehearsed some of their earliest songs; **Mendips** is where Lennon grew up.

The most popular Beatles tour, however, is the two-hour **Magical Mystery Tour** (*year-round daily 2.30pm from the Gower Street bus stop, Albert Dock; extra tour 12.30pm and 3pm most Sats, advance reservations recommended; closed I Jan, 25–26 Dec, £15.95; 0151 236 9091, buy tickets from tourist office; www.beatlestour.org*).

The whole city celebrates **International Beatle Week Festival** every August (*www.liverpooltour.com*).

Across the road, **The Echo Wheel of Liverpool** (*open year-round daily 10am–9pm/Fri–Sat 11pm; £7.50, online £6.38; ♿; 0151 709 8651, www.greatcityattractions.com*) is a 196ft-/60m) high observation wheel.

CITY

Liverpool Anglican Cathedral★★

St James Mount. Cathedral: Open year-round daily 8am–6pm. Contributions welcome. Tower: Open Mon–Sat 10am–4.30pm, Sun noon–2.30pm. Guided tour (1hr) 10am–3pm. £3 suggested donation. Tower, Embroidery Gallery, Great Space Film and audio tour £5. 🅿 *(charge).* ✕. *0151 709 6271. www.liverpoolcathedral.org.uk.*

This monumental edifice in red sandstone is the largest Anglican church in the world. Work began in 1904 and it took most of the century to build, a triumphant reinterpretation of the Gothic tradition by its architect **Sir Giles Gilbert Scott** (1880–1960).

Before entering the church visit the film theatre for the 10-minute panoramic HD

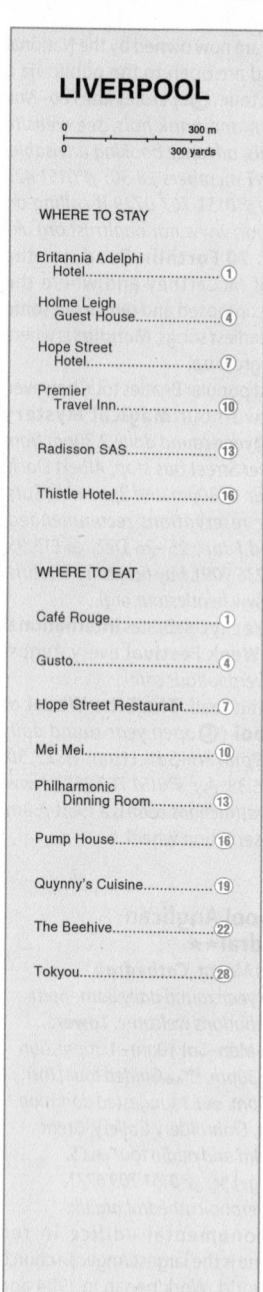

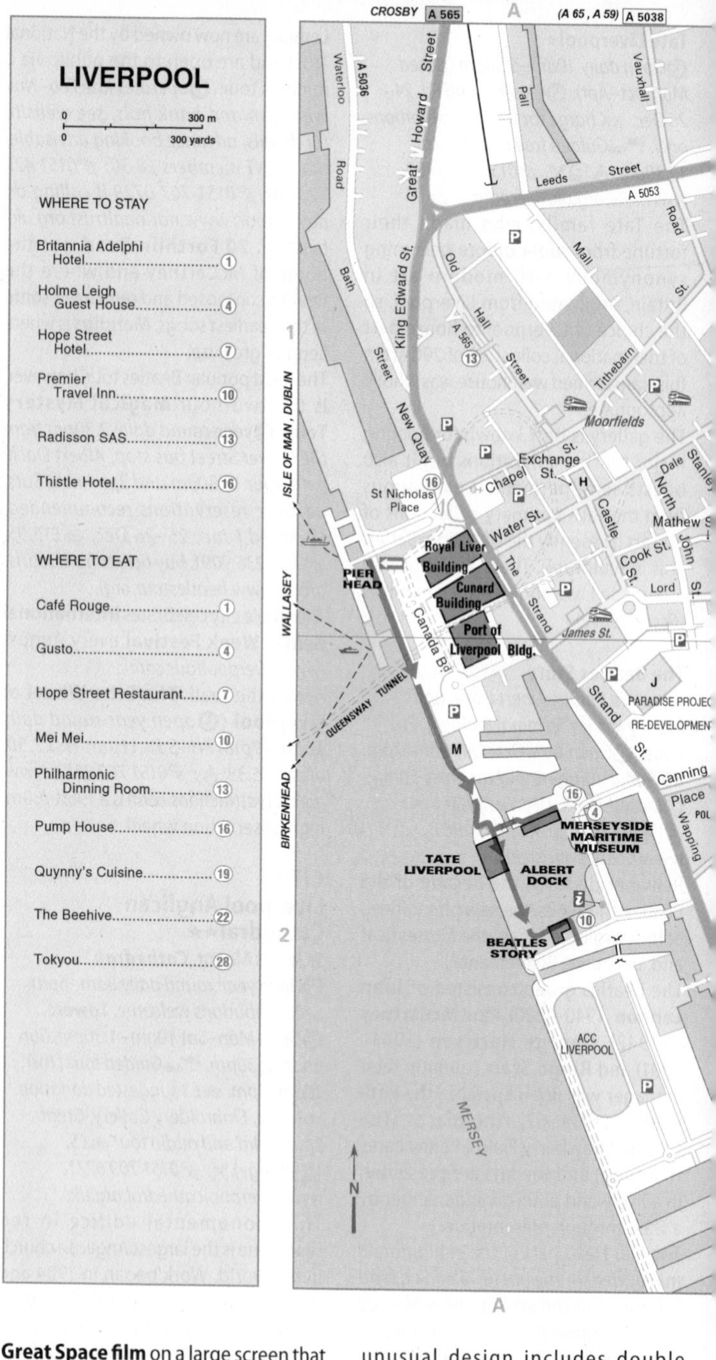
LIVERPOOL
0 300 m
0 300 yards
WHERE TO STAY
Britannia Adelphi Hotel ①
Holme Leigh Guest House ④
Hope Street Hotel ⑦
Premier Travel Inn ⑩
Radisson SAS ⑬
Thistle Hotel ⑯
WHERE TO EAT
Café Rouge ①
Gusto ④
Hope Street Restaurant ⑦
Mei Mei ⑩
Philharmonic Dinning Room ⑬
Pump House ⑯
Quynny's Cuisine ⑲
The Beehive ㉒
Tokyou ㉘
CROSBY
A 565
A
(A 65, A 59)
A 5038
Waterloo Road
A 5036
Great Howard Street
Pall Mall
Vauxhall Road
Leeds Street
A 5053
Bath Street
King Edward St.
Old Hall Street
A 565
Tithebarn St.
Moorfields
New Quay
Exchange St.
Chapel St.
Water St.
Dale St.
North John St.
Stanley
Mathew St.
Castle St.
Cook St.
Lord St.
St Nicholas Place
Royal Liver Building
Cunard Building
Port of Liverpool Bldg.
PIER HEAD
Canada Bd
The Strand
James St.
Strand St.
QUEENSWAY TUNNEL
ISLE OF MAN, DUBLIN
WALLASEY
BIRKENHEAD
PARADISE PROJECT RE-DEVELOPMENT
Canning Place
Wapping
MERSEYSIDE MARITIME MUSEUM
TATE LIVERPOOL
ALBERT DOCK
BEATLES STORY
ACC LIVERPOOL
MERSEY
N
1
2
A

Great Space film on a large screen that fills your field of vision.

On entering, the first impression is of vastness, strength and height. Scott's unusual design includes double transepts and the central "**Great Space**" (15,000sq ft/1,400sq m) under the tower, giving an uninterrupted view of altar

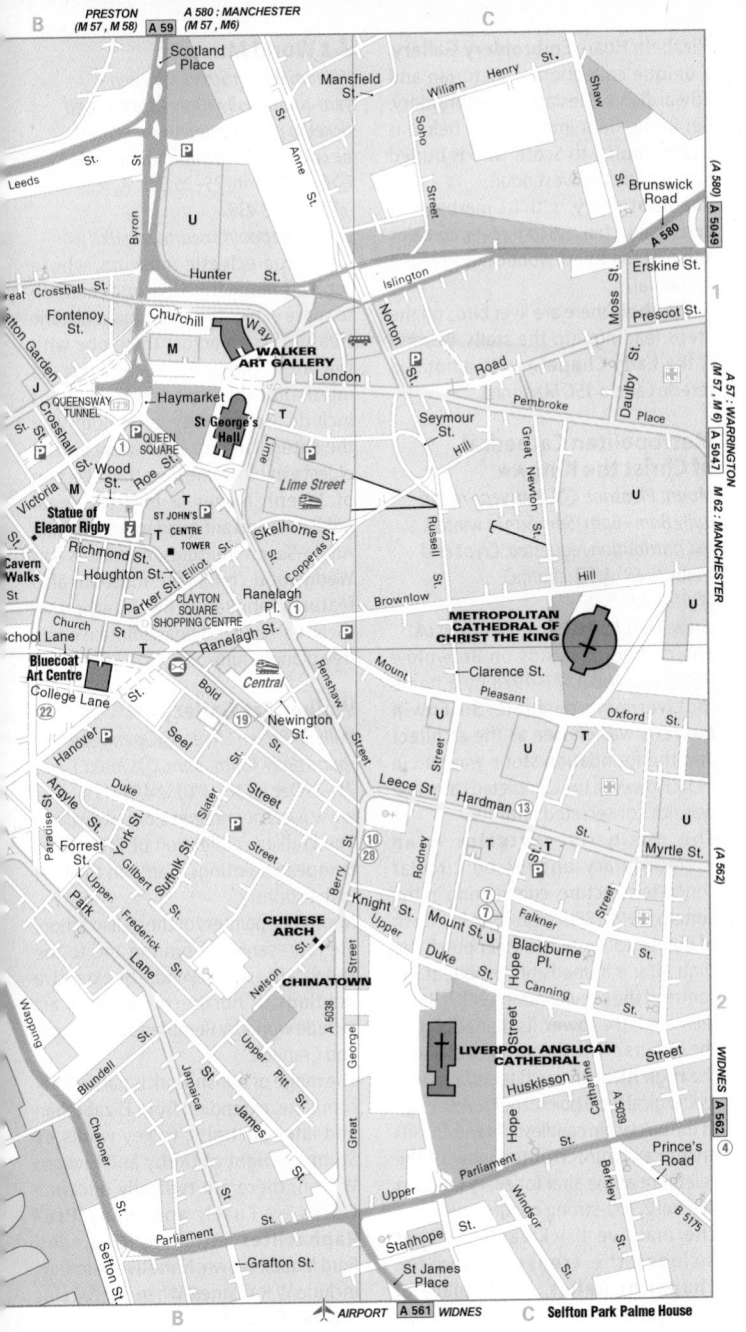

and pulpit. The **tower** is 331ft/100m high but actually rises 500ft/153m above the Mersey and offers wonderful **views**. Reached by 2 lifts and 108 stairs,

it extends across the full width of the building and houses the highest and heaviest (31-ton) peal of bells in the world. Entry to the tower lso includes the

Elizabeth Hoare **Embroidery Gallery**, a unique collection of Victorian and Edwardian ecclesiastical embroidery. Set in the floor immediately below is the memorial to Scott, who is buried just outside the west door.

The **Baptistery**, with its marble font and a baldachin and font cover, contains some of the finest woodcarving in the cathedral.

In the **choir** there are liver birds on the steps leading into the stalls. Beyond is the **Lady Chapel**★ with a notable reredos and a 15C Madonna.

Metropolitan Cathedral of Christ the King★★

Mount Pleasant. ◷*Open year-round daily 8am–6pm (5pm Sun in winter).* ☞*Contribution requested. Crypt and treasury £3.* &. P *(charge).* ✆*0151 709 9222. www.liverpoolmetrocathedral.org.uk.*

The cathedral stands on Brownlow Hill, occupied 1771–1928 by a home for Liverpool's destitute. **Sir Edwin Lutyens** was chosen as the architect and the foundation stone was laid in 1933. However, the completed cathedral was not consecrated until 1967.

The distinctive **exterior** is an extraordinary buttressed circular concrete structure, culminating in the lantern (290ft/88m high) with its crown of pinnacles. From the inner porch the High Altar is immediately visible, at the centre of the circular nave (194ft/59m in diameter). The **tower**, its stained glass in the colours of the spectrum, rises above the **High Altar**, the architectural as well as liturgical focal point. The clever design of the baldachin candlesticks and crucifix ensure an uninterrupted view of the celebrant at the altar for every member of a full 2,300-strong congregation.

The massive brick-vaulted **crypt** includes the **treasury**, and the **Chapel of Relics**, burial place of the archbishops; its door is a six-ton marble disc, which rolls back as did the stone traditionally sealing the tomb of Christ.

👥 World Museum

William Brown Street. ◷*Open year-round daily 10am–5pm. Timed ticket to planetarium (☞free) must be collected from information desk.* ◷*Closed 1 Jan, 25–26 Dec.* &.✗. ✆*0151 478 439. www.liverpoolmuseums.org.uk.*

This large eclectic museum, whose subjects range from live bugs and fish to space exploration, combines historic treasures from across the globe with the latest interactive technology. Its internationally important collections include archaeology, ethnology and the natural and physical sciences. The oldest exhibits come from the collection of Joseph Mayer (a mid-19C local goldsmith and antiquarian) and include Anglo-Saxon treasures, mummies and Wedgwood china. The museum also features innovative live interpretive theatre shows and boasts Britain's only free planetarium.

Walker Art Gallery★★

William Brown Street. ◷*Open year-round daily 10am–5pm.* ◷*Closed 1 Jan, 25–26 Dec.* &.✗. ✆*0151 478 4199. www.liverpoolmuseums.org.uk/walker*

The Walker's collection of British and European paintings is among the best in the country.

Numerous painters of the Italian school are represented, from the 14C to the Renaissance and beyond. The extensive holdings of northern European art include works by Rembrandt, Elsheimer and Cranach.

The range of British work is particularly complete, extending from Elizabethan and later portraits, to key works by Stubbs, Wright of Derby and Richard Wilson; there are typically uncanny works by Fuseli and many **Pre-Raphaelites**, including Millais and Ford Madox Brown. Narrative paintings include W R Yeames' *When Did You Last See Your Father?*

A small number of French Impressionists – Degas, Seurat and Monet – are juxtaposed with their British contemporaries like Sickert.

St George's Hall

🕐Heritage Centre (entrance St John's Lane) open year-round Tue-Sat 10am–5pm. 🕐Closed 1 Jan, Good Fri, 25–26 Dec. ♿. ☎0151 225 6909. www.stgeorgesliverpool.co.uk.

"One of the finest neo-Grecian buildings in the world" (Pevsner), St George's Hall was completed in 1854 and was a multipurpose community building where people could be tried for murder, attend a ball or listen to a concert – all under one roof. It fell into disrepair in the 1980s but was reopened in April 2007 and is now a focal point for cultural, community, civic, corporate and performing arts activities. It contains a circular Concert Room and a vast **Great Hall** of more than Roman opulence. The hall dominates the neighbouring NeoClassical civic buildings, which are a focal point of the city.

A new **Heritage Centre** features imaginative exhibitions, reconstructions and hands-on activities which bring the story of the Hall alive. It offers visitors opportunities to visit the cells used by prisoners awaiting trial and to see the newly refurbished Criminal Court and Judge's Robing Room.

Statue of Eleanor Rigby

Stanley Street.
The statue is the work of former pop singer Tommy Steele, a contemporary of The Beatles; a plaque behind her dedicates the statue "To all the lonely people". Round the corner in Mathew Street is the **Cavern Club**, where the Beatles first performed.

Sefton Park Palm House

Sefton Park, South Liverpool. 🕐*Open year-round daily from 10.30am; Nov–Mar closes 4pm; Apr and Oct closes 5pm; May–Sept closes 6.30pm; may close for special events, see website.* ♿. ☎0151 726 9304. www.palmhouse.org.uk.
This magnificent tiered octagonal Grade-II-listed Victorian glasshouse showcases the Liverpool Botanical Collection.

EXCURSIONS

Southport

▶ *20mi/32km N via the A 565.*
🛈 *112 Lord Street.* ☎01704 533 333. www.visitsouthport.com.
This elegant and dignified seaside resort is distinguished by its tree-lined streets, attractive flowerbeds and famous gardens *(Flower Show held late Aug)*. Broad and spacious **Lord Street**, where the shops have wrought-iron and glass-roofed canopies extending over the pavements, is the epitome of a Victorian promenade. Families enjoy the long sandy beaches – **Crosby Beach** is famous for its haunting Antony Gormley figures staring out to sea – and amusement parks, while **Royal Birkdale** is the best of several first-class golf courses in the locality.

Rufford Old Hall★

NT. ▶ *20mi/32km N on the A 59. Liverpool Road. (DY).* 🕐*Open mid-Mar–Oct and Sept–Oct 11am–5pm; Aug Sat–Sun 11am–5pm.* ☜£6.30. ♿Ⓟ✕. ☎01704 821 254. www.nationaltrust.org.uk.
This is one of the finest 15C houses in Lancashire. The **Great Hall**★ has a magnificent **hammerbeam roof** and ornate carved screen. The Carolean wing was reconstructed in brick in 1662. There is much original furniture, arms and armour, and a folk museum.

Martin Mere Wildfowl and Wetlands Centre

▶ *20mi/32km N on the A 59 to Rufford and W on the B 5246.* 🕐*Open daily Mar–late Oct 9.30–5.30pm; late Oct–Feb 9.30–5pm.* ☜£8.95. ♿Ⓟ✕. ☎01704 895 181. www.wwt.org.uk/martin-mere.
This protected wildfowl habitat covers 350 acres/140ha and provides hides, nature trails, and even a canoe safari for birdwatchers. The mere (lake) is home to over 100 species of rare and endangered ducks, geese, swans and flamingos, and offers a winter haven to thousands of pink-footed geese, Icelandic whooper

swans and Bewick's swans from Russia. There are also beavers and otters here.

🚶 Knowsley Safari Park

▶ 8mi/13km E by the A 5047 and the eastbound carriageway of the A 58 (Prescot bypass). ⏰Open daily 10am/ 10.30am–3pm/4pm. ☞£12, child £9. ♿🅿✕. Rides £1.50 each. ✆0151 430 9009. www.knowsley.com.

It was in the menagerie, established at Knowsley in the 19C by the Earl of Derby, that **Edward Lear** made many of his animal drawings; the tales he told to Lord Derby's grandchildren became his *Book of Nonsense*. Today visitors can drive **safari**-fashion along a 5mi/8km route, passing herds of antelopes, camels, buffalo and white rhino, plus tigers, monkeys, giraffes and more. There is also an elephant paddock, a sea lion show, an **Aerial Extreme** tree-top walkway and amusement rides.

The National Wildflower Centre

▶ Court Hey Park. Just off junction 5 of the M62. ⏰Open daily Mar–Aug 10am–5pm. ☞£3.50. ♿🅿✕. ✆0151 738 1913. www.nwc.org.uk.

Set in a Victorian park within 35 acres/14ha of parkland, this bucolic Millennium Commission attraction features seasonal wildflower displays, demonstration areas with events and activities, and a mix of old and new (award-winning) buildings.

🚶 The World of Glass

▶ 12mi/19km E by the A 5047 (EY) and A 57 to St Helens. ⏰Open Tue–Sun and bank hols 10am–5pm, last entry 3pm. ⏰Closed 1 1 Jan, 25–26 Dec. ☞£5.30, child £3.80. ♿🅿✕. ✆08700 114 466. www.worldofglass.com.

Visitors pass through an inverted brick cone recalling the old furnaces into the modern building on the site of the pioneering Pilkington factory. There's live glass-blowing, a 3-D theatre and lots of interactive stations at this very family-friendly place.

Speke Hall★

*NT. ▶ The Walk. Near airport, 8mi/13km SE on the A 561. **House:** ⏰Open mid-Mar–Oct Wed–Sun and bank hols 11am–5pm. Nov–mid-Dec and first two weeks Mar Sat–Sun 11am–4.30pm. **Garden and grounds:** ⏰Open Tue–Sun 11am–5.30pm (Oct–Mar dusk). ☞£7.27 (garden £4.31). 🅿✕. ✆0151 427 7231. www.nationaltrust.org.uk.*

This black-and-white Elizabethan manor house was built between 1490 and 1612 by successive generations of the Norris family. The **Great Hall** is the oldest part of the building; its panelling, including the Great Wainscot of 1564, is particularly fine. The many smaller rooms reflect the Victorian preference for privacy and comfort. In the courtyard two ancient yews possibly pre-date the house.

Port Sunlight

▶ West-side of the Mersey, south of Birkenhead.

The model village was established in the late-19C by William Hesketh Lever for the workers of his soap factory, giving them a style of life very different from that of the crowded slums of the period. Lord Leverhulme's company became Unilever, one of the world's largest manufacturers of consumer goods.

The **Lady Lever Art Gallery** (⏰*open Mon–Sat 10am–5pm, Sun noon–5pm; ♿🅿✕; ✆0151 478 4136; www.ladyleverartgallery.org.uk*), also founded by Lord Leverhulme and opened in 1922, contains British paintings including Pre-Raphaelite works, period furniture, and a fine Wedgwood collection.

🚶 Blue Planet Aquarium

▶ Cheshire Oaks. M 6, then M56/M6 at junction20, then the M 53 at junction 15. ⏰Open 10am–5pm/6pm. ☞£14.50, child £10.50. ♿🅿✕. ✆0151 357 8804. www.blueplanetaquarium.co.uk.

This claims to be the largest "aquarium adventure" of its kind and has more types of shark (10 species) than anywhere else in Britain. Its shark-infested Aquatunnel is one of the longest in the world at 230ft/70m.

Blackpool

and Lancaster

Since 1846 when the railway first made seaside holidays a possibility for the masses, Blackpool has been one of the most popular and typical (in all except location) British seaside resorts. From the 1950s onwards tens of thousands of holidaymakers from the industrial towns of the North and Midlands traditionally flocked here for their annual week or fortnight holiday. Today short breaks are more popular and around a third of all visitors to Blackpool now come in autumn to see the famous Illuminations.

RESORT

Blackpool Tower★

🕐*Open Easter–Nov daily 10am–11pm; Dec–Easter, Sat–Sun, 10am–11pm.*
🎫*Access to lower levels of Tower free. Individual attraction prices below. Combination Ballroom/Circus/Jungle Jim's tickets available, see website for prices.* ♿✗. *℘0844 856 4000. www.blackpooltower.com.*

Inspired by the Eiffel Tower and opened in 1894, the 518ft/158m-high tower is Blackpool's trademark. It has recently been extensively refurbished and includes old favourites and brand new attractions. The **Circus** (🎫*£9, child £8.10*) features shows most days *(see website)*; at the famous glittering **Tower Ballroom** (🎫*£8.40*) you can dance and/or take tea; **Jungle Jim's** (🎫*child £5.40*) is a highly themed children's play area; **Blackpool Dungeons** is a gruesome and gory horror show (🎫*£14.40, online price £9.60; www.thedungeons.com); The **Blackpool Tower Eye (Skywalk) with 4D Cinema Experience** (🎫*£6 online*) is the Tower's new flagship attraction. Before ascending to the top level, you watch (hear, feel and smell) a 4-D film about the tower and resort. You then progress to the **Skywalk**, a floor-to-ceiling glass observation platform which runs along an entire side of the Tower providing magnificent views out to the Irish Sea, and directly below, between

▶ **Population:** 146,297.
🗺 **Michelin Map:** Michelin Atlas p38 or Map 502 K 22.
ℹ **Info:** 1 Clifton Street, www.visitblackpool.com. *℘01253 478 222.*
📍 **Location:** 55mi/88km due north of Liverpool. The main train Station, Blackpool North, is around 440yds/400m from the centre on Talbot Road. The bus station is on the same road some 50yds/45m away.
👁 **Don't Miss:** A trip up Blackpool Tower; a ride on an old-fashioned tram.
🕐 **Timing:** Allow at least one full day and one night; longer if the weather is good and/or you have children in tow.
👪 **Kids:** The whole of Blackpool is geared to children.

your feet in fact, a bird's-eye view of the famous Blackpool Promenade and coastline over 400 ft/122m below.

Pleasure Beach

Ocean Boulevard. 🕐*Open Apr–Oct daily 10.30am–6pm or later (8pm school hols), mid-Feb–Mar and Nov, Sat–Sun only.* 🎫*See website for prices; book online for significant savings.* ♿✗. *℘0871 222 1234. www.blackpoolpleasurebeach.com.*

With over 6 million visitors a year this huge theme park is Britain's most popular paid-entry tourist attraction, boasting state-of-the-art rides and sideshows. For younger guests there is Nickleodeoen Land; for older, white-knuckle thrill seekers there are some of the fastest, highest, scariest rides in Europe. In between are family rides and no fewer than 15 shows: magic and variety, ice-skating shows, talent searches, and an adult-only circus.

Also on the resort is a small branch of **Ripley's Believe It or Not!** (🕐*open daily from 10am;* 🎫*£8/£4 online, child*

Blackpool Illuminations

Blackpool Illuminations first appeared in 1879 (when they were described as "Artificial Sunshine" attracting 100,000 visitors. Today around 3 million come to town each year for "the lights". The "Big Switch On" is in early September and the light lasts for just over two months, closing down early November. The dazzling display stretches almost 6mi/10km along and around the seafront and comprise lasers, neon, fibre optics, searchlights and floodlighting, plus over 1 million conventional bulbs. In 2010 there were more than 500 scenic designs, tableaux and features. www.blackpool-illuminations.net.

£5/£2 online; ♿; ℘ 01253 341 033; www.ripleys.com/blackpool) boasting its usual offering of weird and wonderful artefacts from around the world.

The Great Promenade Show
South Promenade.
This is an outdoor exhibition of 10 sculptures by some of the UK's leading artists and designers celebrating the character of Blackpool; each exhibits takes a theme – the Illuminations, the Ballroom, the "dirty weekend", the Circus, the freak shows of Victorian Blackpool.

Madame Tussauds
🕐*Open year-round daily 10am– 4.30pm (6pm weekends & school hols).* £12 online. ♿. ℘0871 282 9200. www.madametussauds.com/blackpool.
The Tussaud's formula by the seaside, with five floors of famous (mostly British) music, TV, movie and sports personalities, as well as royalty, politicians and historical figures, all captured in lifelike wax figures.

Sea Life Blackpool
🕐*Open year-round daily 10am–4pm (last entry).* £14.40, child £11.40, *significant discount online .* ♿✕. ℘01253 621 258. www.visitsealife.com/Blackpool.
The Blackpool branch of this successful aquarium chain features over 200 creatures from sharks, octopuses and rays to tiny seahorses, inhabiting over 50 displays including a coral reef, a rainforest and an underwater shark tunnel.

Grundy Art Gallery
Queen Street. 🕐*Open year-round Mon– Sat 10am–5pm (bank hols summer and autumn 11am–4pm).* 🕐*Closed between exhibitions.* ♿🅿✕. ℘01253 478 170.
Blackpool's premier art gallery stages often challenging contemporary visual art exhibitions by established and emerging artists from the UK and abroad. Its permanent collection includes Victorian oils and watercolours, modern British paintings, contemporary prints, jewellery, ivories, ceramics, and interesting old souvenirs of Blackpool.

Stanley Park
This recently restored majestic 256-acre park is a green oasis 2mi/3km from the bustling seafront. It features display gardens, ornate fountains, woodlands, and a boating lake. Immediately west is the **Blackpool Model Village Gardens** 🕐*Open Apr–early Nov daily 10am–dusk;* £6.95, child £5.75; ♿🅿✕; ℘01253 763 827; www.blackpoolmodelvillage.com) in 2.5 acres/1ha of landscaped gardens.

EXCURSIONS
Lancaster Castle
▶ 25mi/40km NE. 🕐*Open all year daily 10am–5pm (last tour 4pm).* 🕐*Closed Xmas/New Year hols.* £5. ℘01524 64998. www.lancastercastle.com.
The Normans built the original castle and the oldest surviving part is the imposing mid-12C keep. It has been a court and prison for centuries and still functions as such today, with only around a quarter of the complex open to visitors. Entertaining tours recall its history as a place of justice (the trial of the famous Pendle Witches took place here in 1612) and punishment.

Isle of Man★

This mountainous island in the Irish Sea was settled by Celts, then by Norsemen, ruled by Scotland, then by England. Its own language, Manx, akin to Gaelic, is now extinct, though the famous tail-less cat survives. The island, a British dependency but not part of the United Kingdom, has its own laws, presented each year to an open-air parliament of the people; this 1,000-year-old descendant of the Norse *Thingvollr* ("assembly field") is held at a central point on the island, Tynwald Green, a site with prehistoric associations. The lowland pattern of unspoiled farmland, small fields bounded by stone walls or high hedgebanks, gives way as the land rises to wild open moorland, bright in late summer with gorse and heather. The highest summit is Snaefell (2,036ft/621m), from which England, Scotland, Ireland and Wales can be seen. Most of the coastline (100mi/160km) is untouched by modern intrusions. The island is no longer as fashionable as it used to be but still attracts significant numbers of holidaymakers, mainly from the north of England. It is most famous for the Isle of Man TT (Tourist Trophy) motorcycle Races (*www. iomtt.com*) held late May–early June. The racecourse is one of the world's most dangerous.

Douglas

The great sweep of Victorian and Edwardian hotels facing promenades and the sandy bay give the island's capital an unmistakable identity. The **Manx Museum** (◐open Mon–Sat 10am–5pm; ◐closed 1 Jan, 25–26 Dec; ▣✕; ℘01624 648 000; www.gov. im/mnh), "the treasure house of the island's story", displays good examples of early Christian sculpture; the Folk-Life Galleries include a reconstructed Manx farmhouse.

The island's halcyon days of mass tourism were the late-19C and early-

▸ **Population:** 69,788.
◔ **Michelin Map:** Michelin Atlas p42 or Map 402 G 21.
▧ **Info:** ℘01624 686 801. www.gov.im/tourism.
◑ **Location:** The Isle of Man Steam Packet Company runs ferries to Liverpool, Heysham (Morecambe), Dublin and Belfast. The island also has an airport.

20C and an extensive network of vintage transport remains. Horse trams – nicknamed "toast racks" – ply the Douglas promenades, narrow-gauge steam railways serve the south and, most remarkable of all, double-track electric tramways lead from Douglas along the high cliffs to the northern resort of Ramsey and to the very summit of Snaefell.

Great Laxey Wheel and Mines Trail★★

Take the Manx Electric Railway N along the coast. Walk up the valley (0.6mi/1km). ◐*Open Easter/late-Mar–late Oct daily 10am–5pm.* ◉*£4.* ▣. ℘*01624 648 000. www.gov.im/tourism.* This giant working waterwheel, a splendid monument of the industrial age, was built in 1854 when the Laxey Valley was the scene of intense lead- and silver-mining activity. Part of the old mines may be visited.

Snaefell Mountain Railway★

Take the Manx Electric Railway via Laxey on the east coast. ◐*Operates (weather permitting) Laxey to summit May–Sept, daily, 10.30am–3.30pm.* ◉*£8.50.* ▣✕. ℘*01624 675 222.*

A vintage tramcar climbs up the side of the glen and on to the mountain slopes to the terminus at the café just below the summit (at 2,036ft/621m). On a clear day there are stupendous **views**★★★ of the lands fringing the Irish Sea.

ADDRESSES

🛏 STAY

MANCHESTER

🛏 **Millstone Hotel** – B1. *67 Thomas Street.* *☏0161 839 0213, www.jwlees.co.uk/ millstone.* 📶. *15 rms* Busy central inn, owned by local brewers J W Lees, managed by "Lees' best tenant 2011", so you should get a warm welcome here. Entertainment four nights per week.

🛏 **Mitre Hotel** – A1. *1-3 Cathedral Gates.* *☏0161 832 2400. http://mitrehotel. manchesterhoteltour.com. 30 rms.* Set in a lovely old Victorian building next to the cathedral, the Mitre offers simple but up-to-date rooms. Good value.

🛏🛏–🛏🛏🛏🛏 **Malmaison** – B2. *Picadilly.* *☏0161 278 1000. www.malmaison.com. 167 rms.* Set in an old warehouse, "Mal Manchester" is one of the most stylish places in town, visited by pop stars and celebrities for its quirky up-to-the-minute "Gothic-lite" fashion, with bold colours, funky furnishings, spa and buzzing music. Great online deals.

🛏🛏🛏🛏 **The Lowry Hotel** – A1. *Chapel Wharf, Salford. ☏0161 827 4000. www.thelowryhotel.com.* 📶. *165 rms.* This boldly designed contemporary five-star hotel at the heart of the Quays is Manchester's most fashionable; indoor pool, spa and wellness facilities.

CHESTER

🛏 **Chester House Guest House** – *44 Hoole Road. ☏01244 348 410. www.chesterhouse guesthouse.co.uk.* 📶. *8 rms.* A 15-min walk from the centre, this modest Victorian house has been impeccably refurbished and offers a warm welcome.

🛏 **Pied Bull** – *57 Northgate Street.* *☏01244 325 829. www.piedbull.co.uk. 12 rms.* Actually set within the city walls this friendly historic 16C inn offers comfortable characterful rooms.

🛏🛏 **Chester Court Hotel** – *48 Hoole Road. ☏01244 320 779. www.chestercourt hotel.com.* 📶. *20 rms* This characterful Victorian house, a five-minute bus journey from town, is a mix of old and new styles, with some rooms in an annex.

🛏🛏–🛏🛏🛏🛏 **Ramada Chester** – *Whitchurch Road, Christleton. ☏0844 815 9001. www.ramadachester.co.uk.* 📶. *126 rms.* Two miles/3km east of Chester in 2 acres/ 0.8ha of grounds, this modern, superior chain hotel boasts a health club and spa.

Rooms are very comfortable. Some very good deals online.

🛏🛏🛏 **The Queen Hotel** – *City Road.* *☏01244 305 000 - www.bw-queenhotel. co.uk.* 📶. *129 rms.* Set in an impressive Victorian building in the heart of town, with a lovely terrace and gardens, bedrooms boast every facility and range from "contemporary-Victorian" to grand luxury antique-carved four-posters.

LIVERPOOL

🛏–🛏🛏 **Holme Leigh Guest House** – C2. *91 Woodcroft Road, Wavertree. ☏0151 734 2216. www.holmeleigh.com. 6 rms.* This modest Victorian redbrick suburban house, 2mi/3.2km from the city centre, is a good base for budget travellers. The owners are very helpful.

🛏–🛏🛏 **Premier Travel Inn** – A2 - *Albert Dock* – *☏0871 527 8622 - www.premiertravelinn.com.* 📶. This highly rated hotel (part of a budget chain) is set in a sensitively converted 19C building with some lovely bedrooms. Perfect location for a short break and great-value.

🛏🛏🛏 **Atlantic Tower** – A1. *Chapel Street.* *☏0871 376 9025/0845 305 8325. www.thistle.com. 226 rms.* Enjoy wonderful views over the Mersey from the restaurant terrace and upper floors of this large modern ship-shape (in every sense) hotel. Smart rooms. Great value online offers.

🛏🛏–🛏🛏🛏🛏 **Hope Street Hotel** – C2. *40 Hope Street. ☏0151 709 3000. www.hopestreethotel.co.uk. 89 rms.* This cosy boutique-design hotel, with gorgeous contemporary rooms, is housed in an 1860 Venetian-style building in a chic part of town. Voted "Best Value Urban UK Hotel 2011" by *The Sunday Times*.

🛏🛏–🛏🛏🛏🛏 **Radisson Blu** – A1. *107 Old Street. ☏0151 966 1500. www.radissonblu.co.uk/hotel-liverpool.* 📶. *194 rms.* A stunning atrium welcomes guests to this contemporary hotel which enjoys magnificent views over the Mersey. Rooms are stylish and good value.

🛏🛏–🛏🛏🛏🛏 **Britannia Adelphi Hotel** – B1. *Ranelagh Place. ☏0871 222 0029. www.adelphi-hotel.co.uk. 402 rms.* Steeped in the history of the city, the Adelphi has played host to all kinds of visiting VIPs, including Roy Rogers and Clark Gable. It is still very grand, including a lovely indoor marble pool and new gym, but some rooms are tired, so choose carefully. Bargains online.

ISLE OF MAN

⊜ **Glen Helen Inn** – *Glen Helen, St Johns.* ℘*01624 801 294. www.glenheleninn.com. 14 rms.* In a picturesque setting near the Rhenass Falls, this small hotel has recently been renovated in contemporary style.

⊜⊜ **The River House** – *Ramsey.* ℘*01624 816 412. www.theriverhouse-iom.com. 3 rms.* This handsome 1820s country house enjoys a perfect, peaceful location, a 10-minute walk from Ramsey, beside the Sulby River, in 3 acres/1.2ha of mature gardens. Classic spacious chintzy bedrooms, each with a lovely outlook.

⅋/ EAT

MANCHESTER

⊛ **Deansgate Locks** is the place for pubs and bars. For Indian restaurants, try **Rusholme**.

⊜ **The Bank** – B2. *57 Mosley Street.* ℘*0161 228 7560. www.nicholsonspubs.co.uk.* Superior pub food is served here, in the grand surrounding of an early-19C Neoclassical library hall.

⊜⊜ – ⊜⊜⊜ **Yang Sing** – B2. *34 Princess Street.* ℘*0161 236 2200. www.yang-sing.com.* Open since 1977 and set on several floors in smart minimalist style, Yang Sing is one of the best Cantonese restaurants in the UK.

CHESTER

⊜ **The Fat Cat** – *85 Watergate Street.* ℘*01244 316 100. www.fatcatcafebars.co.uk.* In the cellar of an old townhouse next to Chester Race Course, low ceilings, oversized comfy sofas and a quirky layout creates a cosy ambience. The simple bistro-style menu includes burgers, salads, pasta and pizza and sharing platters. A popular fun fashionable place.

⊜ – ⊜⊜ **The Coach House** – *39 Northgate Street.* ℘*01244 325 533.* This beautifully refurbished 19C coaching inn in the heart of town serves award-winning gastropub food (and simple traditional pub meals) in attractive "trad-contemporary" surroundings.

⊜ – ⊜⊜ **The Old Harkers Arms** – *1 Russell Street.* ℘*01244 344 525. www.bandp.co.uk/harkers.* Set in the basement of an old warehouse that once fronted the canal, this beautifully furnished atmospheric post-industrial chic pub serves a broad menu of gastropub food and lighter bites.

LIVERPOOL

⊛ Albert Dock, Hope Street and Exchange Street are the main eating and drinking areas. Liverpool's famous Chinatown is on and around Nelson Street, Duke Street and Berry Street.

⊜ **Mei Mei** – C2. *9 Berry Street.* ℘*0151 707 2888.* According to many people this is the best Chinese restaurant in town and certainly one of its most popular.

⊜ **Pump House** – A2. *The Colonnades, Albert Dock.* ℘*0151 709 2367. www.albert dock.com/the-pump-house.* The Albert Dock's former pumphouse, built 1870, has been lovingly converted into an atmospheric cosy pub/bar with a waterside terrace. Expect superior pub grub.

⊜ **The Beehive** – B2. *7 Paradise Street,* ℘*0151 709 5875.* A traditional city pub at the front, a restaurant at the rear, with clubby leather sofas and bookshelves.

⊜ **Tokyou** – C2. *7 Berry Street.* ℘*0151 445 1023.* You can enjoy Cantonese, Thai and Japanese cuisine at this popular noodle bar in the heart of Chinatown.

⊜⊜ **Gusto** – A2. *Edward Pavillion. Albert Dock.* ℘*0151 708 6969. www.gusto restaurants.uk.com.* At the entrance to the docks, in an old warehouse, this classic buzzing atmospheric Italian ristorante has a contemporary stylish interior.

⊜⊜ **Philharmonic Dining Rooms** – C2. *36 Hope Street.* ℘*0151 707 283. www.nicholsonspubs.co.uk.* One of the most lavish pubs in the UK, the "Phil" has dark wood-panelled walls with copper reliefs, Art Deco lighting and a beautiful mosaic floor and bar. On the first floor its dining rooms serve superior pub food.

⊜⊜⊜ **Hope Street Restaurant** – C2. *60 Hope Street.* ℘*0151 707 6060. www.60hopestreet.com.* This elegant family-owned (and -run) restaurant covers three floors of a Georgian townhouse, serving a changing menu of seasonal Modern British food.

ISLE OF MAN

⊜ **China Town** – *7/8 StrathallanCrescent, Douglas.* ℘*01624 673 367. www.chinatown-iom.com.* The oldest and most popular Chinese restaurant on the island.

⊜⊜ **Tanroagan Bistro** – *Ridgeway Street, Douglas* – ℘*01624 612 355. http://tanroagan. co.uk.* This small independent, family-run bistro specialises in fish and seafood.

CUMBRIA AND THE LAKES

The Lake District is regarded by many as England's most beautiful landscape. It has inspired poets and writers for over 200 years and is still one of the most popular holiday regions in the UK. Its fells (mountains) can attract seemingly endless rain and extreme weather changes, adding atmosphere to an already emotive landscape. It is only the weather that stops the summertime crowds from moving in full time. Whatever the time of year, it is a magnificent place for enjoying the simple beauty of nature.

Highlights

1 Cruise peacefully on glassy **Lake Windermere** (p369)
2 Visiting **Brantwood** for its glorious Coniston Water setting (p370)
3 Drive the A 593 via **Wrynose Pass** and **Hardknott Pass** (p372)
4 Walk the "white-knuckle" Via Ferrata trail at **Honister Slate Mine** (p373)
5 Descend the Honister Pass to **Buttermere** (p374)

Lake District National Park

A combination of mountains and lakes, woodland and farmland, this is the largest of Britain's national parks, covering an area of 880sq mi/2,280sq km, of which a quarter is part of the National Trust. Appropriately it is home to Scafell Pike, England's highest mountain, and Wastwater, England's deepest lake.

Ice shaped the troughs and corries, while glacial rubble dammed the valleys and underlying rock dictated whether the hills were softly rounded, like Skiddaw, or wildly rugged, like Scafell Pike and Helvellyn.

The main activity in the Lake District – often shortened to "the Lakes" – is walking, pioneered by local hero, Alfred Wainwright, and there are trails for literally every age and ability. Climbing and mountaineering are other popular, if more specialised pastimes, and latterly windsurfing, mountain biking, daring treetop walks and even a Dolomites-style Via Ferrata have been established. For many visitors, however, simply the sight of the hills reflected in the deep blue waters of the lakes is enough. And if that is viewed from the side of a vintage steamboat, sailing across the lake, then so much the better!

Highlights

Lake Windermere – This is the most famous, and busiest part of the Lakes, made so by eminent literary names such as Wordsworth, Ruskin and Beatrix Potter, all of whose houses are open to the public. The little settlements of Hawkshead, Ambleside and Grasmere are delightful, particularly just out of season.

Eskdale and the northern Llakes – If you want to escape the thick of the crowds and like your landscapes to be more robust, then the lesser-visited lakes of Buttermere and Wast Water and the valleys of Eskdale, Langdale and Borrowdale will not disappoint. Keswick is an interesting old town to use as a break or a base.

Kendal, Furness and South Cumbria – On the southeast fringe of the national park, Kendal is a popular gateway to the region and its excellent museums are a good introduction to the Lakes. The South Cumbria coast may lack the drama and picture-postcard scenery of the national park but with the likeable town of Ulverston, Cartmel Priory and some fine historic houses, does not lack visitor interest.

Eden Valley and Penrith – On the northeast edge of the park, the Eden Valley is a continuation of the dramatic landscapes. The highlight is beautiful Ullswater lake, while the enjoyable small historic towns of Penrith, Appleby-in-Westmoreland and Alston all spring to life on market days.

Carlisle

The only city in the region, and an important border post between England and Scotland, Carlisle has been fought over for many centuries. Its rich history is well documented in its museum and the very fabric of its historic centre.

Food Heroes

Two places that promote all things Cumbrian in their comprehensive **food halls**, and offer café-restaurants to taste there and then, are Cranstons (*www.cranstons.net*) and the Rheged Centre (*www.rheged.com*), both near Penrith. Cranstons is the larger of the two, has the greater pedigree (est 1914), and are master butchers.

The region's most famous meat product is the traditional **Cumberland Sausage** (Cumberland was absorbed into Cumbria in 1974). This long, chunky, textured, peppery pork sausage is characterised by its formation into a rope-like coil, as opposed to being divided into "links". It can be found everywhere in the region, and beyond, but the best come from Cranstons (see above), and Higginson's butchers, Grange-over-Sands.

Cumberland sausage might come served with **Cumberland sauce**, made with oranges, lemons, redcurrant jelly, dijon mustard, portand ground ginger.

In restaurants look out for **Morecambe Salt Marsh Lamb**, and **Cumbrian Mutton**, the latter recently championed by Prince Charles and taken up by many top chefs. In basic terms, mutton is meat from sheep that are older than lambs, though even its aficionados cannot agree on the exact definition. Cumbria's fells and moors are well suited to **sheep farming**, with hardy breeds chosen to weather out the colder months. Mutton was once staple fare in the British Isles, but is increasingly impossible to get hold of, perhaps other than in Cumbria.

On the coast look for **Solway Oysters**, cockles, scallops (the smaller flavourful "**Queenies**" from the Isle of Man are best) and potted shrimps in butter from **Morecambe Bay**. Manx **kippers** are another Isle of Man speciality. **Char** is a tasty lake fish from Coniston, Windermere and Wast Water.

Thornby Moor Dairy (*www.thornbymoordairy.co.uk*) at Thursby make artisan cheese entirely by hand in open vats, including traditional, cloth-bound Cumberland Cheese. The cheesemaking room can be seen through a gallery window and the shop assistant will explain the process to visitors.

The perfect accompaniment to both local cheese and meats is the comprehensive range of traditional preserves, relishes, pickles and chutneys sold by The **Hawkshead Relish Company** (*www.hawksheadrelish.com*) from their shop in Hawkshead. These include Damson Ketchup, made from local Westmorland **damsons**, and old-fashioned **Cumberland Sauce**, once famous nationwide. This rich pungent pouring sauce is made with redcurrants, damson wine, oranges and lemons.

Regional sweet treats include the widely available **Kendal Mintcake** and the much more exclusive **Grasmere Gingerbread**, sold only in Grasmere. A newcomer to the local food scene is **Cartmel Sticky Toffee Pudding** (*www.stickytoffeepudding.co.uk*), hand baked in the back kitchen of Cartmel Village Shop, from which it is also sold.

If you want to see how traditional Cumbrian real ale is brewed, **Jennings Brewery** (*www.jenningsbrewery.co.uk*) at Cockermouth, on its current site since 1874, is open for tours.

Around Lake Windermere you will find **damsons** in great abundance. These small, tart fruits are perfects for the egg-based damson and apply tansy.

Lake District★★★
Cumbria

William Wordsworth said of the Lakes, "I do not know of any tract of country in which, in so narrow a compass, may be found an equal variety in the influences of light and shadow upon the sublime and beautiful."

LANDSCAPE

The region's name comes from the beautiful stretches of water that occupy many of the glaciated valleys radiating out from a high central core of volcanic rocks, presenting abrupt cliffs, crags and precipices. Among the many famous peaks is **Scafell Pike** (3,206ft/977m), the highest point in England. Elsewhere, much of the landscape has been formed by slate: to the north, in the gently-rounded but majestic heights of the Skiddaw group; to the south, in the more broken country reaching its highest point in the commanding presence of **The Old Man**, looming over Coniston Water. The most austere scenery is near the head of Wasdale, where awesome screes plunge to the shore of **Wastwater**, the deepest and most forbidding of the lakes.

The wild drama of the fells is set off by the gentler, pastoral character of the lowland, particularly in the park-like surroundings of Lake Windermere.

Rainfall is high and the many tarns and tumbling becks are well fed. The peaks are often capped in cloud and the slopes shrouded in mist. The rocks are used in the man-made structures of the countryside: in ancient bridges; in the drystone walls which climb high into the fells; in the rough-hewn stone of sturdy barns, cottages and whitewashed farmhouses with massive roofs of slate. Even the towns are mostly built of stone and slate. Until well into the 20C mining was an important activity in Cumbria; coal, iron-ore, lead, copper and graphite, some of which was transported to the coast by rail and made the coastal fishing villages thriving ports. Slate and granite are still quarried on a small scale.

- ⓘ **Michelin Map:** Michelin Atlas p44 or Map 502 K, L 20.
- ⓘ **Info:** www.golakes.co.uk; www.lakedistrict.gov.uk. There are many information centres, listed in the text under the places they are located.
- ▶ **Location:** Oxenholme Station, at Kendal, is the rail gateway to the Lakes with a branch line to Windermere. Buses from all over the Northwest run to the main villages. Ambleside and Windermere make good touring bases; half-day and full-day guided tours in mini-coaches are available. Try Lakes Supertours (℘015394 42751, 015394 88133; www.lakes-super-tours.com) or Mountain Goat tours (t015394 45161; www.mountain-goat.com).
- ☺ **Don't Miss:** A boat trip or walk.
- ☺ **Warning:** Mountain roads are narrow with sharp bends and severe gradients. Walkers and climbers should choose routes suited to their experience.
- ○ **Timing:** At least three days.
- ♟ **Kids:** Hill Top (Beatrix Potter's cottage) for little ones; The Lakes Aquarium.
- ✎ **Walking:** Ask at your tourist information office. It is worth investing in one of Wainwright's walking guides to the region.
- ☍ **Bicycle Trails:** Cycles are readily available for hire. Try Windermere Station.
- ◔ **Sailing:** Lake Windermere has plenty of watersports. Or try Coniston Boating Centre (t015394 41366; www.lakedistrict.gov.uk/conistonboatingcentre).

🚗 DRIVING TOURS

① LAKELAND POETS TOUR
30mi/48km.

The more frequented area round Windermere evokes the memory of the Lakeland poets – **Wordsworth**, **Coleridge** and **Southey** – who were variously inspired by the landscape.

Lake Windermere★★
🛈 *Brockhole. ☎015394 46601. www.brockhole.co.uk*
The longest lake in England (10mi/16km), beautifully framed by wooded slopes and bare fells, is particularly lively and popular for watersports.
The town of **Windermere** was created in the 19C tourist boom and a trip on the water is still de rigueur. **Windermere Lake Cruises** (🕐*cruises daily; onboard catering; ☞£7 to £17.25 full lake cruise; ☎015394 43 360; www.windermere-lake-cruises.co.uk*) offer a choice of cruises, from 45 minutes to a full-day round the lake "hop-on hop-off" pass.

Bowness-on-Windermere
The pretty village is known for its promenade skirting the bay. A **ferry** carries cars and pedestrians across the lake to Sawrey.
The main family visitor attraction is 👪 **The World Of Beatrix Potter** (*Crag Bow;* 🕐*open daily 10am–5.30pm/4.30pm winter;* 🕐*closed last wk Jan–1st wk Feb, 25 Dec;* ☞*£6.75, child £3.50;* ♿🅿✕; ☎*0844 504 1233; www.hop-skip-jump.com*) where all 23 tales by Beatrix Potter are brought to life using the latest audio-visual and interactive techniques, complete with sights, sounds and smells.
Nearby, at Lakeside, the 👪 **Lakes Aquarium** (*Lakeside, Newby Bridge;* 🕐 *open daily 9am–6pm/5pm winter;* 🕐*closed last wk Jan–1st wk Feb, 25 Dec;* ☞*£9.15, child £6.10 (save 25 percent online);* ♿🅿*(charge)*✕; ☎*015395 30153; www.aquariumofthelakes.co.uk*) reveals the aquatic and animal life of the rivers, streams and lakes. There is a walk-through plexi-glass tunnel and displays on piranhas, otters and marmosets.

▷ *In Newby Bridge turn right to Sawrey.*

👪 Hill Top
NT. Near Sawrey. 🕐*Open mid-Feb–Oct Sat–Thu 10.30am–4.30pm (3.30pm Feb–Mar, late May–Aug 10am–5pm). Timed entry ticket system. Try to avoid peak periods, especially during school hol periods when early sell-outs are possible.* ☞*£7, child £3.50.* 🅿*(charge at peak times).* ☎*015394 36 269. www.nationaltrust.org.uk/hilltop.*
This tiny 17C house was the home of **Beatrix Potter**, who created Peter Rabbit, Benjamin Bunny, Jemima Puddle-Duck and many more favourite characters. Unchanged since her death in 1943, it now attracts thousands of visitors seeking the inspiration for their childhood delight. Inside are Beatrix Potter's watercolours, her dolls' house and mementoes.

Lake Windermere

© Karen Town/iStockphoto.com

Hawkshead★

The narrow slate-walled lanes and paths of this traditional Lakeland village are bordered by flower-decked cottages. Wordsworth attended the local grammar school from 1779 to 1787.

The **Beatrix Potter Gallery** *(NT; Main Street;* 🕐 *same as Hill Top (👆see above) entry by timed ticket;* ✂*discount for Hill Top visitors;* ♿*;* 📞*01539 436 355; www. nationaltrust.org.uk)* covers her work as artist, author and local farmer, and displays a selection of her watercolours.

Coniston Water★

The road from Hawkshead provides a fine view of the lake and the surrounding fells dominated by the form of **The Old Man of Coniston** (2,628ft/801m).

Coniston

The little slate-grey town is known for its associations with the author, artist and social reformer John Ruskin (1819–1900), who came to live at nearby Brantwood in 1872. He is buried in the churchyard. Nearby, the **Ruskin Museum** *(*🕐*open mid-Mar–mid-Nov daily 10am–5.30pm; mid-Nov–mid-Mar Wed–Sun 10.30am–3.30pm;* ✂*£5.25;* ♿*;* 📞*015394 41164; www.ruskinmuseum.com)* holds drawings, manuscripts and other mementoes. The museum's new **Bluebird Wing** is dedicated to the world water-speed record-breaking boat *Bluebird*, and its driver, **Donald Campbell**, who set four successive records in the late 1950s on Coniston Water. He was killed when *Bluebird* crashed on Coniston in 1967.

On the northeast shore of the lake is **Brantwood★** *(*🕐*open mid-Mar–mid-Nov daily 11am–5.30pm, mid-Nov–mid-Mar Wed–Sun 11am–4.30pm;* 🕐*closed 25–26 Dec;* ✂*£6.30;* ♿📇✕*;* 📞*015394 41396, www.brantwood.org.uk)*, "the most beautifully situated house in the Lake District". This was the home of **John Ruskin**, one of the greatest figures of the Victorian age. On the walls are exquisite watercolours by himself and by Pre-Raphaelite contemporaries whom he championed. His study turret provides a splendid **view**★ of Coniston in its attractive lakeside setting with the form of The Old Man to the left, perfectly mirrored in the tranquil waters of the lake.

▶ *From Coniston take the A 593; in Skelwith Bridge turn left to Grasmere.*

Grasmere

This beautiful village is synonymous with the great Lake poet **William Wordsworth** (1770–1850). The churchyard of 13C St Oswald's is where Wordsworth, various members of the family and Coleridge's son, David Hartley, are buried. If the wind is blowing your way, you can follow your nose to the **Grasmere Gingerbread Shop** *(*🕐*open daily;* 📞*015394 35428, www.grasmeregingerbread.co.uk)*, tucked away in the corner of the churchyard. A Lakes institution, the fabulous smell of Sarah Nelson's freshly baked gingerbread (sold only here) has been drawing customers to this delightful 17C house-cum-shop since the 1850s.

Dove Cottage & The Wordsworth Museum★

Town End, just off the A 591.
🕐*Open daily 9.30am–5pm last entry (Nov–Feb 4pm last entry).* 🕐*Closed Nov–Feb 9.30am–4pm last entry.* ✂*£7.50.* 📞*01539 435 544. www.wordsworth.org.uk.*

The home of William Wordsworth (1770–1850) and his sister Dorothy from 1799 to 1808, the cottage takes its name from being an early-17C inn (The Dove and Olive Bough) and became a magnet for early-19C literary Romantics such as Coleridge, Southey and De Quincey. In the kitchen, where Dorothy cooked the inhabitants' two meals per day (both porridge), are three chairs embroidered by Dora Wordsworth (the poet's daughter), Sara Coleridge and Edith Southey. The room off it was first Dorothy's, then William's. Upstairs is the sitting room, looking out over the waters of Grasmere, the main bedroom, the Newspaper Room (wallpapered in newspaper to keep it warm), and the pantry-cum-spare room. Behind is a museum containing manuscripts, memorabilia and Lakeland paintings, and the **Jerwood Centre** Reading Room, home to many rare first editions.

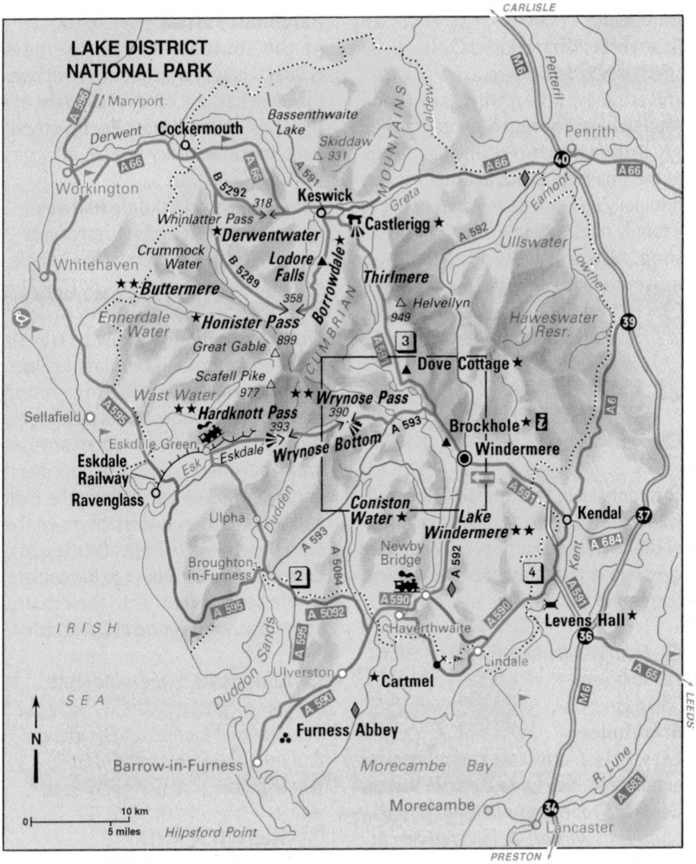

LAKE DISTRICT NATIONAL PARK

(map of the Lake District National Park showing Cockermouth, Keswick, Castlerigg, Derwentwater, Lodore Falls, Thirlmere, Buttermere, Honister Pass, Dove Cottage, Brockhole, Windermere, Hardknott Pass, Wrynose Pass, Coniston Water, Lake Windermere, Kendal, Levens Hall, Cartmel, Furness Abbey, Barrow-in-Furness, and surrounding roads and towns)

Rydal Mount and Gardens

Windermere–Keswick Road.
🕐 *Open Mar–Oct daily 9.30am–5pm, Feb, Nov–24 Dec Wed–Sun 11am–4pm.*
🕐 *Closed 25–26 Dec.* 🎟 *£6.50, 10 percent discount online.*
🅿 ✆ *01539 4 33002.*
www.rydalmount.co.uk.
Overlooking Rydal Water, this 16C cottage, extended in the 18C into a farmhouse, became the home of William Wordsworth (1770–1850) from 1813 until his death in 1850. Here he wrote his most financially successful book, *Guide to the Lakes.* Inside, his library now forms part of the drawing room, and the study ceiling is still painted with the Renaissance design he copied from a visit to Italy. Outside is a beautiful garden.

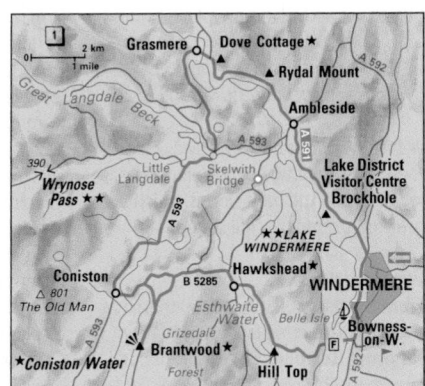

Ambleside

Central Buildings, Market Cross. 0844 225 0544.

This attractive little town makes a good touring base. The much-photographed 17C **Bridge House** is claimed to be one of the smallest houses in Britain. It was originally an apple store, then home to a family of eight, now a National Trust shop. Also worth a visit is the local museum, **The Armitt** (*Rydal Road; open Mon–Sat 10am–4.30pm; £2.80; 015394 31212; www.armitt.com*).

2 ESKDALE VIA WRYNOSE PASS

50mi/80km.

This route leads to the less-frequented, wilder and at times desolate expanses of Ulpha Fell and Furness Fell and goes over two high passes (beware severe bends and gradients).

From Windermere take the A 591 N for 3mi/5km.

Brockhole★

Get your bearings at the comprehensive and imaginative **Lake District Visitor Centre** (*open year-round daily 10am–5pm/4pm winter; (charge); 015394 46 601; www.brockhole.co.uk*), set in a fine country mansion, with large lawns, exhibitions, crazy golf, an indoor play space and adventure playground.

S of Ambleside; left on the A 593. Beyond Skelwith Bridge turn right.

At first the road is enclosed by dykes and then starts to climb up the V-shaped valley between the bare slopes which are grazing grounds for hill sheep.

Wrynose Pass★★

From the pass (1,280ft/390m) there is a **view** back down to Little Langdale. **Wrynose Bottom** – The road runs parallel with the River Duddon along Wrynose Bottom through the wild splendour and gently rounded forms of the fells, which rarely exceed 3,280ft/1,000m but are scarred by steep scree slopes.

Hardknott Pass★★

At the southern end of the pass (1,289ft/393m), which looks west over the more pastoral valley of **Eskdale**, are the ruins of **Hardknott Fort**, a stone-built Roman auxiliary fort (2C AD).

Ravenglass and Eskdale Railway

Operates Apr–Oct daily, rest of year reduced service, see website £7 single journey, £12 day ticket. 01229 71 71 71. www.ravenglass-railway.co.uk. The narrow-gauge railway travels 7mi/11.3km from Ravenglass to Dalegarth. The line, laid in 1875 to carry iron ore and granite, now carries passengers in closed, semi-closed or open carriages drawn by either steam-powered or diesel engines. The line passes from the high fells and tributary waterfalls down the Esk Valley, through the heather, bracken or tree-clad lower slopes to Ravenglass, where seabirds gather in the estuary. There is a visitor centre at Dalegarth.

Either return by the same route or make a long detour via Ulpha, Broughton-in-Furness and Newby Bridge at the southern end of Lake Windermere.

3 KESWICK AND NORTHERN LAKES

29mi/47km.

North of Dove Cottage the road runs parallel to the Rothay up to Dunmail Raise before descending into the valley overshadowed by "the dark brow of mighty" **Helvellyn** (3,114ft/949m). Wordsworth used to walk this route to visit Coleridge and Southey in Keswick. **Thirlmere** – Originally two smaller water bodies, the lake (3.5mi/55km long, 1.2mi/2km wide), enclosed by mountains and forests, is a reservoir, raised 50ft/15m by a dam, surrounded by plantations. **Castlerigg Stone Circle★** – (*Signposts*) The circle is older than Stonehenge and its purpose is unknown. It is set on a grassy outcrop offering far-flung **views** south towards Thirlmere and Helvellyn and west to Derwentwater and Keswick.

Keswick

Keswick, a lakeland town of medieval origin, claims the world's first pencil factory (1832), using the graphite which was mined in Borrowdale as early as the mid-16C. The small, but interesting and child-friendly 👥👤**Pencil Museum** (🕐 *open daily 9.30am–5pm, later at peak times;* 🕐*closed 1 Jan and 25–26 Dec;* 👛*£3.75, child £2.50;* ♿ 🅿; 📞 *01768 773 626; www.pencil museum.co.uk) celebrates the town's 175-plus years of pencil making.

The local **museum** *(Station Road;* 🕐*open Apr–Oct Tue–Sat and bank hols 10am–4pm;* ♿; 📞*01768 773 263; www.allerdale. gov.uk/keswick-museum)* is a real cabinet of curiosities including a 665-year-old cat, the remarkable Musical Stones "pianola", played by Royal Command for Queen Victoria, Napoleon's teacup, the skin of Britain's rarest fish and, more conventionally, manuscripts by both Wordsworth and Southey. Wordsworth used to visit Southey and Coleridge when they and their extended families lived together at Greta Hall (now self-catering holiday accommodation).

▶ *From Keswick take the B 5289 S.*

Derwentwater★

This lake is 3mi/5km long, 1mi/0.6km wide and flanked by clerestories of crags. Southey called it the most beautiful of English lakes.

Lodore Falls

This most literary cascade (according to Southey) "comes thundering and floundering, and thumping and plumping and bumping and jumping and whizzing and hissing and dripping and skipping and grumbling and rumbling and tumbling and falling and brawling and sprawling" but only after heavy rain!

Borrowdale

The attractive valley, where graphite was mined in the mid-16C, leads to the tiny hamlet of Rosthwaite set in a clearing in characteristic Lakeland scenery.

Honister Pass

The road climbs over the pass (1,175ft /358m). To the south are two of the region's most prominent summits – **Great Gable** (2,949ft/899m) and **Scafell Pike** (3,205ft/977m).

On the pass **Honister Slate Mine**★ (🕐 *open year-round daily 9am–5pm; call for times and prices; pre-booking required on all tours;* 📞*017687 77230 or*

Lake Buttermere

© Fantuz Olimpio/Sime/Photononstop

373

77714, *www.honister-slate-mine.co.uk*) is the last of its kind in England and runs fascinating underground tours. Even more of a thrill is its **Via Ferrata** trail (the only one in the country) offering quite literally breathtaking views with only a wire between you and a drop of several hundred feet.

Beyond the pass, the road descends to **Buttermere**★★, which is separated by a glacial delta from Crummock Water, and continues to **Cockermouth**.

Wordsworth House & Garden

NT, Cockermouth. Main Street.
Open mid-Mar–Oct Sat–Thu 11am–5pm £6.50. 01900 824 805. www.nationaltrust.org.uk.

The elegant Neoclassical Georgian house (1745), in which the poet **William Wordsworth** was born in 1770 and spent his early years, is furnished with his own or contemporary furniture and exhibits some of his work, documents and the Wordsworth family tree. His beloved garden contains 18C fruits, flowers and vegetables and leads down to the Derwent.

▶ *From Cockermouth return to Keswick EITHER by the A 66 (the quicker route), OR by the slow steep scenic B 5292.*

The A 66 skirts the west shore of **Bassenthwaite Lake** whereas the slower road climbs over **Whinlatter Pass** (1,043ft/318m) revealing extensive and magnificent views of typical lakeland scenery.

4 KENDAL AND FURNESS

▶ *40mi/64km. From Windermere take the A 591 east.*

Kendal

25 Stramongate. 01539 735 891.
The "Auld Grey Town", built out of the local limestone, is a thriving regional centre. It was birthplace of Henry VIII's sixth wife, Catherine Parr, and before then was famous for its wool trade. Today it is known for its **Mint Cake**, an essential energy-boosting sweet in the backpack of serious walkers.

The fascinating **Kendal Museum** (*Station Road; open year-round Thu–Sat 10.30am-5pm, also Wed in summer. 01539 815 597; www.kendalmuseum. org.uk*) is a shrine to the doyen of Lake District walkers, Alfred Wainwright (1907–91), with his reconstructed office, plus displays on the Lakes' natural history, archaeology and geology.

Abbot Hall★ is an 18C country house, home to two excellent visitor attractions. Occupying the main house, the **Abbot Hall Art Gallery** (*open mid-Jan–mid-Dec Mon–Sat, 10.30am–5pm/4pm Nov–Mar; £6, joint ticket with museum £8; (charge). 01539 722 464; www. abbothall.org.uk*) features important changing exhibitions and works, paintings by George Romney (1734–1802) and a delightful coffee shop.

Set in the old stable block, the **Museum of Lakeland Life & Industry** (*open as art gallery; £5; www.lakelandmuseum.org.uk*) explores the story of the Lake District and its inhabitants before the arrival of the railway and motorcar, with re-created period rooms and workshops, and collections dealing with the Arts and Crafts movement, *Swallows and Amazons* author Arthur Ransome, and the Victorian period.

▶ *Take the A 591 and then the A 590 S.*

Levens Hall and Garden★

Open Apr–mid-Oct Sun–Thu 10am (noon house) to 4.30pm. £11.50. 015395 60321. www.levenshall.co.uk.
An Elizabethan manor has been added to a 13C pele tower to give the present graceful residence, notable for its outstanding carving and **plasterwork**. The dining room, covered in Cordova leather in 1692, has a magnificent set of Charles II walnut dining chairs. The **Topiary Gardens** are some of the oldest in the world, and unique in that the 1690 design has been preserved intact.

▶ *Take the A 590 W to Lindale and then minor roads (signed) to Cartmel and Furness Abbey (see South Cumbria Coast).*

South Cumbria Coast

The Furness Peninsula and the Cartmel Peninsula ("the Lake District Peninsulas") jut into Morecambe Bay and are a quiet, largely rural area. Compared to the national park, the South Cumbria coast receives very few visitors.

> ⏲ **Timing:** Allow a day.
> 🏞 **Don't Miss:** Holker Hall gardens.
> 👫 **Kids:** Cartmel Sticky Toffee Pudding.

CARTMEL PRIORY★

▶ *Cartmel, southern Cumbria, near Morecambe Bay.* ⏲*Open daily, 9am–5.30pm (3.30pm in winter). No visits during services.* 🚶*tours Apr–Oct Wed 11am, 2pm. £2.50.* ♿. ✆*015395 36261. www.cartmelpriory.org.uk.*
Cartmel Priory survived the Dissolution of the Monasteries and is the grandest medieval building (mostly 12C) in the Lake District. It has a curious double tower, one set diagonally upon the other. Inside there is a fine east window and, above the droll misericords in the choir, a beautifully carved screen (1620). The **Priory Gatehouse** (*NT; The Square;* ⏲ *open May–Sept, selected Suns, see website 2–5pm;* ✆*02524 701178; www.nationaltrust.org.uk*), and the 17C and 18C houses give the market square an urbane air.

HOLKER HALL & GARDENS

▶ *Cartmel, southern Cumbria, near Morecambe Bay.* ⏲*Open Apr–Oct Sun–Fri (Hall) 11am–4pm, (Gardens) 10.30am–5.30pm.* 🎟*£11.50. Gardens only, £7.50; Hall only, £7.* ♿🅿✕. ✆*015395 58328. www.holker.co.uk.*
One of the finest country estates in Cumbria, Holker Hall lies in a glorious setting (on land once owned by Cartmel Priory) with gardens that merge into parkland, framed by the Lakeland Hills. The home of the Cavendish family for over 400 years, the present house was built in 1838–42 and according to Pevsner was "the grandest of its date in Lancashire". The award-winning gardens are a succesful mix of formal and informal.

ULVERSTON

▶ *12 mi west of Cartmel.*
ℹ*County Square.* ✆*01229 587 120.*
This attractive old-fashioned market town of grey limestone cottages and cobbled lanes owes its wealth to the cotton, tanning and iron-ore industries which once flourished nearby. Stan Laurel (of Laurel and Hardy fame) was born here in 1890, and the town celebrates the duo in the enjoyable **Laurel and Hardy Museum** (*Brogden Street;* ⏲ *open year-round daily 10am–5pm/Thu, Sat, Sun only Jan.* 🎟*£4;* ✆*01229 582 292;www.laurel-and-hardy.co.uk.*

FURNESS ABBEY

▶ *Barrow-in-Furness, 19mi southwest of Cartmel. EH.* ⏲*Open Apr –Aug daily 10am–5pm;Sept Thu–Mon 10am –5pm; Oct–Mar Sat–Sun 10am–4pm.* ⏲*Closed 1 Jan, 24–30 Dec.* 🎟*£3.80.* 🅿✕. ✆*01229 823 420. www.english-heritage.org.uk.*
The impressive remains of this abbey founded in 1123 by Stephen, Duke of Boulogne (later King of England), include much of the east end and west tower of the church, and the ornately decorated chapter house and cloister buildings. It is currently being rescued from sinking into the soft soil. There is an exhibition on the abbey's history.

Eden Valley and Penrith

The Eden Valley divides the Pennines from the Lake District and is close to both the borders of Scotland and the Yorkshire Dales. It is an area of dramatic landscapes and interesting market towns.

PENRITH

◐ *Northeast of Lake District, beside M6.*
This distinctive red-sandstone market town is the regional centre for the Eden Valley, at its most attractive in the old streets around the **Market Square**. In St Andrew's churchyard lies the **Giant's Grave**, the possible resting place of Owen, King of Cumbria in the 10C. It comprises two pre-Norman crosses and four Norse "hogback" tombstones. You can learn more about this, the town and the region, at the **Penrith and Eden Museum** *(Robinson's School, Middlegate;* ◔*open Apr–Oct Mon–Sat 10am–5pm. Sun 1–4.45pm.* ✆*01768 865105, www. eden.gov.uk/leisure-and-culture).*
Dalemain Mansion & Historic Gardens *(3mi/5km SW of Penrith;* ◔*house and garden open Apr–Sept Sun–Thu 11.15am–1pm and 1.30–4pm/3pm Oct; garden also open Nov–mid-Dec 11am– 3pm;* ☜*£9.50, garden in winter £3;* ✗*;* ✆*017684 86450, www.dalemain.com)* is the area's finest country house. Home to the same family since 1679, it is an intriguing mix of Medieval, Georgian and Tudor buildings and styles.

ULLSWATER★

◑ *9.5mi southwest of Penrith, in the Lake District.*
This is not only England's second-largest lake (after Windermere), but, in many people's eyes, also its most beautiful, twisting its way through spectacular scenery. To one side are mountains, most notably, **Helvellyn**. To the other is a gently curving shoreline of green fields and woodlands, which provided the inspiration for William Wordsworth's famous *Daffodils*.

 ℹ Info: ✆*01768 867 466.*
www.visiteden.co.uk;
www.golakes.co.uk.

Ullswater Steamers *(*✆*017684 82229) www.ullswater-steamers.co.uk)* offers cruises from 35 minutes *(*☜*single journey £5.80)* to round-the-lake day passes *(*☜*£12.70),* departing from Glenridding Pier at the lake's southern tip.

APPLEBY-IN-WESTMORELAND

◑ *15.5mi southeast of Penrith.*
ℹ*Moot Hall, Boroughgate.* ✆*017683 51177.*
The former county town has a broad handsome main street, Boroughgate, shaded by ancient lime trees, which runs from High Cross to Low Cross. At the lower end of the street sits the **12C Church of St Lawrence**, (rebuilt in the 17C) while the sturdy Norman keep of **Appleby Castle** (o━ closed to the public) guards the top of the hill. Halfway along Boroughgate is a picturesque courtyard of **almshouses** built in 1651. In between, the street's architectural styles vary from the Jacobean to Georgian and Victorian.
In the first week of June the **Appleby Horse Fair** is the UK's largest annual gathering of Gypsies and Travellers, attracting around 50,000 to the town.

ALSTON

◑ *20.8 mi northeast of Penrith.* **ℹ***Town Hall, Front Street.* ✆*01434 382 244.*
The highest market town in England, Alston sits at the junction of several trans-Pennine routes; its steep cobbled streets, hidden courtyards and quaint shops invite exploration. Although it's hard to imagine today, 250 years ago this was one of the richest lead mining areas in the country. At the **Nenthead Mines Heritage Centre** *(Nenthead, 4.5mi/7.2km E;* ◔*open daily 10.30am– 5pm;* ✆*01434 382 294; www.npht.com)* you can see reminders of the area's halcyon days. Call ahead and enquire about underground tours *(*☜*£7).*

Carlisle★

Cumbria

The centre of Carlisle is marked by the Market Cross, which stands on the site of the Forum of Luguvalium, founded by the Romans, whose occupation lasted 400 years. The following 500 years of decline and border warfare did not encourage the inhabitants to build grandly or for posterity. The Guildhall (1407) is a rare timber-framed survivor.

CITY
Cathedral★

◷Open year-round daily 7.30am–6.15pm (Sun 5pm). ⊗£2 contribution requested. ♿🅿✕ (Mon–Sat). ☎01228 548 151. www.carlislecathedral.org.uk.
Henry I created the See of Carlisle in 1133, though all that remains of the original Norman building is the truncated nave and the south transept. New work was begun in 1225 and includes the Decorated east window, a fine example of tracery, containing much original 14C glass, and the choir, with its set of sculptured capitals. In the choir, too, is a magnificent **painted ceiling**★, completed in 1360, featuring golden suns and stars on a blue ground. The 16C Brougham Triptych in the north transept is a masterpiece of Flemish craftsmanship.

Tullie House Museum and Art Gallery

Castle Street. ◷Open year-round Mon–Sat 10am–5pm, Sun 11am (Nov–Mar noon–5pm. ◷Closed 1 Jan, 5–26 Dec. ⊗£5.20. ♿✕. ☎01228 618 718. www.tulliehouse.co.uk.
The original house, which dates from 1689 and contains its original oak staircase, has been extended to house the local museum, which presents the long and often turbulent history of the border town through well-presented and lively displays, including Roman occupation, Hadrian's Wall, border *Reivers* (raiders) and the Civil War siege.

▸ **Population:** 72,439.
🖰 **Michelin Map:** Michelin Atlas p44 or Map 502 L 19 – Local map Hadrian's Wall.
🈑 **Info:** Old Town Hall. ☎01228 625 600. www.discovercarlisle.co.uk.
▶ **Location:** 13mi/21km northeast of Calbeck, on the northwest tip of the Lake District and 10mi/16km south of the Scottish border. The compact town centre lies between Town Hall Square and the castle; get your bearings from the view from the ramparts.
☺ **Don't Miss:** The painted ceiling of the choir in the cathedral.

Carlisle Castle

EH. ◷Open Apr–Sept daily 9.30am–5pm. Oct daily 10am–4pm. Nov–Mar Sat–Sun 10am–4pm ◷Closed 1 Jan, and 24–30 Dec. ⊗£5. ☎01228 591 922. www.english-heritage.org.uk.
Established by William II in 1092, the castle served to block the passage of Scots raiders. Opposite the entrance to the keep is the shell of the medieval hall, now home to the Museum of the King's Own Royal Border Regiment *(scheduled to move to another part of the castle late-2012)*. All that remains of the original tower, in which Mary Queen of Scots was once held, is the staircase to the east of the museum building.

Church of St Cuthbert with St Mary

Church: ◷Open year-round daily, dawn–dusk. *Tithe barn:* ◷Open most mornings. ☎01228 521 982. www.stcuthbertscarlisle.org.uk.
The galleried church dates from 1779. Its unique moving pulpit was installed in 1905 to enable the preacher to speak to the galleries. The adjacent **tithe Barn**★(115ft/35m long) was built c.1480.

ADDRESSES

🏠 STAY

WINDERMERE

▢–▢▢ **The Coach House** – *Lake Road.* ☎*015394 44494. www.lakedistrictbandb. com/coach-house.htm.* 🅿. *2 rms.* The unusual contemporary décor is the draw at this late–19C coachhouse cottage, a 10-minute walk from both Windermere and Bowness. A pretty patio looks onto woods.

▢▢ **The Ravensworth** – *Ambleside Road.* ☎*01539 443 747. www.theravensworth. com.* 🅿. *14 rms.* A mile from the lake, this elegant, detached, 1850s-built Lakeland stone residence is a haven of tranquillity with smart modern rooms and a lovely garden terrace. Local five-star spa and wellness privileges offered. Good value.

BOWNESS-ON-WINDERMERE

▢▢ **Laurel Cottage** – *St Martins Square, Kendal Road.* ☎*015394 5594. www.laurel cottage-bnb.co.uk.* 🅿. *4 rms.* This charming 17C cottage is in the heart of Bowness, just a few yards' walk from the lake. Local five-star spa and wellness privileges offered.

CONISTON

▢▢ **Wheelgate Country Guest House** – *Little Arrow.* ☎*015394 41418. www.wheelgate.co.uk.* 🅿. *5 rms.* This charming 17C farmhouse cottage is surrounded by lovely gardens. Free use of local country club facilities.

GRASMERE

▢▢ **Lake View Country House** – *Lakeview Drive.* ☎*015394 35384. www. lakeview-grasmere.com.* 🅿. *4 rms.* Perfectly located at the end of a private lane in Grasmere and within easy walking of the centre, Lake View sits in beautiful open gardens offering stylish traditional rooms.

▢▢▢▢ **Swan Hotel** – *Keswick Road.* ☎*0844 879 9120. www.macdonaldhotels. co.uk/swan.* 🅿. *38 rms.* Built in 1650 as a coaching inn, the Swan is one of the oldest hotels in the Lakes. Cosy, spacious traditional rooms. Access to spa and leisure facilities.

AMBLESIDE

▢▢–▢▢▢ **Drunken Duck Inn** – *Barngates.* ☎*015394 36347. www.drunken duckinn.co.uk.* 🅿. *16 rms.* This splendid modernised family-owned and -run pub, with an acclaimed restaurant, offers lovely trad-modern rooms, a glorious garden and full use of Langdale Spa and Leisure Club. Terrific value during the week.

▢▢–▢▢▢ **The Old Vicarage** – *Vicarage Road.* ☎*015394 33364. www.old vicarageambleside.co.uk.* 🅿. *10 rms.* 🛏 (▢). This beautiful Victorian vicararge, a two-minute walk from town, has its own swimming pool and hot tub, sauna, guest lounge and extensive terrace. Good value.

▢▢▢▢ **Linthwaite House** – *Crook Road.* ☎*015394 88600. www.linthwaite.com.* 🅿. *30 rms. Condé Nast Traveller* recently put this late-19C romantic country house hotel on its Gold List. Its superior luxurious trad-modern rooms are full of character with superb bathrooms. Breathtaking views of Lake Windermere.

KESWICK

▢▢▢▢ **Highfield Hotel** – *The Heads.* ☎*01768 772 508. www.highfieldkeswick. co.uk.* 🅿. *18 rms.* This splendid Victorian hotel is a local landmark with its towers, balconies and veranda. Rooms are large and traditional with modern styling; the gardens are glorious with wonderful views over the lakes and mountains. The tariff includes a four-course dinner in the award-winning restaurant.

WASDALE HEAD

▢▢▢ **Wasdale Head Inn** – *Near Gosforth.* ☎*01946 726 229. www.wasdale.com.* 🅿. *12 rms.* This traditional old pub is a legend among local climbers ("the birthplace of British climbing") who come to ascend Scafell, England's highest mountain. Traditionally decorated modest rooms and award-winning dining await.

BUTTERMERE

▢▢ **Wood House** – ☎*01768 770 208 - www.wdhse.co.uk.* 🅿. The setting of this quiet tastefully traditional luxurious guesthouse may be unsurpassed in the Lakes, with fabulous views. Dinner also available.

CARTMEL

▢▢▢ **Aynsome Manor Hotel** – ☎*015395 36653. www.aynsomemanorhotel. co.uk.* 🅿. *12 rms.* This charming old manor house offers a warm welcome, traditionally styled bedrooms and serves excellent dinners.

GRANGE-OVER-SANDS

◒◒◚◚ **Netherwood & Spa** – *Lindale Road.* ☏*015395 32552. www. netherwood-hotel.co.uk.* 🅿. *36 rms.* Set in extensive grounds overlooking spectacular Morecambe Bay, this large dramatic stately 19C residence sits in beautiful gardens facing Morecambe Bay. Traditional cosy rooms, most with bay views. Its spa facilities are first class.

ULLSWATER

◒◒◚◚ **Leeming House** – *Watermillock.* ☏*0844 879 9142. www.macdonaldhotels.co.uk/leeminghouse.* 🅿. *41 rms.* Set in 22 acres/9ha of grand landscaped gardens (including a croquet lawn) and woodland, this 200-year-old luxury country house hotel boasts direct access to the shores of Ullswater and private fishing.

PENRITH

◒◒ **Hornby Hall Country Hall** – *Brougham.* ☏*01768 891 114. www.hornby hall.co.uk.* 🅿. *7 rms.* This lovely red sandstone Tudor farmhouse off the beaten track retains some of its orignal features.

🍴 EAT

WINDERMERE

◒ **The Lighthouse** – *Main Road.* ☏*015394 88260. www.thelighthouse-restaurant.com.* Set in a handsome Victorian building with fine views from its middle floor, and with a pavement terrace below, this is a good place for a drink and light lunch.

◒◒ **Jericho's** – *College Road.* ☏*015394 42522. www.jerichos.co.uk.* Convivial modern restaurant offering regional produce.

◒◒◚ **Miller Howe** – *Rayrigg Road.* ☏*015394 42536. www.millerhowe.com.* Gourmet cuisine served in a magnificent setting with views of the lakes and mountains. Relaxed.

BOWNESS-ON-WINDERMERE

◒ **Bodega Bar & Tapas** – *Ash Street.* ☏*015394 46825.* This cosy but stylish little place features leather chairs and stripped wooden floors serving tapas until around 10pm, then turning into a party bar later on.

◒◒ **China Boat Restaurant** – *Church Street.* ☏*015394 46326. www. chinaboat.co.uk. Closed Sun winter.*

This was the first Chinese restaurant to open in the Lakes, in 1984, and is still one of the very best.

◒◒–◒◒◚ **The Postilion Restaurant** – *Ash Street.* ☏*015394 45852. www.postilion restaurant.co.uk.* Very stylish restaurant (with separate lounge bar), serving Modern British cuisine. Excellent–value prix-fixe dinner menu.

HAWKSHEAD

◒◒ **Queen's Head Hotel** – *Main Street.* ☏*015394 36271. www.queensheadhotel. co.uk.* This early-17C flag-stone floored, oak-beamed inn serves traditional and Modern British dishes with an emphasis on locally sourced ingredients.

GRASMERE

◒◒ **The Traveller's Rest Inn** – *Keswick Road.* ☏*015394 35604. www.lakedistrictinns. co.uk.* This traditional 16C Lakeland inn is full of character with oak beams and inglenooks, roaring log fires in winter and beer gardens with panoramic views in summer. Traditional favourites and local specialities are on the menu.

AMBLESIDE

◒◒ **Glass House** – *Rydal Road.* ☏*015394 32137. www.theglasshouserestaurant.co.uk.* This beautifully restored, former cloth- and saw-mill, dating from the 15C, now features large glass windows and mezzanine floor. The creative cuisine matches the place with modern and traditional British dishes.

KESWICK

◒ **Lakeland Spice** – *81 Main Street.* ☏*01768 780 005.* This very popular Indian restaurant serves up some of the best curries in the Lake District.

CARTMEL

◒◒◚◚ **L'Enclume** – *Cavendish Street.* ☏*015395 36362. www.lenclume.co.uk Closed Mon–Wed lunch.* Nouvelle cuisine under the supervision of clef Simon Rogan. Reservation required.

ULLSWATER

◒ **The Pooley Bridge** – *Pooley Bridge.* ☏*01768 486 215. www.pooleybridgeinn. co.uk.* This fine old pub with a large traditional bar and original timber ceiling offers open fires in winter and courtyard dining in summer. Superior pub food and a selection of real ales to wash it down.

YORKSHIRE

The largest county in the UK, Yorkshire arouses fierce patriotism among its natives, who affectionately call it "God's own country". For walkers, the thought of the Dales and Moors is a heavenly, if often damp, prospect; fashionistas love Leeds; Goths flock to Whitby; lovers of film and curry beat a path to Bradford; while genteel tourists enjoy a nice cup of tea in Harrogate and Richmond. But no trip to the county is complete without York itself, where the glory of the minster may convince you that God may indeed reside here.

Highlights

1 Choose your weapons at the **Royal Armouries**, Leeds (p383)

2 Combine art and history at atmospheric **Saltaire** (p387)

3 Picnic in the perfect setting of **Fountains Abbey** (p392)

4 Marvelling at the stained glass (and other treasures) in **York Minster** (p397)

5 Train spotting in the **National Railway Museum**, York (p401)

South and West Yorkshire

This traditional coal, steel and textile manufacturing region has long ceased to be an industrial powerhouse and finished the 20C on a low note. However, within the last decade or so its three major cities, Sheffield, Leeds and Bradford, have successfully augmented and revitalised their museums and other visitor attractions, in addition to investing in other major leisure and retail facilities. Industrial heritage is of course key to many visitor attractions, with the UNESCO-listed Saltaire millworkers' village being the prime example. Art, literary and media history are also important. Sheffield and Leeds are particularly strong on 20C art and Bradford is the home of the National Media Museum. Nearby, the Brontë sisters "shrine" of Haworth is an evergreen with visitors.

Yorkshire Dales

In terms of popular imagery, it is the Dales (valleys) of North Yorkshire that most visitors think of when the county's name is mentioned. This unspoiled region is famous for its glorious rolling countryside, perfect for walkers; its attractive patchwork of stone villages,

home to local brewers and cheesemakers; its many romantic religious ruins such as Fountains Abbey (Yorkshire boasted more religious Pre-Reformation establishments than any other English county); charmingly old-fashioned market towns such as Ripon, Masham and Richmond, and the genteel spa of Harrogate. The stately homes of Harewood House, Newby Hall and, above all, grandiose romantic Castle Howard, reflect the great historic wealth of the region.

York

The city of York is without doubt the county's main attraction. Once the second city of the kingdom, it boasts within its ancient compact centre a wealth of historical monuments, museums (particularly its magnificent Railway Museum) and superbly interpreted Roman, Viking and Georgian visitor attractions, that is unrivalled outside London.

North and East Yorkshire

By contrast with York, which in summer fairly teems with visitors, the North Yorkshire Moors and East Yorkshire are mostly unchartered territory. Like York, Beverley has a majestic soaring Minster and Hull boasts a world-class aquarium, while the main attraction of the Moors is its very wildness, punctuated only by long-deserted romantic ruins and villages offering shelter to walkers. The coast however has been popular, despite lack of clement weather, since Victorian times. And, while the fortunes of Scarborough and Bridlington have waned, visitors who make it to Whitby, in the far northeastern corner of the county, are rewarded by one of England's most intriguing resorts, rich in atmosphere and history. Close by, Robin Hood's Bay is another spot which has retained its charm.

Food Heroes

Yorkshire is synonymous with the famous **Yorkshire pudding** (batter), which originated here, and is the staple accompaniment to roast beef. Like the Yorkshire pudding, the term **York ham** is unprotected, and has been copied worldwide by vastly inferior products. You can try the real thing, however, from Ye Olde Pie & Sausage Shoppe *(www.yorksausageshop.co.uk)* in The Shambles.

From the Yorkshire Dales comes the county's most famous cheese, crumbly **Wensleydale** from Hawes. At the Wensleydale Creamery *(www.wensleydale. co.uk)* you can see how it is made and visit their museum, shop, café and restaurant. Artisan cheesemakers, **Shepherds Purse** *(www.shepherdspurse. co.uk)* produce a wide range of local cheeses including blue varieties.

Two excellent shops in **York** that champion local producers are The Yorkshire Pantry *(www.theyorkshirepantry.com)*, stocking exclusively Yorkshire fare, and de'Clare Deli *(http://declaredeli.co.uk)*, which also has a café and offers takeaway food. Elsewhere, **Castle Howard** boasts the award-winning Yorkshire Farm Shop.

Sweet local treats such as **Yorkshire parkin**, a rich, dark loaf made with black treacle, oatmeal and ground ginger; **fat rascals**, which are fruit scones made with almonds, vine fruit, cherries and citrus peel; and **Yorkshire curd tart**, a sweet pastry base covered in a layer of lemon curd and filled with fresh curd cheese, nutmeg and currants; are all best sampled at Betty's Tea Rooms *(www.bettys.co.uk)*. You can keep it local with a cup of Yorkshire tea by Taylor's of Harrogate. Betty's is a Yorkshire food institution in its own right. Alongside their beautiful original café in Harrogate (est 1919) are two more café-tearooms in York and three other branches in the county.

Haver bread, sometimes known as clapbread, is made from fermented oatmeal and milk.

Old Peculiar Cake, made with Theakston's Old Peculiar Ale is just one of the many rich fruit cakes baked in the area. They occasionally take their names from towns such as Ripon and Batley. You may be offered High Tea at dinnertime in Yorkshire, which is made up of a main meal, followed by cakes and tea.

Whitby is a picturesque resort that has retained its fishing fleet, and its Magpie Café *(www.magpiecafe.co.uk)* is reckoned by many to serve the best fish and chips (eat-in or take-away) in Britain. Its sit-down menu offers specialities such as **Lindisfarne oysters**, **Whitby crab** and **Whitby kippers**. The last can be bought exclusively from the rustic shop and smokehouse of Fortune Kippers *(www. fortuneskippers.co.uk)* (est 1872), nestling below Whitby Abbey ruins.

Fish and chips is a popular dish nationwide, but Yorkshire has many of the best fish and chip shops you could find anywhere in the country, with the famous **Harry Ramsden**'s shop and restaurant at Guisley pumping out decent fare for the masses, even if it is somewhat jaded by its fame.

Yorkshire has a wide choice of good beers. The perfect place to see them being made is the village of **Masham**, which has two small traditional breweries offering tours. The official visitor website for Yorkshire offers both ale and tea trails (www.yorkshire.com/delicious).

Bilberries grow in the wild in Yorkshire and you may find them served up in pies, crumbles and pancakes among other desserts.

York Food and Drink Festival *(www.yorkfoodfestival.com)* takes places over 10 days in late September.

Sheffield

and around

The fourth-largest provincial city in England, Sheffield has been known since the 14C for the production of steel and fine cutlery. Today it remains an important manufacturing centre and the commercial and cultural focus of a wide region, with revitalised art galleries, and excellent nightlife and shopping.

▶ **Population:** 431,607.

Michelin Map: Michelin Atlas p35 or Map 502 P 23 – Local map Peak District.

Info: 14 Norfolk Row. ℘0114 221 1900. www.welcometo sheffield.co.uk.

Location: Sheffield is 54mi/86km south of York.

Kids: Weston Park; Magna.

CITY
Millennium Galleries

Arundel Gate. Open Mon–Sat 10am–5pm, Sun 11am–4pm. Charge for temporary exhibitions only. Closed 1 Jan, 24–26 Dec. ℘0114 278 2600. *www.museums-sheffield.org.uk.*

This is the cultural heart of the post-Millennium city, showcasing its heritage alongside contemporary art and design exhibitions. A light, spacious glass-and-white-concrete building is home to four galleries, featuring: craft and design; the Ruskin Gallery with over 900 paintings, watercolours and drawings; metalwork; and world-class touring exhibitions. Adjacent is the **Winter Garden**★ (*open Mon–Sat 8am–11pm, Sun 8am–8pm; www.sheffield.gov.uk)*, one of the largest temperate glasshouses to be built in the UK during the last century, 230ft/70m long and 72ft/22m high, it is home to 2,500 plants from around the world and is a stunning green oasis in the heart of the city. A few yards away, along Pinstone Street, the **Peace Gardens**, featuring eight large water features, are another new award-winning initiative.

Graves Gallery

Surrey Street. Open year-round Wed–Fri 10am–3pm, Sat (and school summer hols) 11am–3pm. Other details as Millennium Galleries (see above).

This attractive suite of galleries features an acclaimed holding of 19C and 20C British and European art, including works by famous names, from Pablo Picasso and Pierre Bonnard to Stanley Spencer and Helen Chadwick.

Kelham Island Museum

Alma Street. Open Mon–Thu 10am–4pm, Sun 11am–4.45pm. £4.50. ℘0114 272 2106. www.simt.co.uk.

Located in one of the city's oldest industrial districts, the museum stands on a 900-year-old man-made island and sets the tone by welcoming visitors with a giant Bessemer converter (used to make steel from iron). Interactive galleries tell the metalworking story of the city from the Industrial Revolution onwards.

Weston Park Museum

Western Bank. 1mi/1.6km from centre. All details same as Millennium Galleries (see above).

This eclectic gallery showcases the city's varied and unusual treasures in a lively populist style, with lots of hands-on exhibits, ranging from Egyptian Mummies to living ants and bees.

EXCURSION
Magna Science Adventure Centre

Sheffield Road, Rotherham. 9mi/14km NE. Open Sept–Mar Tue–Sun 10am–5pm. £10.95, child £8.95 (save 10 percent online). ℘01709 720 002. www.visitmagna.co.uk.

This spectacular interactive discovery centre is housed within a former steelworks with atmospheric lighting and sound and multimedia effects used to evoke the old furnace environment. Exhibits are themed Air, Earth, Fire and Water and there are huge indoor and outdoor play areas.

Leeds★

and around

Set in the heart of northern England, Leeds is one of Britain's great Victorian cities; its population multiplied tenfold between 1800 and 1900 and it ranks third in size among England's provincial cities. Moreover, it is Britain's fastest-growing metropolis. Its docklands area, derelict less than two decades ago, is now thriving and home to a vast array of restaurants, pubs and shops. Heavy industry has been replaced by light engineering and offices, and clothing manufacture by retailers; the precincts and arcades attract shoppers from all over the North. The rich cultural life of this provincial capital ranges from acclaimed opera to the fashionable nightclubs, which bring in multitudes of weekend revellers.

▸ **Population:** 424,194.

◔ **Michelin Map:** Michelin Atlas p40 or Map 502 P 22.

🛈 **Info:** The Arcade, Leeds City train station. ℘0113 242 5242. www.leedslive itloveit.com; www.leeds. gov.uk.

◗ **Location:** 25mi/40km southwest of York. The train and bus stations are in the centre of town.

👪 **Kids:** Royal Armouries Museum. National Coal Mining Museum.

ROYAL ARMOURIES MUSEUM★★★

Armouries Drive. ◔*Open daily 10am–5pm.* ◔*Closed 24–26 Dec.* ✆*Free, but charge for events.* ℘*0113 220 1999 (info-line).* ◔✕. *www.royalarmouries.org*

This purpose-built multi-million-pound citadel in glass, grey brick and marble was inaugurated in 1996 to provide a worthy setting for over 8,500 objects from the superlative collection of weaponry formerly housed in the Tower of London. The quality of the exhibits is matched by an array of advanced and imaginative display techniques which set the items in their context and encourage visitor participation: interactive computers and video screens chatter and hum, and live demonstrations provide movement and drama. A splendid central space, the **Street**, rises between the six floors of the main part of the building to the glazed roof. It terminates in a glazed keep, known as the **Hall of Steel** (over 100ft/30m high), its interior walls hung with a stunning assortment of weaponry arranged in decorative patterns. Five spacious galleries are devoted to War, Hunting, the Tournament, Self Defence and to Oriental Weaponry. The countless treasures include a grotesque grinning face-mask presented to Emperor Maximilian (the museum's emblem), gorgeously inlaid sporting guns, a set of Japanese armour presented to King James I in 1614 and a near-complete set of elephant armour. Among the curiosities is a tiny cyclist's revolver designed to discourage dogs and a monumentally unwieldy punt gun once used by wildfowlers to fell dozens of ducks at a single discharge.

The **Tiltyard**, the first to be built in Britain for hundreds of years, is the setting for thrilling performances of jousting and combat of all kinds.

🎧 WALKING TOUR

Town Hall and Victoria Square

The town hall was the winning design in a competition in 1853. External Corinthian columns, the Baroque tower (225ft/69m) and the splendour of the interior made it a symbol of civic pride when opened by Queen Victoria in 1858. On fine days, chess enthusiasts can be seen playing "Giant Chess" on the boards marked out in Victoria Square.

Leeds Art Gallery★

The Headrow. ◔*Open 10am–5pm (Wed open noon, Sun 1pm).* ◔✕. ℘*0113 247 8256. www.leeds.gov.uk/artGallery*

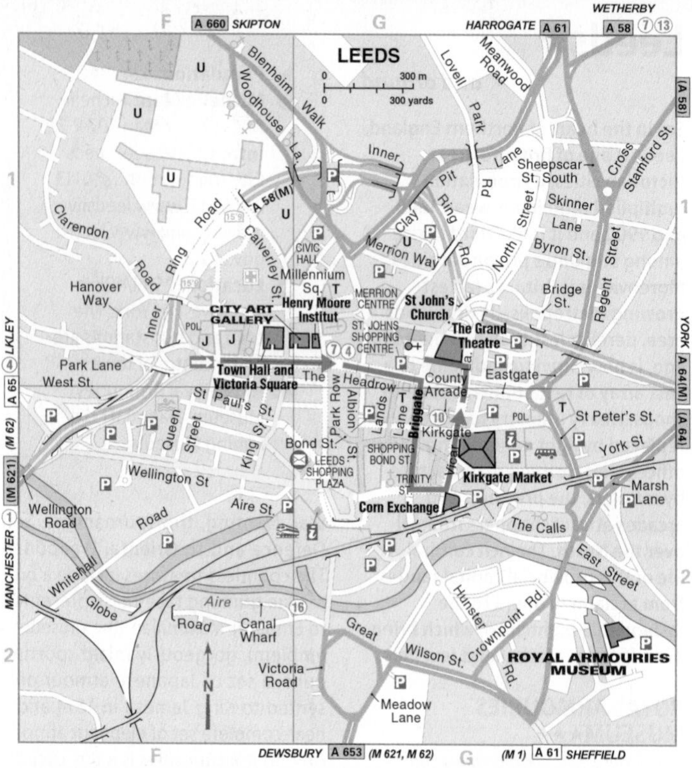

LEEDS

(map with the following labels:)

A 660 SKIPTON — F — G — HARROGATE — A 61 — WETHERBY — A 58 — 7 13

Blenheim Walk — Woodhouse La. — Meanwood Road — Lovell Park — Inner — Lane — Pit — Sheepscar St. South — Skinner Lane — Cross — Stamford Street — A 58(M)

Clarendon — Ring Road — Calverley St. — Clay — Merrion Way — Byron St. — North Street — Regent Street

CIVIC HALL — Millennium Sq. — MERRION CENTRE — ST. JOHNS SHOPPING CENTRE — St John's Church — Bridge St.

Hanover Way — Inner — Ring — Road — CITY ART GALLERY — Henry Moore Institut — The Grand Theatre — Eastgate

Park Lane — West St. — Town Hall and Victoria Square — The Headrow — County Arcade — POL. — St Peter's St. — York St.

St Paul's St. — Albion St. — Park Row — Lands — Bridgate — Kirkgate — Kirkgate Market — Marsh Lane

Queen Street — King Street — Bond St. — LEEDS SHOPPING PLAZA — SHOPPING BOND ST. — TRINITY ST.

Wellington St. — Wellington Road — Aire St. — Corn Exchange — The Calls — East Street

Whitehall Road — Globe Road — Aire — Canal Wharf — Great — Hunslet — Wilson St. — Crownpoint Rd. — ROYAL ARMOURIES MUSEUM

N — Victoria Road — Meadow Lane

DEWSBURY — A 653 — (M 621, M 62) — F — G — (M 1) — A 61 SHEFFIELD

IKLEY — A 65 — MANCHESTER — (M 62) — (M 621) — YORK — A 64(M) — A 64 — A 58(M)

300 m / 300 yards

WHERE TO STAY

Holyday Inn Express City Centre	4
Radisson Blu	7

WHERE TO EAT

Ancestor Pub	1
Browns	4
Erawan Restaurant	7
Harvey Nichols	10
Rico's of Oakwood	13
Simply Heathcotes	16

This is one of the best provincial galleries in Britain, with international-class permanent and temporary exhibitions. Its strength lies in its collection of **19C and 20C British art**, particularly of the early–mid-20C, virtually all major artists of the period being represented. The dominance of British art is relieved by French paintings: a Courbet, several Impressionists and a brilliant Derain of 1905, *Barges on the Thames*. The greatest British sculptor of the 20C, **Henry Moore** (1898–1986), was a Yorkshireman; the range of his achievement, from exquisite small-scale studies to the *Reclining Figure* of 1929 and the powerful post-war *Meat Porters*, is shown in the gallery and at the neighbouring

Henry Moore Institute (✆*open daily 10am –5.30pm/Wed 9pm; ☏ 0113 246 7467; www.henry-moore.org/hmi). The gallery's magnificent Victorian **Tiled Hall** restaurant, with its grand marble columns, ornate tiles, barrel-vaulted mosaic ceiling and original parquet flooring, is alone worth a visit.

St John's Church

✆*Open Tue–Sat 9.30am–5.30pm. ☏ 0113 244 1689.*
The oldest church in central Leeds. Sensitive restoration in 1868 revived its 1630s incarnation.

Leeds City Museum

Millennium Square. ✆*Open bank hol*

*Mons & Tue–Fri 10am–5pm (7pm Wed).
Sat–Sun 11pm–5pm.* ◐*Closed 1 Jan,
25–26 Dec.* &✕. *℘0113 224 3732.
www.leeds.gov.uk/citymuseum.*
Occupying the beautiful old Civic Theatre building and established in 2008, this bright colourful eclectic museum has galleries devoted to Africa, Life on Earth, Ancient Worlds, and The Leeds Story.

EXCURSIONS
Kirkstall Abbey and Abbey House Museum★
▶ *3.5mi/5.6km NW on the A 65.*
Abbey ruins and visitor centre:
◐*Open Apr–Sept Tue–Fri and bank
hol Mon 10am–4pm (Sat–Sun 5pm).
Oct–Mar Tue–Thu 11am–3pm, Sat–Sun
11am–4pm. **Abbey House Museum:***
◐*Open Tue–Fri, Sun and bank hol Mon
10am–5pm, Sat noon–5pm,* &🄿✕.
◐*Visitor centre and ruins free, museum
£3.50. ℘0113 230 5492. www.leeds.gov.
uk/kirkstallabbey.*
Kirkstall was a traditional Cistercian abbey, started in 1152. The austere ruins, which still stand almost to roof height, are dominated by the 16C crossing tower. Across the busy road the former abbey gatehouse is now the **Abbey House Museum**, which re-creates the sights and sounds of life in Victorian Leeds in the year 1880.

Temple Newsam★
▶ *Temple Newsam Road. Near
Whitkirk, 4mi/6km E on the A 63.*
Visitor centre: ◐*Open Tue–Sun and
bank hols 10.30am–5pm (4pm winter).
House and farm:* ◐*Open Tue–Sun &
bank hols (farm also open Mon in school
hols) 10am/10.30am–5pm (4pm winter).*
◐*House £3.70, farm £3.30,/joint £6.*
&🄿*£3.70.* ✕. *℘0113 264 7321.
www.leeds.gov.uk/templenewsam.*
Set within over 1,500 acres/600ha of parkland, woodland and farmland landscaped by Capability Brown in the 18C, this magnificent Tudor–Jacobean mansion was the birthplace of Lord Darnley, husband of Mary Queen of Scots. The brick house, begun in the late-15C and rebuilt in the first part of the 17C, is an attractive setting for a collection of Eng-

lish, European and Oriental **decorative arts★** and for many of the Old Master paintings owned by the City of Leeds. The Home Farm includes re-created workshops, exhibitions and rare breeds of livestock, housed in original buildings.

Nostell Priory★
NT. ▶ *Doncaster Road, Nostell, nr
Wakefield, 18mi/29km SE by the A 61
and A 638. **House:*** ◐*Open late Feb/
Mar–Oct Wed–Sun and bank hols
11am–5pm; open first two weeks Dec,
see website.* ◐*Guided tours 11.15am,
11.30am, 11.45am, 12.15pm.* ◐*£8.50.*
&🄿✕. *℘01924 863 892.
www.nationaltrust.org.uk.*
This Palladian mansion was begun in 1733 by James Paine, then only 19 years old. **Robert Adam** was commissioned in 1765 to complete the State Rooms and they are among his finest interiors. **Thomas Chippendale**, once an apprentice on the estate, designed furniture especially for the house.

≗≗ National Coal Mining Museum for England
▶ *S of Leeds, 6mi/10km W of Wakefield
on the A 642.* ◐*Open daily.*
◐*Closed 1 Jan, 24–26 Dec.*
◐*Underground tours every 10min–
15mins. Book on arrival. During school
hols arrive early as tours are often fully
booked by noon. Advanced bookings
can only be made for tours at 1.30pm
and 3pm, on ℘01924 848 806 before
the day of the tour.* ◐*Tours free, £5.00
fee for booked tours.* &🄿✕. *℘01924
848 806. www.ncm.org.uk.*
Caphouse Colliery contributed significantly to Britain's industrial might until its closure in the 1980s. There are displays, exhibits and an array of old machinery around the pithead buildings, but the highlight of a visit is the donning of helmet and lamp, and the descent (460ft/140m) into the old workings in the company of a former miner.

Yorkshire Sculpture Park★
▶ *West Bretton. 20mi/32km S by the
M 1 to junction 38 and 1mi/1.6km N
off the A 637.* ◐*Open year-round daily*

10am–6pm (5pm Nov–Mar). ⊘*Closed 24–25 Dec.* ♿🅿*(£5).* ✕. ☏*01924 832 631. www.ysp.co.uk.*

Amid lovely parkland lies an outstanding array of modern sculpture, including works by the two most famous British sculptors of the 20C, Henry Moore and Barbara Hepworth (both were born in Yorkshire and both attended Leeds School of Art). An indoor gallery and a fine café provide for wet days.

ADDRESSES

🍴 PUBS/🍷 RESTAURANTS

⊘ Leeds Waterfront, once derelict, is now home to a vast array of restaurants, pubs and shops. The Exchange Quarter along Call Lane and Granary Wharf are also good areas for fashionable cafés, bars and dining.

🛒 SHOPPING

Many of the main high street stores are to be found in **Briggate**, and the elegant **Victoria Quarter**, which boasted the first Harvey Nichols store outside London. For handmade goods head for **Granary Wharf**. For something special or eclectic pay a visit to the **Corn Exchange**, a striking building which has over 50

places to shop, eat and drink. Another splendid historic city centre showpiece building is **Kirkgate Market** (Leeds City Markets); with 800 stalls, it is said to be the largest covered market in Europe.

🎭 ENTERTAINMENT

⊘ Leeds is renowned for its vibrant club culture. If you are in search of more laid-back nightspots, try: **The Wardrobe** (www.thewardrobe. co.uk) with an eclectic programme; the **Hi Fi Club** (www.thehificlub.co.uk), a subterranean bar/club close to Call Lane with DJ-led and live music nights based around jazz, funk, soul and hip hop. They also run a popular comedy night every Saturday.

The **City Varieties Music Hall** (www. cityvarieties.co.uk),the **West Yorkshire Playhouse** (www.wyp.org.uk) and the **Grand Theatre and Opera House** (www.leedsgrandtheatre.com) are the main performing arts venues. Outdoor opera, ballet, pop, jazz and classical music concerts are held in the summer. Leeds also hosts an International Film Festival (www.leedsfilm.com), an International Concert Season (www.leedsconcertseason. com) and an International Pianoforte Competition (www.leedspiano.com). For listings buy a copy of the monthly *Leeds Guide* or read it online (www.leedsguide.co.uk).

Bradford★

West Yorkshire

Bradford prospered through the wool trade and by 1500 it was a bustling market town "which already standeth much by clothing". By 1850 there were 120 mills and Bradford had become the world's capital for worsted (cloth). Among its famous sons are the author J B Priestley (1894–1984), composer Frederick Delius (1862–1934) and the contemporary painter David Hockney (b.1937). The Bradford of today is essentially a Victorian city, but also a UNESCO City of Film. It boasts a large South Asian population, and has become Britain's curry capital, famed for the quantity and

> ▶ **Population:** 289,376.
> ⚲ **Michelin Map:** Michelin Atlas p39 or Map 402 O 22.
> 🛈 **Info:** City Hall. ☏01274 433 678. www.visitbradford.com.
> ◐ **Location:** 9mi/14km west of Leeds. Bradford Interchange just south of the centre, off Bridge Street, is the terminus for buses and trains.
> ◷ **Timing:** Allow one day.
> 👥 **Kids:** The National Media Museum.

quality of its restaurants. The Bradford Mela, now the city's principal festival, is a British-Asian cultural celebration, held in June.

CITY
👥 National Media Museum★ 🔵

Prince's View. 🕐*Open year-round Tue–Sun 10am–6pm, summer daily 9.30am–6pm.* 📷*IMAX £7.75–£9.50, child £5.95–£7.25.* 🍴. 📞*0870 70 10 200. www.nationalmediamuseum.org.uk.*
Part of the same family as London's Science Museum, this lively modern museum is home to over 3.5 million items of historical significance which trace the history and practice of photography, the cinema, television and all new media. There is a huge IMAX cinema and conventional screenings showing arthouse and fringe films; film festivals are also staged

Wool Exchange
Market Street.
🕐*Open shopping hours.*
Built 1867 in grand Italianate/Gothic style, this was once the centre of the world's wool trade. The statues at the entrance are those of St Blaize, patron saint of wool combers, and of Edward III, who did much to encourage the wool industry.
It now houses shops and offices. In Waterstone's you can look up to see the original splendid hammerbeam roof and interior with more excellent interior views from Starbucks on the mezzanine floor.

Bradford Cathedral
1 Stott Hill. 🕐*Open Mon–Sat 9am–4.30pm. Sun for services only.*
♿. 📞*01274 777 720.*
www.bradfordcathedral.co.uk.
The battlemented exterior does not give the impression of a building which, in parts, dates back to the 1440s; the west tower with battlements and pinnacles dates from 1493. The chancel has some fine stained glass, c.1862, by William Morris, Rossetti and Burne-Jones.

Little Germany
Nr the cathedral.
This merchants' district, named after the booming mid-19C trade links with Germany, has been restored to show its fine Victorian architecture (1830–99).

EXCURSION
Saltaire★
🔵 *3mi/5km N.*
With its cobbled streets and honey-coloured stonework, Saltaire village was built as a model village in the 19C by mill owner and philanthropist Sir Titus Salt for the spiritual, physical and moral welfare of his workers. Thanks to its outstanding state of preservation it has been designated a **UNESCO World Heritage Site**.
The vast imposing complex of **Salt's Mill** (🕐*open year-round Mon–Fri 10am–5.30pm, Sat–Sun 10am–6pm; top floor inc Cafe Opera open Wed–Sun;* 🕐*closed 25–26 Dec.*♿ 🅿 🍴; 📞*01274 531 163; www.saltsmill.org.uk*) is still the key feature of the village. **The 1853 Gallery★** is a beautiful space, showcasing the largest collection of art in Europe by **David Hockney**. A major contributor to Pop Art in the 1960s and still active today (in his 70s), Hockney was one of the most influential and is still probably the best-known British artist of his generation. He continues to contribute art to Salt's Mill, emailing his latest works (created on his iPad and iPhone), which are then projected onto the gallery walls.
There is a Saltaire history exhibition, several arty shops, and the building also makes a lovely setting for the Hockney designed **Cafe Opera restaurant** (🕐*open Wed–Sun*).

Salt's Mill by the River Aire

© Darrell Evans/Dreamstime.com

Haworth

North Yorkshire

Haworth (pronounced "HA-wuth") is a Yorkshire hill village, its dark, gritstone cottages crowded together on the edge of the Pennine moors. The long, steep main street is lined with souvenir shops and tearooms, all enjoying the benefits of association with the Brontë sisters, who lived in the parsonage at the top of the hill and wrote most of their stories there.

▸ **Population:** 4,956.
- **Michelin Map:** Michelin Atlas p39 or Map 502 O 22.
- **Info:** 2–4 West Lane. ℘01535 642 329. www.visitbradford. com/bronte-country.
- **Location:** 19mi/31km west of Leeds, 8mi/13km west of Bradford.

VILLAGE

Brontë Parsonage Museum★

Church Street. ◷*Open daily Apr–Sept 10am–5.30pm; Oct–early Jan and Feb–Mar daily 11am–5pm.* ◷*Closed 24–27 Dec.* ✆£6.80. ℘01535 642 323. www.bronte.org.uk.

The parsonage where Patrick Brontë and his family lived conserves furniture, paintings and fascinating memorabilia, such as the children's drawings and home-made books. Here they conceived imaginary kingdoms (Angria and Gondal), wrote poetry and fiction, and here too their brother, Branwell, painted the three sisters.

Brontë Country

The Brontë sisters drew on their local knowledge for descriptions of the places in their novels. Two houses which appear in *Shirley* under other names can be visited near Batley. In the 19C the family of Mary Taylor, one of Charlotte's close friends, lived in an 18C red-brick house, now the **Red House Museum** *(Oxford Road, Gomersal, Cleckheaton;* ◷*open daily 11am/ noon weekends–5pm;* ℘*01274 335 100; www.kirklees.gov.uk)*; the house appears in *Shirley* as Briarmains and is now furnished as it would have been in the 1830s. **Oakwell Hall** *(Nutter Lane, Birstall, near Batley, on the A 638;* ◷*open daily 11am/noon weekends–5pm;* ✆*£1.40;* ✗; ℘*01924 326 240; www.kirklees.gov.uk)* is a dark-stone Elizabethan manor, with impressive latticed windows, furnished as it was for the Batt family in the 1690s; it is surrounded by traces of a moat and a country park with a wildlife garden.

The Tragedy of the Brontë Family

Patrick Brontë was born Patrick Brunty in Northern Ireland and studied for holy orders at St John's College in Cambridge. He came to Haworth as curate in 1820, bringing his wife, Maria and their six children. His wife, who was consumptive, died the following year. In 1825 the two eldest girls, Maria and Elizabeth, fell ill at boarding school in Cowan Bridge and died. In 1846 the first publication by the three surviving sisters appeared, a joint volume of poems by "Currer, Ellis and Acton Bell", names chosen to preserve their initials but conceal that they were women. Next came *Wuthering Heights* (1847) by Emily and *The Tenant of Wildfell Hall* by Anne, who also drew on her experience as a governess for *Agnes Grey* (1847). Also in 1847 Charlotte wrote *Jane Eyre*. All died young: their brother, Branwell, aged 31 in September 1848, Emily (at 30) three months later and Anne (at 29) the following summer in Scarborough, where she is buried. Charlotte married her father's curate in 1854 and died in 1855, aged 39. Patrick Brontë died in 1861, in Haworth, having outlived his wife and all six children.

A gateway (marked by a stone) led from the parsonage garden to the church, where five of the six Brontë children and their mother are buried.

Brontë Weaving Shed: Town End Mill

Town End Mill, North Street.
Open Mon–Sat 10am–5.30pm, Sun 11am–5pm. Closed Easter Sun, 25 Dec. 01535 646 217.

Haworth was originally a weaving village, with over 1,200 handlooms in action at its peak in the 1840s. Here Victorian looms still produce "Brontë tweed" and visitors can try their hand at operating them. There is also an exhibition about Timmy Feather, known as Yorkshire's last handloom weaver. The shop sells knitwear made at the mill.

EXCURSION

Keighley and Worth Valley Railway

Oxenhope. 2mi/3km S on the A 6033. Operates Jul–Aug daily, see website for times. £10 return ticket, £14 Day Rover. 01535 647 777; 01535 645 214. www.kwvr.co.uk.

Steam and heritage diesel engines travel through moor scenery along a branch line linking Oxenhope with Haworth, Oakworth (where *The Railway Children* was set), Damems, Ingrow and Keighley. A re-created Edwardian station is this railway's terminus. At Ingrow is the **Museum of Rail Travel** (*Halifax Road; open year-round daily 11am–4.30pm; £2; 01535 680 425; www.vintage carriagestrust.org*), which preserves traditional wooden rail carriages.

Yorkshire Dales★★

North Yorkshire

Northwest of the great manufacturing towns of Leeds and Bradford lie the Yorkshire Dales (valleys), featuring dramatic limestone scenery, crags, caves, and swallow holes in which streams disappear. In the broad dales such as Airedale, Wensleydale and Wharfedale the stone-built villages are set harmoniously in an ancient pattern of stone-walled fields. Most of the area lies within the protected national park.

WALKING

The Dales are a walker's paradise, crisscrossed with paths and a specially designated cycleway. The four main routes are the **Nidderdale Way** (53mi/85km), starting and finishing in Pateley Bridge; the **Dales Way** (80mi/129km), from Ilkley to Bowness-on-Windermere (in the Lake District), via Wharfedale, Langstrothdale and Dentdale; the challenging **Yorkshire Three Peaks Way** (24.5mi/39km), taking in Penyghent, Whernside and Ingleborough; and the **Pennine Way**,

Michelin Map: Michelin Atlas p39 or Map 502 N, O 21 and 22.

Info: www.yorkshiredales. org.uk; www.yorkshire.com.

Kids: White Scar Caves; Yorkshire Dales Falconry Centre.

at 268mi/431km the ultimate Yorkshire route, passing through Airedale, Malhamdale and the Three Peaks.

SKIPTON

South of Yorkshire Dales, beside A59 and A65. www.skiptononline.co.uk.

This historic town is the Dales' southern gateway and a good base for exploring farther afield. Time your visit for bustling market day (*Mon, Wed, Fri, Sat*).

At the top of the High Street is **Skipton Castle★** (*open Mon–Sat Mar–Sept 10am–6pm, Oct–Feb 10am–4pm; Sun open year-round noon; closed 25 Dec; £6.50; 01756 792 442; www.skiptoncastle.co.uk*), one of the most complete and best-preserved medieval castles in England. Beautiful **Conduit Court** was built by the 10th Earl. Its present appearance owes much to mid-17C restoration.

Skipton sits halfway along the trans-Pennine **Leeds–Liverpool Canal** and 30-minute and 1-hour cruises with **Pennine Boat Trips** (*operate daily Easter–Oct; £6.50 1hr, £3.50 30min; 01756 790 829; www.canaltrips.co.uk*) depart regularly from the centre of town.

WHARFEDALE★

Immediately east of Skipton.
National Park Information Centre, Hebden Road. 01756 751 690.
Wharfedale is one of the most visited dales, largely on account of its geography (it is on the main A 65 road) and for its popularity with walkers. In Bolton Abbey village, **Bolton Priory** (*9mi/14km S of Grassington; open daily 8am–dusk or 4pm–4.30pm; ; 01756 710 238 www.enicholl.com/bolton-priory-church*) was founded by the Augustinians c.1154, in a beautiful setting on a bend of the River Wharfe. Only partially destroyed at the Dissolution, it still functions as a parish church.

MALHAMDALE★

10.8mi northwest of skipton.
Malham Village. 01729 833 200.
This tiny village is a magnet for walkers who come to do the 8mi/13km "cove, tarn and scar" trail. **Malham Cove** is a spectacular natural carboniferous limestone amphitheatre, around 260ft/80m high and 985ft/300m wide. At its summit, walkers are rewarded with great views and an unusual "limestone pavement", deeply fissured and fretted by naturally eroded channels. **Malham Tarn** is an upland lake; **Gordale Scar** is another spectacular cliff formation, carved as a meltwater channel beneath the ice-sheet aeons ago.

The ♦♦**Yorkshire Dales Falconry Centre** (*11mi/18km E; Crows Nest, nr Giggleswick; open year-round daily 10am–4.30pm; £6.70, child £4.70; ; 01729 822 832, www.hawkexperience.com*) overlooks dramatic dales scenery. Eagles, vultures, hawks, falcons, owls and kites give regular flying demonstrations.

RIBBLESDALE

16.5mi northwest of Skipton. Town Hall, Market Place, Settle. 01729 825 192. www.settle.org.uk.
The main settlement in Ribblesdale is **Settle**, the starting point of the very picturesque 72mi/116km **Settle-Carlisle Railway★** (*www.settle-carlisle.co.uk*). The spectacular 24-arch **Ribblehead Viaduct** is known to millions of *Harry Potter* fans as the bridge that the *Hogwarts Express* crosses in the films.

On the western edge of the national park, 12mi/19km north of Settle is ♦♦ **White Scar Cave** (*1.3mi/2km E of Ingleton; guided tours daily Feb–Oct, weekends Nov–Jan, weather permitting, from 10am, last tour 4pm, 80min, 1mi/1.6km; £8.50, child £5.50; ; 01524 241 244; www.whitescarcave.co.uk*), a vast show-cave and the longest in England. It includes a massive ice-age cavern, underground waterfalls, and streams and stalactites galore.

WENSLEYDALE★

Sights along the A684 in the northern Dales. Dales Countryside Museum, Hawes.
The largest of the dales, Wensleydale is famous not only for its eponymous cheese, but as the setting for the *James Herriot* books and TV series which were filmed here, most notably in Askrigg. Fans of the local vet will enjoy a pint in the Kings Arms, which made many appearances as the Drover's Arms.

Hawes

Wensleydale's main town is at its best on market day (*Tue*) when it sells, among many other things, Wensleydale cheese, which has been made locally for centuries.

Around the marketplace are workshops, antiques and speciality shops.

Housed in the old railway station, the **Dales Countryside Museum** (*open Feb–Dec daily 10am–5pm, Jan Tue & weekends 10am–4.30pm. closed 25–26 Dec; £3.50; charge; 01969 666 210, www.yorkshiredales.org.uk/dcm.htm*) looks at the Dales' domestic life, leisure and work over the centuries.

Aysgarth

🛈 *Aysgarth Falls National Park Information Centre.* 📞*01969 662910.*
The main attraction here, **Aysgarth Falls**, lies 0.5/1km out the village. There is a marked trail from the information centre. Another popular walk (*6mi/10km*) leads to 🚶🏛**Bolton Castle★** (🕐*open mid–Feb–Oct 11am–5pm, closing 2pm several Sats during summer;* 💷*£8.50, child £7;* 🅿✕*;* 📞*01969 623 981*). This classic sturdy foursquare fortress is one of the country's best-preserved medieval castles with stunning views over the Dales. Its colourful history includes Mary Queen of Scots being imprisoned here, and Its interiors, complete with sounds and smells, are very atmospheric. A recent addition is a bird of prey centre.

Masham★

Pronounced "mass-em", this pretty little village boasts the largest **market square** in the county, holding a weekly market (Wed, Sat)since 1393.
Masham is famous for **beer** with two very traditional breweries open to the public. The original is the **Theakston's Brewery** (🚶*tours year-round 10am–4.30pm, Jul–Aug 5.30pm;* 💷*£6.25, inc pint of beer/soft drink;* 📞*01765 680 000, www.theakstons.co.uk/visitorcentre*), which has been here since 1827. Just a few minutes' walk away, the **Black Sheep Brewery** (🚶*tours daily 11.30am–3pm/4pm, reduced times in winter;* 💷*£6.95 inc half-pint of beer/soft drink;* ✕. 📞*01765 68 01 01. www.blacksheep.co.uk*) was established in Masham in 1992 by Paul Theakston, as a riposte to the takeover of his family's business by a multinational company. Black Sheep beers rapidly became a regional favourite and, thanks to its location in an old Victorian brewery, it has both heritage and atmosphere.

RICHMOND★

◗*Northeast Dales, near the A1.*
🛈 *Friary Gardens, Victoria Road.* 📞*01748 828 742. www.yorkshiredales.org.*
This attractive country market town enjoys a beautiful location set at the foot of Swaledale on the northeast edge of the Dales National Park.

Richmond Castle★

EH. 🕐*Open Apr–Sept 10am–6pm; Oct Thu–Mon & Nov–Mar Sat–Sun 10am–4pm .* 💷*£4.60.* ✕. 📞*01748 822 493. www.english-heritage.org.uk.*
This ruined castle, begun 1071, stands on a cliff edge high above the river. The **keep**, built of grey Norman masonry (100ft/30m), is stout enough to stand comparison with the White Tower in the Tower of London. An 11C arch leads into the courtyard. **Scolland's Hall**, built in 1080, is the second oldest such building in England. From the roof of the keep there is a splendid **view** across the cobbled marketplace and over the moors.

The Georgian Theatre Royal and Museum★

Victoria Road. 🚶*Guided tours Feb–Dec Mon–Sat 10am–4pm.* 💷*£3.50.* ✕. 📞*01748 823 710.*
www.georgiantheatreroyal.co.uk.
The only Georgian theatre in the country with its original form and features, it was opened in 1787 but fell "dark" in 1848 until being reopened in 1963.

THE BOWES MUSEUM★

◗ *15mi northwest of Richmond via A66. Barnard Castle.* 🕐*Open year-round daily 10am–5pm.* 💷*£9.* ♿🅿✕. 📞*01833 690 606.*
www.bowesmuseum.org.uk.
A French-designed château, set in landscaped gardens (20 acres/8ha) is an unexpected surprise in this area. It was built, from 1869 onwards, to house the extraordinary array of ceramics, pictures, tapestries, furniture and other *objets d'art* amassed by John Bowes and his French wife, Josephine.
Their treasures include novelties like an automated silver swan (*demonstrations once or twice a day; times displayed in the foyer*); its rippling neck, as it swoops to catch a wriggling fish in its beak, is remarkable. There are also paintings of the first rank: a magnificent St Peter by El Greco, part of an extensive collection of 15C–19C Spanish work; two Goyas, two Canalettos and works by Boudin and Courbet.

Fountains Abbey & Studley Royal★★★

and around

Set in the wooded valley of the little River Skell amid glorious North Yorkshire countryside, these Cistercian ruins – the largest abbey ruins in England – are not only famously picturesque but also wonderfully evocative of monastic life. They are beautifully complemented by the spectacular Georgian water gardens of Studley Royal. The whole has been declared a World Heritage Site.

A BIT OF HISTORY

In 1132 a small band of Benedictine monks, revolting against the slack discipline at their abbey in York, were granted land in this "place remote from all the world". They set about transforming their wilderness into the flourishing and productive countryside characteristic of Cistercian endeavour and, within a century, Fountains Abbey was the centre of an enormous enterprise, managing fish-farms and ironworkings, as well as forests and vast tracts of agricultural land, the profits from which paid for an ambitious building programme.

The complex fell into decay following the Dissolution but in 1768 it was bought

- ⓖ **Michelin Map:** Michelin Atlas p39 or Map 502 P 21.
- ⓘ **Info:** ☎01765 608888. www.fountainsabbey.org.uk.
- ⓞ **Location:** 27mi/43km northwest of York.
- ⓞ **Open:** Feb and Oct daily 10am–4pm/dusk; Apr–Sept daily 10am–5pm/dusk. Nov–Jan Sat–Thu 10am–4pm/dusk. 🚶Guided tour (free). £8.15, (NT and EH members free). 🅿(£3, NT members free)✕.

by the Aislabie family, who coveted it as the ultimate in picturesque ruins to complete their lavish landscaping of the adjacent Studley Royal estate.

VISIT

Fountains Hall – Stone from the abbey was used to build the splendid five-storey Jacobean mansion (1598–1611). Behind the striking **façade**★ with its Renaissance details, the interior is laid out to the conventional medieval plan.

Fountains Abbey – The grassy levels of Abbey Green extend to the west front of the roofless abbey church and the monastic buildings adjoining the south side.

The scale and diversity of the monastic buildings suggest the varied activities of

Ruins of Fontains Abbey

© James Emmerson/age fotostock

the great community of monks and lay brothers. The church's tall tower (c.1500) rises above the stately Norman nave. At the east end is the spectacular 13C **Chapel of the Nine Altars** with soaring arches and a huge Perpendicular window.

The most complete and beautiful remains are those of the buildings grouped round the cloister in accordance with the standard Cistercian plan: in the western range is the **Cellarium**, with its astounding 300ft/90m vaulted interior below the lay brothers' dormitory; in the south range is the **Great Refectory**. In the east range is the **Chapter House**, entered through three fine Norman arches.

Studley Royal Water Garden – The gardens were designed to be visited starting from the Canal Gates: choose from a (45min, 1hr 45min, 2hr routes). From 1720 until his death in 1742 John Aislabie, Chancellor of the Exchequer, devoted his vast personal fortune to create a garden at his Yorkshire estate. He remodelled the sinuous valley of the Skell into a spectacular landscape consisting of a series of formal water features and contrived views, embellished with garden buildings and flanked by woodland on the steeper slopes.

The canalised river, emerging from a dark grotto, is led past the **Moon Pond**, overlooked by a Classical **Temple of Piety**, and finally discharges into a lake over a grand cascade flanked by pavilions, known as fishing tabernacles. Along the east side of the valley is a high-level walk which passes through a twisting tunnel, past the **Gothic Tower** and the elegant **Temple of Fame** to **Anne Boleyn's Seat** and the surprise view of the east end of the abbey ruins. The **Seven Bridges Walk** follows the course of the Skell downstream from the lake, zigzagging from bank to bank. In the deer park stands **St Mary's Church**, a masterpiece of High Victorian Gothic by William Burges, on the axis of a long avenue which extends east to the original entrance to the park from the village of **Studley Royal** and aligned on the twin towers of **Ripon Cathedral**.

EXCURSIONS
Ripon★

⬙ *3.7mi/6km N.* ℹ️ *Minster Road.*
☎ *0845 389 0178. www.visitripon.org.*
Ripon's cathedral qualifies its status as one of the smallest cities in England. This, and the large thriving market square (Thursday is the main market day) are the focus. Here, at nine o'clock every night, a horn is blown to "set the watch", an ancient custom commemorating the responsibility of the medieval Wakeman for the safety of the citizens at night.

Ripon Cathedral★

Minster Road. 🕐 *Open daily 8.30am– 6pm.* 💷 *£3 contribution requested.* 🚶 *Guided tours.* ♿ 🅿️.
☎ *01765 603 462.*
www.riponcathedral.org.uk.
The cathedral was started in 1254 on the Saxon crypt of St Wilfrid's Church (AD 672). Pevsner called the imposing Early English west front "the finest in England". The medieval font stands near the west door in the south aisle. Above it are the remains of the great 14C east window shot out in 1643 by the Roundheads. The tiny **Saxon Crypt** (11ft x 8ft x 9ft/3.3mx2.4mx2.7m high) was built by St Wilfrid on his return from Rome. **Misericords** and exquisite **choir stalls** were carved at the end of the 15C. The **Chapel of the Holy Spirit** has a striking modern metal screen, symbolising the Pentecostal "tongues of flame". The **Treasury** displays silverware given to the cathedral, as well as the **Ripon Jewel**, a Saxon gold brooch set with amber and garnets.

Market Square

This is one of the largest squares (2 acres/0.8ha) in the North. The **town hall**, built by Wyatt in 1801, has an Ionic portico and carries along its frieze the motto "Except ye Lord Keep ye Cittie ye Wakeman Waketh in Vain". The **Wakeman's House**, a 14C two-storeyed, timber-framed house, was the home of the last holder of the office, Hugh Ripley, who in 1604 became first Mayor of Ripon.

Yorkshire Law and Order Museums

Open Apr–Oct and school hols daily 1–4pm. Courthouse £1.50, Prison & Police £4, Workhouse £4, joint ticket £8. 01765 690 799. www.riponmuseums.co.uk.

These three museums on the same theme sit in separate historic buildings in very close proximity to each other – the 1830 **Courthouse Museum** (Minster Road); the **Prison & Police Museum** (St Marygate), and the **Workhouse Museum** (Allhallowgate). The Prison & Police Museum, housed in the old Ripon Liberty Prison, built 1816, contains cells, a pillory, a pair of stocks, a whipping post and an old blue police box (very similar to the "Tardis" from *Dr Who*). Saddest of all is the Workhouse, the present building dating from 1855. Together these collections provide a fascinating interwoven insight into law and order and the harsh conditions, for both felons and ordinary folk, in bygone days in this part of the world.

▲▲ Lightwater Valley

North Stainley, 8mi/13km N of Fountains Abbey, off the A 6108. Open mid-Mar–early Sept, then late Oct and Christmas for seasonal events. Gates open 10am, rides open 10.30am, close from 4.30pm onwards, later in peak season. Over 4ft 3in/1.3m tall £21.45, under 4ft 3in/1.3m tall £18.95. Book online, all persons over 3ft 3in/1m tall £15.95 plus £1.50 booking fee, birds of prey centre £1.50 extra. 0871 720 0011. www.lightwatervalley.co.uk.

This is one of the biggest theme parks in the north of England, with over 40 rides and attractions for all ages. "The Ultimate" is the longest roller coaster in Europe.

Adjacent, but accessible without the admission fee, is **Lightwater Country Shopping Village** (*open year-round from 10am; www.lightwatervalley.co.uk/shoppingvillage*), a very popular complex of factory outlet **shops** and eating places, also home to a **Bird of Prey Centre** (*open Apr–Sept 10am–5pm, Mar and Oct 10am–*

3pm, Nov 11am–3pm, Dec 10am–1pm; £3.50, child £2.50, £1.50 all tickets if booked with theme park ticket; 01765 635 010; over 50 birds of prey, wallabies, pythons, dragons, lizards, tarantulas and other "creepy-crawlies".

The World of James Herriot

23 Kirkgate, Thirsk. 16mi/26km NE of Fountains Abbey via the A 61. Open Apr–Oct daily 10am–5pm, see website for winter details. £8. 01845 524 234. www.worldofjamesherriot.org.

A tour of the house and surgery gives a snapshot of life in the 1940s and reveals the dedication of Alf Wight, the vet-turned-author, who wrote under the pseudonym James Herriot. He went on to win international fame and gain the hearts of millions of viewers of the popular television series *All Creatures Great and Small*, based on his series of semi-autobiographical novels.

Newby Hall & Gardens★

7mi/11km E of Fountains Abbey. Open Apr–third week Sept, Tue–Sun & bank hols Mon, daily Jul & Aug 11am–5.30pm. Hall open by guided tour only, noon–4pm each hour (each half-hour Jul–Aug). £12.20 (garden only, £8.70). 0845 450 4068. www.newbyhall.com.

The original 17C mellow-brick mansion, designed by Sir Christopher Wren, and extended and remodelled during the 18C by John Carr and Robert Adam, is renowned for its Adam interiors, collection of Chippendale furniture, Gobelins **Tapestry Room★** and its gallery designed for a rare collection of Classical sculpture brought from Italy by William Weddell in 1765.

From the south front of the house, 25 acres10ha of award-winning **gardens**, including one of Europe's largest double herbaceous borders, descend to the River Ure. A miniature railway runs beside the river. There is also an Adventure Garden for children and a woodland walk.

Harrogate★

and around

Harrogate is a genteel little town. Its heyday as a famous 19C spa town has left a legacy of elegant buildings with fine shops and hotels, which make an excellent base for touring the Yorkshire Dales and Moors.

TOWN

The **Royal Pump Room**, built in 1842, and the **Royal Baths Assembly Rooms**, built in 1897, were the hub of this spa town at its height at the end of the 19C when some 60,000 people a year came to "take the waters" bubbling up from 36 springs in the town centre. At the **Royal Pump Museum** (*Crown Place;* ⏰*open year-round: Mon–Sat 10am–5.30pm/4pm Nov–Mar; Sun 2–5pm, except Aug open noon;* ⏰*closed 1 Jan, 24–26 Dec;* ⊜*£3.60;* &*;* ☏*01423 556 188; www.harrogate.gov. uk*), you can taste the strongest sulphurous water in Europe, wonder at the old spa treatments, discover how Harrogate became a spa town, its Victorian past and take a trip to Ancient Egypt.

An unusual and attractive aspect of the town is the **Stray**, 200 acres/80ha of grassland surrounding the centre.

EXCURSIONS
Harewood House★★

▶ *8mi/13km S by the A 61.*
House: ⏰*Open (Below Stairs) Apr–Oct daily 10.30am–5pm, Feb half-term daily; Mar and Nov Sat–Sun; (state rooms) late Apr–Oct daily noon–5pm. For Christmas details see website.*
Gardens, & grounds: ⏰*Open Apr– Oct daily 10am/10.30am–5.30/6pm; also Feb half-term daily; Mar and Nov Sat–Sun 10am–4pm (Bird Garden 3pm).* ⊜*Grounds, Bird Garden, Terrace Gallery, Below Stairs £7.50–£9. All attractions £11–£13.* ☜*Garden tours Thu 1pm, 2pm, 3pm (*⊜*free); house tours, see website (*⊜*free); Bird Garden tours and beekeeping demonstrations (*⊜*free).* &☐✕ ☏*0113 218 1010 (24hr info). www.harewood.org.*

This splendid pile, "a St Petersburg palace on a Yorkshire hill", was begun in

▶ **Population:** 66,178.
⚖ **Michelin Map:** Michelin Atlas p40 or Map 502 P 22.
▤ **Info:** Royal Baths, Crescent Road. ☏0845 389 3223. www.harrogate.gov.uk.
◑ **Location:** Harrogate is 21mi/34km west of York. Both the bus and train stations are on Station Parade, in the town centre.
♟ **Kids:** Mother Shipton's Cave.

1759 by Edwin Lascelles, and is an essay in Palladian architecture by John Carr of York; its interiors are Neoclassical, one of the greatest achievements of Robert Adam. **Thomas Chippendale**, born at nearby Otley, made the furniture and **Lancelot "Capability" Brown** developed the grounds.

The **Entrance Hall** is the only room to retain its original form, complete with fine plaster-work ceiling. Old Master paintings are hung throughout; there is much rare Chinese porcelain, as well as Sèvres pieces collected at the beginning of the 19C. The **Gallery**★ is perhaps the pinnacle of Adam's work at Harewood.

The **Bird Garden** with over 90 species of threatened and exotic birds housed in sympathetic environments is one of England's most important avian col-

Harewood House
© Lana22/Dreamstime.com

lections *(penguin feeding daily 2pm)*. Family-friendly additions include a huge outdoor adventure playground and **Geopods** housing interactive indoor play areas.

Knaresborough

❯ *2mi/3km E of Harrogate on the A 59.*
This small market town is set on the north bank of the River Nidd. **Knaresborough Castle** *(Castle Yard; ◷ open Good Fri–early Oct daily 10.30am–5pm; ✆ £3.10 inc museum and sallyport; ☞ guided tours through the sallyport underground tunnel 11am, noon, 2.30pm, 3.30pm; 🅿 (charge); ℘ 01423 556 188; www.harrogate.gov.uk/museums)*, now in ruins, was started in about 1130. After the murder of Thomas Becket in Canter-

bury Cathedral in December 1170, the four killers took refuge here. In addition to its underground sallyport it has a rare surviving Tudor courtroom.
Beside the river is ♟ **Mother Shipton's Cave** *(High Bridge; ◷ open daily 10am –5.30pm Apr–Oct; Feb Sat–Sun 10am– 4.30pm, Mar Sat–Sun 10am–5.30pm; ✆ £6, child £4; 🅿 ✗; ℘ 01423 864 600; www.mothershiptonscave.com)*, where Mother Shipton, England's most famous prophetess, b. c.1488, was reputed to have lived and prophesied. Adjacent is the **Petrifying Well**, a geological phenomenon whose cascading waters seem to turn items into stone. In fact they are covering it with a stalactite deposit. It is said to be England's oldest visitor attraction, first opening its gates in 1630.

York★★★

and around

York first came to prominence as a Roman capital, later as capital of eastern England under the Danes, then as a wool trade hub. York is marked by many elegant Georgian buildings that reflect the wealth of those moving from the North into what had become an important centre of social and cultural life. It is the survival of these and many much older buildings that draws hundreds of thousands of visitors here every year and has established the city as the tourist capital of northeastern England. It is famous for its minster, its wonderful railway museum and its many ghost walks.

A BIT OF HISTORY

In AD 71 the Roman Ninth Legion built a fortress, **Eboracum**, later capital of the northern province, and here in AD 306 Constantine the Great was proclaimed emperor. After the departure of the Romans the Anglo-Saxons made **Eoforwic** the capital of their Kingdom of Northumbria. In AD 866 the Vikings captured the city and made it **Jorvik**, one of their chief trading bases.

❯ **Population:** 123,126.
◔ **Michelin Map:** Michelin Atlas p40 or Map 502 Q 22.
🛈 **Info:** 1 Museum Street. ℘ 01904 55 00 99. www.visityork.org.
❯ **Location:** 84mi/135km south of Newcastle-upon-Tyne; 25mi/40km northeast of Leeds. The train station is just outside the city walls. Buses call in the vicinity. Most attractions are within the old walls, easily explored on foot. Try a York City Sightseeing hop-on open-top bus tour *(℘ 01904 655 585; www. yorktourbuses.co.uk; ✆ £10)*.
☺ **Don't Miss:** The stained glass in York Minster; National Railway Museum; The Shambles; Castle Howard.
◷ **Timing:** Two–three days.
♟ **Kids:** National Railway Museum; Jorvik; DIG.

The prosperity of medieval York, a city of 10,000 people and 40 churches, was based on wool. York was once the richest city in the country after London. With the decline of the wool trade after the Wars of the Roses (1453–87) and following the Dissolution of the Monasteries (16C) the city's prosperity waned.

YORK MINSTER★★★

Minster, Undercroft, Treasury, Crypt: Open Mon–Sat 9am (9.30am November–March)–5pm (last entry). Sun noon–3.45pm (last entry). ⃠Closed for sightseeing Good Fri, Easter Sun, 24–25 Dec. All areas (except tower and Glaziers' Studio, see below) £9. Guided tours Mon–Sat (free). ℘01904 557 200. www.yorkminster.org.

The minster is the largest Gothic church north of the Alps (534ft/163m long; 249ft/76m wide across the transepts; 90ft/27m from floor to vault; 198ft/60m to the tops of the towers). The nave, built 1291–1350, is in Decorated style; the transepts of the mid-13C are the oldest visible parts of the present building. The **Chapter House**★★, octagonal with a magnificent wooden vaulted ceiling, is late-13C. The late-15C **Choir Screen**★★ is by William Hyndeley. Its central doorway is flanked by statues of English kings from William the Conqueror onwards. The finest monument in the minster is the **tomb (1)** of the man who began the present building, **Archbishop Walter de Gray**.

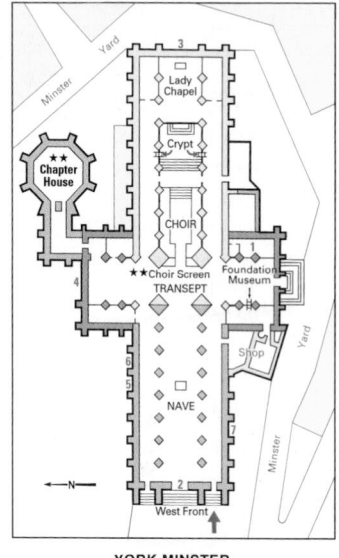

YORK MINSTER

0 — 30 m
0 — 50 feet

1220-1260 Early English
1280-1350 Decorated
1361-1472 Perpendicular

Minster Stained Glass★★★

The minster contains the largest single collection of medieval stained glass to have survived in England. The **West Window (2)** was painted in 1339 by Master Robert. It was the largest in the

City Walls and York Minster

© Warren Chris/Sime/Photononstop

WHERE TO STAY

Alexander House.............①

Bay Tree Guest House.....⑦

Bronte.........................⑧

Coach House Hotel..........⑩

Middlethorpe Hall............⑬

Monkbar Hotel................⑯

The Grange Hotel...........⑲

WHERE TO EAT

Blue Bicycle....................①

Café Concerto.................④

Café n°8 bistro...............⑦

Four High Petergate........⑩

Harkers.........................⑬

Kennedy's......................⑯

Melton's.........................⑲

Melton's Too...................㉒

Rish...............................㉕

The Olive Three
restaurant...................㉘

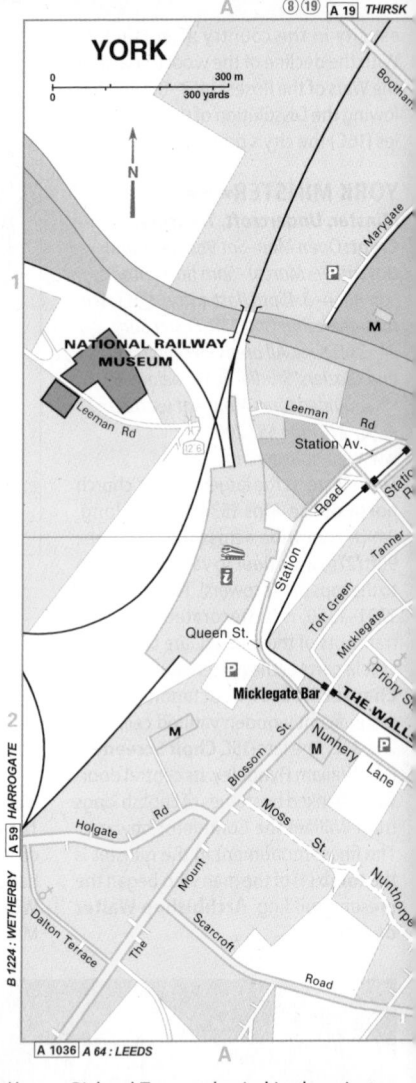

minster at the time but was surpassed by the **East Window** (3) in the Lady Chapel, painted by John Thornton of Coventry 1405–08. It is the largest expanse of medieval glass in the country and revitalised the York school of glass painting. The **Five Sisters Window** (4), lancets of grisaille glass from c.1250, is the oldest window still in its original place in the minster.

The **Pilgrimage Window** (5), c.1312, shows grotesques, a monkey's funeral and scenes of hunting. Next to it is the **Bellfounders Window** (6), given by

Richard Tunnoc, buried in the minster in 1330. He is depicted presenting his window to the archbishop, among scenes of casting and tuning a bell. The **Jesse Window** (7), depicting Jesus' family tree, dates from 1310.

An insight behind the scenes of maintaining and restoring the cathedral's windows is provided in the **Bedern Glaziers' Studio** (👁🔍 *guided tour only, Mon, Wed and Fri 2pm, depart from the group desk in the minster, tours last 1hr and are limited to max 10 people so booking advisable;* ♿; *✆0844 939 0015, or*

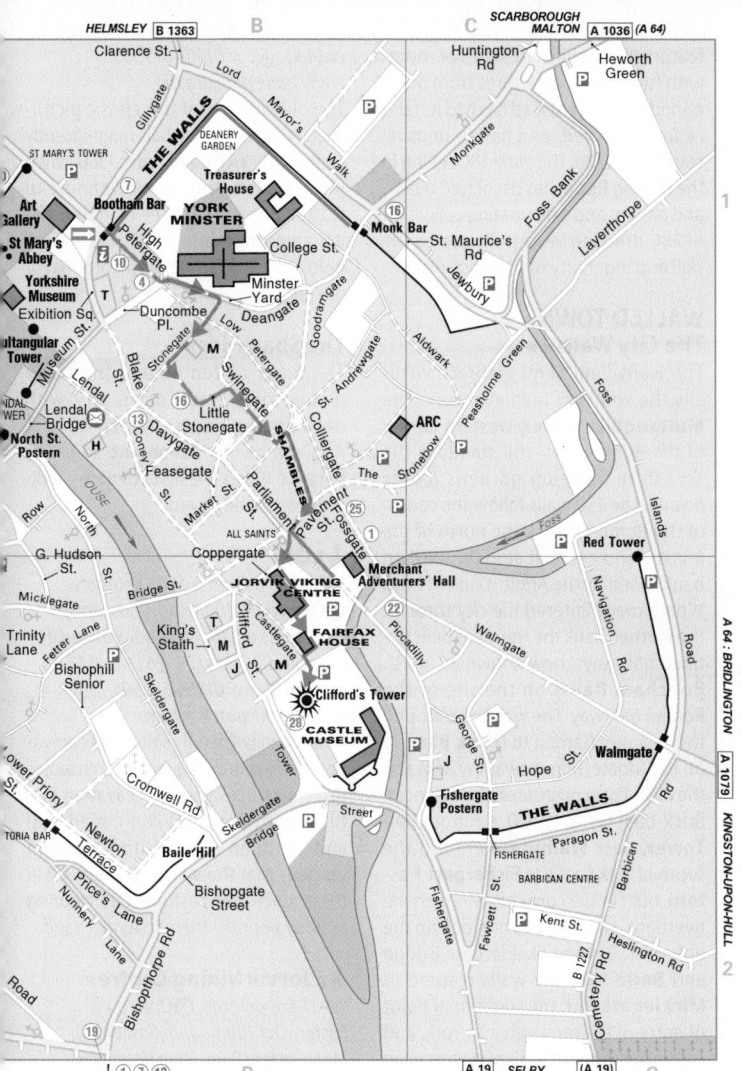

online; £7.50), built in the 13C as the chapel of the College of Vicars Choral. This is now the workshop for the **York Minster Glaziers**, the team of craftspeople who are responsible for the preservation and conservation of the stained glass and go about their delicate work in full view of the public.

Climbing the 275 steps to the top of the minster's central **tower** (open Mon –Sat from 9.45pm/Sun 12.45pm, last trip 4.45pm, later at peak times; Nov–Mar from 10.15am, last trip 30min before dusk; min age 8; £5.50) is an exhilarating, if rather tiring experience. En-route you pass the medieval pinnacles and gargoyles and look over its rooftops. At the top is the best view in town of York's ancient streets.

Treasurer's House

NT. Minster Yard. Open mid-Feb–Nov Sat–Thu 11am–4.30pm (Feb, Nov 3pm). £5.70. Ghost tours of cellar daily £2.40. 01904 624 247. www.nationaltrust.org.uk.

Rebuilt in the 17C and 18C, this fascinating property, renowned for its ghosts,

399

features a magnificent series of rooms with furniture and pictures from many periods. The **Great Hall** has had its false ceiling removed, and has an unusual staircase c.1700. The early 18C ceiling in the **Dining Room** has decorated beams and panels, and a fascinating collection of 18C drinking vessels illustrates the skill and ingenuity of the glass-maker.

WALLED TOWN
The City Walls★★
The walls (3mi/5km) embrace virtually the whole of medieval York. The **Multangular Tower**, western corner of the Roman fort, still stands in the Yorkshire Museum gardens (*see below*). The 13C walls follow the course of the Roman wall to the north of the minster and are built atop the earthen bank raised by the Anglo-Danish kings. Where roads entered the city through the earthen bank the Normans built fortified gateways, now known as "bars". **Bootham Bar** is on the site of the Roman gateway. The walls lead around the Deanery Garden to **Monk Bar** and on to Aldgate; here a swampy area and the River Foss constituted the defences. Brick-built walls, c.1490, run from **Red Tower**, pass **Walmgate** around the south of York Castle to **Fishergate Postern**, built in 1505 on what was then the riverbank. Here York Castle took up the defences. Beyond Skeldergate Bridge and **Baile Hill**, the walls resume to **Micklegate Bar**, the traditional point of entry of the monarch into York, and where the severed heads of traitors were exposed after execution. This is now a **museum** (*open Feb–Sept 10am–4pm, Oct–Dec 11am–3pm; *£3.50; *01904 615 505, www.micklegatebar.com)*, which is run by YAT (*see below Jorvik*).
From here the walls turn northeast and lead to the North Street Postern (BY), where the ferry crossed the Ouse before Lendal Bridge was built.

Barley Hall
2 Coffee Yard, off Stonegate.
Open daily Apr–Oct 10am–5pm (last entry 4pm). Nov–Mar 10am–4pm (last entry 3pm). Closed 24–26 Dec.
*£4.95. . *01904 615 505.*
www.barleyhall.org.uk.
The oldest parts of this classic picturesque timber-framed hall, magnificently restored by **YAT**, date from c.1360, when it was built as the York townhouse of Nostell Priory (*see Leeds*). In the 15C it became the home of William Snawsell goldsmith, Alderman and Lord Mayor of York.

The Shambles★
The most visited among the many picturesque streets of the city, with overhanging timber-framed houses. Also visit nearby **Pavement**, so-called because it was the first street in medieval York to be paved.

👥 DIG
St Saviour's Church, St Saviourgate.
*Open daily 10am–5pm, last entry 4pm, tours are timed so book ahead if possible. Closed 24–26 Dec. *£5.50, child £5. . *01904 615 505.*
www.micklegatebar.com.
At this family-friendly simulated excavation site, a tour by a qualified archaeologist introduces you to excavation pits filled with Roman, Viking, medieval and Victorian finds; visitors then dig up clues that show how people lived in these times, with costumed staff (during holiday periods) there to lend a hand.

👥 Jorvik Viking Centre★
*15–17 Coppergate. Open daily Easter–Oct 10am–5pm (last entry). Nov–Easter 10am–4pm (last entry). Pre-booking recommended in peak season to avoid queues (charge) online or *01904 615 505. Closed 24–26 Dec reduced hours 1 Jan, 31 Dec; *£9.25, child £6.25. . *01904 543 400. www.jorvik-viking-centre.co.uk.*
During building work in Coppergate in the late-1970s, ancient remains were found. A major six-year-long archaeological project, known as the **Coppergate Dig**, went on to make the most remarkable and revolutionary discoveries concerning Viking-age York, or Jorvik. You can see an interpretation of this dig beneath the new **Discover Cop-**

pergate glass-floored gallery, installed in 2010. This includes 1,000-year-old timbers that once formed the wall of a Viking house, and hundreds of the most important objects discovered during the Coppergate excavations. To help interpret what otherwise may be a dry subject are seven lively state-of-the-art animatronics who interact with visitors in Old Norse (happily, also translated into English!).

You then board "Time Capsules" for a journey back into Jorvik, complete with sights, sounds and smells as they might have been on an October day in AD 948. Jorvik is actually part of a family of four visitor attractions run by York Archaeological Trust (YAT). These are Micklegate Bar (♿see above), DIG and Barley Hall (♿see below). If you are visiting two or more properties, joint tickets are available or consider the YAT pass (⊜£16, child £11.25).

In February each year YAT also stages the **Jorvik Viking Festival**, with longship races, feasting and fireworks.

Fairfax House★

Castlegate. ©Open mid-Feb–Dec: Mon by guided tour only, 11am and 2pm; Tue–Sat & bank hol Mon 10am–5pm; Sun 12.30–4.30pm, also by guided tour at 11am. ©Closed 24–26 Dec. ⊜£6. ℘01904 655 543.
www.fairfaxhouse.co.uk.
Perhaps the finest Georgian town house in England, Fairfax House was built in 1755. It houses a collection of Georgian furniture, paintings, clocks and porcelain, and there are displays of eating and dining in 18C England.

York Castle Museum★

©Open daily 9.30am (10am Fri school term)–5pm. ©Closed 1 Jan, 25–26 Dec. ⊜£8. ♿✕. ℘01904 687 687.
www.yorkcastlemuseum.org.uk.
In what was the **Debtors Prison** and the **Female Prison**, two striking buildings from 1705 and 1777 respectively, is now a superb museum of everyday life. The highlight is the re-created **Victorian Street**, which combines real shop fittings and stock, with sound and light effects which evoke the period atmosphere. Half Moon Court is an authentic reproduction of an Edwardian street.

A prize exhibit is the **Coppergate Helmet**, a Saxon relic (c. AD 750), made of iron with brass fittings. It probably belonged to a Northumbrian noble. There are costumes, period rooms, pubs and shops and as part of the entertaining new **York Castle Prison** exhibition area, the actual cell in which legendary highwayman Dick Turpin was held before execution in 1739 (you'll even get to see the virtual Turpin!).

OUTSIDE THE WALLS

Immediately outside the line of the old walls, west of the minster next to the River Ouse, is **Museum Gardens**, home to the ruins of **St Mary's Abbey** and the 14C **Hospitium** (⊶closed to the public access); one of the oldest surviving half-timbered buildings in York, this was originally a guesthouse for the abbey. By contrast, a Classical 19C building houses the **Yorkshire Museum** (©open year-round daily 10am–5pm; ©closed 1 Jan, 25–26 Dec; ⊜£7.50; ♿; ℘01904 687 687; www.yorkshiremuseum.org.uk), which displays some of the city's finest Roman, Viking and medieval treasures. It also has an observatory (©open Sat 11.30am–2.30pm; ♿).

York Art Gallery (BY)

Exhibition Square. ©Open daily 10am–5pm. ©Closed 1 Jan, 25–26 Dec. ♿✕. ℘01904 687 687.
www.yorkartgallery.org.uk.
This extensive collection of paintings spans over 600 years and ranges from 14C Italian panels and 17C Dutch masterpieces to Victorian narrative paintings and 20C works by Lowry and Hockney.

♟♟ National Railway Museum★★★

©Open year-round daily 10am (9.30am summer school hols)–6pm. ©Closed 24–26 Dec. 🅿 (⊜charge). ♿✕. ℘08704 214 001. www.nrm.org.uk.
This magnificent collection, the largest railway museum in the world, presents the history of the railways in the coun-

National Railway Museum

National Railway Museum

try of their invention. The **Great Hall**, a wonderfully spacious former locomotive shed, houses an array of locomotives from clunky early-19C machines to the sleek super-trains of the 21C.

However, the museum's brief extends beyond the glamour of machines like these, to the whole technology and culture of the railway, demonstrated by an extraordinarily rich and varied array of other related objects. The **South Hall** re-creates the atmosphere of a mid-20C mainline station, allowing close inspection of engine cabs, the interiors of coaches, both primitive and luxurious, dining and sleeping cars, goods wagons and road vehicles. Outside are more treasures undergoing or awaiting restoration, plus a mini ride-on railway.

EXCURSION
Castle Howard★★

◯ *15mi/24km NE via the A 64.*
House: ◷*Open late Mar–Oct and late Nov–mid-Dec daily 11am–4pm (last entry).* ***Grounds:*** ◷*Open 10am–5.30pm, winter 10am–4pm/ dusk.* ☞*£13, gardens only, £8.50 (low season £4.50).* ☞*Guided tours house and garden Mar–Oct daily 11am–3pm.* ♿️🅿️✕. *☏01653 648 333. www.castlehoward.co.uk.*
Remarkably Castle Howard, **Sir John Vanbrugh**'s tour de force, was the first building he had ever designed.

The landscaping of the surrounding **park★★★** is one of the most grandiose landscaping projects ever; it consists of a series of compositions focused on some of the most ambitious and beautiful garden structures ever built, notably the **Temple of the Four Winds**, and, crowning a distant rise, a colossal colonnaded **Mausoleum** by Hawksmoor. The woodland garden presents rare trees, shrubs, rhododendrons and azaleas. There is also an adventure playground, and boat trips on the Great Lake.

The striking entrance to the house, topped by a painted and gilded dome (80ft/24m), is familiar to many as the castle was used as the principal location for the TV series *Brideshead Revisited*.

The **statuary** in the **Grand Entrance** is remarkable, particularly the **altar** from the Temple of Delphi.

The heart of the house is the **Great Hall**, which rises through two storeys into the painted dome. In the **Long Gallery** and its **Octagon** are pictures by Lely, Kneller and Van Dyck and two **Holbeins** – the portrait of **Henry VIII** shows a stricken monarch, painted in 1542, just after the execution of Catherine Howard. The magnificent stained-glass windows in the **Chapel** are by the 19C artist Sir Edward Burne-Jones. The **Stable Court** presents period costume (17C on).

East Yorkshire

This is not only the least visited part of Yorkshire but one of the least visited parts of the country by any domestic or foreign tourists. Don't let that deter you, however, as it's worth the detour just for Beverley Minster and The Deep at Hull.

HULL

Once an important centre for fishing and particularly for whaling, Kingston-upon-Hull (to give it its full name) is still a major seaport. Its famous modern landmark is the **Humber Bridge**, built 1972–81, as the longest single-span suspension bridge in the world, measuring 4,626ft/1,410m.

In the city centre on Queen Victoria Square is the **Hull Maritime Museum** (◷ open Mon–Sat 10am–5pm, Sun 1.30–4.30pm. ◷Closed Good Fri, 1 Jan, 25–26 Dec. &. ☎01482 300 300. www.hullcc.gov.uk/museums), covering over seven centuries of maritime heritage with models, artefacts and paintings. Next door, the Ferens Art Gallery (◷as Maritime Museum) holds the city art collection, ranging from European Old Masters to contemporary art, including works by such artists as Hals, Canaletto, David Hockney and Henry Moore. Hull's maritime history is also depicted.

A short walk away is the **old town**, retaining some of the narrow cobbled lanes and ancient inns of medieval and 17C Hull. On the High Street is the **Museums Quarter** (◷all details as Maritime Museum, ℓsee above) with three adjacent collections.

The **Wilberforce House Museum** commemorates the life and work of William Wilberforce (1758–1833), an instrumental player in the abolition of slavery. The **Streetlife Museum**, shows two centuries of transport history and a re-creation of a 1940s high street. The **Hull & East Riding Museum** of archaeology depicts an Iron Age village, a Roman bathhouse with fine mosaics, and a Viking treasure hoard.

Close by is ♣♣**The Deep**★★ (◷open year-round daily 10am–6pm/5pm last entry); ◷closed 24–25 Dec; ⌘£9.95, child £7.95 (save 10 percent online); & ☐£3; ☎01482 381 000, www.thedeep.co.uk). In a stunning building on the Humber estuary, designed by Sir Terry Farrell, this is one of the most spectacular aquaria in Europe, home to over 3,500 fish. A visit culminates in a ride in the world's only underwater lift face to face with sharks and rays.

BURTON CONSTABLE★

◷ Skirlaugh Grounds. 16mi/26km E. ◷Open Easter Sat–late Oct and last week Nov–first week Dec, Sat–Thu 1(grounds 12.30)–5pm (house 4pm Nov–Dec). ⌘£6.75. &☐✕. ☎01964 562 400. www.burtonconstable.com. The house was built c.1600 with a handsome **east front**, brick with mullion windows and projecting wings. The **Entrance Hall**, dates from 1760. In the **Muniment Room**, the remodelling of the house in Georgian times can be followed. The **Long Gallery**, of grand proportions and decoration, contains many family portraits.

BEVERLEY★

Georgian façades hide the ancient timber buildings of a town which in 1377 already boasted one of England's finest churches, a sizeable population of some 5,000 inhabitants and which was the principal town of the area.

Beverley Minster★★

◷Open Mon–Sat 9am–5pm/5.30pm, Sun noon–4.30pm (Nov–Feb daily until

---

ℹ **Info:** 1 Paragon Street, Hull. ☎01482 223 559. 34 Butcher Row, Beverley, ☎01482 391 672. 25 Prince Street, Bridlington. ☎01262 674 474. www.visithull andeastyorkshire.com.

◔ **Don't Miss:** The Percy Tomb and the misericords in the Minster; The Deep; Beverley minster.

♣♣ **Kids:** The Deep.

© Christopher Smith/Dreamstime.com

Flamborough Head

4pm). Guided tours Mon–Sat: ground floor 11am onwards (£5); Roof tours 11.15am & 2.15pm (£5); both tours £7. ✆01482 868 540. www.beverleyminster.org.

The present minster was begun c.1220 and at 332ft/101m long is of cathedral-like proportions. The **Great East Window**, a Perpendicular nine-lighted window containing all the fragments of medieval glass the minster once possessed, was bequeathed in 1416.

The **Percy Tomb** (1340–49) and its canopy, with angels, symbolic beasts and leaf carvings, is the most splendid of funerary monuments from the Decorated period. It probably commemorates Lady Eleanor Percy, who died in 1328. The early-16C **misericords** in the choir stalls are some of the finest in Britain.

St Mary's Church★

Open Apr–Sept Mon–Fri 9.30am–4.30pm, Sat and bank hols 10am–4pm, Sun, 2–4pm. Oct–Mar Mon–Fri, 9.30am–noon and 1pm–4pm. Sun, before and after services only. £2 min contribution requested. ✆01482 865 709. www.stmarysbeverley.org.uk.

Founded c.1120, St Mary's was adopted by the wealthy trade guilds. The tiny (36ft/11m x 18ft/5.5m) Chapel of St Michael with its ingenious "telescopic" **spiral staircase** is contemporary with the Percy Tomb in the Minster.

The Perpendicular west front is comparable with King's College Chapel in Cambridge. By 1524 the addition of the tower completed one of the finest parish churches in the north of England. Look for the extensive collection of **carvings of medieval musical instruments** shared between the minster and St Mary's at Beverley.

All told there are 140, on pew ends, choir stalls, ceiling bosses and in the south porch. The chancel ceiling, painted in 1445, with its pictorial record of 40 English kings, is unique.

Adorning the choir stalls are 23 **misericords** with extraordinary carvings of animals and men, including a "Pilgrim Rabbit" carved c.1325.

THE COAST

Bridlington and **Filey** are the region's two resorts. The former is a typical British seaside family resort, albeit with a pleasant Georgian old town.

Filey is much quieter, retaining vestiges of its Edwardian and Victorian heyday. Both resorts feature excellent sandy beaches, even if they rarely have the weather to match.

Flamborough Head★

A lighthouse marks the headland (215ft/66m), from which there are spectacular sea and coast **views**.

The Cleveland Way coastal footpath follows outstanding chalk-cliff scenery northwards near **Bempton** the cliffs soar to 427ft/130m.

North York Moors

The beauty of this expanse of open moorland lies in its wildness. The heather-covered high ground stretches southeast from industrial Middlesbrough to Whitby and Scarborough on the coast and to Pickering and Helmsley in the south. Much of the land is embraced by the **North York Moors National Park.**

🐾 WALKING

Four regional walking routes have been designed by the National Park Authority with a short holiday/long weekend in mind, and are an easy and enjoyable way to explore the North York Moors National Park. These are the **Esk Valley Walk**, the **Tabular Hills Walk**, the **Hambleton Hillside Mosaic Walk** and the **Newtondale Horse Trail**. These avoid roads wherever possible and link with local services such as bus routes. Maps and specialist guidebooks are available from the park shop or online. You don't have to complete any of these, just dip in and out for as little or as long as you wish. Serious walkers may also like to consider the **Cleveland Way National Trail** and The **North Sea Trail**, both of which have their own websites (*access via www.visitnorthyorkshire moors.co.uk*).

HELMSLEY AREA

The southern gateway to the North York Moors, **Helmsley** is an attractive village boasting the impressive 12C–13C ruins of **Helmsley Castle** (EH; ⏰*open Apr–Sept daily 10am–6pm, Oct Thu–Mon 10am–5pm, Nov–Feb Fri–Sun 10am–4pm, half-term hols open daily;* ✆£4.80; ♿🅿(*charge*); ℘01439 770 442; www. english-heritage.org.uk). Its visitor centre tells the story of how it evolved over the centuries, from a mighty medieval fortress to a luxurious Tudor mansion, to a Civil War stronghold and a romantic Victorian ruin.

Below the castle, **Helmsley Walled Garden** (⏰*open Good Fri/Apr–Oct daily*

ℹ **Info:** Helmsley Castle. ℘01439 770 173. ℘01751 473 791. www.yorkshire. com; www.northyork moors.org.uk

🧭 **Don't Miss:** Rievaulx Abbey; a ride on the North Yorkshire Moors Railway.

👪 **Kids:** The NYMR, Go Ape.

10.30am–5pm, Nov–Mar see website for times; ✆£5; ♿🅿✕; ℘01439 771 427; *www.helmsleywalledgarden.co.uk*), which dates from 1759, is a restored walled garden, conserving old, rare and endangered garden plants. It includes fruit trees, herbaceous borders, herb and ornamental gardens, glasshouses, ponds and fountains.

Neighbouring **Duncombe Park** (⏰*open: house only during craft fairs at Easter, Aug bank hol and Christmas; grounds Jun–Aug Wed–Sun 10.30am–5pm;* ✆£5; ♿🅿🅾♿℘01439 770 213; *www.duncombepark.co*), was built as the seat of the Feversham family in 1713. The Classical landscaped grounds include Doric and Ionic temples, and there is a nature reserve where most of the trees are over 250 years old.

On the B 1257, 3mi/5km northwest of Helmsley, lie the majestic ruins of **Rievaulx Abbey**★★ (EH; ⏰*open Apr–Sept daily 10am–6pm, Oct Thu–Mon 10am–5pm, Nov–Mar Sat–Sun/Feb half-term wk daily 10am–4pm;* ✆£5.60; 🅿✕; ℘01439 798 228; www.english-heritage. org.uk), one of the most complete, and atmospheric, of England's abbey ruins, and one of the most popular visitor attractions in the North. Pronounced "ree-voh", it was the first major monastery built by the Cistercians, founded c.1132 and completed in the late-12C. The ruins – infirmary, chapel, kitchens and a warming house – give an idea of the community's work and show how Rievaulx evolved into one of Britain's wealthiest monasteries. For many the abbey café and beautiful grounds are worth the trip alone.

Adjacent but with no access from the abbey grounds, is **Rievaulx Terrace and Temples** (NT; ⏱open daily mid-Feb–Oct 11am–5pm; ☞£5; ✆01439 798 340, 01439 748 283 (winter); www.nationaltrust.org. uk). This is one of Yorkshire's finest 18C landscape gardens, featuring Classical Georgian temples and a long curving grass terrace with fine views.

Some 12mi/19km east, sheep nibble the grass verges in the charming village of **Hutton-le-Hole**, which gets very busy with summer visitors. The **Ryedale Folk Museum** (⏱open year-round daily 10am–5.30pm/ late Oct–mid-Mar dusk; ⏱ closed early Dec–mid-Jan. ☞£5.50; ♿; ✆01751 417 367; www.ryedalefolk museum.co.uk) is a fascinating collection of local bygones housed in over 20 reconstructed buildings including a school classroom, a Witches' Hovel and an Iron Age dwelling made of mud, horse hair, wood and straw. Some 4mi/6km northeast of the village, at the bottom of a very steep (1:3) slope, lie the fragmentary ruins of 12C **Rosedale Abbey**. From here there is a magnificent panoramic **view**★ across the moors.

PICKERING AREA

The busy market town of Pickering, built on a limestone cliff at the southern edge of the national park, is the regional centre and "Gateway to the Moors". High on a strategic site just north of the centre lie the remains of **Pickering Castle** (EH; ⏱open Apr–Sept 10am–5pm; ☞£3.80; ✆01751 474 989, www.english-heritage. org.uk). This motte-and-bailey castle was a favourite hunting lodge of English kings until the 15C. In town, don't miss the 15C parish **Church of St Peter and St Paul** (Birdgate; www.pickeringchurch. com), famous for its vivid (restored) 15C frescoes. A walk along Birdgate, into Bridge Street, is the **Beck Isle Museum of Rural Life** (⏱open mid-Feb-Oct 10am–5pm; ☞£5; ✆01751 473 653, http://beckislemuseumtrust.wordpress. com), which records local rural life over the last two centuries.

Just around the corner from the museum is Pickering's main attraction, the lovingly preserved ⛺**North Yorkshire Moors**

Railway (⏱for fares and schedule, visit website; on certain days during the summer trains also run along a branch line the full length of the Esk Valley for 24mi/39km. ✆01751 472 508, www.nymr.co.uk). Running for 18mi/29km between Pickering and Whitby, riding the line takes you back some 50 years to the romantic era of steam, complete with cosy wood-panelled carriages, beautifully tended rural stations and smartly uniformed staff. The train stops at **Levisham**, **Newton Dale**, **Goathland** and **Grosmont** before terminating beside the sea at **Whitby** (⏱see opposite). The full journey takes 95 minutes but with a Day Rover ticket (☞£20–£25, child half-price) you're free to break your journey at no extra cost. A popular jumping-off point is the attractive village of **Goathland**. It was popularised as "Aidensfield" in the BBC TV series *Heartbeat*, and the station was the Hogsmeade stop for Harry Potter, though Potter fans should note there is precious little to see to link it with the films. It does, however, boast the refurbished **Warehouse Tea Room** with authentic furniture and artefacts. From Goathland you can walk the signposted **Rail Trail** (3.5mi/5.6km) to **Grosmont**; it runs along the route of George Stephenson's original railway line of 1836. Grosmont, restored to the British Railways' style of the 1960s, is the main depot for the NYMR and its gleaming locomotives can be seen at close quarters in the **Engine Sheds**. There is also a traditional railway buffet café here.

The much-photographed village of **Thornton-le-Dale** lies 2mi/3km east of Pickering and from here minor roads head into the **Dalby Forest** (☞toll road £7). In Low Dalby is the Dalby Forest Visitor Centre (⏱open year-round daily 10am–4.30pm; ✆01751 460 295; www. forestry.gov.uk), where you can pick up information, maps and booklets for various walking and cycling trails (bike hire available from here). There's also a café. Near Low Dalby is the treetop adventure course of ⛺**Go Ape** (⏱open early Apr–Oct daily/closed Tues during term time, Nov Sat–Sun, booking essential; ☞£30, child 10–17yrs £20; ✆0845 643 92 15; goape.co.uk).

North Yorkshire Coast

Given the nature of the weather here, it seems incongruous that this is where the first seaside resort in Britain sprang up; but Scarborough claims that very honour, with its entrepreneurial Victorian residents the first to successfully sell the benefits – proven or otherwise – of seaside breezes, sandy beaches and natural spa waters, well before other seaside towns. Yorkshire's other coastal towns soon followed suit.

> ⚜ **Michelin Map:** Michelin Atlas p47 or Map 502 S 21.
> ▣ **Info:** Brunswick Shopping Centre and Sandside (Harbour), Scarborough. ℘01723 383 636. Langborne Road, Upper Harbour, Whitby. ℘01723 383 636 (all offices). www.discoveryork shirecoast.com.

SCARBOROUGH

◐ *1mi/66km NE of York.*

Scarborough reached its fashionable zenith in the late-19C/early-20C, and despite recent developments remains one of the best places in Britain to savour the Victorian seaside.

Along its **seafront** are promenades, cliff railways, bridges spanning deep denes, pavilions, cafés, chalets, pretty little shelters and the great bulk of the refurbished **Spa** (the waters were declared unfit to drink in the 1930s), now an entertainment and conference centre. The elegant early-19C **Crescent** is home to **Scarborough Art Gallery**, (◐*open Tue–Sun 10am–5pm; ⊛£2; ℘01723 374 753, http://scarboroughartgallery.co.uk*). Just off North Bay Beach is ♟♟**Sea Life and Marine Sanctuary** (*Scalby Mills Road; ⊛£12.95, child £9.95/buy online; ♿✕; ℘0871 423 2110; www.sealife. co.uk*), an underwater safari plus rescued animals.

ROBIN HOOD'S BAY★

◐ *16mi/26km N on the A 171, then a minor road to the right (signposted).*
The little village in this picturesque bay was once the haunt of smugglers.

WHITBY

◐ *47mi/76km NE of York.*
Once a centre for shipbuilding and whaling, Whitby is now a fishing port and holiday resort at the mouth of the River Esk. The east side is overlooked by the atmospheric abbey ruins on the headland; the first few chapters of **Bram Stoker**'s *Dracula* are set here and over the years a veritable industry in ghosts, vampires and Gothic-related aspects has grown up in Whitby.

Whitby Abbey★

EH. ◐*Open Apr–Sept and school half-term hols daily 10am–5pm. Oct Thu–Mon 10am–4pm. Nov–Mar Sat–Sun 10am–4pm. ⊛£6. ♿▣✕. ℘01947 603 568. www.english-heritage.org.uk.*
in AD 657 **St Hilda**, Abbess of Hartlepool, founded the first abbey and earned Whitby an outstanding reputation as a holy place. In 867, however, it was sacked by the Danes. Two centuries later it was re-founded by one of William the Conqueror's knights, Reinfrid, though the present ruins belong to a second rebuilding that took place between 1220 and 1320. It was finally suppressed under Henry VIII in 1539. The innovative visitor centre traces the history of this once-great abbey.

Captain Cook Memorial Museum

Grape Lane. ◐*Open daily Mar 11am–3pm; Apr–Oct 9.45–5pm. ⊛£4. ♿. ℘01947 601 900. www.cookmuseumwhitby.co.uk.*
The late-17C house of shipowner John Walker, where James Cook served as an apprentice, is now a museum celebrating the years Cook spent in Whitby and his achievements as one of the world's greatest navigators. The tour ends in the attic where Cook had his quarters.

ADDRESSES

🏠 STAY

SHEFFIELD

👄👄 **Quarry House** – Rivelin Valley Road, Rivelin Glen Quarry. ☎0114 234 0382. www. quarryhouse.org.uk. 3 rms. This handsome sturdy stone country house, formerly the quarry master's home, is 10mi/16km south of Sheffield (also convenient for the Peak District). It has a bohemian air.

LEEDS

👄👄🍽 **Radisson Blu (The Light) No 1 The Light** – The Headrow, ☎0113 236 6000, www.radissonblu.co.uk. Art Deco style is given a modern twist in this splendid listed building in the centre of town. Rooms and public areas are contemporary, minimalist and very fashionable.

YORKSHIRE DALES

👄👄 **Beck Hall** – Malham. ☎01729 830 332. www.beckhallmalham.com. 18 rms. Ancient and modern rooms in this rambling, rustic early-18C building by the river. Period features include four-posters, carved antique beds, mullion windows and panelling.

👄👄 **Stow House Hotel** – Aysgarth, Leyburn. ☎01969 663 635, www.stowhouse. co.uk. 9 rms. Set apart, overlooking lawns (croquet in summer) and with wonderful open views over Wensleydale, this comfortable characterful Victorian mansion is just five minutes' walk from Aysgarth Falls.

👄👄–👄👄🍽 **Herriots Hotel** – Broughton Road, Skipton. ☎01756 792 781. www.herriotsforleisure.com. This Victorian-listed building is tastefully furnished. Special rooms include four-poster and spa rooms, and those with french doors overlook the canal. Fashionable new Modern British **restaurant** also on site.

👄👄–👄👄🍽 **Ripon Spa Hotel** – Park Street. ☎01765 602 172. www.riponspa.com. 40 rms. A five-minute walk from the cathedral, this elegant building sits in beautiful grounds with croquet lawns and terraces. Modern and traditional rooms. (Note: there is no spa here!)

HARROGATE

👄👄 **The Bijou** – 17 Ripon Road. ☎01423 567 974. www.thebijou.co.uk. 10 rms. Trendy boutique-style accommodation in a bijou Victorian villa in the fashionable neighbourhood of Harrogate's Duchy Estate, a five-minute walk from the centre.

YORK

👄–👄👄 **Acer** – 52 Scarcroft Hill. ☎01904 653 839. www.acerhotel.co.uk. This small pretty boutique guesthouse, complete with four-poster bedroom, is located in a Victorian terrace a few minutes'-walk from the city centre, and offers a warm welcome.

👄–👄👄 **Crook Lodge** – 26 St Mary's, Bootham. ☎01904 655 614. http://crooklodge.yorkwebsites.co.uk. Stylish pretty de-luxe bedrooms in an attractive Victorian house enjoying a quiet city centre location, with private car park.

👄👄 **Coach House Hotel** – Marygate, Bootham. ☎01904 652 780. www.coachhousehotel-york.com. 11 rms. This 300-year-old stone walled oak-beamed hotel was once a coach-builder's house. It Is only 300yds/275m from the minster in a quiet road and has parking facilities. Full bar with beer on tap.

NORTH YORK MOORS

👄 **Cawthorne House** – 42 Eastgate, Pickering. ☎01751 477 364. 5 rms. This handsome sturdy stone house, with a lovely terrace garden, is a five-minute walk from the town centre. Bedrooms are stylish, with a mixed traditional and modern feel. Very comfortable.

👄👄 **No 54** – 54 Bondgate, Helmsley. ☎01439 771 533. www.no54.co.uk. 3 rms. This charming highly popular B&B was built in the early-19C. It has cosy bedrooms, York flagstone floors, real fires in winter and a lovely courtyard garden for the summer. Within walking distance of the centre of Helmsley.

NORTH YORKSHIRE COAST

👄 **Heathfield Guest House** – 22 Prospect Hill, Whitby. ☎01947 605 407. www. bedandbreakfast-whitby.co.uk. 3 rms. Simple but stylish acclaimed small family-run B&B guesthouse a short walk from the town centre.

👄👄–👄👄🍽 **Royal Hotel** – St Nicholas Street, Scarborough. ☎01723 364 333. www. englishrosehotels.co.uk. 118 rms. This classic grand old English seaside hotel (built 1830) overlooking South Bay has moved with the times to include a spa and wellness facilities and rooms with contemporary décor. Offpeak bargains online.

🍴 EAT

SHEFFIELD

👄👄–👄👄🍽 **Rafters** – 220 Oakbrook Road. ☎0114 230 4819. www.rafters restaurant.co.uk. Situated in a leafy suburb 10 minutes from the centre, superchef Marcus Lane's Rafters has been setting the standard for local and regional restaurants for many years. Regular special offers and special menus mean that this otherwise exclusive gastronomic experience is open to most wallets.

LEEDS

For a wide choice of modern bars and restaurants visit the Waterfront.

Fourth Floor Café – *Cross Arcade.* 0113 204 8000. *www.harvey nichols.com.* This chic space on the top floor of Harvey Nichols, with a spectacular view over the rooftops, is spacious, light and airy. By night, subdued lighting and twinkling candles transform it into an inti- mate space. Only seasonal ingredients are used, sourced both locally and from afar.

BRADFORD

Bradford is renowned for the quality of its Indian and Pakistani restaurants.

Karachi – *15-17 Neal Street, Bradford.* 01274 732 015. A short walk from the city centre, the Karachi is one of the oldest restaurants from the Indian continent (it's actually Pakistani) in town, and serves some unusual dishes, such as curried meatballs. Good value.

YORKSHIRE DALES

Cross View Tea Rooms & Restaurant – *38/39 Market Place, Richmond.* 01748 825 897. *www.crossviewtearooms.co.uk.* These lovely traditional tearooms in a listed Georgian building overlook Richmond's historic cobbled marketplace. Open for breakfast, lunch and afternoon tea.

Lockwoods – *83 North Street, Ripon.* 01765 607 555. *www.lockwoods restaurant.co.uk.* Bright, cheerful, laid-back and very stylish, this multi-award-winning brasserie, café and restaurant successfully mixes traditional and contemporary in both its menus, and its décor and art, serving brunch through to dinner. Very family-friendly, it uses the freshest ingredients from local producers and suppliers.

Angel Inn – *Hetton, nr Rylstone. 5mi/8km north of Skipton Angel Inn.* 01756 730 263, *www.angelhetton. co.uk.* One of the country's longest-running gastropubs, parts of the Angel date back 500 years. Choose between the "Bar Brasserie" or slightly more formal "Restaurant", though both are part of the main pub and serve multi-award-winning locally sourced Modern British cuisine.

YORK

The pubs and restaurants along the Riverside (between Lendal

Bridge and Ouse Bridge), Micklegate Bar, Stonegate Walk and Swinegate are all worth exploring.

Café No. 8 Bistro – *8 Gillygate.* 01904 653 074, *www.no8-bistro.com.* Lovely little relaxed café to eat at throughout the day, from a full vegetarian breakfast to spicy Moroccan meatballs for dinner. Outdoor seating at rear.

Blackwell Ox Inn – *Huby Road, Sutton-on-the-Forest (8mi/13km N of York).* 01347 810 328. *www.blackwelloxinn. co.uk.* Worth the journey for the locally sourced food in either the restaurant or the bar of this country-house-like pub.

Melton's Too – *25 Walmgate.* 01904 629 222. *www.meltonstoo.co.uk.* Café-bistro offspring of Melton's (*see below*), set in a charming 17C building and specialising in tapas and other eclectic good-value dishes.

Melton's – *7 Scarcroft Road,* 01904 634 341, *www.meltonsrestaurant. co.uk. Closed Sun, Mon.* Superb Modern British cooking from a husband-and-wife chef proprietors team, using the finest Yorkshire ingredients served in casual, stripped-down surroundings.

HULL

Bars, cafés and pubs can be found mostly in and around Trinity Square.

NORTH YORK MOORS

White Swan – *Market Place, Pickering.* 01751 472 288, *www.white-swan.co.uk.* Everything is home-made and (wherever possible) locally sourced in the gastropub dining area of this cosy characterful 16C coaching inn, on the town's main square.

The Rutland Restaurant – *The Black Swan Hotel, Market Place Helmsley,* 01439 770 466. *www.blackswan-helmsley.co.uk.* Fine dining restaurant with a subtle, modern style, set within a 16C coaching inn recently converted to a boutique hotel. Choose from the table d'hote, the seasonal à la carte, or the Signature menu. Its Brasserie ( ) offers more informal, relaxed dining.

NORTH YORKSHIRE COAST

Magpie Café – *Whitby.*
Marmalade's – *Beiderbecke's Hotel. 1–3 The Crescent, Scarborough.* 01723 365 766. *www.beiderbeckes.com.* This smart brasserie serves simple prix-fixe menus with live jazz every Thursday and Saturday in summer.

NORTHEAST

Like in Yorkshire and Liverpool, folk in the northeast have a fierce sense of place and a dry self-deprecating humour, in part borne out of hardship. The region has suffered much in the late-20C declining from a major industrial powerhouse to little more than a historical footnote. Newcastle-upon-Tyne is the dynamic focus of the Northeast, an exciting city break and a good base to learn about its history and culture. Elsewhere much of this once violently disputed border region has returned to nature.

Highlights

1 Become part of the picture at **Durham Cathedral** (p412)
2 A family day out at **Beamish, The Living Museum** (p414)
3 Stroll the Quayside at **Newcastle**, admiring its bridges and new architecture (p416)
4 Step back in time at Housesteads Fort on **Hadrian's Wall** (p422)
5 Have a wizard time at **Alnwick Castle** and **Garden** (p424)

Durham and Tees Valley

Durham is one of England's most perfectly sited towns. Its magnificent cathedral makes a picture-perfect composition that has graced a thousand travel posters. By contrast to today's genteel cathedral city, around here was mined much of the coal that powered Britain. The area's most enjoyable foray back in time is at family-friendly Beamish The Living Museum. A grittier perspective on the more recent past can be had at Hartlepool, Middlesbrough and Darlington.

Newcastle-upon-Tyne

The regional capital is famous for its spectacular bridges, its black-and-white football team, and its raucous short-sleeved, high-heeled Toon ("town") nightlife. The town is solidly Victorian, though it also boasts much fine Georgian architecture. Its collection of museums and art galleries (∞ *free of charge)* are outstanding. The quayside, once a frenzy of industrial shipping activity, has been regenerated by new iconic landmarks such as the Sage and Baltic music and arts centres, its Millennium Bridge, and hip hotels such as Malmaison and Hotel du Vin. The biggest icon of all, The Angel of the North with its giant outstretched wings, lies just outside the centre, .

Hadrian's Wall Country

The Northeast has always been an important frontier region, from the Romans' Hadrian's Wall (built to keep out the Scots Picts), to the many wars and skirmishes between Scotland and England, from the 14C right through the 16C. Hadrian's Wall, now a World Heritage Site, is still partially intact and many of the most important places along its way feature excellent re-creations and interpretations of life on the Roman frontier. The surrounding area is a paradise for walkers and nature lovers.

Northumberland National Park

Remote from highways and towns, and free from holiday crowds and theme parks, this is (officially) one of England's most tranquil spots. Kielder Water and Forest Park is the favourite day out for walkers, mountain bikers and families who like to keep things natural. For a little more excitement, Chillingham Castle provides a window on both a glorious and a grim past.

Northumberland Coast

The picturesque and very desirable market town of Alnwick boasts a splendid "Harry Potter" castle, and the finest new garden in the country. Close by, Cragside, the former home of the industrialist who did more than anyone to put Newcastle on the map, the Holy Island of Lindisfarne, and the windswept Farne Islands, all make for fascinating and contrasting excursions. England's northernmost town is Berwick-upon-Tweed, fought over so many times between England and Scotland that even today many Brits don't know to whom it belongs! It's worth the journey for its rampart views alone.

Food Heroes

Northumberland beef and lamb are renowned for their quality. In restaurants, look out for breeds of lamb such as **Hexham Blackface**, and **Cheviot**, and beef breeds such as **Gallaway**, and **Welsh Black**. **Alnwick Stew** is a traditional winter dish (not easy to find these days), of gammon or ham, with layers of sliced onion, and potatoes, flavoured with mustard and bay leaf. **Bacon floddies** are a tradtional Gateshead dish, served with sausages and eggs at breakfast or supper.

Pan Haggerty, popular throughout Northumberland, is always served from the pan, its thin sliced potato and onions cooked with a layer of cheese. Its name is perhaps derived from the French *hachis*, meaning sliced. **Celery cheese** is worth trying, as is **Whitley Goose**, which has nothing to do with any sort of bird; it's a dish of onions, cheddar, butter and cream. One of the most famous dishes of the region is **Pease Pudding**, which has its origins in Medieval times. It's a boiled vegetable dish similar to mushy peas, consisting of split yellow peas, salt and spices, cooked in a pot with a bacon or ham joint.

The freshest fish in the region are landed at **North Shields Fish Quay**, and go, among other places, to **Colmans** of South Shields *(http://colmansfishandchips.com)*, voted the best fish and chip shop in England in 2011. Family-owned and operated since 1926 you can eat here or take-away.

The small coastal village of Craster is famous for **Craster Kippers.** L.Robson & Sons *(www.kipper.co.uk)* prepare traditional oak-smoked kippers and salmon in their original 130-year old smokehouses. You can't see inside but you can buy direct or enjoy their products in the company's own Craster Seafood Restaurant on site. There is an even older smokehouse, dating back to 1843, at The Fishermans Kitchen in Seahouses. Now run by Swallowfish *(www.swallowfish.co.uk)* visitors can buy kippers and all kinds of fish and seafood, both fresh and smoked. Historic photos and objects are on display in the shop. Other seafood delicacies of the region include potted salmon and baked herrings.

The holy island of **Lindisfarne** has been famous for its **oysters**, tended by the monks, since around the 14C. The monks, long gone, also introduced mead, a sweet wine made with fermented grape juice, honey and herbs, and fortified with fine spirits. You can taste and buy at St Aidan's Winery (http://lindisfarne-mead.co.uk) who also make and sell Lindisfarne English fruit wines and liqueurs.

Honey lovers can also visit Chain Bridge Honey Farm *(www.chainbridgehoney.co.uk)* on the border in Berwick Upon Tweed. This is the largest natural producer of comb honey in the country, with a visitor centre and café.

The region's most famous drink is **Newcastle Brown Ale**; synonymous with the city it was brewed in from 1927 until 2010 when production moved to Tadcaster, Yorkshire. It has a sweet, nutty taste, somewhere between a bitter and a classic sweet brown ale. You'll find it in every bar. Much less common these days is its traditional working class accompaniment, a ham-and-pease pudding filled **stottie**. A stottie (or stottie cake) is a flat, round doughy bread roll, baked to a local recipe, while pease pudding (see above) is mushy yellow split peas, once popular all over the north east.

EAT! NewcastleGateshead (mid-Jun to late Jun, www.eatnewcastlegates head.com), is a quirky, imaginative and very interactive food festival, which includes street-food markets, a beer and chilli festival and a huge range of (often unusual) events over 10 days.

Durham★★★
and around

The quiet streets of the little medieval city with its castle are the perfect foil for the great sandstone mass of the Norman cathedral rising above the deep wooded gorge of the River Wear in a sublime fusion of architecture and landscape, in what is a truly remarkable setting★★★.

A BIT OF HISTORY

Christianity flourished early in the Saxon Kingdom of Northumbria but conditions were rarely stable in this border country with its coastline exposed to raiders from the east. In 875 the monks of Lindisfarne fled south from Danish attacks, carrying with them the body of **St Cuthbert** (d.687) but it was not until more than 100 years later that his much-venerated remains found their final resting place on easily defended bluffs carved out by the Wear. From the 1070s the site's natural advantages were strengthened by the Normans, who built their castle to command the peninsula's narrow neck. In 1093 the cathedral's foundation stone was laid. Uniquely in England, Durham's bishop was not only spiritual leader but lay lord, the powerful Prince Palatine of a long-troubled province.

The city has remained compact, physically unaffected by the once intense industrial activity all around it. Its scholarly character was confirmed with the foundation in 1832 of the university, after Oxford and Cambridge England's oldest. It is also the county town, an important administrative and shopping centre. On the second Saturday in July, it is thronged with the thousands attending one of Britain's great popular festivals of modern times, the famous **Miners' Gala**.

CATHEDRAL★★★

🕐 *Open mid-Jul–Aug Mon–Sat 9.30–8pm, Sun 12.30–8pm; Sept–mid-Jul Mon–Sat 9.30am–6pm, Sun 12.30pm–5.30pm. For specific opening times of areas within cathedral see website.* 🎧 *Donation requested. Tower £5.*

▶ **Population:** 36,937.
🚗 **Michelin Map:** Michelin Atlas p46 or Map 501 P 19.
ℹ **Info:** ☎0191 384 3720. www.thisisdurham.com.
▶ **Location:** 18mi/29km south of Newcastle-upon-Tyne. The train station and bus station are almost opposite each other on North Road, 10 minutes from the centre. You can see this compact city on foot. Boat trips and rowing boats available.
👁 **Don't Miss:** Chapel of the Nine Altars; riverside views from or near Prebend's Bridge.
🅿 **Parking:** Parking is difficult in the centre.

Temporary exhibitions area, The Story of Saint Cuthbert and Durham Cathedral audio-visual and Monks' Dormitory, joint ticket £5. 🎧 *Guided tours (£4) Mon–Sat 11am, 2pm, sometimes also 10.30am.* ♿✕. ☎0191 386 4266. www.durhamcathedral.co.uk.
Durham Cathedral's beauty lies in its unity: its fabric was mostly completed in the short period between 1095 and 1133 and though added to since, it remains a supremely harmonious achievement of Norman architecture on the grandest possible scale.

Exterior

The usual entrance is the northwest portal, which has many arches and is embellished with the celebrated lion's head **Sanctuary Knocker★**, a 12C masterpiece of expressive stylisation. **Palace Green** is dominated by the cathedral.

Interior

In the **nave★★★** the first impression is one of overwhelming power. Huge deeply grooved columns alternate with massive many-shafted piers to form an arcade supporting a gallery and clerestory. The pointed ribs of the beautiful vault are an important technical and

Durham Cathedral and the Old Fulling Mill viewed from the River Wear

© travellinglight/iStockphoto.com

aesthetic innovation, heralding the lightness and grace of Gothic architecture. The great weight of masonry, its arches enriched with various zigzag patterning, is, however, so well proportioned that the final effect is one of repose, of great forces held in equilibrium. From the crossing there is a stupendous view up into the vault under the central tower, while in the south transept is an extraordinary brightly painted 16C clock. In the choir there are fine **stalls** and the splendidly vain **throne** and **tomb** of the 14C Bishop Hatfield. Beyond the 14C **Neville Screen** with its delicate stonework is the **Shrine of St Cuthbert**.

The 13C **Chapel of the Nine Altars**★★★, an earlier example of which is to be found at Fountains Abbey, is an Early English addition to the cathedral. The sunken floor, designed to gain as much height as possible, and the extravagantly tall lancet windows, which are separated by columns of clustered shafts, reveal a new preoccupation with lightness and verticality. The carved stonework of the bosses and capitals is extremely rich.

At the extreme western end of the building, perched on the very edge of

the ravine, is the **Galilee Chapel**. Twelve slender columns, their arches profusely decorated with zigzag carvings, subdivide the interior, which contains the tomb of the **Venerable Bede** (d.735), England's first historian. From the top of the cathedral's central tower (a long climb of 325 steps: access from south transept) spectacular **views**★ reinforce the full drama of Durham's site.

Monastic Buildings

Around the much rebuilt cloisters are grouped the buildings of the former abbey. They include the monks' dormitory and the **Cathedral Treasury**★, with its collection of Anglo-Saxon embroideries, precious objects and manuscripts and, above all, the evocative relics associated with St Cuthbert – his tiny portable altar, his pectoral cross, fragments of his oak coffin... To the south is the tranquil precinct of the **college**, its mellow, mostly 18C buildings resting on medieval foundations.

CITY AND RIVERSIDE

From the **Market Place**, sited at the very neck of the peninsula, streets descend steeply to the sloping Elvet Bridge on the east and to **Framwellgate Bridge** on the west. From here there is a fine **view**★★ upstream of the cathedral and the stern walls of the castle.

North Bailey and **South Bailey**, with their many pleasant 18C houses, follow the line of the town wall. Nearby is the church of St Mary-le-Bow, now housing the **Durham Heritage Centre** *(North Bailey;* ◷*open Easter weekend, Apr–Jun and Oct Sat–Sun and bank hol Mons 4.30pm, Jul–Sept daily 11am–4.30pm;* &*;* ℘*0191 384 5589; www.durhamheritage centre.org.uk),* telling the story of the city from medieval times to the present day. From here a lane leads downhill to Kingsgate footbridge of 1963, elegantly spanning the gorge to link the city with the uncompromisingly modern building of the University Students' Union, **Dunelm House**. South Bailey ends at the Watergate, from which a track leads down to **Prebend's Bridge**. From here, from the path on the far bank and from the riverside itself are those **views**★★★ which have long captivated writers and artists; a perfect composition of water, trees and humble mill buildings.

Durham Castle★

⌁ *Guided tour all afternoons (2pm, 3pm, 4pm) in university term time, and all mornings (10am, 11am, noon) in term holidays (some afternoons too). Call to confirm or see website for details.* ◷*Closed Christmas holidays.* ⊚*£5.* ℘*0191 334 3800. www.durhamcastle.com.*

The present castle began in 1072 as a simple defensive mound commissioned by William the Conqueror. The Norman architecture of the castle was much modified by successive prince bishops .Today its Norman keep houses **University College** (or Castle as it is known), Durham University's oldest college, founded 1832.

From the courtyard, protected by the much rebuilt gatehouse and overlooked by the keep on its great earth mound, the tour proceeds via the 15C **kitchen** into the imposing **Great Hall**, then to galleries built around the original castle wall, whose fine arched doorway is

still intact. The upper floors are reached by the broad steps of the spectacular **Black Staircase** of 1662. There are two chapels, one of the 16C with humorous misericords including a bagpipe-playing pig and a nagging wife in a wheelbarrow. The **Norman chapel**★, deep below, dates from the castle's earliest days and evokes a more primitive world, with its capitals crudely ornamented with weird figures and savage faces.

Oriental Museum (Durham University)★★

◖ *Elvet Hill, off South Road. From city centre take the A 1050 and A 167 S towards Darlington.* ◷*Open Mon–Fri 10am–5pm, Sat–Sun and bank hols noon–5pm.* ◷*Closed 22 Dec–early Jan.* ⊚*£1.50.* &&&. ℘*0191 334 5694. www.dur.ac.uk/oriental.museum.*

Changing displays range from Ancient Egypt via India and Southeast Asia to Japan; of outstanding interest are its ceramics, jade and other hardstone pieces, and an extraordinary room-like bed, all from China. A new Egyptian gallery has also been designed specifically with children in mind.

EXCURSIONS
♟♟ Beamish, The Living Museum★★

◖ *10mi/16km S by any of the river bridges and the A 692 towards Consett.* ◷*Open Apr–Oct daily 10am–5pm (last entry 3pm); Oct–Nov Tue–Thu and Sat–Sun 10am–4pm/dusk (last entry 3pm).* ◷*Closed 25 Dec.* ⊚*£16 (winter weekdays £8), child £10 (winter weekdays £5).* &&. ℘*0191 370 4000. www.beamish.org.uk.*

This much-loved and hugely popular museum, in a lovely 300-acre/120ha countryside setting, re-creates life in the north of England around the turn of the 20C and also evokes the environment of ordinary people at the start of the 19C, just as the full effect of the Industrial Revolution began to be felt in the region.

Preserved tramcars, supplemented by a pre-second World War motorbus, take visitors through the extensive site to the town, whose shops, houses, bank, working pub, sweet factory, newspaper office and printer's workshop, stocked and furnished authentically, and inhabited by costumed guides, evoke the urban scene of yesteryear. Visitors can also penetrate underground into a real mine (🕐 summer only).

National Railway Museum Shildon (Locomotion)

▶ *Shildon. 13mi/21km S of Durham.*
🕐 *Open year-round daily 10am–5pm (Nov–Mar 4pm).* 🕐 *Closed 22 Dec–early Jan.* ♿🅿✕. *☎01388 777 999. www.nrm.org.uk/locomotion.*
This impressive outpost of York's famous National Railway Museum (👈 *see York*) has a permanent display of over 70 railway heritage vehicles and a busy programme of events and rides on historic trains.

Raby Castle

▶ *19mi/31km SW of Durham.* 🕐 *Open Easter weekend & May–Sept Sun–Wed (Jul–Aug Sun–Fri), park and gardens 11am–5.30pm, castle 1–4.30pm.*
💷 *£9.50.* 🅿✕. *www.rabycastle.com.*
☎01833 660 202.
Built for the powerful dynasty of the Nevills, who still own the castle today, this picturesque medieval lakeside castle exudes a powerful exterior of towers, turrets and fortifications dating back to the 11C. Its interiors range from Medieval, most notably its magnificent Baron's Hall, to Victorian, and its treasures include Meissen porcelain, tapestries, furnishings and paintings by artists such as Munnings, De Hooch, Teniers, Van Dyck and Reynolds.

Tees Valley

Iron and steel (in Middlesbrough), the railways (in Darlington) and shipbuilding (in Hartlepool) made Teesside one of the powerhouses of the UK in the late-19C. All these industries have now disappeared.

Darlington

Darlington's railway museum **Head of Steam** (*North Road Station;* 🕐 *open Apr–Sept Tue–Sun 10am–4pm, Oct–Mar Wed–Sun 11am–3.30pm;* 💷 *£4.95;* ♿🅿✕; *☎01365 460 532, www.darlington.gov. uk/Leisure*) gives pride of place to *Locomotion,* the first ever steam train to carry fare-paying passengers from Darlington (to Stockton-on-Tees) in 1825.

Middlesbrough

Housed in a landmark 2007 building, the town's new pride and joy is **MIMA**, the Middlesbrough Institute of Modern Art (*Centre Square;* 🕐 *open Tue–Sat 10am–4.30pm/Thur 7pm, Sun noon–4.00pm;* ♿🅿✕; *☎01642 726 720; www.visitmima.com*). The town's most famous son, Captain James Cook,

📋 **Info***:*
www.visitteesvalley.co.uk
👪 **Kids:** Hartlepool's Maritime Experience..

is commemorated in the **Captain Cook Birthplace Museum** (*Stewart Park, Marton;* 🕐 *open Mar–Oct Tue–Sun 10am–5.30pm;* ♿🅿✕; *☎01642 311 211, www. captcook-ne.co.uk*).

Hartlepool

In the 19C this was England's third-largest port and its halcyon days are recalled at the lively **Hartlepool's Maritime Experience** (*Jackson Dock;* 🕐 *open daily Apr–Oct 10am–5pm, Nov–Mar 11am–4pm;* ♿🅿✕; *☎01429 860 077,;www.hartlepoolsmaritimeexperience.com*). This excellent award-winning re-creation of an 18C seaport is staffed by guides in authentic period dress and moored here is Britain's oldest warship still afloat, *HMS Trincomalee,* built 1817. Also on site, the **Museum of Hartlepool** includes a superbly restored 1930s paddle steamer.

Newcastle-upon-Tyne★★

and around

Newcastle is an important hub on the busy east-coast route to Scotland. Its dramatic site, rich history and the distinctive dialect spoken by its population of "Geordies" give this undisputed capital of the northeast of England an exceptionally strong identity. Despite recent decline Newcastle retains great vigour as a commercial, educational, entertainment and cultural centre. The city centre shopping complex in Eldon Square was one of the most ambitious of its kind when built, while the gargantuan MetroCentre on the outskirts of Gateshead is billed as one of the largest shopping and leisure complexes in Europe. Post-Millennium, the BALTIC Centre for Contemporary Arts and The Sage music venue are powerful symbols of the city's new cultural ambitions.

A BIT OF HISTORY

The easily defended bridging point where the Tyne enters its gorge was exploited by the Roman founders of Pons Aelius, one post among many along Hadrian's Wall, then by the Normans, whose "New Castle" dates from 1080. Later, abundant mineral resources, particularly coal, stimulated trade, manufacturing and engineering. The great railway inventor **George Stephenson** (1781–1848) was born nearby, as was his son Robert, and in the 19C Tyneside became one of the great centres of industrial Britain, dominated by figures like **William Armstrong**, later Lord Armstrong (1810–1900), whose engineering and armament works at Elswick helped equip the navies of the world.

GATESHEAD

The approach from the south through **Gateshead** reveals an astonishing **urban panorama**★★. The city of Newcastle has spread slowly from the north

▶ **Population:** 189,150.
🔧 **Michelin Map:** Michelin Atlas p51 or Map 502 P 19.
🗄 **Info:** Central Arcade, Market Street. ℘0191 277 8000. www.newcastlegateshead.com; www.gateshead.gov.uk/LeisureandCulture.
◖ **Location:** 84mi/134km due north of York. Central (railway) Station is just that, with a Metro station attached. Haymarket Bus Station is north of the city centre, also linked to the Metro network, which offers fast, efficient travel around Newcastle and Tyneside. Newcastle-upon-Tyne is the city north of the river (where nearly all the major sites are found), while the separate town of Gateshead begins across any of the town-centre bridges. The city centre is best seen on foot.
👁 **Don't Miss:** The BALTIC Centre; views from the city bridges.
🕐 **Timing:** At least two days.
👫 **Kids:** Discovery Museum. Life (Science Centre).

bank of the Tyne via steeply sloping streets and precipitous stairways up to the flatter land to the north. Buildings of all periods and materials are dominated by the castle and the cathedral tower.

BALTIC Centre★

Gateshead Quays. ◷*Open daily Tue 10.30–6pm, Wed–Mon 10am–6pm.* ♿✗. ℘*0191 478 1810. www.balticmill.com.*
Housed in a landmark former flour mill on the River Tyne in Gateshead, this is the biggest gallery of its kind in the world – presenting an ever-changing international programme of contemporary visual art. The views from the top are memorable.

River Tyne with Gateshead Millennium Bridge, The Sage and Tyne Bridge

© Studio Pookini/Fotolia.com

The Sage★

South of the Tyne. ◷Open 9am–9pm/
11pm. ♿🅿✗. ℘0191 443 4661 / 443
4666. www.thesagegateshead.org.

This amazing recent addition to the
riverfront, likened to a giant stainless
steel armadillo, was built 1994–2004,
designed by Sir Norman Foster and Mott
MacDonald, and has already become an
iconic building. It is home to the Northern Sinfonia but hosts all kinds of musical performances taking in every genre.
It is home to a smart café and brasserie,
four bars, and offers wonderful views.

✿◟WALKING TOUR
Quayside★

Newcastle and Gateshead are linked
by seven bridges, which make an outstanding **composition**★ extending
upstream. The oldest is the unusual
High Level Bridge (1848), designed by
Robert Stephenson with railway tracks
above and roadway below. The newest
is the graceful **Gateshead Millennium
Bridge**★, the world's first (and as yet,
only) tilting bridge. The **Swing Bridge**

(1876) designed by Lord Armstrong,
brightly painted and nautical-looking,
follows the alignment of the original
crossing. The monumental stone piers
of the great **Tyne Bridge** (1928) add
drama while the riverside walkways,
with sculpture, pubs, bars and hotels,
are a popular place for a stroll.

Among the tightly packed Victorian
commercial buildings off the Quayside
are a few much older survivors: the 17C
Guildhall, the 18C **All Saints Church**★
and the remarkable timber-framed **Bes-
sie Surtees House** (*EH;* ◷open Mon–
Fri 10am–4pm; ℘0191 269 1200; www.
english-heritage.org.uk) two five-storey
16C and 17C merchants' houses which
boast splendid period interiors.

Castle Keep★

◷Open year-round Mon–Sat 10am–
5pm, Sun noon–5pm. ◷Closed 1 Jan,
25, 26 Dec. ◎£4. ℘0191 232 7938,
www.castlekeep-newcastle.org.uk.

The city took its name from the "new
castle" built by William the Conquer-
or's son, Robert Curthose in 1080. The

PRACTICAL INFORMATION
PUBLIC TRANSPORT

The **Tyne and Wear Metro** runs at
5.30am–11.30pm, linking Newcastle
city with Tyneside and the coast.
Trains run every seven minutes to the
airport and the coast, and every three
minutes at peak times within the
city. For full details on bus and Metro
travel contact **Nexus** (*℘0191 2020 747;
www.nexus.org.uk*).

SIGHTSEEING

For sightseeing on the River Tyne,
River Escapes (*℘01670 785 666; www.
riverescapes.co.uk*) runs regular cruises
from Newcastle Quayside, beside
the Millennium Bridge, during the
summer months, with three themes:
the city, the countryside, out to sea.

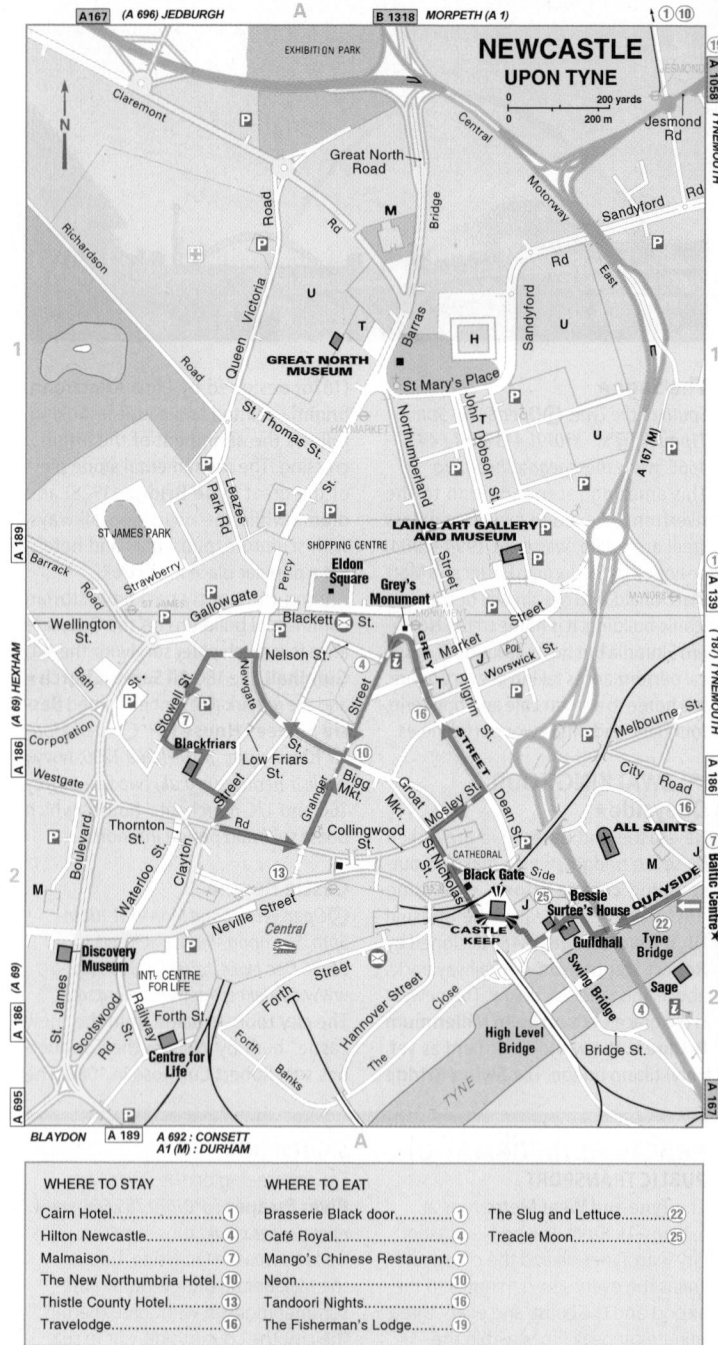

NEWCASTLE UPON TYNE

present keep is all that remains of its 12C successor and is a particularly good example of a Norman keep. From the roof of this massive stone edifice there is an all-embracing panorama of city, river and distant countryside.

City Centre★

Enlightened planning gave 19C Newcastle a new centre of Classical dignity, comprising fine civic buildings, great covered markets and shopping arcades and spacious streets, of which the most splendid is **Grey Street**★, curving elegantly downhill from the high column of **Grey's Monument**, past the great portico of the Theatre Royal.

ADDITIONAL SIGHTS
Discovery Museum

Blandford Square. Open year-round Mon–Sat 10am–5pm, Sun 2–5pm. Closed 1 Jan, 5–26 Dec. (charge). ℘0191 232 6789. www.twmuseums.org.uk/discovery.

This entertaining, colourful museum, full of interactive displays, is the ideal starting point from which to find out all about life on Tyneside, from the domestic to heavy industry, and to inventions which changed the world, including the 115ft-/35m- long *Turbinia* which dominates the entrance. Invented on Tyneside, this was the first ship to be powered by a steam turbine and was once the fastest ship in the world.

Life Science Centre

Times Square. Open year-round daily 10am (Sun 11am)–6pm. £9, child £6.25. (charge). ℘0191 243 8223. www.life.org.uk.

This landmark Millennium project offers live science shows, an interactive theatre, all kinds of hands-on displays, a simulator ride and family-based laboratory workshops. Although it is child oriented it is the public face of a pioneering science village, where scientists, educationalists and businesspeople come together to promote life sciences.

Great North Museum: Hancock★

Barras Bridge. Open year-round daily Mon–Sat 10am–5pm, Sun 2–5pm. Closed 1 Jan, 25–26 Dec. ℘0191 222 6765. www.twmuseums.org.uk/greatnorthmuseum.

On the edge of the university campus, this important museum, boasting 3,500 natural history, archaeological and ethnographical artefacts, recently reopened following a £26 million extension and refurbishment. Its remit is both global history and matters closer to home. Highlights of its 11 galleries include a large-scale, interactive model of Hadrian's Wall, the wonder and diversity of the animal kingdom (including a near-complete life-size T-Rex dinosaur skeleton), life and death in Ancient Egypt, and spectacular objects from the Ancient Greeks. There is also a planetarium.

Laing Art Gallery★

New Bridge Street. Open year-round Mon–Sat 10am–5pm, Sun 2–5pm. Closed 1 Jan, 25–26 Dec. (charge). ℘0191 232 7734. www.twmuseums.org.uk/laing.

This is the region's finest collection, renowned for its English watercolours the sculpture. It emphasises the 19C, with works by eminent Pre-Raphaelites, the apocalyptic works of the visionary **John Martin**.

EXCURSIONS
Angel of the North★

5mi/8km S. Between the the A 1 and A 167, Gateshead. Access off A 167. www.angelofthenorth.org.uk.

Erected in 1998, Antony Gormley's majestic steel Angel, 65ft/20m high, with a wingspan of 175ft/54m and a weight of 208 tonnes, is not only Britain's largest sculpture but its most iconic and best-loved statue of the 21C so far.

Segedunum

Buddle Street, Wallsend. 4mi/6.5km E. Open Apr-Oct 10am–5pm, Nov–mid-Dec and mid Jan–Mar Mon–Fri 10am–3pm. £4.50. ℘0191 236 9437. www.twmuseums.org.uk.

"Segger-doon-um" means strong fort in Roman, and this is the nearest section of **Hadrian's Wall** (*see Hadrian's Wall*) to Newcastle. It features a reconstructed bath-house, a museum of artefacts and a replica full-size section of the wall which once stretched 73mi/117km west from here. A lofty viewing tower looks down on the site.

Hadrian's Wall ★★

In AD 122 the Roman Emperor Hadrian visited Britain and ordered the building of a defensive wall across the northernmost boundary of the empire from Wallsend on the Tyne, to Bowness on the Solway Firth (73mi/117km). Although Hadrian's Wall has come to represent the frontier between England and Scotland, it is well south of the modern border. Parts of this wall can still be seen today and museums, camps and settlements give a picture of military and civilian life on Rome's "Northwest Frontier".

- **Michelin Map:** Michelin Atlas p50, p51, or Map 502 L 19, M, N and O 18.
- **Info:** Wentworth Place, Hexham. ✆01434 652 220. Once Brewed Visitor Centre, Bardon Mill. ✆01434 344 396. www.hadrians-wall.org. www.hadrians wall-northumberland.com.
- **Getting Around:** Bus AD122 (🕐operates Good Fri–Oct daily; ✆0871 200 22 33) runs the length of the wall, stopping at all major points of interest.

A BIT OF HISTORY

The wall – The wall was built by legionaries, citizens of Rome, and garrisoned by as many as 24,000 auxiliaries from conquered territories.

It was defended by a ditch on the north side; on the south side it was paralleled by a military road and "vallum", defining the military zone. The wall was built in stone and turf, with forts, turrets and milecastles (military bases) numbered, from east to west, from Wallsend (0) to Bowness (80).

It follows the best strategic and geographical line and, at places such as Cawfields and at Walltown Crags, commands splendid **views**.

ALONG THE WALL

Follow the B 6318.

The main sites (listed below from east to west) all have car parks and are indicated by light brown signposts.

Corbridge Roman Town★

EH. 🕐 *W of Corbridge.* 🕐*Open Apr–Sept daily 10am–5.30pm; Oct daily 10am–4pm; Nov–Mar Sat–Sun 10am–4pm.* 🕐*Closed 1 Jan, 24–26 Dec.* 👜£5. ♿. ✆01434 632 349. www.english-heritage.org.uk.

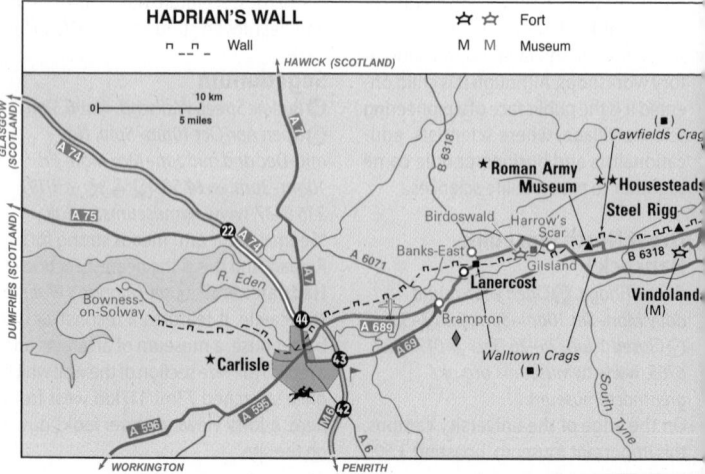

Ruins of the granaries, Corbridge Roman Town

© James Emmerson/age fotostock

This site was occupied for longer than any other on the wall. The **museum** of the Corbridge Roman Town presents the layout with its **granaries**, fountain, headquarters building and temples. From the elevated viewpoint there is a good overall **view** of the visible remains, which represent only a small part of the base and settlement.

Hexham Abbey★

Hexham. ⏰*Open daily 9.30am–5pm.* ⏰*Closed Good Fri.* 🎟*£3 contribution requested.* ♿✕*(Jun–Sept Tue and Sat).* 📞*01434 602 031. www.hexhamabbey. org.uk.*
Stones from the Roman settlement of Corbridge (Corstopitum) were used in

the construction of Hexham Abbey, which was founded in AD 674. All that remains of the original abbey is the **Saxon Crypt★★**.
The fine Early English choir with imposing transepts belongs to the later church (1180–1250). The stone staircase in the south transept was the Night Stair, which led to the canons' dormitory. The **Leschman Chantry★** (1491) has amusing stone carvings on the base and delicate woodwork above.

Chesters Roman Fort and Museum★

EH. Near Chollerford. ⏰*Open daily 10am–6pm Apr–Sept; Oct–Mar 10am–4pm.* ⏰*Closed 1 Jan, 24–26 Dec.* 🎟*£5.*

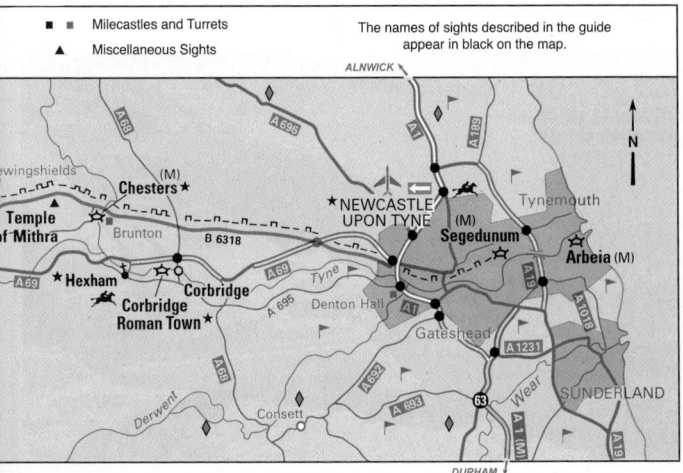

&⃝📇(charge)✖(summer). ℘01434 681 379. www.english-heritage.org.uk.

The best-preserved Roman cavalry fort in Britain lies just west of the point where the wall crossed the River Tyne and remains of the bridge can still be seen on the far bank. The four gateways, headquarters building and barrack blocks of this fort can be traced from their foundations. By the river are the remains of England's best-preserved Roman **bath-house**★. The **museum** contains a selection of sculptured stones collected from and around the wall in the 19C.

Temple of Mithras

Carrawburgh. 5min walk from car park.

This is an unexpected find in such a desolate stretch of moorland. Inside the lobby is a statue of the mother goddess (the original is reconstructed in the Museum of Antiquities in Newcastle). The temple was destroyed early in the 4C, probably by the Christians.

Housesteads Roman Fort★★

EH/NT. ⃝Open Apr–Sept daily 10am–6pm. See website for winter opening. ⃝£5. &⃝📇(charge)✖. ℘01434 344 363/525. www.nationaltrust.org.uk.

This large fort (5 acres/2ha) is perched high on the ridge and is the most complete example on the wall. Still clearly visible are the foundations of the large courtyard house of the commandant,

the granaries, barracks, headquarters building, the four main gateways, the **hospital** and 24-seater **latrine block** as well as part of the civilian settlement.

Vindolanda

Bardon Mill, Chesterholm. ⃝Open daily Apr–Sept 10am–6pm (Oct 5pm). ⃝£6.25, combined ticket with Roman Army Museum £9.50. &⃝📇✖. ℘01434 344 277. www.vindolanda.com.

The fort and civilian settlement on the Stanegate, south of the wall, date from the period before the building of the wall. Full-scale replicas have been built of a stretch of the wall with a stone turret, as well as of the turf wall, which was the earliest barrier, with a timber milecastle. The **Vindolanda Museum**★ holds a unique collection of **writing tablets** (the oldest surviving handwritten documents in Britain), leather goods, textiles and wooden objects.

👥 Roman Army Museum★

Carvoran. ⃝Open daily, as for Vindolanda. ⃝£5, child £2.75. Combined ticket with Vindolanda £9.50. &⃝✖. ℘01697 747 485. www.vindolanda.com.

This is the largest and most modern of the wall museums and presents a lively picture of the wall and its garrison, most vividly in its 3-D film *Edge of Empire*. To the east the quarry viewing-point overlooks one of the finest sections of the Wall, **Walltown Crags**.

Latrines, Housesteads Roman Fort

© Alison Roscoe/iStockphoto.com

Northumberland National Park

and around

Cheviot sheep graze the high open moorland that makes up most of this park, which is popular with walkers, mountain bikers, and for water-sports. On the eastern outskirts lie two outstanding historic properties.

KIELDER WATER AND FOREST PARK

▶ *Centre of Northumberland National Park.*

Not only is Kielder Forest the biggest working forest in England, covering 250sq mi/650sq km, Kielder Water is also the biggest man-made lake in northern Europe. Get your bearings at the Tower Knowe Visitor Centre, where you can jump aboard the *Osprey* for a cruise. It stops at **Leaplish Waterside Park**, where there are various facilities for family fun, including the 👥 **Kielder Water Birds of Prey Centre** (🕐*open daily 10.30am–4.30pm;* ✆£7, child £4.50; ♿; ☎01434 250 400, www.kwbopc.com). Just north of the lake, 👥 **Kielder Castle Visitor Centre**, formerly the hunting lodge for the Duke of Northumberland, is home to a variety of exhibitions, and is the hub for mountain biking.

Kielder Observatory (🕐*visit www. kielderobservatory.org for details*) 1.2mi /2km) west, is housed in a striking modern wooden structure. Its stargazing events take advantage of possibly the darkest night skies in England.

WALLINGTON

▶ *30mi west of Kielder Water, outside the National Park.* 🕐*Open early Mar–Oct Sat–Sun 11am–5pm. During school hols, Wed–Mon 11am–5pm.* ✆£9.70. ♿✕🅿. ☎01670 773 600. *www.nationaltrust.org.uk.*

Wallington is a monument to local industrial magnates, Sir Walter Blackett, who made his fortune from coal- and lead-mining and rebuilt the original late-17C house in the 1740s. It has a splendid interior and fine collections. The land-scaped grounds and enchanting **walled garden** are even more impressive.

🛈 **Info**: Tower Knowe Visitor Centre. ☎0845 155 0236. www.visitkielder.com. Kielder Castle Visitor Centre. ☎01431 250 209. Once Brewed Visitor Centre, Bardon Mill. ☎01434 344 396. Church Street, Rothbury. ☎01169 620 887. www.northumberland nationalpark.org.uk.
👥 **Kids**: Kielder Water Birds of Prey Centre.

CHILLINGHAM CASTLE★

▶ *Northeast, between the national park and A1.* 🕐*Open mid-Apr–Oct Sun–Fri noon–5pm.* ✆£8.50. ♿✕🅿. ☎01668 215359. *www.chillingham-castle.com.*

This splendid medieval castle, with its original battlements, has been much augmented through the ages but retains a real sense of history, some of it very unpleasant. In the 13C it was used as a base by Edward I for his raids on the Scots and its torture chamber contains horrific devices. Partly as a result of this period, it is widely regarded as one of the most haunted places in the country. The Elizabethans added Long Galleries, Capability Brown designed the park in 1752 and the Italian Garden was laid out in the 19C by Jeffrey Wyatville.

Adjacent, but quite separate from the castle, in Chillingham Park, is **Chillingham Wild Cattle Park** (🌸*guided tour only mid-Apr–Oct Sun–Fri; on the hour Mon–Fri 10am until 4pm, Sun 2pm, 3pm, 4pm; Jul–Aug daily, also 5pm; allow 2hrs for the tour;* ✆£6; 🅿. ☎01668 213395, *www.chillinghamwildcattle.com*), featuring the last wild cattle in the world. Numbering around 93 strong, they are the sole survivors of herds that once roamed the forests of Britain. Potentially dangerous, they may only be visited with the warden, who will also tell you their fascinating history.

Northumberland Coast

The charming town of Alnwick (pronounced "ann-ick") is the jewel in the crown of this region. Its castle, like those at Warkworth, Dunstanburgh, and Bambrugh, and the tug-of-war town of Berwick-on-Tweed are reminders that this was once a fiercely disputed border region. More typical of this coast these days, however, is the peace and quiet on Holy Island and the Farne Islands.

ALNWICK★

This attractive grey-stone town grew up around the great medieval castle whose stern walls still seem to bar the route to and from Scotland. Though its streets were laid out in the Middle Ages, Alnwick's present sober and harmonious appearance dates from the 18C when much dignified rebuilding in stone took place. If possible visit on market day, Thursday and Saturday.

▲Alnwick Castle★★

○*Open daily Apr–Oct: grounds 10am–6pm, castle 11am–5pm.* ⊜*£13, child £6. (combined ticket with garden £22).* 🅿️✕. ℘*01665 511 100 (information line). www.alnwickcastle.com.*
Among the many fortifications of this much-contested border country, Alnwick's castle is the most formidable. Begun in Norman times, it was acquired in 1309 by the **Percys**, the region's greatest family, and has remained in their hands ever since. Though much remodelled in the 19C, its basic features are all intact and, in an exquisite setting by the River Aln, it epitomises the romantic ideal of a mighty medieval fortress. It was featured in two *Harry Potter* films and stages various themed activities for children.

▲Alnwick Garden

Denwick Lane. ○*Open Apr–Oct daily 10am–6pm, Nov–Mar 10am–4pm.* ○*Closed 24 Dec.* ⊜*Adult £11, up to four children free.* ⏥🅿️✕. ℘*01665 511 350. www.alnwickgarden.co.uk.*

- ◔ **Michelin Map:** Michelin Atlas p51 or Map 502 O 16/17.
- ℹ **Info:** The Shambles, Alnwick. ℘01665 511 333. 106 Marygate, Berwick-upon-Tweed ℘01289 301 780. Seafield Road car park, Seahouses. ℘01298 30177 or 01665 720844. www.visit northumberland.com.
- ▲ **Kids:** Alnwick Castle (exploring in the footsteps of Harry Potter); Alnwick Garden. The arms and armour at Bamburgh Castle.
- ◎ **Don't Miss**: Alnwick Castle; Alnwick Garden, Holy Island.

Part of the castle estate, this 12-acre/5ha walled plot was rescued from dereliction in 2000 and has developed into one of the most exciting contemporary British gardens in modern times. It features a spectacular water Cascade, a rose garden holding over 3,000 specimens, a Poison Garden (where guides share tales of deadly plants) and a magnificently higgledy-piggledy **tree house** which is one of the largest in the world; don't miss its very popular restaurant and bar (*see Addresses*) .
Alnwick is also unusual among British gardens for being very child-friendly with a Wonderfully Wild project area, water features to get soaked by (on a hot day!), a bamboo labyrinth, and, of course, the tree house to explore, with its walkways in the sky and wobbly rope bridges for bouncing on.

WARKWORTH CASTLE AND HERMITAGE★

EH. ❯ *7.5mi/12km SE of Alnwick on the A 1068.* ○*Castle open: Feb school half-term & Apr–Sept daily 10am–5pm; Oct–daily 10am–4pm. Nov–Mar Sat–Sun, 10am–4pm. Hermitage open Apr–Sept Wed & Sun 11am–5pm.* ○*Closed 1 Jan, 24–26 Dec.* ⊜*Castle £4.80, Hermitage £3.20.* ⏥🅿️. ℘*01665 711 423. www.english-heritage.org.uk.*

Perched high above the river, the castle dates from the 12C and since 1332 has belonged to the Percys. It fell into ruin in the late-16C but has since been preserved. Its only furnished interiors are the **Duke's Rooms** (*open only Wed, Sun and bank hols*). Its general layout can be appreciated from the upper floor of the fine 13C **gatehouse**.

The most prominent feature is the exceptionally beautiful restored **keep**, designed for comfort and convenience as much as for defence.

From the castle the single street of the little planned town runs steeply downhill to the Norman **church of St Lawrence** and to the river crossing with its rare medieval bridge tower.

Don't miss the **Hermitage** (*half a mile upstream, accessible only by boat*), in use between the 14C and the mid-16C.

CRAGSIDE★

NT. ◑ *Rothbury. 12mi/19km SW of Alnwick via the B 6341. NT.* ◐ *Open mid-Mar–Oct Tue–Sun 1–5pm. During school hols, weekends & bank hols 11am–5pm.* ◸£13.20. ▣✕. ℘01669 620 333. www.nationaltrust.org.uk/ cragside.* ◔ *Entry by cash only. On bank hol weekends the property is very crowded.*

The stupendous success of his engineering and armament works at Newcastle enabled **Lord Armstrong** (1810–1900), one of the greatest Victorian inventor/ industrialists, to build this extraordinary country house in which Old English and Germanic styles are romantically combined. It was regarded as a wonder of the age and was the first house in the world to be lit by hydroelectricity, of which Armstrong was a pioneer. The many rooms of its well-preserved **interior**★ give a fascinating insight into the comforts and pretensions of late Victorian domestic life, as well as housing many of Armstrong's ingenious gadgets. This redoubtable man is also hailed as a landscaping genius and Cragside's gardens, laid out under his supervision, are home to the largest sandstone rock garden in Europe.

CRASTER

◑ *8mi/13km NE of Alnwick on the B 1340; after 3mi/5km turn right.*

This dark-stone fishing village is famed for its **kippers** (cured herrings).

From the car park, it is well worth the windy walk (there is no vehicular access) around 1.5mi/2.4km to the skeletal ruin of **Dunstanburgh Castle**★ (*NT/EH;* ◐*open Apr–Oct daily 10am–5pm/4pm, Nov–Mar Sat–Sun 10am–4pm;* ◐*closed 1 Jan, 24–26 Dec;* ◸£4; ℘01665 576 231; www.eng lish-heritage.org.uk, www.nationaltrust. org.uk). Sitting on its lonely crag of volcanic rock this is one of the most stirring sights of the Northumbrian coast. From here there are searching **view** right up and down this wonderfully unspoiled coastline of rocky headlands and sweeping sandy bays backed by dunes.

FARNE ISLANDS★

NT. ◑ *Seahouses. 15mi/24km S by the A 1 and B 1342/1340.* ◐*Boats leave Seahouses harbour once an hour from 10am to 3pm daily. A round trip, including island stop-off, takes between 2½– 3 hours. Landing is permitted May–Jul daily 10.30am–1.30pm (Staple Island), 1.30–5pm (Inner Farne).* ◸*Boat fare £13 to Inner Farne or Staple Island, inc.1hr on island. Landing fee May–Jul (breeding season) £6. Apr & Aug–Oct £5.* ◔*Apr–Jul wear a wide-brimmed hat or baseball cap to protect against dive-bombing birds.* ℘01665 721 099 (Seahouses shop); 01665 720 651 (warden); www.nationaltrust.org. uk, www.farne-islands.com (for boat information).*

In the care of the National Trust, the Farne Islands number 15 to 28 in total, depending upon the tide, and lie between 2mi/3km and 5mi/8km off the coast. They provide nesting sites for 18 species of seabirds, and are home to the largest British colony of grey seals. The wildlife is generally very tame and it is possible to get very close-up views.

⛊ BAMBURGH CASTLE★

◑ *7mi/27km N of Alnwick via the A 1 and B 1341.* ◐*Open third week Feb–Oct daily 10am–5pm, Nov–first week Feb.*

Bamburgh Castle

© Edward Shaw/iStockphoto.com

Sat–Sun 11am–4.30pm. ⏲*Closed 25 Dec –6 Jan.* 💷*£8.50, child £4.* 🅿*(charge).* ✕*.* ☎*01668 214 515.* *www.bamburghcastle.com.*

Beautifully sited on a rocky plateau above a long sandy beach, its original **Norman keep** still dominant, Bamburgh is one of the largest inhabited castles in the country. It was restored in the Victorian era and bought by the redoubtable Lord Armstrong (🔶*see Cragside House, above)* in 1894. It now houses a fine collection of arms and armour from the Tower of London, and Sèvres, Crown Derby, Worcester and Chelsea porcelain. There are exquisite small collections of silver vinaigrettes, Fabergé carvings and jade.

In Bamburgh village, two minutes by car, is the **Grace Darling Museum** (*Radcliffe Road;* ⏲*open Easter–Oct daily 10am– 5pm, Nov–Easter Tue–Sun and bank hols 10am-4pm;* ⏲*closed 1 Jan, 24–26 Dec;* 💷*£2.75;* ♿*;* ☎*01668 214 910, www.rnli. org.uk),* which celebrates the area's most famous person. The daughter of the Longstone lighthouse keeper, Grace was just 22 years old when she risked her life in an open boat with her father, to help save several survivors of the wrecked *SS Forfarshire* in September 1838. The **Longstone lighthouse** still stands and can be seen on boat trips to the Farne Islands (🔶*see above).*

HOLY ISLAND (LINDISFARNE)★

▶ *22mi/35km N of Alnwick to Beal via the A 1, then cross the causeway to Holy Island. This can be crossed only at low tide; timetables posted at either end of the causeway.*

⏲*Lidisfarne Centre open generally 10am–5pm (winter 4pm), according to tides, see website.* 💷*£3.* ♿*.* ☎*01289 389 004. www.holy-island.info.*

Here on this tiny island, the **Lindisfarne Gospels** were written and magnificently illuminated in the Celtic tradition. The original is kept at the British Museum but a (conventional) facsimile and an interactive turning page edition can be viewed here at the centre.

Lindisfarne Priory★

EH. ⏲*Open Feb school half-term & Apr– Sept daily 10am–5pm; Oct daily 10am– 4pm;. Nov–Mar Sat–Sun, 10am–4pm.* ⏲*Closed 24–30 Dec, 1 Jan.* 💷*£4.80.* ☎*01289 389 200.*

The ruins visible today are those of a Benedictine house, founded from Durham in 1093. A visitor centre interprets the ruins and stages occasional events.

Lindisfarne Castle★

Castle: ⏲*Open third week Feb daily and mid Mar–Oct Tue–Sun (Aug daily). Winter, two weekends a month 10am– 3pm depending on tidal access.*

Hours generally 10am–3pm or noon–5pm (visit www.holy-island.info/lindisfarnecastle for details). ⊜£6.30. 🅿. 🚻Emergency WC only; nearest WC in village 1mi/1.6km from castle. 📞01289 389 244. www.nationaltrust.org.uk; www.holy-island.info/lindisfarnecastle. Accessible via a 3mi/5km causeway at low tide only, this 16C castle was restored in 1902 by Edwin Lutyens as a holiday home for Edward Hudson, founder of Country Life magazine. The austere but beautiful interior is in inimitable "Lutyens" style.

BERWICK-UPON-TWEED★★

▷ 30mi/50km N of Alnwick via the A 1.

As a result of its location right on the border – facing northeast to the English, looking southwest to the Scots – the Georgian market and seaside town of Berwick (pronounced "berrick") has been fought over many times, changing hands on no fewer than 14 occasions in the 12C alone.

Today this is England's northernmost town, a fact unknown to many English folk outside the north , who would consider Berwick as Scottish. Their confusion is compounded by the town's football team, Berwick Rangers, who elect to play in the Scottish League.

From 1558 onwards, the **walls**★ (an excellent place to get your bearings), were replaced with ramparts and bastions. The elegant 15-arch **Old Bridge**, built in 1611, is the fifth-known structure to have been built between Berwick and Tweedmouth. The castle has largely been demolished and the railway station was built on part of the site in the 19C. Some of the stone was used for Holy Trinity Church (1651), one of the few to have been built during the Commonwealth, and the remainder was "quarried" in 1720 to build **Berwick Barracks**.

Berwick Barracks & Main Guard

EH. Clock Block, Ravensdowne. ⊙Open Apr–Sept Mon–Fri 10am–5pm. ⊜£3.80. 📞01289 304 493. www.english-heritage.org.uk.

Built in the early-18C, this complex is now home to the King's Own Scottish Borderers Museum, the Berwick Gymnasium Contemporary Art Gallery and the Berwick Borough Museum. The highlights are the excellently crafted pieces collected by the "magpie millionaire" **Sir William Burrell**, which include Imari ware (Japanese porcelain), brassware, medieval religious art, Chinese bronzes and glassware.

View of Berwick-upon-Tweed

© Jose Antonio Moreno/Pictures Colour Library

ADDRESSES

🛏️ STAY

DURHAM

🍽️ **Victoria Inn** – *86 Hallgarth Street . ☎0191 386 5269. www.victoriainn-durhamcity.co.uk .* 📔. *6 rms.* This family-run Grade-II-listed inn, a five minute walk from town, is a much-feted classic Victorian pub with pleasant bedrooms.

🍽️🍽️ **Three Tuns Hotel** – *New Elvet. ☎0191 386 4326. www.swallowhotels. com.* 📔. *50 rms.* This characterful city centre hotel dates back to the 16C and retains many historic features (stained glass, oak panelling/carvings, open fireplaces…). Attractive chintzy bedrooms.

🍽️🍽️ **Farnley Tower** – *The Avenue. ☎0191 375 0011. www.farnley-tower.co.uk.* 📔. *13 rms.* This pretty guesthouse, 10 minutes' walk from town, dates from 1870. Rooms are traditional-modern Victorian style; book a superior for views of the cathedral and castle.

🍽️🍽️ **Cathedral View Town House** – *212 Lower Gilesgate . ☎0191 386 9566. www.cathedralview.com. 6 rms.* This Georgian merchant's house, dating from 1734, is a 10-minute walk from town with sweeping views over the town and countryside.

🍽️🍽️🍽️🍽️ **Durham Marriott Hotel Royal County**. *Old Elvet. ☎0191 386 6821. wwww.marriotthotels.co.uk.* 📔. *50 rms.* Situated on the banks of the Wear, this luxurious property, parts of which date back to the 17C, offers great views of castle and cathedral. Its leisure club includes an indoor pool.

NEWCASTLE

🍽️ **Travelodge** – *Forster Street, Quayside. ☎0871 984 6164. www.travelodge.co.uk.* 📔. *201 rms.* Location and price can't be beaten at this no-frills hotel.

🍽️🍽️–🍽️🍽️🍽️ **The New Northumbria Hotel** – *61/73 Osborne Road. ☎0191 281 4961. www.thenewnorthumbriahotel.co.uk.* 📔. *57 rms.* This recently renovated boutique hotel in Jesmond, a mile from Newcastle city centre, is almost a night out in its own right, including the buzzing Osborne's Bar, informal attractive Scalini's restaurant, and the more sophisticated Louis Restaurant.

🍽️🍽️🍽️ **Hotel du Vin** – *City Road. ☎0191 229 2200. www.hotelduvin.com.* 📔. *42 rms.* On the banks of the Tyne, with outstanding views of Quayside and bridges, the former Tyne Tees Steam Shipping Company HQ has been gloriously converted into timelessly styled bedrooms, a superb trademark bistro, courtyard for al fresco dining and an outstanding wine cellar.

🍽️🍽️🍽️🍽️ **Malmaison** – *Quayside. ☎0191 245 5000. www.malmaison-newcastle. com.* 📔. *20 rms.* Very chic designer hotel next to the Millennium Bridge with an excellent restaurant and superb bar.

🍽️🍽️🍽️🍽️ **Hilton Newcastle** – *Bottle Bank. ☎0191 490 9700. www.hilton.co.uk/ newcastlegateshead.* 📔. *254 rms.* The best river view in town, from the Gateshead side of the water, can be enjoyed from several of the Hilton's luxurious rooms and from its Windows on the Tyne Restaurant. Health club with swimming pool.

HADRIAN'S WALL

🍽️ **Beggar Bog Farm** – *Housesteads. ☎01434 344 652. www.bandb-on-hadrians wall.co.uk.* 📔. *3 rms.* 🍴. Next to Housesteads Roman Fort, this tastefully renovated farmhouse features stripped-back wood-and-stone rooms. Dinner available, good local pubs. Excellent value.

🍽️ **Ashcroft** – *Lanty's Lonnen. Haltwistle. ☎01434 320 213. www.ashcroftguesthouse. co.uk.* 📔. *9 rms.* This elegant Victorian vicarage features spacious high-ceilinged guest rooms. It is located in lovely countryside, near the Wall, on the edge of Haltwhistle village, and stands in 2 acres/0.8ha of award-winning gardens.

🍽️–🍽️🍽️ **Bush Nook** – *Gilsland, Upper Denton. ☎016977 47194. www.bushnook. co.uk.* 📔. *8 rms.* Overlooking Birdoswald Roman Fort and with panoramic countryside views, this old farmstead has been tastefully converted to a very high standard. Attentive friendly hosts, excellent value.

🍽️🍽️🍽️ **Crown & Mitre Hotel** – *English Street, Carlisle. ☎01228 525 491. www.crown andmitre-hotel-carlisle.com.* 📔. *95 rms.* This grand Edwardian landmark hotel has its own bar, modestly priced restaurant and a lovely indoor pool. Good value.

ALNWICK

⊜🛏 **Aln House** – *South Road.* ✆01665 602 265. www.alnhouse.co.uk. 🅿. *7 rms.* This charming modern-styled Edwardian house with gardens is just a short stroll from town.

⊜🛏–⊜🛏🍴 **Greycroft** – *Croft Street (via Prudhoe Street).* ✆01665 602 127. www.greycroft.co.uk. *6 rms.* A short walk from the centre of town, this attractive and spacious Victorian house was beautifully renovated in trad-modern style in 2008, and since then has drawn universally glowing reviews.

BERWICK-UPON-TWEED

⊜🛏🍴 **1 Sallyport** – *Off Bridge Street.* ✆01289 308 827. www.sallyport.co.uk. 🅿. *5 rms.* Located in the heart of Berwick's old town, this super-stylish eclectic "bar and brasserie with rooms", is widely acclaimed as one of the best new places to stay in the North .

⊜🛏🍴 **West Coates** – *30 Castle Terrace.* ✆01289 309 666. www.westcoates.co.uk. *3 rms.* Large elegant Victorian mansion in 2 acres/0.8ha of mature gardens on the edge of town with spacious comfortable traditional rooms. The proprietor runs cookery classes.

🍴 EAT

DURHAM

🐦 Good traditional pubs to try in Durham include the Market Tavern (Market Place) and The Coach & Eight (Framwellgate Bridge).

⊜ **Duke of Wellington** – *Darlington Road.* ✆0191 375 7651. www.emberpuband dining.co.uk. Award-winning food and a range of real ales are served in this traditional pub (a half-hour walk from town), with a smart modern gastropub-style eating area.

NEWCASTLE

⊜ **Mango's Chinese Restaurant** – *43 Stowell Street.* ✆0191 232 6522. www.mangos-uk.com. This stylish place puts a new spin in Cantonese and Thai dishes and also specialises in dim sum.

⊜ **Neon** – *8 Bigg Market.* ✆0191 260 2577. www.neoncafe.co.uk. The darling of Newcastle's café scene, this unpretentious well established little place is as good for a cup of real coffee as it is for authentic Greek and Mediterranean food at bargain prices.

⊜ **Tandoori Nights** – *17 Grey Street.* ✆0191 221 0312. Opposite the Theatre Royal, this stylish Indian restaurant specialises in Balti cuisine, vegetarian dishes and sharing *thali* plates.

⊜🍴 **Café Royal** – *8 Nelson Street.* ✆0191 231 3000. *Open 8am–6pm. Closed Sun.* This light contemporary European café-bar is as good for weary shoppers as it is for impressing a lunch date.

⊜🍴🍴–⊜🍴🍴🍴 **The Fisherman's Lodge** – *Deep Dene House, Jesmond Dene.* ✆0844 809 0992. www.fishermanslodge. co.uk. Save up and treat yourself to the Modern British piscean delights at one of Newcastle's longest-established restaurants, in the heart of leafy Jesmond.

HADRIAN'S WALL

⊜🍴 **Angel Inn** – *Corbridge.* ✆01434 632 119. www.angelofcorbridge.co.uk. This fine old 18C coaching inn has been handsomely restored to become a stylish gastropub serving Modern British cuisine.

⊜🍴 **Ristorante Adriano** – *1 Rickergate, Carlisle.* ✆01228 599 007. www. adrianoristorante.co.uk. Carlisle's top Italian restaurant serves pizzas pastas classic national dishes.

ALNWICK

⊜🍴 **Tree House** – *Alnwick Garden.* ✆01665 511 852. www.alnwickgarden.com. *Closed dinner Mon–Wed.* Dine in the magical surroundings of a tree house, for either a simple lunch or a special candlelit dinner, on excellent locally sourced British cuisine.

BERWICK-UPON-TWEED

⊜🍴 **Amaryllis** – *5–7 West Street.* ✆01289 331 711. www.amaryllisberwick.co.uk. Berwick's most popular restaurant serves high quality locally sourced food in fashionable minimalist contemporary surroundings.

SCOTLAND

There are few countries which offer so much instant popular imagery as Scotland: lochs and mountains, tweed and tartan, kilts and bagpipes, haggis and whisky. It may fuel the tourist trade but this fiercely patriotic nation entered the 21C bearing a new identity, most vigorously represented by the new Scottish Parliament, a symbol of a modern country intent on self-rule. The old cultural trappings remain, but are now joined by many modern icons, and the country as a whole has become a fashionable destination for both short city breaks and get-away-from-it-all holidays, often in the great outdoors.

Highlights

1 Stroll **Edinburgh**'s Royal Mile from castle to palace (p440)

2 Discover the secrets of the **Burrell Collection** (p454)

3 Ascend **Cairn Gorm** and walking or skiing its slopes (p476)

4 Cruise the bonny bonny banks of **Loch Lomond** (p461)

5 Take in the scenery from **Kyle of Lochalsh** to **Gairloch** (p482)

Southern Scotland

The romance of the gentle rolling **Scottish Borders** is encapsulated in the words of Walter Scott – whose Abbotsford home is a highlight – and the many evocative ruins of abbeys and castles littering the landscape.

Robert Burns took his poetic inspiration from **Ayrshire**, **Dumfries and Galloway**, which remain largely unspoiled. Across the water from Ayr, the Isle of **Arran**, known as "Scotland in miniature", is a tonic for the stresses of modern life. **Edinburgh** is the gateway and perfect introduction to almost every aspect of Scottish history and culture. Not only is it the nation's most beautiful and sophisticated city, during Festival season is also the most exciting place in Britain. Its hinterland, the **Lothians** is home to some of Scotland's most famous sights, while across the Firth of Forth is the ancient kingdom of **Fife**, not only the ancestral home of Scottish monarchs, but, in St Andrews, also the cradle of golf.

Due west of Edinburgh, the buzzing, sometimes gritty metropolis of **Glasgow** is a vibrant mix of year-round arts and culture, world-class museums, stylish places to eat and stay, and some of the best shopping in the UK.

Central Scotland

Heading north, **Stirling and Argyll** is the glorious Scotland of the popular imagination and stunning landscapes, home to Rob Roy, William ("Braveheart") Wallace, the Mull of Kintyre, Tobermory, and Loch Lomond, among many other national icons. **Dundee**, Scotland's fourth city, has recently spruced itself up for visitors. **Angus** is famous for Glamis Castle and its Pictish legacy. The picturesque central region of **Perthshire** was Scotland's ancient royal heartland; today it is one of the adventure-sports capitals of Europe. The **Grampians** are famous for their turreted castles, malt whisky distilleries, dramatic mountains rugged coastlines, and Royal Deeside. Less traditionally known is Aberdeen, Scotland's third city, today grown wealthy and sophisticated on oil wealth.

Northern Scotland

Picture-postcard Scotland comes to life in the **Highlands** with majestic scenery, awesome wilderness, towering mountains, and broad expanses of shimmering water, none more famous than Loch Ness. The west coast islands known as the **Western Isles** have a magic and identity all their own, with elemental beauty and stern weather, well-known to walkers and nature watchers.

Beyond the isolated edge of the wild mainland lie the remote archipelagos of the **Orkneys** and **Shetland Islands** respectively; the latter feels almost Scandinavian. Both island groups have a deep sense of history and local culture, are surprisingly varied, and boast some of Europe's oldest prehistoric monuments.

Scottish Borders★★

The gentle rolling countryside of the Borders makes an easy transition from England but its multitude of ruins and castles tell of a turbulent history. Ironically, these very places where destruction and death were meted out are now some of the region's favourite beauty spots.

TWEED VALLEY★★

▷ *The River Tweed rises in the Tweedsmuir Hills to the W of the Borders and flows eastwards acting as the frontier with England for the latter part of its journey, ending at Berwick-upon-Tweed, some 97mi/156km E.* ⊙*Allow three days.*

The Tweed Valley has long been a favoured area of settlement. Ancient forts and monastic houses are found all over the region. It was much fought over and the troubled times are remembered in many a Border ballad and poem. Today, the valley is primarily agricultural, though the traditional woollen and knitwear industries are the mainstay of the towns. On its long and beautiful course the Tweed flows past several famous landmarks – castles, abbeys and great houses – making the exploration of its banks a delight.

🚗 DRIVING TOUR

▷ *139mi/210km.*

Moffat

At the head of the Annan Valley, the small town of Moffat makes a good base from which to explore the area.

▷ *Take the A 708 Selkirk road.*

Grey Mare's Tail★★

At the head of Moffat Water Valley is the Grey Mare's Tail, a spectacular waterfall (200ft/60m drop). The road leads on up the now narrow V-shaped valley to cross the pass and then descends the valley of the Little Yarrow Water. Here, by St

Michelin Map: Michelin Atlas p50 or Map 501.

Info: www.scot-borders.co.uk.

Mary's Loch, is Tibbie Shiel's Inn, meeting place of **James Hogg** (1770–1835), "the Ettrick Shepherd" and his friends.

▷ *Take the road to the left, signposted Tweedsmuir, past Megget Water; turn right into A 701.*

Broughton

In this trim roadside village is the **John Buchan Centre** (*Old Church;* ⊙*open Easter weekend and May–mid-Oct daily 2–5pm;* ⊛*£2;* 🅿; ✆*01899 880 258; www.johnbuchansociety.co.uk*), a tribute to the author (of *The Thirty-Nine Steps*) and statesman **John Buchan**, Lord Tweedsmuir (1875–1940).

▷ *Take the B 7016 E and the B 712 N, parallel to the Tweed. At the junction, turn right into the the A 72.*

One mile short of Peebles, on a rocky outcrop overlooking the river is **Neidpath Castle** (⊶ *closed to the public*), a 14C L-plan tower house, typical of the fortified dwellings needed in the days of border and clan warfare.

Peebles

The former spa town is a good centre from which to explore the Tweeddale countryside, or to fish for salmon. The author **Robert Louis Stevenson** and the explorer **Mungo Park** lived in the town. **William Chambers**, publisher of the famous dictionary, who was born here, donated the Chambers Institute, a library and a museum to the town.

▷ *6mi/10km down river, by the A 72; cross the Tweed at Innerleithen*

Traquair House★★

⊙*Open Jun–Aug daily 10.30am–5.30pm; Easter Mon–May and Sept daily 11am–5pm; Oct daily 11am–4pm; Nov*

Sat–Sun 11am–3pm. ☞£7.60, grounds only, £4. ♿🅿✖. ✆01896 830 323. www.traquair.co.uk.

There was a royal hunting lodge here as early as 1107, which was transformed into a Border "peel", or fortified tower house, during the Wars of Independence. The wings were added in the late-17C. This typical tower house has a wealth of relics, treasures and traditions and many Jacobite associations and personal belongings of Mary Queen of Scots. Also of interest are the **vaulted chamber** where cattle used to be herded in times of raids, a priest's room and a **brew-house** whose ale is highly regarded. In the grounds are a maze and craft workshops.

▶ Return to the A 72; head E on the B 7060, then the A 7 left to Abbotsford.

Abbotsford★★

♿⏰House closed until May 2013. Visitor centre & gardens open mid-Apr–mid-Oct 9am–6pm Oct 4pm. ⏰Closed Mons from last Mon in Jun–last Mon Jul. ☞Visitor centre free, gardens £3.50 🅿✖. ✆01896 752 043. www.scottsabbotsford.co.uk.

Abbotsford is a fantasy in stone, typical of **Sir Walter Scott** (1771–1832), the man who did so much to romanticise and popularise all things Scottish. He bought the house in 1812 and transformed it. Unfortunately, it is closed for major restoration until May 2013, during which time a new **visitor centre** interpreting Scott's life and achievements, and Abbotsford gardens will be open to the public. When reopen, visitors can see his massive writing desk and a collection of some 9,000 rare books and many items relating to Scotland and its history, collected throughout Scott's life.

▶ Take the A 7 to the A 72; turn right.

Melrose★

The pleasant town, grouped around the abbey ruins, is overshadowed by the **Eildon Hills**. Their strange triple peak – of volcanic origin – was believed to have been the work of Michael Scott, a 13C wizard, who is buried in the abbey. David I founded **Melrose Abbey★★** (open year-round daily 9.30am–5.30pm, Oct–Mar 4.30pm; ☞£5.50; 🅿; ✆01896 822 562; www.historic-scotland.gov.uk) in 1136. Once one of the richest abbeys in Scotland, the original buildings were damaged in the 14C, notably in 1322 by Edward II's retreating army. Robert the Bruce, whose heart is reputedly buried here, ensured their rebuilding. The ruins date from the late-14C to the early-16C and are distinguished by a profusion of **decorative sculpture★★★**: delicate tracery, canopied niches, intricate vaulting and ornate gables.

▶ Leave Melrose by the B 6361 running along the Tweed. Past the viaduct, turn left onto the A 68, then, once over the river, right on a minor road to Leaderfoot, then up Bemersyde Hill and turn right onto the B 6356.

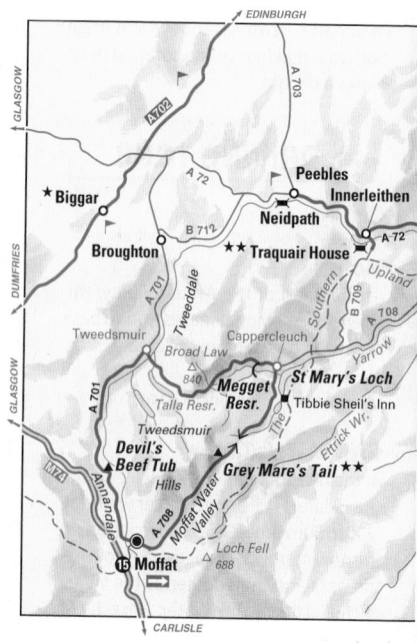

Scott's View★★

The magnificent viewpoint (593ft/181m) faces west across the winding Tweed to the three conical peaks of the Eildons.

▶ *Local road to Dryburgh Abbey.*

Dryburgh Abbey★★

🕐*Open daily 9.30am–5.30pm (4.30pm Oct–Mar).* ◉*£5.* ♿🅿. *☎01835 822 381. www.historic-scotland.gov.uk.*
One of the group of Border abbeys founded by David I, begun in 1150, Dryburgh was repeatedly attacked by the English in the 1300s and badly damaged when the town was razed in 1544. A sheltered meander of the Tweed provides a splendid **setting**★★★ for the majestic ruins of the abbey in mellow red stone. Sir Walter Scott is buried in the east chapel.

▶ *Return to the B 6356; take the B 6004 to St Boswells; turn left on A 699 by the Tweed.*

Kelso★

Standing at the confluence of the Tweed and the Teviot, Kelso grew from a fording place into a thriving market town. Here again are the ruins of a fine **abbey**, founded 1128, but many times destroyed. The town has some remarkable Georgian architecture and the cobbled town **square**★★ features an elegant 19C **town hall**. The graceful bridge was built in 1803 by John Rennie. On the outskirts of Kelso is **Floors Castle**★ (🕐*open Good Fri–Oct daily 11am–5pm;* ◉*£8, grounds only, £4.50;* ♿🅿✕; *☎ 01573 223 333; www. roxburghe.net).* The distinctive pinnacled silhouette stands on a terraced site overlooking the Tweed. The main block, built to the designs of William Adam, was extended in the 19C when William Playfair added the wings. Many of the rooms were refurbished early this century to accommodate an outstanding collection of **tapestries** and **furniture**.

Mellerstain★★

6mi/10km NW of Kelso via the A 6089.
🕐*Open 12.30pm (gardens 11.30am)– 5pm: Good Fri–Easter Mon; May, Jun & Sept Sun, Wed & bank hol Mons; Jul & Aug, Sun, Mon, Wed, Thu; Oct, Sun only.* ◉*£8.50. Gardens only, £5.* ♿🅿✕. *☎01573 410 225. www.mellerstain.com.*
The glory of this 18C mansion is the deli-

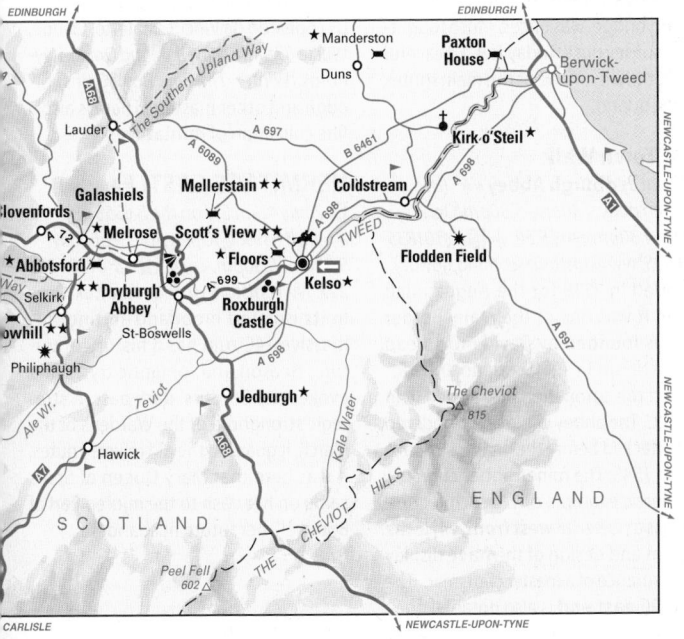

cacy of Robert Adam's interior decoration. The **ceilings**★★★ in delicate pastel colours are complemented by matching fireplaces, woodwork and furniture. The **Library**★★★ is a masterpiece.

▷ *Return to Kelso and continue on the A 698 to Coldstream. Follow the A 697 to Cornhill-on-Tweed then Branxton.*

Flodden Field

A monument inscribed "To the brave of both nations" marks Pipers Hill, the centre of the English positions. In two hours, on 9 September 1513, the English army, of around 20,000 men, slaughtered around 10,000 of their Scottish opponents who numbered 25,000. This included most of the generation of Scotland's nobility and their king, James IV, who had led them into battle in support of his recently renewed "Auld Alliance" with the French. By contrast the English suffered around 1,700 deaths.

JEDBURGH★

▷ *10mi/16km N of the border.*
🖽*Murray's Green.* ✆*01835 863 170. www.scot-borders.co.uk.*
The royal burgh of Jedburgh, spanning the Jed Water with a mid-12C triple-arched bridge, was once a much fought-over border post. Today it is a peaceful market town on one of the main routes into Scotland.

🐾 Town Walk

Begin at **Jedburgh Abbey**★★ *(HS;* 🕒*open daily 9.30am–5.30pm/Oct–Easter 4.30pm);* ◷*£5.50;* ♿️🅿️*;* ✆*01835 863 925; www.historic-scotland.gov.uk),* founded in 1138 for the Augustinian order. It was one of the many Border abbeys founded by David I to spread monasticism in 12C Scotland and witnessed the coronation of Malcolm IV in the 12C. The abbey was often plundered and attacked before the final destructive raid in 1545. The ruined abbey church is a majestic example of 12C architecture and has a powerful **west front**, while the rhythm and design of the **nave** display the assurance of a master craftsman. The mid-12C **east end** is also notable.

Continue north on Abbey Bridge End and turn down High Street. On Queen Street is the **Mary Queen of Scots Visitor Centre**★ (🕒*open Mar–Nov daily 10am/Sun 11am–4.30pm;* ✆*01835 863 331; www.scotborders.gov.uk/museums),* a fine 16C tower house where Mary stayed in 1566. Engraved glass panels, paintings and documents relate the life of this tragic queen.

Head back down High Street and continue on Castle Gate. **Jedburgh Castle Jail and Museum** (🕒*open late-Mar–Oct Mon–Sat 10am–4.30pm; Sun 1pm–4pm;* ✆*01835 864 750; www.scotborders.gov. uk/museums),* built in 1823 on the site of the original castle, was one of the most modern jails of its day.

BOWHILL★★

▷ *19mi/31km NW by the A 68, A 699, A 7 and A 708.* **House:** 🕒*Open Jul–Aug daily from 1pm, last tour 3.30pm.*
Country Park: 🕒*Open Easter–Aug, see website for days/times.* ◷*£8. Park only, £3.50.* ✆*01750 22204. www.bowhill.org.*
Among the many treasures which grace Bowhill are fine pieces of French **furniture**, Mortlake tapestries, relics of the Duke of Monmouth and an important collection of paintings including works by Leonardo da Vinci, Canaletto, Claude, Wilkie *(George IV in Highland Dress)*, Reynolds *(Winter, The Pink Boy)*, Gainsborough and other masters. There is also a fine collection of **miniatures**.

HERMITAGE CASTLE★

▷ *26mi/42km SW on the B 6358 and A 698, B 6399.* 🕒*Open Apr–Sept daily 9.30am–5.30pm.* ◷*£4.* 🅿️*.* ✆*01387 376 222. www.historic-scotland.gov.uk.*
In its isolated moorland setting this massive 14C ruin has a history of torture, treason and romantic trysts and evokes the Borders' dark past. A strategic stronghold of the Wardens of the March, it guarded the old reivers' routes. It was here that Mary Queen of Scots came on her dash to the injured Earl of Bothwell, her future husband.

Ayrshire and Arran★★

Aside from Burns' pilgrims and keen seaside golfers, few visitors have Ayrshire as a "must see" on their itinerary. Most of the visitors who come to the west coast are Irish (from just across the sea) though many American holidaymakers also make their first Scottish footfall just outside Ayr, at the confusingly named Glasgow Prestwick Airport. Most head east, to Edinburgh, but they could do worse than turn west, and cross the water to the Isle of Arran for an equally fine introduction to the country.

ISLE OF ARRAN★★

Arran is the largest of the islands in the Firth of Clyde, measuring some 20mi/32km long by 10mi/16km wide and with a population of just under 5,000. Cut in two by the Highland Boundary Fault, it is said to present "Scotland in miniature". A mountainous northern part (Goat Fell 2,866ft/874m) has deep valleys and moorlands, while the southern half consists of lowland scenery. Sheltered bays and sandy beaches, together with ample facilities for yachting, swimming, golf, sea-angling and fishing, make tourism the island's principal industry.

🚗 ISLAND TOUR

▶ *56mi/90km.*
Allow about half a day, not including visiting time. 🖐*Make sure the fuel tank is full before setting out as there are few filling stations.*

Mainly a coastal route, the road affords views of the diversity of scenery; but as well as the coast road, try the 10mi/16km String Road across the "waist" of the island, between Blackwaterfoot and Brodick. The first highlight is outside the port and bay from which it takes its name. **Brodick Castle**★★ *Castle: (*🕐*open Apr–Oct daily 11am–4pm/3pm Oct;*

> ♿ **Michelin Map:**
> Michelin Atlas p48,
> p53 or Map 501 E 17.
> 🛈 **Info:** The Pier, Brodick.
> 22 Sandgate, Ayr.
> 📞0845 225 5121.
> www.ayrshire-arran.com.
> 👁 **Don't Miss:** Brodick
> Castle's rhododendron
> garden in bloom (late
> spring). Culzean Castle
> for its clifftop setting.

grounds: 🕐 *open year-round daily 9.30am–dusk;* 💷*£11;* 🅿 ♿*£2)*✗*;* 📞*0844 493 2152; www.nts.org.uk)* is the historic stronghold of the Hamiltons, Earls of Arran. The 13C red sandstone castle was extended by Cromwell in 1652 and again in the Baronial style in 1844. The Hamilton and Beckford treasures comprise a fine collection of silver, porcelain, furniture and family portraits as well as paintings by Watteau, Turner and Herring. The gilded heraldic ceiling is remarkable. An 18C formal walled garden and a 65-acre/26ha **rhododendron garden**, one of the finest in Britain, benefit from the mild local climate. Arran was on the main migration route for Neolithic agriculturalists up the western seaboard of Scotland and around 1.5mi/2.4km inland off the road north of Blackwaterfoot, lie the **Machrie Moor Stone Circles** (🕐*accessible at all times; www.historic-scotland.gov.uk)*. Built about the same time as the later parts of Stonehenge, these remnants of five Bronze Age stone circles remains enjoy a powerful setting of moorland backed by mountains.

As the road swings round Arran's southern tip, the granite island of **Ailsa Craig** (1,000ft/300m high) can be seen to the south. The road from Lamlash Bay, sheltered by Holy Island, back to Brodick gives a spectacular view of its castle, dominated by Goat Fell.

SOUTH AYRSHIRE

▶ *Ayr is 36mi/58km SW of Glasgow. Ayr station is 1mi/1.6km from the town*

A Moving Landmark

According to tradition, Ayr's Auld Brig (13C), a narrow cobbled bridge immortalised by the Scottish bard, Robert Burns, was financed by two sisters who lost their fiancés when they drowned trying to ford the river in spate.

centre. The bus station is at Sandgate in the centre.

Ayr is a pleasant market town that has grown up around a medieval core. Today it is a thriving resort on Scotland's southwest coast with splendid sandy beaches as well as a famous racecourse and golf courses which host international competitions. It is probably most notable, however, as the hub of **Burns Country**.

Burns Country Alloway★

3mi/5km S of Ayr by the B 7024.
Alloway is famed as the birthplace of the poet Robert Burns (1759–96), whose birthday on 25 January is celebrated throughout the world. Within the **Burns National Heritage Park** are a number of sites: the spartan **Burns Cottage and Museum**★ (*open daily Apr–Sept 10am–5.30pm, Oct–Mar 10am–5pm; closed 1–2 Jan, 25–26 Dec; £4; combined ticket to all other Burns attractions; 01292 443700;* evokes his humble origins and displays an extensive collection of manuscripts and relics; the **Burns Monument** overlooks the River Doon and the 13C **Brig o'Doon**; The **Tam O'Shanter Experience** (*entry*

details as Burns Cottage and Museum; £2) presents the bard's life and times as well as an introduction to southwest Scotland. **Alloway Kirk** also has Burns associations.

Culzean Castle★

NTS. 16mi/26km SW of Ayr by A 719. **Castle:** *Open Easter/Apr–Oct, daily 10.30am–5pm; Nov–Mar Thu–Sun 11am–4pm.* **Country Park:** *Open daily 9.30am–dusk. Castle and country park £12, country park only £8. 0844 493 2149. www.nts.org. uk. www.culzeanexperience.org.*
Culzean Castle (pronounced "cullane") enjoys a dramatic clifftop **setting-★★★**. The castle was the work of **Robert Adam** (1728–92). Though a Classicist, Adam added arrow slits and battlements to this most spectacular castle, to complete the mock-medieval touch. The harmonious interior is enhanced by friezes, chimney-pieces and delicately patterned ceilings. The elegant **Oval Staircase**★★ and **Saloon** are good examples of the architect's original style. He also designed the splendid furnishings. The Eisenhower exhibition traces the castle's connection with the former American president.
The grounds include a Victorian walled garden comprising the Pleasure Garden with extensive herbaceous borders, the restored Victorian Vinery and Peach House, a Fountain Court Garden (including the Orangery), a herb garden, wildlife garden and an adventure playground.

Culzean Castle

Dumfries and Galloway

If Scotland has an unknown corner, then it is probably the western borders region of Dumfries ("dum-frees") and Galloway. It is less polished than its better-known neighbour, the Borders, due east, but has many of the same appealing ingredients, some truly wild areas, much fewer visitor numbers and a distinct lack of coach parties on the "Shortbread & Tartan" heritage trail.

DUMFRIES★

The "Queen of the South", Dumfries is the chief town of Scotland's southwest, best known for its historical associations. **Robert the Bruce** (1306–29) started his long campaign to free Scotland from Edward I in Dumfries by killing John Comyn, one of the competitors for the crown, and having himself crowned at Scone in 1306. Eight years later, his victory at Bannockburn was key to achieving Scotland's independence. **Robert Burns** is Dumfries' most famous son.

DRUMLANRIG CASTLE★★

▶ *18mi/29km northwest of Dumfries on the A 76.* **Castle:** *Open Good Fri/Apr–Aug daily 11am–4pm; gardens Good Fri/Apr–Sept daily 10am–4pm.* *Castle £9. gardens only, £5.* &▣✕. *01848 600 283. www.drumlanrig.co.uk.*
The castle was a 14C–18C Douglas stronghold and stands impressively with four square towers quartering the courtyard structure. Innovation comes with the main façade and its terraces, horseshoe staircase, dramatic turreted skyline and rich sculptural detail. The interior holds a superb collection of paintings (including a Holbein and a Rembrandt), fine furniture and clocks. In the oak-panelled Dining Room, carved panels attributed to Grinling Gibbons alternate with 17C silver sconces and family portraits.

NEW ABBEY

▶ *8mi/13km southwest of Dumfries on the A 710.*

- ▶ **Population:** 21,164.
- **Michelin Map:** Michelin Atlas p49 or Map 501 J 18.
- **Info:** *01387 253 862.* www.visitdumfriesand galloway.co.uk.
- ▶ **Location:** Southwest Scotland, 33mi/53km northwest of Carlisle across the border. Both the train station (Station Road, off English Street) and the bus station (Whitesands) are in the town centre.
- **Timing:** Allow two days.

This pretty little one-street village with ducks on the millpond grew up to service **Sweetheart Abbey★** *(HS; open Apr–Oct daily 9.30am–5.30pm/Oct 4.30pm, Nov–Mar Sat–Wed 9.30am–4.30pm; £4; ▣; 01387 850 397; www. historic-scotland.gov.uk).* Founded in 1273 by Lady Devorgilla of Galloway, in memory of her husband John Balliol, this was the last Cistercian abbey in Scotland. The name derives from the fact that the foundress was laid to rest together with a casket containing the embalmed heart of her husband. The beauty and charm of the ruins are enhanced by the contrast between warm red sandstone and the clipped green of surrounding lawns.
A short walk away is the **New Abbey Corn Mill** *(HS; open Apr–Oct 9.30am–1pm & 2–5.30pm, Oct closes 4.30pm Nov–Mar Sat–Wed 9.30am–4.30pm; £4.50; ▣; 01387 850 260; www.historic-scotland.gov.uk),* a fully restored water-powered corn mill built around the end of the 18C and in service unit just after the Second World War. Now a charming time capsule, it operates in summer.
The village is also home to the **National Museum of Costume★** *(Shambellie House; open Apr–Oct daily 10am–5pm; £4.50; ▣✕; 0300 123 6789; www.nms. ac.uk)* with lively displays of costumes from the Victorian era to the 20C, in the charming setting of a mid-19C Baronial house.

CAERLAVEROCK CASTLE★

HS. ◗ 9mi/15km southeast of Dumfries on the B 725. ◷Open daily year-round 9.30am 5.30pm (Oct–Mar 4.30pm). ☞£5.50. ♿✕🅿. ☏01387 770 24. www.historic-scotland.gov.uk.

Overlooking the Solway Firth, this imposing medieval castle is girt by a moat and earthen ramparts.

Its formidable exterior is in contrast to the harmonious **Renaissance courtyard façade★★**. It suffered many border conflicts and it was besieged by Edward I in 1300 (there is a siege warfare exhibition in the castle visitor centre). It was besieged again in 1640, and following its surrender to the Covenanters was demolished.

RUTHWELL CROSS★

HS. Ruthwell Parish Church.
◗ 8.5mi/13.5km southeast of Dumfries. ◷Open byappt only. Call for opening time, ☏01387 550 7612. www.historic-scotland.gov.uk.

The late-7C Ruthwell Cross is regarded as one of the major monuments of early medieval Europe and depicts the Life and Passion of Christ, complete with detailed tracery, animals and birds, and runic inscriptions.

It is an outstanding example of **early Christian art**. The cross was demolished in 1642 by the General Assembly; the pieces were re-assembled and installed here in 1887.

KIRKCUDBRIGHT★

◗ 26.5mi southwest of Dumfries.

Now promoted to visitors as an "artist's town", Kirkcudbright (pronounced "cur-coo-bree") has historically depended on farming and fishing, and is the only town in the region to retain its fishing fleet. The attractive town centre dates from the Georgian and Victorian periods and boasts several historic properties open to visitors.

Kirkcudbright's artistic legacy, which developed in the late-19C–early-20C, is outlined in the **Tolbooth Art Centre** (◷open Mon–Sat 10/11am–4/5pm, May–Oct, Sun 2–5pm; ☏01557 331 556, www.dumgal.gov.uk).

Robert Burns (1759–96)

The bard lived and farmed in and around Dumfries and a statue stands at the north end of the High Street. The **Robert Burns Centre** (Mill Road; ◷open Apr–Sept Mon–Sat 10am–5pm, Sun 2–5pm; Oct–Mar Tue–Sat 10am–1pm–5pm; ☞charge for audio-visual theatre only, £2; ♿✕; ☏01387 264 808; www.dumfriesmuseum.demon.co.uk) is an excellent introduction. Burns spent his final years just across the river, at **Burns House**, now a museum (Burns Street; ◷open hours/website as Robert Burns Centre; ☏01387 255 297). He had moved here after giving up his former home at **Ellisland Farm** (Hollywood Road; ◷open Apr–Sept daily 10am–1pm, 2–5pm/Sun 2–5pm, Oct–Mar Tue–Sat 2–5pm; ◷closed early Dec–early Jan; ☞£4; ☏01387 740 426; www.ellisland-farm.co.uk), just north of Dumfries, in order to take up a post with the Excise. Back in town, a few yards from Burns House, the churchyard of St Michael's is home to the **Burns Mausoleum** where Burns, his wife (Jane Armour) and several of their children are buried. **Alloway** (3mi/5km S of Ayr), his birthplace, is also on the **Burns Trail** (leaflets from tourist information centres).

THREAVE ESTATE★★

NTS. Castle Douglas, 17mi southwest of Dumfries. ◷Open Apr–Oct daily 10am–5pm, Nov–Dec 23 & Feb–Mar Fri–Sun 10am–5pm. House: Apr–Oct, Wed–Fri & Sun 11am–3.30 ; ⬤house by guided tour. ☞£11; garden only, £6.50. ☏0845 493 2245. www.nts.org.uk.

Best known for its magnificent display of springtime daffodils, **Threave Garden** is worth a visit in all seasons. Highlights include the rose garden, the herbaceous perennials, and the walled garden with its outstanding temperate glasshouse collection. The principal rooms of the Scottish Baronial Threave House have been restored to the way they were in the 1930s.

Edinburgh★★★

City of Edinburgh

Edinburgh, capital of Scotland, lies on the Firth of Forth, a deep inlet gouged into the east coast. The city is located on a series of volcanic hills, each giving a different and often spectacular vantage point. Most famous of these is Arthur's Seat (823ft/251m), overlooking Holyrood Park. Edinburgh boasts a colourful history; the Old Town, huddled for years on the ridge running down from the Castle Rock, contrasts with the New Town, with its elegant Georgian streets and squares.

A BIT OF HISTORY

The Castle Rock had been a secure refuge for generations when in the late-11C Malcolm Canmore and Queen Margaret chose the site for their residence. Their son, David I, favoured the site by founding the Abbey of the Holy Rood. During the reign of the early Stuarts Edinburgh gradually assumed the roles of royal residence, seat of government and capital of Scotland. With the Union of the Crowns (1603) and subsequent departure of James VI of Scotland and I of England for London, Edinburgh lost much of its pageantry and cultural activity. In 1707 self-rule came to an end with the Union of the Parliaments.

It was in the late-18C during the Enlightenment, a period of intellectual ferment, that plans were mooted for a civic project of boldness and imagination: the creation of the Georgian New Town. The town has gained further status as the

PUBLIC TRANSPORT

Bus services are frequent and usually run on time. A new tram service in the city centre was installed in 2009. Visit the *Tourist Information Centre* or the *Transport Information Centre at 1 Cockburn Street* for timetables.

The two main operators are **Lothian Buses** (*℘0131 555 6363*) and **First Buses** (*℘08708 72 72 71*).

▶ **Population:** 418,914.

🗺 **Michelin Map:** Michelin Atlas p56 or Map 501 K 16.

ℹ **Info:** 3 Princes Street (above Waverley Station). ℘0845 2255 121. www.edinburgh.org.

▶ **Location:** Edinburgh is compact. You can visit nearly all the centre on foot. Waverley Station, at the heart of the city, accommodates all main bus and train services. Haymarket Station is 2mi/3km west of the centre and also services Glasgow, Fife and the Highlands.

🧭 **Don't Miss:** The Royal Mile; a ghost tour; the Scottish Parliament Building; the views from the Nelson Monument and Arthur's Seat; Charlotte Square; the Fringe Festival; Royal Museum and Museum of Scotland; Royal Yacht *Britannia*; Forth Bridges view.

🕐 **Timing:** At least three days.

👪 **Kids:** Edinburgh Zoo; Our Dynamic Earth; Deep Sea World (North Queensferry).

🚶 **Walking Tours:** The Edinburgh Literary Pub Tour (*℘0800 169 7410; www.edinburghliterarypub tour.co.uk*); Mercat Tours (*t0131 225 5445; www. mercattours.com*); City of the Dead Tour (*℘0131 225 9044; www.blackhart. uk.com*; (not for children).

Bus Tours: City tours depart daily every 15–20 minutes from Waverley Bridge (*£12; ℘0131 220 0770; www. city-sightseeing.co.uk*).

🅿 **Parking:** Difficult and expensive. Walk or use the bus and tram.

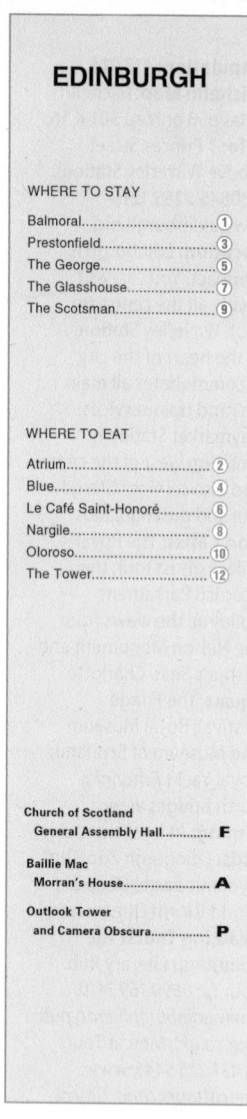

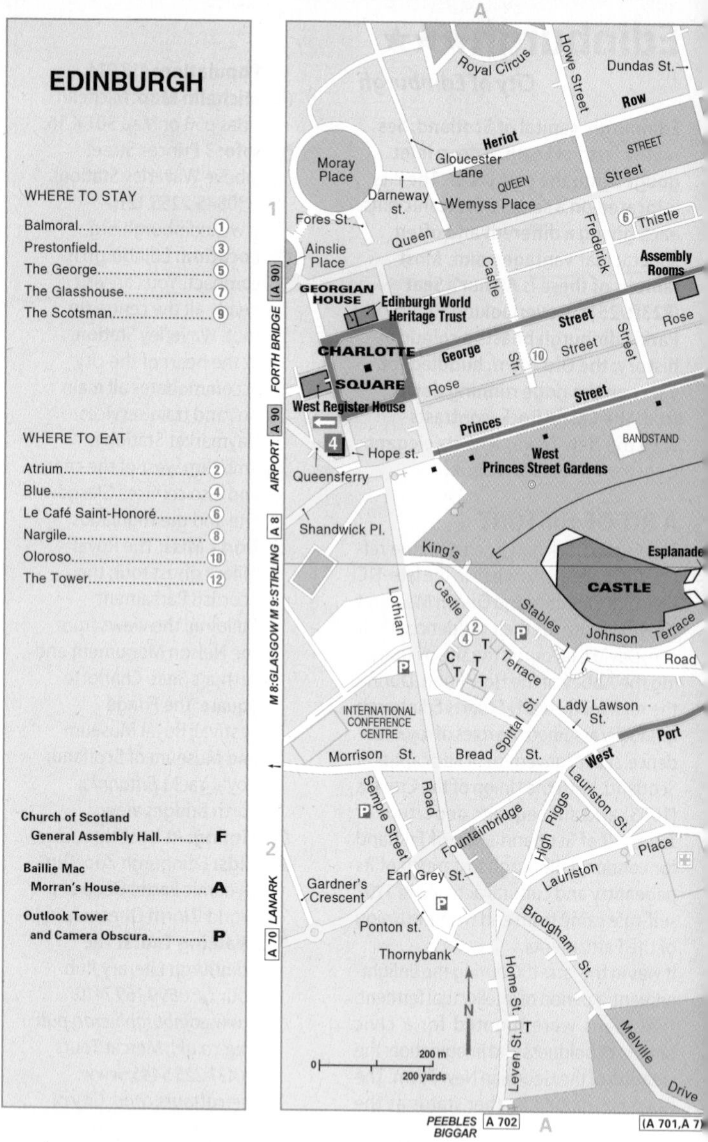

EDINBURGH

WHERE TO STAY

Balmoral .... ①
Prestonfield .... ③
The George .... ⑤
The Glasshouse .... ⑦
The Scotsman .... ⑨

WHERE TO EAT

Atrium .... ②
Blue .... ④
Le Café Saint-Honoré .... ⑥
Nargile .... ⑧
Oloroso .... ⑩
The Tower .... ⑫

Church of Scotland
  General Assembly Hall .... F

Baillie Mac
  Morran's House .... A

Outlook Tower
  and Camera Obscura .... P

seat of the Scottish Assembly, which sits in the new Parliament building next to the Palace of Holyroodhouse.

⇝ OLD TOWN

① THE ROYAL MILE★★★

The principal thoroughfare of Old Edinburgh runs from the castle down the ridge through Castle Hill, Lawnmarket, High Street and Canongate to the abbey and Palace of Holyroodhouse. For two centuries the city's Flodden Wall (16C) restricted the spread of Edinburgh, confining expansion to the 10- and 12-storey "tenements", with narrow wynds and closes, so typical of the Old Town. The few original buildings which remain can still today give the impression of what medieval and 17C Edinburgh must have looked like.

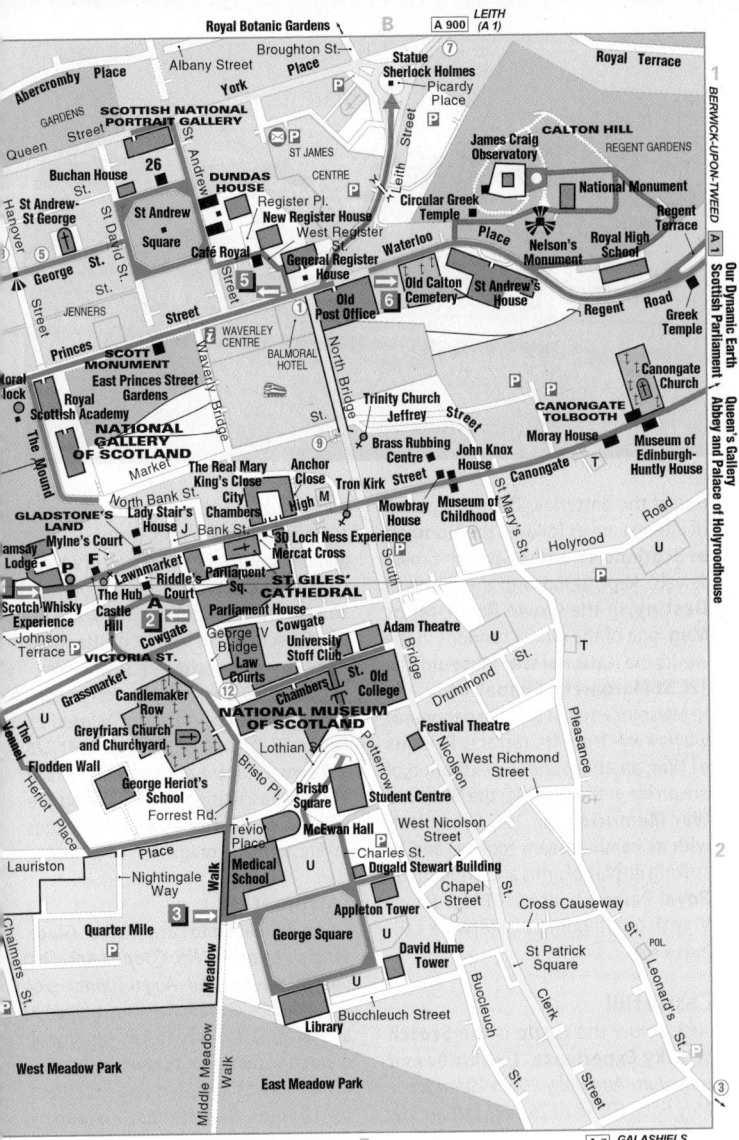

Castle★★

HS. ◷Open year-round daily (subject to state and military events and the Tattoo) Apr–Sept 9.30am–6pm; Oct–Mar 9.30am–5pm. ◷Closed 25–26 Dec. ☞Guided tour (free). ☞£15 peak, £14 off-peak (buy online to save waiting in line). ⚙✕. ✆0131 225 9846. www.edinburghcastle.gov.uk.

The iconic silhouette of the castle on its strategic site atop Castle Rock★★★ is the best-known view of Edinburgh. Though a royal residence since the 11C, the castle and most of the buildings today are basically those resulting from its use as a military garrison over recent centuries. The esplanade, an 18C parade ground, is the setting for the Edinburgh Festival's most popular event, the Military Tattoo. The fortifications afford splendid **views** across Princes Street to the New Town. The **one o'clock salute** is fired from

Edinburgh Castle

© Vitaly Titov/Dreamstime.com

one of the batteries. The main points of interest are as follows: the **Honours of Scotland**★★★ (the Scottish Crown Jewels), kept, along with the **Stone of Destiny**, in the Crown Room; **Mons Meg**, one of the oldest cannons in the world; the **National War Museum**; the 12C **St Margaret's Chapel**, dedicated to Malcolm's queen and the panoramic views★★★ from its terrace; **Prisons of War**, an atmospheric re-creation of prison life in the late-18C; the **National War Memorial**; the 16C **Great Hall** with its hammerbeam roof★★, and its striking display of arms and armour; the **Royal Palace**, built in 1617 for James VI with outstanding plasterwork ceilings★★★.

Castle Hill

Just below the castle is the **Scotch Whisky Experience** (◔*entry by tour only, Jun–Aug daily 10am–5pm/Sept–May 6pm; ◔closed 25 Dec; ⊜from £12; ♿✕; ℘0131 220 0441; www.whisky-experience.co.uk)*, with a ride through a replica distillery and various clever audio-visual exhibits on the art of whisky distilling. Opposite stands the Outlook Tower housing Edinburgh's ♿**Camera Obscura and World of Illusions** (◔*open year-round daily 9.30am/10am–5pm/6pm/Jul–Aug 8.30pm ; last presentation 1hr before closing; ◔closed 25 Dec; ⊜£9.95, child £6.95; ♿; ℘0131 226 3709; www.camera-obscura.co.uk)*, which affords a fascinating ever-changing live window on the city, as well as galleries on illusions and magic.

Lawnmarket

Castle Hill leads into Lawnmarket. **Gladstone's Land**★ (NTS; ◔*open Apr–Oct daily 10am–5pm/Jul–Aug 6.30pm; ⊜£6; ♿; ℘0844 493 2120; www.nts.org.uk)* is a typical narrow six-storey tenement erected within the city walls in the 17C; in 1617 it was acquired and extended by Thomas Gledstanes, a wealthy merchant. The atmospheric restored

Edinburgh International Festival★★★

This prestigious festival held every August has provided a top-quality programme in all the art forms since 1947. The **Military Tattoo** presents a spectacle rich in colour, tradition, music and excitement, under the floodlights of the Castle Esplanade. **The Fringe** spills out onto the streets and squares of Edinburgh, with performers from all over the globe presenting over a thousand productions, often avant-garde, sometimes just plain eccentric. Also held during this period is the **International Book Festival**. Visit www.eif.co.uk for full details.

premises comprise a shop with living quarters above, complete with original painted ceilings and furnishings.

A few yards downhill, along the narrow alleyway of Lady Stair's Close, the **Writers' Museum** (◑*open year-round Mon–Sat 10am–5pm; also Aug Sun noon–5pm; ℘0131 529 4901; www.edinburgh museums.org.uk*) showcases three of Scotland's greatest literary figures: Robert Burns (1759–96), Sir Walter Scott (1771–1832) and Robert Louis Stevenson (1850–94).

High Street

Lawnmarket leads into High Street and **St Giles' Cathedral**★★ (◑*open year-round Mon–Fri 9am–5pm/May–Sept 7pm, Sun 1–5pm; ☞£3 contribution requested; ✕; ℘0131 225 9442; www. stgilescathedral.org.uk*). The present High Kirk of Edinburgh is probably the third church to occupy this site. Alterations and restorations have, however, drastically changed its character since its rebuilding in the 14C. The only original exterior feature is the crown **spire**★★★ dating from 1495. Inside, it is the monuments and details that provide much of the interest.

Behind the cathedral on Parliament Square is the 17C **Parliament Hall** (◑*open Mon–Fri 10am–4pm; ◑closed bank hols; ⓖ; ℘0131 348 6852*), which was decreed by Charles I and in which the Scottish Parliament met from 1693 to 1707. It is now behind a Georgian façade. Its magnificent **hammerbeam roof** is an original feature. Nearby is a 17C equestrian statue of Charles II. At the east end of the square stands the **Mercat Cross**, formerly the hub of Edinburgh life, meeting place of traders and merchants and scene of royal proclamations, demonstrations and executions. Opposite the cathedral are the **City Chambers**, formerly the Royal Exchange built in 1753. Adjacent, part of the same complex is the entrance to **The Real Mary King's Close** (*Warriston's Close; ⬦tours Apr–Oct daily 10am–9pm/Aug 9am–11pm, Nov–Mar Sun–Thu 10am–5pm, Fri–Sat 10am–9pm; ◑closed 25 Dec; ☞£12.50; ✕; advance booking essential.*

℘0845 070 6244. www.realmarykings close.com). Hidden beneath the Royal Mile lies a warren of "closes" (narrow alleyways) where people lived, worked and died. As the Old Town expanded ever upwards, these closes became built over, or as legend has it, deliberately sealed up, inhabitants and all, whenever the dreaded plague visited (which it did frequently). For centuries they lay forgotten and abandoned, until the late-1990s when tours were licensed to reintroduce them to the general public. The Real Mary King's Close, complete with its many ghosts, is now the most popular of these.

Further down High Street is the picturesque **John Knox House** (◑*open year-round Mon–Sat 10am–6pm, also Jul–Aug Sun noon–6pm; ☞£4.25; ⓖ✕; ℘0131 556 9579; www.scottishstorytellingcen tre.co.uk*) built in about 1490, associated with both John Knox, the religious reformer, and with James Mossman, the goldsmith to Mary Queen of Scots. An exhibition incorporates details on both men and re-creates the atmosphere of 16C Edinburgh.

Next door is the early-17C **Mowbray House**, while across the road is the ⬦⬦**Museum of Childhood** (◑*open year-round Mon–Sat 10am–5pm, Sun noon–5pm; ⓖ; ℘0131 529 4142; www. edinburghmuseums.org.uk*), a fascinating collection devoted to anything and everything to do with local childhood.

Canongate

High Street leads into Canongate. Just before Canongate Church stands the attractive 16C **Canongate Tolbooth**★, home to **The People's Story Museum** (◑*open year-round Mon–Sat 10am–5pm; also Aug Sun noon–5pm; ⓖ; ℘0131 529 4057; www.edinburghmuseums.org. uk*). which uses oral history, reminiscence and written sources to tell the story of the lives, work and leisure of the ordinary people of Edinburgh, from the late-18C to the present day.

Opposite stand three 16C mansions known as Huntly House, occupied by the **Museum of Edinburgh** (◑*same as The People's Story; ⓖ; ℘0131 529 4143*) offering some fascinating local exhibits including the true story of the famously faithful dog, "Greyfriars Bobby".

Just before you arrive at the Scottish Parliament Building, take a right on Reid's Close to **Our Dynamic Earth** (👥; ⏱open Apr–Oct daily 10am–5.30pm/ Jul–Aug 6pm, Nov–Mar Wed–Sun 10am– 5.30pm; last entry 1hr 30min before closing; ₤10.80; child £7.20; ♿✕; ☏0131 550 7800; www.dynamicearth.co.uk). Occupying what appears to be a giant marquee just below the dramatic Salisbury Crags, Edinburgh's major Millennium visitor attraction gallops through the natural and geological history of the earth via a series of often spectacular exhibits, a 3-D and a 4-D film, and many hands-on displays.

At the end of Canongate is Britain's most controversial post-Millennium building, the **Scottish Parliament**★ (⏱see website for visiting details; 🎫free guided tours Mon and Fri when Parliament is not sitting, and year-round Sat & public hols; ♿✕; ☏0131 348 5200. www.scottish. parliament.uk/vli), where members of the public can attend debates, and visit both this remarkable building and exhibitions staged here. It was designed by the Spanish architect Enric Miralles (1955–2000), who died before its completion in 2005, four years late and ten times over budget. Its unusual design and outlandish features make it not only a must-see for students of modern architecture but also recommended viewing for anybody remotely interested in the subject.

Palace of Holyroodhouse★★

Palace: ⏱Open Apr–Oct daily 9.30am–6pm; Nov–Mar daily 9.30am–4.30pm. *Gardens:* ⏱Open summer only. ⏱Closed third week Jun–first week Jul, late Jul, 25–26 Dec and during Royal and State visits, see website. ₤10.75 (joint ticket with Queen's Gallery £15.10). ♿. ☏0131 556 5100. www.royalcollection.org.uk

At the east end of the Royal Mile, amid the green slopes of Holyrood Park, leading up to Arthur's Seat, stands the Pal-

ace of Holyrood, official residence of the monarch in Scotland.

The abbey was founded by David I, in 1128. James IV started to transform the guesthouse of the abbey into a royal palace but it was Charles II's architect Sir William Bruce who created a magnificent building in the Palladian style. On arrival you will find the **Queen's Gallery** (⏱same hours as palace with separate entrance; ₤6, joint ticket with palace £15.10; ♿), which stages a programme of changing exhibitions of pieces from the Queen's private Royal Collection.

The inner court elevations are outstanding Renaissance work of the Stuart period and among Scotland's earliest examples. The decoration and craftsmanship in the **State Apartments** is outstanding, particularly the **plasterwork ceilings**★★★, the fruit of 10 years' labour by "gentlemen modellers".

The **Historic Apartments** in the 16C round tower have close associations with Mary Queen of Scots and contain tapestries from the Mortlake workshop founded by her son; the painted ceilings are magnificent. In the small room adjoining the bedchamber Mary's secretary, Rizzio, was murdered in 1566.

The roofless nave is all that is left of this once-great **abbey** (⏱same opening times as the palace; visitors are free to visit on their own at the end of the guided tour), dating from the late-12C and early-13C. Here lie David II, James II, James V and also Lord Darnley, father of James VI of Scotland, who united the crowns.

②/③ SOUTH OF THE MILE

Grassmarket was once one of Edinburgh's main markets, as well as the setting for public executions. Today it is a popular area for student accommodation and busy pubs and restaurants. Off here are the remains of the **Flodden Wall**, built following the disastrous battle in 1513. Follow the route marked on the map to see **Edinburgh University**, laid out around George Square, before continuing to the National Museum of Scotland.

National Museum of Scotland★★★

Chambers Street. ⏰*Open year-round daily 10am–5pm.* ⏰*Closed 25 Dec.* ♿✕. ✆*0131 247 4422. www.nms.ac.uk.* The elaborate Venetian Renaissance-style façade of the main building contrasts with the interior. The spacious, well-lit Main Hall is a masterpiece of Victorian cast-iron and plate-glass construction. The museum, recently refurbished to great effect, has all-encompassing collections, devoted to the arts and sciences, from natural history to sculpture, and decorative arts from all over the world.

A sandstone drum tower highlights the innovative design of the **Scotland Galleries**, which traces the story of the country from 3,500 years ago to the present day with the unique collections placed in their historical perspective and with the help of an interactive computer system. The exhibits explain the natural landscape and geological foundation, the peopling of the country, the independent kingdom (1100–1707), the modern state and various other aspects of Scotland.

NEW TOWN★★★

When the decision had been taken to extend the Royalty of Edinburgh, the development was organised by a then unknown architect, James Craig, whose design had won the competition. The **North Bridge** was built across the valley and the New Town was laid out on a grid-iron pattern, with vistas and focal points. The wealthy soon took up residence in these splendid squares and elegant streets.

④ GEORGE STREET

The principal street of Craig's plan is closed at either end by Charlotte and St Andrew squares. From the street intersections there are good views away to the Forth or down to Princes Street Gardens with the castle as backdrop. George Street ends at St Andrew Square. Head north from here on St Andrew Street to the recently refurbished **Scottish National Portrait**

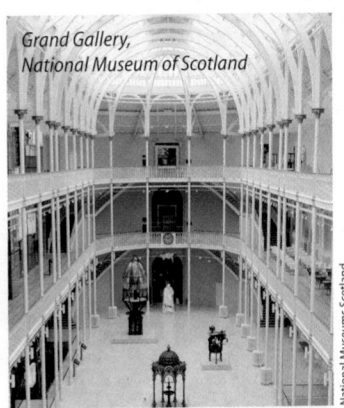

Grand Gallery, National Museum of Scotland

National Museums Scotland

Gallery★ (*1 Queen Street;* ⏰*open year-round daily 10am–5pm/Thu 7pm;* ⏰*closed 25–26 Dec;* ♿✕; ✆*0131 624 6200; www.nationalgalleries.org*). Housed in a splendid Victorian building with wonderful mosaics at the entrance, it "illustrates Scottish history by likeness of the chief actors in it". This includes masterpieces of portraiture of royalty, statesmen, politicians, literary figures, sportsmen and musicians past and present, with some superbly innovative modern works.

In 1791 Robert Adam was commissioned to design **Charlotte Square**★★★, the New Town's most elegant ensemble. On the square, the National Trust for Scotland has magnificently refurbished no. 7, the **Georgian House**★ (*NTS; 7 Charlotte Square;* ⏰*open daily Mar 11am–4pm, Apr–Jun and Sept–Oct 10am–5pm, Jul–Aug 10am–6pm;* ∞*£6;* ♿; ✆*0844 493 2117; www.nts.org.uk*), is filled with Georgian treasures: furniture, silver, porcelain and fine paintings, while its lower floors give a good impression of domestic life in the period 1790–1810.

⑤ PRINCES STREET

Princes Street has grown from a totally residential street, looking out onto gardens in the newly filled-in Nor'Loch, into Edinburgh's prime shopping street. The gardens, famous for the **Floral Clock** composed of 20,000 annuals, opened to the public in 1876.

Following Sir Walter Scott's death in 1832, a public appeal was launched

View of Edinburgh from Calton Hill with Dugald Stewart Monument

and the foundation stone of the **Scott Monument**★ (*Princes Street;* 🕐 *open; Apr–Sept Mon–Sat 10am–7pm, Oct–Mar Mon–Sat 9am–4pm; Sun all year 10am–6pm;* £3; 🕿 *0131 529 4068; www.edinburghmuseums.org.uk*) was laid in 1840. The 200ft-/61m-tall Gothic spire shelters a marble statue of **Scott** and is surrounded by 64 characters from his novels and by the busts of 16 Scottish poets. A viewing platform (*287 narrow stairs to the top*) affords a magnificent **view**★ over central Edinburgh.

Dividing Princes Street Gardens into East and West are two imposing Classical buildings, the National Gallery and the Royal Scottish Academy. The **Royal Scottish Academy** (*entrance on Princes Street;* 🕐 *open Mon–Sat 10am–5pm, Sun noon–5pm;* 🕐 *closed in between exhibitions;* ☞ *free unless otherwise stated;* &✗; 🕿 *0131 225 3922, www.royalscottishacademy.org),* stages temporary exhibitions of contemporary art.

National Gallery of Scotland★★

The Mound. 🕐 *Open year-round daily 10am–5pm (Thu 7pm).* 🕐 *Closed 25–26 Dec.* &✗. 🕿 *0131 624 6200. www.nationalgalleries.org.*

An imposing Classical building houses masterpieces of European art (15C–19C) by Raphael, Rembrandt, Vermeer, Poussin, Claude Lorrain, Boucher, Monet, Van Gogh and many more.

The British tradition is represented by Turner, Gainsborough and Constable, among others. There is a fine collection of **Scottish paintings**, including Ramsay, Raeburn, McTaggart and the Glasgow school.

6 CALTON HILL

East of Princes Street, beyond elegant Waterloo Place, rises **Calton Hill** crowned by Classical monuments and follies which gave rise to the nickname "Edinburgh's acropolis": the porticoed **National Monument**, a **Greek temple** and the 18C **Old Observatory**. There are wonderful views from here but for Edinburgh's best **panorama**★★★ climb to the top of the **Nelson Monument**, a folly in the shape of an upturned telescope (🕐 *open Apr–late Oct Mon–Sat 10am–6pm/7pm, also Sun Jul–Sept noon–5pm; late Oct–Mar Mon–Sat 10am–3pm* ☞ *£3;* 🕿 *0131 556 2716; www.edinburghmuseums.org.uk*). The harmonious sweep of **Regent**, **Calton** and **Royal terraces** (19C) is enhanced by its fine architectural and ironwork features.

OUTSKIRTS
Royal Botanic Garden★★★

▶ *1mi/1.6km from city centre by Broughton Street.* 🕐 *Open year-round daily 10am–6pm (Nov–Feb 4pm).* 🕐 *Glasshouses close 5.30pm (Nov–Feb 3.30pm).* ☞ *Garden free; glasshouses £4.* &✗🅿 *West Gate, Arboretum Road.*

ℰ0131 552 7171. www.rbge.org.uk.
The 70 acres/28ha of the Royal Botanic
Garden are a refreshing haven from the
city bustle.

In 1670, when Edinburgh was emerging
as a centre for medical studies, a physic
garden was established by the university. The original plot was situated near
Holyrood Abbey but around 1820 it was
moved to the present site.

Highlights include: the rhododendrons;
the modernistic Exhibition Plant Houses
(1967), which provide unimpeded interiors where winding paths lead through a
series of landscaped presentations; the
Exhibition Hall, devoted to changing displays; the Tropical (1834) and Temperate
(1858) palm houses; the beautiful view
from the café terrace.

Scottish National Gallery of Modern Art★

▶ *West of the centre, on Belford
Road beyond the Belford Bridge over
the Water of Leith (signed footpath).*
🕒*Open year-round daily 10am–5pm
(Aug 6pm).* 🕒*Closed 25–26 Dec.*
ℰ*0131 624 6200, 0131 624 6336
(recorded information).* ♿🅿✕. *www.
nationalgalleries.org.*

In a garden setting with sculptures by
Epstein, Hepworth and Moore, among
others, the SNGMA has fine examples
of 20C art ranging from Fauvism and
Cubism, with highlights by Matisse and
Picasso, to Russian Primitivism, Nouveau
Réalisme, Pop Art and a collection of
Scottish art, in particular by the Scottish
Colourists and Edinburgh school.
Immediately across the road is the **Dean
Gallery**★ (🕒*same opening details and
facilities as SNGMA*), famous for its giant
Vulcan sculpture by Edinburgh-born
Eduardo Paolozzi (among other works
by him), and a world-class Dada and
Surrealist collection, including works by
Dalí, Miró, Ernst, Magritte and Picasso.

Royal Yacht Britannia★

▶*Ocean Terminal Centre, Port of Leith.
2mi/3km N of city centre.* 🕒*Open
daily Oct–Jun 10am–3.30pm/4pm
(last entry), Jul–Sept 9.30am–4.30pm
(last entry).* 👁*£11, booking by phone*
(small charge) advisable to avoid
queueing in Aug. 🕒*Closed 1 Jan, 25
Dec.* ♿🅿✕. ℰ*0131 555 5566. www.
royalyachtbritannia.co.uk.*

The Royal Yacht was launched from a
Clydebank shipyard in 1953. By the time
she was decommissioned in 1997 she
had sailed more than a million miles on
nearly one thousand official engage-
ments, carrying Queen Elizabeth II and
her family all over the world. Aboard
visitors can see the royal apartments,
crew's quarters, bridge and wheelhouse
and engine room. The fascinating audio
tour and visitor centre brings it to life.

🧍‍🧒 Edinburgh Zoo★★

▶ *2mi/3km W on Corstorphine Road.*
🕒*Open daily 9am–6pm (Oct & Mar
5pm, Nov–Feb 4.30pm).* 👁*£15.50, child
£11.50 (see online for special offers).*
♿🅿 *(£4)*✕. ℰ*0131 334 9171. www.
edinburghzoo.org.uk.*

One of Britain's finest and most successful zoo parks (in terms of breeding),
Edinburgh is home to over 1,000 animals
and is famous for the largest penguin
colony in captivity. Its collection of big
cats and the African Plains Experience
are other highlights.

Craigmillar Castle★

HS. ▶ *3mi/5km SE.* 🕒*Open Apr–Sept
daily 9.30am–5.30pm (Oct 4.30pm).
Nov–Mar Sat–Wed 9.30am–4.30pm.*
🕒*Closed 1–2 Jan, 25–26 Dec.* 👁*£4.20.*
ℰ*0131 661 4445. www.historic-
scotland.gov.uk.*

Even in ruins Craigmillar has an air of
impregnability. The 14C tower house
rises massively above two curtain walls.
The outer wall encloses a courtyard in
front and gardens on either side. The
inner curtain built in 1427 is quartered
with round towers, pierced by gunloops
and topped by attractive oversailing
machicolated parapets. The Great Hall,
(at first floor level) is a grand apartment.
where, it is said, Mary Queen of Scots
sought refuge after the murder of Rizzio,
and plotted the murder of Darnley.
Climb to the top to appreciate the strategic excellence of the castle layout.

Lothians

The Lothians is both a dormitory region and countryside playground for Edinburgh, with first-class beaches, golf links, coastal scenery and Scotland's sunniest weather.

MIDLOTHIAN
Forth Bridges★★

❯ *Best viewed from the esplanade at South Queensferry, 9mi/15km W of Edinburgh on the A 90.*

The first ferry across this point (being the narrowest part of the Forth) was operated around 1070 by the monks of Dunfermline, for pilgrims travelling to the abbey. By the 17C it was the busiest ferry crossing in Scotland. The **Forth Rail Bridge** was begun in 1883 and was opened in 1890. The **Road Bridge**, a slimline suspension bridge with its amazing "curve", was built 1958–64.

Just on the Fife side of the bridge stands **Deep Sea World** (*open year-round daily 10am–5pm/6pm; ☞£12.50, child £8.25; save £2/ticket booking online; ☎01383 411 880; www.deepsea world.com*), a spectacular aquarium boasting the longest underwater viewing tunnel in Britain. Fearless visitors can book a shark dive (*additional charge*).

Rosslyn Chapel★★

❯ *Roslin village (signposted). 7mi/11km S.*
Open year-round Mon–Sat 9.30am–6pm (May–Sept 5pm), Sun noon–4.45pm. Last entry 30mins before

closing. Closed 1 Jan, 24–25, 31 Dec. ☞£7.70. Guided talks throughout the day. ☎0131 440 2159. www.rosslynchapel.org.uk.

One of the most mysterious and mythologised sites in Britain, famously starring in Dan Brown's *The Da Vinci Code*, Rosslyn Chapel stands on the edge of the Esk Valley and is a bewildering example of master craftsmanship. It was built by order of Sir William St Clair, third and last Prince of Orkney (1396–1484). Work lasted from 1446 until 1486, just after Sir William's death. Among the intricate, rich decoration, the best-known single item is the **Apprentice Pillar★★★**.

Legend has it that while the master mason was abroad, his apprentice carved the pillar. On his return, seeing the quality of craftsmanship, the master killed his apprentice in a fit of jealousy.

Dalmeny★★

❯ *6mi/10km W by A 90.*

The village is famous for its parish **Church of St Cuthbert★** (*open Apr–*

Detail of the Apprentice Pillar, Rosslyn Chapel

© David Lyons / Alamy

ℹ **Info:** www.edinburgh.org; www.visiteastlothian.org; www.visitmidlothian.org.uk; http://visitwest lothian.co.uk.

🕐 **Timing:** Allow at least three days.

👪 **Kids:** Deep Sea World, Falkirk Wheel, New Lanark.

Sept Sun 2–4pm, otherwise key obtainable at post office or 5 Main Street, opposite church; ℘0131 331 1479), an exceptionally fine example of Norman architecture, with an intricately carved south **doorway**★★. To the east of the village is **Dalmeny House**★ *(South Queensferry; ↠guided tour only, first Sun Jun–late Jul/early Aug, Sun–Tue, 2.15pm, 3.30pm; ⊚£6; ♿️🅿️✕; ℘0131 331 1888; www. dalmeny.co.uk)*, home of the Earls of Rosebery. Of particular interest are the Rothschild collection of 18C French furniture, porcelain and tapestries.

EAST LOTHIAN
Haddington★
◆ *18min/29km E.*

This handsome market town grew up in the 12C around a royal palace and by the 16C it was the fourth-largest town in Scotland. In the 18C it entered a golden age based on agricultural wealth. Follow The Sands past the 16C **Nungate Bridge** with its pointed cutwaters up to the **High Street**★ and its continuous line of frontages, often gable ended. The 14C–15C **St Mary's Parish Church** enjoys a peaceful riverside setting. Its impressive dimensions are a reminder of its history as a great burgh church. The historic house of **Lennoxlove**★ *(1mi/0.6km S on the B 6369; ↠ guided tour only, Easter Sun–Sept, Wed, Thu & Sun 1.30-3.30pm; ⊚£5; 🅿️✕; ℘01620 828 605; www.lennoxlove.com)* has associations with Mary Queen of Scots, and boasts several fine **portraits** and **furniture**.

WEST LOTHIAN
Hopetoun House★★
◆ *South Queensferry. 1mi/18km W on the A 90 and A 904.* ◷*Open Good Fri– late Sept daily 10.30am–5pm.* ⊚£9.20. ♿️🅿️✕. ℘0131 331 2451. www.hopetounhouse.com.

A mansion of contrasts set in beautiful landscaped grounds, the house (built 1699–1707) displays the mature Classicism of **Sir William Bruce**, its main staircase richly embellished with carving leading the eye upwards to the painted cupola. The flamboyant extensions and frontage (1721–67) are the work of William Adam, completed by his son John. The grandeur of the State Apartments is complemented by the original furnishings, magnificent plaster ceilings and a notable art collection.

Linlithgow Palace★★
HS. ◆ *19mi/31km W by the A 8 and M 9.* ◷*Open year-round daily 9.30am–5.30pm (Oct–Mar 4.30pm).* ⊚£5.50. 🅿️✕. ℘01506 842 896. www.historic-scotland.gov.uk.

The history of the town is that of its royal palace, around which it grew from the 12C. Following the rebuilding of the palace in 1424 it enjoyed over a century of grandeur as the centre of Scotland's court until the Union of the Crowns (1603). The roofless and forbidding four-square ruin still shelters several delicate features, notably the 1530s **fountain**★ in the courtyard and a superbly carved **fireplace**. Alongside the palace stands the 15C–16C late Gothic **St Michael's Church**★ *(◷open daily May–Sept 10.30am–4pm (Oct–Apr 1pm). ℘01506 842 188. www.stmichaelsparish.org.uk)* with its controversial defiantly modern spire (1964).

♟️Falkirk Wheel★★
◆ *28.5mi W. Tamfourhill.* ◷*Open daily Mar–Oct 10am–5.30pm. Nov–Feb Wed–Sun 11am–4pm (no boat trips Nov).* ⊚*Visitor centre free; mini-cruise £7.95, child £4.95.* ♿️🅿️✕. ℘08700 500 208. www.thefalkirkwheel.co.uk.

The Falkirk Wheel is one of Scotland's most ingenious modern engineering achievements, designed to relink the Forth and Clyde Canal to the Union Canal. The problem was that the latter lay 115ft/35m above the level of the former. Historically, the two had been joined at Falkirk by a flight of 11 locks that stepped down across a distance of 0.9mi/1.5km, but these have been dismantled in 1933, thus breaking the link. The wheel, the world's first and only rotating boat lift, was thus created (2002) to lift a canal barge 115ft/35m high from one canal to the other. This was opened in 2002.

Glasgow★★★

Scotland's most populous city is an important industrial centre and port, lying 44mi/74km west of Edinburgh. Many of Scotland's leading businesses make Glasgow their home. In recent years the city has had a cultural renaissance.

A BIT OF HISTORY

It was to this part of the embattled Kingdom of Strathclyde that **St Mungo** came in the mid-6C: he set up his wooden church on the banks of the Molendinar Burn, and became the first bishop of the city. In the 17C Glasgow became the centre of the Protestant cause. By the 18C the city was rich from trade in textiles, sugar and tobacco, her wealth increasing in the 19C through banking, shipbuilding and industry.

The arts prospered amid the wealth: neither the **Glasgow Boys** (W Y MacGregor, James Guthrie, George Henry and John Lavery, who advocated realism in an age of romanticism), nor the pioneer Modern movement led by **Charles Rennie Mackintosh**, could have so flourished in any other city. The realist and radical traditions have been adopted by the Glasgow painters of the 1980s (Steven Campbell, Ken Currie, Peter Howson, Adrian Wisniewski and Stephen Conroy). Today Glasgow is the home of the Scottish Opera, Scottish Ballet and several notable **art collections**.

1 CITY CENTRE
Gallery of Modern Art★

Royal Exchange Square. ◐*Open daily 10am/Fri & Sun 11am–5pm (Thu 8 pm).* ◗*Free guided tours.* ♿✗. ℘*0141 229 3050. www.glasgowmuseums.com.* This landmark 18C Neoclassical mansion houses a wide-ranging collection of contemporary art. It has a massive Corinthian portico and a magnificent main hall with a barrel-vaulted ceiling.

Glasgow School of Art★

167 Renfrew Street. Mackintosh Gallery. ◗*Visit by guided tour only each hour, Apr–Sept daily 10am–4pm, Oct–Mar*

- ▸ **Population:** 662,853.
- ⛁ **Michelin Map:** Michelin Atlas p55 or Map 501 H 16.
- ▯ **Info:** 11 George Square. ℘0141 566 0800. www.seeglasgow.com.
- ◗ **Location:** 46mi/74km west of Edinburgh via the M 8. Trains from England arrive at Central Station; from Edinburgh at nearby Queen Street Station. Neighbouring Buchanan Street Bus Station is the terminus for regional, intercity and local buses. Underground stations are indicated on our map. Open-top hop-on hop-off bus tours leave from George Square. (℘*0141 204 0444. http://city sightseeingglasgow.co.uk).*
- ⊛ **Don't Miss:** The Burrell Collection; Glasgow Cathedral; Hunterian Art Gallery Mackintosh Wing; Museum of Transport; an excursion to New Lanark.
- ◷ **Timing:** Allow at least three days in the city.
- ≜ **Kids:** Glasgow Science Centre; New Lanark.

Mon–Sat 11am, 2pm, 3pm. Booking advisable. ◉£8.75. ♿✗. ℘*0141 353 4526. www.gsa.ac.uk.*
Charles Rennie Mackintosh designed this building, regarded as his masterpiece, in 1897–1909. It holds his acclaimed library with three-storey-high windows and suspended ceiling, plus the furniture gallery with items from Miss Cranston's Tearooms.

Tenement House

NTS. 145 Buccleuch Street. ◐*Open Mar–Oct daily 1–5pm.* ◉£6. ℘*0844 493 2197. www.nts.org.uk.*
This two-room flat, with kitchen and bathroom, portrays turn-of-the-century tenement life and is a piece of important Glasgow social history.

PUBLIC TRANSPORT

Buchanan Bus station (*℘0141 332 3708*) gives information on travel passes for the metro, bus and trains. The **SPT (Strathclyde Partnership for Transport) Discovery** ticket valid for one day allows visitors to discover the varied aspects of Glasgow starting from different metro stations. Their range of tickets *(www.spt.co.uk/tickets)* also includes the **Mackintosh Trail Ticket** *(⊜£16)* offering combined entry to all paying (Charles Rennie) Mackintosh attractions in the city, the Hill House in Helensburgh, as well as unlimited travel on Subway and FirstBus services in Greater Glasgow.

SIGHTSEEING

PDG Helicopters (*℘0870 607 9000; http://tours.pdg-helicopters.co.uk)* offers helicopter rides which afford spectacular views of the city and of Loch Lomond.

Boat trips "doon the watter" along the Firth of Clyde are also very popular.

② CATHEDRAL–THE BARRAS

Start at the **cathedral**★★★ (⊙*open Apr–Sept Mon–Sat 9.30am–5.30pm, Sun 1–5.30pm; rest of year closes 4pm;* ●*free guided tours May–Sept;* ⊙*closed 1–2 Jan, 25–26 Dec;* &*;* *℘0141 552 8198; www.glasgowcathedral.org.uk)*, the fourth church on the site of St Mungo's original building, best viewed from the heights of the nearby Necropolis. The cathedral is mostly 13C and 14C with 15C additions. The **nave** is late Gothic; its elevation of richly moulded and pointed arches, more numerous at each level, rises to the timber roof. Beyond the 15C stone screen is the **choir**, mid-13C in the finest early pointed style. Beyond the ambulatory, through one of the four chapels leading off from it, is the upper chapter room (rebuilt in the 15C) where the medieval university held its classes. The lower church is another Gothic delight, where light and shade play effectively amid the piers enshrining the **tomb of St Mungo**, Glasgow's patron saint, whose legend is illustrated on the St Kentigern Tapestry (1979). The 15C **Blacader Aisle** is an extension by Glasgow's first archbishop with ribbed vaulting and carved bosses.

Follow the High Street, then Duke Street to reach **George Square**. Though started in 1782 George Square is magnificently Victorian. Of special interest are the 1869 **Merchants' House** and, opposite, the **City Chambers**★ (&●*guided tour, official functions permitting, Mon (excl. bank hols)–Fri 10.30am, 2.30pm;* *℘0141 287 4018; www.glasgow.gov.uk)*, where the grandeur and opulence of the loggia, council and banqueting halls are reminders that Glasgow was the second city of the Empire in Victorian times. Follow the route marked on the map to reach the **Glasgow Cross**. The heart of Glasgow until Victorian times, the **Tolbooth Steeple**★ is the last reminder of its faded elegance.

Further along this walk you come to the **People's Palace and Winter Gardens** *(Glasgow Green;* ⊙ ***People's Palace:*** ⊙*open year-round Tue–Thu and Sat 10am–5pm, Fri and Sun 11am–5pm, **Winter Garden:*** ⊙*open daily 10am–5pm;* &🅿✕*;* *℘0141 276 0788; www.glasgowmuseums.com)*. This social history museum with exotic gardens is sited on Glasgow Green, a place used for grazing, jousting, parades, public hangings and, above all, free speech. From the gardens, follow the route marked on the map to see **The Barras**, a famous century-old colourful weekend street market.

③ KELVINGROVE/WEST END

The area around Kelvingrove Park is home to two impressive museums and a park with a famous 1924 bandstand.

Hunterian Museum, Art Gallery and Mackintosh House★★★

⊙*Open Mon–Sat 9.30am–5pm.* ⊜*Mackintosh House £3 (free Wed after 2pm), other areas free.* &✕*.* *℘0141 330 4221 museum;* *℘0141 330 5431 for art*

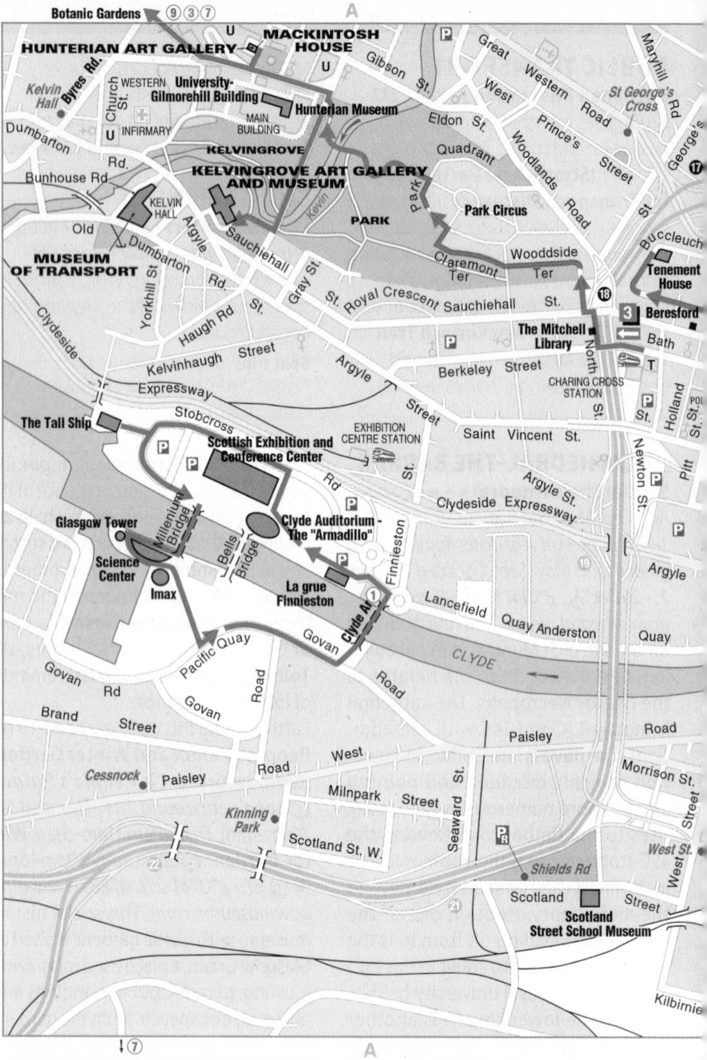

Botanic Gardens ▸ ⑨③⑦

HUNTERIAN ART GALLERY **MACKINTOSH HOUSE**

University-Gilmorehill Building

Hunterian Museum

WESTERN

Church St.

Byres Rd.

Kelvin Hall

Dumbarton

INFIRMARY

MAIN BUILDING

Gibson St.

Great Western Road

West

Prince's

Eldon St.

Quadrant

St George's Cross

Maryhill Rd

George's

Woodlands Road

Street

⑰

KELVINGROVE

KELVINGROVE ART GALLERY AND MUSEUM

Bunhouse Rd.

KELVIN HALL

Old Dumbarton Rd.

MUSEUM OF TRANSPORT

Yorkhill St.

Argyle St.

Sauchiehall

PARK

Park Circus

Kelvin

Park

Wooddside Ter

Claremont Ter

Sauchiehall St.

Buccleuch

Tenement House

③ **Beresford**

Bath

Riverside Museum

Clydeside

Haugh Rd.

Kelvinhaugh Street

Gray St.

Royal Crescent

Argyle

North St.

The Mitchell Library

CHARING CROSS STATION

Holland St.

POL

Expressway

Stobcross

Berkeley Street

Saint Vincent St.

The Tall Ship

Scottish Exhibition and Conference Center

EXHIBITION CENTRE STATION

Newton St.

Argyle St.

Pitt St.

T

Glasgow Tower

Science Center

Imax

Millennium Bridge

Bells Bridge

Clyde Auditorium - The "Armadillo"

La grue Finnieston

Clydeside Expressway

Finnieston

①

Argyle

Lancefield Quay

Anderson Quay

Pacific Quay

Govan Quay

Govan Road

Clyde Av.

Govan Rd

Brand Street

Govan Road

CLYDE

Road

Paisley

Road

Cessnock

Paisley

Road

West

Milnpark Street

Seaward St.

Morrison St.

West St.

West Street

Kinning Park

Scotland St. W.

P R

Shields Rd

Scotland

Scotland Street

Scotland Street School Museum

Kilbirnie

▾⑦

A

WHERE TO STAY

City Inn	①	Marks Hotel	⑤	The Town House	⑨
Malmaison	③	Sherbrooke Castle	⑦	

---

gallery and Mackintosh House;
℘0141 330 4772 Zoology Museum.
www.hunterian.gla.ac.uk.
These University of Glasgow museums hold an eclectic and fascinating collection including medicine and anatomy, one of the world's great **coin** collections, and Roman and Egyptian artefacts. There is a separate zoology museum.

The art gallery★★ includes an important holding of works by **James McNeill Whistler**★★★ (1843–1903), as well as portraits and 19C and 20C Scottish art. The **Mackintosh House**★★★ is a reconstruction of the home of Charles Rennie Mackintosh.

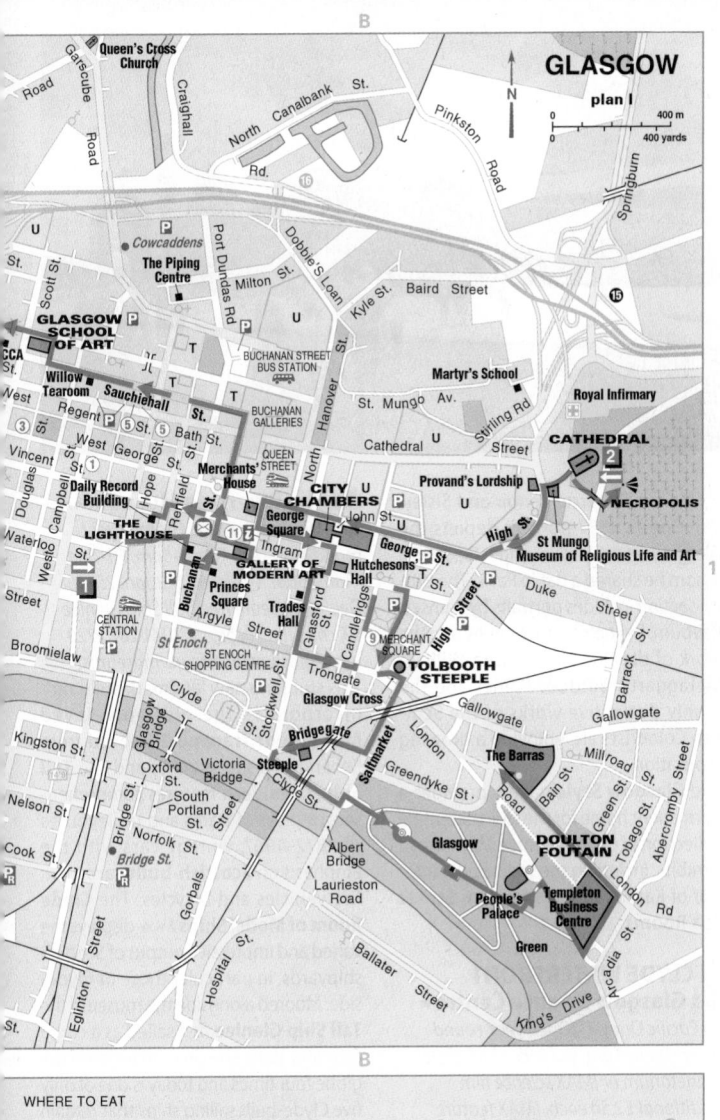

GLASGOW

plan I

0   400 m
0   400 yards

WHERE TO EAT

Gamba	①	Manna	⑤	The Dhabba	⑨
La Parmigiana	③	Stravaigin 2	⑦	Urban	⑪

Kelvingrove Art Gallery and Museum★★★

🕐Open year-round Mon–Thu and Sat 10am–5pm, Fri and Sun 11am–5pm. 🕐Closed 1–2 Jan, 25–26 Dec. ⬩Free guided tours. ♿🅿✕. ☎0141 276 9599. www.glasgowmuseums.com.

The building opened in 1902, financed by the 1888 Glasgow International

Exhibition. The European art section is displayed in the first-floor galleries. The Dutch and Flemish holding includes works by Jordaens, Rubens, Brueghel the Elder and Rembrandt, as well as Ruisdael landscapes. French 19C and early-20C movements are represented by Millet, Fantin-Latour and Courbet; and the Impressionists

The Riverside Museum

© Glasgow City Council (Museums) 2011/photo: Ian Watson

by Monet, Pissarro, Renoir and Sisley. Van Gogh's 1887 portrait depicts the Glasgow art dealer, Alexander Reid, with whom he shared a flat in Paris. The British section includes portraits by Ramsey, Raeburn, Reynolds and Romney and the work of the Pre-Raphaelites. William McTaggart's outdoor scenes and the highly distinctive works of the Scottish Colourists are enjoying a growing reputation.

The **Glasgow Style** gallery provides a permanent home for the city's extensive collection of Charles Rennie Mackintosh exhibits, including the spectacular interior of Kate Cranston's **Ingram Street Tea Rooms**.

④ CLYDE WATERFRONT
Glasgow Science Centre★

50 Pacific Quay. ⏱Open year-round daily 10am–5pm. ≈£9.95, child £7.95. Planetarium or IMAX science film additional £2.50 each, IMAX feature film additional £9.95, child £7.95. ♿🅿(£3). ✕. ☏0141 420 5000. www.glasgowsciencecentre.org.

Housed in three stunning modern buildings of real architectural merit this modern hands-on science centre contains hundreds of interactive exhibits in its Science Mall, a Science Show Theatre, a Climate Change Theatre plus a planetarium and an IMAX cinema. Visitors can also take a ride to the top of the rotating **Glasgow Tower**, at 416ft/127m high, for a splendid view of the city.

The Riverside Museum★★

100 Pointhouse Place. ⏱Open year-round Mon–Thu 10am–5pm, Fri–Sun 11am–5pm. ⏱Closed 1–2 Jan, 25–26 Dec. ≈Museum free, Tall Ship Glenlee £7, child free. ♿✕. ☏0141 287 2720. www.glasgowlife.org.uk/museums.

This stunning new landmark building incorporates the old much-loved **Museum of Transport** (moved from Kelvingrove site in 2010) and the **Tall Ship, Glenlee**. It features comprehensive displays of trams and trolleybuses of 1872–1967, vintage cars with the emphasis on **Scottish-built cars★★★**, fire vehicles and bicycles. The **Clyde Room of Model Ships★★★** displays the varied and impressive output of Scottish shipyards, in particular those of Clydeside. Moored alongside the museum the **Tall Ship Glenlee** first sailed as a cargo carrier in 1896. She circumnavigated the globe four times and today is one of only five Clyde-built sailing ships that remain afloat in the world.

BURRELL COLLECTION★★★

▶ 3mi/5km SW on the M 77. Pollok Park. ⏱Open year-round Mon–Thu & Sat 10am–5pm, Fri and Sun 11am–5pm. ⏱Closed 1–2 Jan, 25–26 Dec. ⏱Guided tour (free). ♿🅿✕. ☏0141 287 2550. www.glasgowmuseums.com.

The collection of shipowner **Sir William Burrell** (1861–1958) is spaciously laid out in a custom-built gallery, surrounded by parkland. The **Ancient Civi-**

Charles Rennie Mackintosh (1868–1928)

The city's famous architect, designer and artist developed his original style combining the Scottish vernacular tradition and Art Nouveau influences. Glasgow takes great pride in its legacy of fine buildings and interiors by Mackintosh: **Glasgow School of Art**, the **Mackintosh House**, **The Willow Rooms** *(217 Sauchiehall Street)*, **Queens Cross Church** *(270 Garscube Road)* and **Scotland Street School** *(225 Scotland Street)* as well as the offices of the *Daily Record (Renfield Lane)* and the **Glasgow Herald** *(Mitchell Steet)*. **Hill House** in Helensburgh is a must for fans of domestic architecture. An unusual recent addition is the **House for an Art Lover** *(Bellahouston Park)* built to Mackintosh's original design for a competition. See also the recently redesigned **Kelvingrove** collection.

lisations section includes items from Egypt, Mesopotamia, Italy and Greece. **Oriental Art** incorporates ceramics, bronzes and jades from the third millennium BC to the 19C, and features the enamelled Ming figure of a **lohan**, or disciple of Buddha, which is dated to 1484. Burrell's particular interest was in **Medieval** and **post-Medieval European Art** and there are some outstanding examples. Of the early works to be found in **Paintings**, **Drawings and Bronzes**, Bellini's *Virgin and Child* is notable. The **Hutton Castle Rooms** are complete with medieval and antique furnishings.

Pollok House★

NTS. Pollok Park ◐*Open year-round daily 10am–5pm.* ◐*Closed 1–2 Jan, 25–26 Dec.* ⊛*£6, Nov–Mar free.* ♿🅿✕. *℘0844 493 2202. www.nts.org.uk.*
The highlight of this 18C mansion is the collection of **Spanish paintings**★★ acquired by Sir William Stirling Maxwell (1818–78). These include portraits by El Greco and etchings by Goya as well as works by Tristan, and Murillo.

EXCURSIONS
Hill House, Helensburgh★

NTS. Upper Colquhoun Street.
◐*21mi/34km NW via the A 82 and A 814.* ◐*Open Apr–Oct 1.30–5.30pm.* ⊛*£9. ℘0844 493 2208. www.nts.org.uk.*
On a hillside overlooking the Clyde, built 1902–04, this is the finest of Charles Rennie Mackintosh's domestic creations.

New Lanark★★

◐*20mi/32km SE via the M 74 and A 72.* ◐*Visitor centre open year-round daily 10am (Oct–Mar 11am)–5pm.* ◐*Closed 1 Jan, 25 Dec.* ⊛*£8.50, child £6.* ♿🅿✕. *℘01555 661 345. www.newlanark.org.*
In the deep gorge of the River Clyde, an 18C planned industrial village comprising four cotton mills, housing and amenities for the workforce was the acclaimed achievement of the Glasgow manufacturer and banker David Dale and his son-in-law Robert Owen, a social reformer. The village, still partly residential, has been declared a UNESCO World Heritage Site.

Mill no. 3, which houses the **visitor centre**, including the Annie McLeod Experience Ride, is the most handsome of the four units. Other points of interest include the Nursery Buildings (for pauper apprentices), the village store, the counting house, Robert Owen's School for Children, Robert Owen's house, and a working textile machinery. There is also a beautiful **Roof Garden** to enjoy.

The riverside **Dyeworks** has displays on the wildlife of the **Falls of Clyde**, a beauty spot which has inspired painters (including Turner) and poets (such as Scott and Wordsworth) alike. A footpath *(1mi/1.6km)* leads to the Falls.

Angus and Dundee

Dundee is Scotland's fourth largest city and trying hard to break into Scotland's tourist destination major league. It boasts first-class maritime and industrial heritage attractions, a splendid revitalised art gallery and museum, and a burgeoning cultural, restaurant and shopping scene. Predominantly agricultural, the most famous landmark in Angus is Glamis ("glarms") Castle, made famous by Shakespeare. The region is also famous for its Pictish remains, while on a sunny day, its glory is the beautiful gardens at Edzell Castle.

DUNDEE★

With a population of around 166,000, Dundee is a busy seaport, an educational centre and the capital of Tayside. The area has been continuously occupied since Mesolithic times. Traditional historic activities (such as whaling and jute milling) have given way to modern high-tech industries. The city centre blends fine Victorian buildings with modern shopping facilities.

City Walk

Just east of the Tay Bridge in Victoria Dock is **HM Frigate Unicorn★** (*open Apr–Oct daily 10am–5pm, Nov–Mar Wed–Fri noon–4pm, Sat–Sun 10am–4pm; closed 23 Dec–4 Jan; £5; 01382 200 900; www.frigateunicorn. org*), which was launched in 1824 as a 46-gun frigate for the Royal Navy. She is now the oldest British-built ship still afloat. Visitors can explore the main gun decks, with their 18-pounders, and the captain's and officers' quarters, and discover the flavour of life in the Royal Navy in the golden age of sail.

West of the Tay Bridge near the railway station is **Discovery Point★** (*Discovery Quay, Craig Harbour; open Apr–Oct daily 10am (11am Sun)–6pm, Nov–Mar 10am (11am Sun)–5pm; closed 1 Jan, 25–26 Dec; £8, child £5, joint ticket with Verdant Works (see below) £12, child*

- **Michelin Map:** Michelin Atlas p62 or Map 501.
- **Info:** Discovery Point, Discovery Key, Dundee. 01382 527 527. www.angusanddundee.co.uk.
- **Kids:** Discovery Point; Sensation.

£7.50; 01382 309 060; www.rrsdiscovery.com) and the pride of the city, the **RRS Discovery★**, which was custom built in Dundee in 1901 for scientific exploration. The ship forms the centrepiece of an exciting exhibition, with a spectacular audio-visual presentation devoted to Captain Scott's epic Antarctic Expedition (1901–04), including the vessel's dramatic rescue and other journeys and actual artefacts of the crew.

On the other side of the tracks, on Greenmarket, is **Sensation** (*open daily Apr–Oct 10am–5pm; closed 1 Jan; £7.25, child £5.25; 01382 228 800; www.sensation.org.uk*), Dundee's award-winning hands-on science centre with over 80 interactive stations, shows, demonstrations and special exhibitions. Just north of here is the University of Dundee and beyond, on West Henderson's Wynd, is **Verdant Works★** (*open Apr–Oct daily 10am (11am Sun)–6pm; Nov–Mar Wed–Sat 10.30am–4.30pm, Sun 11am–4.30pm; £7.25, child £4.25, joint ticket with Discovery Point, above; 01382 225 282; www.verdantworks.com*), which tells, in lively fashion, the story of how jute (a natural fibre using for weaving) became a major industry in Dundee, featuring original working machinery alongside the latest hands-on exhibits. Northwest of the Tay Bridge, a splendid recently refurbished Victorian Gothic building is home to **The McManus★** (*Albert Square; open year-round Mon–Sat 10am–5pm, Sun 12.30–4.30pm; 01382 307 200; www.mcmanus. co.uk*), Dundee's principal art gallery and museum. Its galleries cover prehistory; "the Making of Modern Dundee" (from 1850 to date); "Dundee and the World" (housed in the stunning Albert Hall, with its magnificent wooden ceiling and spectacular stained glass); an authentic Victorian Art Gallery; contemporary art, and the city's nationally significant collection of 20C art.

GLAMIS★

⏵ *12mi/19km N of Dundee.*
Set in the rich agricultural Angus Glens countryside, this picturesque small village (pronounced "glarms") was made famous by Shakespeare, its castle the residence of Macbeth.

Angus Folk Museum★

NTS. Kirkwynd. ⏱*Open Apr–Jun, Sept-Oct Sat–Sun & all bank hols noon–5pm. Jul–Aug daily noon–5pm.* ⬤£6. 🅿 ♿. ☎*0844 493 2141. www.nts.org.uk.*
Six charming 18C cottages and a farm house this fascinating collection of domestic and agricultural bygones, from the last 200 years, including a schoolroom and Victorian parlour.

Glamis Castle★★

Dundee Road. ☞ *Guided tour only (every 10min–15min), daily; 10am–6pm (last tour 4.30pm). Nov–Dec 10.30am–4.30pm (last tour 3pm).* ⬤*£9.50.* ♿🅿✕. ☎*01307 840 393. www.glamis-castle.co.uk.*
Glamis is the archetypal Scottish castle; its massive sandstone pile bristles with towers, turrets, conical roofs and chimneys. It has a fascinating history includ-

ing a ghost (Lady Glamis, burned as a witch), literary associations (Macbeth was Thane of Glamis) and Royal Family connections since the 14C; most recently it was the childhood home of the late Queen Mother.

Exterior – The 15C L-shaped core of the castle has been added to and altered, apparently at random through the centuries. Statues of James and his son, Charles I, flank the driveway. To the side is a beautiful Italian Garden.

Interior – Guided tours take visitors throughout the castle's 10 principal rooms. Jacobean armour and furniture, Mortlake tapestries and interiors of many periods are on display. The chapel has a series of paintings of the Apostles and scenes from the Bible by Jacob de Wet (1695–1754), a Dutch artist who also worked at Blair and Holyroodhouse. The splendid **Drawing Room** is adorned by a **plasterwork ceiling** (1621) and a magnificent fireplace.

EXCURSIONS

Aberlemno Stones★

HS. ⏵ *12mi/19km NE via the A 94 and B 9134.* ⏱*Open May–Oct. The stones are boarded up from last working day Sept–first working day Apr. www.historic-scotland.gov.uk*
These Pictish sculptured stones depict animal and abstract symbols, hunting and battle scenes and a cross with flanking angels. They stand at the roadside and in the churchyard.

Glamis Castle

© P. Tomkins/VisitScotland/ScottishViewpoint

Meigle Sculptured Stone Museum★★

HS. ❯ *Meigle. 7mi/11km west by A 94.* ⏱*Open Apr–Sept daily 9.30am–5.30pm.* ⬤*£4.* ♿. *✆01828 640 612. www.historic-scotland.gov.uk.*

The former village school displays an outstanding collection of 26 early **Christian monuments**★★ in the Pictish tradition, all found locally. The carving is full of vitality and shows a high degree of skill.

Edzell Castle & Garden★

HS. ❯ *25mi/40km NE by the A 94 and B 966 to Edzell village.* ⏱*Open Easter/ Apr–Sept daily 9.30am–5.30pm; Oct daily 9.30a,–4.30pm. Nov–Mar Sat–Wed 9.30am–4.30pm.* ⬤*£5.* ♿🅿. *✆01356 648 631. www.historic-scotland.gov.uk.*

The ruined castle is an early-16C tower house but the highlight here is the formal walled garden known as **The Pleasance**★★★, which is without equal in Scotland. Sir David Lindsay (c.1550–1610) created this garden in 1604; it is a product of the Renaissance ideas he had absorbed on his wide travels. The blaze of summer colour against the rich red of the walls diverts attention from the rich heraldic and symbolic **sculptures** on the surrounding walls, but these, too, reward closer inspection.

Stirling and Argyll

This is the most romanticised area of all Scotland, in both fact and fiction. Who hasn't heard of "the bonnie bonnie banks" of Loch Lomond, Rob Roy, Scott's "Lady of the Lake", the Holy Isle of Iona, Bannockburn and – as recently as the late-20C – Mull of Kintyre, "Balamory" (Tobermory on Mull) and "Braveheart" William Wallace? The scenery is familiar from chocolate boxes and jigsaws: the hills and glens of the Trossachs and the many glorious lochs make for unmissable quintessential Scottish viewing.

STIRLING★★

Controlling the route between Edinburgh (69mi/70km SE) and the Highlands, and the crossing of the Forth at its tidal limit, Stirling has been strategically important from time immemorial. Most of its long history has therefore been essentially that of the castle and former royal residence perched on its well-nigh impregnable crag. Today it is an ideal touring centre.

From its redoubtable site Stirling has seen many battles, the most important being the two victories over the English

◔ **Michelin Map:**
Michelin Atlas p54–55, p59–60 or Map 501.

▤ **Info:** Old Town Jail, Stirling ✆01786 449 272. Ancaster Square, Callander ✆1877 382 352. Balloch ✆01389 753 533. The Pier, Craignure ✆01680 812 377. Tobermory ✆08707 200 625. Main Street, Tobermory, Isle of Mull ✆08707 200 625. Front Street, Iona ✆01499 302 063. Argyll Square, Oban ✆01631 563 122. www.visitscottishheartlands. com; www.lochlomond-trossachs; org. www.isle-of-iona.com; www. inveraray-argyll.com; www.oban.org.uk.

👪 **Kids:** Loch Lomond Sea Life Centre; Old Town Jail, Stirling.

at Stirling Bridge in 1297 and Bannockburn in 1314. Stirling became a permanent royal residence with the accession of the **Stewarts**, and its golden age came under **James IV**. After his death at Flodden Field, in 1513, his queen, Margaret, brought her son to Stirling, where he was crowned as James V. His daughter, **Mary Queen of Scots**, was crowned in the Chapel Royal, and her infant son, the future **James VI** of Scotland and I of England, was baptised here in 1566. It was with his departure to Whitehall that Stirling's role as a royal residence ended.

Stirling Castle★★

HS. ⏰Open year-round daily 9.30am–6pm (5pm Oct–Easter). £13, Argyll's Lodging £2 extra. Guided tours (free). Buy timed tickets online to avoid queues. ♿P£4, max stay 4 hrs. ✕. ℘01786 450 000; www.historic-scotland.gov.uk/stirlingcastle, www.stirlingcastle.gov.uk

The approach is through the old town. A statue of Robert the Bruce stands guard on the esplanade.

Begun by James IV in 1496, the palace is a masterpiece of Renaissance ornamentation, completed by his son in 1540. Its outstanding feature is the elaborate design of the **external elevations★★★** – best admired from the Upper Square. The castle has recently undertaken major interpretive improvements including a new exhibition telling its story, in the Queen Anne **Casemates**. Beneath the palace lie the atmospheric medieval vaults, now home to a series of family-friendly interactive displays all about the lives of people at court such as jesters and musicians.

Rob Roy MacGregor (1671–1734)

Much of the rugged terrain of the Trossachs is closely associated with the daring exploits of the outlawed clan leader and hero of Sir Walter Scott's novel *Rob Roy* (1818). Rob was a real person; Glen Gyle at the head of Loch Katrine was his birthplace and he and his wife and two of their sons lie in the churchyard of Balquihidder on Loch Voil.

The façade of the **Great Hall** (1460–88) is lit by four pairs of embrasured windows; the noble interior is notable for its **hammerbeam oak roof**, minstrels' gallery and dais flanked by oriel windows. In contrast the **palace** itself (1496–1540) is decorated with original figure carvings in recessed arches and above the cornice. The **royal apartments**, recently returned to their mid-16C appearance following a major refurbishment, boast fine 16C oak medallions known as the **Stirling Heads★★**. The early Renaissance **Chapel** (1594) features round-headed windows framing the elaborate doorway and an ornate interior.

The 500-year-old King's Old Building houses the **Argyll and Sutherland Highlanders Regimental Museum★** (⏰closes 45min before castle), presenting 200 years of regimental history.

Stirling Castle

© P. Tomkins/VisitScotland/ScottishViewpoint

Old Town

The medieval town, with its narrow wynds and steep streets, spills downhill from the castle. **Argyll's Lodging**★ (HS; ☞entry only to Stirling Castle ticket holders, by guided tour, daily 12.15pm, 2.45pm, 4.15pm; ☞£2; ℘01786 450 000.;www.historic-scotland.gov.uk/stirlingcastle, www.stirlingcastle.gov.uk) was built in 1632 by Sir William Alexander, founder of Nova Scotia and contains wonderful examples of fine **Scottish Renaissance decoration**★.

In the **Church of the Holy Rude**★ (Ⓛopen daily Easter–Oct 11am–4pm; ☞contribution requested; ℘01786 475 275; www.holyrude.org) the infant James VI was crowned, in 1567, with John Knox preaching the sermon. It retains its 15C oak **timberwork roof**.

Beyond **Bothwell House** (39 St John's Street) with its projecting tower, stands the ♣♣**Old Town Jail** (Ⓛopen Easter–Oct daily 10am–5pm; ☞£6.65, child £4.10; P; ℘01786 450 050; www.oldtownjail. com), where the harshness of prison life can be experienced courtesy of lively actor guides.

At the bottom of Broad Street, formerly the centre of burgh life, with its mercat cross and tolbooth, is **Darnley's House**, a 16C townhouse (now a café) where Mary's husband, Lord Darnley, is said to have stayed.

EXCURSIONS
Dunblane★

▶6mi/10km N on the A 9.
A mainly residential town of some 6,000 inhabitants, modern Dunblane gained tragic notoriety in 1996 for a massacre of 16 schoolchildren.

An ecclesiastical centre since Celtic times, the old town is grouped round its beautiful 13C Gothic **cathedral**★★ (HS; Ⓛopen Apr–Oct Mon–Sat 9.30am–12.30pm, 1.30–5.30pm, Sun 2–5.30pm; winter open throughout day, closes 1hr earlier; ☞donation requested; ℘01786 825 388; www.historic-scotland.gov.uk), which survived the Reformation intact. The vigorous carving of the canopied 15C **Chisholm stalls** and their misericords is remarkable. In the glorious choir is the ornate **Ochiltree stalls**. The **Lady Chapel**, the oldest part of the building, has ribbed vaulting and carved bosses. Adjoining the south side of the nave is a 12C tower, and the magnificent **west front**★★, overlooking the Allan Water.

Doune Castle★

HS. ▶10mi/16km on the A 84. Ⓛopen Apr–Sept daily 9.30am–5.30pm; Oct daily 9.30am–4.30pm; Nov–Mar Sat–Wed 9.30am–4.30pm. Ⓛclosed 25–26 Dec. ☞£5. P. ℘01786 841 742. www.historic-scotland.gov.uk.
This late-14C fortress with its 100ft-/30m-high **keep-gatehouse** stands apart from the village. With elaborate accommodation on a semi-royal scale, it is an example of a truly self-contained, secure residence of its period.

Monty Python fans will be amused to hear that Holy Grail was filmed here, and can take an audio tour of the castle narrated by Terry Jones.

Bannockburn

NTS. ▶2mi/3km S by the A 9.
ⓁSite open daily (Heritage Centre open Mar–Oct daily 10am–5pm/5.30pm). ☞£6. ♿PX. ℘0844 493 2139. www.nts.org.uk.
An equestrian statue of **Robert the Bruce** marks the king's command post on the eve of the battle. By 1313 Bruce had retaken most of the kingdom lost to Edward I, who had died in 1307. On 24 June 1314, he routed a numerically superior English army, ineptly led by Edward II. After Bannockburn, independence for Scotland was assured. An audio-visual presentation tells the dramatic story.

National Wallace Monument★★

▶1mi/1.6km NE by the A 9 and B 998.
Ⓛopen daily Apr–Jun and Sept–Oct 10am–5pm; Jul–Aug 10am–6pm; Nov–Mar 10.30am–4pm. Ⓛclosed 1 Jan, 25–26 Dec, 2 days Jan for maintenance. ☞£7.75. PX. ℘01786 472 140. www.nationalwallacemonument.com.
This towering 140-year-old five-storey

landmark commemorates **William Wallace** (1270–1305) the national hero, mythologised in the epic film *Braveheart*, who rallied Scottish forces against English rule. He recaptured the castle from Edward I's forces after his victory at Stirling Bridge in 1297, but following the Scots' submission in 1304, Wallace was captured and died a traitor's death in London in 1305.

An audio-visual presentation depicts Wallace and his place in Scottish history. From the viewing platform *(246 steps)* atop Abbey Craig (362ft/110m) there is a **panorama**★★ of Stirling surroundings.

TROSSACHS★★★

▶ *18mi/29km NW of Stirling.*

Occupying Scotland's midriff area, the Trossachs stretch between Loch Venachar in the east to the shores of Loch Lomond and take in some of Scotland's most famous scenery, with rugged mountains and wooded slopes reflected in the waters of many lochs. Sir Walter Scott's romantic poetry and novels did much to popularise the Trossachs, reinforced by Wordsworth and Coleridge, who followed in his footsteps in 1830.

Callander★

This busy summer tourist centre, popular with visitors for over a century, is the main eastern gateway to the Trossachs. It became known to millions of British TV viewers in the 1960s as the Tannochbrae of *Dr Finlay's Casebook*.

Loch Venachar

The Trossachs road *(A 821)* skirts the lower slopes of **Ben Ledi** (2 884ft/879m) overlooking the banks of Loch Venachar, before reaching the scattered settlement of **Brig o'Turk**. The village has artistic associations, favoured by Ruskin and Millais and, later, the **Glasgow Boys**.

Loch Katrine★★

The best way to see this lovely loch is to take a **boat trip** (⌚*operates from Trossachs Pier Apr–Oct daily, see website or call for times;* ⛵*2hr scenic cruise £14.50;* ♿; ✆*01877 332 000; www.lochkatrine. com*) on the *SS Sir Walter Scott*. The loch isles, Ellen's Isle and Factor's Isle figure respectively in works by Sir Walter Scott's *The Lady of the Lake* and *Rob Roy*. To the south of Loch Katrine looms the twin-peaked form of **Ben Venue** (2,385ft/727m). Beyond, a hilltop viewpoint affords a magnificent **panorama**★★★ across the Trossachs.

Aberfoyle

The attractive much-visited village was where Rob Roy abducted Baillie Nicol Jarvie. A road leads west through the forest park to Loch Lomond.

Loch Lomond★★

The blue waters of this famous loch (656ft/200m deep) are flanked by rugged mountains in the north and pastoral woodlands in the south.

Loch Lomond Shores is the area's main

View of Loch Lomond and Ben Lomond with snow

© Martin McCarthy/iStockphoto.com

visitor centre (*open daily 10am–5pm;* ♿ 🅿 ✕; *01389 751 031; www.loch lomondshores.com*) with upmarket shops, a café and restaurant, and canoes, kayaks, aquarollers and bikes for hire. It is also home to ♿ **Loch Lomond Sea Life Centre** (*open daily from 10am, closing times vary. £13.20, child £9.60, buy online to save up to £5 per ticket*) ♿; *01389 721 500; www.vistalife.com*) with Scotland's only Giant Sea Turtle, shark tunnel, touch pool, otters, large-screen cinema and more. There are also spectacular views from its roof terrace.

A short walk away, **Sweeney's Cruise** offers loch cruises (*operates Easter– Sept; see website for times and prices; ♿; 01389 752 376; www.sweeney.uk.com*) calling at the attractive village of **Luss★** with its mellow stone cottages.

The **West Highland Way** follows the east shore northwards to Fort William passing on the way the lower slopes of **Ben Lomond★★** (3,196ft/974m), the most southerly of the Highland "Munros" (mountains over 3,000ft/914m).

ISLE OF MULL★

CalMac ferries (www.calmac.co.uk) connect Mull with Oban (40min), Iona, Kilchoan and Lochaline on the mainland. This narrow island (max 26mi/42km across) sits at the mouth of Scotland's Great Glen. It is dominated by the mountain Ben More (3,169ft/966m), with a long deeply indented coastline, rang-

ing from rocky cliffs to sandy beaches and superb sea views. Inland, pastoral crofting landscapes contrast with desolate moorlands.

The colourful little main town and ferry port, **Tobermory** (star of BBC children's TV as *Balamory*), fringes the yachting centre of Tobermory Bay, 22mi/35km north along the coast from Craignure, the island's main ferry terminal.

From Craignure follow the coast road 3mi/5km to **Duart Castle** (*open Apr Sun–Thu 11am–4pm, May–mid-Oct daily 10.30am–5.30pm; £5.50;* 🅿 ✕; *01680 812 309; www.duartcastle.com*), home of the Chief of the **Clan MacLean**, perched on a rocky crag guarding the Sound of Mull, with magnificent views. The keep dates from c.1250 but the 13C castle was burned in the late-17C. Sir Fitzroy MacLean, the 26th Chief, restored the stronghold to its present appearance in 1911.

Isle of Staffa★★

NTS. Open daily. Ferries Apr–Aug from Iona, Fionnphort Ulva and Mull, see website for operators. 08444 493 2215. www.nts.org.uk.

This basaltic island, now a National Nature Reserve, is known for its amazing rock formations and spectacular caves, made famous by Mendelssohn's overture *Fingal's Cave*, composed following his visit in 1829. Its awesome beauty has inspired poets and painters alike.

Fingal's Cave, Isle of Staffa

© TT/iStockphoto.com

ISLE OF IONA★

▶ *West coast, off southwesterly tip of the Isle of Mull. CalMac ferries (www.calmac.co.uk) make the short journey between the islands. www.ionahistory.org.uk.*

St Columba established his monastic settlement here 1,400 years ago, and even today it is one of the most venerated places in Scotland.

The saint's community flourished until brought to an end by the Norse raids of the 8C and 9C. Intricately carved crosses and grave slabs are a testament to its prior artistic accomplishments. A Benedictine monastery was re-established in the early-13C but disappeared at the Reformation. In 1938 a third religious brotherhood – now an ecumenical community – came to the isle and a major restoration programme was completed in 1966. The abbey today is a place of hospitality, reflection and worship, while a small community of around 270 crofters inhabits the fertile island.

☙☙ WALKING TOUR

Take the road from the old Benedictine **nunnery** with its medieval church and conventual buildings. Go through the gate past the intricately carved 15C **Maclean's Cross**★ and the early Christian burial ground, **Reilig Odhrain** (where Scotland's kings from Kenneth MacAlpine to Malcolm III were buried) to the 12C **St Oran's Chapel**★, the oldest building on the island, with a fine Norman west door. Walk down the **Street of the Dead**, where three **High Crosses** catch the eye (an 8C **Cross of St Martin**★, a 9C–10C truncated shaft of St Matthew and a replica of the 8C St John's Cross).

On the other side of the Street of the Dead is St Columba's cell, Tor Abb. The **abbey** (HS; ⏱ *open year-round daily 9.30am– 5.30pm/Oct–Mar 4.30pm; ⬡£5.50; ♿; ✆01681 700 512; www.historic-scotland. gov.uk; www.ionahistory.org.uk*), stands on the site of its Columban predecessor. To the north of the west front is St Columba's shrine. Beyond the abbey is the **Infirmary Museum**★ (⏱*open daily*

9am–5pm ✆*01681 700 404*) with an outstanding collection of early Christian and medieval stonework including the ornate 8C **Cross of St John**★ (restored), medieval effigies and grave slabs.

INVERARAY★★

▶ *37mi/60km SE of Oban.*

This delightful small Georgian whitewashed township lies halfway along Scotland's west coast on the shores of Loch Fyne, a short distance from its castle, the seat of the Clan Campbell.

Inveraray Castle★★

⏱*Open Apr–Oct daily 10am– 5.45pm. ⬡£9.20, save £1 booking online. ☐☒. ✆01499 302 203. www.inveraray-castle.com.*

The exterior is in Gothic Revival style. The 5th Duke refurbished the interiors in the Neoclassical style after the fashion of Carlton House in London. In particular, the **dining room** is a masterpiece of delicately detailed plasterwork and painting. The Tapestry Drawing Room reveals an Adam-designed compartmented ceiling, decorative panels and overdoors by Girard. The **armoury hall** with its decorative display of polearms, Lochaber axes and broadswords is where the duke's personal piper plays a medley of Campbell tunes to awaken the household.

☙ DRIVING TOUR

LOCH FYNE TO LOCH AWE

The great sea-loch of **Loch Fyne**★★ stretches from the heart of the Argyll mountains down the arm of Loch Gilp where it turns due south to reach the open sea. In the 19C this was a successful herring fishery. Today Loch Fyne is famous for its oysters.

Some 6mi/10km south of Inveraray, on the A 83 is the **Auchindrain Museum**★ (⏱*open Apr–Oct daily 10am–5pm, Nov– Mar Mon–Fri 10am–2pm ⬡£5.95, free in winter; ☐☒; ✆01499 500 235; www. auchindrain-museum.org.uk*), an openair museum evoking life in the typical

River Coupall in Glen Coe, Buachaille Etive Mor in the background

bygone communal-tenancy farms. Follow the loch south and round the headland to Lochgliphead, then take the A 816 and B 841 to **Crinan**★, a delightful hamlet at the western end of the Crinan Canal. From Crinan, picturesque roads *(the A 819 N to Cladich and the lochside B 840)* lead to scenic **Loch Awe**★★. This is Scotland's longest lake (over 25mi/40km long), the third-largest freshwater loch in Scotland and the site of two hydro-electric projects. The loch is famous for trout fishing, while its islands include several ruined castles. **Kilchurn Castle** juts out on the northern shore. This 15C stronghold, built by Sir Colin Campbell, with late-17C extensions, was abandoned in the mid-18C.

OBAN★

A busy tourist centre and service town for the hinterland and islands, Oban lies opposite the Isle of Mull at the southern end of the Great Glen. It owes its development to the railways and steamboats. The outstanding landmark is **McCaig's Tower** (1897), a replica of the Colosseum, built to relieve unemployment, but never finished.

On the shores of picturesque Loch Creran, 12mi/19km north, the ▲▲**Scottish Sea Life Sanctuary**★ *(Barcaldine; ○ open Mar–Oct daily 10am–5pm, reduced hours in winter; ○ closed 25 Dec; ◎£13.20, child £10.80, save up to £4 by booking online; & P ✕; ℘01631 720 386; www.sealsanctuary.co.uk)* is a busy rescue and rehabilitation facility for both common seals and grey seals.

Glen Coe★★

The dramatic approach to Glen Coe (11mi/18km long) – the stark and grandiose setting where the infamous **Glen Coe massacre** occurred in 1692 – is heralded by the **Meall a Bhuiridh** (Hill of the Roaring Stags, 3,636ft/1,108m), the **Buachaille Etive Mor** (Big Herdsman of Etive, Glen Etive, between them.

The flat-topped rock known as The Study pinpoints the head of Glen Coe. Beyond the waterfall rise the mighty rock-faces of the **Three Sisters**. These are the outliers of the **Bidean nam Bian** (Peak of the Bens), which soar to 3,743ft/1,141m one side; the serrated ridge of **Anoach Eagach** is to the other, while Loch Achtriochtan spreads out on the valley floor. **Glencoe and Dalness Visitor Centre** *(NTS; ○ open Apr–Oct daily 9.30am–5.30pm, Sept–Oct closed Fri-Sat, Nov–Mar Thu–Sun 10am–4pm; ◎£5.50; &; ℘0844 4932222; www.nts.org.uk)* interprets the massacre and provides information on local walks and climbs. The village of **Glencoe** itself nestles on the shores of Loch Leven and is home to the charming **Glencoe and North Lorn Folk Museum** *(○ open Easter–Oct Mon–Sat 10.30am–4.30pm; ◎£3; & P; ℘01855 811 664)*, set in two 18C thatched croft houses and three other ancient buildings.

The picturesque road south *(A 82, A 828)* skirts the south shore of Loch Leven and descends along the east coast of **Loch Linnhe**, the largest sea-loch in Scotland, and cuts across to Loch Creran and back to Oban.

Kingdom of Fife

Fife's regal connections began with the 4C Kingdom of the Picts and ended with the Union of the Crowns in 1603. Ever since then the "Kingdom of Fife" has been a relative backwater. However, with St Andrews' perennial golfing popularity, the stunning Forth bridges, and the naval dockyard at Rosyth, it is hardly a forgotten corner. Where Fife resonates with modern visitors is its well-kept memories of its halcyon royal and aristocratic days, at Dunfermline, Culross and Falkland Palace. Its quaint fishing villages are another big draw.

ST ANDREWS★★

This Fife coast resort is most famous as the home of golf, but is also known for its long-established university with its strong recent links to the Royal Family. In the 12C a priory, and later a cathedral were established, leading to the foundation of the university. By 1472 St Andrews was the ecclesiastical capital of Scotland. Its importance declined in the 17C, owing to the switch in trade from the Baltic to the American colonies, and after the Act of Union in 1707.

The 19C, however, saw St Andrews return to prominence as a tourist and golfing centre, an importance it has kept to this day.

- ▶ **Population:** 11,136
- **Michelin Map:** Michelin Atlas p56 or Map 501 L 14.
- **Info:** 70 Market Street. ℘01334 472 021. www.visitfife.com. 1 High Street, Dunfermline., ℘01383 720 999. Scot. Fisheries Museum, Anstruther. ℘01333 311 073. Caril Museum. ℘01333 450 869.
- ▶ **Location:** St Andrews is 54mi/87km northeast of Edinburgh. The nearest train station is 5mi/8km northwest at leucars, linked to St Andrew by bus. Buses from Edinburgh and Dundee terminate at the central City Road bus station.
- **Don't Miss:** Abbey church; Culross Village.

St Andrew's Cathedral★

At the eastern end of St Andrews' two main streets. Open year-round daily 9.30am–5pm (4.30pm Oct–Mar). £4.50, combined ticket with castle £7.60. ℘01334 472 563. www.historic-scotland.gov.uk.

The imposing **St Regulus Church** may have been originally intended to house the relics of St Andrew. Robert of Scone built the church, with its lofty

Ruins of St Andrew's Castle

© Afunbags/Fotolia.com

tower, between 1127 and 1144. The tower *(151 steps)* affords a magnificent **panorama**★★ across St Andrews and its main monuments. St Regulus' was replaced from 1160 by the later cathedral, the largest church ever built in Scotland. After the Reformation this once-noble building was used as a stone quarry, and reduced to the ruin on view today. The **museum** has a good collection of early Christian sculptured stones. Now in ruins, the 13C **St Andrew's Castle** *(HS;* 🕐 *open same hours/prices as cathedral;* ✆ *01334 477 196; www. historic-scotland.gov.uk),* overlooking the foreshore, was once a part of the palace of the archbishop. Visitors can explore its Mine and Counter-mine – unique underground passages which give a palpable sense of the horrific nature of medieval siege warfare – and the Bottle Dungeon – one of the most infamous castle prisons in medieval Britain, cut out of the solid rock.

EXCURSIONS
Scotland's Secret Bunker
▶ *Crown Buildings, Troywood.* *10mi/16km SE on the B 9131 and B 940.* 🕐 *Open mid-Mar–Oct daily 10am–6pm (last entry 5pm).* ◉*£9.90.* 🅿️&✕. ✆ *01333 310 301. www.secretbunker.co.uk.*

Around 130ft/40m below the surface of Fife's farmlands, this now-not-so-secret bunker was built as an early warning radar station and later converted to a nuclear command centre. Protected by 10ft/3m of reinforced concrete, all stages of operational life are brought hauntingly to life with audio-visual displays, a large selection of military vehicles and even a Russian anti-aircraft missile evoking the menace of the Cold War era.

East Neuk★★
▶ *Crail is 10mi/16km SE of St Andrews on the A 917.*

The East Neuk (neuk means corner) coastline is dotted with picturesque fishing villages, each clustered around its harbour and with a wealth of vernacular architecture. These were the ports once visited by the Baltic and Dutch trade.

Crail★★ is the most attractive village, particularly around the **old centre** sloping down to the harbour; don't miss the cottages (nos. 22–28) on Shoregate; the three-storey Custom House (no. 35 Shoregate); and the charming buildings at 32 Castle Street and at 1 Rose Wynd.

In **Anstruther** is the **Scottish Fisheries Museum**★★ *(St Ayles Harborhead;* 🕐 *open Apr–Sept Mon–Sat 10am–5.30pm, Sun 11am–5pm; Oct–Mar Mon–Sat 10am–4.30pm, Sun noon–4.30pm;* 🕐 *closed 1–2 Jan, 24–25 Dec.* ◉*£6;* &🅿️✕; ✆ *01333 310 628; www.scotfishmuseum.org).* Don't be misled by its

---

Golf: A Royal and Ancient Game

Since the 15C St Andrews links – with its swards of springy turf and sand bunkers – has been a place for playing golf or at least the early ball and stick version of this sport. So popular was the game that by 1457 an Act of Scottish Parliament was passed requiring that "futeball and the golfe be utterly cryit down" in favour of kirk attendance and archery practice. Mary Queen of Scots was an occasional player; her son James VI popularised the game in England. Founded in 1754, the Society of St Andrews Golfers had the title **Royal and Ancient** conferred on it by William IV in 1834. It is now recognised as the ruling body. To meet the increasing popularity of the sport, new courses were laid out supplementing the **Old Course**, established several centuries ago. By the beginning of the 20C St Andrews was firmly established as golf's mecca. The town now regularly hosts the British Open and Amateur Championships, Walker Cup Matches and other tournaments, bringing huge crowds. Visit the **British Golf Museum** *(Bruce Embankment;* 🕐*open daily year-round 9.30am/10am–4pm/5pm;* &; ✆*01334 460 046, www.britishgolfmuseum.co.uk).*

apparently small setting as behind the façade is a large courtyard full of buildings, including the 16C Abbot's Lodging, a fisherman's cottage, the Merchant House (1724) and a covered historic boatyard. Aside from its huge collection of smaller artefacts are 19 historic boats, some berthed in the harbour opposite.

Pittenweem is the least picturesque of the East Neuk's three main fishing villages but is Fife's busiest fishing port and still has some fine old properties.

Head north on Church Street for around 3mi/5km to **Kellie Castle and Garden**★(NTS; *Castle:* ◷*open Apr–Oct Thu–Mon/daily late May–Aug 12.30–5pm/Oct 4pm; Gardens and grounds:* ◷ *open daily 10am–6pm/Nov–Mar 3.30pm;* ◉£9; ♿🅿£3; ✖; 𝒫*0844 493 2184; www.nts.org.uk),* a fine example of unspoiled 16C–17C traditional Scottish architecture featuring corbelled turrets with conical roofs, pedimented dormers, and crow-stepped gables. The 17C **plasterwork ceilings** are notable.

DUNFERMLINE★

◉ *36mi/58km SW of St Andrew's.*

Dunfermline, the former capital of Scotland, lies immediately north of the present capital, Edinburgh, across the Firth of Forth. Its great abbey and royal palace figure frequently in Scottish history. The town has long been a thriving industrial centre, with coal mining and linen weaving, and new industries maintain this tradition today.

In 1066, **Malcolm III** (Canmore) sheltered the heir to the English throne, **Edgar Atheling** and his family, fleeing from William the Conqueror after defeat at Hastings, in his Dunfermline Tower. Edgar's sister **Margaret** married the Scots king in 1070. She was a devout Catholic and was largely responsible for introducing the ideas which gradually supplanted the rituals of the Celtic church. The Benedictine abbey was founded by **David I**, son of Queen Margaret. **Robert the Bruce** (1274–1329) helped with the reconstruction of the abbey in 1034 and is buried here. After the Reformation, King James VI (James I of England) had an impressive new

palace built to the west of the old cloister. He gave the palace to his queen, Anne of Denmark, and Charles I was born here. There were fleeting royal visits thereafter, but following the Union of the Crowns in 1603, the palace was never again a regular royal residence.

◔ Town Walk

Northwest of the train station is **Dunfermline Abbey**★ (HS; ◷*open late Apr–Oct daily 9.30am–5.30pm Oct 4.30pm), Nov–Mar Sat–Thu 9.30am–12.30pm and 1pm–4.30pm/closed Thu pm, Sun am;* ◉£4; 🅿; 𝒫*01383 739 026; www.historic-scotland.gov.uk),* an 11C Benedictine abbey founded on the site of a Celtic church. The Norman nave of the **abbey church**★★ with its massive pillars and round-headed arches is one of the finest in Scotland. The east end (rebuilt in the early-19C) serves as the parish church; a memorial brass marks the tomb of Robert the Bruce. There are few remains of the great monastic ensemble.

Nearby, **Abbot House** *(Maygate;* ◷*open year-round daily 9.30am–4.30pm (Nov–Feb Sun–Fri closes 4pm);* ◷ *closed 1 Jan, 25–26 Dec;* ◉£4 *inc. guided tour;* ♿🅿✖; 𝒫*01383 733 266; www.abbothouse.co.uk)* is now an attractive heritage centre. Head south from here on St Margaret Street, which leads to Moodie Street and the **Andrew Carnegie Birthplace** (◷*open Mar–Nov daily 10am (2pm Sun)–5pm;* ♿🅿✖; 𝒫*01383 724 302; www.carnegie*

birthplace.com). The self-made steel baron and great philanthropist, Andrew Carnegie (1835–1919) was born in this house before emigrating to America with his family in 1848. An exhibition traces his life and work.

EXCURSIONS
Culross★★

▶ *13mi/21km E on the A 944 and B 9037.* According to legend, St Mungo, patron saint of Glasgow, was born in this small burgh (pronounced "coo'ross") on the north shore of the Firth of Forth.

A Cistercian house was founded here in the 13C and trade with the Low Countries, salt panning and coal mining brought prosperity.

Today Culross is famous for its fine examples of Scottish vernacular architecture of the 16C and 17C in all its rich detail. The small buildings in the **village**★★★ feature inscribed lintels, decorative finials, skewputts, crow-stepped gables, forestairs, harling and rubble stonework with door and window trims. The **Town House** *(NTS; same ticket to Study and palace; ◷Open Apr–May and Sept, Thu–Mon noon–5pm; Jun–Aug, daily noon–5pm; Oct Fri–Mon, noon–4pm; Study and Town House by guided tour only, from palace reception every hour, last tour 4pm/Oct 3pm; garden year-round 10am–6pm or dusk; ☞£8.50;* 🅿️♿️✕*;* ☎*0844 493 2189; www.nts.org.uk)* is a stone-and-slate building erected in 1625 in Flemish style; it contrasts with the white harling and red pantiles of the surrounding buildings. The Back Causeway, behind, has

a central line of raised paving stones for the exclusive use of local notables. Opposite, the **Study**★, which has a 17C painted ceiling (restored) and original panelling, is the oldest house in Culross with a replica of the 1588 mercat cross in front of its gable end. The **palace**★★, a comfortable house built (1597–1611) by George Bruce, a rich merchant and coalmine owner, boasts pine-panelled rooms and 21 fireplaces which burned coal rather than logs. Dutch tiles carried as ballast in his ships were used for flooring and roofing.

Falkland Palace★

NTS. ▶ *31mi/50km NE by the M90, A 91 and A 912.* ◷*Open Mar–Oct Mon–Sat 11am (Sun 1pm)–5pm.* ☞*£11.* ☎*0844 493 2186. www.nts.org.uk.*

In 1425 this hunting-seat of the Earls of Fife passed to the crown and became one of the Stewarts' favourite royal palaces. The gatehouse and street façade built in Gothic style by James IV, a Renaissance monarch who entertained a splendid court, is in sharp contrast with the Renaissance ornament of the courtyard façade of the south range added by his son, James V. A tour of the interior includes the keeper's gatehouse apartments, adorned with royal portraits, coats of arms and elegant furnishings. The lovely **gardens**★ feature a large collection of scented early summer blooms and also boast the original Real (Royal) Tennis court. Built for James V in 1539, it is the world's oldest tennis court still in use today.

Culross Palace with a view to the Forth estuary

© Foto/MICHELIN

Perthshire★

Situated in the very heart of Scotland, Perthshire boasts some of the finest and most accessible scenery anywhere in the Scottish Highlands. It has long been a retreat for the royal and well heeled – from ancient Scone Palace to modern Gleneagles – and nowadays is also a mecca for adrenalin junkies and white-knuckle outdoor activities.

PERTH

◔ *42mi/67km due N of Edinburgh.*

This former Royal Burgh, situated on the River Tay, retains the atmosphere of a country town, with many fine examples of **Georgian architecture★** and is an ideal touring base. The Tay is famous for salmon fishing and for freshwater mussels which produce beautiful pearls. The "Fair City" has played a prominent role in Scottish history and might well have become the capital had not James I been assassinated here in 1437. Other tumultuous events included the murderous Clan Combat of 1396 and the destruction of the monasteries following John Knox's heated sermon of 1559.

Black Watch Regimental Museum★

Balhousie Castle, Hay Street. ◷*Open year-round Mon–Sat 9.30am–5pm. Apr-Oct–Apr also Sun 10am–4pm* ◷*Closed festive period.* 🅿. ⊚*£5.* ☎*01738 638 152; www.theblackwatch.co.uk.*

In the early-18C General Wade enlisted and armed independent companies of Highlanders which became known as the **Black Watch**, for the "watch" they kept on the Highlands, and for their dark tartan. The museum, set in Balhousie Castle (1860), traces the often turbulent history of this elite regiment.

Perth Museum & Art Gallery★

78 George St. ♿◷*Open year-round Mon–Sat 10am–5pm.* ◷*Closed festive period.* ☎*01738 632 488. www.pkc.gov.uk.*

Displays of local glass, silver and clock-making industries, and natural history. Work by Scottish artists predominates.

ℹ **Michelin Map:** Michelin Atlas p62 or Map 501 J 14.

🚩 **Info:** Lower City Mills, West Mill Street, Perth. ☎01738 450 600. www.perthshire.co.uk. 22 Atholl Road, Pitlochry. ☎01796 472 215. The Cross, Dunkeld. ☎01350 727 688. The Square, Aberfeldy. ☎01887 820 276. The Mews, Braemar. ☎013397 41600.

The Waterworks (Fergusson Gallery)

Marshall Place. ♿◷*Open year-round Mon–Sat 10am–5pm.* ◷*Closed festive period.* ☎*01738 783 425; www.pkc.gov.uk.*

This handsome circular building, formerly the city's waterworks, is a new cultural highlight, home to a rotating exhibition of the works of J D Fergusson (1874–1961), foremost among the Scottish Colourists.

EXCURSIONS
Scone Palace★★

◔ *2mi/3km NE by the A 93.* ◷*Open Apr–Oct daily 9.30am–5pm, Sat 4pm (last entry).* ⊚*Palace £9.60, rounds only, £5.50.* ♿🅿✕. ☎*01738 552 300. www.scone-palace.co.uk.*

One of Scotland's most hallowed sites, Scone (pronounced "skoon") was the centre of Kenneth MacAlpine's Scotto-Pictish kingdom from the mid-9C.

Moot Hill, now occupied by a 19C chapel, was where Scottish kings were enthroned on the **Stone of Destiny** (also known as the Stone of Scone). Wrecked in the wave of destruction of 1559, the abbey became the seat of the Earls of Mansfield. The present Gothic Revival palace dates from 1808. Its richly furnished apartments contain a splendid array of porcelain and ivories, unusual timepieces, busts and portraits, and collection of papier mâché *objets d'art*. The grounds include a maze, children's playground and 50-acre/20ha pinetum.

The Stone of Destiny

According to legend, the Stone of Destiny was Jacob's pillow, which eventually reached Ireland by way of Egypt and Spain and is believed to have served as a coronation stone for the High Kings at Tara. Kenneth MacAlpine was the first king to be crowned on the stone at Scone and it subsequently served for the coronation of all Scottish kings until 1296 when the Scots were defeated by Edward I. He carried off the stone, which was placed beneath the Coronation chair in Westminster Abbey, where for 700 years it played an integral part in the coronation rituals. It was stolen in 1950 but was later recovered in Arbroath Abbey. From early days controversy has raged about the authenticity of the stone. Some believe the original stone never left Scotland. In 1996 the people of Scotland greeted the return of the Stone of Destiny, which is the symbol of Scottish nationhood, with great emotion. It is now on display with the Honours of Scotland in Edinburgh Castle but will be returned (temporarily) to Westminster Abbey for use in future coronations.

Dunkeld★

▶ *14mi/23km N on the A 9.*

Dunkeld was the site of a monastic establishment from AD 700 and later a majestic Gothic **cathedral** (*Cathedral Street;* ⊙*open Apr–Sep, daily, 9.30am–6.30pm; Oct–Mar, daily, 10am (2pm Sun) to 4.30pm;* ✎*guided tours (free) Jun–Sept Mon–Fri 10.30am–12.30pm;* ℰ *01350 727 249; www.dunkeld cathedral.org.uk*) set in an attractive riverside precinct.

PITLOCHRY★

▶ *26mi/42km N of Perth on the A 9.*

This attractive town, set in the Tummel Valley, makes a fine touring centre to enjoy the magnificent scenery of mountains, lochs and moors. It hosts a famous festival of drama, music and art in summer and in recent years has become the adventure-sports capital of Scotland with a wide range of activities.

EXCURSIONS
Queen's View★★

▶ *10mi/16km W by the B 8019.*

This beauty spot was named after Queen Victoria's visit in 1866, and commands a wonderful view up Loch Tummel.

Blair Castle★★

▶ *Blair Atholl. 7mi/11km N on the A 9.*

⊙*Open Apr–late Oct daily 9.30am–4.30pm (last entry). Nov–late Mar Sat–Sun 10am–3pm (last entry).* ⊙*£9.25,*

winter £7.40. ♿🅿✕. ℰ*01796 481 207. www.blair-castle.co.uk.*

Blair Castle was the centre of the ancient kingdom of Atholl and the home of the Duke of Atholl until the death of the last of the line in 1996. It is still home to the only private army left in the British Isles, the **Atholl Highlanders**, sole survivor of the clan system. A large part of the tower built here in 1269 still remains, and the castle with its turrets and parapets continues to command a strategic route into the Central Highlands.

The 18C interiors include sumptuous stucco ceilings, family **portraits** (by Lely, Jacob de Wet, Hoppner, Zoffany and Landseer), collections of armour and porcelain, Jacobite and other historic relics. The grounds include nature trails and a deer park.

Aberfeldy★

▶ *10mi/16km SW*

Burns wrote: "Come let us spend the … days, In the birks of Aberfeldy" and the deep pools and majestic waterfalls of the Birks (birches) remain one of Aberfeldy's most popular attractions.

They also power the big overshot waterwheel in the **Water Mill** (⊙*open Mon–Sat 10am–5pm/5.30pm, Sun 11am–5pm.* ✕; ℰ*01887 822 89, www.aberfeldywatermill.com*). This now houses the largest bookshop in the rural Highlands, a contemporary art gallery, a music shop and cafe, set in an early-19C watermill.

Grampians★

Comprising the Cairngorms, Moray and Aberdeenshire, the Grampians are Britain's finest mountain scenery. As wild as the Arctic or as tame as a family railway ride, they are accessible to any visitor. The delights of Royal Deeside are well known, those of Aberdeen less so, and the Granite City is often the Grampians' surprise package; few tourists expect city-slick culture this far north of Edinburgh. Outside the city are some of Scotland's best castles, finest fishing villages and a tempting malt whisky trail.

ABERDEEN★★

⊙ *126mi/203km NE of Edinburgh.*

The dignified and prosperous "Granite City" developed from two fishing villages on the Dee and the Don and also prospered from its rich agricultural hinterland. During the latter part of the 20C Aberdeen gained new riches thanks to its proximity to the North Sea oilfields and became the oil and gas capital of Europe. Today the oil is running out but the city is still a major offshore centre.

A Bit of History

An episcopal city by the 12C, Old Aberdeen had a large secular community outside its precincts; in the late-15C Bishop Elphinstone founded a uni-

Michelin Map:
Michelin Atlas p61–62, p67–69 or Map 501.

Info: 23 Union St. ℘01224 288 828. www.aberdeen-grampian.com. The Mews, Mar Road, Braemar. ℘01339 741 600. www.braemarscotland. co.uk. 14 The Square, Grantown-on-Spey. ℘01479 873 535. www.cairngorms.co.uk; www.visitcairngorms.com (for Eastern Cairngorms). 17 High Street, Elgin. ℘01343 542 666. www. aberdeen-grampian.com. www.elginscotland.org;

Don't Miss: The heraldic ceiling in St Machar's Cathedral; Aberdeen Art Gallery; Pitmedden Gardens; Grampian castles; a Highland Games gathering; the view from Cairn Gorm (on a clear day) and a sunset meal in their award-winning Ptarmigan restaurant at 3,540ft/1079m.

Kids: Cairngorm Reindeer Centre; Landmark Forest Adventure Park.;Strathspey Steam Railway.

View of Aberdeen with the harbour and the docks

© P. Tomkins/VisitScotland/ScottishViewpoint

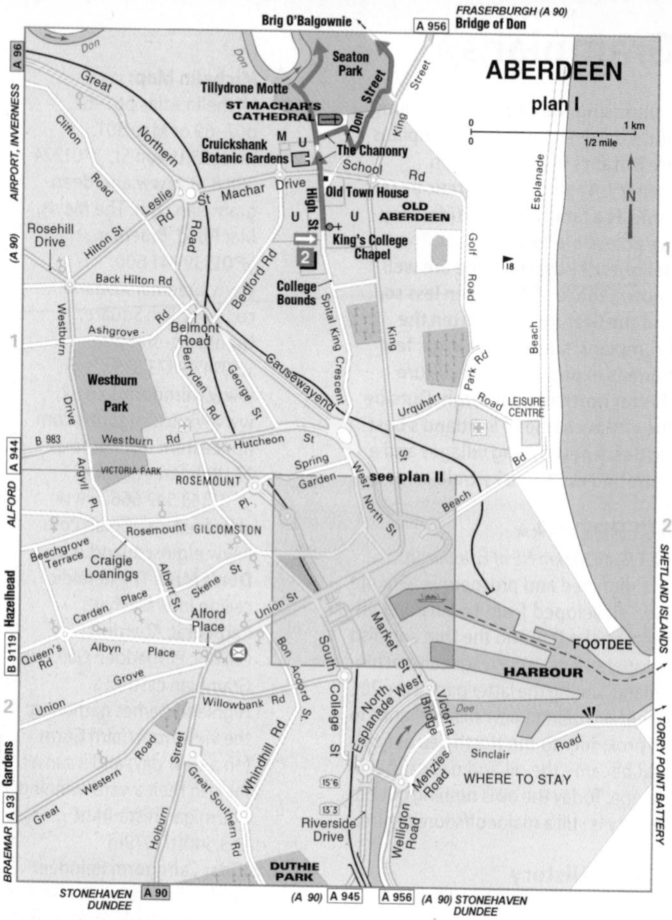

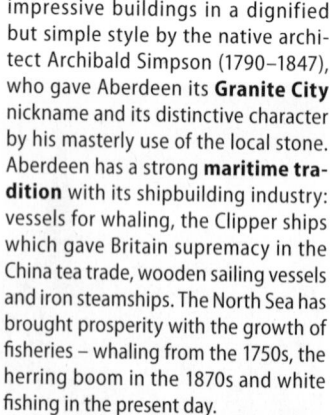

ABERDEEN
plan I

FRASERBURGH (A 90)
A 956 Bridge of Don

Brig O'Balgownie

Seaton Park

Tillydrone Motte

ST MACHAR'S CATHEDRAL

Cruickshank Botanic Gardens

The Chanonry

School Rd

Old Town House

OLD ABERDEEN

King's College Chapel

College Bounds

Westburn Park

ROSEMOUNT

GILCOMSTON

Rosemount Pl.

Beechgrove Terrace

Craigie Loanings

Alford Place

FOOTDEE

HARBOUR

WHERE TO STAY

DUTHIE PARK

STONEHAVEN DUNDEE A 90 (A 90) A 945 A 956 (A 90) *STONEHAVEN DUNDEE*

versity. A second distinct burgh grew around the king's castle and became an active trading centre. As the city expanded the streets were lined with

impressive buildings in a dignified but simple style by the native architect Archibald Simpson (1790–1847), who gave Aberdeen its **Granite City** nickname and its distinctive character by his masterly use of the local stone. Aberdeen has a strong **maritime tradition** with its shipbuilding industry: vessels for whaling, the Clipper ships which gave Britain supremacy in the China tea trade, wooden sailing vessels and iron steamships. The North Sea has brought prosperity with the growth of fisheries – whaling from the 1750s, the herring boom in the 1870s and white fishing in the present day.

More recently Aberdeen has become the "offshore capital of Europe" for the North Sea oil industry and exploration and supply-base activities continue to

Aberdeen, "Flower of Scotland"

Aberdeen's parks and gardens are justly famous. Try to see: **Union Terrace Gardens** (off Union Street) with their celebrated floral displays including Aberdeen's coat of arms; the splendid **Winter Gardens** in Duthie Park; the rose garden and maze at **Hazlehead**; the delightful **Johnston Gardens** and the university's **Cruickshank Botanic Gardens**.

play an important role.

Most visitor attractions are clustered in Old Aberdeen and the city centre.

⚓ WALKING TOURS

2 OLD ABERDEEN ★★

Aberdeen's medieval streets capture the essence of the old town, which became a burgh of barony in 1489, a status retained until 1891. The North Sea provided growth in the 18C–19C in the form of fisheries.

Start at **King's College Chapel**★ (*entry by door in Quadrangle, 25 High Street; ⊙ open Mon–Fri; ⊙ closed Christmas and New Year; &; ℘01224 272 137; abdn. ac.uk*), the only original building left of Bishop Elphinstone's university in its campus setting. Outstanding features are a delicate Renaissance **crown spire**★★★, the tinctured arms on the west front buttresses (including those of James IV and his queen, Margaret Tudor) and rare, richly carved **medieval fittings**★★★.

At the crossroads stands the **Old Town House**, an attractive 18C Georgian house. Beyond is The Chanonry, a walled precinct for the residences of the bishop and other clerics.

From the chapel, walk up the High Street past the **Old Town House**, **Chanonry** and **Cruickshank Botanic Gardens** to get to **St Machar's Cathedral**★★ (*The Chanonry; ⊙ open daily Apr–Oct 9am–5pm, Nov–Mar 10am–4pm; &; ℘01224 485 988; www.stmachar.com*), whose twin spires have long been one of the landmarks of Old Aberdeen.

The cathedral, which dates from the 14C and 15C was built "overlooking the crook of the Don" in compliance with instructions from St Columba. The impressive exterior is complemented by a splendid 16C **heraldic ceiling**★★★.

The brightly coloured coats of arms present a vision of the European scene around 1520.

The early-14C **Brig o'Balgownie**★ (*approach via Don Street – V*), with its pointed Gothic arch and a defensive kink at the south end, is one of Aberdeen's most important medieval structures.

1 CITY CENTRE

Start at the **Maritime Museum**★ (*Provost Ross's House, Shiprow; ⊙ open Tue–Sat 10am–5pm, Sun noon–3pm; &; ℘01224 337 700; www.aagm.co.uk*). The museum is located in two 16C town houses bordering Shiprow, a medieval thoroughfare winding up from the harbour. Ship models, paintings, artefacts and interactive displays trace local maritime industries.

Follow Shiprow round to Union Street and turn right towards **Castlegate**. The medieval market place was situated here. Notable features are the Mannie Fountain (1706), a reminder of the city's first water supply, and the splendid **Mercat Cross**★★ dating from 1686 and decorated with a unicorn, a frieze, and royal portrait medallions and coats of arms. It was the place for public punishment and proclamations.

Behind the 19C **Town House** on Castle Street rises the tower of the 17C **Tolbooth** (*⊙ open early Jul–2nd wk Sept Tue–Sat 10am–4pm, Sun 12.30–3.30pm; &; ℘01224 621 167; www.aagm.co.uk*), which houses exhibits on the history of crime and punishment within the city.

Handsome **Marischal Street** extends south from Castle Street. It was laid out in 1767–68 with houses built to a uniform three storeys and attic design. Return to Castle Street and turn left, then right on Broad Street for **Marischal College**★, founded in the 16C by and amalgamated with the older King's College to form Aberdeen University; it has a striking 20C granite façade. **Marischal Museum** (*⊙ closed until further notice; ℘01224 274 301; www.abdn. ac.uk*) tells the history and prehistory of Northeast Scotland with fine ethnographical collections.

At the end of Broad Street turn left onto Upper Kirkgate for **Provost Skene's House**★ (*Guestrow, between Broad Street and Flourmill Lane; ⊙ open year-round Mon–Sat 10am–5pm; ⊙ closed 1–2 Jan, 25–26 Dec; ✕; ℘01224 641 086; www. aagm.co.uk*), a 17C townhouse containing tastefully furnished 17C, 18C and early-19C rooms with elaborate plasterwork ceilings and panelling. The chapel boasts an outstanding 17C painted **ceiling**★★ of New Testament scenes. Continue on Upper Kirkgate towards the **Aberdeen Art Gallery**★★ (Schoolhill; ◷open Tue–Sat 10am–5pm, Sun 2–5pm; ♿✖; ✆01224 523 700; www.aagm.co.uk), whose permanent collection has a strong emphasis on contemporary art. Various works of art are displayed in its elegant marble-lined interior. The **Scottish Collection** includes important works by local artists. The **Macdonald Collection**★★ of British artists' portraits is a survey of the art world in the 19C.

EXCURSIONS
Deeside★★
▶ *The heart of Deeside is around 50mi/80km W of Aberdeen via the A93.*
The splendid valley of the salmon-rich Dee flows from its source 4,000ft (1, 219m) high in the Cairngorms to the sea at Aberdeen.

Some 30mi/48km west of Aberdeen, the green at **Aboyne** forms the setting for colourful **Highland Games** in August. About 19mi/31km further lies **Balmoral Castle** (◷open Apr–Jul daily 10am–5pm; ⬤guided tour (1hr) 2nd Sat Nov–2nd Sat Dec, Sat only, 11am, noon, 1pm, 2pm; ⬤£9; ♿🅿✖; ✆01339 742 334; www.balmoralcastle.com). This has been the summer residence of the Royal Family since Queen Victoria's reign when Prince Albert bought it in 1852. It was then immediately demolished as it was too small for Albert and the present building was designed under the prince's supervision and completed in 1856. Victoria described Balmoral as "my dear paradise in the Highlands" and the current Royal Family spend August, September and early October here. Before they arrive, however, the Ballroom (the largest room in the castle) its grounds and gardens, plus exhibitions, are open to the public.

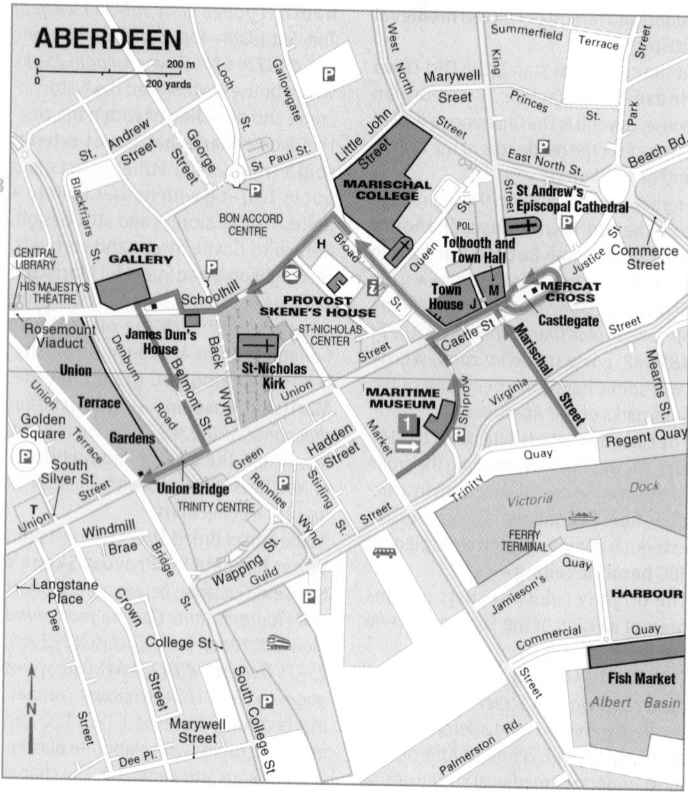

ABERDEEN

0 — 200 m
0 — 200 yards

(Map of Aberdeen city centre showing streets and landmarks including Marischal College, Art Gallery, St Andrew's Episcopal Cathedral, Tolbooth and Town Hall, Mercat Cross, Castlegate, Provost Skene's House, St-Nicholas Kirk, Maritime Museum, Union Bridge, Harbour, Fish Market, Albert Basin and various named streets such as Union Street, George Street, Schoolhill, Castle St, Marischal St, Regent Quay, College St, South College St, Marywell Street.)

Balmoral Castle

©Louise McGilvray/Fotolia.com

Continue on the A 93 for 10mi/16km to **Braemar**. It too boasts a **castle** (○*open Apr–Oct Sat–Sun, also Jul–Aug Wed 11am–4pm;* ◎*£5;* □; ✆*013397 41600 ; www.braemarcastle.co.uk),* albeit much humbler than its famous neighbour, and dates mostly from the 18C and 19C. The village is best known for its **Highland Gathering**, held annually in September and normally attended by royalty. At the road's end is the famous beauty spot **Linn o'Dee**, where, in season, salmon may be seen leaping.

Pitmedden Garden★★

NTS. ▷ *14mi/23km N by the A 92.* ○*Open May–Sept daily 10am–5.30pm.* ◎*£6.* ♿□✕. ✆*0844 493 2177. www.nts.org.uk.*

Sir Alexander Seton (c.1639–1719), possibly influenced by the Versailles designs of Le Nôtre, or the gardens of Sir William Bruce at Holyrood, laid out the original formal gardens. Honeysuckle, jasmine and roses create a succession of fragrances, while fountains, topiary, sundials, and a fascinating herb garden add to the sense of discovery around the walled garden. The garden is seen at its best in July and August, from the Belvedere, when 30–40,000 annuals are in bloom. A Museum of Farming Life relives the agricultural past of the region.

THE CAIRNGORMS★★

▷ *Aviemore is 90mi/145km W of Aberdeen from the centre.* ◉*The mountains are remote and can be a treacherous place to all but well-equipped and experienced walkers and mountaineers.*

This granitic range between the Spey Valley and Braemar features some of Britain's wildest and most dramatic mountain scenery. Much of it lies above 3,000ft/almost 1,000m, with Ben Macdui (4,296ft/1,309m) as its highest point even though the region is named after the lower peak of Cairn Gorm (4,084ft/1,245m).

The **Cairngorms National Park** covers 64,000 acres/26,000ha, making it the biggest national park in Britain, with the largest area of arctic mountain landscape in the UK at its heart. The severe climate of the windswept summits allows only an Arctic-Alpine flora to flourish. The mountains are the home of the golden eagle, ptarmigan, snow bunting, dotterel and of the rare osprey (RSPB observation hide at Loch Garten). The only reindeer herd in Britain, numbering around 150, is to be found in the Glenmore Forest Park at the 👥**Cairngorm Reindeer Centre** (♿○*Exhibition nd Paddocks: open early-Feb–early-Jan (weather permitting);* ⟲*guided tour available daily 11am, also May–Sept 2.30pm, Jul–Aug Mon–Fri 3.30pm;* ◎*paddock only, Apr–early-Jan £3.50 adult, £2.50 child; tour (includes Exhibition and Paddocks) £10, child £5;* ⊙*wear warm and waterproof clothing and sturdy footwear;* ✆*01479 861 228; www.cairngormreindeer.co.uk).*

The centre has an Exhibition and Paddocks with a small number of deer (Easter–early Jan), but most visitors make the short journey out into the wild to find the herd, which ranges freely in the open. The deer are very friendly and can be stroked and hand-fed.

Mountain biking in the Cairngorms National Park

© P. Tomkins/VisitScotland/ScottishViewpoint

Cairn Gorm★★★

Happily, for non-mountaineers, a modern **funicular railway** (*operates year-round daily from 10am, every 15–20min, last train 4.30pm/5pm depending on weather, see website or call; £9.95, includes exhibition, book online to save 10 percent); ; 01479 861 261; www.cairngorm-mountain.com*) provides an easy way of appreciating something of the magic and beauty of the mountains. The railway transports visitors to two levels. The first is Base Station, with a Mountain Garden. The Ptarmigan Top Station, nestled just below the summit of Cairn Gorm, includes a shop, a bar, the excellent Ptarmigan restaurant and a mountain exhibition.

The already excellent view from the car park unfolds further as the train ascends. At the terminal, at 3,600ft/1,100m, there is an extensive view★★★ westwards of the Spey Valley. A path leads up another 500ft/150m to the summit of Cairn Gorm (4,084ft/1,245m), which affords a wonderful panorama★★★ in all directions, well beyond the Cairngorm mountains. For conservation reasons, during the summer months there is no exit out onto the mountain from the top for walking unless you are booked on a **Walk @ the Top** guided tour (*£14*). In winter you can exit but are restricted to a small area. The northern and western slopes of Cairngorm are ideal for skiing, and the construction in the 1960s of the **Aviemore Centre** – a complex of shops, hotels and entertainment facilities with an "après-ski" flavour – transformed the **Aviemore**★ village into Britain's first winter-sports resort. There are ice-rinks for skating and curling, a dry-ski slope and a swimming pool. Winter-sports facilities are also available at Grantown-on-Spey, an elegant 18C town.

The **Strathspey Railway** (*; Dalfaber Road; daily service Easter–Sept, times vary rest of year; ; ; (on-board train); 01479 810 725; www.strathspeyrailway.co.uk*) operates a steam service on a line 5mi/8km from Aviemore to Boat of Garten and Broomhill.

Highland Wildlife Park★

Kincraig. 12mi/19km S of Aviemore. Open Apr–Oct daily 10am–5pm/ Jul–Aug 6pm, Nov–Mar (weather permitting) 10am–4pm. £12.60, child £9, save £2 online. . 01540 651 270. www.highlandwildlifepark.org.

Home to Scottish wildlife as well as internationally endangered animals, this park is run by the Royal Zoological Society of Scotland and includes tigers, bison and the only polar bear living in a British zoo.

Highland Folk Museum

Newtonmore, Kingussie. 15.5mi /25km S of Aviemore, Open mid-Apr–Aug daily 10.30am–5.30pm, Sept-Oct 11am–4.30pm. . 01540 661 307. www.highland folk.com.

This award-winning collection relates the life of the Highlanders (dress, musical instruments, farm implements, old crafts) and includes a "black house" typical of the Western Isles, and a water-powered mill.

Landmark Forest Adventure Park

Landmark, Carrbridge. 6mi/10km N of Aviemore. Open year-round daily 10am-5pm (Apr–mid-July 5pm/6pm, mid-Jul–late Aug 7pm). Several rides/ attractions close in winter. ☜*Apr–Oct £12.60, child £10.50; winter £4.10, child £3.05.* ⚬🅿✕*;* ✆*0800 731 3446; www. landmarkpark.co.uk)*

A favourite family day out with adventure climbs, watersplash rides, a mini-roller coaster, a high-wire challenge course and nature-themed activities.

ELGIN★

◗ *Elgin is 38mi/61km NE of Inverness.*

Elgin stands on the banks of the Lossie just off the northeast coast. The original town plan has been well preserved, with the main street linking the two mainstays of any medieval burgh – the cathedral and the castle.

Elgin Cathedral★

HS. ⚬🕐*Open Apr–Sept daily 9.30am–5.30pm (Oct 4.30). Nov–Mar Sat–Wed 9.30am–4.30pm.* ☜*Guided tours (free) Mon–Fri.* ☜*£5.* ⚬*.* ✆*01343 547 171. www.historic-scotland.gov.uk/elgin.*

The diocese dates back to 1120, but the ruins here are those of a cathedral built in 1270. In 1390 Alexander Stewart, the **Wolf of Badenoch**, second son of King Robert II, destroyed both cathedral and town. Both were repaired, and the 13C **chapter house**★★ was reconstructed in the 15C. The cathedral suffered further deterioration after conservation was begun in the early-19C.

EXCURSIONS
Speyside

◗ *Dufftown is 18mi/29km S of Elgin.*

A brown-and-white signposted **Malt Whisky Trail** *(approx 70mi/112km; www. maltwhiskytrail.com)* through the glens of Speyside, takes in eight famous distilleries and a cooperage, all of which offer a fascinating glimpse into the production of Scotland's "sovereign liquor". The basic tour is often complimentary, with a charge for tasting tours where more than a wee dram or two is sampled. The trail centres on Dufftown; the following are essential stops. **Glenfiddich Distillery** *(0.5mi/0.8km) north of Dufftown;* 🕐*open year-round Mon–Sat 9.30am (noon Sun)–4.30pm; winter,*

weekends only; ⚬*;* 🅿*;* ✆*01340 820 373, www.glenfiddich.co.uk/distillery)* is a perfect example of a working distillery, little changed since 1886.

Picturesque **Dallas Dhu Distillery** *(HS; 1.2mi/2km S of Forres, 14mi/ 23km W of Elgin;* 🕐*open Apr–Sept daily 9.30am–5.30pm/Oct 4.30pm, Nov–Mar Wed–Sat 9.30am–4.30pm;* ☜*£5.50, includes a free dram;* ⚬*;* 🅿*;* ✆*01309 676 548, www.historic-scotland.gov.uk)*, dating from 1898, is no longer in production but is a fascinating time capsule.

Speyside Cooperage *(Dufftown Road, Craigellachie, 4mi/6km N of Dufftown);* 🕐*open year-round Mon–Fri 9am–4pm;* ☜*£3.30;* ⚬🅿✕*;* ✆*01340 871 108; www. speysidecooperage.co.uk)* is the only working cooperage in the UK where you can witness the ancient craft of barrel making.

Sueno's Stone★★

◗ *13mi/21km W of Elgin. Just east of Forres off the A96.*

This huge superbly carved Pictish sandstone slab (some 20ft/6m high) is unique in Britain. It is probably a funerary monument commemorating a battle. Three sides are decorative – one carved with a wheel cross. The fourth side, the most spectacular, shows horsemen, warriors and headless corpses.

Brodie Castle★

NTS. ◗ *Brodie, near Forres. 16mi/26km W of Elgin.* 🕐*Open 10.30am–4.30pm/ 5pm: daily Apr, Jul–Aug. May–Jun & Sept–Oct Sun–Wed.* ☜*£9.* ⚬🅿✕*.* ✆*08444 932 156. www.nts.org.uk.*

The seat of the Brodies since the 11C, the castle developed from a 16C towerhouse to the present building. Interiors of various periods are the setting for a splendid collection of paintings, exquisite timepieces and French **furniture**. The ornate **plasterwork ceilings** date from the 17C.

BANFF★

◗ *40mi/64km N of Aberdeen.*

This small royal burgh town, set on the coast at the mouth of the River Deveron, on Banff Bay, boasts many attractive

18C buildings, none more so than Duff House (*see below*). With magnificent views of cliffs and headlands all along this splendid coastline, Banff is an excellent base for excursions: west to the picturesque fishing villages of **Portsoy**, **Cullen** and **Buckie**; east to **Macduff**, **Gardenstown**, **Crovie** and **Pennan**.

Duff House★★

Overlooking the Duff House Royal Golf Club beside the River Deveron. see website or call for opening times. £6.85. &⊟✕. ℘01261 81 81 81. www.duffhouse.org.uk.

This splendid Baroque mansion designed by William Adam has been restored to its former glory. A double curving staircase rises up to the great central block and Corinthian pilasters support a richly decorated pediment. Small intimate rooms surround the spacious vestibule dominated by a grandiose painting by William Etty, and the Great Drawing Room hung with Gobelins tapestries and pastoral paintings by Boucher.

GRAMPIAN CASTLES★★

Aberdeen's hinterland is rich in castles, both complete and ruined from the early Norman to the Scottish Baronial style; many of these characterise the golden age of castle-building, which occurred between the 16C and the 17C.

Haddo House★

NTS. 26mi/42km N of Aberdeen by the A 92 and B 9005. **House:** *Open Good Fri–Jun and Sept–Oct Fri–Mon by guided tour only, 11.30am, 1.30pm, 3.30pm; Jul–Aug daily 11am–5pm.* **Garden and country park:** *Open year-round daily 9am–dusk.* £9. &⊟✕. ℘08444 932 179. www.nts.org.uk.

The present house was designed by William Adam in 1469. George Hamilton Gordon (1784–1860), prime minister during the Crimean War, still found time to repair the house and to landscape the parkland. Its superb late Victorian interiors feature elegant rooms with coffered ceilings and wood panelling, a perfect setting for family portraits and mementoes. The country park offers splendid vistas.

Fyvie Castle★

NTS. 26mi/42km N of Aberdeen by the A 947. Castle open Apr–Jun and Sept–Oct Sat–Wed noon–5pm; Jul–Aug daily 11am–5pm. £11. &⊟✕. ℘08444 932 182. www.nts.org.uk.

Alexander Seton, Lord Chancellor (c. 1639–1719), remodelled Fyvie creating the spectacular **south front** (150ft/46m long), an impressive example of 17C Baronial architecture, and the **wheel stair**. In the late-19C Fyvie was refurbished in opulent Edwardian style, decorated with portraits by the Scottish master of this art, **Henry Raeburn**.

Crathes Castle★★

NTS. 15mi/24km SW of Aberdeen by the A 93. Open Apr–Oct daily 10.30am–4.45pm; Nov–Mar Sat–Sun 10.30am–3.45pm. £11. &⊟✕. ℘08444 932 166. www.nts.org.uk.

The wonderfully crowded and detailed skyline of this 16C tower house, including fairy-tale-like turrets and gargoyles of fantastic design, is a striking example of the inventive Baronial tradition. The interiors include some fine early vernacular furniture as well as some outstanding examples of **painted ceilings**. Stone pendants and armorial paintings adorn the barrel-vaulted **High Hall**, where the **Horn of Leys** – the original token of tenure dating from 1322 – has pride of place above the fireplace. The oak-panelled roof decorated with armorial devices and the horn motif is a unique feature of the **Long Gallery**.

The series of **separate gardens**★★★ are a delight in the wealth and colour of the planting.

Castle Fraser★

NTS. 15mi/24km W of Aberdeen by the A 944 and B 993 at Dunecht. Open Apr–Jun and Sept–Oct Wed–Sun and bank hols noon–5pm; Jul–Aug daily 11am–5pm. £9. &⊟✕. ℘08444 932 164. www.nts.org.uk.

Castle Fraser, built 1575–1636, is a traditional tower house with highly individual decoration. The **exterior**★★ is remarkable. The local style with its harmonious combination of traditional features – turrets, conical roofs, crow-stepped gables, chimney stacks, decorative dormers and gargoyles – was Scotland's unique contribution to Renaissance architecture. The **central block** of this Z-plan castle is distinguished by a magnificent heraldic achievement. The refurbished interiors bring to life the simple lifestyle of a 17C laird.

Dunnottar Castle★★

18mi/29km S of Aberdeen via the A 92. *Open daily Apr–Oct 9am–6pm, Nov–Mar 10am–dusk/5pm.* *£5.* *01569 762 173.* *www.dunnottarcastle.co.uk.*
Set on an almost inaccessible **promontory**★★★ with sheer cliffs on three sides, the castle dates from the 14C and was the last castle remaining in Royalist hands during the Commonwealth.
Here the Honours of Scotland (royal regalia) were held during an eight-month siege by Cromwell's troops in 1651–52, being finally smuggled out and hidden in a nearby church. The fortified **gatehouse** and **keep** contrast with

the 17C **Waterton's Lodging** and the **16C–17C buildings** arranged around a quadrangle.

Tolquhon Castle★

HS. *17mi/27km N of Aberdeen via the B 999.* *Open Apr–Sept daily 9.30am–5.30pm; Oct–Mar Sat–Sun 9.30am–4.30pm.* *£4.* *01651 851 286. www.historic-scotland.gov.uk.*
Pronounced "tol-hoon", this is one of the most picturesque castle ruins in the Grampians. The present structure dates from 1574. Its gatehouse is a gem, built not to deter, but to impress. The main house is a charming composition at the far end of the courtyard, with a good "below stairs" and family rooms above to explore. In the laird's bedchamber on the second floor is a secret compartment below the floor where Sir William Forbes, the builder of the castle, hid his valuables.
In the nearby parish church in the village of Tarves, Sir William also built the **Tolquhon Tomb** burial vault. This is one of the best examples of Scotland's so-called "Glorious Tombs" from the Jaco-bean age, finely decorated with beguil-ing stone effigies Forbes himself (d.1596) and his wife, Elizabeth Gordon.

Dunnottar Castle

© P. Tomkins/VisitScotland/Scottish Viewpoint

Highlands and Western Isles

If there were only one region that could fly the flag for Scotland abroad, then it would probably be the Highlands. It not only not only boasts Scotland's most awe-inspiring landscapes of dark lochs and snow-capped peaks, but also some of the most remote and extensive wilderness in Europe. There is island romance, on Skye and in the Hebrides, history aplenty (Glencoe, Bonnie Prince Charlie, standing stones), legends (Nessie, Macbeth), wildlife (dolphins, whales, eagles and deer), and a whole host of sporting opportunities in both summer and winter.

INVERNESS★

○ *156mi/251km N of Edinburgh, 119mi/191km SW of John O'Groats.*
Standing at the northern end of the Great Glen, astride the River Ness (flowing from Loch Ness), Inverness is the traditional capital and hub of the Scottish Highlands. It services much of northern Scotland on a daily basis, while its legendary loch attracts many boating visitors.

WALKING TOUR
Just east of the Young Street bridge on Castle Wynd is the **Inverness Museum and Art Gallery**★ (○open Mon–Sat 10am–5pm; ○closed 25–26 Dec, Dec 31–Jan; ℅; ℘01463 237 114; http://inverness.highland.museum), an imaginative well-presented exhibition interpreting the region's rich heritage (and present day arts and crafts) including the Great Glen, the Picts, General Wade's roads and Telford's Caledonian Canal.
Immediately to the south on Castle Street, is 19C **Inverness Castle**, sitting on a low cliff, overlooking the River Ness and the cathedral on the opposite bank. It now houses the Sheriff Court and is closed to the public, though a good **view** of the town and the River Ness may be enjoyed from its esplanade.
Across the bridge, follow the road

Michelin Map:
Michelin Atlas p65–67, p74 or Map 501.
Info: Castle Wynd, Inverness. ℘01463 234 353. www.inverness-scotland.com. Gairloch. ℘01445 712 130. Kyle of Lochalsh. ℘01599 534 276. Ullapool. ℘01854 612 135.
The Car Park, Broadford. Bayfield House, Bayfield Road, Portree. ℘(both) 01845 225 5121. Wick: ℘0845 225 5121. County Road. John O'Groats: ℘01955 611 373. www.visithighlands.com.
Kids: Loch Ness Exhibition Centre at Drumnadrochit.

to Ardross Street and take a left for **St Andrew's Cathedral** (○open daily; ℅; ℘01463 233 535; www.inverness cathedral.com), a richly decorated neo-Gothic Revival church of 1866–69. Its nave piers are of polished Peterhead granite.

EXCURSIONS
Cawdor Castle★
○ *13mi/21km NE on the A 96 and B 9090.* ○Open Easter–early Oct daily 10am–5.30pm. ⊚£9. Gardens and grounds only, £5. ☐℅. ℘01667 404 401. www.cawdorcastle.com.
Built in the late-14C by the Thanes of Cawdor (the title, meaning nobleman, Shakespeare's witches promised to Macbeth), the castle was added to in the 17C. Note the lovely 17C Flemish and English tapestries and, amid the many portraits, one of the 18C thane, splendidly dressed in an assortment of tartans. Outside, there are three gardens to enjoy – the oldest being the Walled Garden, c.1600) – the Big Wood, a putting green and a nine-hole golf course.

Fort George★
HS. ○ *20mi/32km NE on the A 96 and B 9006.* ○Open Apr–Oct daily 9.30am–

5.30pm, Oct–Mar daily 9.30am–4.30pm. £6.90. ☒🅿✗. 𝒫01667 460 232. www.historic-scotland.gov.uk.

Set on a peninsula jutting out into the Moray Firth, this is the most impressive artillery fortress in Britain, and was built between 1745 and 1746 on the orders of George II, to prevent his law and order from being disrupted by the Highland clans. Highlights include the historic barrack room, the grand magazine, the garrison chapel and the **Queen's Own Highlanders Regimental Museum** (Ⓞ*closed winter Sat–Sun and third week Dec–early Jan*).

Cromarty★

▶ *26mi/42km NE via the A 9 and A 832.*

On the northern tip of the Black Isle, at the mouth of the Cromarty Firth, guarded by the Sutors Stacks, the tiny port of Cromarty has been aptly described as "the jewel in the crown of Scottish vernacular architecture". Learn more at the elegant 18C **Cromarty Courthouse Museum** (*Church Street;* Ⓞ*open May–Sept Sun–Thu daily 11am–4pm; 𝒫01381 600 418; www.cromarty-court house.org.uk*).

Dornoch★

▶ *55mi/88km NE on the A 9.*

A scenic route cuts across the Black Isle, passes along the north bank of the Cromarty Firth, near the pretty little town of **Tain**, formerly an important pilgrimage centre, and crosses the Dornoch Firth to reach this charming burgh which boasts miles of sandy beaches and famous golf courses. The medieval cathedral dominates the town.

Culloden

NTS. ▶ *6mi/10km E by the A 9 and B 9006.* Ⓞ*Visitor centre open daily Apr–Sept 9am–6pm (Oct 5pm); Nov–Mar 10am–4pm.* Ⓞ*Closed 24 Dec–late Jan.* £10. ☒🅿✗. 𝒫08444 932 159. *www.nts.org.uk/Culloden.*

Here, on 16 April 1746, the Jacobite army of Bonnie Prince Charlie was slaughtered by government troops under the command of George II's younger son "Butcher Cumberland", finally ending

the hopes of a Stuart restoration to the British throne. An excellent new **visitor centre** interprets the battle.

🚗 DRIVING TOURS

GREAT GLEN★

▶ *65mi/105km SW on the A 82.*

The geological fault of the Great Glen cuts across the Highlands, linking the Atlantic Ocean with the North Sea through a series of narrow lochs joined together by part (22mi/35km) of Thomas Telford's **Caledonian Canal** (1803–22). The lochs and canals are now used principally for pleasure craft (operators offer "Monster Hunting" trips on Loch Ness). At the southern end of the glen, **Fort William★** marks the northern tip of Loch Linnhe, sitting in the shadow of Britain's highest mountain, **Ben Nevis** (4,406ft/1,344m). The town makes an ideal touring centre.

Heading north from here on the A 82 you come to Torlundy, where cable cars (Ⓞ *see website for times;* return trip £11; 🅿☒✗; 𝒫01397 705 825. *www. nevis-range.co.uk*) rise to the **Nevis Range** ski resort with great **views★★** en route. From here the A 82 will take you past Loch Lochy and Loch Oich until you arrive at Loch Ness.

LOCH NESS★★

The dark waters of this loch (754ft/230m deep) are renowned the world over as the home of the elusive "monster", **Nes-**

Nessie

The initial sighting of a large snake-like, hump-backed monster with a long thin neck in Loch Ness was made in the 8C by a monk. Despite various expeditions, some highly equipped with submarines, helicopters and sonar electronic cameras, the loch has failed to reveal its secret (the true identity of Nessie). The tradition is hardly surprising in a country where the kelpie or water-horse was common in the tales and legends of the past.

sie. First spied in the 8C by a local monk, Nessie has continued to captivate and mystify and, despite modern technology, remains an enigma.

From Fort Augustus and its canal lock, travel north on the west side of the loch on the A82 to see the much-photographed ruins of **Urquhart Castle**★ *(HS; ⊙open daily Apr–Sept 9.30am–6pm (5pm Oct), Nov–Mar 9.30am–4.30pm); ⊜£6.36; ⊡; ℘01456 450 551; www.historic-scotland.gov.uk)*, strategically set on a promontory jutting into the loch. This former stronghold was one of a chain of defences controlling this natural route. An exhibition and audio-visual display in the new visitor centre traces its history, including an outstanding array of medieval artefacts found at the castle. Next stop on the A 82 is the pretty little village of **Drumnadrochit**. Here you can satisfy your curiosity in all things Nessie at the ♣♣**Loch Ness Exhibition Centre**★ *(⊙open daily; Easter–Oct 9.30am–5pm/Jun–Aug 9am–5.30/6pm; Nov–Easter 10am–3.30pm; ⊜£6.50, child £4.50; ♿⊡✕; ℘01456 450 573; www.lochness.com).*

WESTER ROSS★★★

The main touring centres are Kyle of Lochalsh, Gairloch and Ullapool, respectively, 78mi/125km, 69mi/111km and 57mi/92km W of Inverness.
The Atlantic seaboard of Wester Ross is wild and dramatic, with magnificent mountains and placid lochs.

Kyle of Lochalsh to Gairloch★★★

120mi/193km. Allow a whole day.
The route covers some of the finest scenery in the Wester Ross region – Loch Maree studded with islanpds, the Torridon area and the Applecross eninsula. Some of the roads will be busy in high season, but many stretches will allow the luxury of enjoying the scenery in solitude. **Kyle of Lochalsh** is the ferry port for Skye and a busy place in summer.

Eilean Donan Castle★

9mi/15km E of Kyle of Lochalsh by the A 87. ⊙Open Mar–Oct daily 10am (9am Jul and Aug)–6pm.⊜£6. ⊡✕. ℘01599 555 202. www.eileandonancastle.com. This much-photographed castle enjoys an idyllic **setting**★★ on an island in the loch and is now linked to the shore by a bridge. After two centuries of disuse, following a Jacobite raid in 1719, it was completely reconstructed 1911–31 according to its earlier layout The ramparts afford **views** of three lochs.

▷ *Return to Kyle and leave by the road running along the coast to the north.*

Plockton★

Once a "refugee" settlement at the time of the Highland clearances, Plockton, with its palm-lined main street and sheltered bay, is a sailing centre.

▷ *At Achmore, take the A 890 to the left, and at the junction with the A 896, go left again, towards Lochcarron. At Tornapress, the visitor can elect to continue on the A 896 to Shieldaig, but the minor road across the peninsula, via Bealach-na Bo, well repays the effort. It has hairpin bends and 1:4 gradients, and is not recommended for caravans or learner drivers.*

Bealach-na-Bo

On the way up to the pass (2 053ft/626m) the hanging valley frames spectacular vistas of lochs and mountains, while from the summit car park, the **views**★★★ westward, of Skye and its fringing islands, are superb.

▷ *Either continue north along the coast, via Fearnmore, to Torridon, or the return to Tornapress, for Torridon by the A 896.*

Torridon Countryside Centre

NTS. ♿⊙Open Apr–Sept, Sun–Fri 10am–5pm. ⊜£3.50. ⊡. ℘0844 4932 229. www.nts.org.uk.
The centre interprets the area's spectacular geology and nature and includes

Loch Maree with a view to Ben Slioch

© David Woods/iStockphoto.com

a deer enclosure and deer museum. Information is available on walking and climbing.

▷ *At Kinlochewe, take the A 832 to the left.*

Loch Maree★★★
Loch Maree epitomises the scenic beauty and grandeur of the west coast. It lies between Beinn Eighe and the towering **Ben Slioch** (3,217ft/980m) to the north. To the north is the **Letterewe Estate**, one of Scotland's great deer forests.

Victoria Falls★
A platform and the riverside path give good views of these falls, named after Queen Victoria's visit in 1877.

Gairloch
The ideal centre for touring the Torridon area, exploring the hills and enjoying the sandy beaches of this part of the west coast, and admiring the splendid views of the Hebridean Islands. The pier at the head of the loch still has all the bustle of a fishing port.

Gairloch to Ullapool★★
56mi/90km . Allow 4hrs.
This route runs along the coastline with its bays, beaches and headlands and a backdrop of breathtaking mountain scenery.

▷ *Take the A 832 across the Rubha Reidh peninsula.*

Stop before descending to the River Ewe and look back from the roadside **viewpoint★★★** at the superb view of Loch Maree with its forested islands.

Inverewe Garden★★★
NTS. ⏱*Open year-round daily from 10am. Closes: Apr and Sept 5pm; May 5.30pm; Jun–Aug 6pm; Nov–Mar 3pm.* ⛽*£9; winter, by donation.* ♿🅿⛽✕. ✆*0844 4932 225. www.nts.org.uk.* These outstanding 50-acre/20ha gardens enjoy a magnificent coastal setting on the same latitude as Leningrad. Their profusion so far north is made possible by the influence of the Gulf Stream. Colour is found at most seasons, from azaleas and rhododendrons in May to heathers and maples in the autumn.

▷ *Continue on the A 832; left onto A 835.*

Falls of Measach★★
The waters of the River Droma make a spectacular sight as they drop over 150ft/45m in the wooded cleft of the **Corrieshalloch Gorge★**. The road follows the north shore of **Loch Broom★★** in a particularly attractive setting.

▷ *Continue NW on the A 835.*

Ullapool★

The village was laid out in the 18C and flourished during the herring boom. Fishing still plays an important part in the local economy. Ullapool is an ideal touring centre; the car ferry terminal for Stornoway, a haven for yachtsmen and an unrivalled centre for sea angling. Various boats sail to the **Summer Isles** to watch seals and sea birds.

ISLE OF SKYE★★

Skye is joined to the mainland by the Skye Bridge at Kyle of Lochalsh and has two mainland ferry (www.calmac.co.uk) connections, from Mallaig and Glenelg to Armadale.

In Norse and Gaelic tales, Skye is known as the "Island of Cloud", or the "Winged Isle". Mystery and enchantment still lie heavy here. Skye is the largest of the Inner Hebrides group, just off the north-west mainland. Crofting, tourism and forestry are the principal occupations of the 9,000 or so islanders, 85 percent of whom still speak Gaelic.

The Cuillins★★★

The scenic splendour of the Cuillins makes these peaks the isle's most famous feature. The **Black Cuillins**, a 6mi/10km arc of sharp peaks, encircle Loch Coruisk; many of these peaks are over 3,000ft/914m in height, with Sgurr Alasdair (3,258ft/993m) the highest. On the other side of Glen Sligachan the softly rounded forms of the pink granite **Red Cuillins** contrast with their neighbours.

Portree★

Skye's pleasant little capital, arranged around a sheltered bay, is a popular yachting centre.

Kilmuir

The town stands on the north coast of the **Trotternish Peninsula★★**, the most northerly of Skye's peninsulas, with lovely seascapes and a basalt rock pinnacle. The small churchyard has a monument to **Flora MacDonald** (1722–90), known for her part in the escape of Bonnie prince Charlie after the collapse of the Jacobite cause at Culloden. She brought the Prince, disguised as her maid, from Benbecula in the Outer Hebrides to Portree. From here he escaped to exile in France.

Skye Museum of Island Life★

Open Easter–Oct Mon–Sat 9.30am–5pm. £2.50. ₺P. 01470 552 206. www.skyemuseum.co.uk.

The Skye Museum is a collection of thatched cottages – a crofter's house, a weaver's house, a smithy and a *ceilidh* house – depicting, as closely as possible, the conditions of a small township at the close of the 19C.

Dunvegan Castle

Open Apr–mid-Oct daily 10am–5.30pm. £9. ₺PX. 01470 521 206. www.dunvegancastle.com.

This Hebridean fortress, seat of the MacLeods, is set on a rocky platform overlooking Loch Dunvegan, and until 1748 the only entrance was by a sea

View to the Black Cuillins across Loch Scavaig

gate. Most notable of the treasures kept here is the fragment of silk, known as the **Fairy Flag**.

Legend has it that the flag, given to the 4th Chief by his fairy wife, has the power to ward off disaster to the clan, and has twice been invoked.

Popular **seal-spotting** trips depart from the castle in summer (⏱operate mid-Apr–mid-Sept; ⊜£6).

WICK
▶ 16mi/26km S of John O'Groats.

This thriving market town was once Scotland's main herring port. Only a small fleet now operates, but in its heyday over 1,000 boats sailed from Wick and neighbouring Pulteneytown.

John O'Groats
▶ 19mi/31km N on the A 9.

Traditionally this is the northeastern-most point in mainland Britain, some 876mi/1,410km from the southeastern-most point, Land's End.

The settlement takes its name from a Dutchman, Jan de Groot, who started a ferry service to the Orkneys in the 16C.

Duncansby Head★
▶ 2mi/3.2km E of John O'Groats.

The northeastern headland of mainland Scotland, Duncansby Head, overlooks the treacherous waters of the Pentland Firth. The **scenery** is spectacular. Standing just offshore, the **Stacks of Duncansby**★★, pointed sea stacks, rise 210ft/64m up from the water. A variety of seabirds flock to the rocks.

WESTERN ISLES
The chain of islands known as the Western Isles extends around 130mi/210km north–south. The Outer Hebrides share a history of Norse control with the Isle of Man much further south.

Traditional activities include peat working and the weaving of Harris tweed. Buffeted by Atlantic waves, the islands are treeless and windswept, but rejoice in glistening *lochans* (small lochs), superb sandy beaches, and crystal-clear waters. The islands' isolation has

helped to preserve the still flourishing Gaelic culture.

Mods (special events and festivals of Gaelic art and music), *ceilidhs* (gatherings often with music and dancing), concerts, Highland Games and agricultural shows are staged year-round. And, of course, Gaelic is still widely spoken.

Isle of Lewis
Stornoway
Stornoway, the capital and only sizeable town, is the base for excursions inland where hotels (and petrol) are scarce. The land-locked harbour is overlooked by a 19C castle. Eye peninsula to the north has some fine sandy beaches.

Callanish (Calanais)
Standing Stones★★
HS. ▶ 6mi/26km west of Stornoway, signposted off A 858. ⏱Open Apr–Sept daily 10am–6pm. Oct–Mar Wed–Sat 10am–4pm). ☎01851 710 395. www.historic-scotland.gov.uk

Over 4,000 years old and contemporary with Stonehenge, the stones, of Lewisian gneiss, form a circle, while approach avenues form the points of the compass. It is assumed that they were used for astronomical observations.

Carloway Broch (Dun Carloway)★
▶ 5mi/8km beyond Callanish Standing Stones, signposted off A 858.

This is an incomplete example of a broch (small fortified farm c.500 BC), though enough remains of the galleried walls and entrance chamber for the builders' skill to be admired.

Arnol Black House
HS. ▶ 6mi/10km beyond Carloway, signposted off the A 858. �⏱Open year-round Mon–Sat, 9.30am–5.30pm (4.30pm Oct–Mar). ⊜£4. ☎01851 710 395. www.historic-scotland.gov.uk.

This typical basic dwelling has been preserved as a reminder of ancient island life as it was until half a century ago.

Orkney and Shetland Islands★

The archipelago of the Orkney Islands is located off the northeast tip of Scotland – the nearest island is just 6mi/10km offshore – where the North Sea and the Atlantic Ocean meet. It is made up of 67 islands, about half of which are inhabited. The largest island, known as "Mainland", is home to most of the population. The islands are mainly low lying, with a gently rolling landscape of green fields, heather moorland heaths and lochs. Battered by sea and wind, the Sheltland Islands coastline is wildly indented with a savage beauty; in places rugged and rocky, elsewhere sandy and smooth. Here on the very edge of the British Isles you will find remains of the earliest human settlements and a Viking heritage that is still alive today. The islands are closer to the Arctic Circle than to Manchester, closer to Bergen in Norway than to Edinburgh, and many aspects of the local culture feel more Scandinavian than Scottish.

⚙ **Michelin Map:** Michelin Atlas p74–75 or Map 501.

🗎 **Info:** ✆08701 999 440. www.visitshetland.com. West Castle Street, Kirkwall. ✆01856 872 856. www.visitorkney.com.

⊗ **Don't Miss:** St Magnus Cathedral, Kirkwall; Skara Brae; Old Man of Hoy.

SHETLAND ISLANDS★

Daily sailings from Aberdeen to Lerwick and regular flights from Aberdeen, Edinburgh, Glasgow, Inverness and London to Sumburgh. The capital, Lerwick, is on the east coast of Mainland, which is 50mi/81km long north to south, and 20mi/32km across at its widest. Population: 22,522.

There are 100 or so Shetland Islands but fewer than 20 are inhabited. Shetland is hilly and has many inlets (voes), the most famous of which, **Sullom Voe**, is home to Europe's largest oil and gas terminal. Nonetheless, the oil industry still takes second place to fishing in importance, while the area directly affected by oil and gas exploration is bordered by beautiful, wild spaces. The islands also hold important evidence of early human settlement.

Up Helly Aa★★★

This colourful and rousing fire festival is the most spectacular reminder of the Viking heritage. Explanations for the pageant held on the last Tuesday in January are various, from spring rites to placating the Norse gods, or up-ending of the holy days. The principal figure, the **Guizer Jarl** (earl) and his

©Jeff J. Mitchell/Reuters/Corbis

warriors, all clad in the finery of Viking war dress, head the great torchlit procession in their Viking longship. A thundering rendering of the *Galley Song* precedes the burning of the galley and the final song, *The Norseman's Home*. Celebrations continue throughout the night.

LERWICK

The Shetlands' capital sits in a natural harbour sheltered by the Island of Bressay. Local attractions include the ruined **Clickhimin Broch**★ and the **Shetland Museum and Archives** (Hay's Dock; ♿ 🕐 open year-round Mon–Sat 10am–5pm, Sun noon–5pm. ✕; ☎01595 695 057; www.shetland-museum.org.uk).

This waterfront centre, opened in May 2007 is the perfect starting point to learn about Shetlands heritage and culture. As well as museum displays there is a lively programme of events including storytelling, a popular islands' tradition.

Jarlshof★★

HS. ◗ Mainland. 25mi/40km S of Lerwick by the A 970. 🕐Open daily Easter–Sept 9.30am–5.30pm; Oct 9.30am–4.30pm. ⬚£4.70. 🅿. ☎01950 460 112. www.historic-scotland.gov.uk.

The site of Jarlshof has been occupied from the middle of the 2nd millennium BC until the 17C.

There are six Bronze Age houses, and a late Iron Age broch with other dwellings clustered around it. Numerous Viking longhouses tell of several centuries of occupation. There was a farmstead here in the 13C; the New Hall was built in the 16C.

Mousa Broch★★★

HS. ◗ Mousa Island. 12mi/19km S on the A 970. Motor boat (15min) from Sandwick jetty. 🕐Open daily Apr–Sept 9.30am–5.30pm; winter 9.30am–4.30pm, call ☎01856 841 815 (Skara Brae) to confirm. 🕐Closed 24–25 Dec. ⬚Ferry charge around £12. ☎01950 431 367 (ferry operator); 01856 841 815 (Historic Scotland). www.historic-scotland.gov.uk.

Small fortified farms, brochs, were peculiar to Scotland, the culmination of a tradition stretching back to 500 BC. Most have crumbled, but Mousa, probably dating from the 1st or 2nd century AD, still stands to a height of over 43ft/13.3m and is the finest surviving Iron Age broch tower.

Broch tower, Mousa Broch

© Lars Johansson/Fotolia.com

A staircase, chambers and galleries were built into the thickness of the walls of this imposing kiln-shaped **tower**, which is more than 40ft/12ft across at its base. In the courtyard are a hearth and lean-to structures.

ORKNEY ISLANDS★★

◗ The main island of Orkney is divided into the Eastern Mainland and the Western Mainland. Several British airports service Orkney and mainland ferries run here from Aberdeen (6hrs), Scrabster (90min), Gills Bay (1hr) and John O'Groats (40min), which is 10mi/16km S of the islands. Orkney Ferries (☎01856 8720 44) and Loganair (☎01856 872 494) service the other islands. Population: 19,612.

Lying off the northeast tip of mainland Scotland, the Orkney archipelago comprises 67 islands of which fewer than 30 are inhabited. The cliffs are home to countless seabirds, and seals and otters are common. The first Neolithic settlers came in the 4th millennium BC. Some of their dwellings remain and their fine stone tombs can be seen throughout the islands. From the early Iron Age – around the 5C BC – fortified villages grew up round the massive stone buildings known as brochs. The Vikings came to Orkney from the late-8C AD, sweeping away the culture of the Pictish Orcadians. Orkney's culture still has Scandinavian elements, though the islands were pawned to King James III of Scotland in 1468, as part of the dowry of his Danish bride.

Kirkwall★★

A capital since Viking days, Kirkwall stands on the isthmus separating the eastern and western parts of the island. Handsome townhouses (now shops), some emblazoned, line the stone-flagged main street and pends (alleyways) lead to attractive paved courtyards.

St Magnus Cathedral★★ dominates the skyline of Kirkwall (◔*open Apr–Sept daily 9am–5pm, Oct–Mar Mon–Fri 9am–5pm;* ☁*guided tour including tower;* ♿🅿; ☏*01856 874 894*). Built by Earl Rognvald, 1137–1152, and dedicated to his murdered uncle, Earl Magnus, the cathedral is an outstanding example of Norman architecture. The red stone exterior is severe and plain. The three west front **doorways** added later show confident originality in their combination of red and yellow sandstone.

Inside carefully controlled proportions create a sense of vastness belying the building's modest dimensions. The square pillars on either side of the organ screen enshrine the relics of St Magnus *(right)* and Earl Rognvald *(left)*.

Opposite on Broad Street in the fine 16C townhouse of Tankerness House is **The Orkney Museum★** (◔*open Apr–Sept Mon–Sat 10.30am–5pm, Sun 2pm–5pm, Oct–Mar Mon–Sat 10.30am–12.30pm, 1.30pm–5pm;* ☏*01856 873 191; www.orkney.org*), with excellent displays on the islands' prehistory.

Walk south from here on Broad Street and go left on Palace Road for **Earl's Palace★** (♿◔*open Easter–Oct daily 9.30am–5.30pm (Oct 4.30pm);* ◔*closed 1–2 Jan , 25–26 Dec;* ☁£3.62; ☏01856 871 918; www.historic-scotland.gov.uk. The remains of this early Renaissance palace have splendid corbelling on the windows, chimney breast and corbel course, and sculptured panels above the main entrance and oriel windows. It was built c.1600–07 by **Earl Patrick Stewart**. The vaulted chambers on the ground floor hold exhibitions of Orkney history from the early Middle Ages to the present, while the grand staircase leads to the Great Hall and apartments.

🚗 DRIVING TOUR

WESTERN MAINLAND★★

Leave Kirkwall west by the A 965 for the **Rennibister Earth House** *(behind the farmhouse, access by trapdoor and ladder)*, by the southeastern shore of Bay o' Firth. The oval chamber has five wall recesses and an entrance passage. Human bones were found in it, though its purpose remains uncertain.

Further west, approximately 550yds/500m from the southeastern shore of the Harray loch is **Maes Howe★★** (◔*open Apr–Sept daily 9.30am–5pm, Oct–Mar 9.30am–4pm;* ◔*closed 1–2 Jan, 25–26 Dec;* ☁£5.20; 🅿✗; ☏*01856 761 606; www.historic-scotland.gov.uk*). This Neolithic burial cairn dates from pre-2700 BC and was covered by a mound (26ft/8m high and 115ft/35m wide). The cairn was broken into in the 12C by Norsemen, who left runic marks.

Maes Howe is part of the Heart of Neolithic Orkney World Heritage Site. West of Maes Howe, the **Stones of Stenness** sit at the base of a neck of land separating the lochs of Stenness and Harray. The **Ring of Brodgar** Stone Age circle stands on this neck. It still has 27 of its original 60 stones standing. Two entrance causeways interrupt the encircling ditch. West of the Stones of Stenness on a promontory jutting into the loch is **Unstan Cairn**, a Stone Age chambered tomb from the mid-4th millennium.

Further west on the A 965 is **Stromness★**, the second-largest town and principal port. Stromness grew from its original Norse settlement to become a whaling station in the 18C and the last port of call for the Hudson Bay Company ships sailing to Canada. The **Pier Arts Centre** *(Victoria Street;* ♿◔*Open year-round Mon–Sat 10.30am–5pm;* ☏*01856 850 209; www.pierartscentre. com)* has a permanent collection of abstract art based on the work of the St Ives artists, Ben Nicholson and Barbara Hepworth. Aspects of Orkney's natural and maritime history are presented in the **Stromness Museum** *(52 Alfed Street; ⚡🕐 open Apr–Sept daily 10am–5pm; Oct–mid-Feb and mid-Mar Mon–Sat, 11am–3.30pm; ⊜£3; 🅿; 📞01856 850 025; www.scbf.co.uk).*

North of Stromness on the A967 is **Skara Brae**★★ *(⚡🕐 open Apr–Sept daily 9.30am–5.30pm, Oct–Mar 9.30am–4pm; ⊜£5.58 (winter: site partially closed); 🅿✕, picnic area; 📞01856 841 815; www.historic-scotland.gov.uk)* on the southern shore of the Bay o' Skaill. This 5,000-year old settlement was buried in sand for a long period. The seven best-preserved Stone Age dwellings are rectangular with coursed flagstone walls and a hearth in the middle, and are connected by a subterranean sewer system.

Further north, separated from the mainland by the waters of Brough Sound is the **Brough of Birsay**★ *(access on foot across causeway at low tide; 🕐open mid-Jun–Sept 9.30am–5.30pm, when tides permit; ⊜£3.13; 📞01856 841 815 or 01856 721 205; www.historic-scotland.gov.uk).* The earliest remains are Pictish. In the 10C Norse farmers occupied the island and Earl Thorfinn the Mighty (c.1009–65) built a church after a pilgrimage to Rome. It became a cathedral and was the initial resting place of St Magnus before the construction of Kirkwall Cathedral. Excavations show a small oblong nave, short narrow choir and rounded apse, surrounded by a Norse graveyard. A little to the southwest is a collection of stone-and-turf **Norse long houses**.

Return to Kirkwall. About 10mi/16km south by the A 961, past St Mary's, is **Scapa Flow**. From the **Churchill Barriers**, built in the Second World War by Italian prisoners of war to link the four islands with the mainland, there is a good view of the naval base where the German Grand Fleet scuttled itself in 1919. Beyond the first barrier is the **Italian Chapel**★, a unique and moving testament to faith in adversity, built by the same prisoners inside two Nissen (prefabricated corrugated iron) huts.

Pentland Firth Crossing

The crossing (a very choppy two-hour car ferry journey operating between Stromness and Scrabster) is an ideal way of seeing the outstanding cliff scenery of Hoy. The name means high island and its highlights are the sheer cliffs of St John's Head (1,140ft/347m) and the famous **Old Man of Hoy**★★★, a breathtaking red sandstone sea stack (450ft/137m) rising sheer out of the turbulent waters. It is the domain of myriad screeching and hovering seabirds.

Old Man of Hoy

© Alan Majchrowicz/age fotostock

ADDRESSES

🏠 STAY

BORDERS

🛏🍽 **Fauhope House** – *Off Monkswood Road, Gattonside, Melrose.* ☎01896 823 184. *www.fauhopehouse.com. 3 rms*. Melrose Abbey is just visible from this stylish and charming 19C Arts-and-Crafts–type house with antiques and fine furniture.

🛏🍽 **Edenwater House** – *Off Stichill Road, Ednam.* ☎01573 224 070. *www. edenwaterhouse.co.uk. 4 rms*. This charming house enjoys an idyllic rural location next to a 17C kirk, 2mi/ 3km north of Kelso. Bedrooms and lounges boast antique furniture. Modern Scottish cuisine is served in the elegant **dining room** (🛏🍽).

AYRSHIRE AND ARRAN

🛏🍽 **Kilmichael Country House** – *Glen Cloy, near Brodick, Arran.* ☎01770 302 219. *www.kilmichael.com. 7 rms/suites.* The oldest dwelling on Arran, this elegant mansion house offers luxury with character. Set in delightful tranquil countryside, all rooms are individually styled with antique furnishings; there is also an award-winning **restaurant** (🛏🍽) and self-contained cottages.

DUMFRIES & GALLOWAY

🛏🍽 **Baytree House** – *110 High Street, Kirkcudbright.* ☎01557 330 824. *www. baytreekirkcudbright.co.uk. 3 rms.* This elegant Georgian house, surrounded by a beautiful garden, is five minutes from the centre of town in the historic harbour conservation area.

🛏🍽 **Rivendell** – *105 Edinburgh Road, Dumfries.* ☎01387 252 251. *www. rivendellbnb.co.uk*. Attractive Charles Rennie Mackintosh-style villa with parquet floors, distinctive woodwork and brass fittings. The comfortable bedrooms have views over a large garden.

EDINBURGH

🛏🍽 **Prestonfield** – *Priestfield Road.* ☎0131 225 7800. *www.prestonfield. com.* This superbly restored 17C country house on the edge of Holyrood Park offers 22 rooms and a gourmet restaurant, **Rhubarb** (🛏🍽).

🛏🍽 **The George** – *19–21 George Street.* ☎0131 225 1251. *www.principal-hayley.com.* Beautifully appointed Classic New Town hotel that makes the most of Robert Adams-listed 18C design. Its **Tempus Bar & Restaurant** (🛏🍽) sits beneath a magnificent glass dome.

🛏🍽 **The Glasshouse** –*2 Greenside Place.* ☎0131 525 8200. *www.theeton collection.com.* The city's most unusual and trendy boutique hotel mixes ultra-modern styling (glass themes with great views onto park and city) and all the latest gadgets behind a 19C church façade.

🛏🍽 **The Scotsman** – *20 North Bridge Street.* ☎0131 556 5565. *www.theeton collection.com.* The grand marble offices of Edinburgh's principal newspaper now host this stunning modern hotel. Its beautiful **North Bridge Brasserie** (🛏🍽) is recommended.

GLASGOW

🛏🍽 **The Town House** – *4 Hughenden Terrace.* ☎0141 357 0862. *www.townhouse hotelglasgow.com.* Elegant personally run centrally located townhouse with nice Victorian touches, spacious rooms and an inviting lounge with a real fire. Good value.

🛏🍽 **Marks Hotel** – *110 Bath Street.* ☎0141 354 7705. *www.markshotels.com.* The spacious attractive rooms in this ultra-trendy 103-bedroom hotel (with a stunning penthouse) are excellent value.

🛏🍽 **Mint Hotel** – *Finnieston Quay.* ☎0141 240 1002. *www.minthotel.com.* Wide range of prices and good-value deals available in this recently relaunched super-smart functional contemporary-styled hotel with excellent café-bar-restaurant

🛏🍽 **Sherbrooke Castle Hotel** – *11 Sherbrooke Avenue, Pollokshields.* ☎0141 427 4227. *www.sherbrooke.co.uk.* A splendid celebration of late-19C Baronial style with romantic and rich furnishings, country house refinement and a panelled dining room, just five minutes from the city centre. Great value deals online.

🛏🍽 **Malmaison** – *278 West George Street.* ☎0141 572 1000. *www.malmaison. com.* Visually striking former Masonic chapel with ultra-stylish rooms in bold patterns and colours. Superb French-themed **Brasserie-restaurant** (🛏🍽).

ANGUS AND DUNDEE

🛏🍽 **Shaftesbury Hotel** – *1 Hyndford Street, Dundee.* ☎01382 669 216. *www. shaftesburyhotel.net. 6 rms.* In a quiet street with views over the Tay and the park, set in a fine old Baronial-style Victorian house, the Shaftesbury offers spacious and very attractive traditional contemporary rooms. A wide selection of malt whiskies in the Garden Bar. Very good value.

STIRLING AND ARGYLL

🛏 **Number 10** – *Gladstone Place, Stirling.* ☎01786 472 681. *www.cameron-10.co.uk. 3 rooms.* Set in a pleasant suburb within walking distance of the old town, this 19C terrace house is deceptively spacious and offers modern-traditional bedrooms.

⊜⊜ **Dunmor House** – *Leny Road, Callander.* ℘*01877 330 756. www.dunmor callander.com. 5 rms.* This large Victorian house nestles underneath Callander Crags on the village's fringes. It has been refurbished to provide elegant high-quality contemporary accommodation at very reasonable prices.

⊜⊜ **Lomond View** – *Tarbet.* ℘*0130 170 2477. www.lomondview.co.uk. 3 rms.* Spacious light airy bedrooms tastefully decorated in tartan, with pine furniture; terrace with panoramic loch views.

⊜⊜⊜ **The Park Lodge Hotel** – *32 Park Terrace, Stirling.* ℘*01786 474 862. www. parklodge.net. 9 rms.* This charming Georgian house, with splendid castle views, was built in 1825. Its bedrooms (some with four-posters) have style and period furnishings. There is also a lovely walled garden. Good value. **Restaurant** (⊜⊜⊜) recommended.

FIFE

⊜⊜ **Aslar Guest House** – *120 North Street, St Andrews.* ℘*01334 473 460. www.aslar.com. 5 rms.* This Victorian guesthouse features good-value homely bright modern-traditional bedrooms with DVD players; most overlook a quiet garden.

⊜⊜⊜ **The Russell Hotel** – *26 The Scores, St Andrews.* ℘*01334 473 447. www.russell hotelstandrews.co.uk. 10 rms.* This charming small hotel is set in a Victorian terraced townhouse by the sea (four rooms have sea views). Very good value. Its award-winning **restaurant** (⊜⊜⊜) delivers Modern Scottish cuisine.

PERTHSHIRE

⊜–⊜⊜⊜ **Dunmurray Lodge** – *72 Bonnethill Road, Pitlochry.* ℘*01796 473 624. www.dunmurray.co.uk. 4 rms* This charming immaculately kept 19C cottage has a homely sitting room and cosy cream-shaded bedrooms. Excellent value.

⊜⊜ **Taythorpe** – *Isla Road, Perth.* ℘*01738 447994. www.taythorpe.co.uk. 3 rms.* An immaculately kept modern guesthouse, a short walk from the city centre and close to Scone Palace, with cosy bedrooms, an inviting lounge and communal breakfasts.

⊜⊜⊜ **Parklands Hotel** – *2 St Leonard's Bank, Perth.* ℘*01738 622 451. www. theparklandshotel.com. 14 rms.* Near the station, this hotel has won national awards for its contemporary accommodation (with every mod con) and its excellent bistro, **No 1 Bank** (⊜⊜); terrace dining in summer.

GRAMPIANS

⊜⊜–⊜⊜⊜ **Highland Hotel** – *91–95 Crown Street, Aberdeen.* ℘*01224 583 685. www.highlandhotel.net. 50 rms.* Charming and very comfortable good-value family-run hotel a short walk from the city centre.

⊜⊜ **Atholl Hotel** – *54 King's Gate.* ℘*01224 323 505. www.atholl-aberdeen. co.uk. 34 rms.* This Baronial-style hotel is set in the leafy West End, close to the city centre. Rooms are light and airy with Tartan décor. Its popular restaurant serves fresh local produce and the lounge bar has a wide selection of malt whiskies

⊜⊜ **Pittodrie House** – *Chapel of Garioch, Inverurie.* ℘*08701 942 111. www.macdonaldhotels.co.uk/pittodrie. 27 rms.* Set within its own ancient 2,000-acre/810ha estate extending as far as the eye can see, this luxury hotel offers a tranquil retreat with romantic Scots Baronial turrets, mysterious passageways and stone spiral staircases. Recommended **restaurant** (⊜⊜⊜).

⊜⊜⊜ **Raemoir House Hotel** – *Raemoir, 12mi/3km from Banchory.* ℘*01330 824 884. www.raemoir.com. 20 rms.* Built in 1750 and converted into a hotel in 1943, the house, voted Scotland's Country House Hotel of the Year in 2011, stands in a beautiful 10-acre/4ha park. Antique furnishings adorn the traditionally decorated bedrooms. Award-winning Modern British restaurant (⊜⊜⊜⊜).

HIGHLANDS AND WESTERN ISLES

⊜⊜ **MacDonald House Hotel** – *1 Ardross Terrace, Inverness.* ℘*01463 232 878. www.macdonaldhouse.net. 11 rms.* The MacDonald House is family owned and run with the atmosphere of a B&B. It enjoys a superb situation in one of the most picturesque areas of Inverness, on the River Ness opposite the cathedral.

⊜⊜⊜ **Glen Mhor Hotel** – *Ness Bank.* ℘*01463 234 308. www.glenmhor.co.uk. 50 rms.* Beneath the castle and on the river, this very smart hotel consists of six Victorian townhouses and offers a range of traditional contemporary rooms, each with their own character and varying prices. It has a particularly good bar and excellent **Nico's Seafood & Grill House** (⊜⊜⊜).

SHETLAND ISLANDS

⊜⊜ **Busta House Hotel** – *Busta.* ℘*01806 522 506. www.bustahouse.com. 23 rms.* Close to the geographical centre of Shetland and dating mostly from the 18C, this characterful friendly place is the best hotel on the archipelago. Try the fresh local food on offer. Along with some of its 160 malt whiskies.

ORKNEY ISLANDS
🛏🍽 **The Sands** – *Burray.* ☎*01856 731 298. www.thesandshotel.co.uk. 6 rms.* A former fishing store, totally modernised with stylish rooms (all with sea view), a popular bar and spacious dining room also with views of the bay.

🍽 EAT
In addition to the establishments listed below we also recommend places to eat in the *STAY* section (🕯*see above*).

BORDERS
🍽 **Oscar's** – *35–37 Horsemarket, Kelso.* ☎*01573 224 008. www.oscars-kelso.com.* This stylish wine bar *(open for lunch)* and restaurant *(open for dinner)* successfully combines Scottish and Mediterranean flavours.

🍽 **The Hoebridge Inn** – *Gattonside, Melrose.* ☎*01896 823 082. www.the hoebridgeinn.com.* This charming rustic converted 19C bobbin mill serves top-class traditional Scottish fare (among other dishes) with a modern twist.

AYRSHIRE AND ARRAN
🍽🍽 **Creelers Restaurant** – *Home Farm, near Brodick, Arran.* ☎*01770 302 797. www. creelers.co.uk. Closed Mon.* Superb choice of local fish and seafood as well as smoked-from-next-door salmon, duck and Arran venison, from the island's unique red deer.

DUMFRIES AND GALLOWAY
🍽 **Bruno's Restaurant** – *3 Balmoral Road, Dumfries.* ☎*01387 255 757. Closed Tue and lunch.* Bruno's is the town's original and authentic Italian restaurant, serving traditional freshly prepared dishes, run by the same family for over 40 years and still getting rave reviews.

EDINBURGH
🍽🍽🍽–🍽🍽🍽🍽 **The Tower** – *Museum of Scotland, Chambers Street.* ☎*0131 225 3003. www.tower-restaurant.com.* Expect top-class game, grills and seafood at this stylish contemporary restaurant on the top floor of the museum; stunning views from window tables and terrace.

🍽🍽🍽–🍽🍽🍽🍽 **Oloroso** – *33 Castle Street.* ☎*0131 226 7614. www.oloroso.co.uk.* Very stylish third-floor restaurant with great views of the castle, serving up Modern Asian-influenced dishes.

🍽🍽🍽–🍽🍽🍽🍽 **The Witchery by the Castle** – *325 Castlehill, The Royal Mile.* ☎*0131 225 5613. www.thewitchery.com.* Next door

to the castle, Edinburgh's most atmospheric and spectacular dining destination occupies a 16C merchant's house, re-created to appear as it was 500 years ago. Theatre suppers and lunch menus put it within most budgets.

🍽🍽🍽 **The Grain Store** – *30 Victoria Street.* ☎*0131 225 7635. www.grainstore-restaurant. co.uk.* Set on Edinburgh's prettiest street, diners sit beneath the cosy rustic stone vaulting and archways of the original storerooms. Authentic Scottish cuisine using local produce is served.

🍽🍽🍽 **Le Café Saint-Honoré** – *34 North West Thistle Street Lane.* ☎*0131 226 2211. www.cafesthonore.com.* A bustling atmospheric, typical and authentic French bistro, celebrating the Auld Alliance. Booking essential.

GLASGOW
🍽 **La Parmigiana** – *447 Great Western Road, Kelvinbridge.* ☎*0141 334 0686. www.laparmigiana.co.uk.* Compact traditional establishment serving a sound repertoire of tasty Italian food.

🍽🍽 **Stravaigin 2** – *8 Ruthven Lane.* ☎*0141 334 7165. www.stravaigin.com.* "Think Global Eat Local" is the message of this long-established trend-setting unfussy bistro; contemporary menu with an eclectic range of original dishes.

🍽🍽–🍽🍽🍽🍽 **Urban** – *23–25 St Vincent Place.* ☎*0141 248 5636. www.urbanbrasserie. co.uk.* This stunning Grand Café-brasserie is set in the former Bank of England's Scottish headquarters, serving Modern British cuisine using seasonal and locally sourced products.

🍽🍽🍽 **Gamba** – *225a West George Street.* ☎*0141 572 0899. www.gamba.co.uk.* Long established but very stylish modern restaurant, with a strong claim to being the best seafood restaurant in Glasgow.

ANGUS AND DUNDEE
🍽 **Metro Bar and Brasserie** – *Apex City Quay Hotel, Dundee.* ☎*0845 365 0002. www.apexhotels.co.uk.* This contemporary brasserie and bar, right on the city quay, offers a "global-local" menu with influences from around the world.

STIRLING AND ARGYLL
🍽🍽 **The River House** – *Castle Business Park, Craigforth, Stirling.* ☎*01786 465 577. www.riverhouserestaurant.co.uk.* Based on the design of a traditional Scottish *crannog* (ancient loch-dwelling), this stunning traditional-modern restaurant is set on a loch at the foot of the castle and offers great value with its excellent Scottish-Mediterranean dishes.

Callander Meadows, 24 Main Street. Callander. ☎01877 330 181. www. callandermeadows.co.uk. Closed Tue–Wed. This lovely early-19C townhouse restaurant with charm and character is run by Nick and Susannah Parkes, chefs with many years' experience in high-class restaurants including The Gleneagles Hotel. Expect high-quality bistro-style dishes with fresh, seasonal food, sourced locally.

Lade Inn – Kilmahog, E of Callander. ☎01877 330 152. www.theladeinn.com. Bright lively attractive traditional modern pub where they brew their own beer and cook up modern variations on pub classics. Eating and drinking options include a garden room and a nice garden. Regular live music.

Highland Cottage – Raeric Road (by Back Brae), Tobermory. Closed late Oct–mid-Mar. ☎01688 302 030. www.highland cottage.co.uk. This modern small luxury hotel by the harbour features a pretty dining room and an excellent locally sourced menu. It also has lovely individually styled rooms (🛏🛏🛏🛏), with sea views and four-poster beds.

FIFE

The Vine Leaf – 131 South Street, St Andrews. Closed Sun–Mon and lunch. Established 1987 ☎01334 477 497. www.vineleafstandrews.co.uk. and still owned and managed by the same husband and wife team, The Vine Leaf probably serves the best Scottish food in town and has a top wine list.

The Cellar – 24 East Green, Anstruther. ☎01333 310 378. www.cella ranstruther.co.uk. Closed Sun–Mon and Tue–Thu lunch. Booking essential. Near the harbour, this renowned award-winning seafood restaurant has a warm, romantic ambience with open fires and exposed brick and stone. Bold, original dishes

The Seafood Restaurant – The Scores, St Andrews. ☎01334 479 475. www.theseafoodrestaurant.com. Floor-to-ceiling glass on all four sides of this spectacular award-winning restaurant ensures a sea view for all. Excellent service accompanies the changing seafood menus.

PERTHSHIRE

Deans @ Let's Eat – 77–79 Kinnoull St., Perth. ☎01738 643 377. www.letseatperth. co.uk. Closed Sun, Mon. Vibrant award-winning Modern Scottish cuisine with a firm focus on flavour and seasonability in a relaxed contemporary setting, a short walk from the centre.

Kerachers – 168 South Street, Perth. Closed Sun–Mon and lunch. ☎01738 449 777. www.kerachers-restaurant.co.uk. The Keracher family have been involved in the fish business since 1925 though the extensive locally sourced menu is not exclusively based on seafood.

GRAMPIANS

La Lombarda – 2–8 King Street, Aberdeen. ☎01224 640 916. www.la lombarda.co.uk. Claimed to be the oldest Italian restaurant in the UK (established 1922), Lombarda serves classic Italian dishes, pasta, pizzas, meat and seafood dishes, mainly sourced from local suppliers, in a friendly, traditional atmosphere.

HIGHLANDS AND WESTERN ISLES

Crannog – The Underwater Centre, An Aird, Fort William. ☎01397 705 589. www.crannog.net. This lakeside seafood restaurant was converted from a bait store by its former fisherman owner and enjoys wonderful views over Loch Linnhe.

Applecross Walled Garden Cafe and Restaurant – Applecross, Strathcarron. ☎01520 744 440. www.applecrossgarden. co.uk. Closed Nov–late Mar, see website for opening times. This delightful, quirky place on the beautiful Applecross Peninsula is one of the best (and very best value) places to eat in the Highlands. Fresh seafood is their forte and everything is homegrown or comes from very near by.

Three Chimneys & House Over-By – Colbost, Dunvegan, Skye. ☎01470 511 258. www.threechimneys.co.uk. This renowned restaurant is set in an atmospheric crofter's cottage on the shore of Loch Dunvegan. It serves accomplished Skye gourmet seafood dishes and Highland-sourced meat. It also has six beautiful romantic rooms (🛏🛏🛏), enjoying spectacular views of the sea.

SHETLAND ISLANDS

Monty's Bistro – 5 Mounthooly Street, Lerwick. ☎01595 696 555. Closed Sun. Intimate and atmospheric with exposed stone walls and stripped floors, this is agreed by many to be the Shetlands' finest restaurant serving accomplished uncomplicated locally inspired dishes.

ORKNEY ISLANDS

Creel – Front Road, St Margaret's Hope, South Ronaldsay. ☎01856 831 311. www.thecreel.co.uk. This contemporary restaurant serves flavourful dishes using local produce; try their seafood specials and home-made ice creams. They also have stylish rooms (🛏🛏🛏).

WALES

There are many traditional Welsh icons: male voice choirs, rugby, coal pits, slate mines, medieval castles, Mount Snowdon and, of course, sheep, which still outnumber people over three to one. Since around the turn of this century many new icons have added to and updated Wales' offering to the world: outstanding national museums in stunning new buildings that interpret past industries; the striking new Welsh Senned (parliament) building and redevelopment of Cardiff's docks; pioneering coastal adventure activities such as coasteering and RIBs (rigid inflatable boats) in Pembrokeshire; Cardiff's Millennium Stadium and Mount Snowdon's 21C visitor centre. Add to this near-deserted roads, wild walks, charming little seaside towns, some of Britain's most beautiful beaches, and it's easy to see why Wales is back on the tourist map.

Highlights

1 Brave the miners' underground tour at **Big Pit Museum** (p498)
2 Chill out on glorious **Gower Peninsula** beaches (p501)
3 Climb the walls of mighty **Caernarfon Castle** (p510)
5 Ascend **Snowdon** (p515)– by whichever means sui t you best!
6 Explore the ultimate architectural folly, **Portmeirion** (p517).

South Wales

South Wales is where Welsh industry began and "The Valleys" have entered not only into national lore but have become symbolic of a way of life and Welshness far beyond. After many lean years, national pride has returned to the region with Cardiff in the vanguard of the Welsh renaissance.

Pembrokeshire

The lovely golden beaches of the Pembokeshire Peninsula are just about as far as you can get from the cities of north and central England, and with no motorways, it is perhaps no surprise that crowds are rare in this lovely part of the world. It boasts a wonderful variety of beaches, some delightful seaside towns, and a cliffline that is often spectacular.

Mid-Wales

In the 19C English travel writers coined the term, the "Green Desert" to describe Mid-Wales, on account of its lack of infrastructure. It still is the most deserted part of the Principality, though there's enough life in the delightful little border towns and the main settlements which serve the hills of the Brecon Beacons, famous among walkers.

North Wales

Dominated by Snowdonia and its surrounding hills, pastoral North Wales is very much a place for walking and the Great Outdoors. For sightseeing however its castles are legendary and it has a rich, industrial heritage which can be explored at some of the finest visitor attractions in the Principality. One of Wales' best-kept secrets is the beautiful seaside holiday coastline stretching along the Lleyn Peninsula.

National Parks

Snowdonia –Around half a million people reaching Snowdon's summit each year and only a quarter of them admit to using the railway! The Aran Mountains in the south and the rugged Rhynogydd are less crowded.

Pembrokeshire Coast – For much of its length this narrow park is less than three miles wide. Steep cliffs display spectacularly folded and twisted rock formations; sheltered bays invite bathing and scuba-diving. Offshore islands such as Skomer and Skokholm support huge colonies of seabirds.

Brecon Beacons – High red sandstone mountains divide the ancient rocks of mid-Wales from the coalfields and industrialisation farther south. Along the southern edge of the park, a limestone belt provides a dramatic change in scenery and there are hundreds of sink-holes and cave systems.

South Wales

The south is the heartland of Welsh industry with The Valleys, just north of Cardiff, traditionally providing coal to Britain and the world, and the iron and steel works of Port Talbot, adjacent to Swansea, powering British Imperialism and industrialisation from the 1830s until around 50 years ago.
Today, where there was once over 600 mines burrowing deep into the earth, a mere handful of small drift mines pick over the pieces.
The history and sacrifices of the miners is recalled at the evocative Big Pit (the industrial landscape around here has been designated as a World Heritage Site) and at the Rhondda Heritage Park.
By contrast, the port cities that grew rich on coal and metal, are enjoying something of a renaissance. Cardiff –"Europe's newest capital" (since 1955) – boasts cultural attractions, shopping, entertainment, restaurants and nightlife, particularly around Cardiff Bay, commensurate with that status. Swansea too has revitalised its moribund docks; its Maritime Quarter is home to all kinds of new places to eat, drink and visit, including the splendid new National Waterfront Museum. Its revitalised promenade leads west to Swansea's seaside resort, The Mumbles, and out to the glorious landscapes of the Gower Peninsula with its beautiful golden sands.

Don't Miss: National Museum Cardiff; the exotic interiors at Castell Coch and/or Cardiff Castle; Big Pit; St Fagans; Caerphilly Castle; Swansea's Maritime Quarter and the Gower Peninsula beaches.

Timing: Allow a couple of days for Cardiff and a day for Swansea.

Kids: The National Museum Cardiff; Techniquest; Rhondda Heritage Park; Big Pit; The Mumbles; the beaches of the Gower Peninsula.

Tours: The route marked on the Cardiff map offers a pleasant stroll.

CARDIFF★★★

On the Severn estuary opposite Weston-Super-Mare. High-speed InterCity trains link most cities with Cardiff. Both the train and bus station are on/just off Central Square. Sights are spread out; use the City Sightseeing hop-on hop-off bus tour to get around (year-round daily; £10; 07808 723 908; www.city-sightseeing.com). Big events at the Millennium Stadium will mean heavy congestion on the roads and booked-up central accommodation. Pop: 262,313. Michelin Map: Michelin Atlas p16 or Map 503 K 29. Wales Millennium Centre, Cardiff Bay, 029 2087 7927. Old Library, The Hayes. 029 2087 3533. www.visitcardiff.com.

Cardiff, capital of Wales, arose around the Roman fort guarding the crossing of the Taff, on the road between Caerleon and Carmarthen. By the start of the 20C it was the world's principal coal port and much of its appearance today can be directly attributed to this era. At the end of the 20C a series of major projects – most notably the Welsh National Assembly Building, the redevelopment of the Cardiff Bay dockside, and the magnificent **Millennium Stadium** – have helped revitalise the city.

National Museum Cardiff★★★

Museum Avenue, Cathays Park. (charge) Open year-round Tue–Sun & most bank hols 10am–5pm. (charge, . 029 2039 7951. www.museumwales.ac.uk.

The magnificently refurbished and extended headquarters of the National Museum and Gallery of Wales is situated in **Cathays Park**, the spacious early-20C

Welsh Landscape Gallery, National Museum Cardiff

Amgueddfa Cymru–National Museum Wales

civic centre, which is the outstanding example in Great Britain of Beaux-Arts planning and architecture. There are impeccably arranged displays of archaeology, glass, silver and porcelain; the picture galleries and the natural history collections are among the finest in the UK. Outstanding works in the **picture galleries★★**, include masterpieces by Manet, Renoir, Monet, Cézanne and Van Gogh; European painting and sculpture from the Renaissance onwards, with fine works by Italian masters; works by Claude and Poussin; and by modern greats such as Oskar Kokoschka and Max Ernst. However, the great strengths of the gallery lie in its collections of **British art** and in works by the **French Impressionists** and **post-impressionists**.

Other galleries include the archaeology section, **Origins: in search of early Wales; The Evolution of Wales, from the Big Bang to dinosaurs;** and the popular hands-on **Clore Discovery Centre**.

Cardiff Castle★

Kingsway. ○*Open year-round daily 9am–6pm (Nov–Feb 5pm), last entry/ tour 1hr before closing.* ○*Closed 1 Jan, 25–26 Dec.* ⊙*£11; inc guided tour of additional apartments £14.* ✕. ℘*029 2087 8100. www.cardiffcastle.com.*

The first known fortifications at Cardiff Castle were built by the Romans at the end of the 50s AD. After Hastings (1066), William the Conqueror gave Robert Fitzhamon a free hand in the southern borderlands, and he built a timber motte-and-bailey castle here within the ruins. The 12-sided stone keep is 12C. It was the 3rd **Marquess of Bute** (1847–1900), reputedly the richest man in Britain at the time, who in 1868 commissioned the architect **William Burges** (1827–81); his romantic imagination was given free rein in an extraordinary series of exotic **interiors** – Arab, Gothic and Greek – to create the unique monument to the Victorian age we see today.

An **interpretation centre** explains the history of the castle with a film presentation. From its open-air roof terrace, there are fine views of the castle and city skyline. Also in the grounds are the **Welch Regiment Museum** and the **Queen's Dragoon Guards Museum**.

Cardiff Bay★

South of the castle, the decline of Cardiff's extensive docklands, once the outlet for much of the coal dug from the South Wales Valleys, has been largely reversed by an ambitious programme of conservation and restoration and by the creation of major new cultural and recreational facilities. Today it is Europe's largest waterfront development. The project's keystone is the barrage con-

Cardiff Bay

© Eurasia Press/Photononstop

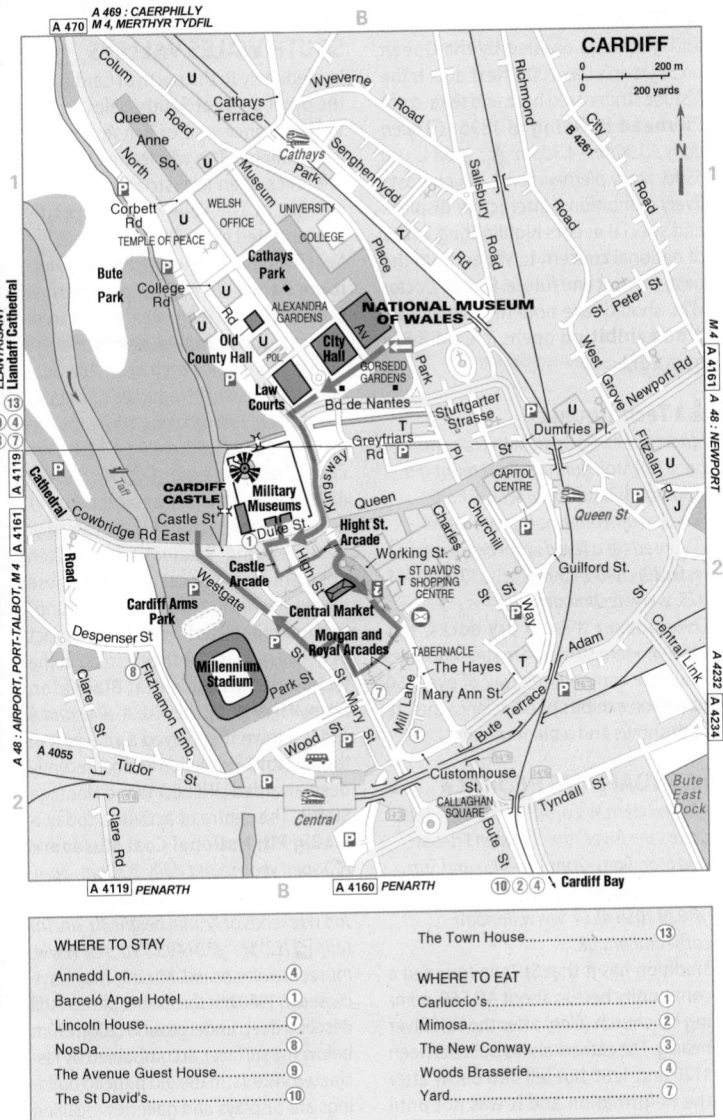

A 469 : CAERPHILLY
A 470   M 4, MERTHYR TYDFIL

B

CARDIFF

Colum

Wyeverne Road

Richmond

Queen Road

City

B 4261

Cathays Terrace

Cathays Park

Senghennydd

Anne North Sq.

Museum

Salisbury

Road

St. Peter

Corbett Rd

WELSH OFFICE

UNIVERSITY

Place

M 4 A 4161

Bute Park

TEMPLE OF PEACE

College Rd

COLLEGE

West Grove Newport Rd

A 48 : NEWPORT

Cathays Park

ALEXANDRA GARDENS

NATIONAL MUSEUM OF WALES

St.

Fitzalan Pl.

Old County Hall

City Hall

POL.

GORSEDD GARDENS

Park Av.

Stuttgarter Strasse

Dumfries Pl.

Law Courts

Bd de Nantes

Greyfriars Rd

Capitol Centre

U

CARDIFF CASTLE

Military Museums

Pl

Kingsway

St

Queen

Charles

Churchill

Queen St

J

Castle St

Duke St.

Hight St. Arcade

Working St.

St

Way

Guilford St

Central Link

A 4232 A 4234

Cowbridge Rd East

Taff

Westgate

Castle Arcade

High St

ST DAVID'S SHOPPING CENTRE

Cardiff Arms Park

Despenser St

Central Market

Morgan and Royal Arcades

TABERNACLE

The Hayes

Adam

Millennium Stadium

Park St.

St. Mary St.

Mary Ann St.

Wood St

Mill Lane

Bute Terrace

Tyndall St

A 4055

Tudor St

Customhouse St.

Bute East Dock

Clare St

Fitzhamon Emb.

Central

CALLAGHAN SQUARE

Bute St

Clare Rd

A 4119 PENARTH

B

A 4160 PENARTH

⑩②④ Cardiff Bay

LLANTRISANT Llandaff Cathedral

Cathedral Road

A 4119 A 4161 A 48 : NEWPORT

A 48 : AIRPORT, PORT-TALBOT, M 4

WHERE TO STAY	
Annedd Lon	④
Barceló Angel Hotel	①
Lincoln House	⑦
NosDa	⑧
The Avenue Guest House	⑨
The St David's	⑩
The Town House	⑬

WHERE TO EAT	
Carluccio's	①
Mimosa	②
The New Conway	③
Woods Brasserie	④
Yard	⑦

structed across the estuary of the Taff to create a freshwater lake with an 8mi/13km waterfront.

Butetown, named after the first promoter of the docks (the 2nd Marquess of Bute) was the core of the harbour area; its buildings, slowly being rescued from dilapidation, include the huge Renaissance Revival pile of the **Coal Exchange**, completed in 1866, now used as a concert and entertainment venue. By way of total contrast is the contemporary white

tube-like building, home to the **Cardiff Bay Visitor Centre**, where you will find the tourist office.

Pride of place bayside goes to the **National Assembly (Senedd)** building, the Welsh Government's new debating chamber and committee rooms (○*public may attend debates Tue–Wed 1.30–6pm; booking ahead advisable as there are only 120 seats;* &; ✗; ℘*0845 010 5500 www. assemblywales.org/visiting*). This stunning construction of timber, steel, slate and glass was opened by the Queen on St David's Day 2006. Next door is the historic strident red brick and terra-cotta **Pierhead Building** of 1896 (⏰*open daily 10.30am–4.30pm;* &.; ℘*0845 010 5500, www.pierhead.org),* which hosts lively exhibitions, interactive displays and special events highlighting issues of national concern to Wales, from the past, present and future. Fans of *Doctor Who* should take note that a major **Dr Who exhibition** opens in Cardiff Bay from 2012.

👤👤 Techniquest★

Stuart Street. ⏰*Open Mon (Tue and bank hol Mon during school term)–Fri 9.30am–4.30pm (5pm school hols), Sat–Sun and bank hols 10am–5pm.* ⏰*Closed for a few days over Christmas.* 👓*£6.30, child £4.50.* &.✕. ℘*029 20 475 475. www.techniquest.org.*

Overlooking the old dry docks, this ultra-modern structure in steel and glass houses a compelling array of over 150 hands-on exhibits plus a science theatre with shows and a planetarium.

LLANDAFF CATHEDRAL★

▷*7mi/11km W Cardiff Castle by A 4119, across the River Taff.* ⏰*Open Fri–Sat and Mon 9am–7pm,Tue–Thu and Sun 7am–7pm/8pm.* 🅿(limited). ℘*029 2056 4554. www.llandaff cathedral.org.uk.*

Tradition has it that St Teilo founded a community here in about AD 560, naming his church *(Llan)* after the Taff River nearby. The cathedral was built between 1120 and 1280 but fell into decay after the Reformation and it was not until the 18C that John Wood was chosen to restore the cathedral.

Almost the whole of his work was destroyed by a land-mine which fell to the south of the cathedral on 2 January 1941. The chancel is now divided from the nave by a concrete arch embellished with some of the 19C figures from the choir stalls and by a huge aluminium *Christ in Majesty* by Epstein. In the Memorial Chapel of the Welch Regiment is Rosetti's *The Seed of David.*

SOUTH WALES VALLEYS

Immediately to the north of Cardiff and the other ports of South Wales lie **The Valleys**, once one of Britain's greatest coalfields. The whole area is rich in the relics of an industrial age but the essence of The Valleys is particularly concentrated in the Rhondda area.

Near Pontypridd, the 👤👤**Rhondda Heritage Park★** *(Trehafod, Lewis Merthyr Colliery;* ⏰*open year-round daily, except Mon Oct–Easter, 9am–4.30pm; children's "Energy Zone" play area open Apr–Sept daily 10am–5pm;* ✎*guided tours daily 10am, noon, 2pm, booking advised as limited spaces;* 👓*£5.60, child £4.30, Energy Zone £2 per child extra;* &.🅿✕; ℘*01443 682 036; www.rhonddaheritagepark.com),* developed around the old Lewis Merthyr mine, tells the "fascinating and often poignant story of coal mining in these valleys and includes an "underground" visit (part simulated). Retired miners act as genial guides – as they also do in the far east of the coalfield, at **Blaenafon** *(28mi/45km NE by the M 4, A 4042 and A 4043),* a town that played a vital part in the Industrial Revolution and has recently been awarded UNESCO World Heritage Status. The centre of activities today is 👤👤**Big Pit: National Coal Museum**★ (⏰*open year-round daily 9.30am–5pm;* ✎*underground tours 10am–3.30pm, Jan weekends only; min height 3ft 3in/1m tall;* 🅿*(£2)*✕; ℘*01495 790 311; www. museumwales.ac.uk).* Mining may have ceased in 1980 but the former pitmen still descend deep underground (300ft/90m below the surface), accompanied by fascinated visitors. In the old pithead buildings are displays and galleries recalling the harsh realities and dangers of this ancient industry.

ST FAGANS NATIONAL HISTORY MUSEUM★★

St Fagans. ▷*4mi/6km W of Cardiff.* ⏰*Open year-round daily 10am–5pm.* ⏰*Closed 24–26 Dec.* &.🅿*(£3.50)*✕. ℘*029 2057 3500. www.museumwales.ac.uk.*

One of the finest collections of vernacular buildings in Britain stands in the parkland of St Fagans Castle, an Elizabethan mansion. There are over 40 re-erected

buildings from all over Wales, including cottages, farmhouses, a chapel, bakehouse, school, corn mill, woollen mill, tannery, a village store and, more unusually, a toll house and a cockpit. A unique collection of coracles, a working farmstead and an award-winning terrace of miners' cottages add to the variety of the exhibits, while a number of traditional craftsmen demonstrate their skills in their craft workshops. Modern galleries present the traditional domestic, social and cultural life and there are displays on costume and agriculture.
St Fagans Castle itself was built c. 1580 on the site of an earlier castle. It has been restored to its 19C appearance and furnishings. Its fine formal gardens include a mulberry grove and there are fishponds, stocked as in the 17C.

CAERPHILLY CASTLE★★

CADW. ▷ *7mi/11km N of Cardiff by A 470 then the A 469.* ○*Open Mar–Oct daily 9.30am–5pm, Nov–Feb 10am (Sun 11am)–4pm.* ⊚*£4.* ℘*029 2088 3143. http://.cadw.wales.gov.uk.*
This massive stronghold, the largest in Wales, sits behind its extensive water defences, reducing the busy town gathered round the outer limits of its vast site to relative insignificance.
Begun in 1268 by the powerful baron Gilbert de Clare, the castle was the first in Britain to be built from new on a regular concentric plan; the design of its walls, towers and gateways embodied many innovative features too and it served as a model for the castles of Edward I shortly to be built in North Wales.
The castle's decay was accelerated in the Civil War by deliberate destruction, of which the half-ruined "leaning tower" in the southeast corner of the main ward is a poignant reminder. The present state of the impressive complex is largely due to the general restoration carried out in the 19C and 20C. The approach to the castle is via the great gatehouse; this is set in the immensely long **East Barbican**, a fortified dam separating the outer moat from the inner moat and its flanking lakes to north and south. Behind these defences is the castle's core, an outer ward with semi-circular bastions and an inner ward with drum towers, mighty gatehouses and the **Great Hall**, the last rebuilt c.317. Protecting the western gatehouse, the original entrance, is an extensive western outwork and beyond this, the 17C redoubt on the site of a Roman fort.

CASTELL COCH★★

CADW. ▷ *5mi/8km N on the A 470.* ○*Open as Caerphilly Castle (ⓒsee above).* ⊚*£3.80.* ℘*029 2081 0101. http://.cadw.wales.gov.uk.*
A pseudo-medieval stronghold, Castell Coch ("Red Castle") was created, like Cardiff Castle, by the wealth of the Marquess of Bute and the imagination of William Burges, who in 1875 started to build a fantasy 13C castle, with turrets inspired by Chillon and Carcassonne in France, complete with drawbridge, portcullis and "murder holes". French, Gothic and Moorish influences combine in the fantastic interior decorations.

CAERLEON★

▷ *12mi/19km NE by the M 4 to junction 25, then follow signs.*
Caerleon, ("City of the Legions" in Welsh), was home to between 5,000 and 6,000 men of the Legio II Augusta, from AD 75 until AD 300. At the **Caerleon Amphitheatre, Roman Fortress & Baths**★★ *(CADW;* ○*open as Caerphilly Castle (ⓒsee above);* ℘*01633 422 518; http://.cadw.wales.gov.uk)* you can see the remains of the enormous **Fortress Baths**★, now roofed over and filled with water. On the High Street in the **National Roman Legion Museum**★ (○*open daily 10am (2pm Sun)–5pm;* ○*closed 1 Jan, 24–26, 31Dec;* &; ℘*01633 423 134; www.museumwales.ac.uk)* are the remains of the fortress, which includes the most complete **amphitheatre**★ in Britain and the only remains of a Roman Legionary barracks on view anywhere in Europe. The amphitheatre, just outside the fortress walls, was built about AD 90. The **barrack buildings** are in pairs, with verandas onto a central street, accommodating eight men to a room, with the centurion at the end of the block.

TREDEGAR HOUSE★★

▶ *11mi/18km E of Cardiff via the M 4.*
Guided tour only, Easter–Sept,
Wed–Sun & bank hols 11am–4pm
(last entry). £6.95. ♿ ♿ ✕.
01633 815 880. www.newport.gov.uk.
One of the finest houses to be built in
England or Wales in the expansive years
following the Civil War, this great mansion of 1664–72 was the residence of the
fabulous wealthy Morgan family – landowners, entrepreneurs and the develop-
ers in the 19C of the docks in Newport.
Many of the interiors have been refur-
nished, in part with original pieces;
among the most striking are the Brown
Room with its exuberant carving, the
Gilt Room and the Cedar Closet with its
scented panelling. The **grounds**★ retain
something of their original formal layout, with superb ironwork gates and
geometric parterres.

SWANSEA★

▶ *Swansea is 40mi/64km W of Cardiff.*
Frequent trains run direct from London,
Bristol, Manchester and Cardiff. The
train station is a 10-min walk N, the bus
station is in the centre by the Quadrant
Shopping Centre. Pop: 172,433.
Michelin Atlas p15 or Map 503 I 29.
Plymouth Street. 01792 468 321.
www.visitswanseabay.com.
Swansea is the lively urban centre for
southwest Wales and, after Cardiff, is the
country's second city. Three centuries of
industrial activity in the **Lower Swansea
Valley** resulted in one of Britain's most
spectacularly derelict landscapes. Since
the late-1960s, however, a programme
of reclamation has succeeded in transforming the area, which now comprises
parkland, light industry, and commercial and retail developments, with few
traces left of its industrial past. Over the
next decade, Swansea city centre is also
undergoing restoration with up to £1
billion of investment promised.

Maritime Quarter★

The recent (and ongoing) developments, along and behind Swansea's
5mi/8km bayside promenade, are recognised as one of the top three waterside
developments in Europe. The mid-19C
South Dock has been renovated as a
600-berth marina, the centrepiece of a
new "inner-city village" of nightclubs,
bars, pubs, restaurants, spruce apartments, public squares and quayside
walks. The **Dylan Thomas Theatre**
(and statue) commemorates poet **Dylan
Thomas** (1914–53). Fans of Thomas may
like to visit **Number 5 Cwmdonkin
Drive, Birthplace of Dylan Thomas**
(*guided tour only, daily 10.30am–
6pm; last tour 4.30pm; £4.95; 01792
405 331, www.5cwmdonkindrive.com*) in
the town centre.
The jewel in the crown of the Maritime
Quarter is the **National Waterfront
Museum**★ *(Oystermouth Road; open
year-round daily 10am–5pm; Closed
1 Jan, 25–26 Dec; ♿ ✕; 01792 638 950;
www.museumwales.ac.uk)* housed in a
magnificent building, opened 2005, that
elegantly combines old and new architecture. Its varied exhibits include a complete, re-erected woollen mill; several
retired vessels, among them a lightship,
are moored at the quayside, and historic
vehicles of the Mumbles Tramway can
be seen in the tramshed. Beyond its displays, the museum explores the way of
life for ordinary people at the time of the
Industrial Revolution in Wales.
Adjacent the **LC** *(www.thelcswansea.
com)* leisure centre is home to Wales'
largest waterpark, a four-storey aquatic-
themed play-area for young adventur-
ers, a 30ft/9m climbing wall, and one of
the largest exercise and wellness arenas
in the Principality.

Glynn Vivian Art Gallery★

*Alexandra Road. Open Tue–Sun and
bank hols 10am–5pm. ♿. 01792 516
900. www.swansea.gov.uk.*
Built on the fortune made from copper-
smelting, this acclaimed gallery is one
of the best places in the country to see
a wide variety of Welsh art, from 1700
to the present day. It also boasts a fine
collection of Swansea pottery.

GOWER PENINSULA★★

Heading west from Swansea, a chain of
superb beaches and magnificent cliffs

extend along the south coast of the peninsula (14mi/23km), Britain's first designated Area of Outstanding Natural Beauty.

The Mumbles, Swansea's very own seaside resort *(www.mumbles.co.uk)*, is overlooked by the spectacular shell of **Oystermouth Castle** (⏰*open mid-Jul–Sept daily 11am–5pm;* ⬛*£1;* ✆*01792 635 075, www.swansea.gov.uk)*. The resort's many outdoor activities include sailing, surfing, waterskiing and parascending. The approach to the tiny village of **Rhossili**★★ in the far southwestern corner of the peninsula hardly prepares the visitor for the breathtaking **views** which open up from the coast-guard cottages housing the **National Trust Rhossili Visitor Centre** (⏰*open Apr–Oct 10.30am–5pm/6pm, Nov–Mar 10.30am/11am–4pm/4.30pm;* ⏰*closed 2 wks Christmas;* ♿; ✆*01792 390 707, www.nationaltrust.org.uk)*.

The cliffs fall dramatically away to the great arc (3mi/5km) of **Rhossili Bay** with the surf crashing on its wonderful sandy beach. High above is Rhossili Down (633ft/193m); to the south is **Worms Head**, 1mi/1.6km-long sea-serpent-shaped rock, accessible only at low tide.

ABERDULAIS TIN WORKS AND WATERFALL★

NT ▶ *1mi/17km NE of Swansea by the A 483, A 48 and A 465.* ⏰*Open Good Fri, mid-Mar–Oct daily 10am–5pm, rest of year Sat–Sun and bank hols 11am–4pm.* ⬛*£4.50.* ♿⬛✖. ✆*01639 636 674. www.nationaltrust.org.uk.*

In a pretty wooded gorge, the waters of the River Dulais crash down among huge boulders and past the remains of the works of the Aberdulais Tinplate Co., founded 1830.

The site's industrial history goes back to 1584, when copper smelting began, and a new exhibition and interpretation project shows how the falls played an important role in the industrialisation of South Wales. It was also frequented by artists (including Turner) who found it an appropriately picturesque subject. Today the waters of the Dulais are used to make Aberdulais self-sufficient in

environmentally friendly energy, with its waterwheel – the largest in Europe – generating electricity. Lifts enable visitors to access the upper levels for excellent views of the falls and to see the waterwheel and turbine in action.

KIDWELLY (CYDWELI)★

CADW. ▶ *21mi/34km NW of Swansea via the A 483, A 4070 and A 484.* ⏰*Open Mar–Oct daily 9am–5pm (6pm Jul–Aug). 10am Nov–Feb (11am Sun)–4pm.* ⏰*Closed 1 Jan, and 24–26 Dec.* ⬛*£3.50.* ♿⬛. ✆*01554 890 104. http://.cadw.wales.gov.uk.*

The **castle** ruins date from the 1280s. The walls enclosed the Norman town to form a "bastide", as also found in North Wales at Conwy and Caernarfon.

In town, **St Mary's Church** (✆*01554 890 295, www.stmaryskidwelly.org.uk)*, built c.1320, in Decorated style, originally served a Benedictine monastery.

NATIONAL BOTANIC GARDEN OF WALES★

▶ *20mi32km north of Swansea by the M4, then the A48.* ⏰*Open year-round daily 10am–6pm (4.30pm Oct–Mar).* ⏰*Closed 25 Dec.* ⬛*£8.50.* ♿⬛✖. ✆*01558 668 768. www.gardenof wales.org.uk.*

The gardens were a Millennium project opened in May 2000, on the site of MIddleton Hall and its historic parkland, dating back some 400 years

Its centrepiece is the **Great Glasshouse**, the largest single-span glasshouse in the world. The 10,000 or so plants here (representing around 1,000 species) come from six areas of the world: California, Australia, the Canary Islands, Chile, South Africa, the Mediterranean Basin; and the Great Glasshouse is zoned to reflect this. The surrounding grounds were originally laid out in the Regency period with five lakes, herbaceous borders and a double-walled garden.

The Millennium Project rescued them from dereliction. The latest addition to the garden is the **Tropical House**, sited within the Double Walled Garden.

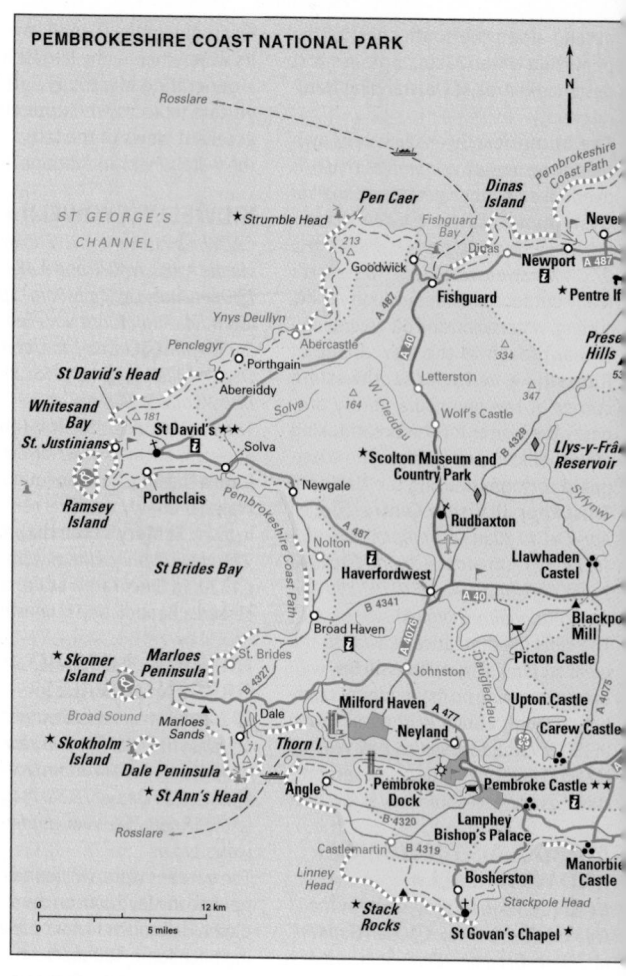

PEMBROKESHIRE COAST NATIONAL PARK

Pembrokeshire

Travelling the inland roads of the westernmost part of the Principality, even in high summer, can feel like a step back to a quieter time.
And in the lonelier places dolmens, megaliths and Celtic crosses remain. But it is the Pembrokeshire Coast which attracts most visitors.
The shoreline changes quickly from ragged rocks to glorious beaches with a rich bird- and animal life including puffins, seals, whales and dolphins. Tiny St David's is not only home to Wales' finest church,

but in and around here a number of young adventure tour operators are bringing a whole new, and very different, set of pilgrims to this part of the world, pioneering coasteering and offshore white-water RIB rides. Beautifully located and very picturesque, historic Tenby is Pembrokeshire's established and deserved favourite resort with families seeking classic bucket-and-spade holidays, but is just one of many beaches to choose from on this stretch of coast. The Pembrokeshire Peninsula, the most

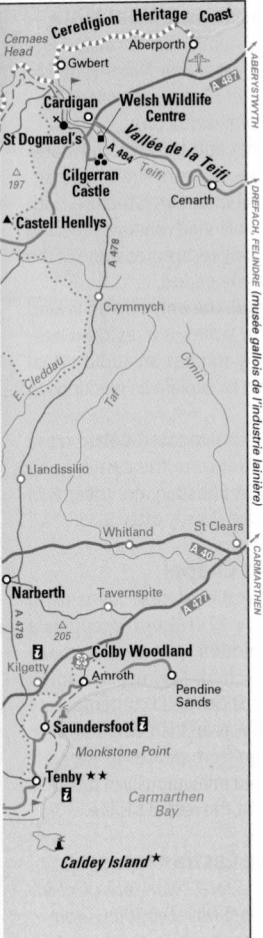

🔵 **Michelin Map:** Michelin Atlas p14 or Map 503 E, F 27, 28 and 29.

ℹ️ **Info:** Haverfordwest. ✆01437 763 110. Town Hall, Fishguard. ✆01437 776 636. Fishguard Harbour. ✆01348 874737. Pembroke. ✆01437 776 499. Saundersfoot. ✆01834 813 672. www.visitpembrokeshire.com.

👁️ **Don't Miss:** The Cathedral in St David's, or an excursion aboard an RIB.

SOUTH COAST★★ (85mi/137km)
Tenby★★

▶️ *53mi/85km W of Swansea.* Pop: 5,226. *Michelin Atlas p14 or Map 503 F 28.* ℹ️Unit 2, Upper Park Road. ✆01834 842 402. www.visitpembrokeshire.com. This little medieval town on its rocky promontory, near the country's south-westernmost point, combines all the ingredients of a popular seaside resort in a compact attractive centre. During the Victorian era Tenby was eagerly visited for its "restorative qualities" and walkways were built here for seaside strolls.

Harbour and seafront★★ – This is a perfect composition of jetty, massive retaining walls, Fishermen's Chapel and rugged warehouses, backed by pretty Georgian and Regency houses, crowding together and rising to crown the low cliff. Superb sandy beaches extend north and south. On Castle Hill is **Tenby Museum and Art Gallery** (🕐open year-round daily 10am–5pm; winter Mon–Fri only; ✕; 🕐closed Christmas period; ⊚£4; ✆01834 842 809; www.tenbymuseum.org.uk), with paintings by Augustus and Gwen John and other Tenby artists.

Town – A good stretch of the **town walls** encloses a characteristically intricate web of medieval streets, widening out at **St Mary's** (🕐open daily 9am–5pm; ✆01834 842 068), one of Wales' most substantial parish churches, with a spire over 150ft/45m tall. The **Tudor**

western part of Wales and part of the old Kingdom of Dyfed, abounds not only in the dolmens and megaliths of prehistory but also in the splendid stone crosses of Celtic Christianity. In 1952 the coastline was designated the Pembrokeshire Coast National Park, the smallest of the national parks of Wales and England; its wonderful variety of beaches is backed by cliffs revealing a complex, sometimes spectacular geology and harbouring a rich birdlife.

Offshore Exploration

A boat trip, watching seals, dolphins and (hopefully) whales, is an essential part of exploring the Pembrokeshire Coast, There are several boat excursions that depart from St Justinian, a few minutes' drive from St David's, in search of marine wildlife. Choose from a conventional boat or a jet-powered rigid inflatable boat (RIB), which can be bumpy but is a real thrill: **Thousand Islands Expeditions** *(Cross Square, St David's; ℘01437 721 721; www.thousandislands. co.uk);* **Voyages of Discovery** *(1 High Street, St David's; ℘01437 721 911; www.ramseyisland.co.uk).*

Merchant's House *(NT;* ⏰*open mid-Mar–Oct Sun–Fri, daily half-term Feb hol and during other hols, 11am–5pm/ Feb 3pm; ℗£3; ℘01834 842 279; www. nationaltrust.org.uk)* is a late-15C town dwelling, virtually unchanged externally and well preserved inside, with period furniture.

Manorbier (Maenorbyr)

"The most delectable spot in Wales", according to Giraldus Cambrensis, traveller and historian born here c.1146. When seen from the bay, the mighty walls of **Manorbier Castle** *(*⏰*open early Apr–Sept & Oct half-term week, daily 10am–6pm; closed some Sats summer for private functions, see website; ℗£4; ⏰ 🅿; ℘01834 871 394; www.manorbiercas tle.co.uk),* which belonged to his family, recall the great Crusader strongholds of the Levant.

The spectacular stretch of coastline between St Govan's Head and Linney Head features high cliffs, arches (including the **Green Bridge of Wales**), sea-caves, blow-holes and stacks, including two impressive pillars, **Stacks Rocks**★ (Elegug Stacks). Near Bosherston, the **chapel**★ first established as a hermit's cell by St Govan in the 6C seems almost a part of the cliffface *(*⏰*note: this area is part of the Castlemartin artillery range; check locally in advance for accessibility).*

Carew Castle and Tidal Mill★

⏰*Open mid-Apr/Easter–Oct daily 10am–5pm, rest of year 11am–3pm. ℗£4.75, winter £3. ⏰. ℘01646 651 782. www.carewcastle.com.*

Much of what still stands today dates from the late-13C–early-14C. The magnificent Elizabethan architecture, with rows of tall mullioned windows reflected in the mill pool, recaptures some of the elegance of the period.

The **tidal mill**, the only one of its kind remaining in Wales, is a restored late-18C building and has an audio-visual presentation to explain its workings to visitors.

The heavily ornamented **Celtic cross** near the entrance to the castle is one of the earliest Christian monuments in Wales, erected shortly after 1035.

St Govan's Chapel

This tiny medieval cell, measuring 18ft/5.5m by 12 ft/3.6m, occupies a delightful hidden spot and has many legends attached. The most common story is that St Govan (a contemporary of St David) was an Irish Christian who found refuge from pirates in the cleft which opened miraculously in the rock. Here he spent the rest of his life.

Pembroke Castle★★

⏰*Open Apr–Sept 9.30am–6pm, Oct & Mar 10am–5pm Nov–Feb 10am–4pm.* ⏰*Closed 1 Jan, 24–26 Dec. ℗£4.75. ⏰✕(summer only). ℘01646 681 510. www.pembrokecastle.co.uk.*

This powerful ancient castle has for centuries guarded the strategically sited town of Pembroke and its safe anchorage. Soon after the Battle of Hastings in 1066 the Normans looked to Wales, but not until 1093 did Earl Roger of Montgomery build the first Pembroke Castle. The castle we see today was built in the 1190s and enlarged a century later.

The massive **keep**, 70ft/21m high with walls 19ft/6m thick at the base, is the crowning glory of the castle. The **Wogan Cavern**, below the Norman Hall, is unparalleled in British castles; a natural vaulted cavern, 60ft/18m by 80ft/24m, probably used as a store and boathouse.

Marloes Sands

This broad sandy beach separates the Dale and Marloes Peninsulas. On the beach, note the **Three Chimneys**, Silurian rocks up ended by powerful earth movements.

Visits can be made to the bird sanctuary islands of **Skomer★**, **Skokholm** and Grassholm, with their colonies of seabirds (including the charming puffin, the emblem of this National Park). Contact **PembRokeshire Island Boat Trips** (℘01646 603 110, www.pembrokeshire-islands.co.uk) who depart from Dale and Martin's Haven

Haverfordwest (Hwlffordd)

The former county town with its hilltop castle ruin is still the regional urban centre.

Newgale

One of several holiday villages on this coast, its splendid 2mi/3km stretch of sand, backed by a storm ridge of shingle, makes this a family favourite.

Solva (Solvach)

The picturesque harbour at Lower Solva was built to be out of sight of sea-raiders. Today it shelters pleasure boats as well as fishing craft.

NORTH COAST★★ (55mi/88km)
St David's (Tyddewi)★★

Pop: 1,428. Michelin Atlas p14 or Map 503 E 28 – Local map Pembrokeshire Coast. ⓘOriel y Parc, Landscape Gallery. ℘01437 720 392. www.visitpembroke shire.com.

Were it not for its splendid cathedral, St David's would rank as a mere village. Instead it is famous as Britain's tiniest city and a thriving tourist-oriented community, at the westernmost point of the **Pembrokeshire Coast Path**.

There has been a Christian community and daily worship on this site for more than 14 centuries and in the 12C Pope Callixtus II decreed that two pilgrimages to St David's were the equivalent of one to Rome – a privilege shared only with Santiago de Compostela.

St David's Cathedral

© Gail Johnson/Dreamstime.com

Cathedral★★

🕐*Open year-round daily, 7.30am (12.45pm Sun)–6pm. ⊛£4 contribution requested. ➤ Guided tours Aug Mon 11.30am, Fri 2.30pm. ⅊🅿✕. ℘01437 720 202. www.stdavidscathedral.org.uk.*

Wales' greatest church, built in lichen-encrusted purple stone, sits in a secluded hollow, revealing itself with dramatic suddenness as you pass through the gatehouse into the precinct containing both cathedral and Bishop's Palace.

The present building was started in 1180 by Peter de Leia (1176–98), a Florentine monk and the third Norman bishop. Up to the wall behind the high altar, what we see today is substantially his cathedral. The whole building slopes upwards from west to east (approx 14ft/4m) and presents a unique and striking impression to a visitor entering the south porch, at the western end of the nave. The late-15C **nave roof** is a magnificent piece of work, in Irish oak, incorporating the dragon of Wales on the pendants. In the south choir aisle is the tomb of the historian **Gerald of Wales** (1146–1223). Before the high altar is the table tomb of **Edmund Tudor**, grandfather of Henry VIII, who ordered it to be moved here

Port and the beach in Tenby

© Foulkes Justin/Sime/Photononstop

from Greyfriars at Carmarthen after the Dissolution. The remains of St David's shrine, built in 1275, are on the north side of the presbytery.

Bishop's Palace★

CADW. ○*Open Mar–Oct daily 9.30am–5pm (Jul–Aug 6pm). Nov–Feb daily 10am (Sun 11am)–4pm.* ○*Closed 1 Jan, 24–26 Dec.* ⊛£3.20. ℘*01437 720 517 http://.cadw.wales.gov.uk.*
This mighty ruin comprises three buildings, surrounding a courtyard. The **Bishop's Hall** and **Solar**, with kitchen and chapel, appear to have been the main residence; the **Great Hall** to the south, with its elaborate porch and stairs from the courtyard, was reserved for entertaining important guests. The main buildings date chiefly from the 13C and 14C and are the work of Bishop Thomas Bek (1280–93) and Bishop Henry de Gower (1328–47). Open-air theatre performances are occasionally staged here.

Fishguard (Abergwaun)

The lower town offers a pretty haven for pleasure craft. Brunel planned to make Fishguard a trans-Atlantic port to rival Liverpool and for a brief period great liners like the *Mauretania* berthed here. Today the only significant traffic are the ferries to and from Rosslare (Ireland).

Newport (Trefdraeth)

Trefdraeth means town by the beach in Welsh and Newport is locally famous for its golden sands, protected by craggy headlands. Quiet and pretty with a small ruined Norman castle and church the village is a good base for walkers.

Nevern (Nanhyfer)

Among the yews in the churchyard of St Brynach's Church stands a splendid 11C Celtic wheelhead **cross** (13ft/4m high), richly carved in interlacing patterns.

Pentre Ifan★

This massive *cromlech* (dolmen), overlooking Newport Bay, consists of four great upright stones, three of which support a massive capstone.
It stands on the lower slopes of the rounded, heather-clad **Presely Hills** (Mynydd Preseli), from whose eastern crests came the bluestones of Stonehenge, probably transported across from Newport Bay.

Castell Henllys

Meline. ○*Open Easter/Apr–Oct daily 10am–5pm. Nov–Mar daily 11am–3pm.* ○*Closed around 20–31 Dec.* ⊛£4.75, winter £3. ℘*01239 891 319. www.castellhenllys.com.*
This hilltop fort (its name means Castle of the Old Court) is the setting for a partial re-creation of an Iron Age community with storage pit, cultivated areas and three picturesque Hobbit-like conical thatched huts with smoky interiors. Inside you can grind flour and make bread just like the Celts used to. Living history re-enactments *(see website for details)* also bring the site to life.

Mid-Wales

The area now called Mid-Wales and the Brecon Beacons approximates to the old kingdom of Powys (by far the largest county in Wales) and occupies the mid eastern part of the Principality, butting up to the English border. South of here lie the hills and mountains of the Brecon Beacons National Park. The park – which spills into other counties, and even England – takes in some of the more remote parts of Wales, and is very popular with walkers. There are, of course, many well-trodden ways, but off the beaten track, you're more likely to meet sheep, or the odd mountain pony, than fellow humans. Attractive little towns near the English border, the National Showcaves, and (farther afield) the magnificent gardens of Powis Castle offer other distractions. On the west coast of Mid-Wales, Aberystwyth is the Principality's most agreeable summer holiday resort, maintaining an elegant and unspoiled air.

BRECON BEACONS★★

▶ *The main centres in the Brecon Beacons are Aberdare, Abergavenny, Brecon, Crickhowell and Hay-on-Wye. For outdoor types the best starting point is the National Park Visitor Centre at Libanus, 5mi/8km SW of Brecon (℘01874 623 366; www.breconbeacons. com). Michelin Atlas p15–16 or Map 503 I, J, K 28.* ☺*Although walking is the best way to discover the Brecons, these are real mountains, so take sensible precautions.*

Black Mountains

To the east the **Black Mountains** form a natural border with Herefordshire. **Hay-on-Wye** (☺*see Herefordshire*), at the northern end of the range, is famous for its numerous bookshops. South is **Hay Bluff**★★ *(4mi/6km by the B 4423 and a single-track road)*, an escarpment offering incomparable **views** over the Wye Valley and far into central Wales. Some 8mi/13km south of Hay-on-Wye

🛈 **Info:** Cattle Market Car Park, Brecon. ℘01874 622 485. Hay-on-Wye: ℘01497 820 144. http://tourism. powys.gov.uk; www.brecon beacons.org; www.brecon-beacons.com.

☺ **Don't Miss:** The National Showcaves; Powis Castle; hire a narrowboat on the Monmouthshire and Brecon Canal (details from tourist office); in Aberystwyth, the Light Railway to Devil's Bridge Falls.

🕑 **Timing:** Two days minimum for the Brecon Beacons.

👪 **Kids:** The National Showcaves. These red sandstone mountains culminate in a spectacular north-facing escarpment overlooking the lesser uplands of Mid-Wales. South from this great barrier (highest point Pen-y-Fan, 2,907ft/886m) extend high rolling moorlands cut by lush valleys, the broadest of them formed by the River Usk. Downstream from Brecon, centrally placed for exploring the Brecon Beacons National Park, the river is accompanied by the most delightful of waterways (33mi/53km), the Monmouthshire and Brecon Canal.

is **Llanthony Priory**★★ (🕑*open year-round daily 10am–4pm; http://cadw. wales.gov.uk).* The ruins of this late-12C Augustinian priory stand in the Vale of Ewyas beside the River Honddu. Eight splendid arches, topped by the ruined triforium, still stand beside the remains of the crossing tower and the east end of the church; parts of the monastic quarters now house a small hotel *(www. llanthonyprioryhotel.co.uk).*

Llanthony Priory

© Sime/Photononstop

Central Beacons

The **Central Beacons** dominate the skyline south of **Brecon** (Aberhonddu), rising to 2,907ft (886m) at Pen y Fan, the highest point in southern Britain. The Normans constructed a castle at Brecon, the ruins of which overlook the meeting of the rivers Honddu and Usk; they also built a priory whose church is now the cathedral. The stone-built former county town has kept its intricate medieval street pattern and numerous dignified 18C houses.

Fforest Fawr Geopark

Continuing west is the sandstone massif of **Fforest Fawr** (*www.fforestfawrgeopark.org.uk*) – meaning Great Forest in English – and its hills, which are known as "Fans" (Fan Fawr is 2,408ft/734m). Water run-off from these hills formed steep river valleys with spectacular waterfalls. The park is known for its waterfalls, including the 88ft/27m **Henrhyd Waterfall** and the falls at **Ystradfellte**★, and its caves, such as **Ogof Ffynnon Ddu**.

The **Black Mountain**, **Y Mynydd Du** (not to be confused with the Black Mountains, *see above*), is the most westerly peak, culminating in the summit of **Fan Brycheiniog** at 2,631ft (802m) and the glacial lakes of **Llyn y Fan Fach** and **Llyn y Fan Fawr**.

⚑ National Showcaves Centre for Wales/Dan-Yr-Ogof★

▶ *19mi/31km SW of Brecon via the A 40 and A 4067.* ◷*Open Apr–Oct 10am –3pm (last entry); extended hours in high season, call for details.* ⚋*£13.50, child £7.50.* 🅿🗙. ℘*01639 730 284. www.showcaves.co.uk.*

This 11mi-/17km-long underground complex includes the largest as well as the longest single-chamber cave open to visitors in Britain. Only the first section of the cave system is open to the public. Bones of humans and animals have been found in nearby chambers and human occupation of the caves dates back to the Bronze Age. They were formed in the permeable limestone which underlies this southern part of the Beacons, and include swallow-holes and underground rivers, examples of which can be seen in the "waterfall country" around the village of **Ystradfellte**★. There are archaeological displays, an interpretive exhibition and several areas themed for children, including a dinosaur park.

MID-WALES NORTH
Powis Castle & Garden★★

NT. Welshpool. ▶*68mi/109km N of Brecon. NT.* **Castle:** ◷*Open Mar–Oct Wed–Mon 1–4pm, Apr–Sept 5pm.* **Garden:** *late Feb–Oct 11am–4/4.30pm (Apr–Sept 5.30pm).* ⚋*£11.20 (garden only £8.20).* ♿🅿🗙. ℘*01938 551 929. www.nationaltrust.org.uk.*

The town of Welshpool (Y Trallwng) lies at the northern end of the ridge on which Powis Castle is built. The massive twin towers of the gateway date from the late-13C. Highlights include the Long Gallery, with its mid-17C *trompe l'œil* panelling; the Dining Room and Oak Drawing Room were remodelled in the early-20C. The castle houses the collections of Clive of India (1725–74) and many fine paintings.

The world-famous garden, overhung with clipped yews, shelters rare and tender plants. Laid out under the influence of Italian and French styles it was created towards the end of the 17C, has not been remodelled and is one of the rare remaining masterpieces of the period.

MID-WALES WEST
Aberystwyth★★

▶ *121mi/195km due W of Birmingham. The railway station and bus station are a 10min walk from the centre of town. Pop: 8,636. Michelin Atlas p24 or Map 503 H 26. ▯Terrace Road. ✆01970 612 125. www.tourism.ceredigion.gov.uk.*

Set roughly halfway along the west coast, Aberystwyth successfully combines the difficult balancing act of being the liveliest seaside resort in the Principality with being a prestigious university town and maintaining its unspoiled Victorian appearance. Despite its popularity with "foreign" (English) visitors the town retains a real sense of Welshness.

The **Vale of Rheidol Light Railway**★ (♾*Apr–Oct most days, see website for schedule; ∞return £14.50; ▯✕; ✆01970 625 819; www.rheidolrailway.co.uk)*, built in 1902 to service the lead mines in the valley, shares the mainline station with National Rail services. The narrow-gauge steam train runs from Aberystwyth through the lovely wooded Vale of Rheidol to the waterfalls at **Devil's Bridge**★. The journey (12mi/19km) takes an hour as the train climbs slowly up to the terminus (639ft/195m). The engines and rolling stock are all original.

Terrace Road leads from the railway station to the seafront via the **Ceredigion Museum** (♾*open year-round Mon–Sat 10am–5pm. Oct–Mar noon–4.30; ⚓; ✆01970 633 088, www.museum.ceredigion.gov.uk)*, next to the tourist office. The restored Edwardian Coliseum Theatre is now one of the most unusual and striking museum interiors in Britain. Objects of all ages are on display with the focus on the Victorian period and later.

Continuing on to the **seafront**★, you will find few modern intrusions to mar the Victorian harmony of Marine Terrace. To the north, the **Cliff Railway** of 1896 *(Cliff Terrace; ♾operates daily mid-Mar–early Nov 10am–5pm, rest of year Wed–Sun; ∞£3.50 return; ✕; ✆01970 617 642; www.aberystwythcliffrailway.co.uk)* scales the heights of Constitution Hill, home to the world's largest **Camera Obscura** (♾*opening times vary, ✆01970 617 642; ∞£1)*. On the promontory beyond the pier is the ruin of the castle begun in 1277 by Edward I.

To the east of the centre, follow Penglais Road (A 487) and turn right for the **National Library of Wales** *(Reading Room: ♾open Mon–Fri 9.30am–6pm, Sat 5pm; ⌁guided tour weekly Mon 11am, Wed 2.15pm; ⚓▯ (charge);✕; ✆01970 632 800; www.llgc.org.uk).* Set on top of Penglais Hill with a magnificent **view**★ across town, this is one of the UK's most important libraries. Its **permanent collection**★ is priceless.

Elan Valley★★

▶ *34mi/55km E of Aberystwyth via the A 44 to Rhayader; circuit of lakes 25mi/40km.*

Reservoirs were built in the Elan Valley, 1892–1904, to supply water to Birmingham. The Claerwen Dam, built to increase the supply, was opened in 1952. The **Elan Valley Visitor Centre** *(Rhayader; ♾open mid-Mar–early Nov daily 10am–5.30pm; ⚓▯ (£1); ✕; ✆01597 810 898, 01597 810 880 (winter); www.elanvalley.org.uk)* at the foot of the Caban-coch dam, has displays explaining the construction and operation of this great engineering feat, as well as the ecology of the surrounding woods and high moorlands, habitat of the rare red kite. The reservoirs have created a landscape of great beauty. The dams are best seen in flood conditions.

Cardigan (Aberteifi)

▶ *38.5mi/62km SW of Aberystwyth via the A 487.*

Tucked into the southwest corner of Mid-Wales, bordering Pembrokeshire, Cardigan is an excellent place for nature lovers. Its bay is home to Europe's largest population of bottlenose **dolphins** and various boat trips depart daily. The area is also excellent for birdwatching, particularly at the **Welsh Wildlife Centre** *(Teifi Marshes, Cilgerran; ♾open Easter–Oct daily 10.30am–5pm, Nov & Dec Wed–Sun 10.30am–4pm; ⚓▯£3; ✕ ✆01239 621600, www.welshwildlife.org)*. Its visitor centre is a spectacular wood-and-glass construction offering panoramic views and an acclaimed café-restaurant.

North Wales

North Wales is a land of picture-book fortresses: Harlech, Conwy, Beaumaris, and in particular mighty Caernarfon Castle. Built by Edward I in the 13C, they may resemble giant rough hewn children's sandcastles, but this deadly serious "Iron Ring" was constructed to intimidate the locals, to prevent and crush rebellion in the region. Collectively they have been designated as a World Heritage Site.

Towering above all is mighty Snowdon, the highest point in England and Wales, and kingpin of an area unequalled in Britain for its majestic scenery. Snowdonia is not only a magnet for walkers; its railway and the small-gauge railways of Ffestiniog are evergreen attractions. Nearby, Portmeirion is the most extravagant folly village in Britain, an architectural Disneyland in the best possible taste. Moving west the (relatively) remote golden sands and unspoiled villages and resorts of the Lleyn Peninsula have a real Welsh charm.

Inland, Llangollen is world famous for its summer Eisteddfod, when Welsh music and voices ring out most proudly, but is worth a visit at any time of year for its stunning Pont Cysyllte "waterway in the sky" aqueduct.

The north coast resort of Llandudno has been a family favourite since Victorian times. Heading out to the Principality's northwest extremity, the Isle of Anglesey (now home to Prince William and Kate Middleton) is mostly pastoral and peaceful. Last-stop west, before Ireland, is Holy Island's spectacular coast.

CAERNARFON★★

 On the NW tip of mainland Wales. The nearest railway station is Llanfairpwll 8mi/13km N. Climb the castle walls and battlements to get your bearings across town. Pop: 9,271. Michelin Atlas p32 or Map 503 H 24.

 Don't Miss: The view of Caernarfon Castle from the water; Beaumaris Castle; Plas Newydd; Conwy Castle; Penrhyn Castle; the ascent to the Great Orme; Bodelwyddan Castle; Snowdon Mountain Railway and the view from the summit; Llechwedd Slate Caverns; Centre for Alternative Technology; the beaches of the Lleyn Peninsula; Harlech Castle.

 Timing: Allow two hours for Caernarfon, a full day for Anglesey, a minimum three days for Snowdonia.

 Oriel Pendeitsh, Castle Street. 01286 672 232. www.gwynedd.com. www.visitcaernarfon.com.

The strategic importance of Caernarfon (Welsh for "fort on the shore") has long been appreciated. It was the most westerly position of the Roman Empire in Wales, who built their fort of Segontium nearby. The Normans chose the castle's present site, overlooking the Menai Strait, for their wooden stronghold. It was probably replaced by a stone castle even before Edward I began his mighty structure, bristling with towers and turrets, designed as a seat of power whose walls imitated those of mighty Constantinople. The town today, still watched over by the castle and partly encircled within its walls, is a centre for visitors to Snowdonia and for yachtsmen eager to make use of its proximity to the waters of the strait and Caernarfon Bay. There are good beaches nearby.

Caernarfon Castle★★★

CADW. *Open Mar–Oct daily 9.30am–5pm (Jul-Aug 6pm). Nov–Feb daily 10am (Sun 11am)–4pm.* *Closed 1 Jan, 24–26 Dec.* £5.25. *01286 677 617. www.caernarfon.com, http://cadw. wales.gov.uk.*

Building work on this impressive structure started in 1283 under Master James of St George (c.1235–1308), who built for his royal patron a castle with walls decorated with bands of coloured stone and polygonal towers like those of Constantinople. Grandiose in design, it was to serve as the seat of English government in the Principality. The appearance of the castle today is due to the vision of the constable in the 1840s, **Sir Llewelyn Turner** (1823–1903), who cleared, restored, re-roofed and renewed, in the teeth of local opposition. Massive curtain walls link the towers to form a figure of eight with the lower bailey to the right and the upper to the left. The great twin-towered gatehouse, **King's Gate**, was defended by five doors and six portcullises.

The **Eagle Tower**, crowned by triple turrets, each, as in Constantinople crested with an eagle, had accommodation on a grand scale. It now houses exhibitions. It was at the castle that the first English Prince of Wales – Edward of Caernarfon, later Edward II – was born in April 1284, and in 1969 the castle hosted the investiture of **Charles**, **Prince of Wales**.

The **Queen's Tower** houses the Regimental Museum of the Royal Welch Fusiliers. In **Castle Square** is the statue of the legendary Welsh politician **David Lloyd George** (1863–1945), Liberal MP for Caernarfon for 55 years and prime minister 1916–22.

Old Town

The old town hugs close to Edward I's castle, occupying the land just north. The circuit (800yds/732m) of **town walls** and towers encircling the medieval town was built as a single operation at the same time as the castle. The walls are punctuated at regular intervals by eight towers and two twin-towered gates.

On St Helen's Road is the station for the **Welsh Highland Railway**★ (*operates Apr–Oct daily, see website for full schedule; £32 return; P ; 01766 516 024; www.festrail.co.uk)*, the starting point for a spectacular 25mi/40km journey, hauled by the world's most powerful narrow-gauge steam locomotives. These climb from sea level to over 650ft/200m on the foothills of Snowdon, before zigzagging dramatically down the steep hillside to reach Beddgelert, then through the magnificent Aberglaslyn Pass and on to Porthmadog.

SEGONTIUM ROMAN FORT

SE of Caernarfon on the A 487. Beddgelert Road. Open year-round Tue–Sun & bank hol Mon 12.30–4.30pm. Closed 1 Jan, 24–26 Dec. P . 01286 675 625. www.segontium.org.uk.

The scant remains of the Roman auxiliary fort of Segontium overlooks Caernarfon. Finds excavated are now in the National Museum Cardiff.

ISLE OF ANGLESEY★★

Across the Menai Strait from Bangor. Bangor and Holyhead are on the main rail route with connections and services from most parts of the UK. Beaumaris is a good base on Anglesey. Michelin Atlas p32 or Map 503 G, H 23, 24. Station

Beaumaris Castle, Snowdonia in the background

© Gail Johnson/Dreamstime.com

Site, Llanfairpwll. *01248 713 177. Port Terminal, Holyhead. *01407 762 622. www.visitanglesey.co.uk.

Anglesey is separated from the northwest tip of mainland Wales by the **Menai Strait**. Its landscape of low undulating hills, rich in prehistoric remains, makes it and popular with walkers as with yachtsmen.

Thomas Telford (1757–1834) built the **Menai Suspension Bridge** (A 5) to carry his road to Holyhead. The Admiralty insisted upon a clearance of 100ft/30m between water and roadway, and the bridge, with its span of 579ft/176m between towers, was the longest iron bridge in the world when it was opened in 1826. It gives its name to the small town on the other side. Modern traffic also flows to the island over the Britannia Bridge (A 55).

Head 4mi/6km northeast from Menai Bridge on the A 545 to **Beaumaris**★★. One of the fortress towns founded in the late-13C by Edward I, Beaumaris is now a peaceful little resort, with a wonderful prospect across the Menai Strait to Snowdonia. **Beaumaris Castle**★ (CADW; *open Apr–Oct daily 9.30am–5/6pm, Nov–Mar daily 10am/Sun 11am–4pm; *closed 1 Jan, 24–26 Dec; *£3.70; *01248 810 361; http://cadw.wales. gov.uk) was the last and the largest of Edward's Welsh strongholds. Though never finished, Beaumaris is the finest example in Britain of a concentric castle. A moat surrounds it and there was once a defended dock, capable of taking ships of up to 40 tons. The Great Hall, impressive enough today, was once twice its present height.

Heading southwest from Menai Bridge on the A 5, turn left in **Pentre Uchaf** onto the A 4080 and continue for 1.5mi/2.4km to **Plas Newydd**★★ (NT; *open Apr–Oct Sat–Wed and Good Fri, 11.15am–5pm. Garden same dates (rhododendron garden open early Apr) 10am–5.30pm; *guided tour (*free) 11am–1pm; *£9.30, garden only, £7.30; *01248 714 795, 01248 715 272 (infoline); www.nationaltrust.org.uk/plas-newydd). This magnificently sited late-18C mansion in extensive parkland and gardens (169 acres/68ha), once home to the Marquess of Anglesey, looks over the Strait to the mountains of Snowdonia. In 1936 the artist **Rex Whistler** decorated the long dining room with a whimsical masterpiece of *trompe l'œil*.

Head west from Menai Bridge on the B 5420 to Llangefni and turn right onto the B 5111 for Rhosmeirch and **Oriel Ynys Môn**★ (*open year-round daily 10.30am–5pm; *; *; *01248 724 444; www.visitanglesey.co.uk). This modern museum and gallery succeeds admirably in explaining the island's special identity. Imaginative displays evoke Anglesey's rich past as well as current issues and there is a reconstruction of the studio of **Charles Tunnicliffe** (1901–79), one of the very finest British wildlife painters of the 20C.

PENRHYN CASTLE★★

*NT. Bangor. ▶ 11mi/18km NE of Caernarfon via the A 487 and A 55.
*Open mid-Mar–Oct Wed–Mon noon (11am Jul–Aug)–5pm. Grounds open 1hr earlier. *£9; grounds and stable-block only, £5.60. *. *01248 353 084. www.nationaltrust.org.uk/penrhyncastle.*

This extraordinary evocation of the Middle Ages was built in the 1820s and 30s for George Dawkins Pennant, heir to the enormous wealth produced by the Penrhyn slate quarries. Its mighty keep (124ft/38m high) gives it the very image of an impregnable Norman fortress, but in fact it was a country home of the utmost luxury, providing hospitality to the members of the Anglo-Irish Ascendancy on their way to and from the port of Holyhead.

The décor of the interior is a *tour-de-force* of traditional craftsmanship, filled with furniture of an opulence seldom seen since. The paintings on show in the Dining Room include an array of Old Masters (Rembrandt, Canaletto, Jan Steen, Van der Velde…) unparalleled in North Wales. Its grandiose outbuildings house a fascinating industrial railway museum, a model railway museum, a dolls museum and large restored Victorian kitchens.

View from Conwy Castle

© Traci1002/Dreamstime.com

The extensive parklands include a walled garden with many unusual plants.

CONWY★★

▶ *23mi/37km NE of Caernarfon, via the A 487 and A 55. Pop: 3,649. Michelin Atlas p33 or Map 503 1 24. 🚹 Castle Buildings, Conwy. ☎01492 592 248. www.visitconwy.org.uk.*

Viewed from the east bank, the walled town and massive castle, bristling with towers, make a breathtaking sight against the mountain background. Astride the River Conwy (pronounced "con-oo-ee") is the famous Conwy Suspension Bridge, designed and built by Thomas Telford in 1826, fitting seamlessly into the defensive ensemble.

Town

The 13C **town walls**★★ (35ft/11m high and 6ft/2m thick) girdle the town on three sides, and were built at the same time as the castle. The circuit is defended by 22 towers and three gateways and provides a good wall-walk between Upper Church Gate and Berry Street.

The original founder of Conwy, Llywelyn the Great, dominates all from his column in Lancaster Square.

Farther down the High Street at the corner of Crown Lane is **Plas Mawr**★★ (CADW; ⓞopen Tue–Sun and bank hols: Apr–Sept 9am–5pm, Oct 9.30am–4pm; ☜£5.20, joint ticket with Conwy Castle £7.30; ♿; ☎01443 336 000; http://.cadw. wales.gov.uk), a mansion built in 1577 by Robert Wynne, a true Elizabethan adventurer. Its rooms still evoke the more gracious moments of the age in which it was built.

At the junction with Berry and Castle streets is **Aberconwy House** (NT; ⓞ open mid-Mar–Oct Wed–Mon Jul–Aug & mid-late-Feb 11am–5pm; ☜£3.40; ☎01492 592 246; www.nationaltrust. org.uk), a remarkable surviving medieval timber townhouse, c.1300.

Conwy Castle★★

CADW. ⓞOpen Mar–Oct daily 9.30am– 5pm (Jul–Aug 6pm), Nov-Feb 10am (Sun 11am)–4pm. ☜£4.80, joint ticket with Plas Mawr (♿see above) £7.30. ☎01492 592 358. http://cadw.wales.gov.uk.

This masterpiece of medieval architecture (1283–87) was supplied from the sea, as were Edward I's other Welsh castles. Eight massive drum towers with pinnacled battlements protect the two wards of the castle, set on its rocky ridge. The inner ward with the royal apartments was approached by water and the large outer ward from the town.

BODNANT GARDEN★★

▶ *8mi/13km S of Conwy via the A 470. ⓞOpen late Feb–mid-Nov daily 10am– 5pm (4pm Nov). ☜£7.65. ♿🅿✗. ☎01492 650 460. www.bodnant garden.co.uk.*

The garden (99acres/40ha), laid out largely in the late-19C and early-20C, comprises formal terraces around the house and The Dell, an area for woodland walks. Noted for rhododendrons, camellias and magonlias, it is also justly famed for its golden Laburnum Arch, which flowers in late spring.

LLANDUDNO★

▶ 4.5mi/7.2km N of Conwy.
To get your bearings take a ride on the tramway, or for a bird's-eye view jump aboard the Llandudno cable car. Pop: 13,202. Michelin Atlas p33 or Map 503 I 24. ⊞Library Building, Mostyn Street, Llandudno. ℘01492 577 577. Castle. www.visitconwy.org.uk.

Safe sandy Blue-Flag beaches with views of Snowdonia, Punch and Judy shows, a Victorian pier and other traditional British seaside trappings make Llandudno an evergreen family summer holiday resort. The Victorian **pier★** of 1875, a delicious confection in the Anglo-Indian style, is, unlike many contemporary structures of its kind, splendidly shipshape.

The family of Alice Liddell, inspiration for Lewis Carroll's immortal Alice in Wonderland, spent most of their holidays in Llandudno and a delightful statue of the White Rabbit stands on the West Shore. The hill above town, known as the **Great Orme** (679ft/207m), can be reached either by the 1903-vintage cable-hauled **Great Orme Tramway★** (Victoria Station, Church Walks; ◷operates late Mar–late Oct daily 10am–6pm, Mar and Oct 5pm; ⊚£5.80 return; ℘01492 879 306; www.greatormetramway.com); by the **Llandudno Cable Car★** (Happy Valley; operates mid-Mar–Oct daily 10am–5pm; ⊚£6.50 return; ℘01492 877 205; www.llandudnoattractions.com); or by road. It offers superb views across the water, town and Snowdonia.

Far underground are the caves and passageways of the **Great Orme Ancient Copper Mines** (◷open mid-Mar–Oct daily 10am–5pm; ⊚£6.50; ℗; ℘01492 870 447, www.greatormemines.info), first worked by Bronze Age miners.

BODELWYDDAN CASTLE★★

Bodelwyddan. ▶ 11mi/18km E of Llandudno on the A 470 and A 55.
◷Open mid-Apr–Oct Wed–Sun 10am–5pm (daily during school hols). Nov–Mar, Easter Sat–Sun and Thu (daily

during school hols) 10.30am/11am–
◷Closed 2 wks over Christmas. ⊚£
℗℗✕. 01745 584 060.
www.bodelwyddan-castle.co.uk.

Transformed in the course of the 1 resemble a medieval stronghold, elwyddan Castle has become a s setting for a magnificent selecti **Victorian portraits** from Lon **National Portrait Gallery**. The p ings are hung in rooms whose fit and furniture have been carefully entertainingly chosen and arra to evoke various themes. The ga have been restored to their Edwa character.

RHUDDLAN CASTLE★★

CADW. ▶ 6mi/26km E of Llandudn by A 470, A 5 and A 547. Castle Stree ◷Open Apr–Oct daily 10am–5pm. ⊚£3.20. ℘01745 590 777. http://.cadw.wales.gov.uk.

Diggers from the Fens (◓see East A and East Midlands) and elsew laboured for three years during war of 1277 to divert the River C so that a castle which could be sup from the sea could be built. A town up which, in the war of 1282, repl Chester as the main base of opera against the Welsh in Snowdonia. In the "Statute of Wales" was issued "securing to the Principality of Wal judicial rights and independence" castle was partly demolished afte Civil War. Entry to the remains is b **west gatehouse**, the best-surv feature.

First and second floors provided fortable apartments with firepl Similar suites must have existed i east gatehouse. The concentric of the castle within its wide dry n with lower walls to the outer ward a defended river wall and dock, ca be traced on the ground.

ST ASAPH CATHEDRAL★

▶ 15mi/24km E of Llandudno on th B 5155 and A 55. High Street. ◷Ope Mon–Sat 9am–6.30pm, Sun 7.30an 4pm. ℗℗ (charge). ℘01745 583 42 583 597. www.stasaphcathedral.org

Rhuddlan Castle

©Christopher Moncrieff/Dreamstime.com

This is the second-smallest cathedral city in the country, after St David's. St Kentigern founded a monastic community here in AD 560. The present cathedral, mainly 13C, houses the Bible used at Prince Charles' investiture in 1969.

SNOWDONIA★★★

◗ *SE of Caernarfon. Betws-y-Coed, Beddgelert, Blaenau Ffestiniog and Llanberis all make good bases. Michelin Atlas p32 or Map 503 I 24.* 🛈*Royal Oak Stables, Betws-y-Coed,* ℘*01690 710 426. Ty Meirion, Stryd Fawr, Dolgellau,* ℘*01341 422 888. Canolfan Hebog, Beddgelert,* ℘*01766 890 615. www.snowdonia-npa.gov.uk.*

Snowdonia National Park covers about 840sq mi/2,180sq km of wild beauty among the scenic mountains of North Wales. Mount Snowdon, at 3,560ft/1,085m, is the highest mountain in England and Wales, dominating the north. Cader Idris at 2,930ft/893m towers south. In all there are 96 peaks over 2,000ft/600m here.

Betws-y-Coed★

Beautifully set amid tree-clad slopes at the junction of the rivers Conwy and Llugwy, Betws-y-Coed (Chapel in the Woods) is the gateway to Snowdonia. A sturdy stone bridge, Pont y Pair, spans the Llugwy downstream from its romantically wooded ravine, where cascades form the famous **Swallow Falls**. Note Telford's ornate cast-iron bridge over the Conwy, built in 1815.

Llanberis★

The starting point for the **Snowdon Mountain Railway** (ك*see below*), this little slate-quarrying town is also home to the excellent **Welsh Slate Museum**★ (🕐*open Easter–Oct daily 10am–5pm, Nov–Easter Sun–Fri 10am–4pm;* ♿🅿✕; ℘*01286 870 630; www.museumwales. ac.uk*), housed in the engineering workshops of the great Dinorwig Quarry.

In fact you can penetrate far into the depths of the mountain itself at the **Electric Mountain Visitor Centre** (🕐*open daily 10am–4.30pm, Jun–Aug and all school hols 9.30am–5.30pm,* ⬦*tours Easter–Oct daily;* ꙭ*visitor centre free, underground tour £7.75, booking advisable, "sensible" footwear required;* ♿🅿✕; ℘*01286 870 636; www.electricmoun tain.co.uk*) to see where the turbines of the **Dinorwig Power Station** are housed in great man-made caverns.

Snowdon★★★

The easiest ascent is from Llanberis aboard the **Snowdon Mountain Railway**★★ (🕐*operates, weather permitting, late Mar–early Nov, 9am–5pm every 30min; summit trains early May onwards;* ꙭ*summit return £19 if 9am train booked, £25 other times, (£18 one way)* ك*;*

515

Beddgelert

Three valleys meet here and the village looks south to the Pass of Aberglaslyn. The dramatic scenery is enough to attract the tourist, but in the 18C the local innkeeper, anxious to encourage trade, embroidered an old legend, and created "Gelert's Grave".

The tale has it that Llywelyn the Great had a hound called Gelert. He left Gelert guarding his baby son and returned to find the child missing and the dog covered in blood. Llywelyn, believing Gelert had killed his son, slew the poor beast before he discovered that it had in fact saved the boy from a wolf, whose body was discovered nearby.

P (£4); ✕; ℰ 0871 720 0033; www.snowdonrailway.co.uk), a rack-and-pinion steam-powered line built in 1896 and the only one of its type in Britain. Principal footpaths are fully described in the leaflets and maps published by the Park Authority. The most straightforward path follows the ridge used by the railway, while the most scenic begins at the Pen-y-Pass car park on Llanberis Pass. For experienced walkers, the scramble along the knife-edge of Crib Goch is an exhilarating experience. In fine weather, the **panorama**★★★ from the summit of Snowdon takes in all Anglesey, the Isle of Man, and the Wicklow Mountains in Ireland. Take it all in from the comfort of Hafod Eyri, the striking £8.3million **Snowdon Summit Visitor Centre**, completed in 2009

Blaenau Ffestiniog★

Slate is still quarried here albeit on a lesser scale than in the past. In the **Llechwedd Slate Caverns**★★ (🕐 open year-round daily, tours 10.15am–5.15pm/4.15pm Oct–Mar, Victorian Village Apr–Sept only; 🕐 closed 1 Jan, 25–26 Dec; ⬤ one tour £10, child £7.90; two tours £16.30, child £12.10; P ✕; ℰ 01766 830 306; www.llechwedd-slate-caverns.co.uk) the story of Welsh slate is told on film and visitors are carried by train through two individual sets of caverns, where tableaux depict working conditions. Above ground, a working pub, shops, a workshop and house replicate Victorian and early-20C village life.

Blaenau Ffestiniog is linked to Porthmadog on the coast by the **Ffestiniog Railway**★★ (🕐 operates Apr–Oct daily 9am–5pm, Nov–Mar certain days only, see website for full schedules and fares; ♿ P ✕; ⬤ £19 all day rover; ℰ 01766 516 024; www.festrail.co.uk), built in 1836 to haul slate from quarry to port. The traditional narrow-gauge line (13mi/21km) now takes tourists through the splendidly wooded scenery of the Vale of Ffestiniog, past lakes and waterfalls, to the "city of slate" among the mountains.

Snowdon Mountain Railway

© Snowdon Mountain Railway

Portmeirion Village

© Portmeirion Ltd

♣♣ Centre for Alternative Technology★★

◗ *3mi/5km N of Machynlleth on the A 487.* ◷ *Open 2nd week Jan–late Dec daily 10am–5pm/5.30pm (6pm summer hols).* ∞*£6.50–£8.50, child £4.* ♿🅿✕. ℘*01654 705 950. www.cat.org.uk.*

Pioneers in inventing and promoting ecological systems since 1973, there are working examples of environmentally responsible buildings, renewable energy generation, sustainability in the home, organic growing, composting, waste management, and a host of other "green initiatives" on display at this family-friendly place. Interactive displays for kids and grown-ups make it fun as well as educational.

PORTMEIRION★★★

◗ *20mi/32km S of Mt Snowdon. Population: 4,187. Atlas p32 or Map 503 H 25.* ◷ *Open daily year-round 9.30am–7.30pm.* ◷ *Closed 25 Dec* ∞*£9, half-price after 3.30pm; Nov–Mar free with website voucher); free entry year-round if lunch is pre-booked at Hotel Portmeirion. Free guided tours (20min) 10.30am–3.30pm.* ♿🅿✕. ℘*01766 770 000. www.portmeirion-village.com.*

Built on a wooded peninsula, with wonderful views over the shining waters and sweeping estuary sandbanks, and with the mountains of Snowdonia (some

20mi/32km distant) as a backdrop, this fantasy village was created by the architect and pioneer preservationist Sir Clough Williams-Ellis (1893–1978). Many films and TV programmes have been shot here, the most famous being the cult-hit series *The Prisoner* (1966–67). "The Village" is an extraordinary mixture of fantasy, theatrical effects and visual tricks; Sir Clough claimed that it was to serve "no useful purpose save that of looking both handsome and jolly", sufficient incentive to attract the large number of visitors who come for the day, or those who stay longer, either in the hotel, or in one of the other many delightful Baroque-, Rococo- or Mediterranean-influenced buildings.

Archways lead to **Battery Square** with some of Portmeirion's earliest buildings, while the Citadel area is dominated by the **Campanile**, which looks much taller than its actual height (80ft/24m) because of Sir Clough's mastery of illusionism. In the valley leading down to the shoreline is the **Piazza**, the green heart of the village, with shops and restaurants and views to the **Pantheon** and the **Bristol Colonnade**, rescued from demolition and re-erected here.

HARLECH CASTLE★★

CADW. ◗ *18mi/29km E of Portmeirion by the A 487 to Maentwrog then S by A the 496.* ◷ *Open Mar–Oct daily 9.30am–5pm*

(Jul–Aug 6pm). Nov–Mar daily 9.30am (11am Sun)–4pm. £3.80. 01766 780 552. http://.cadw.wales.gov.uk.

Harlech Castle was built 1283–89, during Edward I's second campaign in Wales. Its impressive outline rises on a rocky crag, 200ft/60m above the plain; with panoramic views to Snowdonia, across the Lleyn Peninsula and out to the open sea. Pause to look at the massive east front with its daunting **gatehouse**, and solid drum towers, which confronted would-be attackers. Enter by the modern wooden stairs, at the spot where a second, inner drawbridge pivoted to come down. Once inside, the strength and importance of the gatehouse soon becomes apparent.

LLEYN (LLYN) PENINSULA★★

W of Portmeirion by the A 487 and A 497.

Geologically a continuation of the mountains of Snowdonia, this remote peninsula with its wild scenery and splendid coastline is one of the strongholds of Welshness.

At the base of the peninsula is the charming Victorian seaside resort of **Criccieth** with the ruins of its 13C Welsh **castle** (CADW; open Apr–Oct daily 10am–5pm, Nov–Mar Fri–Sat 9.30am (11am Sun)–4pm; £3.20; 01766 522 227; www.cadw.wales.gov.uk), and the nearby resort of **Pwllheli**. Near the end of the peninsula, at Rhiw, sheltered from the winds among the trees of the westernmost woodland, are the gardens of **Plas-yn-Rhiw**★ (NT; open May–Sept Wed–Mon noon–5pm/late Mar–May & Oct Thu–Sun; Sept Thu–Mon; £4; ; 01758 780 219; www.national trust.org.uk), an endearing little country house, part Tudor, part Georgian, with spectacular bay views.

The other attractions of the peninsula are mostly natural, particularly its wonderful golden sandy **beaches**. Most beautiful is **Porthor** ("Whistling Sands") on the northern side; other good beaches include, Porth Nefyn; Porth Ceiriad, picture-postcard Portdinllaen, The Warren at Abersoch, backed by huge dunes with wonderful mountain views. It is nearly always warmer and more sheltered on the southern side of the peninsula.

Near the tip, by the attractive seaside fishing village of **Aberdaron**, the rugged hill of **Mynydd Mawr** overlooks the pilgrims' island of **Bardsey**★. Visitors to the island can see the remains of the 13C abbey of the Augustinians, who took over from the ancient Celtic foundation of the 6C; legend has it that 20,000 saints are buried on Bardsey. Today it is renowned for its flora and seabirds including the rare Manx Shearwater. Day-trip cruises, lasting around four hours, are run by Bardsey Boat Trips (see website for schedule; £30 includes a talk on history and wildlife; 07971 769 895, www.bardsey boattrips.com) from Porth Meudwy.

LLANGOLLEN★

12mi/19km S of Wrexham.
Population: 2,546. Michelin Atlas p33 or Map 503 K 25.

The verdant Vale of Llangollen and the valley of the Dee have long formed a convenient route for travellers from England on their way to North Wales. This little market town, dominated by the dramatically sited ruins of the 12C Castle Dinas Brân, is still a popular stopping place. Llangollen hosts the **International Eisteddfod** (Festival) and many other events in and around the spectacular tent-like structure of the **Royal International Pavilion**.

Plas Newydd★ (10min on foot from the town centre, Hill Street; open April, Good Fri–Oct Wed–Sun & bank hol Mon 10am–5pm; £5.50; ; 01978 861 314; www.denbighshire.gov.uk) was the home of "**The Ladies of Llangollen**" from 1780 when they arrived from Ireland and set up house together. The lesbian relationship of Lady Eleanor Butler and Miss Sarah Ponsonby caused considerable comment in Regency Britain's high society, though they entertained a constant stream of distinguished visitors at their home. They began the transformation of a humble cottage into the eccentric "black-and-white" building it is today. They are buried together in nearby St Collen's Church.

Llangollen Railway

🕐*Operates daily Jun–Oct & most week-ends throughout the year, see website for schedule.* ⬭*£11 Dayrover ticket.* ♿🅿✕. ✆*01978 860 979 (enquiries). www.llangollen-railway.co.uk.*
This is the only standard-gauge pre-served steam railway in Wales, explor-ing the Vale of Llangollen upstream for 7.5mi/12km as far as Glyndyfrdwy.

Llangollen Wharf

Llangollen Wharf. 🕐*Operates daily Easter–Oct 11am. Times may vary, call ahead.* ⬭*Horse-drawn barge £6 (45min), booking advisable; or £11 (2 hrs), Sun and Tue school hols only, 11am, booking required. Aqueduct £12 (2hrs), booking required.* ♿🅿✕. ✆*01978 860 702. www.horsedrawnboats.co.uk.*
Probably the most relaxing way of enjoying the scenery around Llan gollen is to take a ride on a **horse-drawn barge**, on the winding Llangol-len branch of the Shropshire Union Canal built by Thomas Telford. The towpaths follows the narrowing canal westward to join the Dee at Telford's **Horseshoe Falls**, a curving elegant weir in a roman-tic setting. You can also take motorised **aqueduct cruises** from here to cross the spectacular **Pont Cysyllte**★★ "stream in the sky" (🍂*see below*), or if you're in a group, hire your own barge to cross the bridge.

ERDDIG★★

NT. 🕽 *2mi/3km S of Wrexham, off the A 525.* **House:** 🕐*Open daily: mid-Mar–Oct 12.30–4.30pm, Nov–Dec 11am–3.30pm.* **Garden:** 🕐*Open year-round 11am–4pm: Jan–late Feb Sat–Sun only; late Feb–Dec (Mar–Oct 5.30pm).* ⬭*£9.90, garden and outbuildings only, £6.30.* ♿🅿✕. ✆*01978 355 314. www.nationaltrust.org.uk.erddig.*
This late-17C house was rescued in 1973 from dereliction due to mining subsidence. It contains much furniture of outstanding quality, supplied for it in the 1720s, as well as magnificent por-celain, tapestries and paintings. There is also a unique collection of portraits, photographs and poetic descriptions of staff. The restored joiner's shop, sawpit, laundry, bakehouse, kitchen and serv-ants' hall all furnish an insight into the complex running of a country estate. The **State Bedroom** with 18C Chinese wallpaper contains a magnificently restored bed from 1720. The early-18C formal garden survives, at least in out-line, and has now been restored.

CHIRK CASTLE★★

NT. 🕽 *7mi/11km E of Llangollen on the A 5.* 🕐*State Rooms, garden and tower open Jul–Oct daily 10am (11am State Rooms)–5pm. For other times through-out the year, see website.* ⬭*£9. Garden and tower only, £7.20.* ♿🅿✕. ✆*01691 777 701. www.nationaltrust.org.uk.*
Chirk Castle, or Castell y Waun, was built to a design similar to that of Beaumaris (🍂*see Isle of Anglesey*), started the same year, 1295. It has been in continuous occupation from then until the present day and shows the adaptation of a great fortress to the changing needs of later times. The **State Rooms** in the north wing are the great glory of Chirk.
The castle stands in a landscaped park of great splendour and extent, in part laid out in the late-18C by William Emes, a follower of Lancelot "Capability" Brown. Close to the house, topiary and hedging recall the formal gardens swept away by Emes, but the most distinctive feature of the grounds are the **wrought-iron gates**★, a Baroque masterpiece made at the nearby Bersham ironworks.

PONT CYSYLLTE★★

🕽 *4mi/6km E of Llangollen on the A 539.*
One of the great monuments of the industrial age, this magnificent aque-duct was built 1795–1810 by the great engineer Thomas Telford to carry the Ellesmere Canal over the River Dee. It is now on the UNESCO World Heritage List. Throughout its length (1,007ft/307m) it is accompanied by a towpath protected from the drop (121ft/37m) by iron rail-ing. You can actually cross the bridge by barge (🍂*see above*).

ADDRESSES

🏠 STAY

CARDIFF

Annedd Lon – *157 Cathedral Road. ☏029 2022 3349. www.anneddlon.co.uk.* Friendly centrally located guesthouse in an elegant Victorian-Gothic building in a conservation area.

Lincoln House – *118 Cathedral Road. ☏029 2039 5558. www.lincolnhotel.co.uk.* Beautifully renovated and sympathetically furnished 23-bedroom Victorian house in an ideal central location. Friendly owners, good service.

SWANSEA

Morgans Hotel – *Somerset Place. ☏01792 484848. www.morganshotel.co.uk.* This stunning luxury boutique hotel is set in a historic building previously home to the port authority, in the Maritime Quarter. The food (🍴–🍴) is fashionable, served in a choice of rooms or alfresco, in sleek but casual surroundings.

PEMBROKESHIRE

The Esplanade – *1 Esplanade, Tenby. ☏01834 842 760. www.esplanadetenby. co.uk.* Rather old-fashioned but very comfortable rooms in a traditional seaside hotel with great sea views directly over the main town beach.

St Brides Spa Hotel – *St Brides Hill, Saundersfoot. ☏01834 812 304. www.stbridesspahotel.com.* Contemporary luxury spa hotel, located on a headland overlooking. Saundersfoot harbour with elevated views over Carmarthen Bay. At the Cliff Restaurant sea views accompany contemporary dining (🍴).

BRECON BEACONS

The Old Post Office – *Llanigon, nr Hay-on-Wye. ☏01497 820 008. www.oldpost-office.co.uk.* This small, beautifully converted characterful former 17C inn mixes smart modern ambience with exposed beams and antique fittings.

Old Black Lion – *Lion Street, Hay-on-Wye. ☏01497 820 841. www.oldblacklion.co.uk.* Parts of this 17C inn date back to the 1300s with original exposed timbers. The menu uses the best of British produce including locally reared meat, seasonal vegetables and herbs from the pub's own gardens. Ten attractive bedrooms (🍴).

Plough Inn – *Rhosmaen, Llandeilo. ☏01558 823 431. www.plough rhosmaen.com.* This charming ex-farmhouse four-star boutique hotel offers a new gym, a sauna and panoramic countryside views; its restaurant serves Modern British cuisine (🍴).

ABERYSTWYTH

Gwesty Cymru – *19 Marine Terrace. ☏01970 612 252. www.gwesty cymru.com.* Enjoy breathtaking views of Cardigan Bay while enjoying a seasonal selection of contemporary Welsh food and drink in the beautiful rustic restaurant of this charming small boutique hotel (🍴).

CAERNARFON

Celtic Royal Hotel – *Bangor Street. ☏01286 674 477. www.celtic-royal.co.uk. 110 rms.* The best hotel in town, highly rated by its guests, recently refurbished and tastefully decorated in trad-modern style with a chic Art Deco bar and leisure club.

ANGLESEY

Neuadd Lwyd – *Penmynydd, Llanfairpwllgwyngyll. ☏01248 715 005. www.neuaddlwyd.co.uk.* The old Victorian Rectory-cum-Country-House has been skilfully restored and refurbished to an exceptionally high standard. It is located in a beautiful rural setting with spectacular views of Snowdonia and the Isle of Anglesey. Enjoy Modern British gourmet dining on local produce (🍴).

CONWY

Castle Hotel – *High Street, Conwy. ☏01492 582 800. www.castlewales.co.uk.* This part 15C coaching inn with its unusual brick façade is one of Conwy's most-photographed buildings. The interior is elegant and contemporary; its dining room, **Dawson's** (🍴) offers locally inspired brasserie classics.

SNOWDONIA

Tan y Foel – *Capel Garmon. 1.6mi/2.5km from Betws-y-Coed. ☏01690 710 507. www.tyfhotel.co.uk.* Dating in part from the 16C, this five-star country guesthouse has been sympathetically refurbished and exquisitely styled to fuse period charm with contemporary design.

HARLECH

Castle Cottage – *Pen Lech, Harlech. ☏01766 780479. www.castlecottageharlech.co.uk.* Attractive cottage behind Harlech Castle, with cosy contemporary luxury interior. Bedrooms are spacious and comfy; some have stunning castle/mountain views.

Daily changing menus (🍽🍽🍽) display passionately sourced local produce and modern touches.

⍿/ EAT

CARDIFF

🍽🍽 **Laguna Restaurant and Bar** – *Park Plaza Hotel, Greyfriars Road.* ☎*02920 111 103. www.parkplazacardiff. com.* Smart modern restaurant serving interesting Modern (local) British dishes.

🍽🍽 **Woods Brasserie** – *Pilotage Building, Stuart Street, Cardiff Bay.* ☎*02920 492 400. http://knifeandforkfood.co.uk/woods.* Modern brasserie dishes are served from an open kitchen with full-length windows offering bay views.

SWANSEA

🍽🍽–🍽🍽🍽 **Didier & Stephanie's** – *56 St Helens Road.* ☎*01792 655 603. Closed Sun–Mon.* Cosy, neighbourhood-styled restaurant in the Maritime Quarter with a strong Gallic influence. Welcoming owners provide tasty, good-value, seasonally changing menus with lots of French ingredients.

🍽🍽🍽 **The Welcome to Town** – *Llanrhidian.* ☎*01792 390 015. www.the welcometotown.co.uk. Dinner only Tues-Sat and Sun lunch.* This converted 18C pub is set on a picturesque part of the Gower Peninsula. It has a cosy, traditional interior, where top-quality seasonal dishes are served from an award-winning menu.

PEMBROKESHIRE

🍽–🍽🍽🍽 **The Shed** – *The Quay, Porthgain (halfway between Fishguard and St David's).* ☎*01348 831 518. www.theshedporthgain. co.uk.* At the tip of the harbour in a charming spot, this locally renowned rustic "fish-and-chip bistro" with harbour sea views started life as a lobster pot store and now serves simply prepared, tasty seafood dishes.

🍽🍽🍽 **Cwtch** – *22 High Street, St David's.* ☎*01437 720 491. www.cwtchrestaurant. co.uk. Closed Sun, Mon in winter.* Pronounced "cutsh", this friendly rustic-style restaurant was voted best in Wales by readers of the *Which? Good Food Guide 2012.* It features hearty portions of honest British classics, crafted from local produce and arriving with large sides of veg; old-school desserts.

🍽🍽🍽🍽 **The Grove** – *Molleston, Narberth. 10mi/16km N of Tenby.* ☎*01834 861934. www.thegrove-narberth.co.uk.* This multi-award-winning restaurant in a charming boutique country house hotel serves gourmet Modern British food using locally sourced ingredients.

BRECON BEACONS

🍽🍽 **Nantyffin Cider Mill Inn** – *Brecon Road West, Crickhowell.* ☎*01873 810 775. www.cidermill.co.uk.* Originally a drovers' inn dating back to the 16C and then a cider mill during the 19C, the building has been stunningly restored and serves Modern British cooking.

CAERNARFON

🍽🍽–🍽🍽🍽 **Stones Bistro** – *4 Hole in the Wall St, Caernarfon.* ☎*01286 671 152. Dinner only. Closed Sun–Mon.* Occupying a 17C temperance house, this fashionable French-style bistro specialises in fish and lamb.

🍽🍽🍽 **Rhiwafallen** – *Llandwrog, 4.4mi/7km S of Caernarfon.* ☎*01286 830 172. www.rhiwafallen.co.uk.* Oak flooring and furniture combine with rich fabrics and contemporary artwork to create sleek, luxurious and contemporary rooms. The restaurant serves a seasonally changing three-course fixed-price menu (Tue–Sat dinner, Sun lunch 🍽🍽🍽).

ANGLESEY

🍽🍽–🍽🍽🍽 **Ye Olde Bull's Head Inn** – *Castle Street. Beaumaris.* ☎*01248 810 329. www.bullsheadinn.co.uk.* Contemporary decor merges with ancient stone and timbers whether you choose to dine from the bistro menu in the **Brasserie** (🍽🍽), or on the imaginative Modern British cooking served in the **Loft Restaurant** (🍽🍽).

🍽🍽🍽 **The Moody Goose** – *Cleifiog Uchaf Hotel, Spencer Road, Valley.* ☎*01407 741 888. www.cleifioguchaf.co.uk. Closed Sun, Mon.* An interesting menu of locally-sourced dishes with a twist is served in the slate-floored, homely unfussy bistro-style dining room of this small country house hotel, fronting onto the Inland Sea.

SNOWDONIA/CONWY

🍽🍽🍽 **Castle Deudraeth Brasserie** – *Portmeirion Village.* ☎*01766 772 400. www.portmeirion-village.com.* Expect locally sourced seafood, fish and lamb, classic gastropub puddings and unusual beers in this most unusual of village settings.Garden terrace for alfresco meals. Note: free entry to Portmeirion Village to customers who have a two-course lunch.

🍽🍽–🍽🍽🍽 **The Groes Inn** – *3mi/5km ß of Conwy.* ☎*01492 650 545. www.groesinn. com.* Beautifully refurbished multi-award-winning 16C hotel inn serving locally sourced Modern British cuisine and superior pub food, either in its lovely dining room or in the bar. Beautiful trad-modern rooms (🍽🍽🍽).

INDEX

INDEX

INDEX

INDEX

INDEX

INDEX

INDEX

INDEX

MAPS AND PLANS

Great Britain Maps: This material is Crown Copyright and is reproduced with the permission of Land and Property Services under delegated authority from the controller of Her Majesty's Stationery Office. © Crown Copyright 2010. Permit number 110034

MAP LEGEND

Highly Recommended	★★★
Recommended	★★
Interesting	★

Tourism

Sightseeing route with departure point indicated

Ecclesiastical building

Synagogue – Mosque

Building (with main entrance)

Statue, small building

Wayside cross

Fountain

Fortified walls – Tower – Gate

AZ B Map co-ordinates locating sights

Tourist information

Historic house, castle – Ruins

Dam – Factory or power station

Fort – Cave

Prehistoric site

Viewing table – View

Miscellaneous sight

Recreation

Racecourse

Skating rink

Outdoor, indoor swimming pool

Marina, moorings

Mountain refuge hut

Overhead cable-car

Tourist or steam railway

Waymarked footpath

Outdoor leisure park/centre

Theme/Amusement park

Wildlife/Safari park, zoo

Gardens, park, arboretum

Aviary, bird sanctuary

Additional symbols

Motorway (unclassified)

Junction: complete, limited

Pedestrian street

Unsuitable for traffic, street subject to restrictions

Steps - Footpath

Railway - Coach station

Funicular - Rock-railway

Tram - Metro, underground

Bert (R.)…

Post office - Telephone centre

Covered market

Barracks

Swing bridge

Quarry - Mine

Ferry (river and lake crossings)

Ferry services: Passengers and cars

Foot passengers only

Access route number common to MICHELIN maps and town plans

Abbreviations and special symbols

C	County council offices		T	Theatre
H	Town hall		U	University
J	Law courts			Park and Ride
M	Museum		M 3	Motorway
POL.	Police		A 2	Primary route

COMPANION PUBLICATIONS

MAPS OF GREAT BRITAIN
Michelin maps 501, 502, 503, 504 –
Scotland; Northern England, The Midlands;
Wales, The Midlands, South West England;
South East England, The Midlands, East
Anglia (Scale 1: 400 000 -1cm = 4km - 1in:
6.30miles) cover the main regions of the
country, the network of motorways and
major roads and some secondary roads.
they provide information on shipping
routes, distances in miles and kilometres,
major town plans, services, sporting
and tourist attractions and an index of
places; the key and text are printed in
four languages.

COUNTRY MAPS
The Michelin Tourist and Motoring Atlas -
Great Britain & Ireland (Scale 1: 300 000 -
1cm = 3km - 1in: 4.75 miles) covers
the whole of the United Kingdom and
the Republic of Ireland, the national
networks of motorways and major
roads. It provides information on route
planning, shipping routes, distances
in miles and kilometres, over 60 town
plans, services, sporting and tourist
attractions and an index of places; the
key and text are printed in six languages.

INTERNET
Michelin is pleased to offer a route-
planning service on the Internet:
www.travel.viamichelin. com.
www. viamichelin. com.
Choose the shortest route, a route
without tolls, or the Michelin
recommended route to your
destination; you can also access
information about hotels and
restaurants from The Red Guide, and
tourist sites from The Green Guide.

YOU ALREADY KNOW THE GREEN GUIDE, NOW FIND OUT ABOUT THE MICHELIN GROUP

MICHELIN
A better way forward

The Michelin Adventure

It all started with rubber balls! This was the product made by a small company based in Clermont-Ferrand that André and Edouard Michelin inherited, back in 1880. The brothers quickly saw the potential for a new means of transport and their first success was the invention of detachable pneumatic tires for bicycles. However, the automobile was to provide the greatest scope for their creative talents. Throughout the 20th century, Michelin never ceased developing and creating ever more reliable and high-performance tires, not only for vehicles ranging from trucks to F1 but also for underground transit systems and airplanes.

From early on, Michelin provided its customers with tools and services to facilitate mobility and make traveling a more pleasurable and more frequent experience. As early as 1900, the Michelin Guide supplied motorists with a host of useful information related to vehicle maintenance, accommodation and restaurants, and was to become a benchmark for good food. At the same time, the Travel Information Bureau offered travelers personalised tips and itineraries.

The publication of the first collection of roadmaps, in 1910, was an instant hit! In 1926, the first regional guide to France was published, devoted to the principal sites of Brittany, and before long each region of France had its own Green Guide. The collection was later extended to more far-flung destinations, including New York in 1968 and Taiwan in 2011.

In the 21st century, with the growth of digital technology, the challenge for Michelin maps and guides is to continue to develop alongside the company's tire activities. Now, as before, Michelin is committed to improving the mobility of travelers.

MICHELIN TODAY

WORLD NUMBER ONE TIRE MANUFACTURER
- 70 production sites in 18 countries
- 111,000 employees from all cultures and on every continent
- 6,000 people employed in research and development

Moving
for a world

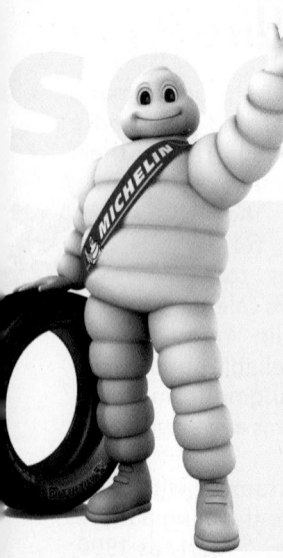

Moving forward means developing tires with better road grip and shorter braking distances, whatever the state of the road.

CORRECT TIRE PRESSURE

RIGHT PRESSURE

- Safety
- Longevity
- Optimum fuel consumption

-0,5 bar

- Durability reduced by 20% (- 8,000 km)

-1 bar

- Risk of blowouts
- Increased fuel consumption
- Longer braking distances on wet surfaces

forward together
where mobility is safer

It also involves helping motorists take care of their safety and their tires. To do so, Michelin organises "Fill Up With Air" campaigns all over the world to remind us that correct tire pressure is vital.

WEAR

DETECTING TIRE WEAR

The legal minimum depth of tire tread is 1.6mm. Tire manufacturers equip their tires with tread wear indicators, which are small blocks of rubber moulded into the base of the main grooves at a depth of 1.6mm.

Tires are the only point of contact between the vehicle and road.

The photo below shows the actual contact zone.

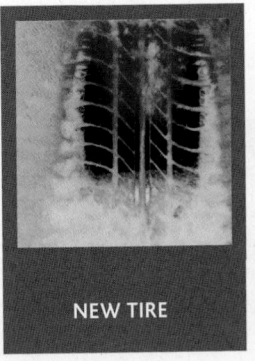

If the tread depth is less than 1.6mm, tires are considered to be worn and dangerous on wet surfaces.

NEW TIRE

WORN TIRE
(1,6 mm tread)

Moving forward
means sustainable mobility

By 2050, Michelin aims to cut the quantity of raw materials used in its tire manufacturing process by half and to have developed renewable energy in its facilities. The design of MICHELIN tires has already saved billions of litres of fuel and, by extension, billions of tons of CO_2.

Similarly, Michelin prints its maps and guides on paper produced from sustainably managed forests and is diversifying its publishing media by offering digital solutions to make traveling easier, more fuel efficient and more enjoyable!

The group's whole-hearted commitment to eco-design on a daily basis is demonstrated by ISO 14001 certification.

Like you, Michelin is committed to preserving our planet.

Chat with Bibendum

Go to
www.michelin.com/corporate/en
Find out more about
Michelin's history and the
latest news.

QUIZ

Michelin develops tires for all types of vehicles.
See if you can match the right tire with the right vehicle…

Michelin Apa Publications Ltd

58 Borough High Street, London SE1 1XF, United Kingdom

No part of this publication may be reproduced in any form
without the prior permission of the publisher.

© 2012 Michelin Apa Publications Ltd
ISBN 978-1-907099-56-4
Printed: December 2011
Printed and bound in Germany

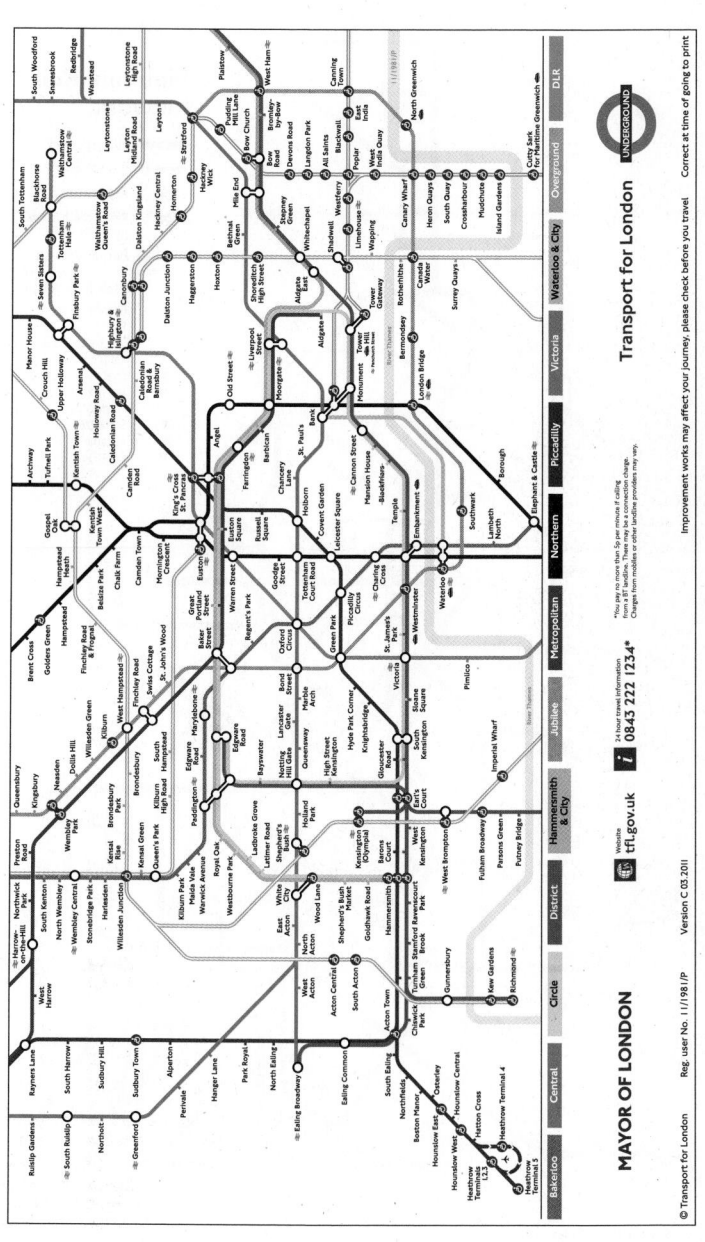

National Rail network

- ▬▬ Principal routes
- ── Other selected routes
- ⊗ Airport interchange
- ✈ Railair coach link with Heathrow Airport
- ⛴ Ferry interchange

LONDON TERMINALS

- C Charing Cross
- E Euston
- F Fenchurch Street
- K Kings Cross
- L Liverpool Street
- M Marylebone
- P Paddington
- S St Pancras
- V Victoria
- W Waterloo

Channel Tunnel services
LILLE, BRUSSELS, PARIS

National Rail Enquiries
08457 48 49 50
www.nationalrail.co.uk

© ATOC 2000. All rights reserved. MCD/BAJS-1S 11/00

⬤ National Rail